Theoretical Logic in Sociology

Men do not always take their great thinkers seriously,
even when they admire them.

Sigmund Freud,
*Group Psychology and the
Analysis of the Ego*

Theoretical Logic in Sociology

Volume Two

THE ANTINOMIES OF CLASSICAL THOUGHT: MARX AND DURKHEIM

Jeffrey C. Alexander

University of California Press
Berkeley · Los Angeles

University of California Press
Berkeley and Los Angeles, California
© 1982 by
The Regents of the University of California
First Paperback Printing 1985
ISBN 0-520-05613-2
Printed in the United States of America

1   2   3   4   5   6   7   8   9

Library of Congress Cataloging in Publication Data

Alexander, Jeffrey C.
  Theoretical logic in sociology.

  Includes bibliographical references and index.
  v.1. Positivism, presuppositions, and current
controversies.—v. 2. The antinomies of classical
thought: Marx and Durkheim.
  1. Sociology—History—Collected works.
2. Sociology—Philosophy—Collected works.
3. Sociology—Methodology—Collected works.
HM24.A465   301   75-17305
                           AACR1

CONTENTS—OVERVIEW

Volume Three
THE CLASSICAL ATTEMPT AT
THEORETICAL SYNTHESIS: MAX WEBER

THE ANTINOMIES
OF CLASSICAL
THOUGHT:
MARX AND DURKHEIM

Contents
VOLUME TWO
THE ANTINOMIES
OF CLASSICAL
THOUGHT:
MARX AND DURKHEIM

Part Three
One-Dimensional Theory and Its Discontents

Preface to Volume Two

This is the second part of a four-volume work. Naturally, I hope that the work will be read in its entirety, but I recognize that this may not be possible, and so have written each volume in such a way that it can be read independently of the others.

Since the work is of one piece, it is inevitable that each successive volume will in some important ways build upon the arguments made in those preceding. The present volume draws upon the framework and arguments laid out in volume 1, *Positivism, Presuppositions, and Current Controversies*. In that volume, I made certain statements about the nature of science and the relationship of its components, about the status of contemporary theoretical debate in sociology, about the qualities of good theorizing, and about the possibility for objectivity in postpositivist social-scientific theory. I cannot hope to summarize those statements fully here, but I will try to provide the reader with enough background so that the understanding of the present volume can proceed apace. I will, of course, be returning to these themes throughout the course of this volume, and many of the questions considered abstractly in volume 1 will here be thought through in a more concrete way. Many, however, will not, and the very concreteness of the present treatment makes a brief

NOTE: I have not reproduced, either here or in subsequent volumes, the acknowledgments which prefaced volume 1, in which I thank the numerous individuals—teachers, colleagues, students, editors, family, and friends—who have helped me in vital ways throughout this long project. In specific connection to the present volume, however, I would like to thank Kenneth Rasmussen for the invaluable assistance he provided in checking and translating German texts.

abstract that much more necessary. Needless to say, for those who have read the preceding volume, this abstract is redundant and unnecessary.

In volume 1, two simultaneous polemics were conducted. First, I argued against the positivist persuasion in contemporary understandings of science, evident not only among philosophers and sociologists of science but among its practitioners as well. The crucial proposition of the positivist persuasion, I argued, is the belief that factual statements can be ontologically separated from nonfactual statements or generalizations. From this central tenet, the other components of the positivist persuasion inevitably follow: The notions that philosophical or metaphysical issues play no essential part in a true empirical science, that theoretical disputes must be decided by reference to crucial empirical experiments alone, that methodological techniques of verification or falsification are of critical and ultimate importance. In opposition to these positivist tenets, I suggested that general as well as specific thinking is crucial to science and defined this "theoretical" as contrasted to "methodological" or "empirical" logic as the concern with the effects of more general assumptions on more specific formulations. It is this more general concern with theoretical logic that is the focus of the entire work.

The second polemic was directed against theoretical arguments that have occurred within the nonpositivist framework itself. I argued that recent debates in sociological theory have sought to reduce—to "conflate" —theoretical argument to one or another particular set of nonempirical commitments. Theoretical empiricism has, for example, sought to reduce sociological theory to assumptions about methodology, conflict theory to assumptions about the relative equilibrium of the empirical world at a specific time, antifunctionalist critique to assumptions about the nature of scientific models, and ideological criticism—practicing a "strong program" in the sociology of knowledge—to the political components of a theorist's perspective.

I proposed, to the contrary, that science be conceived as a multilayered continuum, one that stretches from the most general, metaphysically oriented presuppositions, to more specific ideological assumptions and models, to still more empirical assumptions and methodological commitments, and finally to empirically related propositions and "facts." Each of these levels, I insisted, has relative autonomy vis-à-vis other kinds of scientific commitments, although each is powerfully interrelated to others at the same time. It is the task of *theoretical* logic in sociology to explicate what each of these commitments entails and how they are interrelated. Only with such a differentiated understanding of science, moreover, can the dichotomy of idealist versus positivist, or materialist, understandings of science be resolved, for with this understanding it becomes clear that every scientific statement is the product of the interaction between pressures from both environments, the

Figure 1

THE SCIENTIFIC CONTINUUM AND ITS COMPONENTS

Metaphysical
environment

Empirical
environment

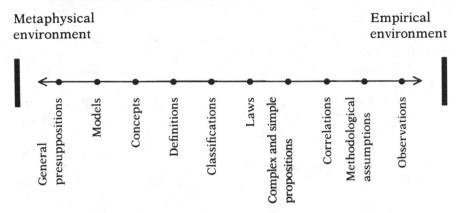

empirical and the metaphysical. Figure 1 is my schematic representation of the scientific continuum which I presented in volume 1 and repeat here for the reader's convenience.

As part of this second polemic I also made a final point: not only have recent theoretical arguments been reductionistic, or conflationary, but taken together they have usually ignored the most generalized elements of social scientific argument. I called these elements "presuppositions" and defined them as the assumptions any social scientist makes about the nature of human action and how it is aggregated into patterned arrangements.

These presuppositional assumptions address the problems of action and order. In the first place, and here I must unfortunately simplify complex issues which were treated earlier at some length, action can be defined either in an instrumental, rationalizing way or in a manner that pays more attention to nonrational, normative or affective components. The former is to take up the materialist path, the latter the idealist, although there is also, of course, the possibility for a more integrated and synthetic, or multidimensional, position. Secondly, theory must also adopt an orientation to order. Are social arrangements the results of individual negotiation or do they present themselves as collective structures that have sui generis or emergent status? Individualistic approaches often reveal important elements of empirical interaction, but they ignore the invisible parameters within which such action takes place, parameters which, indeed, often inform the substance of action itself. If one emphasizes collective order, on the other hand, individual action remains vitally important, for assumptions about the nature of action will determine how such collective order shall be described. In line with the idealist approach to action, collective order has often been given a normative hue. This position has the advantage of allowing collective structures to be combined with the voluntary agency of individuals, for normative order rests upon internal, subjective commitments. Yet taken by itself, this approach exaggerates the responsiveness of the collectivity to individual subjective concerns. But if action is assumed, in the name of greater realism, to be instrumentalizing and rational, collective structure will be described as external and material, for if motives are always calculating and efficient, action will be completely predictable on the basis of external pressure alone. Subjectivity and the concern with motive drops out: order is then viewed in a thoroughly deterministic way. These two solutions to the problem of collective order form the traditions of *sociological* idealism and *sociological* materialism, traditions that must be sharply separated from idealism and materialism in a purely epistemological sense. Of course, once again, there remains the theoretical possibility that more synthetic and multidimensional understandings of collective order may be achieved.

It is within the contexts of these various polemics that I introduced certain technical arguments which might at first glance elude those who are reading the present volume alone. These are: (1) the dangers of "conflation" in scientific argument; (2) the importance of multidimensional thought at the most general presuppositional level; (3) the dangers of "reduction" within this presuppositional level itself. Within the context of the preceding summary, however, these technical points should now be more accessible. (1) Conflationary arguments attempt to make each of the components of the scientific continuum primarily dependent on one particular differentiated commitment. Thus, "conflict sociology" is conflationary, as are so many of the arguments for "critical sociology" and the arguments for or against "functionalist sociology." In other words, each of the arguments I previously mentioned represents a dangerous, conflationary strategy. (2) Within the presuppositional level—the most general and ramifying level of scientific reasoning—I insisted on the theoretical power of multidimensional thinking over either its idealist or materialist counterparts. Critical benefits accrue to both forms of one-dimensional thought, but there are also debilitating weaknesses which make each, taken by itself, theoretically unacceptable. (3) I suggested that one-dimensional thinking was often camouflaged by a form of reductionism within the presuppositional level itself: the reduction of the problem of action to the problem of order. Sociological idealists and materialists often—in fact, almost invariably—argue that a collective rather than individualistic approach can be achieved only if action is perceived either in an instrumentalist or normative way. This reduction is false. The questions of action and order are themselves relatively autonomous, although, once decided, they profoundly affect one another.

Normative and instrumental understandings of action each can be collectivist and, conversely, each can be individualistic.

I have made other arguments in volume 1. Most importantly, I suggested that nonpositivistic thought does not have to be merely relativistic, that it can attain its own kind of objectivity. The strong assertion of a fully generalized and inclusive theoretical criterion—multidimensionality—is basic to maintaining such an objective, universalistic position. I hope to demonstrate this objectivity in the following pages.

I have summarized the main points of my earlier discussion in an unforgivably foreshortened way. I trust, however, that this presentation will be sufficient for the reader to see the context within which the following analysis of Marx and Durkheim takes place. Without further ado, let us proceed to this first phase of the examination of the classical founders of sociology.

Chapter One

PROLEGOMENA. GENERAL THEORETICAL ARGUMENT AS INTERPRETATION

The Critical Role of "Readings"

In the preceding volume, I have argued for the importance of certain elements of the scientific continuum over others, or at least for the uniquely ramifying effects of particular, "presuppositional" contributions. Within the presuppositional level itself, I argued for the significance of one particular kind of commitment over the others. How, then, shall we now proceed?

I have decided to take what may at first glance seem a rather controversial course: I will continue my theoretical argument by engaging in interpretation, by making "readings" in which I attempt to understand what central texts in the history of sociology actually "mean." But why engage in readings rather than embark on a more straightforward and contemporary discussion of telling empirical problems, demonstrating, perhaps, the strength of the multidimensional position in relation to such empirical grounds? Why, moreover, devote my interpretive efforts to sociologists of the past, to sociological theorists, indeed, who are no longer even alive, three of whom concluded their contributions more than half a century ago? I do so because, in certain critical respects, it is by interpreting and reinterpreting "classical" works that fundamental argument is conducted in the social sciences. In volume 1, it was noted

NOTE: In addition to the citation of sources, the backnotes include numerous substantive discussions—refinements of points that occur in the main text and digressions about relevant issues and secondary literature. To enable the interested reader to turn immediately to this substantive annotation, I have distinguished these substantive notes by marking them with a dagger[†] following the note number. A ribbon bookmark is provided to facilitate such referral.

1

that a major difference between social and natural science is not the fact of subjective orientation, but the relative lack of consensus in any given phase of social science about what the proper subjective orientations are. This lack of consensus makes communication and mutual understanding difficult. It is for this very reason, indeed, that generalized argument in the social sciences needs "classics," that despite the undeniable fact of empirical accumulation theoretical argument so often moves "backward" from discussion of contemporary reality to debates over the thought of founding figures. Only in this way can generalized, abstract debates occur on some common ground. Only in this way, too, can "philosophical" debate take a form that is concrete and specific enough to be easily understood. To illustrate this issue, one might, in fact, employ my model of the scientific continuum (fig. 1) as a metaphor. If social scientific argument extends from more general to more specific statements, one may also say that the continuum stretches from debates about current empirical controversies, on the one side, to arguments about the general presuppositions of the founders of social science on the other. In many instances, it is upon the most general presuppositional side of this continuum that critical social scientific development rests, and it is to this most generalized side that I devote the remainder of this work.

The positivist persuasion in sociology would certainly deny to readings of classical works the status of theoretical argument. If they are to have any continuing status at all, classical works must function as "exemplars," as methodologically and propositionally precise models of how scientific research is to be done.[1†] The most articulate and influential statement of this perspective is Robert K. Merton's argument for the "systematics" over the "history" of sociological theory.[2] The epigraph Merton chooses for his essay is Whitehead's statement that "a science which hesitates to forget its founders is lost," and on the basis of an empiricist and accumulationist understanding of sociology he differentiates between a "scientific" approach to a discipline's founders and a "humanistic" one. In the humanities, where subjective interpretation is fundamental, the continual rereading of great works is necessary. In science, to the contrary, the sign of maturity is that such earlier great works can be ignored. Science is an objective discipline, and for this reason the kind of "erudition" supplied by rereadings is often in conflict with "originality." If historical works are still to be studied, in Merton's view, they should be read only in a truly historical context: to find new factual chronologies in the intellectual prehistory of science. To read historical works in a general interpretive way, however, is "mere commentary." Interpretive commentary is banal precisely because in trying to straddle scientific and humanistic orientations it merges systematics with history.[3] There is, in fact, only one legitimate reason for social scientists to reread the classics, and that is if they can discover new concrete empirical ideas, discoveries that develop as the result of the scientist's own newly increased empirical knowledge.[4] The classics may be reread, therefore, because they present "unretrieved information" that may still be "usefully employed" in an explanatory way.[5]

In the preceding volume we have seen how generalized, nonempirical debate is often decisive within natural scientific development itself. In fact, on certain important occasions, it is even true that to make such advances natural science turns to the reinterpretation and reunderstanding of earlier, historical work.[6†] In social science, however, generalized reference becomes a much more frequent form of independent argument, and it is in social science that earlier works, therefore, become luminous and classical. Merton tried to extend the model of natural to social science. The best argument against this position is to look at the actual practice of social science itself.

How, indeed, are the central commitments in sociology actually made, and how are other social scientists persuaded to accept them? In the postwar era, every major new form of theoretical argument has been offered, in part, as a pivotal reading of classical works. The arguments for conflict theory, for ideological determinism, for institutional over systems theory, and even for the elimination of theoretical consideration itself—all the reductionist arguments considered in volume 1—have been offered in terms of what Marx, or Durkheim, or Weber, or Parsons "really meant." These supposedly backward-looking interpretive gestures, moreover, have usually played the critical role in carrying the day.[7†] If possible, such reliance on rereading has been even more central at the most general presuppositional level. There has been no more powerful argument for a particular version of general theorizing than to demonstrate that these presuppositions actually informed the theorizing of a venerated classical figure, or conversely that they did not appear in the work of a figure whom the contemporary theorist and his followers consider anathema. Every major mode of presuppositional thought has, of course, been embodied in empirical propositions and exemplars; but each has also rested its case upon highly skillful and often highly tendentious readings of sociology's founding works. It is for this reason that readings are always, implicitly, polemical statements. They are not simply objective empirical assessments but are launched from presuppositions of their own. Every reading, then, is a critical reading, a theoretical argument written from a particular perspective in order to demonstrate a particular theoretical effect.

If both specific and generalized social-scientific arguments often occur in the context and in the form of reinterpretations, then it should not be surprising that critical shifts in social-scientific opinion involve the same kind of interpretive process. Social-scientific change does not respond simply to empirical anomalies but to shifts in general assumptions. These general assumptions, in their turn, are often challenged by innovative or revolutionary readings of classical works. Just as new empirical critiques may reflect shifts in general assumptions, they may be stimulated by shifts in "historical" interpretation. It is always true, moreover, that they are accompanied and sustained by them. Every attempt at empirical revision in social science will follow one of the generalized presuppositional paths laid out in volume 1. Social-scientific change will be created or legitimated either by "revisionism" within a particular classical tradition or by overthrowing one classical tradition for another.

Finally, if it is structured disagreement that creates social-scientific classics in the first place, then in times of greater and more intense theoretical conflict rereadings become even more intellectually critical. One does not have to accept the totalistic and conflationary notions of "crisis" proposed by Robert W. Friedrichs and Alvin W. Gouldner in the wake of the 1960s to recognize that periodic feelings of crisis are empirical facts of intellectual life. If readings are central to generalized argument, then a crisis in generalized argument can fairly be seen as a crisis of interpretation. In such periods there is even less agreement and mutual understanding about what the classical founders actually said, and perhaps even stronger contention about who the founders actually were. It is not coincidental, therefore, that major works which sought to address themselves to the turbulence of sociology in the late 1960s— Gouldner's *The Coming Crisis in Western Sociology* (1970), Friedrichs' *A Sociology of Sociology* (1970), and Anthony Giddens' *Capitalism and Modern Social Theory* (1972)—all initiated wide-ranging "revisions" of classical texts even as they portrayed themselves as arguing from social rather than independent intellectual grounds. Friedrichs conducted a revisionist history of postwar sociology as prelude to his polemical reading for the conflict school. Taking explicit issue with Merton's insistence that " 'history' offers no instruction regarding the substantive viability of a 'theoretical' posture," he argued that his own enterprise would be "justified by the light it sheds on today's internecine battles over the discipline's paradigmatic base."[8] Gouldner's strategy was even more ambitious. He produced a revisionist history of all sociology itself, using this ideological backdrop to reread the entire sociological tradition, and particularly Talcott Parsons, as having a conservative and idealist intent. Polemically justifying a reduction to ideology and the production of a radical social science, Gouldner tried to insist, at the same time, that his critical arguments were rooted in interpretations of classical work.[9†] Giddens offered a more neo-Marxist reading of the ideological underpinnings of the classical tradition, explicitly connecting the crisis of sociology to a crisis of interpretation. Reconsidering Marx, Durkheim, and

Weber in a strongly anti-Parsonian way, he insisted that such a new reading would be critical to any theoretical resolution.[10†]

Any strategy of interpretive readings, of course, leads directly to the question of "history," that is, to the relation of history and theory as the issues were so precisely defined by Merton's classic essay. Yet despite the fact that theoretical efforts are directed at historical figures, at classical works rooted in the sociological past, it must be insisted, all the same, that every reading is unhistorical in a fundamental sense. I reject the distinction between history and systematics, for it is based on the false notion of a presuppositionless science and of a presuppositionless history as well. Any attempt to reconstruct the "true" historical meaning of a classical work is bound to be a useless one, for our judgments are and must inevitably be evaluative, inspired by a theoretical goal that is rooted in contemporary time. "History," indeed, might even be considered a dangerous illusion when combined with theory, for it is too often whiggish history, the account of how past theories converge with the author's own present position. Arguments for the historical convergence of classical theorizing invariably use "history" merely as legitimation.[11†] There is an ironic and latent positivism in such arguments, for they imply that the contemporary, quintessentially "modern" theorist has discovered the truth, which must, perforce, be henceforth undisputed. Convergence arguments inevitably undermine the possibility for a full consideration of general theoretical questions, for the assertion of contemporary historical agreement allows the writer to avoid facing those theoretical positions which have been historically defeated.

The problem, of course, is that history is not itself objective, and it can be invoked in radically different ways. H. Stuart Hughes and Parsons describe the triumphant emergence of normative and psychological theorizing in the generation of the 1890s; Robert N. Nisbet asserts the same triumph in the reaction to modernity more than fifty years before.[12†] Yet normative theory surely cannot be historically inevitable if it can be effectively demonstrated as having arisen at two very different historical times. Even more revealing, there is an argument for convergence that reads intellectual history in precisely the opposite way. For Halévy and Horkheimer, for example, what characterized "modern" theorizing was its drastic break with Romantic ideas, its embrace of instrumental and technical modes of analysis.[13†] As the very existence of such contradictory arguments suggests, there has, in fact, been no linear historical development. To argue for any such convergence—in either positive or negative terms—is to reduce theoretical to empirical argument. Historical evidence cannot substitute for theoretical argument. Theoretical debates have not been settled once and for all with the emergence of this most modern of times. Presuppositional conflicts continue to provide the axes of dispute throughout different historical periods. Although one position may be stronger at one point in time, there are usually sufficient historical carriers to assure the survival of every theoretical strand.[14†]

Behind theoretical arguments for convergence, then, there is a vulgar kind of consensus history. For my part, I believe no consensus exists, and I intend in the following chapters to illustrate the origins of the conflicting sociological traditions. In this sense, I do not reject history at all, only "history." An honest and truly historical understanding of the circumstances of social theory will reveal strong conflicts, and strong points of agreement as well. We must know something about the historical context within which a theory was constructed if we are to understand that theoretical language itself, yet that language cannot be understood simply by knowledge of its history alone.

But just as I must reject the convergence argument, I must argue against the equally distorted use of history that presents theory as in unprecedented crisis. In a strange way, "crisis" theory is actually the other side of the convergence argument, its mirror image. Where convergence is optimistic and whiggish history, crisis argument is apocalyptic. It foresees the imminent transformation of theoretical debate, a transformation which will leave nothing familiar, a millenium in which theoretical disagreement will be no more. In fact, however, while theoretical crises may indicate greater analytic disagreement, this is not the actual source for the acute feelings of distress. What a "crisis" suggests, rather, is that these analytic disagreements have become superimposed on ideological ones. It is this superimposition that creates the sense of fissure and fragmentation throughout a discipline. Proponents of crisis theory argue that this empirical fact of superimposition is actually a structural inevitability: "history" has produced ideological configurations whose respective theories are bound to talk past one another. But this dramatic narrative distorts the true nature of sociological thought, creating a much tighter relationship between cognitive and ideological elements than theoretical logic actually allows.[15†] Crisis arguments, then, actually undermine further the possibilities for common communication, rational argument, and critique. As in the misuse of history presented by the convergence school, the effect of "crisis theory" is to divert intellectual attention from the actual theoretical issues involved and to focus it on the social origins of the crisis itself. If social and historical developments have created theoretical crisis, then it is only natural that they will provide the map for their resolution. But like any other interpretive reading, crisis theorists have a polemical bias of their own. They refer to the forces of history, but history is always on their own analytical side. If "history" were actually so decisive, after all, why should they engage in such vigorous reinterpretations of texts?

I have earlier laid out the grounds upon which one can hope to engage in more objective argument (vol. 1, ch. 4). I approach interpretation in terms of the distinctive presuppositional criteria established above. I will try to demonstrate that it is these very generalized questions which have informed the basic structures of classical thought, that it was by virtue of certain presuppositional decisions that the founding fathers achieved what they regarded as their greatest contributions, and that it was the limitations of their presuppositional insight that created the problems they could not resolve. These classical theorists, I will demonstrate, were far from the objective fact-mongerers which the positivist persuasion has portrayed. Nor did they focus only on the more specific levels of scientific commitment, as other reductionist arguments would contend. These theorists searched also for answers to general questions, for "solutions" to the enigma of human action and the riddle of social order. They studied the empirical world, I contend, in part to document and specify the answers they developed and presupposed.

My readings of classical sociology will not hinge on new discoveries of buried texts, or translations of heretofore untranslated works, or rely on "recent scholarship" to justify claims—though I do hope to make some textual "discoveries," to offer new translations if they are warranted, and certainly to utilize recent scholarship whenever I can.[16†] My contribution, rather, rests upon the nature of theoretical argument itself. I will evaluate and criticize the founding fathers from the perspective of a multidimensional theory; for it was, I believe, the failure to understand and fully embrace a truly synthetic logic that marked the barriers of classical thought. The failure to achieve multidimensionality, I will demonstrate, defined the apparently inexplicable residual categories of their work. It also defined the tasks of their students and successors. The mark of an outstanding student is his sensitivity to the unresolved theoretical tensions in his master's legacy. Revision is made under the cover of loyal exegesis, but it is structured—often unconsciously—by the strains in the original work, and in the greatest students it involves the attempt to overcome them.

If one were to insist that the validity of interpretive readings must stand or fall on a single "crucial experiment," it would be the challenge to explain the course of the exegesis and apparently devoted "isms," or schools, that have grown up around the major figures of classical thought. If the perspective that informs my reading is sufficiently generalized, and the reading itself sufficiently responsive to the shifting course of the actual texts, my interpretation should explain not only the tensions in the work of the original theorist but of his school as well and, indeed, the conflicts and divisions in the secondary literature which has sought to explicate both in turn.[17†] It is to this task that I now turn.

Part One

COLLECTIVE ORDER AND THE AMBIGUITY ABOUT ACTION

Chapter Two

MARX'S FIRST PHASE (1)

From Moral Criticism to External Necessity

If the theoretical significance of "readings" were ever in doubt, one need only observe the crucial significance that rereadings of Marx have had for successive generations of Western social thinkers. The relationship between interpretation and social theory announces itself not only directly, as in Louis Althusser's *Reading "Capital,"* but in the more camouflaged manner by which each generation of Marxist thought has presented its most important theoretical revisions as simply defining, once again, the contents of Marx's original work, from Labriola's *Essays in the Materialist Conception of History* and Plekhanov's *The Materialist Conception of History* to Lefebvre's *Dialectical Materialism* and Sartre's *Critique of Dialectical Reason.*

The central problem in Marx's work, all agree, is the relation between freedom and necessity. I will argue that in Marx's mature writing this relationship manifests itself as a tension between Marx's ideological commitment to the expansion of freedom and his theoretical commitment to the determination of individual acts by an external collective order. It is the determination by such a collective order that produces the paradox which haunts Marx's theory and stimulates its continual reinterpretation: Marxism is an antivoluntaristic social theory which functions, ideologically, to stimulate active, voluntaristic change. It was, nevertheless, in his depiction of the rational structures of this collective order that Marx took the greatest pride; it was his propositions about the evolution of this collective order, and its ineluctable effects on individuals and groups, that qualified him, in his view, as a true social "scientist."

Of late, this description of Marx as the pioneer of an antivoluntaristic structuralism has been thrown into great doubt, and the younger generation of his interpreters has not simply salvaged some antideterministic strands but often declared Marx's theory to be fully multidimensional. I will dispute these interpretations, and argue that they misperceive Marx by confusing certain crucial issues in the generalized logic of presuppositional reasoning. Before entering into this debate, however, I must refer to theoretical errors of a much more common variety, namely, the failure to perceive the significance of generalized reasoning at all.

1. REDUCTION AND CONFLATION IN MARXIST INTERPRETATION

Until the most recent generation of Marxist scholarship, the deterministic view of Marx was widely accepted, yet it was almost always justified or criticized by reference to non-presuppositional levels of theoretical commitment. At the most specific level, positivist interpreters linked the crucial character of Marx's theory to observational statements, and ultimately, to the nature of the empirical world which he observed and within which he worked. In the 1890s, Engels and Kautsky praised Marx for his revolutionary science of economic determinism.[1†] Karl Korsch echoed this evaluation in the 1930s, arguing that Marx's fame rested upon the accuracy of his economic predictions and upon his acute depiction of the course of class struggle.[2†] Yet as early as the mid-1890s, Marx's critics based themselves on such a positivist level as well. Edward Bernstein argued that economic developments such as the effect of economic monopoly disproved Marx's immiseration theory and consequently cast doubt on his emphasis on the determinism of economic crises under capitalism.[3] A generation later, Robert Michels argued that the development of hierarchy in socialist parties disproved Marx's mechanistic theory of class revolution.[4] In the postwar period, analysts like Serge Mallet, David Lockwood, John A. Goldthorpe, and André Gorz have argued that late capitalism created forms of embourgeoisement that would force revolutionary strategies to shift to a more subjectivist concern with worker alienation.[5] T. B. Bottomore, one of the most preeminent positivist sociologists in the Marxist tradition, has also supported this kind of empirical critique, reasoning that it is the fate of the ideological orientation of new middle classes that must decide the fate of contemporary radical movements.[6]

I have argued that such purely "evidentiary" arguments are not, in fact, theoretical at all. Despite the wealth of empirical evidence contrary to Marx's original propositions, Marxism has continued to be a vital theoretical movement. Given the impact of generalized commitments, empirical propositions can be revised, and the integrity of apparently "falsified" theories can remain very much intact. Perhaps the best indication of the weakness of this positivist approach is, indeed, the way interpretation has continued to focus on considerations of much more generalized import.

At the opposite end of the continuum from the positivist persuasion, interpreters have explained—often rationalized—Marx's determinism by pointing not to the state of the evidence but to the social conditions within which this evidence was pursued. Lewis A. Coser argues that it was the backwardness of Germany, with its legal exclusion of the working class, that produced Marx's belief in the inevitably revolutionary effect of class struggle.[7] Anthony Giddens takes this sociology of knowledge in a different direction. Starting from the postulate that the fundamental ideas of the classical thinkers are not as divergent as many have suggested, he claims that particular historical circumstances, namely, the unusual nature of English development, led Marx to emphasize economic over political factors, and that his more general theory is not economic at all.[8] Conservative critics have offered explanations which, though ideologically incompatible, follow from the same theoretical logic. Robert A. Nisbet, for example, argues that Marx's determinism proceeds from his revolutionary drive for power and his antihumanitarian acceptance of coercion.[9] Since the logic of such sociological reduction leads ultimately to ad hominum argument, it is not surprising that critics have also explained Marx's determinism as the projection of a neurotic mind.[10] Finally, the attempt to reduce Marx's determinism to its social base has often taken an indirect course. Critics like George Lichtheim, Shlomo Avineri, and Jürgen Habermas argue that it was not Marx himself but actually prewar German social-democracy, with the immobility produced by its bureaucratized party structure, that produced the antivoluntaristic qualities of Marxist thinking in the twentieth century.[11]

While these two kinds of arguments present perhaps the classical genres of Marxist explanation, the tradition has also been strongly affected by more recent modes of theoretical debate. More than any other contemporary critic, Ralf Dahrendorf is responsible for the argument that Marx is, most of all, a "conflict" theorist. It is from his perception of empirical conflict, Dahrendorf argues, that the most crucial aspects of Marx's determinism, for example his antinormative emphasis, derive.[12] Piotr Sztompka, in contrast, argues that the crucial commitment in Marx's work is to a functional model, and links Marx's notion of rational-purposive action to his systems theory.[13] The wellsprings of Marx's thought have also been linked to his metamethodological commitments. Althusser defends the later writings as the beginning of modern positive science, and sees Marx's economic determinism as linked inextricably to this scientific commitment to explanation.[14] Habermas and Albrecht Wellmer make a similar judgment but draw opposite conclusions: it is the problem of positivism that leads Marx's later writings to the brink of determinism.[15]

While these arguments accept, either implicitly or explicitly, a view of Marx's theory as deterministic, what is crucial for the present argument is that they have supported or criticized this view in an insufficiently generalized way. Each writer conflates Marx's theory with one of its parts. I would argue, to the contrary, that such particularized kinds of evaluations are incapable of justifying or refuting Marx's theory as such. For this task more generalized reference is required.

It is one of the great merits of most of the recent Marxist interpretation that it has based its argument for an antideterminist Marx precisely on an interpretation of his presuppositional stance. It is true, of course, that this generalized argument for voluntarism still can become mired in traditional kinds of confusions. Thus, within the existentialist tradition, Sartre and those influenced by him, like Dick Atkinson, often link Marx's theoretical voluntarism to his recognition of the autonomy of the individual act, to his recognition of the chance and randomness involved in any particular event.[16] That Marx recognized this kind of autonomy, however, should never have been in doubt; the question of voluntarism rests upon the resolution of more complex and problematic issues in theoretical logic.

Most of Marx's recent interpreters, quite correctly, link voluntarism more directly to questions of epistemology and to the logic of social causality. Cognizant that voluntarism depends on subjectivity, they point to the social and interactional, not rational and reflective, quality of Marx's epistemology. It is from this epistemological clarification that they move to the issue of social causality, arguing that Marx evidenced a strong concern with consciousness and with the ideological and cultural elements that distort it. For its most influential contemporary interpreters, indeed, Marx's thought is prototypically multidimensional. Giddens describes Marx as "break[ing] through the traditional philosophical division between idealism and materialism" and declares that the question of whether "ideas are mere 'epiphenomena' which have no 'independent' part to play" in Marx's thought is, by now, essentially a dead issue.[17] Bertell Ollman, who has offered the most detailed and original investigation into Marx's social philosophy, argues: "Though Marx . . . emphasizes the effect until then neglected proceeding from material factors, the full cloth, Marxism, is the product of the dialectical intertwining of the two."[18]

In making this claim, interpreters have stressed the continuity between Marx's "mature" work (typically considered as beginning with *The Communist Manifesto* in 1848) and his "early" writings (generally, the pre-1848 work), for it is the younger Marx who most directly considers subjectivity and its relation to the supra-individual world. In my discussion of Marx's thought, I will, therefore, turn initially to these early writings. I will indicate, first, that they are much more complex than has traditionally been assumed and that in the course of even this early development Marx's theoretical logic becomes increasingly ambiguous. More importantly, I will argue that by the time Marx approaches the end of this early period, in the famous manuscripts of 1844, his theoretical logic evidences a decidedly deterministic bent. Indeed, in the last of these early writings—in the three transitional works written between 1845 and 1847—Marx creates the generalized basis for his more specific, empirically oriented theory of historical materialism, the "Marxism" that the world came to know only with the publication of *The Communist Manifesto* in 1848.

2. "EARLY WRITINGS": FROM NORMATIVE TENSION TO UTILITARIAN CALCULATION

There are three distinct stages in Marx's early thought, stages which are not usually differentiated from one another, let alone considered separately from Marx's more fully developed later work.

With Marx, one must assume from the outset a critical ideological intention. Whether from psychological predisposition, intellectual milieu, or historical circumstances, radical opposition characterized his intellectual work at least from the period of his doctoral dissertation in 1839, the point at which his sophisticated writing begins. Of course, in ideological terms this oppositional stance changes in significant ways, most importantly from radical democracy to humanistic socialism and, later still, to more class-oriented socialism. From the standpoint of the present argument, however, the crucial point is the theoretical logic by which these oppositional, critical impulses were expressed, the presuppositions which encapsulate not only Marx's ideological criticisms but also his empirical observations of inequality and alienation and his model of the contradictory capitalist system. It is these presuppositions, we will find, which undergo the most crucial changes and which play the most ramifying role in the evolution of Marx's early writings into the "Marxism" which was to change the world.

2.1. MORAL CRITICISM AND THE APPEAL TO UNIVERSAL NORMS: THE STARTING POINT

In the period 1839 through 1842, Marx engaged in a form of Hegelianism. He certainly was not simply a follower of the great idealist theorist; he was conscious of a radical break from Hegel and, even in this early period, was concerned to save the "rational kernel" of Hegel's thought and discard the system as a whole. Yet while Marx sharply challenged Hegel's ideological commitments and empirical propositions, he accepted, in good part, Hegel's general presuppositions.

For Hegel, while man is inevitably confined to particular conditions, as a thinking subject he can lift himself beyond these particular circumstances to achieve a universalistic perspective on his world. This connection to universal thought provides for the achievement of human freedom and also, in Hegel's view, man's relation to divinity.[19] It was this access to divine universality that inspired the "young Hegelian" movement of the 1830s, a movement that radicalized Hegel's understanding by stressing the separation and tension between universalism, which was of divine inspiration, and mankind's actual circumstances, which remained particularistic. Given this inspiration, it was not accidental that these radical humanists focused primarily on the critique of religion, which, they believed, perpetuated an artificial separation between divine and human nature. It was in their religious critique, which had strong political overtones, that the young Hegelians practiced the philosophical activity of "criticism," a term most clearly associated with Marx's future teacher and older colleague, Bruno Bauer.

In the four-year period which is our present concern, Marx produced a doctoral dissertation and a series of articles which, though printed as "journalism," are much more essays on social philosophy than sociological discussions of current events. Though Marx develops here a distinctive theoretical position of his own, his links to the young Hegelians remain clear. In terms of the problem of order, Marx is, from the very beginning, anti-individualist. Yet he is also decidedly anti-materialist; he believes that a spiritual or normative order undergirds the apparently private and materialistic activity of institutional life, both domestic and political. While marriage, for example, seems to be a matter "only of *individual will*," subject to "the caprice of the spouses," in actuality it has a supra-individual reality, an "ethical substance."[20] The same is true for the state. Contrary to public perception, the legislator "does not *make* law"; this would imply an individualism which does not, in fact, exist. Rather, the legislator "expresses the inner principles [or inner laws] of spiritual relationships in conscious, positive laws."[21]

Marx believed that in the unique historical period of post-Hegelian Germany this normative order had assumed a universalistic form. There existed a general morality over and above particular interests. This "morality as morality, as the principle of a world with its own laws" stood in sharp contrast to such particularistic normative standards as "discipline, morals, and outward loyalty" as they were so often embodied in concrete institutions as "police-regulated honorability." True, these latter, particularistic standards also represented forms of supra-individual moral obligation. Yet they were "laws without objective norms."[22] More universalistic, objective norms, therefore, often had to present themselves in forms that opposed traditional morality. Thus, in contrast to actual religion, "morality recognizes only its own universal and rational religion."[23]

This universalistic morality manifests itself in "reason." For the Hegelianized Marx, the rationality which reason provides for action means that action is regulated by a specific set of normative standards, but this does not mean that people act rationally in an instrumental, antinormative sense.[24†] Marx is committed, at this point in his thought, to the depiction of a collective order that rests upon an anti-instrumental perception of action.

In certain historical periods, Marx believed, normative order becomes articulated by philosophy. At these "nodal points" in history, philosophy embodies "abstract principles" which "turn against the apparent world."[25] In these periods, "philosophy asks what is true . . . for *all* men, not what is true for individuals; its metaphysical truths do not recognize the boundaries of political geography."[26] Because "spiritual existence has become . . . enriched to universality," the "totality of the world is implicitly split."[27] It is to this split in normative order that philosophy addresses itself as a form of normatively rational action.

Philosophy, Marx emphasizes, has primarily a subjective reference, as it must to prefigure a normative rather than external order: "Philosophy as *subjective* consciousness relates itself to actuality." It is this inner reference, indeed, that allows philosophy to be critical, to espouse "the general principle of all religions; the sacredness and inviolability of subjective conviction."[28] It is because Marx conceives of actors as referring to an inner, normatively structured order that he can so strongly emphasize the voluntary quality of action. "It is a psychological law that the theoretical mind," having become in certain circumstances "free in itself," emerges as *"will"* and "turns against the worldly actuality which exists outside of it."[29] In these periods, therefore, criticism is the most perfect form of philosophical activity. It presents the prototypical case of how universal normative references can forge the subjective roots of voluntarism. "The *practice* of philosophy," Marx writes, "is itself *theoretical*. It is *criticism* which measures individual existence against essence, particular actuality against the Idea."[30]

In 1842, when Marx was forced to pursue a career outside the academe, it was only natural, given these theoretical commitments, that he would pursue a career of public criticism. In his intellectual journalism Marx could bring the universalistic ideals embodied in philosophy into the public domain, for the normative order which regulated philosophy certainly applied as well to everyday life. "The same spirit that builds philosophical systems in the brains of the philosophers," Marx argues, "builds railroads by the hands of the workers."[31]

Marx's crusading intellectual journalism takes aim at the pollution of public morality by the sources of reaction which had popularized particularistic morality. His criticism of Prussian newspaper censorship clearly reveals the collective and normative presuppositions of this early work. The danger of censorship is not simply that it affects the *"behavior of individual* citizens,"* he writes, but that it affects the "behavior of the public mind."[32] Censorship is effective not because of its physical force, but because through its power it can establish a distorted, particularistic kind of normative order: "Censorship is official criticism; its norms are critical norms." It is, therefore, the morality established by censorship which must be subjected to radical criticism.[33]

If the masses of citizens are as sensitive to normative order as philosophers, Marx's strategy is clear. Through his journalistic philosophizing, Marx will unleash the "clarifying words of public rationality." By referring to the universalistic elements in the public morality, he will appeal to "the test of doubt."[34] Such critical reformulation of the public mind is, he argues, the crucial strategy in any attempt at practical reform:

> Dangerous practical attempts, even those on a large scale, can be answered . . . but *ideas*, which have conquered our intelligence and our minds, ideas that reason has forged in our *conscience* are *chains* from which we cannot tear ourselves away without breaking our hearts.[35]

Public criticism must break these internalized moral chains and create new, more universalistic affective attachments. It can do so, however, only in a voluntaristic way, by appealing to the "troubled conscience" produced by the encounter between an individual's universalistic ideals and the limited circumstances of his objective reality.[36]

Public criticism consists precisely in exacerbating this tension through public suasion that appeals to universalistic morality. Thus, in an article directed both to public officials and citizens alike, Marx criticizes press censorship in the following terms:

> You order us to have trust, and [yet] you bestow legal powers on distrust. . . . You demand of the officials that they act impersonally, without anger, passion, narrow mindedness and human frailty. But you suspect that impersonal *ideas* are full of personal intrigues and subjective baseness.[37]

In another piece, he argues against the historical, or positive, school of law on the grounds that "what is *positive* [i.e., what exists empirically] . . . is *uncritical*." "If *reason* were the norm of what is *positive*," Marx insists, "then what is positive would not be the norm of reason." On these grounds he can argue that positive law "*desecrates* everything that is *sacred* to lawful, moral, political man."[38] And in a later article, which remained unpublished, Marx argues against the notion that religious education should be supported by the state. If the state relies on actual religion for its instruction, he claims, it ignores the true moral order, which is more universalistic than any particular religion. The "true 'public' education of the state" must rest, therefore, on a less explicit and more generalized process of moral socialization: "The state educates its members . . . by transforming the aims of the individual into universal aims, by transforming raw impulses into ethical articulation."[39] In the terms that we shall later find articulated by another great classical theorist, Marx would promote change by increasing the tension between sacred and profane morality.

2.2. NATURAL NECESSITY AND THE APPEAL
TO SELF-INTEREST:
THE INITIAL TRANSITION

By the end of 1842, Marx's social theory began to undergo a clearly discernible shift in emphasis. Though the biographical events associated with this period can in no sense validate our purely theoretical analysis, they can, nevertheless, serve to make this theoretical movement more comprehensible. A variety of factors, in fact, coalesced in these months to push Marx's general orientation in a more instrumentalist direction: the increasing censorship of the *Rheinische Zeitung*, of which Marx had been editor; his participation in a study group on "social questions" organized by the communist Moses Hess; the intensity and radicalism of the political climate in Cologne; finally, the appearance in 1842 of Lorenz von Stein's *The Socialism and Communism of Present-Day France*, which Marx and his associates studied assiduously.[40]

In this movement away from his earlier theoretical position, two phases are clearly discernible. In late 1842 and January 1843, Marx was called upon to write about aspects of a series of controversial economic issues for the *Rheinische Zeitung*. He perceived these facts through lenses that were decidedly more instrumentalist than the ones he had worn in his previous work. The first of these articles dealt with the legal problems of Rhineland farmers, who had traditionally been free to gather wood from common land. With industrialization and the increasing scarcity of wooded land, these traditional rights were violated, and the farmers were increasingly prosecuted for theft. Marx objected to this prosecution, in part, on the grounds that the economic circumstances of the farmers left them no choice; insofar as this violation was not voluntary, they had not violated any truly universalistic standards of morality.[41]

Marx expanded on this theme more forcefully in a companion article, where he investigated the increasing impoverishment of the Moselle winegrowers in an effort to corroborate a correspondent whose accuracy had been questioned by a Prussian political authority. In response to the authority's doubts about the validity of the winegrowers' complaints, Marx argues that these complaints were objective, not subjective, and that they derived from material, not spiritual, sources. The contrast with his earlier perception of order and action could not be more striking. While he continues to argue that social issues must be seen in terms of social relationships, not individuals, this collective order is now external and opposed to individual will.

> In the investigation of political conditions one is too easily tempted to overlook the objective nature of the relationships and to explain everything from the *will* of the persons acting. There are relationships, however, which *determine* the actions of private persons as well as those of individual authorities, *and which are as independent as are the movements of breathing*.[42]

The latter, physical reference is not coincidental, for Marx has shifted radically in his approach to rebellion. Oppositional activity is no longer voluntary and willed, but rather a natural necessity produced by the exteriority of collective constraint. "As soon as it is demonstrated that something was *necessitated* by conditions," Marx writes, "it will not be difficult to figure out under which *external* circumstances this thing actually *had* to come into being."[43] For the first time, an analogy is employed which will become only too familiar in his subsequent work. Marx compares himself to a natural scientist and, correspondingly, parallels external social processes with natural, physical dynamics: "One can determine this with almost the same certainty as a chemist determines under which *external* circumstances some substances will form a compound."[44] Such positivism, of course, neatly reinforces Marx's dependence on deterministic presuppositional logic.

Still, in neither of these two articles does Marx offer a completely instrumentalist approach. In both, he remains at least partly committed to his earlier logic. It is this ambiguity that makes the articles transitional; rather than seeing Marx as giving up his earlier commitments, it would be more correct to say that while remaining true to them he has entered into a new realm whose contradictory implications he has not yet fully understood. The earlier presuppositional perspective is most clearly seen in the solution Marx offers to the problems he has described in such a distinctively instrumental way. The local authorities, he argues, must more fully institutionalize the universalistic morality which is already a significant, if not yet dominant, part of the normative order. In his discussion of wood theft, for example, Marx defends the validity of customary, tradition-bound law against administrative decree, and recommends that law should be connected to the "whole complex of civic reasoning and civic morality" rather than to economic consideration and interests.[45] In the article on the Moselle winegrowers, he offers a similarly normative resolution: "To resolve the difficulty, the administrator and administered both need a third element . . . which at the same time represents the citizen [*ist bürgerlich*] without being directly involved in private interests." This resolving element, he argues, is the free press, which is composed of "a political mind and a civic heart [*bürgerlichen Herz*]."[46]

A second phase of this transition appears in early 1843, when Marx begins to give his new intellectual sensibility a more formal and explicit theoretical form. With the shift in late 1842, Marx had initiated a break from Hegel much more radical than the conflict over ideological and empirical issues which had demarcated the "young Hegelian" group. He was moving now toward an instrumentalist position that rejected the most generalized elements of Hegel's thought, particularly Hegel's commitment to a collectivity informed by normatively governed action. Marx's essays of 1843 directly confront Hegel's political, social, and religious philosophy at the most generalized level.

If any single catalyst marked this new phase of Marx's transition it was his encounter with Feuerbach. Though certainly Marx was familiar with Feuerbach's earlier writings, it was the *Preliminary Theses for Reform of Philosophy*, published in February 1843, that made a deeper impression on him.[47] Feuerbach, indeed, generated immediate and widespread controversy by launching a quasi-materialist critique of Hegel. Arguing that Hegel placed too much emphasis on the "spiritual" subject, he claimed that this contributed to Hegel's undue optimism about the social realization of universal order. A more realistic position, Feuerbach proposed, would reverse this emphasis and place the "predicate" —material being—in a position ontologically prior to the spiritual realm. Like the French materialists who had so influenced his thought, Feuerbach could now argue that being determined consciousness. What was more, by so radically separating the universal qualities of the human spirit, or "species-being," from natural being, he could now argue that man's present condition was one of alienation: Feuerbach's thought was a naturalism stripped of any spiritual qualities.

Although Feuerbach did not create Marx's movement toward an instrumentalist position, he gave this movement a form which allowed Marx to develop his instrumentalism within the formal conceptual vocabulary of Hegelianism, in terms of the tension between subject and object, universalism and particularism, objectification and alienation. Biographical factors were also significant, and they "overdetermined" this intellectual shift. The *Rheinische Zeitung* was shut down by Prussian authorities, and Marx left for Paris with the hope for another editorship there. In France, he moved for the first time within an almost exclusively socialist circle, an international group which included Mauer, Proudhon,

Blanc, and Bakunin, and which emphasized, in contrast with Marx's early "radical democracy," the determinate role of economics in social life.[48] Finally, it was in 1843 that Marx began his first serious readings in social and political history, particularly that of America and France. None of these personal facts, of course, "explains" Marx's changing theoretical orientation; they simply provide contextual corroboration for the kinds of rapid shifts which are readily observable in his intellectual life.

In the writings of 1843 there emerges for the first time the division between material life and consciousness which later becomes formalized in Marx's base-superstructure model. Though in this early work Marx describes the split in terms of a "civil society" opposed to political or religious life, the logic of the division is basically similar. More importantly, however, Marx roots this social model in presuppositions that directly contradict his earlier assumptions. His argument appears first in the "Contribution to the Critique of Hegel's *Philosophy of Right*" in the form of paragraph-by-paragraph commentaries on this crucial Hegel text. Only in the "Essay on the Jewish Question," however, does this new theoretical orientation emerge in full-blown form.

Addressing himself to the order question, Marx refers first to the normative community and individual interdependence implied by democratic political society. Yet while such political life might appear to realize "species being" —and certainly did once so appear to Marx himself—it is, he now argues, actually an "unreal universality."[49] In civil society, which constitutes the real concrete stage for human existence, there is no collective normative order. Indeed, Marx employs the terms "material life" and "civil society" [*bürgerliche Gesellschaft*] interchangeably.[50†] Normative order cannot exist, because Marx views the individual as an "isolated monad" radically separated from his fellow man.[51] In civil society, the individual leads an "egoistic life"; "he acts simply as a private individual."[52] There is no possibility here for the spiritual, or normative, order that Marx earlier described as the basis of institutional life: "Man is separated from the community, from himself, and from other men."[53] The legal rights to individual freedom and political equality, which Marx once connected to the universalistic normative order, are now declared merely ephemeral. Normative order, after all, is not really order at all. "The so-called rights of man," he contends, are simply the reflection of material separation, "of egoistic man, of man separated from other men and from the community."[54]

The logical corollary to this negation of normative order is an instrumental, technical understanding of action, and this is precisely what Marx describes. "The only bond between men," he argues, "is . . . private *interest*."[55] Action is reduced to instrumentality: man "treats other men as *means*."[56]

Because he retains his commitment to collective order, Marx must move, ineluctably, toward an antivoluntarist position. "Degrad[ing] himself to the role of a mere means," man is powerless against an order that is external to his volition. Man becomes "the plaything of alien powers."[57] Far from asserting their autonomy through the application of universalistic reason, men now live in the realm of "natural necessity."[58]

This position is basically reiterated in Marx's "Contribution to the Critique of Hegel's *Philosophy of Right*," written at the end of 1843. It is amplified, however, in one particularly crucial way. There exists an economic class, Marx now asserts, that embodies in itself the demand for renewed community and normative action. Moreover, this class understands that in order to achieve this new form of action and order, private property must be abolished through the institutionalization of socialism.[59] With his discovery of the proletariat as the empirical specification of his more generalized presuppositions, Marx is ready for his marriage with political economy, a relationship that is consummated in the manuscripts of 1844.

The writings of 1843, however, still mark a transitional phase in Marx's presuppositional development; they contribute to a transformation that is not yet complete. And, indeed, alongside this strongly-stated instrumentalist position one still finds, as in the immediately preceding journalistic pieces, references to normative order and anti-instrumental action which give evidence of Marx's earlier commitments. In one sense, these references might be called residual categories, for they certainly have no positively defined role in the logic of civil society which Marx has described. Yet in another and equally valid sense these are not residual; they stand on their own as pieces of self-contained theorizing in continuity with Marx's earlier work.

In terms of causal reasoning, the most significant contradictory element appears in the famous paragraph on religion in Marx's "Contribution to the Critique of Hegel's *Philosophy of Right*." It is true that this passage may be read as simply reaffirming the dualism of the "civil society" conception; thus, Marx describes religion as the "inverted world consciousness" that is the "reflex" of an "inverted world." Yet this analysis of religion actually says much more:

> Religion is the *general theory* of this world, its encyclopedic *compendium*, its *logic* in popular form, its spiritual *point d'honneur*, its enthusiasm, its moral sanction, its solemn complement, its *general basis* of consolation and justification. It is the fantastic realization of the human being inasmuch as the human being possesses no true reality.[60]

According to this analysis, social life demands a general theory, a metaphysical rationalization which also has a popular form, in sum, a normative order which springs from internal as well as external sources. Moreover, this order, once created, will follow a certain logic of its own. It will impose solemn moral sanctions while allowing the release of enthusiasm and providing consolation; it will complement the material world while realizing, at the same time, some utopian fantasies of fulfillment.

All this recalls Marx's earlier, more normative presuppositions. Action is portrayed here in an anti-instrumental way. If it is consciousness that inverts the world, "reason" still exists, for action must have reference to an order, or promise, beyond immediate circumstance. In this sense, alienation becomes an active rather than passive variable, for individuals have an "interest" in reason, the achievement of universalism which, even in the most constricting situation, will transmute human needs into universalistic ideals. In this way, society sustains enthusiasm, notions of spiritual honor, and commitments to moral justification, all of which have pretensions to universality and present implicit points of tension with more particularistic institutions.

On the basis of this anti-instrumental perspective, Marx can reaffirm another theme from his earlier work: the social significance of moral criticism. Religion must be criticized by philosophy, which embodies universalism in a more direct and less compromised way. By reference to this higher normative order, man can become more active and free. "The criticism of religion," Marx insists, "disillusions man so that he will think, act and fashion his reality as a man who has lost his illusion and gained his reason."[61] Moral criticism of religion, then, constitutes independent leverage against the material world: "The struggle against religion is, therefore, indirectly a struggle against *that world* whose spiritual aroma is religion."[62]

Marx now sets out a program in which such religious criticism serves as a model for the kind of universalistic judgments which should be made against other social spheres, a process by which "the criticism of heaven is transformed into the criticism of earth."[63] In the revolutionary struggle for communism, he believes, such theoretical, normative reasoning will be a vital force. Though it is true that "material force can only be overthrown by material force," Marx insists that the division of normative and material order is not absolute because "theory itself becomes a material force when it has seized the masses."[64] A revolution, of course, needs a material base, and for this reason it must depend upon the proletariat. Yet this material force presents only the "passive element."[65] It is ideas, acting in reference to the philosophically articulated normative order, that create the active dimension of the revolutionary movement. For historical precedence, Marx points to the Protestant Reformation. "Just as [in the Reformation], it was once the *monk*," he writes, "so it is now the *philosopher* in whose brain the revolution begins."[66]

Marx notes approvingly the "monstrous discrepancy between the demands of German thought and the answers of German reality."[67] Indeed, the strategy of criticism will succeed as a revolutionary force precisely because German thought has created internalized norms and commitments that are in tension with actors' material environments. If this tension is sufficiently magnified, the result will be an internally rooted revulsion against conservatism. "The burden [of civil society]," Marx argues, "must be made still more irksome by awakening a consciousness of it, and shame must be made more painful still by rendering it public."[68] From this shame, the internal resources of voluntarism can develop: "The nation must be taught to be *terrified* of itself, in order to give it *courage*."[69] It is no wonder that Marx argues that the revolutionary struggle must be waged as much against the self as against external forces: "It is no longer a question, therefore, of the layman's struggle against the priest outside himself, but of his struggle against his *own internal priest*, against his own *priestly nature*."[70]

The striking ambiguity of Marx's thought in 1843 is even more clearly revealed in a series of public letters he wrote later that year to his friend and associate, Arnold Ruge, which appeared in the first, and last, issue of the *Deutsch-Französische Jahrbücher* in February of 1844. During the same period in which he was setting out a philosophical rationale for the atomism and determinism of bourgeois civil society, these letters again reaffirm the themes of transcendent order and voluntaristic action.

The revolution, Marx contends, founders because of volitional weakness more than from external barriers: "Even greater than the external obstacles seem to be the inner ones."[71] Socialist practice, unfortunately, usually ignores this element in its attention to material factors. "The entire socialistic principle," Marx writes, "is only *one* side of the reality of true human nature. We have to be concerned just as much with the *other* side, the *theoretical* existence of man."[72] Theory can activate the masses only by awakening their emotional and moral commitment to the idea of freedom.

> Freedom, the *feeling* of man's dignity, will first have to be awakened again in these men. Only this feeling, which disappeared from the world with the Greeks and with Christianity vanished in the blue mist of heaven, can again *transform society* into a community of men to achieve their highest purposes, a democratic state.[73]

The road to revolution, therefore, leads through criticism, and Marx writes to Ruge that "what we have to accomplish at this time is . . . clear: *relentless criticism of all existing conditions*."[74] Criticism appeals to reason, and reason rests, in turn, on the universalistic order that is partly—

only partly—camouflaged by civil society. By forcefully appealing to this transcendent order, criticism heightens the tension between official norms and particularistic institutions.

> The critic, therefore, can start with any form of theoretical and practical consciousness and develop the true actuality out of the forms inherent in existing actuality as its ought-to-be and goal. As far as actual life is concerned, the political state especially contains in all its modern forms the demands of reason, even where the political state is not yet conscious of its socialistic demands. And the political state does not stop here. Everywhere it claims reason as realized. Equally, however, it everywhere gets into the contradiction between its ideal character and its real presuppositions.[75]

Marx reaffirms, once again, the emphasis on consciousness and self-change that follows from the theoretical inclusion of normative order.

> Our slogan, therefore, must be: Reform of consciousness. . . . The world has long dreamed of something of which it only has to become conscious in order to possess it in actuality. . . . Therefore, we can express the aim of our periodical in one phrase: A self-understanding (critical philosophy) of the age concerning its struggles and wishes. . . . To have its sins forgiven, mankind has only to declare them for what they are.[76]

If Marx seems to cross the line here into a radical form of one-dimensional idealist voluntarism, this confusion will be clarified in his writing of 1844, when his transition to an instrumental collectivist perspective on modern society is much more substantially achieved.

2.3. ALIENATION AND THE SUBMISSION TO MATERIAL ORDER: THE AMBIVALENT ACCEPTANCE OF POLITICAL ECONOMY IN THE 1844 MANUSCRIPTS

Marx was already acquainted with political economy in 1843, as his references to the proletariat and private property in the "Contribution to the Critique of Hegel's *Philosophy of Right*" clearly indicate. Still, it was not until he encountered Friedrich Engels' essay, "Outline of a Critique of Political Economy," which appeared alongside Marx's essay in the *Deutsch-Französische Jahrbücher*, that Marx began to give economic thought his full attention. This critical work by Engels, which Marx later called a "brilliant sketch," introduced Marx to a mode of discourse that perfectly fitted the shifting direction of his own theoretical development.

By the end of 1843, when he first read Engels' essay, Marx had already sharply criticized Hegel's presuppositional commitments. Although Feuerbach's work had allowed him to continue to employ the

Hegelian tensions of subject-object, universalism-particularism, and objectification-alienation, Marx had also followed Feuerbach in his effort to materialize these Hegelian concepts. For Marx, the members of civil society were individual monads conducting themselves in an egoistical, purely self-interested way. Without reference to a transcendent moral order, the members of civil society were powerless against external force.

Marx turned to political economy because he believed it provided powerful empirical evidence for this new understanding of action and order, evidence which, because of its scientific status, presented a much more compelling case than mere philosophic casuistry or moral argument. If political economy was the truth of capitalist society, then it was no wonder that community and subjectivity were nowhere to be found. Henceforth, "capitalism" increasingly replaced "civil society" in Marx's formulations, and his earlier, purely humanistic treatment of the promise of the proletariat gave way to more firmly realistic accounts of proletarian struggle and to more empirical predictions of its eventual success.

Even now, however, Marx did not completely reject his earlier commitments. The assumption of normative community and subjectivity remained central to important aspects of Marx's discussion, though its position in his general theoretical system was now overshadowed by utilitarian elements. It is this very combination of normative Hegelianism and political economy that constitutes the riddle of this transitional period in Marx's thought.

2.3.1. The Challenge of the "Theses on Feuerbach": Philosophical Multidimensionality Reaffirmed as Species-Being

To begin to explore the complex position which emerged after Marx's encounter with political economy, one must turn first to the "Theses on Feuerbach," the famous notes that Marx sketched early in 1845 which have occupied such a central role in the debate over voluntarism in his work. In these "Theses," Marx argues that human action must be viewed as "praxis," and he defines praxis in a strikingly multidimensional way.[77†] Feuerbach viewed activity too mechanistically; he did not recognize the role of subjectivity.

> The main shortcoming of all materialism up to now (including that of Feuerbach) is that the object, the reality, sensibility, is conceived only in the form of the *object* [and] not as sensuous human activity, *practice*, not subjectively.[78]

Marx then asserts that without subjectivity there can be no opportunity for voluntarism and activism, a theoretical problem that is particularly bothersome for anyone committed, as Marx was, to a revolutionary ideology. In order to justify their political activity, revolutionary theorists emphasize the power of objective circumstances over individuals, but if these circumstances are conceived as themselves partly subjective it soon becomes evident that these circumstances are only as strong as the men behind them. "The materialistic teaching on the changing of circumstances and education forgets," Marx writes, "that the circumstances are changed by men."[79] Indeed, the one-sided objectivist emphasis in the revolutionary, materialist tradition has created a peculiar situation, for it is only in idealism that will and subjectivity have become significant theoretical elements. But this conservative idealism, from Marx's point of view, is hopelessly unrealistic: "The *active* side was developed abstractly in opposition to materialism by idealism, which naturally does not know the real, sensuous activity as such."[80] The only way to account realistically for external barriers while emphasizing the voluntarism created by human subjectivity is to define human action as praxis: "The concurrence of changing of the circumstances and of the human activity, or *self*-changing, can be conceived and rationally understood as revolutionary practice."[81]†

This argument strongly recalls the position of Marx's earliest writings. He rejects here any sharp dichotomy between subject and object, arguing that every object is invested with subjectivity and that every subject remains part of the material world. The bond, then, between actors and their environment, human or nonhuman, cannot be reduced simply to external control; correspondingly, action toward this subjectively familiar world cannot be considered simply as the utilitarian calculation of behavioral consequences. It is not by accident that Marx concludes his first and most important thesis with the statement that only by conceiving of action as praxis can one envision "practical-critical" activity.[82] It was active philosophical criticism, one may recall, that was the major proposal in Marx's earliest, subjectivist program.

Marx is now in a rather paradoxical position. On the one hand, he has argued that human activity is, on some level at least, multidimensional praxis, that the materialists are wrong about utilitarian motivation and atomistic objectivity. On the other hand, in his writings as early as 1843 he portrays civil society precisely in such mechanistic terms, as composed of isolated individuals bent on self-interested and antinormative action. In fact, Marx had worked out the solution to this theoretical dilemma in his manuscripts of 1844 (posthumously published as the "Economic and Philosophical Manuscripts"), although, as we will see, his solution is not itself devoid of theoretical ambiguity.

2.3.2. The Tentative Solution: "Natural Man" and the Instrumental Logic of Political Economy

As Marx came to see it, the key to resolving this latent dilemma lay in the contrast between human potential and social reality, in the contrast between a general mode of orientation and the contents of this orientation in a particular historical period. In the "Economic and Philosophical Manuscripts" of 1844, Marx defines the general orientation of man, his epistemology, in terms of "species-being." Qua species, human action is praxis. In the first place, it is resolutely subjective. Men have consciousness, and it is this consciousness that converts the external world into his objects:

> Man makes his life activity itself an object of his will and consciousness.... Conscious life activity distinguishes man from the life activity of animals. Only for this reason is he a species-being.[83]

It is this subjective capacity that allows men to go beyond simple utilitarian motives, that enables them to theorize about the world before them. "Man is a species-being," Marx writes, ". . . because he practically and theoretically makes the species . . . his object."[84] If it were not for such theorizing, human action would be a "determination"; man would be "completely identified" with his environment. Subjectivity, then, allows for voluntarism: "Because he is a species-being . . . his activity [is] free activity."[85]

Marx emphasizes, moreover, that the freedom provided by such a subjective approach to action does not necessarily imply an individualistic approach to order. "It is above all necessary to avoid postulating 'society' once again as an abstraction confronting the individual. The individual *is* the *social being*."[86] The distinction between the individual actor and society, therefore, must be viewed as an analytic, not concrete, distinction. "Individual human life and species-life," Marx asserts, "are not different things."[87] But how can an individual and society not be viewed as separated, when they do involve differentiated entities? This vision can be sustained only by postulating a subjective, internal bond between individuals. Indeed, this is precisely Marx's point. "Though man is a unique individual," Marx believes, "he is equally the whole, the ideal whole, the subjective existence of society as thought and experience."[88] For collective order to be complementary to freedom, it must be internal order: "As society itself produces man as man, so it is *produced* by him."[89] "Man exists in reality," Marx writes, "as the representation . . . of social existence."[90] If the concrete individual can be viewed as a subjective "representation" of social life, to that degree social life may be viewed as resting upon subjective foundations.

Yet this species-capacity is not realized in civil society, which Marx now calls capitalism—the society of private property. It is this exceptionalism that allows Marx to resolve his theoretical paradox and which provides him, in addition, with the basis for his radical ideological indictment. In capitalism, he argues, species-man has been replaced by "natu-

ral man." This reversal has occurred because of "alienation." It is not
that human life has returned completely to the condition of animal life.
Marx defines epistemological reflexivity as the very point of distinction
between man and animals, and it remains for him a constant of human
existence. What changes in capitalism is the way this human knowledge
of the external world has been formulated. Alienated action seems to be
nonhuman because knowledge has become simply utilitarian:

> Private property has made us so stupid and partial that an object
> is only *ours* when we have it, when it exists for us as capital or
> when it is directly eaten, drunk, worn, inhabited, etc., in short,
> *utilized* in some way.[91]

When an object is viewed simply from the perspective of utilization, the
end of action, the reference supplied by its inherent subjectivity, effectively disappears: action "*appears* to man only as [a] means,"[92] as focusing only on the most efficient relation to the external world. "Private
property," Marx writes, "only conceives these various possessions as a
means of life, and the life for which they serve as a means is the life of
private property."[93]

Without the reference to ends, the subjectivity of action is lost. "Just
as alienated labour transforms free and self-directed activity into a
means," Marx argues, "so it transforms the species-life of man into a
means of *physical* existence."[94] Without subjectivity, moreover, the internal bond that potentially unites actors is broken. Private property "alienates species-life and individual life."[95] The concrete separation of
empirical individuals now reflects a real analytic rupture: "The statement that man is alienated from his species-life means that each man is
alienated from others."[96]

The questions of action and order, however, are independent, and
while utilitarian, alienated individuals are necessarily atomized and discrete, this does not mean that Marx now accepts an individualistic approach to social order. He remains committed to a collectivist vision.
However, without the possibility for internalization—for the interpenetration of individual and society that is inherent in species-being—
this supra-individual order can no longer be a voluntary one. "The alienation of the worker," Marx writes, "means not only that his labour becomes an object . . . but that it exists independently, outside himself," and
that it "stands opposed to him as an autonomous power."[97] Such collective order can only be an antivoluntary one. Instead of a praxis which
creates freedom and sociality at the same time, consciousless action can
create order only as "servitude to the object."[98] In Marx's mind, one must
remember, the superiority of human to animal labor rests upon the normative character of human work. While man "knows how to apply the
appropriate *standard* to the object," he writes, animals "can produce

only under the compulsion of direct physical needs."[99] In alienated labor, this normative reference is eliminated. As physical need becomes the driving force, "[man's] work is not voluntary but imposed, *forced* labour."[100]

Marx's point could not be more explicit or his judgment more harsh. While species-capacity endows man with subjectivity and felt community, capitalism alienates man from both these qualities: "He is . . . reduced both spiritually and physically to the conditions of a machine and from being a man becomes merely an abstract activity and a belly."[101] Motivated only by utilitarian considerations and subject only to external controls, alienated man is "crude and misshapen." Alienated man is "barbarous," the quintessence of "stupidity and cretinism."[102] Still, this is a perversion of human nature, not human nature itself. The utilitarianism of capitalist society subverts what is uniquely human in man's epistemology, but does not eliminate it. Man is not, in fact, an animal, though it is true that he "*feels* himself to be freely active only in his animal functions."[103] Praxis remains the epistemological position of man, but because the alienation of praxis makes motivation exclusively rational, praxis in capitalist society appears "as if" it had no subjective, voluntary component.[104†]

It should now be clear how this decisive encounter with political economy allowed Marx to resolve the theoretical paradox he faced. Through his acceptance of political economy, Marx found empirical justification for the more generalized, anti-Hegelian commitments which had grown increasingly significant in the course of his development.

On the one hand, this acceptance was empirical. Throughout the "Manuscripts," and in his later writings as well, Marx relies heavily in his propositional analysis on the empirical laws formulated by the great political economists, like the laws of wages and capitalist competition.[105†] It is true that these laws proceed only on the assumption that action is purely utilitarian, but that, indeed, is precisely the point. Marx insists that "political economy has merely reformulated the laws of alienated labour."[106] Since he himself accepts alienation as a fact of capitalist life, he can argue that the propositions of political economy are to be viewed as valid: "We have accepted its terminology and its laws."[107] That these great traditional economists have left human morality out of their account is merely a testimony to the acuity of their empirical insight.

> M. Michel Chevalier reproaches Ricardo with leaving morals out of account. But Ricardo lets political economy speak its own language; he is not to blame if this language is not that of morals. . . .
> If there is no [moral] relation, can Ricardo be held responsible?[108]

To the contrary, in fact, Marx asserts that "it is a great step forward by

Ricardo, Mill, et al., as against Smith and Say, to declare the existence of human beings . . . as indifferent or indeed harmful."[109]

But Marx's positive approach to political economy is not limited solely to important aspects of their empirical findings, for he accepts significant elements of their presuppositional stance as well. "We have begun from the presuppositions of political economy," Marx writes, and he refers here to one presuppositional question in particular, namely, the assumption about the instrumental character of action. It is true that "political economy conceives the worker only as a draught animal, a beast whose needs are strictly limited to bodily needs," but that, after all, is the way that human nature has been perverted in capitalist society.[110] As alienated men, workers do care only about pleasure and pain. It is true that political economy argues that the worker is motivated only by calculations of utility: "It . . . proposes the thesis that he, like a horse, must receive just as much as will enable him to work."[111] But in making this assumption political economy is only doing justice to the true nature of proletarian action, for, after all, "political economy treats the proletarian . . . merely as a worker."[112] Similarly, the propositions of political economy are accurate only if individuals are assumed to be discrete and atomized. "In all political economy," Marx writes, "we find that the hostile opposition of interests, struggle and warfare are recognized as the basis of social organization."[113] But Marx can accept this, too: Is not the atomization of individuals the inevitable result of describing action as purely efficient and instrumental?

Marx's acceptance of political economy's orientation toward action could not be more forthright. Indeed, time and time again he cites its formulations as proof that alienation actually does exist. The following sequence is a familiar one in Marx's argument: while species-man subjectively controls his material production, "alienated labor reverses this relationship";[114] thus, in capitalism, the material world controls man, and the empirical law formulated by political economy, that wages are inversely related to the length and intensity of labor, is correct. For example, Marx introduces his chapter on alienated labor as follows: "We shall begin from a contemporary economic fact."[115] He follows this sentence with a discussion that moves from empirical law to an argument for alienation and, finally, to the justification for an instrumental and collectivist presuppositional position.

> The worker becomes poorer the more wealth he produces and the more his production increases in power and extent. The worker becomes an ever cheaper commodity the more goods he creates. The devaluation of the human world increases in direct relation with the increase in value of the world of things. . . . This *fact* simply implies that the object produced by labour, its

product, now stands opposed to it as an alien being, as a power
independent of the producer. The product of labour is labour
which has been embodied in an object and turned into a physical
thing.[116]

In other words, political economy works: it formulates the specific empirical results of instrumental action.

> The alienation of the worker in his object is expressed as follows
> in the laws of political economy: the more the worker produces
> the less he has to consume; the more value he creates the more
> worthless he becomes; the more refined his product the more
> crude and misshapen the worker; the more civilized the product
> the more barbarous the worker; the more powerful the work the
> more feeble the worker; the more the work manifests intel-
> ligence the more the worker declines in intelligence and be-
> comes a slave of nature.[117†]

But Marx was not simply another political economist. He rejected
certain crucial elements in their empirical calculations, and he based
this disagreement on a criticism of a fundamental aspect of their presuppositional position. In purely empirical terms, the problem was that political economy was more descriptive than explanatory.

> Political economy begins with the fact of private property; it
> does not explain it. It conceives the material process of private
> property, as this occurs in reality, in general and abstract for-
> mulas which then serve as its laws. It does not comprehend these
> laws; that is, it does not show how they arise out of the nature of
> private property. Political economy provides no explanation of
> the basis for the distinction of labour from capital, of capital
> from land.[118]

In one sense, this is an ideological problem. Because political economy
wants, implicitly or explicitly, to present the laws of capitalist society as
natural and unchangeable, its analysis is unhistorical. Envisioning neither past nor future, political economy cannot envision a society based
upon a nonutilitarian, or nonalienating, approach to action. Unable to
comprehend the true capacity of human nature, it "naturalizes" the theoretical assumption of instrumental action. "Political economy," Marx
writes, "conceals the alienation in the nature of labour."[119†] But in a
deeper sense, this failure is a presuppositional one. Political economy
sees only the surface of capitalist society. Deceived by the formal individualism of bourgeois life, it develops a purely individualistic mode of
explanation. The only motor-forces political economy identifies, Marx argues, are individual motives, like human "avarice" and "competition";[120]
it does not understand that the "apparently accidental conditions" of

bourgeois society actually represent "the expression of a *necessary* development."[121]

Political economy, then, is not sufficiently collectivist. While Marx endorses its presuppositions about action in capitalist society, he rejects its assumptions about the nature of order. The laws of capitalism are not the result of individual decision. Marx criticizes Ricardo, for example, for believing that "economic laws rule the world blindly," the unforeseen results of contracts freely entered into.[122] To the contrary, actual conditions are far from the kind of "lottery" that even the best political economists describe.[123] The truth is that the basic contractual relationships of capitalism are far from free: "Labour is not the *free product of a free market*."[124]

The source of order in capitalist society, Marx insisted against the political economists, is social class, not the individual. This is clear, first of all, in terms of the divergent interests that classes have in bourgeois society itself. "The worker does not necessarily gain," Marx argues, "when the capitalist gains."[125] If individuals freely entered into social relations, a natural identity of interest would occur. Since, however, class relations actually create the context for individual decisions, such an identity of interests is hardly likely. "It is absurd," Marx says, to conclude as Adam Smith does, that "the interest of the landlord is always identical with that of society"; for the interest of the landowner, "far from being identical with that of society, is bitterly opposed to the interest of the tenants, the agricultural labourers, the industrial workers and the capitalists."[126] As this argument implies, behind such divergence of interest is the domination of one class by another. It is the supra-individual force of class power that actually creates the laws which political economy describes. Thus, Marx argues that "the demand, upon which the worker's life depends, is determined by the caprice of the wealthy and the capitalists."[127] The landowner and the capitalist "prescribe laws for him [the worker]."[128]

If such an emphasis on collective order is combined with a utilitarian, antinormative understanding of action, the result can only be the elimination of voluntarism and the disappearance of individual activism. This is of course exactly the situation that, Marx believes, results from the class arrangements of capitalist society.

> Capital is the *power of command* over labour and its products.
> The capitalist possesses this power, not on account of his personal or human qualities, but as the owner of his capital. His power is the purchasing power of his capital, *which nothing can withstand*.[129]

With the evidence of political economy before him, Marx has justified his rejection of reason and subjectivity as motivating forces in capitalist society. He does not deny that praxis still operates at the purely epistemological level. Men are not animals, they still have intentionality. But the alienation of praxis makes men focus only on means, and this perversion of intention makes action look "as if" it were purely objective. For without reference to ideal ends, action is oriented to the external environment of action in a purely instrumental and efficient way. If the capacity for subjectivity is eliminated by alienation, the sociological analysis of action in capitalist society need not involve a subjective reference. Praxis is therefore rejected as an appropriate "sociological epistemology," as a source for the presuppositions that guide the social analysis of action in a particular historical period.[130†]

On the other hand, while Marx accepts political economy's assumptions about action, he decisively rejects its understanding of order. The rational action he sees is not the product of free individuals; it is, rather, the result of a coercive, supra-individual order. To the degree that political economy does not comprehend this collective order, its empirical predictions are incorrect.

2.3.3. The Hanging Thread: The Subjective Foundations of Alienation and the Problem of the Transition to Communism

Marx's position in the 1844 manuscripts is, however, still more ambiguous. Despite, perhaps, his own self-conscious intention, and despite the role which the theoretical logic I have described was destined to play in his later work, Marx's manuscripts, taken as a whole, do not simply appropriate the modified logic of political economy. The picture is more complicated because Marx chose to establish the hegemony of instrumental action by employing an idea that had deep roots in the anti-utilitarian, Romantic tradition, namely, the notion of subjective estrangement from self. While Marx argued, of course, that it is this very estrangement that makes subjectivity irrelevant, by invoking this particular rationale he has, simultaneously, suggested a line of argument that is antithetical to any materialist position. Is the materialist theory of society based, ultimately, on certain subjective conditions? Does this materialist theory remain valid only so long as certain phenomenological limitations—that is, alienation—are maintained?

There is one sense—the sense usually taken by recent Marxist interpreters—in which Marx's invocation of alienation does not involve him in a theoretical dilemma. It is true, this argument goes, that Marx argues that political economy is valid only because of the alienation of man. But since he maintains that this alienation is itself the product of an objective situation, that it is created by the determinate laws of capitalism and by the existence of private property upon which these laws depend, he does not intend this subjective condition of emotional estrangement to become a cause in itself. According to this rendition of Marx's argument, as long as the objective conditions of capitalism exist, so will alienation. Once this objective situation ends, alienation will also cease. Subjective alienation, then, is not a true intervening variable because it does not have independent value. If A (private property) causes B (alienation), and B causes C (utilitarian action), then A causes C. According to this logic, the fundamentally utilitarian logic that Marx presents in the "Manuscripts" is not in danger.

There is, indeed, the strong sense in the "Manuscripts" that Marx is moving toward this kind of argument. He does, after all, invoke alienation to justify the elimination of the subjective aspects of action and to rationalize a collectivist form of instrumental theory. Why, then, should he not relate this alienation to an objective, economic cause, particularly when the failure to do so would allow subjectivity to reenter his theory in an ad hoc, residual way? The fact, however, is that Marx does *not* explain alienation in this manner, no matter how common-sensical it would have been for him to do so. Although alienation is utilized to justify the relevance of an utilitarian theory, it is not linked causally to an exclusively objective, external force. While Marx uses private property and the laws of capitalism to corroborate and give evidence of alienated action, he does not actually argue that they create it. In failing to make this direct connection, he has opened up his theoretical logic to major contradictions.

"It is easy to understand," Marx allows, how the "whole revolutionary movement" finds its "empirical, as well as . . . theoretical, basis in the development of private property, and more precisely in the economic system."[131] It is easy to understand, as he puts it, but it is not correct. For to argue this way, he believes, is to be deceived by appearances. Marx acknowledges that he has "derived the concept of alienated labor (alienated life) from political economy, from an analysis of the movement of private property,"[132] but he insists that this derivation has been only a logical one rather than an effort to establish any true historical or sociological relationship. In fact, he argues, "the analysis of this concept [alienation] shows that although private property *appears* to be the basis and cause of alienated labour, it is rather a consequence of the latter."[133]

Since Marx consistently identifies labor with life activity as such, for him to argue that private property derives from alienated work is not only to link property arrangements to the structure of the labor process but to connect private property with the more general conditions of "alienated life and estranged man."[134] The objective fact of private property, he insists, is rooted in "self-alienation":[135] "Private property is only the sensuous *expression* of the fact that man is at the same time an objective fact *for himself* and becomes an alien and non-human object *for himself*."[136] Alienation ultimately depends, therefore, on the perception of the actor himself. In defining "what constitutes the alienation of labor,"

Marx's analysis depends heavily on whether or not an actor actually feels estranged.

> [The worker] does not fulfill himself in his work but *denies* himself, has a *feeling* of misery rather than well-being, does not develop freely his mental and physical energies but is physically exhausted and mentally debased. The worker, therefore, *feels* himself at home only during his leisure time, whereas at work he *feels* homeless.[137]

It is this subjectively oriented approach that allows one to understand the phenomenological explanation that Marx offers for the existence of the capitalist itself. While he does not retract the notion that the capitalist assumes a coercive position vis-à-vis the passive worker, he suggests that it is the self-alienation of the worker himself that actually allows this capitalist to come into being. Psychologically and morally degenerated, the worker creates the capitalist as a projection of his own internal need for domination.

> Through alienated labour the worker creates the relation of another man, who does not work and is outside the work process, to this labour. . . . Private property is, therefore, the product, the necessary result, of alienated labour, of the external relation of the worker to nature and to himself.[138]

This analysis is, quite simply, an anticapitalist variation on the idealist notion that social structures are merely material forms for the expression of consciousness.[139]†

Marx suggests here a theoretical position radically opposed to the logic of political economy. Still, this suggestion need not necessarily contradict his analysis of contemporary capitalist society, for, as I have argued above, Marx asserts that it is the very alienation of action in this situation which allows the laws of political economy to hold sway. Marx's counter-logic must intrude, however, into any analysis of the transition away from a capitalist society. If capitalism and private property rest upon alienation, and if alienation is the result of self-estrangement, then the transformation of capitalism cannot depend upon the elimination of private property alone. True, this objective negation may be considered a necessary precondition of communism—Marx acknowledges at one point that the relation between alienation and private property is reciprocal[140]—but it certainly is not sufficient. In fact, Marx's "Manuscripts" discussion of communism concentrates exclusively on the self-oriented struggle against subjective estrangement.

Marx first attacks the notion that abolishing material inequality between capitalist and worker is at the basis of communism. "The equality of incomes," he argues in a criticism of Proudhon, "would only change the relation of the present-day worker to his work into a relation of all men to work."[141] Since subjective relationships would remain alienated in a society which had transformed only such material arrangements, this society would still be capitalist in substance, if not in form: "Society would then be conceived as an abstract capitalist."[142]

To establish communism, then, it is not enough simply to reform the external environment of action; rather, it is the nature of action itself which must be transformed. It is "the way in which they [workers] *react* to [the] object," not the object itself, which must be attacked.[143] To change the motivational underpinnings of capitalism is to transform the instrumental character of action. "Need and enjoyment," Marx insists, must lose "their *egoistic* character and nature . . . its mere *utility.*"[144] This process, he stresses, is relatively independent of shifts in the objective environment. An "enforced increase in wages" can do nothing by itself; communism must concentrate, instead, on restoring to the worker his "human significance and worth."[145] The problem, then, with the demand for the "abolition of private property" is that it focuses only on mere "physical possession" rather than on "the personality of man."[146] To transform personality is to transform *"all* his [man's] human relations to the world," his powers of thinking, feeling, observing, and acting.[147] It is the "subjective aspect,"[148] then, which must become the focus of activity in creating a communist society: "The supercession of private property is, therefore, the complete emancipation of all the human qualities and senses . . . from the subjective as well as the objective point of view."[149]

Most analysts in the Marxist tradition, even those sensitive to the special status of Marx's early writings, have interpreted this discussion as relevant simply to Marx's vision of the future communist society.[150]† We have seen, however, that this can hardly be the case. Marx is led to this subjectivist approach to the future society because of the tension in the logic that informs his analysis of the present one. When Marx discusses communism, the contradictory underpinnings of his early theoretical position become explicit. While capitalism may still operate according to the logic of a critical political economy, the achievement of communism depends on processes which can be analyzed only in terms of more subjective, internally-oriented presuppositions.

Insofar as Marx can apply these contradictory frameworks to different historical periods, the theoretical tension that marks this early work remains muted. The problem, however, is the empirical demarcation of "capitalism" from "communism." Is there a "transition" to communism? If so, does it obey the laws of the future society or the past one? If the logic of political economy applies to the entire capitalist period—to the entire historical time characterized by private property or alienation that precedes the communist revolution—then the two divergent theoretical logics can be neatly separated: Marx can safely conduct his analysis of the contradictions and struggles of capitalist society within an exclusively instrumentalist framework. If, however, the transition to communism begins with the struggle against capitalism itself, then Marx would have to bring his normative, future-oriented analysis into his theory of the contradictions of capitalist society and into his analysis of the class struggles which such a society generates. Unable to separate these different theoretical perspectives temporally, he would have to find some way to interrelate them analytically.

In the 1844 "Manuscripts" Marx never explicitly addresses the transition problem. For the most part, he maintains the concrete separation of his two presuppositional positions. He locates the strains of capitalist society in the external, objective environment, and relates the effectiveness of these strains to the fact that actors respond to this environment in an instrumental and efficient way. Still, Marx's position on this issue is not without ambiguity. There is, indeed, some evidence that he brings his anti-utilitarian theory to bear upon his sociological analysis of strains and struggles within capitalism itself. "When communist artisans form associations," Marx writes at one point, "their association itself creates a new need—the need for society—and what appeared to be a *means* has become an *end*."[151] Though he acknowledges here that external strains provide the initial source of conflict—communist artisans form associations in response to economic exploitation—he is arguing, implicitly, that utilitarian motivation is superseded within the very heart of capitalist society. Action, for a whole class of people, becomes noninstrumental and end-oriented, and individuals are connected by internal bonds rather than by external force.

> The most striking results of this practical development [i.e., association] are to be seen when French socialist workers meet together. Smoking, eating, and drinking are no longer simply *means* of bringing people together. Society, association, entertainment which also has *society* as its aim, is sufficient for them; the brotherhood of man is not an empty phrase but a reality.[152]

From this perspective, any analysis of working-class struggle would have to draw heavily on an anti-utilitarian approach to action and order. How, for example, does this internally generated need for solidarity ("association") become structured in different situations? How does the need for expressive activity ("entertainment") relate to the need for solidary moral regulation within the working class movement? Certainly the "reality" of this growing solidary community would seriously undermine any predictive laws that were related only to the external criteria of political economy. Simply to raise these issues is to indicate the kinds of potential theoretical strains that Marx's attention to alienation created for his growing commitment to an instrumentalist position.

In the "Manuscripts" of 1844, Marx found a way to connect his increasingly materialist theoretical position with the most significant social science of his day, political economy. Marx had once believed that subjectivity and intention were still operative in the society of his time, that the tension between particularistic morality and the universalistic judgments of philosophy and religion transformed subjective feelings of alienation into a revolutionary force. Although he had already moved significantly toward a more objectivist position in 1843, he remained committed to the idea that subjective discomfort and moral outrage had enormous political potential. In 1844, however, Marx discovered political economy, and he believed this new social science verified his shift toward a more materialist position. In accepting political economy, Marx moved one step further away from his convictions about the importance of subjective dissatisfaction. The alienation of reason no longer constituted the principal focus of his analysis of capitalism, and the subjective protest to restore reason no longer provided the primary means to transcend capitalist society.

The "Manuscripts," nonetheless, was a work of transition, and the concept of alienation continued to play an important role in the logic which Marx developed. This commitment to the alienation concept indicates that Marx had not yet fully resolved his theoretical ambivalence. Subjectivity and internal order form the primary presuppositions for his analysis of communism, and at least in one significant instance they entered into his analysis of capitalism itself. Even as he completed the 1844 "Manuscripts," then, Marx was still involved in contradictory modes of theoretical discourse.

Marx's emphasis on the alienation concept diminishes in his subsequent writing. Indeed, those contemporary theorists most committed to a thoroughly objectivist Marxism deny there is any continuity between the "Manuscripts" and Marx's later work, pointing to what one interpreter sees as an "epistemological break" in 1845.[153] Although the discontinuity after 1844 was not, in fact, epistemological, nor even particularly radical, we will see that it was, nonetheless, decisive.

Chapter Three

MARX'S FIRST PHASE (2)

The Attack on Moral Criticism and the Origins of a Historical Materialism

1. THE YEARS OF TRANSITION

In the three years between 1844 and 1847, Marx completed his transition to an instrumentalist sociology of capitalism. Biographically, this involved three works: *The Holy Family*, where Marx settled accounts with the radical Hegelianism which had inspired his earlier, normatively oriented work; *The German Ideology*, where he not only continued this critique of German idealist philosophy but also produced his first concrete empirical studies in historical materialism; and *The Poverty of Philosophy*, where he utilized a scathing attack on Proudhon to develop the critique of political economy which would occupy so much of his later work.[1†] Analytically, the work of this period marks two important departures. First, Marx makes great strides in specifying the rationalist and collectivist presuppositions he had outlined in the earlier "Economic and Philosophical Manuscripts" of 1844, producing not only coherent general propositions about classes and modes of production but also a new methodological position and the first steps toward a model of capitalist society. Second, and perhaps most importantly, Marx moves to resolve the presuppositional ambiguity that still lingered in those earlier manuscripts. He does not give up on the idea of alienation, but he now radically separates any attack on the subjective bases of alienation from his analysis of capitalist society. The more utopian aspects of his theory of communism, with its potentially normative and self-oriented thrust, are firmly relegated to some indefinite historical future. In its place, a much more practical approach to communism appears, one which is keyed solely to the conditional problem of property. Once this is accomplished, the transition to communism is no longer theoretically problematic and the analysis of class conflict in capitalist society can proceed entirely upon utilitarian ground.

1.1. THE ATTACK ON CULTURAL "GENERALITY" AND THE END OF PHILOSOPHY

In his early writings, Marx argued that cultural practice, like religious activity and philosophy, possesses an inherent movement toward universalism. In certain historical periods, at least, these intellectual products could provide a standard of critical reason by which to judge other, more particularistic moralities. Important institutional spheres, like the state and the legal order, would reflect this cultural conflict, embodying contradictory normative tendencies. For these reasons, moral criticism, which could seize the masses and make them conscious of this normative tension, could become a major revolutionary force.

In the transition period, one of the most striking features of Marx's writing is its full-throated attack on the very possibility of such normative generalization. In one sense, of course, this merely carries through the logical implications of his earlier acceptance of political economy. Yet this attack actually goes much further. By providing the grounds for rejecting the role of radical theory and criticism, Marx undermines one of the primary nonutilitarian forces which in the "Manuscripts" he had described as playing an active role in the transition to communism.

Far from linking universalistic norms to specifically cultural processes, Marx now denies that such universalism has any autonomy whatsoever. Indeed, the very existence of principles whose scope extends beyond concrete institutional life is due simply to the power of certain interest groups: "The 'general interest' is created by individuals who are defined as 'private persons.' "[2] Far from relating to the organization of ends and reflecting the existence of normative order, the notion of a general interest must be viewed as no more than a means, the result of a calculation by the ruling class. "In order to carry through its aim," Marx writes, "each new class . . . is compelled . . . to represent its interest as the common interest of all the members of society . . . expressed in ideal form: it has to give its ideas the form of universality."[3]

The reference point of such a hypocritical, purely utilitarian attempt at generalization must be the external environment, the material position of the ruling class itself. "The ruling ideas are nothing more," Marx asserts, "than the ideal expression of the dominant material relationships, the dominant material relations grasped as ideas."[4] Social ideas, then, are the result of a calculation to defend material position; they are produced when those who possess, in Marx's words, the material "means of mental production" apply them to their conditions of existence. Themselves the product of the material environment, cultural notions certainly can provide no independent leverage for change: "[Since] the so-called 'general,' is constantly being produced by the other side, private interest," it "by no means opposes the latter as an independent force with an independent history."[5†]

If there is no possibility for culturally rooted generalization, then institutions like the state and law certainly cannot reflect principles of organization at variance with private interest and particularistic morality. The modern state is simply another expression of the ruling class's calculation of interest. With its formal adherence to universalist norms, the state is an excellent device to legitimate the status of a new and perhaps unpopular economic group. "Every class which is struggling for mastery," Marx suggests, "must first conquer for itself political power in order to represent its interest in turn as the general interest."[6] Indeed, as with any purely rational calculation, this action is, in effect, an objectively necessary one. The ruling class, Marx writes, is forced to establish the state simply to maximize the interest of its members.[7] Because the interests of the class as a whole often run counter to the immediate interests of any single capitalist, the identity of class interest must be established in an artificial way.

> Because individuals seek *only* their particular interest, which for them does not coincide with their communal interest, the latter will be imposed on them. . . . The *practical* struggle of these particular interests, which constantly *really* run counter to the . . . communal interests, makes practical intervention and control necessary through the illusory "general" interest in the form of the state.[8]

But external necessity is also related to the new, more impersonal form of class domination, not simply to the need of the new class to rationalize its control. "By the mere fact that it is a class and no longer an estate," Marx writes, "the bourgeoisie is forced to organize itself no longer locally, but nationally, and to give a general form to its mean average interest."[9] To achieve this national domination, the bourgeoisie, in effect, buys the pre-existing state apparatus: "The modern state, which [was] purchased gradually by the owners of property by means of taxation, has fallen entirely into their hands through the national debt, and its existence has become wholly dependent on the commercial credit which the owners of property, the bourgeois, extend to it, as reflected in the rise and fall of the State funds on the stock exchange."[10] Thus, although the state may appear to be an autonomous entity from the perspective of an individual property owner, it is no more than an instrumental means writ large, the product of certain determinate conditions. "Through the emancipation of private property from the community," Marx writes, "the state has become a separate entity, beside and outside civil society; but it is nothing more than the form of organization which the bourgeois necessarily adopt both for internal and external purposes, for the mutual guarantee of their property and interests."[11] The modern legal system, with its emphasis on individual rights and responsibility, assumes the integrity—the relative autonomy—of universalistic social norms, and the formal neutrality of law is derived from its connection to an institution, the state, whose "public" character expresses this normative autonomy. If the state's autonomy is illusory, then, so is the autonomy of the legal order. In fact, the political mediation of the legal order is simply another device to camouflage particularistic interest.

> Since the state is the form in which the individuals of a ruling class assert their common interests . . . it follows that the state mediates in the formation of all common institutions and that the institutions receive a political form. Hence the illusion that law is based on the will, and indeed on the will divorced from its real basis—on *free* will.[12]

Law reflects the same external conditions as the state. "If power is taken as the basis of right," Marx reasons, "then right, law, etc. are merely the symptom, the expression of other relations upon which state power rests."[13] Far from presenting an exalted, almost sacred organization of ends—the status it held in his earlier writing—law is now reduced by Marx merely to another form of the organization of means.

With these denials of any normative basis for the state and the legal order, Marx has set the stage for his reductionistic, base-superstructure model of society. "The social organization evolving directly out of production and commerce," he writes at one point, "in all ages forms the basis of the state and of the rest of the idealistic superstructure."[14] We find in *The German Ideology* the first concrete, empirical descriptions of the "unreality" of cultural institutions. Once material life has achieved a certain productive level, Marx asserts, "consciousness *can* really flatter itself that it is something other than consciousness of existing practice, that it *really* represents something without representing something real; from now on consciousness is in a position to emancipate itself from the world and to proceed to the formation of 'pure' theory, theology, philosophy, ethics, etc."[15] Regarding philosophy, for example, Marx argues that Kant's emphasis on free will merely reflected the weakness of the German bourgeoisie and its fear of carrying out the revolutionary economic role of the French middle classes. The "whitewashing spokesman" of the German burghers, Kant "separated [the] theoretical expression [of free will] from the interests it expressed," converting the "materially motivated determinations of the will of the French bourgeoisie into *pure* self-determinations . . . and moral postulates."[16] The same insistence on epiphenomenal culture occurs in Marx's discussions of art, where he argues, for example, that the emergence of an artistic style "depends wholly on demand, which in turn depends on the division of labor and the conditions of human culture resulting from it."[17]

With this elaboration of his mechanical model, Marx is ready to specify his instrumental-collectivist presuppositions in a more empirical way, and in *The German Ideology* he produces, for the first time, the outlines of his materialist theory of history. He formulates, first, man's original historical condition, and in describing this primordial state he takes a decisive, indeed fateful step. Men are distinguished from animals, Marx insists, not by their capacity for meaningful expression, by their focus on ends, but rather by their ability to produce particularly efficient means. "Men can be distinguished from animals by consciousness, by religion or anything else you like," Marx writes, but "they themselves begin to distinguish themselves from animals as soon as they begin to *produce* their means of subsistence."[18†] The problem of subsistence is a problem of direct adaptation to the material environment; it directs theory to external conditions and to the problem of necessity. As Marx writes: "[Men's] means of subsistence depends first of all on the nature of the actual means of subsistence they find in existence and have to reproduce."[19] Viewing action as resting on such "natural bases," it is no wonder that Marx explains order as primarily "conditioned by . . . physical organization."[20] Although physical organization and material conditions are historically variable, their singular analytic importance remains constant: "The 'history of humanity,' " Marx insists, "must always be studied and treated in relation to the history of industry and exchange."[21] Whatever specific form it takes, individual action is always externally determined: "The nature of individuals thus depends on the material conditions determining their production."[22]

In the transitional period, Marx elaborates this material order by emphasizing the crucial coordinating role of the division of labor. "The production of life," he writes, "appears as a double relationship: on the one hand as a natural, on the other as a social relationship."[23] The social relationship is the "cooperation of different individuals" which is established by the exigencies of production.[24] Participation in the division of labor, Marx emphasizes, is not a matter of individual desire or will. Drawing on the same distinction between natural and species, or conscious, action that he articulated in his earlier work, he argues that "cooperation is not voluntary but has come about naturally." It has no relation to individual ends: men are "ignorant" of the "origin and goal" of the division of labor. Such a seemingly natural force functions, inevitably, as "an alien force existing outside of them," which men "cannot control." The different stages of productive development, Marx asserts, are "independent of the will and the action of man, nay even the prime governor of these."[25] And

while he does not deny human intentionality, he argues that this purpose
is structured not by consciousness but by necessity.

> What is society, whatever its form may be? The product of men's
> reciprocal action. [But] are men free to choose this or that form
> of society for themselves? By no means. Assume a particular
> state of development in the productive forces of man and you
> will get a particular form of commerce and consumption. As-
> sume particular stages of development in production, com-
> merce, and consumption and you will have a corresponding
> social constitution, a corresponding organization of the family,
> of orders or of classes.[26]

It is no wonder that Marx's historical discussion in this period finds its
independent variables exclusively in such conditional factors as economic demand, economically-oriented political force, economically-rel-
evant population shifts, and productive technology.[27] These are the
factors which determine the economic division of labor, and though
Marx's causal analysis will shift slightly in his later writing toward more
purely economic factors, the more general emphasis on exclusively conditional force will remain firm.

With this instrumental approach to history, it would be highly inconsistent if Marx were to argue that moral criticism has a role to play in the
transformation of capitalism. Earlier, he had justified the importance of
such criticism by arguing that the real chains of man were the "inner
chains" that distorted self-consciousness. Now he ridicules this metaphor, arguing that it is a figment of the young Hegelians' imagination:
"*Criticism* has . . . transform[ed] *real, objective* chains existing *outside me*
into *merely ideal*, merely *subjective* chains *in me*."[28†] In doing so, this
young Hegelian criticism had transformed real, material struggles—the
conflicts over means—into "mere struggles of thought," into mere struggles over ends.[29]

In his attack on criticism, Marx follows two distinct strategies. First,
on the basis of his critique of cultural generalization, he argues that criticism is impotent because it directs itself to a phenomenon, ideas, which
has no independent reality. "*Ideas* can never lead beyond the established
situation," Marx now affirms; "they only lead beyond the ideas of the established situation."[30] Thus, "to have rebuked them [capitalist ideas]
morally and *exposed* them as the antithesis of spirit and progress" is to
make no reference to their real origins.[31] To combat the "phrases of this
world" is "in no way combatting the real existing world." Since ideas
merely mirror pre-existing structures, society can be changed only by
the "practical overthrow of the actual social relations," and Marx concludes that "not criticism but revolution is the driving force in history."[32]

The "liberation" of "man" is not advanced a single step ... by liberating man from the domination of these phrases, which have never held him in thrall.... "Liberation" is an historical and not a mental act, and it is brought about by historical conditions, the development of industry, commerce, agriculture, the conditions of intercourse.[33]

Alongside this argument, Marx introduces another extension of his anti-generalization position. This second strategy involves a revision of his earlier approach to the nature of radical social theory. Attacking the very validity of speculative philosophy, Marx now argues that for a radical theory to be true it must be based exclusively on empirical observation. Marx ridicules, for example, a review by Bauer, his former colleague, which lauds Proudhon's anticapitalist analysis of private property for its faith in justice rather than applauding Proudhon's reliance upon scientific observations of the nature of material reality.[34] The whole idea that radical communist theory rests upon culturally rooted, universalistic norms is now dismissed as an absurdity; it denies the empirical, scientific status of communist theory. "The theoreticians of the proletarian class," Marx asserts, "no longer need to seek science in their minds; they have only to take note of what is happening before their eyes and to become its mouthpiece."[35] If critical theory itself simply reflects the material world, it does not constitute an independent element in social transformation.

Since theory does not refer to any independent normative order, the very notion that the success of communist writing rests upon its transformation of consciousness—upon "truth brought to consciousness"[36]—must be in error. Communist theory does not address the "depths of soul" but rather "empirical interest." Revealing the (already self-evident) organization of means, it stimulates "empirical action" against the external pressures that condition such efficient action.[37] Compared with such realistic incentives, "the opinion and conceptions of the philosopher," his "speculative imagination," count for naught.[38] Indeed, to argue for the independent importance of moral criticism is like trying to argue that it is the idea of gravity, rather than the physical force of gravity itself, which causes a drowning man to go down. "Once upon a time," Marx writes, "a valiant fellow had the idea that men were drowned in water only because they were possessed with the idea of gravity."

If they were to knock this notion out of their heads, say by stating it to be a superstition, a religious concept, they would be sublimely proof against any danger from water. His whole life long he fought against the illusion of gravity, of whose harmful results all statistics brought him new and manifold evidence. This

honest fellow was the type of the new revolutionary philosophers in Germany.[39†]

With this apocryphal story, Marx concludes his preface to *The German
Ideology*. The moral of the story is a simple one: if capitalism produces
"natural" men, the transformation of capitalism can only be based upon
naturalistic force.

1.2. TRANSFORMING THE STATUS OF "ALIENATION": THE ATTACK ON SUBJECTIVITY IN THE TRANSITION TO COMMUNISM

Much more forcefully than in the 1844 "Manuscripts," Marx has
now developed the instrumental and collectivist line of his thought. His
attack on cultural generalization, his denial of superstructural autonomy to the state and law, his exposition of a purely materialist history,
and his argument for a purely empirical, antiphilosophical communist
theory all achieve this result. He has thus moved toward a resolution of
the major ambiguity which marred that earlier work, namely the emphasis on subjectivity and normative order that issued from his theory of
communist society. In this crucial period of intellectual transition Marx
finally lays to rest this ghost of his Hegelian past.

As I have emphasized throughout the earlier discussions, Marx's
movement toward instrumental logic in no way involves the denial of
alienation in capitalist society. To the contrary, since he continues to accept the subjectivity of human epistemology, the concept of alienation actually enables him to invoke successfully an instrumentalist sociology of
capitalism. It is not surprising, then, that the familiar dialectic of con-
sciousness-alienation-instrumentalism continues to inform the work of
this transitional period. Thus, while Marx argues that the proletariat is
"conscious of its misery," "conscious of its dehumanization," this does
not in the least prevent him from explaining, in the same breath, that the
dissolution of the source of this misery, private property, is "brought
about by the very *nature of things*."[40] The linkage between these apparently contradictory statements is, once again, Marx's assertion that alienation makes consciousness sensitive only to means, not ends. The
objectification of consciousness, itself a product of material forces,
means that the proletarian can be responsive only to material pressures.
Marx is well aware that such an exclusive focus on means and external
conditions eliminates the possibility for voluntaristic proletarian action:
"Man's own deed becomes an alien power opposed to him which
enslaves him instead of being controlled by him," a power "which is
forced upon him and from which he cannot escape."[41†] Marx continues
to accept political economy as, simultaneously, an empirical verification

of alienated society and the only valid basis for an empirical analysis of its transformation. After all, he reasons, it was capitalism that first created the materialist theory on which political economy is based,[42] and if its conceptual language portrays action in a coarse and narrow way it is only because such coarseness is prescribed by capitalist society itself. The laws of political economy accurately reflect the nature of action in the capitalist period.

> Doubtless, Ricardo's language is as cynical as can be. To put the cost of manufacture of hats and the cost of maintenance of men on the same plane is to turn men into hats. But do not make an outcry at the cynicism of it. The cynicism is in the facts and not in the words which express the facts. . . . If they [some critics] reproach Ricardo and his school for their cynical language, it is because it annoys them to see economic relations exposed in all their crudity, to see the mysteries of the bourgeoisie unmasked.[43]

Once again, however, this acceptance is qualified. Political economy is ideological: it treats private property, money, and exchange as givens of social life instead of explaining them in a historically specific way.[44] Behind this conservatism is the bourgeois inability to embrace collectivist rather than individualist presuppositions about the nature of social order. Marx had made a similar criticism in the early "Manuscripts," but he now specifies this objection in a way that lays out the empirical questions that will preoccupy him for the rest of his life. Because political economists accept at face value the individualistic notion of a free contract, Marx argues, they mistakenly view every exchange relationship as a reciprocal and equal one. The price a capitalist receives for his product, then, will be said to equal the costs he has incurred in making it.[45] From this error it is clearly but a short step to the favorable judgment of capitalism itself. If profit is proportionate to actual cost, wages will be viewed as proportionate to profit. Exploitation—the element of profit which accrues simply from property ownership—becomes invisible.[46] Machines, for example, will be viewed as complementary to human labor on the grounds that because they have increased profit they must also have benefited labor, while in fact the machines benefit the property owner not the laborer. Marx argues that once economic relationships are accepted as free, the power element is lost, and with this loss the tension between the economic potential of industrial society and its narrowly capitalist form disappears.[47] If political economy misses the role of private property and its carrier, the capitalist class, it will be deluded by the appearance of equality in capitalist society. This individualism often goes so far as to view consumption itself as a matter of personal "judgment" and "estimation," ignoring the obviously determinate effects of the economic division of labor.

True, the worker who buys potatoes and the kept woman who buys lace both follow their respective judgments. But the difference in their judgments is explained by the difference in the positions which they occupy in the world, and which themselves are the product of social organization.[48†]

Expanding upon his earlier arguments, Marx emphasizes the relation between alienated instrumentalism and the hegemony of political economy. The alienation concept, however, no longer serves the same implicit function for Marx as it did in the "Manuscripts" of 1844. It is no longer the Trojan horse by which subjectivity is smuggled into his theory of capitalism. Marx's earlier theoretical predicament was created because he failed to identify private property as the cause of alienation. In the writings of his transition period, this ambivalence is systematically rectified.

Marx prepares the ground for his new, purely objectivist interpretation of alienation by arguing for its differential application. Although he still acknowledges that the propertied class is alienated in the technical sense of the term, he now insists that despite their alienation they retain "the semblance of a human existence." "Comfortable and confirmed" in their alienation, the members of this class can exercise their human power in a purposive and ruthless way.[49] The proletariat, in contrast, is "ruined" and made "impotent" by its alienation and for this reason is abject before the powers of the market and ruling class.[50] According to this reasoning, the possession of property can, in itself, neutralize the most important effects of alienation. Yet in the earlier "Manuscripts," Marx had rejected this very proposition, employing the epithet "abstract capitalist" to designate the alienation that would continue in a property-oriented communist society.

Marx even more directly identifies alienation with private property by linking them both to the division of labor. In his view, alienation is produced by the division of labor, and the division of labor is inseparable from private property.[51] "The division of labour and private property are," he now insists, "identical expressions: in the one the same thing is affirmed with reference to activity as is affirmed in the other with reference to the product of the activity."[52] If the cause of alienation is private property, then communism, which means the abolition of alienation, must be identified also with the abolition of private property.

Only at this [communist] stage does self-activity coincide with material life, which corresponds to the development of individuals into complete individuals and the casting-off of all natural limitations. The transformation of labour into self-activity corresponds to the transformation of the earlier limited intercourse into the intercourse of individuals as such. With the appropriation of the total productive forces through united individuals, private property comes to an end . . . Individuals are no longer subject to the division of labour.[53]

Although Marx no doubt continued to adhere privately to the vision of unalienated society as the liberation of the human senses—one which would depend upon the spiritual transformation of the self—he has now decisively eliminated this vision from his scientific, theoretical formulations. Later, he will introduce the distinction between early and later phases of communism—which subsequent theorists termed the distinction between socialism and communism—to differentiate his more spiritual vision from more mundane concerns. But even then the theoretical point will remain the same: the historical period which immediately succeeds capitalism is based upon the transformation of the external environment of action, not action itself.[54†]

Once Marx has firmly identified the postcapitalist society with purely material change, alienation no longer plays havoc with his analysis of capitalist society itself. The subjectivity of some future society no longer intrudes upon the struggle to transform the present one. Marx's analysis of the proletarian struggle against capitalism now proceeds entirely within the rubric of alienated action and external order. Ends and self-conscious purpose no longer are relevant to the class struggle. "It is not a question," Marx now asserts, "of what this or that proletarian or even the whole proletariat momentarily *imagines* to be the aim."[55] "Communism is . . . not a *state of affairs* to be established, an ideal to which reality [will] have to adjust itself."[56] If Marx now believes that "individuals must appropriate the existing totality of productive forces . . . merely to safeguard their very existence," it is the external, not the internal reference that governs his analysis of proletarian struggle: "This appropriation is first determined by the *object* to be appropriated, the productive forces."[57] External necessity produces revolutionary change, whether or not this necessity is imagined or willed.

> It is a question of *what* the proletariat *is* and what it consequently is historically compelled to do. Its aim and historical action is prescribed, irrevocably and obviously in its own situation in life.[58] . . . We call communism the *real* movement which abolishes the present state of things. The conditions of this movement result *from the premises now in existence.*[59]

Marx specifies this new general theory of class struggle by developing a purely instrumentalist explanation of class "association," the very concept which in the "Manuscripts" had provided him with his principal opportunity for normative theorizing. "Separate individuals form a class," he now insists, "only insofar as they have to carry on a common battle against another class; otherwise they are on hostile terms with each other as competitors."[60] If order is primarily external, in other words, any new social arrangements must be instrumentally motivated. Marx applies this general proposition to bourgeois and proletarian alike. He devotes a good deal of time, for example, to describing the origins of the late medieval guilds and burgher-dominated cities which, he believes, were "true 'associations,' called forth by direct needs."[61] In contrast to his discussion in the "Manuscripts," however, such "need" is described in purely material terms. The "necessity for association" that produced the guilds was a response, first, to the "need for communal markets in an age where the industrialist was at the same time a merchant" and, second, to the "growing competition of the escaped serfs swarming into the rising towns."[62] Town development represented simply an extension of these same factors. Basically, the causes were three: the "care of providing for the protection of property," the concern for "multiplying the means of production," and the need for maintaining the "defense of the separate members."[63] In a word, Marx concludes, "the citizens in each town were compelled to unite against the landed nobility to save their skins."[64]

Despite his greater moral sympathy for the proletarians, Marx applies the same general propositions to explain the association that furthers their cause. While at first "competition divides their interests," less competitive association remains possible because the proletarians also have objective interests in common: "the maintenance of wages." Association, then, begins as the most efficient strategy to combat the capitalist's control of wages. "This common interest which they have against their boss," Marx writes, "unites them in a common thought of resistance: combination,"[65] and "this combination always has a double aim, that of stopping competition among the workers, *so that* they can carry on general competition with the capitalist.[66]

While at first these associations are concerned only with the economic issues of wages, the maintenance of the workers' organizations gradually becomes an end in itself: "If the first aim of resistance was merely the maintenance of wages, [then] combinations, at first isolated, constitute themselves into groups."[67] The reason for this, once again, is an instrumental one, for the capitalists themselves have "unite[d] for the purpose of repression of workers' organizations." To external threat, the maintenance of workers' organizations becomes the only rational response. "In the face of always united capital," Marx writes, "the maintenance of the association becomes more necessary to them than that of wages."[68] The worker actually has no choice but to associate, and the "end" of association assumes, in effect, the theoretical status of a mere means.

Because of this emphasis upon external necessity, Marx has been accused of failing to distinguish between a divided class situation and a united one, between purely economistic class action and more political activity. In fact, he does distinguish between a class which is merely against capital and a class which is "for itself," one which strives to maintain organizational solidarity and integration.[69] The significant theoretical point, however, is not that this distinction is made, but how. The theoretical logic that informs Marx's description of this associational development is purely instrumental. In sharp contrast to many of his current interpreters, Marx himself readily admits that his explanation leaves no room for voluntarism and choice. At least until capitalism itself has been thoroughly transformed, "the last word of social science will always be: 'Combat or death: bloody struggle or extinction. It is thus that the question is inexorably put.' "[70]

1.3. THE RESIDUAL CATEGORY OF LATER MARXISM: INEXPLICABLE NORMATIVE ACTION

In the early period of Marx's theoretical development, when he worked within a radicalized Hegelianism, instrumental force never entered into his theoretical explanations. The consistency of his normative theoretical logic, which provided the framework for every more specific statement, simply excluded such material elements from the field of social activity. When such elements began to enter Marx's thinking, with the empirical investigations of 1842, they could do so only with the introduction by Marx himself of a general theoretical framework which presupposed the possibility of antinormative behavior and instrumental order. For a certain period of time, therefore, when Marx's observations of the empirical world were informed by two competing general theories, neither normative nor instrumental facts were residual to his theorizing. Each could find a secure home in Marx's work, if not in the emerging materialist framework then in the older, Hegelian line of his thought. True, reference to normative phenomena—self-change, philosophy, cultural universalism, solidary association—now occupied a minority position in Marx's writing. Nonetheless, they remained one part of his theoretical logic, as was clearly indicated by the way he used "alienation" to subjectivize his treatment of private property and communism.

In his transitional writings, however, Marx resolved this theoretical ambivalence. If the concrete materialist theory was not yet fully elaborated, the general analytic framework was now fully in place. In terms of theoretical logic, this transition transformed the analytic status of certain empirical "facts." Phenomena which in the "Manuscripts" had still been defined in a normative way were now viewed as manifestations of an instrumental logic. This represented an important accomplishment, for empirical phenomena like universalism, cosmopolitan law and political ideals, and critical class consciousness could now be explained in ways that reinforced rather than contradicted the materialist perspective. Through this transformation of theoretical logic, the supposedly subjectivist concepts like "alienation" and "class for itself" —concepts which have become so controversial in recent Marxist interpretation— were purged of all reference to normative order or cultural action. Indeed, they are the best illustrations of Marx's enormous success in transforming empirical phenomena from one kind of theoretical framework to another. More than any of the other creators of classical sociological theory, Marx actually succeeded in developing from his presuppositional base a logically closed system of theoretical propositions, one which could explain virtually any empirical fact in a systematic and consistent way.[71] As we will see even more clearly in later chapters, Marx was unusually sensitive to the problems which certain kinds of empirical facts posed to theoretical consistency. To encompass these potential challenges, he elaborated a complex and strategic empirical model that "covered the bases." With this model he could encompass a wide variety of empirical phenomena while maintaining his commitment to instrumental action and external order.

Still, even in this later, post-"Manuscripts" period, one finds occasional residual categories in Marx's writing, references to empirical facts which presuppose general assumptions that are outside his carefully developed theoretical framework.[72] Not surprisingly, Marx's residual categories are normative phenomena: nonrational forms of behavior that are explicitly, and masterfully, denied autonomy by the consciously constructed systematic theory. Such residual references appear most often in Marx's casual writings—his letters, newspaper articles, reports on current events, speeches to political groups. Indeed, I will argue later that they appear so frequently in Marx's informal analyses of class struggle and organization that they amount to a significant and revealing contradiction in his political thought. Nonetheless, empirical references remain residual unless they are incorporated into the general concepts that inform theoretical work. Not only are such casual normative references never formally included in Marx's writing, but they rarely appear at all in his self-consciously "scientific" statements, even in such a residual way.

In the three major works of Marx's transitional period, indeed, residual categories amount to no more than a few paragraphs. In every instance, they completely contradict not simply the developing thrust of Marx's general theoretical logic but also the specific, more empirical elaborations he has so painstakingly constructed.

Marx twice introduces residual categories in his analysis of the bourgeois revolution. Once, in the middle of his discussion of English economic development in the seventeenth and eighteenth centuries, Marx notes in passing that "there already existed in England the . . . pre-conditions of this new phase: freedom of competition inside the nation, [and] the development of theoretical mechanics."[73] In parentheses, he elaborates this statement very briefly by explaining, first, that Newton's physical mechanics "was altogether the most popular science" in eighteenth-century England and, second, that "free competition inside the nation had everywhere to be conquered by a [political] revolution—1640 and 1688 in England."[74] At an earlier point in his analysis of Europe's early economic development, Marx briefly notes a similar kind of fact. "The possibility of commercial communication transcending the immediate neighborhood," he writes, depended among other things on "the crude or more advanced needs (determined by the stage of culture attained) of the region accessible to intercourse."[75]

But these ideas are clearly anomalous. To talk about the independent role of science and politics after devoting page after page to detailed attacks on cultural and political universalism is simply to introduce categories outside the central line of argument. Not only do they refer to no prior theorizing about science or political revolution, but they directly contradict Marx's conclusions in several crucial empirical discussions that are, in fact, grounded in his general theory. The same kind of criticism must be leveled against his argument about culture. If the stage of cultural needs is to be a mediation for economic development and competition, it is strange that Marx constructs his entire analysis of early modern capitalism on purely material arguments, and stranger still that he makes physical needs of subsistence the crucial variable in the development of new productive systems.

Anomalous empirical qualifications also appear in Marx's theory of the proletarian revolution. At one point, for example, he tries to explain how radical ideas can occur in backward countries like Germany by introducing a notion of evolutionary survivals. "Consciousness can sometimes appear further advanced than the contemporary empirical relationships," he asserts, because radicalism often draws upon traditionalistic, premodern ideas that continue to affect the capitalist period. Such ideas can influence individuals "even apart from their pecuniary circumstances." To explain how traditionalistic ideas could survive in this way, Marx states that "various [productive] stages and interests are never completely overcome, but only subordinated to the prevailing interest and trail along beside the latter for centuries."[76] This line of explanation, however, completely contradicts the mechanical, economic interpretation of German radicalism that Marx developed for the good part of two major books, *The Holy Family* and *The German Ideology*. It also goes entirely against the argument that consciousness is simply consciousness about empirical interests that Marx so painstakingly develops throughout this transitional period. Indeed, if earlier ideas were, in fact, to continue to influence later periods of history, Marx's base-superstructure model of consciousness and society would be in theoretical shambles.

These occasional references, then, are simply not explained by the theory Marx has developed. In fact, far from indicating Marx's continuing commitment to a normative, voluntaristic framework—a position so often taken by Marx's recent interpreters—I would suggest precisely the opposite. Since these references are entirely residual, they actually illustrate the consistency and sureness of Marx's overriding commitment to an instrumental form of collectivist theory. Rather than representing the continuity of old commitments, these extraneous categories indicate the lines of strain that Marx's new, thoroughly instrumentalist position must inevitably encounter. In the great debate over Marx's ideas that began with his death, such normative references surfaced time and time again, as his followers tried to avoid determinism and rationalism while maintaining their commitment to "Marxist" theory. Usually these references remained residual; sometimes they formed the basis for covertly anti-Marxist theories. I will consider these revisions at a later point. Here it is enough to say that such occasional references are certainly not integrated into Marx's new, much more thoroughgoing materialism. Indeed, he developed his new theory to refute the kind of "idealism" which they implied. The transitional work of 1844–1847 represented the first fruits of this materialist theory. *The Communist Manifesto*, published in 1848, represented its maturity.

2. MATURITY: RATIONAL ACTION AND COERCIVE ORDER IN *THE COMMUNIST MANIFESTO*

Telescoping four years of research and analysis, *The Communist Manifesto* put Marx's thinking into its final form. It is not an exaggeration to say that Marx devotes the rest of his career to more fully elaborating different sections of this historical document.[77†]

Marx would have us consider the *Manifesto*, its obvious polemical purposes aside, as a purely empirical document. As in the rest of his work, he concentrates here on presenting the facts, historical and contemporary, and devotes no time at all to conceptual elaboration or to explicitly generalized argument. Our knowledge of Marx's personal history, however, his long philosophical struggle to develop a satisfactory and consistent general framework, belies this presentation of self. It is also contradicted by the inherently multidimensional nature of scientific thought itself: every sociological statement is theoretically informed. The facts in the *Manifesto* must, then, be read theoretically. When they are, they reveal that Marx has ordered the empirical world in a manner that effectively illustrates the presuppositional logic he has struggled to create. To read the *Manifesto* theoretically is to discover, in astonishingly economical and systematic form, the specification of Marx's instrumental and collectivist metaphysics.

Central passages in the *Manifesto* have become famous; they are inscribed in the literature, philosophy, and monuments of human beings around the world. For this reason they have often been interpreted as rhetoric. I would contend, to the contrary, that these phrases have a very precise theoretical meaning.

The *Manifesto* first of all addresses the question of action. Like every social theorist, Marx presupposes the nature of action, and a good deal of his empirical work is devoted to providing evidence for his position. What motivates individual behavior in capitalist society? Are people rational or nonrational? Marx comes right to the point. Once the bourgeois has got the upper hand, he writes, there is no "religious fervor."[78] In capitalist society, there can be no reference to an ideal order which transcends concrete interaction— "all that is holy is profaned"[79]—and certainly no emotional, extrarational excitement about it. Neither is there "chivalrous enthusiasm," for emotionality cannot be directed in an altruistic direction.[80] Individuals, furthermore, do not "honor" one another, nor do they have "reverent awe" for any special position or occupation, for "the physician, the lawyer, the priest, the poet, the man of science."[81] These motives too would clearly violate any presupposition of instrumentality, for they would destroy the "efficient" relation between actor and environment. In Marx's view, prejudices of all kinds are similarly absent from capitalism. Not only is capitalist man—particularly the proletarian who makes up the "vast majority" — "stripped . . . of any trace of national character," but law and morality are now seen for what they are, shibboleths which fail to camouflage the utilitarian character of everyday life.[82] With these "facts" established, Marx has ruled out every possible source of behavioral inefficiency. Action can now be seen, empirically, for what it must be theoretically, namely, "egotistical calculation."[83] In capitalism, men act toward each other only with "sober senses," in a "naked, shameless, direct, and brutal" way. There is, Marx concludes, "no other nexus between man and man than naked self-interest, than callous 'cash payment.' "[84]

Marx is careful to indicate, however, that this kind of action does not necessarily mean that no order binds men at all, and for "nexus" in the phrase preceding one should undoubtedly read "moral nexus." While rationality means that individuals do not morally interpenetrate—that individual separateness is viewed as a concrete and empirical, not simply an analytical division—it does not mean that there is no supra-individual order at all. To the contrary, Marx asserts in the opening sentences of the *Manifesto* that "we almost always find a complicated arrangement of society into various orders."[85†] Since action is viewed as entirely in-

strumental, however, this collective order can be portrayed only in a coercive, antivoluntaristic way. Indeed, the common denominator among
the various orders into which societies have been divided is this: they
have all reflected the relationship between "oppressor and oppressed."[86]
Social order, then, is accomplished through external domination, and
while the exact nature of this oppression varies with the mode of production, the oppressing group is always differentiated by its possession of
the crucial means: property. In capitalism, order is established by the
class with access to capital.

Marx portrays this coercive general order of capitalist society as carried into its specific institutional life. As a microcosm of class domination, the factory is the central institution of capitalist society. In
describing the order of factory life, Marx compares it to the prototype of
coercive force, the army. "As privates of the industrial army," he writes,
"they [the laborers] are placed under the command of a perfect hierarchy of officers and sergeants."[87] Indeed, a direct line can be drawn
from the most general origins of class order to the minute details of life
in the factory. "Not only are they slaves of the bourgeois class," Marx
writes about the proletarians, but "they are daily and hourly enslaved by
the machine, the over[seer], and, above all, the individual bourgeois
manufacturer himself."[88] He emphasizes that this order is purely instrumental, concerned only with the organization of means: it is a "despo-
tism" which "proclaims gain to be its end and aim."

But if this institutional analysis is to be consistently supported by empirical fact, Marx must not only emphasize the great importance of factory life but instrumentalize noneconomic institutions as well. It is no
doubt for this theoretical reason, as well as for empirical and ideological
ones, that he so sharply attacks the effectiveness of institutions that are
not so directly specialized in the organization of means. Of all the institutions of capitalist society, the family would be most likely to promote normative order. Against this possibility Marx argues that "the bourgeois
has torn away from the family its sentimental veil, and he has reduced
the family to a mere money relation."[89] If the irrational emotions and
moral loyalties generated by the family are eliminated, so must the solidary bonds that such families generate, particularly stratification by age
and sex. "Differences of age and sex have no longer any distinctive social
validity for the working class," Marx asserts. "All are instruments of labor, more or less expensive to use."[90] Marx must take a similar position in
regard to the state, the institution so often associated with notions of abstract right. It is to this theoretical necessity that we owe the famous
phrase which has become epigrammatic: "The modern state is only an
executive committee for administering the common business of the
bourgeois class."[91]

If Marx's institutional sociology specifies the coercive imperatives of his instrumental approach to order, it is not surprising that his historical sociology follows firmly along the same track. "The modern bourgeoisie," he writes quite reasonably, is "the product of a long course of development."[92] This "development," however, is rather narrowly defined, for it consists solely in the reorganization of social means, in a "series of revolutions in the modes of production and of exchange."[93] At every step in Marx's analysis of the creation of capitalism, the motivating action is assumed to be purely rational, and the crucial independent variable is the external factor of economic demand.[94†] Individual or group action is pictured, at every point, as the result of such conditional pressure, not as its creator. The initial discovery of large overseas markets— "the increase in the means of exchange and in commodities generally" —gave the newly emerging bourgeois "an impulse never before known."[95] Because the closed guilds of medieval society could not meet the "growing wants of the new market," guild masters were "pushed to one side by the manufacturing class." After all, the "division of labor *in* each single workshop" was far more efficient than the "division of labor *between* the different corporate guilds."[96] Yet "the markets kept ever growing, the demand ever rising," and in response to this continuous external stimulus "steam and machinery revolutionized production" and ushered in the large industrial bourgeoisie.[97] This class, in turn, established a great world market, and it was "this market [which] has given an immense development to commerce, to navigation, to communication by land." These economic and economically induced developments then "reacted on the extension of industry" and "in proportion as industry developed . . . in the same proportion the bourgeoisie [further] developed, increased its capital, and pushed into the background every class handed down from the middle ages."[98]

Once modern capitalism has been established, the rule of external necessity holds with even greater force. The actions of the bourgeoisie are completely involuntary. Since they "cannot exist without constantly revolutionizing the instruments of production," competition among capitalists, which relies heavily on wage cutting, becomes a "life and death question."[99] The laborers, for their part, are equally without control over their fate. Without productive means of their own, they must adapt to every reorganization of their economic environment: "They are consequently . . . exposed to all the vicissitudes of competition, to all the fluctuations of the market."[100]

From these initial circumstances, the movement toward socialism is a matter of course. Given the social relations of private property, the fluctuations of the capitalist market must become increasingly wild and uncontrolled. Because the competition among capitalists is so intense, the worker's life is now focused entirely on means: "The cost of production of a workman [i.e., his wage] is restricted, almost entirely, to the means of subsistence that he requires for his maintenance, and for the propagation of his race."[101] This same competition, moreover, makes the possession of even this minimal means highly tenuous, for "commercial crises" appear increasingly to "cut off the supply of every means of subsistence."[102] The modern laborer, therefore, "instead of rising with the progress of industry, sinks deeper and deeper below the conditions of existence of his own class."[103] The laborer "becomes a pauper, and pauperism develops more rapidly than population and wealth."[104]

The proletariat revolts because the bourgeoisie "is incompetent to assure an existence to its slave within its slavery."[105] That this revolt becomes political in form does not mitigate the instrumentalism of its motivation, for each step in the workers' political organization is a response to the imposition of new external demands. It is only "in proportion as machinery obliterates all distinctions of labor" that "the various interests ... within the ranks of the proletariat are more and more equalized."[106] And only as "the wages of the workers [become] ever more fluctuating" and "their livelihood more and more precarious" do the "collisions between individual workmen and individual bourgeois take on more and more the character of collisions between classes." *"Thereupon,"* Marx writes, "the workers begin to form combinations (Trades' Unions) against the bourgeoisie; they club together *in order to* keep up the rate of wages; they found permanent associations *in order to* make provision beforehand for these occasional revolts."[107] He concludes that "the proletariat during its struggle with the bourgeoisie is compelled to organize itself as a class."[108†] True, this union is helped by the "improved means of communication," but this too is "created by modern industry."[109] Eventually, in response to the continuing external exigencies, this ever expanding union of workers forms not just a class but a political party, and the civil war between bourgeois and proletarian breaks out into open revolution.[110]

> The advance of industry, whose involuntary promoter is the bourgeoisie, replaces the isolation of the labourers, due to competition, by their revolutionary combination, due to association. The development of Modern Industry, therefore, cuts from under its feet the very foundation on which the bourgeoisie produces and appropriates products. What the bourgeoisie, therefore, produces, above all, is its own grave-diggers. Its fall and the victory of the proletariat are equally inevitable.[111]

Moreover, the rule of this victorious proletariat, and the nature of socialist society it promotes, cannot help but be emancipatory, for only by the provision of property for all, by the socialization of property, can the proletariat abolish the external circumstances whose pressure forced its initial revolt. It is because the proletarians "have nothing of their own to secure and to fortify" that their dictatorship will be altruistic.[112] This amoral morality is not self-interest "rightly understood"; it is straight self-interest ordered by a set of fortuitous external circumstances.

Just as Marx instrumentalizes the family and state in his institutional materialism, so can he systematically account for the role of ideas in his historical materialism. Ideas for Marx are mere ideology, the instruments of class rule. In response to the claim that a communist society threatens "freedom," Marx replies that communism abolishes only "bourgeois freedom," for "by freedom is meant, under the present bourgeois conditions of production, free trade, free selling and buying."[113] Part 3 of the *Manifesto*, in fact, is a discursus on the subordination of ideas to class interest, as Marx links every current in contemporary socialist and communist thought to the strategic, instrumental needs of different economic groups. If a strand of socialism is nostalgic for the cooperation of the rural past, such a misguided conception can only be explained as the socialism of the aristocracy. It was *"in order to* arouse sympathy," according to Marx, that "the aristocracy *were obliged* to lose sight, apparently, of their own interests, and to formulate their indictment against the bourgeoisie in the interest of the exploited working class alone." The resulting ideology, "half lamentation, half lampoon," is only hypocritically proletarian, for it was "only *in order to* rally the people to them" that the aristocracy "waved the proletarian alms-bag in front for a banner."[114] If another strand envisions socialism as restoring individual property and agricultural independence, this must be the socialism of the petty bourgeoisie. Because the "individual members of this class . . . are being constantly hurled down into the proletariat by the action of competition," it is only natural that their writers should side with the proletariat and "should use, in their criticism of the bourgeois regime, the standard of the petit-bourgeoisie."[115] If members of the bourgeoisie themselves advocate socialism, it can only be because a "part of the bourgeoisie is desirous of redressing social grievances, *in order to* serve the continued existence of bourgeois society."[116] If German socialism deemphasizes economic issues and focuses instead on the alienation of humanity, this can occur only because the still backward nature of the German class struggle has failed to specify sufficiently the economic interests of the disaffected intellectuals.[117] The same kind of economic problem flaws the more critical and anti-capitalist utopian socialism espoused by reformers like Fourier and Owens, who wrote about the transformation of capitalism before the economic situation "offer[ed] to them the [actual] material conditions for the emancipation of the proletariat."[118]

In this systematic refutation of opposing socialist theories, it is their economic origins, not the ideas themselves, that hold Marx's attention, but the mechanical quality of this exercise should not blind us to the importance of the argument. What is at stake here is nothing less than the legitimacy of *The Communist Manifesto* itself. If ideas are simply the means to achieve interests, then the only way to evaluate socialist theories is to evaluate the interests which they represent. Since the *Manifesto* is more expressly directed to the interests of wage laborers than are the other socialist traditions of its day—more expressly directed, that is, to interests which are not only more morally legitimate but which appeal to the vast majority—the ideas it espouses must, pari passu, have the greater validity. But while this method of evaluation conveniently eliminates the autonomy of normative, scientific standards, it poses a difficult problem for Marx himself. What is the position of the author of this manifesto, himself a middle-class, highly educated intellectual of German extraction? Was it not the product of long years of study and philosophical innovation? Is the document not a testimony to the independence of ideas from immediate material interests?

The ultimate test for Marx's antivoluntaristic theory lies in his explanation of himself as a revolutionary ideologist. Given the systematic quality of Marx's mature theory, it should not be surprising that he can, indeed, account for himself in strictly instrumentalist terms. It is true, he acknowledges, that a "small section of the ruling class," a "portion of the bourgeois ideologists," cuts itself adrift and joins the revolutionary class.[119] They do so, however, only after economic proletarianization has already forced entire sections of the bourgeoisie to assume a working-class existence if they are to survive—only after the "process of dissolution going on within the ruling class" has assumed a "violent and glaring character."[120] It is, then, economic conditions themselves which have produced the ideas of the *Manifesto*, not the cleverness or creative will of any intellectual. "The theoretical conclusions of the Communists," Marx asserts, "are in no way based on principles that have been invented, or discovered, by this or that would-be reformer."[121] To the contrary, the ideas of the *Manifesto* are there for all to see. "They merely express in general terms," according to Marx, "actual relations springing from an existing class struggle, from a historical movement going on under our very eyes." Not only is the determinism of Marx's theory preserved, but he has found a way to allow scientific standards to remain intact while undermining their analytic autonomy. For the propositions of the *Manifesto* are surely verified by the empirical reality which they inevitably reflect.

As the first mature statement of his objectivist, antivoluntary logic, *The Communist Manifesto* brings to a conclusion Marx's movement away from the subjectivism of his early writings. "Alienation" as a self-consciously employed theoretical concept virtually disappears from this essay, forced out of the picture by Marx's ferocious attack against anti-instrumental institutions, the autonomy of cultural causation, and all forms of nonrational motivation. It is not true, however, that Marx no longer believes in, or cares about, alienation in capitalist society.[122] While he leaves no doubt about his conviction that social action in capitalism is devoid of normative intention, he just as clearly judges this rationalization to be a tragic loss. Instrumental action is consistently described in terms of its contrast to the nonalienated condition Marx earlier called species-being: personal worth has become mere exchange value;[123] men have become commodities;[124] craftsmen have been transformed into appendages of nonhuman machines.[125] The good society means the reconciliation of subject and object, a free association which is at once voluntary and cooperative.[126]

Ironically, Marx's very acceptance of empirical alienation allows him to adopt a purely objectivist theoretical logic. Although he surely still perceives the existence of alienation, he no longer assigns it an independent role in his sociological theory. Flatly attributing alienation to private property, Marx in the *Manifesto* follows the course which he laid out in his earlier work. While he continues to envision communist society as abolishing alienation, in sharp contrast to the 1844 "Manuscripts" he now argues that the achievement of communism depends not on the transformation of human motivation and the ends which organize it, but simply upon the reorganization of means. "The distinguishing feature of communism," he argues, "is . . . the abolition of bourgeois property."[127]

Throughout the *Manifesto*, Marx insists that the source of misery in capitalist society—the misery which he now views as confined to the working class alone—is the privatization of ownership, the capitalist "relations of production." Private property distorts the "forces of production." It is private property that creates democratic poverty instead of wealth and is the cause of class conflict and revolution. No wonder, then, that every practical movement toward the creation of communism which Marx describes is focused entirely upon the reorganization of means. Through such devices as the abolition of inheritance and the nationalization of the means of production, transportation, and communication, Marx would create a socialist version of Bentham's "artificial identity of interests." With completely public property, the material basis for division and conflict is abolished, and with this different external environment for action, altruistic free association will follow forthwith.[128†]

While it is legitimate, then, to argue that Marx does not lose sight of subjective feelings of alienation in his mature writings, this perspective ignores the significant shift in his emphasis which *The Communist Manifesto* formalizes. Although Marx recognizes the existence of such estrangement, his sociological theory now focuses exclusively on antisubjective, collective force, on the "laws" which structure individual volition in capitalist society. To make alienation itself a theoretical focus would point to the inclusion of subjective categories, a step which would reverse the path along which Marx has traveled since his earliest work. Marx has now adopted the logic of a radical, collectivist political economy. It is the great public struggles which now interest him, the instrumental struggles for economic equality and public ownership. Marx always believed that collective forces impinged heavily on individual life, but for a long transitional period he was unsure about what kind of action, instrumental or normative, such forces implied. With the conclusion of the *Manifesto*, this ambiguity about action is firmly resolved. Marx's conversion to instrumentalism is complete.

3. CONCLUSION: INTERPRETIVE ERRORS AND MARX'S TRUE CONTRIBUTION

Now that the first phase of Marx's development has been presented in some detail, the nature of his contribution to sociological theory can be truly understood. To offer such an evaluation, however, one must first enter the thicket of Marxist interpretation.

Until the mid-1950s, an economistic portrait of Marx was widely accepted, in Marxist and non-Marxist circles alike; Marx was generally considered to be within the rationalistic strand of Western intellectual history. With the diffusion of his early writings, and the more general shifts in the intellectual and political environments, this understanding has been gradually modified and even reversed, particularly but by no means exclusively within Marxist and neo-Marxist circles. As a result, Marx has come to be viewed as a radical variant of the Hegelian tradition. He appears, if not as a Romantic, then as highly affected by Romanticism, as one who emphasized the emotional and cultural undergirdings of capitalist society.

The most influential contemporary interpreters of Marx promote a "dialectical" reading. They argue that Marx never adopted a one-sided materialist position and, correspondingly, that no really significant shift marks the transition between the early and the later Marx. Giddens claims that Marx gives full play to ideas in his later work.[129] Atkinson asserts that Marx's sensitivity to the causal role of alienation allows him to understand that "how property is used must depend on how men *feel* about it, what they *understand* by it, and what subjective significance it has for them."[130] Ollman takes a similar path, arguing that the external "laws of capitalism" in Marx's theory of capitalism are voluntaristically conceived: "They become necessary in [*sic*] virtue of everyone thinking and acting as if they are." Marx views objective conditions, Ollman claims, merely as the projections of alienated consciousness.

> To *conceive* of machines as needing workers is to accord machines the power to need workers. Likewise, to *conceive* of money as having the power to buy everything is indeed to have money which has the power to buy everything.[131]

Avineri makes similar claims, arguing that in the later writings Marx views the motor force of capitalism in the same way as in his Hegelian phase, namely, as a tension between normative universalism and economic particularism. According to Avineri, it is Marx's position that "in a modern society, man must lead a double life and conform to two conflicting standards of behavior."[132]

These interpretations, however, overlook the radical shift that occurs in Marx's attitude toward alienation during his early period.[133†] I have shown that, eventually, Marx used alienation to justify rather than to confront the instrumentalist position, and that he comes to articulate a theory which denies autonomy to human volition and to the kinds of normative ideals upon which it depends.

There are obvious extra-intellectual reasons for this common interpretative error. If Marxism is to be maintained as a revolutionary ideology, Marxist theory must be corrected in a way that does nothing to undermine the authority of Marx himself. The solution, of course, is to "read" Marx as if he had offered a different and more satisfactory theory all along. Such strategic reasoning has without doubt played an important role in the contemporary revision of Marxist interpretation, and it will be discussed at much greater length in the concluding chapter of this volume. At this point, however, I am more interested in the sources of theoretical confusion per se; and, indeed, the errors of recent interpreters can be seen as deriving from significant errors in theoretical reasoning itself.

First and most importantly, analysts have failed to distinguish Marx's epistemological position in the purely philosophical sense from the way this epistemology informs his specifically sociological reasoning.[134†] Thus, if Marx can be shown to criticize materialism in his abstract epistemological writings, he must, it is argued, reject an exclusively economic approach to action and an exclusively material order in his sociological theory. The problem here is that interpreters have lost sight of the fact that while theoretical presuppositions are philosophically informed, they represent what I have called (vol. 1, ch. 3) "sociological epistemology," not epistemology per se. In the consideration of action in *society*, the problems of subjectivity/objectivity and voluntarism/determinism take on a different character from that which they possess in abstract, strictly philosophical debate. In strict philosophical terms, the epistemological problem of freedom hinges merely upon acknowledging the independent existence of internal motivation. The problem of "sociological epistemology," however, concerns, first, the specific nature of that subjective factor—whether or not subjective action is conceived in purely instrumental and efficient terms—and, second, the way in which plural actions are arranged in social order. If a theorist commits himself to a collective source of social order, and if he perceives motivation as purely efficient, then he will have to approach social action *as if* it were controlled exclusively by external material force. Whether or not his formal epistemology acknowledges subjectivity, therefore, his sociological epistemology will be mechanical and materialist.

Insofar as interpreters have often failed to make this vital distinction, they have speculated about epistemological elements in Marx's work which have nothing to do with his sociological writing about the nature of action and order in capitalist society. It is for this reason that a radical disjunction so often develops between discussions of "Marx's philosophy" and his sociology, for this reason that recent interpreters have so often either ignored the specifically sociological elements of Marx's work or have failed to connect his empirical, propositional writing to the more philosophical presuppositions which inform it.

The second kind of interpretive error which has produced such misunderstanding in recent Marxist scholarship is the tendency to conflate levels of sociological thought which have to be viewed as relatively independent. Recent critics have too often conflated Marx's ideological commitment to human emancipation with his presuppositions about action and order, arguing that if Marx wanted to create a voluntaristic and normatively ordered society, he must also have embraced this perspective in his sociological theory of contemporary society. In the growing effort to "humanize socialism," associated not only with the New Left but with the movement of dissent in Eastern Europe, this conflation has increasingly taken on a strongly moral imperative. But, in fact, there is no necessary correlation between these different levels of sociological theorizing. To deny the possibility for tension between the theory and the ideology is to deny one of the major sources of tension within the socialist movement itself.

These kinds of errors in theoretical logic permeate the work of Marx's recent interpreters. For example, after asserting, quite reasonably, that Marx's philosophical position "does not involve the application of a deterministic *philosophical* materialism,"[135] Giddens claims that Marx readily accepts the notion that individuals form societies, in part, because of shared moral commitments.

> [According to Marx,] the "isolated individual" is a fiction of utilitarian theory. . . . Each individual is thus the recipient of the accumulated culture of the generations which have preceded him. . . . It is, then, man's membership of [*sic*] society, together with the technological and cultural apparatus which supports that society and which makes it possible, which serves to differentiate the human individual from the animal.[136]

Giddens moves, in other words, from Marx's philosophical position in the abstract directly to his presupposition about the nature of human society. But without seeing how praxis in capitalist society is defined in a purely instrumental way, without seeing that Marx's epistemology must be applied to the problems of action and order if it is to serve as the basis for sociological theory, the roots of Marx's theory of society are impossible to perceive. Giddens argues, quite rightly, that Marx rejects philosophical materialism. But Marx's rationalist assumptions about action in capitalist society effectively eliminate subjectivity from his theory of capitalism nonetheless.

Avineri similarly conflates different levels of Marx's thought. Demonstrating that even in the earlier writings he never adopted a philosophically idealist position, Avineri argues that the materialism, or more accurately the realism, shared by the early and the later Marx demonstrates the theoretical similarities of the two periods.[137] But he ignores the strikingly diverse ways that the abstract epistemology of praxis comes to be defined in each case. Further, he argues that the forthright humanism of Marx's maturity—his ideological desire to place the human actor at the center of the social universe—provides support for a voluntaristic theoretical interpretation of this later work: "the dichotomy between a young, 'humanistic,' 'idealist' Marx vis-à-vis an older, 'determinist,' 'materialist' Marx," Avineri insists, "has no foundation whatsoever in the texts themselves."[138] The conflation of ideology, abstract epistemology, and sociological presuppositions could not be more clear.

In Ollman's case, the difficulties stem more from a misunderstanding of presuppositional issues than from failing to distinguish them from epistemological or ideological ones. Because he adopts an overly broad definition of rationality as involving simply reasoning, or the weighing of means against ends, Ollman can argue that consciousness— "obviously a constituent relation of reason in this sense" —is central to Marx's sociological theory.[139] But only if he had seen, to the contrary, that the crucial assumptions about action revolve around questions of instrumentalism versus normation, around the precise nature of the relationship between means and ends rather than the fact of their relation as such, could he have accurately understood the true role of consciousness in Marx's later work. This role, of course, is undermined precisely by the alienation which Ollman acknowledges but cannot reconcile with his simultaneous assertion that Marx proposes a broader, noninstrumental rationality.

Such theoretical errors create unexplained inconsistencies in the interpretations themselves. After presenting disclaimers about Marx's reductionistic materialism and arguing for Marx's social rather than utilitarian orientation toward the individual, Giddens launches into a ten-page description of Marx's theory of social development which focuses exclusively on the relationship between utilitarian need and changes in productive systems.[140] Similarly, after arguing that subjective estrangement is a major factor in Marx's analysis of changes in modern society, he remarks, nonetheless, that for Marx "the overcoming of alienation ... hinges upon the supercession of private property."[141] Giddens fails to recognize the inconsistency of these two positions because he ignores crucial issues in theoretical logic. By failing to differentiate sociological presuppositions from general epistemology, he has created a sharp disjunction between his discussion of Marx's philosophy and his social theory. An anti-utilitarian approach to action and order, if it were really to have presuppositional status, would have to be connected to empirical propositions about social development of other than purely economic concern. Similarly, if subjective estrangement were actually the effective cause of action in capitalist society, the liberation of communism would necessarily hinge on transformations other than those of private property. Not unexpectedly, Giddens can only weakly explain why alienation drops out as a systematic focus in the later Marx. He simply accepts at face value Marx's own rationale that, after 1844, he was no longer interested in abstract philosophy.[142]

Similar inconsistencies disturb Avineri's argument. Despite the basic contention of his book that a voluntaristic and anti-objectivist theory of capitalism grows out of Marx's philosophy, Avineri makes, in the midst of his argument, a surprising admission: "Marx thinks that present circumstances still make it impossible to produce" subjectively oriented knowledge and action in the social world. As a consequence, Avineri admits, "the validity of traditional mechanistic materialist modes of consciousness" may, indeed, still hold good for Marx's description of capitalist society.[143] Shortly afterward, Avineri resumes the main thread of his argument, asserting that Marx did not, in fact, give up on human intentionality and on the subjective component of knowledge even in capitalism. The problem, he feels, is simply that Marx neglected to "spell out" the process by which such volition is actually carried.[144] These two statements are never reconciled, nor could they be. I would suggest that if Marx actually did continue to accept mechanistic materialism this would certainly explain why he failed to spell out the process by which human volition occurs. It is revealing that Avineri concludes his book by acknowledging that his analysis has concerned Marx's "philosophical system" alone, not his concrete, explanatory sociological theory.[145†] This admission suggests that intentional praxis, the elaboration of which has been the subject of Avineri's entire explication of Marx, may not, after all, inform Marx's actual sociological theory. If it does not, then Avineri's claim that normative tension is at the center of Marx's theory of change is certainly in error, and alienation may function to ensure an instrumental approach to action in the later writings after all.

We have already noted the basic inconsistency in Ollman's work, that while he emphasizes, on the one hand, the reifying projections created by alienated action, he argues, on the other, that "whatever their degree of alienation," men act with purposive, voluntaristic rationality.[146] If workers have such broad powers of rationality, however, it is difficult to explain their lack of revolution and revolt. To deal with this anomaly, Ollman resorts at crucial points in his argument to residual categories. To explain the empirical facts of worker passivity and irrationality, he refers to concepts which are completely outside Marx's theoretical framework. It is "character structure," Ollman asserts, that explains irrationality, and character structure consists in normative internalizations from family, sex roles, and generational groupings.[147] "The idea of character structure," Ollman claims, "does little violence to Marx's basic framework; the interactions he describes go on as before except that something now stands between conditions and response."[148] But if Marx's own analysis of interaction consists simply in condition and response, with no extra-economic mediation, then we are back to an instrumental interaction of the kind that is based neither on reified projection nor on broad, volitional rationality.[149]†

These confusions and self-contradictions can be avoided only by clarifying theoretical logic. General epistemology cannot be substituted for specifically sociological presuppositions, nor can these presuppositions be identified too closely with ideology. Very few interpreters, in fact, have succeeded in making these distinctions. While contemporary observers have distorted Marx's thought by overemphasizing the centrality of the alienation concept, other commentators have argued that alienation has no role at all. Bell argued in 1960, for example, that with *The German Ideology* Marx gives up any conception of human nature as transcending capitalist instrumentalism and that he no longer sees the abolition of the division of labor as an historical possibility.[150] While this perspective at least recognizes the enormous shift that occurs in Marx's perspective, it makes the separation between the two periods overly hermetic. Not only is the later role which alienation plays in legitimating instrumentalism completely obscured, but the continued humanism of Marx's ideological commitment is quite wrongly denied.[151]†

Althusser, who distinguishes sharply between "*theoretical* anti-humanism" and the acceptance of humanism "as an *ideology*,"[152] has initiated a more accurate attack on the role of alienation in the later writings. He emphasizes, correctly, that the later Marx rejected humanism as a theoretical perspective because it implied a voluntaristic approach to social change. Marx never believed, he asserts, "that the knowledge of an object might ultimately replace the object or dissipate its existence."[153] Such a subjectively oriented understanding, Althusser argues, is confined to Marx's early writings alone, where projected feelings of alienation are in fact perceived as the source of the material power of things.[154]

Althusser falters, however, in denying any relation whatsoever between the early and the later writings, in denying to the mature Marx a trans-historical perspective on human nature and by implying that such an emotional question as human alienation is foreign not simply to Marx's mature empirical theory but to his ideology as well. By arguing that an "epistemological break" occurred in Marx's work in 1845,[155] Althusser can ignore the crucial role that alienation plays in rationalizing the rejec-tion of voluntarism in the later writings, for it is not the rejection of a dialectical epistemology as such but rather its specification as alienated, purely efficient rationality that creates the objectivism of Marx's matu-rity. Althusser fails, then, to recognize the continuing, if radically differ-ent role that "alienation" plays in the later work.[156]†

Only among certain representatives of the Frankfurt school of Marx-ism do we find an understanding of the continuity between early and late Marx that recognizes, at the same time, the deterministic nature of the later work. Though Marcuse's famous *Reason and Revolution* has usu-ally been taken as an argument for Marxism as moral criticism, it is, in fact, nothing of the kind: Marcuse grasps theoretical issues involved in Marxian theory more firmly than have many of his contemporary fol-lowers. The entire point of "alienation" in Marx's mature writing, Mar-cuse argues, is to demonstrate the unattainability of normative as opposed to instrumental reason in capitalist society. In contrast with later analysts who have tried to see nonrational action in Marx's accep-tance of alienation, Marcuse understood forty years ago that Marx's point was precisely the opposite: "Marx emphasizes time and time again that his materialistic starting point is forced upon him by the materialis-tic quality of the society he analyzes."[157] Indeed, Marcuse's entire analy-sis of Hegel's theory of objectification is intended to indicate that Marx rationalizes Hegel by identifying the ahistorical process of objectification with alienation, and that it is Marx's greater insight into the brutalizing nature of the capitalist economy that allows him to do so. Without hesita-tion, Marcuse asserts that Marx's recognition of the alienation of reason justifies his acceptance of mechanistic order. "Marx's analysis showed him," Marcuse argues, "the law of [economic] value as the general 'form of Reason' in the existent social system."[158] Further, this "law of value . . . operate[s] as a blind mechanism outside the conscious control of indi-viduals."[159]

While Marcuse enthusiastically accepts the determinism of the later Marx as demonstrating the true inhumanity of capitalist society, the most important current representative of the Frankfurt tradition, Habermas, develops this interpretation into a critique of Marx. Habermas dis-tinguishes between Marx's epistemological commitment to reflexivity and his theoretical description of action in capitalist society by criticizing

Marx's reduction of praxis to labor. "Marx deludes himself about the nature of reflection," Habermas writes, "when he reduces it to labor."[160] While most other contemporary analysts view this identification of praxis and labor as testifying to the voluntaristic elements in Marx's approach to work, Habermas is more realistic. He realizes that in the face of the restraints Marx places on labor in capitalist society, such an identification eliminates the intentionality of praxis, not the instrumentality of labor.

> Marx reduces the process of reflection to the level of instrumental action. By reducing the self-positing of the absolute ego to the more tangible productive activity of the species, he eliminates reflection as such as a motive force of history, even though he retains the framework of the philosophy of reflection.[161]

In contrast to Marcuse, however, Habermas qualifies his position in certain crucial ways, arguing at various points that such reduction occurs only in Marx's formal statements. "At the level of his material investigations," Habermas argues, "Marx always takes account of social practice."

> The productive activity of individuals and the organization of their interrelations . . . are subject to norms that decide, with the force of institutions, how responsibilities and rewards, obligations and charges to the social budget are distributed among members. The medium in which these relations of subjects and of groups are normatively regulated is cultural tradition.[162]

But this statement neglects the role of alienation in Marx's work, and it is impossible to reconcile it with Habermas' earlier critique. Not surprisingly, Habermas never substantiates this claim for the multidimensionality of Marx's later writings.[163†]

If the function of alienation in mature Marxism is, after all, to legitimate a sociology of instrumental action and coercive order, one must look to the rationalistic tradition of social theory if one is to discover the real theoretical contributions effected by Marx's transition to maturity. Indeed, the upshot of my earlier analysis of this transition is not only that Marx accepted the logic of the instrumentalist tradition but that he faced the theoretical challenges to this tradition more squarely than any theorist before or since.

The tradition of instrumental rationalism in Western culture has always faced a crucial dilemma. Its historical roots were tied to the movement toward individuality and voluntarism in early modern Europe—in the Renaissance, the Reformation, and the French and English revolutions. This historical relationship between rationality and individualistic voluntarism—which is not a necessary one in purely theoretical terms—presents rationalism with two equally unpleasant choices. If it remains so tied to individualism, rationalism must leave the problem of order unresolved. The question "what holds society together?" can then be answered only in terms of uncoordinated individual decisions or in terms of residual categories like the invisible hand. On the other hand, if the rationalistic tradition abandons individualism for a collective solution, its voluntaristic qualities are lost, for it can now describe collective control only through external coercion.[164†]

The history of instrumental thought moves back and forth between the poles of this dilemma.[165] Hobbes' theory may be viewed as prototypical of the collectivist strategy. His rigorous theorizing clearly revealed that, given the assumption of scarce resources, instrumental action among discrete individuals must produce the war of all against all. Hobbes' Leviathan emerges as a response to this chaos, as the coercive source of order external to the individual which operates as a determining condition devoid of any normative aspect.[166†] The disadvantage of this Hobbesian solution lay in its extinction of freedom. While the liberal theorists who followed Hobbes were not inclined to follow him along this path, few were prepared to deviate from the rationalist tradition itself. Faced with these constraints, order could be resolved only by some kind of theoretical subterfuge. Locke's contract theory established just such a contraband solution and it did so in a paradigmatic way. Because Locke implicitly changed the state of nature from hostile to cooperative, he could describe the organized society which emerged from the social contract as achieving order and harmony without sacrificing individualism. Locke could, apparently, resolve the order problem without resorting to Hobbes' drastic restrictions of voluntarism. The problem, of course, was that this solution rested upon a certain sleight of hand. If Locke had no recourse to external force, it was because he altered his assumption about action without acknowledging that he had done so, substituting for a purely instrumental efficiency behavior that was more altruistic and cooperative.

Classical economics, from Locke himself to Smith and, to some extent, Ricardo, was rooted in this Lockean solution to the rationalist dilemma. From the conception of mutually advantageous, yet rational individual interaction there emerged the notion of the mutual and voluntary exchange of goods and service. When this first great empirical theory of society came under fire, it was attacked by radicals who were intent on remaining within the rationalist tradition but, at the same time, felt compelled to reject Locke's assumption about the natural identity of social interests. These critics, in effect, took up the earlier solution of Hobbes, though in the process they transformed its ideological content. The eighteenth-century French philosophes developed materialist theories about the supra-individual, empirical sources of social problems. By the early nineteenth century, the strand of this writing informed by Rousseau had evolved into socialist theory. On the English side of the Channel, the most important assault on Locke's individualism began with Bentham's "philosophical radicalism." The radical, often socialist political economists who emerged as the left wing of the Benthamite school merely transformed Bentham's understanding of the "artificial identity of interests" into an attack on institutions like inherited wealth and private capital.

It was under the influence of these two anti-individualist tendencies in the rationalist tradition that Marx made the transition to his mature theoretical position. Until Marx, the anti-individualistic response to Lockean theory was fragmentary; either it was too burdened with philosophical speculation to function as an alternative sociological paradigm—as with the works of the philosophes and Bentham—or it was too exclusively concerned with economic life, as with the French and British political economists. Before Marx, there existed no systematic, empirically-based rationalist theory that could compete with the Lockean model in its own terms as a theory of the social whole.

Marx addressed the Lockean challenge in the guise of traditional political economy, and while he accepted its rationalism he launched a ruthless attack on its individualism. For the logic of this critique as well as for much of its empirical content, Marx drew upon both the French socialists and the Benthamite utilitarians. In effect, he presented himself with a more empirical and critical version of the Hobbesian problem. Bourgeois society, for Marx, was composed of alienated men who pursued their own interest with no concern for shared communal life. What, he asks, can be the source of order in this brutal world? Without Hobbes' political motives and with, certainly, a disinclination to take seriously the independent power of political force, Marx could not take up the cause of Hobbes' sovereign. He did, however, postulate an order that was equally forceful in its controlling power. Marx proposed as sovereign the forces of the market, governed as they were, in turn, by the various orders of property division, social class, and coercive institutional life. Men did not have the "equal faculties" under capitalism which Locke described, nor did they "share all in one community of nature," as Locke had proposed.[167] To the contrary, capitalism alienated men from their species capacity and distorted the community's relationship to nature through disproportionate wealth. Because of capitalism, Hobbes was right: "If two men desire the same thing, they become enemies."[168] As long as people were not furnished with communal facilities, they would be, not perhaps in a state of war of all against all, but in a war of class against class. If such an order eliminated man's control over his own actions, that was precisely the price of order in capitalist society.[169†]

This was the logic of the purely instrumentalist position that Marx developed in the transition away from his Hegelian past. Marx faced the order problem more clearly than other rationalist theorists before him, and he was more willing to accept the costs of establishing instrumental order than most rationalist theorists have been since. Still, there were paths to collective order other than the one taken by Marx, and it is to a theorist who eventually promoted a radically different resolution, one equally paradigmatic for sociological theory, that we now turn.

Chapter Four

DURKHEIM'S FIRST PHASE (1)

The Ambiguous Transition from Voluntary Morality
to Morality as External Constraint

Contemporary readings of great theorists are geared to contemporary times. Just as Marx has recently been decisively reinterpreted, so has Durkheim. On one thing most readers of Durkheim, past and present, have always agreed: he, like Marx, emphasizes social structure. Durkheim helped to create classical sociology because he located social forces outside of the individual actor. But at this point the serious theoretical problems only really begin. The problem for Durkheim, as for Marx, is what structure means: How does structure hold individuals within its limits? Of what are these limits composed? If structure exists, somehow, outside of the individual, can it act only in opposition to freedom? The problematics of Durkheim interpretation, then, are precisely the ones around which Marxist inquiry has also revolved. The fundamental question has always been how Durkheim stipulates the relation between determinism and free action. People keep reading Durkheim, and arguing about him, to find out whether the determinateness of social structures must involve the sacrifice of voluntary control and, conversely, whether the postulate of individual control can be purchased only at the price of denying the realities of external force. How generations have understood Durkheim has fundamentally shaped the pattern of their sociological discourse. The debates over Durkheim's work are, inevitably, arguments about the most basic directions of sociological thought.

Understanding the central issues in Durkheim's thought, of course, involves much more than simply reading it. Every reading is an exercise in theoretical logic, and, no less than with Marx, the crucial barriers to understanding Durkheim stem from the analytical confusion that distorts theoretical thinking in sociology.

1. REDUCTION AND CONFLATION IN DURKHEIMIAN INTERPRETATION

Durkheim has suffered perhaps even more than Marx from the inveterate desire of sociologists to reduce the scientific continuum to one of its parts, a weakness that Durkheim himself, as we will see, shares with his later interpreters. The most striking example of such reduction has been the continuing suggestion by advocates of the positivist persuasion that Durkheim's greatness lies in his steadfast commitment to empirical manipulation. Merton sees Durkheim's subsequent impact on sociology as linked to his focus on middle-range propositional generalizations.[1] Stinchcombe lauds *Suicide* as the greatest statistical experiment in sociological history and presents Durkheim's generalizations as if they were simply inducted directly from his data about voluntary deaths.[2] Pope criticizes these generalizations on the same logical grounds, arguing that his own statistical reexamination of Durkheim's data has produced propositional questions that make Durkheim's theoretical innovation groundless. From a logically similar position, Evans-Pritchard dismisses Durkheim's theories of religion as based on flimsy evidence and second-hand data.[3] For these interpreters, whatever Durkheim's theory turns out to be—too determinate, too ideal, too voluntary—it must be viewed as a product of specific observational statements.[4†]

But Durkheim's interpretation has been just as forcefully distorted from the other, much more generalized side of the sociological continuum. Ever since the publication of his first book, critics have argued that Durkheim's work was far from observational and scientific, that it must be viewed rather as the immediate product of the social environment within which it was written. Not objective norms but political values constitute the real formative layer of Durkheim's theory according to this view, and if his conception of structure leads in one direction or another it is for ideological reasons, not for scientific ones. This reduction has been emphasized particularly by Durkheim's critics on the left, who have regarded his emphasis on social morality as equivalent to a call for acquiescence to capitalism. In 1932, the French Marxist Paul Nizan accused Durkheim of formulating a "doctrine of obedience, of conformism, and of social respect."[5] Another French Marxist, Georges Kagan, made the same claim in 1938, calling Durkheim "the antirevolutionary par excellence in the sense that he is profoundly attached to tradition."[6] For Benoît-Smullyan, writing after the war, Durkheim was "anti-individualist in ethics and conservative in politics," hence his allegedly anti-individualistic realism.[7] For a more contemporary critic, Irving Zeitlin, the conceptual innovations of Durkheim's work are also quite secondary. What was new, what separated Durkheim so sharply from Marx, was his counterrevolutionary political stance, and it is from this ideological commitment alone that Durkheim's emphasis on the power of social solidarity derives.[8] Coser's much more nuanced interpretation is, nonetheless, theoretically much the same: he directly derives the normative aspects of Durkheim's theory from the social situation of the Third Republic.[9]

Between these extremes of theoretical reduction, Durkheim's thought has been tied to other kinds of overly narrow and specific theoretical issues. Discussions of Durkheim have, for example, been overwhelmingly concerned with the functionalist organic model he employed. Analysts from Radcliffe-Brown to Pope have seen this functionalist commitment as the generative conceptualization of Durkheim's work, responsible both for the strength and the weaknesses of his approach to the problem of social structure.[10] More recently, as the debate over functional models has given way to arguments about conflict versus consensus, Durkheim's propositions about empirical stability and equilibrium have been singled out as the most decisive feature of his sociology.[11]

These different reductionist interpretations are so cross-cutting that each throws the other into doubt. Whereas the functionalist model will be invoked to explain Durkheim's conservatism, the same political position will, just as often, be invoked to explain his functionalism. Where both functional models and political ideology seek to account for Durkheim's alleged bias against social conflict, his propositions about the crucial empirical role of consensus will, conversely, be pointed to as the basis for his functionalism and his conservatism. The circularity of these interpretations reveals the inadequacy of reducing Durkheim's theory to any one of its parts.

More important than such ambiguity, however, is the fact that such reductionism ignores altogether the most generalized level of theoretical argument. For these critics, Durkheim's solutions to the fundamental problems of social determinism and individual freedom can be found exclusively in the lower levels of the scientific continuum: in his perception of empirical fact, in his sensitivity to conflict or stability, in his choice of model, in his political evaluation of the status quo. But the most important and ramifying theoretical decisions that Durkheim made are addressed to the presuppositional questions of action and order. The answers he gives to these questions establish the basis for each of the more specific levels of his theory.

Yet for Durkheimianism as for Marxism, it has been disagreement and misunderstanding on the presuppositional level itself which has constituted the basis for competing schools of criticism. Durkheim's presuppositional commitments have been presented in such various ways as to legitimate entirely different approaches to sociology. It is, most of all, the problem of order, not action, which has proved so intractable to Durkheim's interpreters, to both his critics and his sympathizers. There is, in the first place, a strong temptation to take the "order" issue out of its presuppositional context altogether and to conflate it with the kinds of more specific theoretical questions I have just described. By falsely identifying the "problem of order" with a concern for stability or with conservatism, influential interpreters have dismissed it as irrelevant to Durkheim's theoretical strategy. Giddens, for example, points out that Durkheim was preoccupied with change and historicity and was far from being a political conservative, and then goes on to conclude that "it can perfectly well be said that it [the problem of order] was not a problem for Durkheim at all."[12] Others similarly point to Durkheim's "practical-humanistic concerns" and his "evolutionary emphasis" as evidence that the problem of order must not have concerned him.[13] Conversely, more conservative interpreters have used the same conflationary distortion to argue that order was indeed Durkheim's fundamental concern. Thus, Nisbet acknowledges that Durkheim was liberal by political choice and modernist by method, but argues, nonetheless, that his sociology constitutes a "massive attack on the philosophical foundations of liberalism."[14] With the term "philosophy," Nisbet wishes to invoke the most general, presuppositional level of Durkheim's thought. He ends up, however, by defining this concern very narrowly as a preoccupation with order in the conservative sense of an interest in social harmony, consensus, and obedience to established authority. To a certain extent, Parsons makes a similar error; indeed, much of the confusion about order in Durkheim responds to Parson's initial conflationary usage. In contrast to Nisbet, Parsons sharply differentiates the concern with empirical stability from any necessary ideological orientation. But he often conflates Durkheim's truly generalized solution to the order problem—which Parsons himself did so much to illuminate—with a preoccupation with concrete empirical equilibrium.[15]

I will contend, against both these arguments, that the problem of order must be firmly distinguished from the empirical question of equilibrium and from the ideological evaluation of change. As an approach to the fundamental nature of social relationships, the order problem focuses on the question of the random versus the structured quality of human events, on whether the aggregation of individual acts derives from individualistic or collectivist sources. As will be seen, Durkheim's answers to these questions are relatively independent of his approaches to conflict and political action. His presuppositions imply neither conservatism nor liberalism, stability nor change. To the contrary, they provide the crucial framework within which such issues take on their specific theoretical meaning.

But even when order is accorded its truly presuppositional status, Durkheim's interpreters continue to treat it in a less than fully generalized way. On the basis of their own presuppositional biases, analysts read Durkheim, either critically or deferentially, to legitimate tendentious positions of their own. The most widespread interpretive error develops from the notion that supra-individual order is necessarily antivoluntarist. From this perspective the particular type of collective order—which hinges, in my terms, on the kind of action that is believed to inform collective structures—becomes irrelevant. Whether normative or instrumental, internal or external to the concrete individual, collective order must for these analysts inhibit self-expression and autonomy.

This understanding informs a range of otherwise antithetical readings of Durkheim's work. "Group mind" critics hold, for example, that insofar as Durkheim views order as external to the isolated individual his work must be viewed as an example of "deterministic" social theory.[16] While these nominalist theorists usually read Durkheim as a collective-idealist, another school of interpretation makes essentially the same error while reading him in quite the opposite way, as a kind of materialist. In this case, Durkheim's antivoluntary determinism is seen as deriving from his emphasis on the actual instrumental force of group pressure, not just from his supra-individual emphasis per se. According to Blau, for example, Durkheim could not have emphasized internal value commitments, since all such "psychological" elements are inherently individualistic; the only true collective order is the external kind engendered by "fear of sanctioning."[17] If Durkheim emphasizes social control, then he must be a theorist of coercive social organization, and his understanding of action is implicitly instrumentalized.[18] Strongly influenced by the nominalism of existentialist thought, Aron offers a similar reading: Durkheim must be an antivoluntarist because the locus of his collective order is the concrete human group.[19]

Most recently, this reading has been formulated in particularly revealing ways by those who argue that Durkheim must be seen as a "structuralist." According to this perspective, which is an implicit polemic against contemporary normative functionalism, Durkheim's theory differs little in essentials from that of Marx. One analyst points, for example, to a convergence between Marx and Durkheim, which is a "natural and necessary consequence of their common assumptions concerning the systematic character of society and the need for a group unit of analysis."[20] Once again, it is the simple fact of collective order, not its specific nature, that is conceived here as the crucial theoretical determinant. But, as I tried to demonstrate in my initial discussion of Marx, the notion of "structure" is where classical sociological theory begins, not where it ends. The most crucial issues in theoretical logic are lost if Durkheim's and Marx's common collectivism is taken to exhaust their theoretical relationship. To do so is to make utterly incomprehensible the generations of debate and reformulation within both Marxism and Durkheimianism.

In opposition to this diffusely nominalist-cum-materialist understanding of Durkheim's sociological collectivism, there is another tradition of interpretation which recognizes, much more accurately, that by positing collective order Durkheim hoped to eschew only the most radically individualist type of voluntarism. This understanding, classically formulated by Parsons and most recently by such commentators as Filloux, Bellah, Lukes, La Capra, and Giddens, avoids the determinist error through its insight that the individual actor is necessarily social, an insight gained partly from the tutelage of Durkheim himself.[21] Yet in making this important insight into Durkheim's theoretical intention these analysts have too often assumed his theoretical success. I will contend, to the contrary, that it is the gap between Durkheim's intentions and his ability to develop a fully satisfactory theory in accord with them which defines the drama of his theoretical development.

These analysts usually go on to argue, moreover, that Durkheim not only successfully criticized mechanistic materialism but that he transcended an overly voluntaristic idealism as well. In part, they have confused Durkheim's acceptance of methodological materialism—his "naturalistic" approach to social analysis—with his acceptance of the materialist dimension in a sociological and presuppositional sense.[22] They also argue for such a Durkheimian synthesis of materialism and idealism on the grounds that the critique Durkheim made of philosophical idealism necessarily implied his rejection of idealism in sociological theory. This argument mirrors the strategy employed by recent Marxian critics to argue against materialist interpretations of Marx.[23†] Neither view yields a picture of Durkheim as a truly multidimensional theorist. The presuppositional synthesis of sociological idealism and materialism is essentially independent of either strictly methodological or strictly philosophical considerations.

A fully multidimensional theory of society, I will argue in the following pages, emerges clearly only with the confrontation of Durkheim and Marx. A consideration of Durkheim illuminates the problematic aspects of Marxian theory and, at the same time, a reading of Marx is indispensable for the discovery of the weaknesses in Durkheim's thought. The present chapter shows that—despite his best theoretical intentions and some crucial initial formulations—Durkheim could not free himself in the early part of his career from the deterministic theoretical framework that Marx had himself embraced. When Durkheim does finally construct a theory that is at once collectivist and voluntary—in his later writings— he avoids the determinism of Marx's later work only at the cost of making the "structures" of his own theory overly dependent on the very voluntarism they were designed to protect. This dialectic between Durkheim and Marx illuminates the central dilemmas of sociological thought.

2. DURKHEIM'S EARLY WRITINGS: THE UNSUCCESSFUL SEARCH FOR A VOLUNTARY MORALITY

Like Marx, Durkheim was a theorist committed to practical ends, ends which involved the fundamental restructuring of modern society. Durkheim, too, viewed socialism as the form this future society must take. In pursuing these practical goals, moreover, Durkheim drew from the same intellectual traditions as Marx himself, from French socialism, German Romanticism, and English utilitarianism. Durkheim was, finally, also a dialectician. Like his revolutionary predecessor, he intended to produce a new theoretical synthesis by incorporating the best elements of these widely divergent perspectives and discarding the worst.

We have seen how Marx's relation to these various traditions changed sharply in the course of his movement to intellectual maturity. We will find similar discontinuity in Durkheim's intellectual growth, though his development is not as linear as Marx's. Marx began with an antipositivist and voluntaristic theory strongly influenced by German Romantic Idealism. When, under the influence of French socialism and English utilitarianism, he later moved to a more scientific and materialist stance, this early Romantic commitment reverberated in his later work in ways that have often turned out to be confusing for later interpreters. While the starting point of the young Durkheim is more ambiguous, the direction of his initial movement is surprisingly similar. Durkheim accepted certain currents in French socialism, but he was profoundly torn between utilitarian and Romantic approaches to the institutionalization of state control. In his earliest formulations he emphasized voluntarism and normative control, but by the end of his early writings he had articulated almost as deterministic and antivoluntaristic a vision as the maturing Marx. From the beginning, however, Durkheim reinforced this perspective with a scientistic positivism which Marx, at a similar stage of development, had forcefully rejected. The first work of Durkheim's maturity, *The Division of Labor in Society*, specifies this general instrumental position, although it does so in an extraordinarily ambivalent way. There exists, therefore, a profound parallel not only between the paths that Durkheim and Marx followed in their early writings but in their first great works as well.

The *Division of Labor* functioned for Durkheim, however, not as the confirmation of his ideological vision but as its denial, not as the fulfillment of his theoretical ambition but as its frustration. This first mature work confronted him with the implications of his instrumental vision, and he turned back from it to a voluntaristic and idealistic vision. In direct contrast to the consistent line of Marx's later development, Durkheim's theory undergoes a second conceptual upheaval. Where the echoes of Marx's early Romanticism provided an illusory voluntarism for his later theorizing, the remnants of Durkheim's determinism gave to his later theorizing a misleadingly antivoluntaristic slant.

It has become fashionable in the Durkheim literature, as with recent interpretations of Marx, to deny these abrupt shifts and self-contradictions, and to stress, instead, the continuity of Durkheim's theorizing. If Durkheim was a "group mind" theorist, he was always so; if a "structuralist," then continuously structuralist; if multidimensional, then consistently so synthetic.[24†] In demonstrating the fallacy of such readings, I will turn first, as I did with Marx, to Durkheim's earliest work, writings which in contrast to Marx's famous "Manuscripts" have not received nearly the attention they deserve.[25†]

2.1. SOCIAL CRISIS AND THE SEARCH FOR A RESPONSIVE COLLECTIVISM

As with Marx, Durkheim's earliest theoretical decisions must be seen against the background of his social commitment. The years during which he came to his vocation as a sociologist were marked by extraordinary social conflict, and from the perspective of the French left, which Durkheim shared, the dangers of civil strife were balanced only by the hopes for a republican renewal. As a young teen-ager in Alsace, Durkheim had directly experienced the threat posed by the Franco-German war of 1870-1871. He observed less directly but no doubt as keenly the effects of the class war that triggered and eventually guaranteed the bloody repression of the Paris Commune in 1871. Throughout the rest of this decade the very existence of the Third Republic was an open question. The French Senate, for example, ceased to be a bastion of Monarchist sentiment only in 1879, the year Durkheim was admitted to the Ecole Normal Supérieure. Struggles over secular education wrenched the ideological foundations of the Republic in the beginning of the 1880s, when Durkheim, as a young baccalaureate, took his first positions teaching philosophy in provincial lycées. As this decade progressed, the Boulangist movement exacerbated political instability, and the dynamics of rapid industrialization created increasingly bitter conflict between classes and regions.[26]

It is no wonder that when Durkheim's first sociological articles began to appear in the mid-1880s they demonstrated such sensitivity to the problem of social cohesion: A "society whose members are not bound to one another by some solid and durable link," he wrote in 1886, "would resemble a loose pile of dust which could at any time be dispersed by the slightest wind to the four corners of the world."[27] His early writings reveal a strong curiosity about the sources of this type of transient and divided condition, not only in the problems generated by capitalism but in the weakness of political authority and the failure of normative consensus. By attacking these sources of national instability, Durkheim would encourage more effective social regulation. He wished to reconstruct the unity and harmony of the French nation.

Yet this commitment to national integration and social control was counterbalanced, in Durkheim's mind, by an equally strong commitment to the democratic expansion of liberties for individual citizens. The instability he feared was produced, after all, by the severe political conflicts between left and right, and in this struggle Durkheim definitely took the Republican side. Harmony must be established, then, but not at the cost of sacrificing individual freedom. In 1885, Durkheim approvingly characterizes Fouillée's belief that "the individual must be his own master and determine his own destiny," and with this statement he indicates his firm rejection of the ideological principles of French conservative thought.[28] For Durkheim, the resolute secularist, the cosmological conception proposed by conservatives like Comte and Bonald to legitimate deference to authority over individual liberty was completely out of the question.[29] He posited, in contrast, a sharp break between the traditionalism of medieval society and modernity, and argued that the liberation of the individual was part of an irresistible historical trend: "With progress, the individual is more and more distinguished from the physical and social milieu which surrounds him, and develops increasing consciousness of himself."[30]

Such freedom demands a restriction in external coercive force. Yet Durkheim realized that if the sources of national strife were to be controlled the restoration of social harmony would require vast institutional force. He follows the preceding argument about the historic inevitability of individualism, for example, with the assertion that "it is, however, certain that the activity of the state is extending itself further and further without the possibility of assigning it, once and for all, a definite limit."[31] That such value commitments were in tension with one another, if not downright contradictory, Durkheim was not unaware. Indeed, he insists on this paradox: "The liberty which the individual enjoys grows at the same time as his social obligations."[32]† The contradiction, if it is one, must be squarely acknowledged, for it is a social reality even if it can hardly be explained or understood. "Social progress has two sides," Durkheim writes, "which seem to be mutually exclusive: since most of the time only one of them is seen."[33]

His efforts to do justice to both sides of historical progress guided Durkheim's response to the two great ideological movements of the French Republican left, socialism and solidarism. Socialism had, of course, been a significant current in France since Saint-Simon, and, as such, French socialism had nothing to do with the scientific socialism of Marx. By the late 1870s, however, a more self-consciously working-class socialism had begun to recover from the debacle of the Commune, and by the late 1880s more Marxian forms of socialism had assumed a central place in French political and intellectual debate.[34] Durkheim's personal interest in socialism can be traced back at least to 1881 when, after graduating from the Ecole Normale Supérieure, he decided to devote his doctoral dissertation to the study of socialism and modern society.[35] It can also be clearly seen in his first published article, four years later, where he argued that the repression of the medieval corporation had produced an economic struggle that was "crushing the weakest and reducing them to misery."[36] No wonder Durkheim sharply criticized the French conservative tradition for underplaying the challenge to social cohesion presented by industrial capitalism and for rejecting the socialist antidote which, he thought, capitalism inevitably required. Thus, in 1886, Durkheim attacked Comte for omitting from his sociological theory the "two most essential factors in the progress made by sociology, understanding economic change and the development of socialism."[37]

Yet, for all of this, Durkheim would not happily embrace the kinds of restraint on individual action so often implied by socialist theory. He particularly objected to the coercive approach to socialism that he viewed as endemic to Marxian thought. Although it is not clear how well Durkheim actually knew Marx's work, his reservations about Marx's mature political theory were—as has been demonstrated in the preceding chapter—certainly justified.[38†] Even in the most ambiguous sections of his earliest writings Durkheim was far more concerned with maintaining the voluntarist impulse than was the mature Marx. For example, although his doctoral thesis investigated the application of socialism to industrial society, it did so—as his early provisional title indicated—from the perspective of "the relationship between individualism and socialism."[39] And while he decried the effects of unrestrained capitalism on the powerless worker, he was equally alarmed by the prospect of state intervention in the name of socialist control. If the state should intervene, "taking in its hand the general interests which have not been able to organize and defend themselves" and "meddling, consequently, in all the details of collective life," according to Durkheim, individual freedom would be gravely threatened.[40] From the [rule of the] proletariat, he warns, "we fall into a despotic socialism." Excessive freedom for selfish social groups on the one hand, excessive coercion in the socialist solution on the other—"these are, in effect, the two chasms between which civilized societies today seem to waver."[41]

It was to resolve this ideological dilemma that Durkheim turned to the socialism of certain writers in the German historical school. If the contradictory elements in Marxian socialism had developed because its regulation would "impose itself by force on individuals," a socialist solution would have to be found that could establish regulation and control without force.[42] Durkheim was attracted, for this reason, to the emphasis on moral suasion of the German "socialists of the chair"—Schmoller, Wagner, and Brentano. Yet he was highly critical of them, at the same time, for too easily embracing the authoritarian notion of socialism from above; such an acceptance of state power, Durkheim believed, would have the same despotic effects as the Marxist conception of socialism as class dictatorship. These criticisms, in turn, led Durkheim to the socialists associated with the tradition of the historical school of jurisprudence and economics, who he thought were more critical of the German statist tradition and much more self-consciously concerned with the freedom of the individual.[43†] One of the most forceful spokesmen for this tradition was the historical economist Schaeffle, whose admittedly utopian proposals made a great impression on Durkheim, both immediately before and after his extended trip to Germany in the academic year 1885/86. What Durkheim said about Schaeffle he would surely have said about himself, namely, that the concept of socialism "could be unburdened of all internal contradiction" if only "the fundamental principles of Marx's theory [were] renounced."[44†] Of course, socialism had to be "authoritarian" in some sense, since it must exert collective control over the anarchy created by capitalist individualism and social conflict. Yet Schaeffle had demonstrated to Durkheim that socialism need be authoritarian only in the sense of being "organized," in the sense of subjecting industrial forces to explicit rules.[45] Instead of imposing itself by force on individuals, socialist authority, in Schaeffle's vision, "emanates ... from the free will of individuals" themselves. The internal contradiction of socialism—its coercive imposition of human freedom—could now be resolved, for "collective activity does not create itself or organize itself out of nothing, but is a resultant of individual activities."[46] The social harmony and national reconstruction promised by socialism could in this way be collective and individual at the same time.

If Durkheim was critical of contemporary socialist movements for being too authoritarian, for ignoring the historical movement toward individualism, he sharply criticized French solidarism for being too individualistic and for underestimating the long-term movement toward collectivism and control. Solidarism was a middle-class movement that, like more working-class socialism, opposed the abuses of unrestrained capitalist development. An ideology that eventually became the semi official doctrine of the Third Republic, its most important intellectual foundations were established by Fouillée in the 1880s.[47] Fouillée critiqued traditional individualist thought by insisting that Rousseau's contract theory be combined with the much more organismic understanding formulated by Comte and Darwin. The abuses of unrestrained capitalist entrepreneurialism must be counterbalanced, he believed, by a conception of "society" to which individual actors owed debts and obligations. Despite these reformist sentiments, however, Fouillée held private property sacrosanct and believed that the state's role in establishing such social obligations should remain minimal. Since free contracts among conscious individuals must remain the basis for all collective life, the payment of social debts remains for Fouillée a matter of unforced agreement.

Durkheim rejects this solidarist vision, not simply because it is too moderate but because it is overly individualist. While he acknowledges and applauds Fouillée's rejection of the doctrine of economic individualism, he argues that Fouillée continues to accept the basic image of man as isolated and free. As a result, Fouillée pays insufficient attention to the need for strong state control.

> Society [for Fouillée] is composed of free individuals. Universal suffrage permits collective life without affecting this liberty [and so Fouillée supports it]. Society [for Fouillée] is an association, a sort of limited holding company where all the interested parties [*les intéressés*] must be consulted on the management of the business.[48]

If such consultation were made, of course, effective social regulation would be completely impossible.

Durkheim rejected solidarism, then, for not going far enough toward restructuring French society. This reconstruction, Durkheim believed, would require a much more thoroughgoing socialization than solidarists like Fouillée were willing to concede. Solidarists rejected socialism because they believed, incorrectly, that individualism and social control were antithetical. Marxian socialists, in Durkheim's view, shared the same belief. They agreed with solidarists that socialist reforms would have to be instituted by an authoritarian state; they differed only in the fact that they accepted such a sacrifice of individual liberty as a cost worth bearing. Durkheim wanted to believe this dilemma was a false one, that this ideological confrontation between socialists and solidarists was unnecessary. He admitted, however, that just how collective control and voluntary choice could be reconciled remained theoretically "obscure"; this combination, so "contradictory in appearance," was something "which has never yet been explained."[49] He would devote his career to finding a way to explain it.

2.2. THE CRITIQUE OF CLASSICAL ECONOMY: MORALITY AS THE COLLECTIVIST ALTERNATIVE

Like most of his generation in the 1880s, Durkheim felt compelled to move beyond ideology to science, to transform political discourse into sociological thought. From the very beginning of his sociological writings, therefore, Durkheim searched for the theoretical meaning of his political dilemma. How can the individual actor be reconciled with collective order without damaging, irrevocably, the voluntary scope of his activity? Although Durkheim's ideological interest made this presuppositional question central to his theoretical concerns, the answer which he offered certainly cannot be seen simply as a reflection of his ideology. Durkheim believed, as the young Marx had, that ideological and political positions depended upon certain crucial theoretical developments. It is no wonder that Durkheim, like Marx, turned with such a sense of urgency to the task of establishing the nature of social order and the kind of action upon which it depended.[50†]

Durkheim tries to establish his position on these vital questions by simultaneously criticizing and incorporating the answers provided by widely diverse scientific traditions. Like Marx, he begins with classical economics, and he praises it as the first truly empirical social science: "The economists were the first to proclaim that social laws are as necessary as physical laws and to make this axiom the basis of a science."[51] He also lauds classical economics for the value it places upon individual action and self-control.[52] At the same time, however, Durkheim criticizes these English writers for failing to differentiate between their ideological emphasis on the individual and the status of the individual in a theoretical sense. Reifying their personal commitment to individual choice, the economists offer a seriously distorted vision of social order. For them, Durkheim writes, there is "nothing real in society but the individual"[53]: "It is by him and it is for him that all is done."[54] The economists portray society, correspondingly, merely as a "mechanical aggregate of juxtaposed individuals,"[55] and regard any more organic vision as a "metaphysical entity that the scientist can and must neglect."[56]

> That which is called by this name [of society] is only the connecting together of each individual activity; it is a composite which is nothing more than the sum of its parts.[57]

Durkheim rejects the economists' position because it can achieve voluntarism only at the expense of social regulation. Since he believes that individual action occurs within a collective order, he insists that the line between individual and society cannot be drawn in nearly as clean cut and concrete a manner as the economists would like. True, part of their position must be accepted if individualism is to be preserved. But society, too, "is a real being," and Durkheim insists that to recognize the centrality of the individual in no sense excludes social control. Despite its rootedness in the individual, the social entity "nonetheless has its own nature and personality."[58] Durkheim emphasizes that order itself assumes a supra-individual form, even while he appreciates that the decisions of individual actors somehow form its foundation. He can argue, therefore, that the failure to comprehend collective order implies also a failure to understand the true nature of individual action. He concludes with the ironic suggestion that classical economics "does not perceive that in proceeding so [individualistically], it contradicts itself," because "the ideal at which it aims, to know the highest level of liberty and individual initiative, can never be achieved on the basis of its isolated individual."[59]

Durkheim, then, mounts an attack on classical economics that differs appreciably from Marx's. Where Marx was concerned to argue against the economists' approach to order simply on collectivist grounds, Durkheim carefully formulates his own collectivist critique in a way that continues to reflect his greater concern about individual control. Yet Durkheim does not, for that, necessarily reject Marx's much more instrumentalist critique of economic individualism. His own socialist rejection of capitalist economic activity might seem to indicate, indeed, a similar interest in the instrumental aspects of collective control. The possibility remains that Durkheim is building upon and extending Marx's critique of classical economics rather than completely rejecting it.

There is some evidence in the early writings that Durkheim is of just such a mind. At one point, for example, he specifies his presuppositional critique by attacking classical economics for ignoring the vast differences of instrumental power between worker and capitalist.

> What can the unfortunate worker, reduced to his own resources, do against the rich and powerful boss, and is there not a real and cruel irony putting these two so manifestly unequal forces in the same category? If they enter into combat [en lutte], is it not clear that the second will always and without difficulty crush the first? What does such liberty amount to?[60]

Capitalist and worker, then, must not be regarded simply as independent individuals but as representatives of socially structured, unequal forces. This was, of course, precisely the argument made by Marx.[61†] In another essay, Durkheim further agrees with Marx that this unequal social position is the source of the social conflict that classical economists do not see, for "interests of the individual and those of society are far from always coinciding."[62] And at still another point, he points to this inequality of means and the conflict it engenders as the rationale for socialist intervention. "Instead of starting with human nature and deducing science from it as the orthodox economists did," it must be recognized that "economic facts transcend the individual's sphere of action." Once it is understood that economics "constitutes a function which is not domestic and private but social," it becomes clear that "society [cannot] abandon this function to the free enterprise of individuals."[63]

If Durkheim had continued in this direction, he would have entered, unequivocally, the realm of radical political economy. Indeed, at one point he applauds, much as Marx himself once did, "the new economic school" that, in sharp contrast to orthodox economics, recognizes the powerful role which collective factors, particularly the state, play in economic life.[64] From a concentration on this institutional source of collective order, Durkheim might have moved into the Marxian topography, into the discussion of the division of labor and social classes, the distribution of wealth, and social conflict.

Yet in his ideological evaluations, as the earlier discussion demonstrated, Durkheim rejected Marxian socialism as overly deterministic. And though it is not certain that he understood the finer points of Marx's socialist theory, he certainly perceived correctly that Marxists conceived of the socialist state as a purely economic instrument for the equalization of social wealth. Durkheim translated these ideological reservations into a critique of economic individualism that sought much more than Marx's critique to maintain the economists' respect for individual volition. It should not be surprising, then, that Durkheim does not continue to follow the Marxian path in his collectivist critique of economic individualism, although, as I will show later, his rejection of a generally instrumental approach is, in the end, far from complete.

A sign of this parting of the ways can be seen in Durkheim's suggestion that "social economy" might be a more appropriate term for the collectivist school of economics than "political economy."[65] Better social than political because the collective order that Durkheim would explain is, apparently, more moral and nonrational than economic and instrumental. The German economists Durkheim would follow turn out to be much more interested in the divergence of the ends that regulate economic life than in its distortion by the unequal distribution of means. If Marxian socialism is despotic, the source may be its willingness to accept the orthodox English economists' narrow vision of action, even if it rightly rejects their individualistic negation of order. Durkheim himself will not make this mistake. Arguing that "the need for abundant food is not the only one that is felt by the social organism," Durkheim writes that the state, capitalist or socialist, must not be conceived in a purely materialist way. "Could one say," he asks, that the state's "only aim was to assure their [individual citizens'] security and to arrange their well being?"[66] Durkheim brings a presuppositional critique of rationality to bear on the problem of a voluntaristic socialism. He applies it also to his dissatisfaction with economic individualism. Classical economists are wrong not simply because they ignore collective power, he now argues, but because "they are so taken with liberty they misunderstand and deny the need . . . for solidarity."[67] Moral solidarity, then, appears to be the collective force upon which Durkheim's social science will focus. Morality must be the collective force that can preserve order without threatening freedom.

Yet Durkheim's early writings reveal only a rudimentary understanding of how morality might effect this reconciliation of individualism and determinism. He was sure of one thing: morality was part of the natural world. For this reason it must be studied in a scientific manner. This constituted one fundamental reason for Durkheim's rejection of Kantianism in its pure form, a rejection in which he followed the path laid out for him by the two French philosophers who had influenced him most, Renouvier and Boutroux.[68] In Durkheim's view, the naturalistic quality of morality implicitly gave to it a collective, supra-individual status. But collective in precisely what sense?

To acknowledge the sui generis character of morality and its distinction from purely individualistic phenomena did not in itself yield an understanding of how it actually worked in society. Durkheim was torn, even after his rejection of the English economists, between different presuppositional perspectives on morality, even between conflicting strands of different intellectual traditions. Once again, this conflict revolved around his effort to combine collectivism with voluntarism. He accepted, for example, Comte's notion that society constituted a real living organism in which moral consensus played a preeminent part.[69] He later interpreted the French organicist critique of individualism in the following way: actual men have little in common with the abstract, isolated entities that are the subject of political economy. Real individuals are subject to rules of action which they did not create but which they nonetheless respect.[70] Yet Durkheim was less inclined to adopt Comte's emphasis on social deference and his proposals for anti-individualistic controls. These reservations made him particularly receptive to the work of a later French organicist, Espinas, who broadly argued in his book *Les Sociétés animales* that moral conscience rose out of individual action itself.[71]

The same tension informed Durkheim's reading of the German historical school, which he hailed as the first great attempt to make the study of morality an empirical science.[72] On the one hand, he applauded Wundt for realizing that the rejection of metaphysical realism—the reification of society as an entity over and above the heads of individuals—need not imply an acceptance of the isolated individual as the source of morality.

> From the fact that collective phenomena do not exist outside of individual consciences it does not follow that they come from them; but rather they are the work of the community. They do not emerge from individuals in order to spread themselves

through society, but rather they emanate from society and are then diffused in individuals.[73]

Yet this collectivist approach is immediately hedged, and Durkheim adds in the sentence following that while "individuals receive them [collective phenomena] more than they make them," each individual "collaborates a little if only to an infinitesimal extent." His treatment of Schaeffle's sociological, as opposed to his socialist, program is similarly ambiguous. Even while he praises Schaeffle's analysis of morality for superceding a purely economic emphasis on individual choice, Durkheim qualifies the collective emphasis.[74] He returns to the importance of the individual actor and tries to articulate his naturalistic perspective on society in an emphatically antideterministic way. Reminding his readers that "the collective mind is only a component of individual minds," he insists that, since the sociologist is not a metaphysician, social consciousness cannot be conceived of as a "transcendent being, soaring above society."[75]

Finally, Durkheim is ambivalent even about the English tradition itself. The orthodox economists, of course, are unacceptable. But Durkheim's response to the utilitarian tradition more generally is much less antagonistic. Throughout these early writings, Spencer is a singularly important point of reference. This utilitarian was not, after all, an economist. He conceived himself to be, much as the other utilitarians before him, a moral philosopher. Although he conceived of morality in a rather instrumental way, he never denied its existence or importance, even insisting that the state act in a way that preserved the moral good, however defined. And in contrast to the French and Germans, Spencer demonstrated a concrete and empirical grasp of social morality which Durkheim greatly appreciated.[76]

Pushed by his value commitments and practical interests, Durkheim formulated his early presuppositional position through the search for a science that could emphasize collective regulation without sacrificing individual choice. Classical economics was, Durkheim believed, both highly scientific and strongly individualistic, but it failed to appreciate the necessity for, and the fact of, social control. Seeking a more effective synthesis, Durkheim ruled out a purely materialist position on order as too anti-individualist in turn. He decided that collectivist theory must make "morality" its essential focus, something which materialism could not do. Yet, in important respects, this initial solution to Durkheim's dilemma was no solution at all. The social role of morality could still be conceived in a number of contradictory ways. I turn now to a more detailed consideration of the presuppositional solutions Durkheim considered in this early work. We will see that his approaches to order are so various that his sociology ends up embracing the very theoretical dangers that his concentration upon morality was designed to avoid.

2.3. DURKHEIM'S CONTRADICTORY APPROACHES TO MORAL ORDER: THEORETICAL AMBIVALENCE AND THE MOVEMENT TOWARD AN ANTIVOLUNTARISTIC DETERMINISM

Durkheim knew what he wanted to do but he did not yet know exactly how to do it. The autonomy of the individual must be recognized, but, at the same time, so must the collective and controlling nature of society. As a first step toward this goal, philosophical realism must be rejected. Nothing exists ontologically, Durkheim stressed time and time again, except the individual. From this insight he was led to a crucial recognition, one which would play a fundamental role in all of his later work: the very nature of social control somehow develops from the process of individual interaction itself. In one of Durkheim's earliest essays, published in 1885, the logic of this theoretical reasoning—and its relation to Durkheim's ideological concerns—is already evident. In contesting the solidarist attack on socialism, Durkheim argues against the false assumption that social control can be achieved only through the coercion of a centralizing state. He contends, to the contrary, that socialist control can be conceived of as voluntary if it is correctly understood as derived from the aggregation of individual decisions: "Collective life must not be understood as created out of nothing by a decree from on high; it is a resultant, the reverberation in a common center of millions of elementary lives that vibrate dispersed throughout the organism."[77] In a later essay, this important understanding is formulated more strictly in terms of presuppositional logic. Invoking his by now familiar reservations about social realism, Durkheim places this critique in a new and much more powerful context. Instead of arguing abstractly that society can have no existence apart from the individual parts which compose it, Durkheim begins to explain how this movement from individual to social force can come about: "These parts have between them definite relations, are assembled in a certain manner, and . . . there results from this assembly something new . . . which has special properties."[78]

If Durkheim, then, is to resolve the dilemma that haunts his intellectual life he must investigate the nature of individual interaction and the implications for social order which result from it. The obvious place to start is with the problem of action. Since order rests upon the interaction of individuals, the nature of action becomes central to any conceptualization of order. Durkheim has discovered one of the most fundamental principles of theoretical logic.

2.3.1. The Problem of Action: Durkheim's Ambiguous Critique of Egoistic Rationality

Yet while he acknowledges its central importance, Durkheim can conceptualize action only in the most halting way. The base line is his commitment to the existence of morality and the critique of egoistic rationalism which this existence implies. Durkheim must reject the notion that moral ends reflect a simply individual choice. He is, indeed, sharply critical of the conception of actors as proto-scientists who are fully knowledgeable about the environment within which they act, fully cognizant of the effects their actions will produce. It is a "psychological truth," Durkheim asserts in 1887, "that the greatest part of social institutions is due not to reason and calculation but to more obscure causes," to "motives without relation to the effects they produce and which, as a result, they cannot explain."[79] The view of an all-knowing consciousness is unrealistic. For as often as not "we act without knowing why, or the reasons we give ourselves are not the real ones."[80]

If the ends of action cannot, then, be deduced from an actor's conscious reflection about his environment, two possibilities remain. The first is that such reflection is mediated by normative factors which transcend the immediate context. To adopt this alternative is to argue for moral as against instrumental action. There is, in fact, one important strand in Durkheim's early writings that takes precisely this approach, and which can be viewed as a direct challenge to the kind of "realistic" thinking about action so enthusiastically adopted by Marx—for example, in *The Communist Manifesto*. The most important political economists, Durkheim complains, "have not hesitated to declare that national feelings were only the remains of prejudices destined to disappear one day."[81] Indeed, this is not only an empirical prediction but actually the economist's fondest hope: "He had believed that critical spirit was sufficient to dissolve instincts and moral sentiments."[82] But if this is the case, then "economic action can have resort to nothing but egoism, and in this way, political economy is separated completely from morality."[83] If this is so, the very existence of morality is called into question. Once all social ties are assumed to have been broken—as they are in this purely economic approach to action—Durkheim wonders whether any moral ideal remains to humanity at all.

If the existence of morality is to be preserved, such a completely instrumental view must be rejected. Action must be seen as mediated by considerations other than efficiency, considerations which are not less normative for being unscientific. Man "partakes of an age and a country," Durkheim affirms in direct opposition to Marx's view of alienated man, and "he has prejudices and beliefs."[84] In fact, "he has aspirations of all sorts and many concerns other than keeping an economical budget."[85] The economic and rationalizing dimension of action must, therefore, be carefully isolated. "It is not exact to say that the essential object of social life is the 'collective search for subsistence,' " Durkheim argues against a position which was at the heart of *The German Ideology*.[86] If action is to be characterized in terms of different kinds of motives, material concerns will be only one among many. "The phenomena of sympathy," Durkheim insists, "are not subordinate to the need for nourishment and are not less strong."[87] At another point, he speaks of the role of "subconscious sentiments." There seems no doubt that Durkheim has tried to differentiate these nonrational dimensions of action to demonstrate that order can be of a distinctively normative rather than mechanistic type.[88]

In logical terms, however, there is another theoretical alternative that Durkheim can choose, even if he continues to reject the notion that human ends are the result of purely individual reflection. This stricture, after all, denies only that people can muster complete knowledge of the results that a given action may produce. One can accept the image of the rational actor, however, and still contest the postulate that actors have perfect knowledge of their environment. One can stress, for example, that this environment is too complicated to fully comprehend, that no single individual, no matter how rational, can follow out the intricate repercussions produced by action in a complex society. This kind of argument takes aim, implicitly, at an overly simplified understanding of action's external conditions; it is not directed against the conception of rational action itself. It is exactly this kind of reasoning that Marx himself invokes in his famous warning that while (rational) men make history, they make it only in the circumstances which are given to them.[89†]

It is crucial to the understanding of Durkheim's theoretical development to see that he does, in fact, embrace this second alternative to purely individual ends as well. If institutions are not the results of consciously intended action, Durkheim argues, it is not because men act in nonrational ways but because "facts are too complex to be embraced completely by human intelligence."[90]

> We can never comprehend anything except the most immediate consequences of even the simplest of our actions; how could we grasp the distant and obscure effects of a phenomenon whose ramifications spread throughout the organism?[91]

Significantly, on certain occasions Durkheim even couches his ideological criticism in precisely this kind of presuppositional language. He argues, for example, that it was such a failure to perceive how complex the external environment actually is—not the failure to perceive the moral rootedness of action itself—that led the individualistic solidarists astray. Since Fouillée and his followers overestimated an actor's possible knowledge of his social situation, it is no wonder, Durkheim believes, that they so radically underestimated the need for social restructuring, and committed themselves instead to a modified kind of laissez-faire perspective.[92†]

Even the most democratically minded socialists make much the same mistake, in Durkheim's view, for they root their argument for a responsive socialism on the notion that socialist institutions could be constructed in a completely conscious way. In Schaeffle's theory, Durkheim complains, "everything happens in broad daylight." The individual's consciousness is considered omnipresent: "It . . . clarifies all, penetrates all, moves all."[93] Schaeffle can conceive socialism as the result of free individual decisions because he believes that the rational individual "has a clear conception of the group to which he belongs and the ends which it is appropriate to pursue." The individual, Schaeffle believes, "compares, discusses, and yields only to reason."[94] Durkheim rejects this position, just as strongly as he rejected the theoretical individualism of solidarism. He argues that socialism, like any other collective force, inevitably exerts its influence in less direct ways. Given the complexity of the environment, the impact of individual acts cannot easily be foreseen. If action is to be redirected or reformed, the source of this reformation must be external to the individual actor, who may himself still be conceived in a purely rational way.

Does such an approach to action differ from Marx's? True, Durkheim believes this rational action is controlled for an ultimately moral purpose. For Marx, in contrast, its external, coercive control has no moral justification. Nonetheless, the logic of these approaches to action is similar, their conception of the relation between action and environment directly parallel.

Durkheim insists that the ends of action be conceived in a way that is not purely individualistic, in a manner which allows for collective morality. Yet as alternatives to individualism he embraces theories of action that imply strikingly divergent portraits of social order. If ends are mediated normatively, a moral order would be a voluntary one. But if ends are collective simply because interaction ramifies in ways that are too complex for even rational actors to comprehend, moral order itself can be conceived as the mechanical result of external force.

2.3.2. The Problem of Order: The Tortuous Path toward Collective Control

As Durkheim addresses the problem of order in his early writings, his options are severely limited even if they are not completely consistent. Order must involve morality, but it may invoke this morality either directly or indirectly. Order cannot be based on individualistic rationality, but instrumental action is permitted if the environment is perceived as sufficiently complex. Finally, while order implies regulation by social force, this force can, indeed must, be viewed as the direct reflection of individual interaction itself. It is no wonder that Durkheim tries first one resolution then another. He moves back and forth between what are often contradictory theoretical strategies, between more individualistic solutions and more social ones, between instrumental orders and orders that are normatively mediated.[95†]

ORDER AS THE NATURAL IDENTITY OF INTEREST:
MORALITY AS VOLUNTARISM

All of Durkheim's proposals about order have one thing in common: they reject the philosophically idealist position that order can be achieved through a metaphysical deus ex machina.[96] Durkheim finds such a proposal not only in the writings of "spiritualists" who would link order to a divine source, but in Kant as well. "How is it possible," he asks, "that pure reason, without the benefit of experience, conceals in itself a law that is found to regulate exactly domestic, economic, and social relations?"[97] Kant, Durkheim complains, makes morality a transcendent fact which escapes science. In contrast, morality must be conceived as a "social function, or, more likely, a system of functions which is formed and consolidated little by little under the pressure of collective needs."[98]

Yet one of the first approaches to order that Durkheim considers in his early writings, while not idealist in the philosophical sense, is very much in the Kantian tradition. Collective morality, Durkheim sometimes professes, can be imbedded in the innate structure of human motivation itself. If this were true, it would certainly offer an easy solution to the theoretical problems Durkheim faced, and he did not hesitate to recognize the advantages. A theory that emphasized natural sentiments of sociability would avoid the paradox that independent individuals often associate in ways that are detrimental to purely utilitarian calculation.

> There exists, or at least there is formed in the course of evolution, a need of sociability and social instincts which are absolutely disinterested. It is to satisfy them that individuals form larger and larger societies and do that sometimes to the detriment of their interests properly so-called.[99]

There is no doubt, Durkheim writes, that "every man ... instinctively understands that he does not suffice unto himself."[100] Social order, then, is the result of such social sentiments as "honor, respect, and affection."[101] Whether or not the individual benefits materially, the collective nature of interaction is assured: "The child *senses* that he depends on his parents, the merchant on his clients, the worker on his boss, the boss on his workers."[102] The "struggle for domination [*la lutte pour la domination*]," then, is far from being the "fundamental fact of social life." Rather than a struggle "without scruples, without loyalty," social life is conducted by actors with an innate sense of loyalty and mutual sympathy.[103]

Moreover, while these sentiments are embodied in the individual actor, they are in no sense individualistic. To the contrary, they are compellingly social. The attraction that men feel for each other is not a matter of conscious reflection. It is based upon ideas, Durkheim insists, "that consciousness does not perceive."[104] Such sympathetic sentiments, in fact, have the same analytic status as the social instincts that guide animal life.[105] For this reason, the social sentiments are true "resources against individualism."[106]

Yet while not individualistic in the sense of being asocial, these social sentiments express themselves in the form of purely individual decisions, and this of course is the greatest theoretical advantage of all. If social instincts are inherent in individuals, society certainly cannot be viewed as antithetical to voluntary control. Because we are "*predispose[d]. . .to devotion and sacrifice*," society is not the kind of "artificial combination" that can direct individual action only at the expense of freedom.[107] Against this Benthamite vision, Durkheim would propose order as a natural identity of interests, composed of spontaneous sentiments which "leave my autonomy and personality almost intact." "No doubt," he admits, "they tie me to others, but without taking much of my independence from me."[108†]

Yet, while this conception of natural sympathy seems to resolve certain fundamental problems, Durkheim concludes that it would only open up others. To the degree that he emphasized natural sentiments of association, Durkheim was undoubtedly taking up the work of Espinas, whose publication of *Les Sociétés animales* in 1877 caused a minor sensation in French intellectual circles. Espinas drew an elaborate analogy between human societies and animal ones in order to demonstrate the organic quality of social life. Concerned to construct an antimaterialist theory of order, Espinas wrote that "instead of rendering consciousness by the material organism we have especially tried to explicate material organization by consciousness."[109] Yet Espinas tried to root this social consciousness in purely individual sentiments; he claimed that for humans, as for animals, there was a "law of attraction of like for like, and of sympathy."[110] Thus, while he was one of the first to employ the term "collective conscience," Espinas could explain it only in an individualistic way, as the result of psychological relations among complex organisms."[111]

Whether or not he was actually aware of these incongruities in Espinas's position, Durkheim eventually concluded that the theory of natural sympathy failed to resolve the individual/society dilemma. While he agreed that individuals may act more instinctually than reflectively, he also saw the great theoretical dangers that would occur if sentiments were tied too closely to the isolated actor. If sympathetic sentiments were innate, then morality would be perceived as a spontaneous achievement. Without access to the source of his cooperative feelings, the unreflective actor would have the misleading impression that his own individual decisions actually constituted society. From the individual's perspective, then, it would appear as if association were totally free.

> Most intellects are able to embrace only a restricted horizon. . . .
> If I do not *perceive* the invisible bonds which link me to the rest
> of the society, I will think that I am independent of it and I will
> act accordingly.[112]

"The question," Durkheim asks, is not whether some social instinct exists
or not but "whether this sentiment can go so far as to include society in
its entirety."[113] The answer he gives, finally, is that it cannot. While the
theory of innately social sentiments admirably allows for voluntarism, it
cannot plausibly explain the anti-individualistic control and regulation
that society needs. The social connections it proposes are, in the end, simply too precarious.[114]

ORDER AS COLLECTIVE NORMS:
MORALITY WITH VOLUNTARISM

It was perhaps in response to the inadequacies of the concept of this
natural identity of interest that Durkheim also offered in his early writings a particular kind of collectivist solution to the order problem. While
continuing to draw upon his anti-instrumental conception of action,
Durkheim argues here—much like the early Marx—that subjective ends
can be socially produced, that they are in some sense supra-individual:
"Moral ends have the particular character that they are conceived as
obligatory."[115] Thus, while moral constraint is internal, it exercises on us
a public influence that we are bound to respect.[116] Yet Durkheim stresses
that this external compulsion need not necessarily be anti-voluntary. He
emphasizes, as Marx himself once did, that the differentiation between
what is individual and social is not so easy to make, that the individual,
even if apparently independent, must be seen as a social being.[117] The
individual is not simply "integrated" with society; society actually "penetrates" him. It is absurd, therefore, to try to conceptualize voluntarism
by negating what is external to the individual, for "to isolate oneself from
it, to abstract from it, is to diminish oneself."[118]

Like Marx in his radical Hegelian years, Durkheim points to essentially spiritual phenomena as examples of this order which is at once collective and voluntary—to the social conscience, the collective spirit,
language, love between husband and wife and familial affection, the mu-
nicipal spirit, patriotism, and love of humanity.[119] These forms of normative order present effective theoretical alternatives to social force
conceived in a more materialist way, for while they are equally anti-individualistic their moral status allows collective control to be maintained
without sacrificing voluntarism. Durkheim presents the issue as a theoretical choice, one which does not allow any possibility for synthetic,
multidimensional solution. "Solidarity comes from within and not from
without," he asserts in opposition to the instrumentalist position.[120] At

another point, in a discussion that could not be more antithetical to the logic of mature Marxism, Durkheim argues that the "conditions of existence" to which social structure responds are spiritual, not material ones. Rather than being viewed as referring to conditions that are "indispensable to survival pure and simple," the minimum conditions of existence must be understood to include whatever makes life worth living. For example, while "honor is not a condition necessary for life" in any material sense, "what man of heart, what people would want life without honor?"[121] Social action depends, then, on a voluntary impulse, an impulse that corresponds to invisible yet nonetheless powerful social bonds.

Durkheim sketches an institutional portrait of this social order in a highly polemical way, positioning himself in direct opposition to the kinds of social structures which are considered prototypically materialist. In even more general terms than the early Marx, Durkheim argues that law presents an abstract, universalistic norm against which to measure particularistic action. It is not sufficient, he writes, to trace the law to physical milieus like climate, or to purely behavioral facts like the number of inhabitants.[122] Nor is it correct—as Marx's later thinking would suggest—to see the law simply as an efficient means, something like a peace treaty which "only translates and sanctions the results of the [class] struggle."[123] The law must be seen as relating to a different order entirely, to the "average tastes, ideas and culture of the nation."[124]

This normative approach to the law naturally implies a critique of the materialist theory of the state. In a crucial transitional essay, one may recall, Marx argued that state-imposed duties on firewood were to be seen as economic instruments of class domination. Durkheim takes the opposite view, and he bases his position on his critique of instrumental action. To describe state-imposed taxes like customs and stamp duties as part of a struggle over the means of subsistence, he writes, is to "confound the ends and the means."[125] He offers a simple analogy to amplify his argument. While one must eat in order to live, it is not necessary to eat any particular kind of food. In the same way, if the state is to perform its special function it must procure for itself financial resources through taxation; but what kinds of resources, and from where, are not themselves material issues. They depend on what ends the state is trying to realize.[126] The state, therefore, must not be viewed in a completely instrumental way, as "nothing more than a means to insure the power of the minority,"[127] or as a "vast machine destined to repress [the] multitude of unsociable beings."[128] To the contrary, the state represents simply the "exterior and visible form" of the moral solidarity by which individual ends are shaped.[129]

While the early Marx concentrated on the legal and political orders, Durkheim carries his critique into the very center of the materialist argument, to the economy itself. In a striking discussion that is diametrically opposed to the path Marx later followed, Durkheim declares that the economy is itself a moral fact. He praises the German historical economists for their effort to prove "that these two orders of fact [i.e., economics and morals], while being distinct from one another, are, however, of the same nature."[130] The economic order gains its determinate power not through instrumental coercion but by the same obligatory strictures as morality itself. Economic life is merely one form of moral obligation.

> What difference is there, then, between morality and political economy? It is that the one is the form of which the other is the content. What belongs properly to morality is this form of obligation which comes to attach itself to certain ways of acting and to mark them with its imprint. Economic phenomena can under certain conditions invest themselves with morality as can all other social facts. This is not to say, assuredly, that they themselves constitute the entire content of morality: but they are a very important part of it.[131]

In an early review of Schaeffle's work Durkheim becomes more specific. Paraphrasing one of Schaeffle's own arguments, he specifies what particular moral function money performs. Wealth, he writes, must be viewed as a special kind of highly flexible symbol. Since it can be so easily exchanged, it serves as a means of communication that can unite diverse social elements.[132]

If the economic, political, and legal spheres embody moral obligation and depend upon subjective compliance, then social change itself must be a voluntary process. The young Marx argued that even the most revolutionary change depended upon awakening individual consciences to universalistic norms and that any really permanent changes must proceed from internal transformations of the self. Durkheim's argument is similar. Social change, he insists, must focus on the spiritual order, not the material one: "Social evolution is not directed from the outside inside, but from the inside to the outside."[133] Only in this way can change occur without sacrificing individual control.

Imprisoned by the logic of their instrumentalist position, the classical economists were forced to describe change in a way that directly contradicted their commitment to individual freedom. By invoking economic laws which they conceived as "not less natural than the laws of gravity and electricity," their theories effectively counseled fatalism and resignation. If contingency and independence are to be restored to historical development, purely material causes like the increase of population and the quantity of supply and demand must be avoided.[134] Not that such material factors are not real; to argue without any reference to the external environment would be idealist in the philosophical, not simply the sociological sense. Durkheim contends, rather, that such external facts affect action only if they change moral standards. Thus, while the growth in demographic volume is an important fact, its main effect is a moral one: it forces the collective conscience that binds men to one another to be less personal. As volume increases, social ideas become more impersonal, more independent of time and space; they raise themselves above particular societies and become ideas that apply to humanity in general.[135] Far from being a material fact, then, social density is an intrinsic part of the movement toward normative universalism. Durkheim finally argues, much like the early Marx, that conscience must be at the center of any important historical change.

> If wars, invasions, and class struggles have an influence on the development of societies, it is by the condition of acting first upon individual consciences. *It is through them that everything proceeds, and it is from them, in a word, that everything emanates.*[136]

It is not surprising that Durkheim concludes his discussion of social change by suggesting that "the study of social psychology is not, therefore, merely an appendix of sociology: it is the very substance of it."[137]

Yet throughout these discussions of moral order, Durkheim worries that he has gone too far in an anti-individualist direction. If collective order consists in pressures on the individual conscience, how can it still be voluntary? To resolve this seeming paradox, Durkheim continually returns to the insight which he derived from his critique of philosophical realism: collective force, no matter what kind, must be viewed as the result of individual interaction itself. It was this understanding, more than any other, that attracted him so powerfully to Schaeffle. Schaeffle realized, according to Durkheim, that the internal impulsion of morality results from a "spontaneous movement of the conscience," from the "free burst of will."[138] Since "society is only a composite of individual minds," it is individuals themselves, not some abstract and external entity, that produces moral order.

> *They* are in perpetual interaction through the exchange of symbols; *they* interpenetrate with one another. *They* group themselves according to their natural affinities; *they* coordinate and systematize themselves.[139]

In a later essay on the German psychologist Wundt, Durkheim gained his most sophisticated understanding of why this individual, subjective contribution to moral order had so often been ignored.[140] The problem is that social theory has viewed the individual as a concrete "thing," impervious to internalized social controls.[141†] Yet "representing the self like a transcendent being" is as antithetical to voluntarism, Durkheim insists, as the converse error, representing society only as a concrete material force. The metaphysical understanding of the individual, as a transsocial thing, results from the false analogy between material entities and living beings. To represent to ourselves material things, we form concepts that are completely devoid of subjectivity, since the content of "things" is, by definition, formed without reference to the senses. This is the origin of the "substantial" concept of matter. The problem is that "once this concept is formed, the mind is tempted to apply it equally to interior phenomena, for which, however, it has not been made and to which it is not suited."[142] In contrast to material subjects of scientific investigation, "states of conscience [i.e., interior phenomena] ... *are* known by us directly and we immediately see how they are linked to one another without there being any need for recourse to a metaphysical hypothesis." Since human actors are very much the product of subjective experience, "phenomenological reality is sufficient in itself, and there is nothing to look for outside of it." Having avoided the concrete, substantialist understanding of the individual, it no longer appears as if our personalities have sharply marked contours that make "reciprocal penetration" impossible. To the contrary, it becomes clear that individual personalities substantially overlap, and that social order can be based upon the subjective feelings of individuals.

But as soon as Durkheim has successfully argued for the voluntaristic status of moral order he just as quickly begins to worry that this moral order is simply not collective enough. His insight into the interactional basis of society and the complementarity of individual choice and social control were still not sufficiently developed. He is still the same person, after all, who tried to reconcile order and individualism by making social sentiments instinctual, an individualistic approach, one must not forget, that was temporally coterminous with the much more sophisticated individual-society conceptualization I have just described. It is the fear that individual choice and social control are irreconcilable that leads Durkheim away from his vision of a voluntaristic moral order. Retrenching to the more traditional understanding of the individual which he so strongly criticized in his Wundt review, Durkheim himself offers a reified and "substantialist" approach to social control. Order, he now says, is "not dependent on the caprice of each person, but result[s] from the nature of things." Dichotomizing individual and society, he reverts to an anti-phenomenological, mechanistic conception of force. If order is obligatory, it is "not because [it] satisfies certain individual tendencies ... but because it is the very condition of social life."[143]

Durkheim's ambivalence is so marked that his retrenchment can be observed in the very essays that first established his argument for a voluntaristic moral order. Thus, after lauding Schaeffle's insight into the reconcilability of individual action and moral control, Durkheim wonders whether "it is not to singularly restrain morality to make it consist only in the free disposition of will," and he protests that morality cannot be so exempt from constraint.[144] His other discussion of Schaeffle reveals the same contradictory quality. He praised Schaeffle, one must remember, for seeing that moral order proceeds from the actual decisions of individuals. Schaeffle knows that "the ideas or the impressions spontaneously emitted from all points in the society" are part of the "free intercourse" which is the "heart and soul of society."[145] Yet Durkheim immediately follows these passages with an argument based on the idea that the individual himself cannot be a social unit. If spontaneous activity is not to remain sterile, he writes, it must be "regulated and ordered," and he describes this order as effective only if it directly opposes individual will. Authoritative order requires submission; it is sustained through directives which "everyone follows without question."[146] Authority, he insists, "is made to command and it must be obeyed."[147] If individual action is an inherently antisocial force and social order can be maintained only in an anti-individualistic way, then voluntarism can be created only in direct opposition to society. Social pressure, Durkheim warns, "warps and perverts everyone's will." Freedom exists only because "there is within us . . . something intimate and personal which is our own creation," a "world in which the individual reigns supreme and into which society does not penetrate."[148] Nothing could be further removed from his insight into the reconcilability of order and freedom.

In this vein, Durkheim criticizes and finally rejects the antisubstantialist, analytic approach to the individual proposed by Wundt. Instead of seeing Wundt's emphasis on the subjective status of the individual as facilitating an understanding of social control, he now complains that Wundt's approach leads to individualism: it makes the individual's attachment to society appear to be an outgrowth of his need to feel part of the social whole.

> [For Wundt,] morality results from the efforts that man makes to find a durable object to which he can become attached. . . . Once [he has set about to] look for it, the first objects of this he encounters are the family, the city, the nation, and he stops with them. However, they do not, even so [i.e., by virtue of their obvious "social" status] have value by themselves, but only because they symbolize, albeit in an imperfect manner, the ideal which he pursues.[149]

Although Durkheim will, at a much later stage in his career, accept precisely this kind of formulation as a more satisfactory way to interrelate individual and society, his present state of theoretical confusion makes it impossible for him to find here any such thing. A choice must be made between individual freedom and social control. If the individual is viewed as initiating social order, it becomes impossible to conceptualize external obligations.

> We cannot oblige ourselves to ourselves! . . . To whom do we owe our duty? To ourselves? This is a play on words! What is a debt where we are debtor and creditor at the same time?[150]

Durkheim still has not discovered, then, how individual liberty and social regulation can be reconciled. While he contemplated the notion of innately moral sentiments, he eventually rejected this solution as insufficiently social. In response to this failure, he established morality as a socially-produced collective order. This strategy confronted him, in turn, with the problem of how to maintain voluntarism. To meet this challenge, he argued that moral order must be rooted in individual interaction, and that individual volition was antithetical to social control only if it was viewed in a reified, overly concrete way. Yet Durkheim immediately drew back from this insight, expressing doubt that such individualistically based activity would be collective enough. Having rejected a theory of innate sentiments as too precarious, Durkheim was determined not to postulate a social control that was too voluntaristic in turn. What was the solution? If individually-produced moral control was too subjective, too open to individual caprice, then morality would have to be conceived in a manner that was not subjective. Social psychology, Durkheim had decided, must be considered only one part of sociology, and not a very important one at that.[151] We are now ready to consider the third and final approach to order that Durkheim makes in his early work.

ORDER AS COLLECTIVE FORCE:
MORALITY WITHOUT VOLUNTARISM

Shortly after Durkheim had concluded the discussion of economic order as a form of moral obligation, he proceeded to demonstrate the nature of this obligation in a particularly revealing way. As a society gets more populous, he wrote, it must produce more from the soil. In response to this need, the soil will be more intensively cultivated, but a precondition for this economic advance is the institutionalization of individual rights in property. This dynamic, Durkheim writes, explains why private property becomes more and more a sacred right in the course of social evolution.[152] What Durkheim has explained here is how economic order produces moral obligation, not how this order is itself a form of morality. He argues from necessity to morality, from objective force to subjective will. Without being aware of it, he radically shifts the grounds of his theoretical logic.

Marx was pushed to an objectivist position because the increasingly economistic character of his radicalism convinced him that moral action in bourgeois society was impossible. Durkheim's shift toward objectivism, paradoxically, was motivated by precisely the opposite sentiment, by his conviction that collective morality, even in bourgeois societies, could greatly restrict individual action. In both cases, however, the theoretical formulation of this objective control exacted the same price: the effective elimination of voluntary action. For Marx, this determinism complemented his ideological vision as well as his empirical judgment, and it remained his generalized orientation throughout his career. For Durkheim, this new determinist position was neither ideologically nor empirically compatible, and we will see later how the reaction against it produced far-reaching changes in his theoretical development. We must first, however, examine the new determinist logic itself.

To understand fully this radical disjunction in Durkheim's approach to moral order, we must understand more than the simple fact that he ultimately judged his first two, more voluntaristic, approaches to order as failures. Although certainly this judgment in itself would have been sufficient to produce a crisis in Durkheim's thought, we must understand, in addition, certain important facts about his general theoretical background. These facts explain the resources which he brought to bear on this crisis and were crucial in determining the particular course his theoretical revisions would take.[153†]

The first important point of reference, one not yet discussed, is that from the beginning of his intellectual career Durkheim identified his critique of presuppositional individualism with an argument for the theoretical importance of social equilibrium. Individualistic theory was wrong, he believed, not just because it failed to explain order as the result of collective arrangements but because it did not understand the sources of empirical stability. Social order referred, then, both to the fact of collective force and to the condition of stability. This conflation emerged, in part, from Durkheim's own ideological preoccupation with the cohesion of the new French Republic.[154†] It also followed naturally from his critique of the classical economists, whose presuppositional individualism coincided with a facile belief in the automatic harmony of individual interests. Criticizing the economists as "happy optimists who perceive only perfect concordance and providential harmony," Durkheim clearly considered his own conflation of collective order with social harmony a healthy corrective. It is difficult to see, Durkheim writes, how a "spontaneous play of egoisms results miraculously in the harmony of interest."[155] Only with a more collectivist approach to social theory, he asserts, could society be understood as "better harmonized [*mieux equilibré*]."[156]

But no matter how understandable, this conflation of different levels of theoretical argument was a serious theoretical error. It put "equilibrium" at the center of Durkheim's theorizing in a fundamentally flawed way. The point is not that equilibrium is, in itself, a harmful theoretical concept, but rather that it should not be the criterion for presuppositional order. If it becomes so, it can establish certain criteria for order that are incompatible with other, more distinctly presuppositional commitments. For Durkheim, we will see, this was precisely the problem.

The other fact we must keep in mind, which at first glance seems unrelated to the problem just described, is that Durkheim's thinking reflected a fundamental ambivalence about action. As we have seen in the earlier discussion, while there is one dimension of Durkheim's argument that opposes utilitarianism by describing action as normatively mediated activity, another strand of his argument takes a much different path. Instead of opposing the efficient calculation of ends and means, Durkheim criticizes the notion that this calculation occurs within an environment that is completely known. Durkheim's argument subtly shifts, in other words, from a critique of action to an argument about order, from an attack on instrumental action per se to an argument that it be placed within a broader, more determinate environment.

It was the combination of these theoretical commitments that led Durkheim to resolve his problems with "order" by moving to an objectivist logic. His objection to an individually-produced moral order, we recall, was that it was insufficiently determinist. This determinism, Durkheim now realized, could be attained in a way that also guaranteed equilibrium. Moral order could be conceived as the result of an external force that articulates the environment within which rational action proceeds; it could be conceived, in other words, as the result of a force that creates an "artificial identity of interests."[157†]

In one of the earliest examples of this presuppositional shift, Durkheim elaborates his critique of individualistic theory in the following way:

> Moral laws are made in our day-to-day social relations. . . . They express the conditions of our mutual adaptation. Now these conditions can neither be predicted nor calculated a priori; they can be observed only after equilibrium has been produced and has fixed them with as much precision as possible.[158]

This statement is revealing for the way it combines Durkheim's earlier concerns with his new ones. In the first place, he continues to accord morality a prominent position and to argue that it is rooted in individual interaction itself. This was the very conceptual orientation, of course, that laid the foundations for his anti-utilitarian approach to order. Yet what is strikingly new about this passage is that individual interactions and the moral laws they produce are no longer the real focus of Durkheim's argument. They are now merely the expression of other conditions, which themselves provide the reference point for nonmoral, instrumental adaptation. These external conditions are not subject to individual will; to the contrary, they come about as the result of equilibrium-seeking shifts in the individual's environment.

In this solution, then, Durkheim does not deny moral order as such. He sees it, however, as a fact accomplished by nonmoral means. If he believes that the "collective conscience is nothing but an integrated system, a harmonic consensus,"[159] and if he can accept rational action if only it is collectively regulated, it is not surprising that his approach to morality can become quasi-utilitarian. "The essential function of morality," he writes in 1887, "is to adapt individuals to one another, to assure thus the equilibrium and survival of the group."[160] Morality is reduced to its "practical function," which is, quite simply, "to make society possible, to allow men to live together without too much pain and conflict."[161] This practical achievement is accomplished through practical means, and it is not necessary to alter the substance of instrumental action itself. "Egoistic motives eliminate each other," Durkheim insists, "because they are contradictory," not because they are transformed into altruism. What is produced from the clash of such egoistic acts is not moral solidarity as such but "a kind of equilibrium and spontaneous regularization of these [egoistic] sorts of propensities."[162]

This new approach to moral order clearly implies the most radical transformation in Durkheim's approach to institutional life. The ramifications are already visible in the earliest essays, where his approach to the state is sometimes at great variance with what was at that time his dominant anti-utilitarian emphasis. In one early review, for example, Durkheim justifies his apparently anti-individualist argument for state intervention on the following grounds. The state, he insists, is itself committed to individualism, to enhancing the pursuit of individual interests. The only justification for the state's intervention into individual lives, therefore, is an instrumental one: its centralized position allows it to see individual interests better than the individuals themselves. Instead of being immersed in the individual parts of society, the state is able to see the whole.[163] Durkheim does not argue here that the state can be regulated by a humanistic morality, although this would certainly be one way that voluntarism and determinism could be resolved. He advances, instead, a much more mechanistic reconciliation, arguing that the environment of action is too complex for the individual to know his own interest. Another rationale for a utilitarian political theory is provided, the following year, in an argument Durkheim makes against political individualism. "The individual," he asserts, "is not separated from his fellow man by an abyss."[164] Whereas in other writings of this period such a metaphor would be invoked to introduce Durkheim's argument for moral solidarity, he argues here that the "abyss" must be bridged by collective coercion.

[The individuals] are so pressed one atop the other that one of them cannot move in any way without the others feeling the effects. There is not, therefore, one of our actions which is not without interest to someone else, which cannot harm him and which, consequently, cannot become the object of legislative measures.[165]

Once again, the state is viewed simply as a device to provide the kind of artificial identity of interest necessary to achieve equilibrium, a position that could not be more different from Durkheim's analysis of the state as the external manifestation of moral solidarity. We will see that Durkheim elaborates this instrumental approach to institutions much more fully in his sociological theorizing of 1888-1890. Before addressing this work, however, we must examine a final strategy Durkheim employs for reconciling morality with instrumental milieu.

Durkheim's new emphasis on the mechanical basis of moral order clearly complements his approach to action as rational calculation in a complex environment. The adaptation he emphasizes portrays an actor who, no matter how reflective, must adjust himself to the web of circumstances in which his action is enmeshed: "To live is not to think but to act, and the course of our ideas only reflects the flow of events around us."[166] It is the equilibrium of external conditions that establishes the ends of action, that forces us to "act without knowing the end of our act." Thus, though Durkheim calls such action "unconscious adaptation," it is clear that he utilizes "unconscious" only to indicate that even the most reflective action is produced by factors outside individual control and produces unintended consequences in turn.

Despite this clear-cut relationship between his new approach to moral order and his proto-utilitarian approach to action, Durkheim is not completely satisfied. His understanding of action is, after all, highly ambivalent, and he is aware of the shortcomings of the efficiency postulate even as he invokes it. Although he is determined to move toward a more constraining, less precarious approach to social order, he would like to reconcile this approach with noninstrumental action as well, with a notion of "unconscious" more in line with the traditional notion of irrational activity. This is precisely the direction that Durkheim's thinking takes as he moves toward his instrumental position. The key to this reconciliation is the concept "habit."[167] By employing the notion of habit, Durkheim can connect nonrational action to instrumental and coercive order: the notion of habit itself implies mechanical adaptation.

Once we have repeated a certain number of times a certain action, *by the effect of habit, our conduct takes a form which is imposed on our will with an obligatory force. We feel as if we must cast all of our action in the same mold.*[168]

Initially triggered by external circumstances, habit will reproduce non-reflective adaptive responses as long as the habit continues to be reinforced.

> Social phenomena derive from practical causes. . . . Every act of human conduct, individual as well as social, has for its aim the adaptation of the individual to his milieu. . . . If certain modes of action persist and especially if they are generalized, one can be nearly certain that either they are useful [*utile*] or they have become so.[169]

The external stimuli that habits respond to are the conditions of equilibrium. By forcing the will into an involuntary adaptation to milieu, they guarantee the utility of voluntary choice.[170†] Once Durkheim has effected this reconciliation of nonrational action with instrumental force, he is ready to formulate his own sociological theories.

2.4. INVOLUNTARY MORALITY AND DURKHEIM'S FIRST SOCIOLOGY

The first three years of Durkheim's writings consisted of critical commentaries on the state of sociological work in France, England, and Germany. Although the notion of instrumental order makes its appearance in this period, these writings are dominated by the anti-utilitarian moral solution in its individualist and collectivist forms. Yet Durkheim had serious reservations about both these anti-utilitarian solutions, and these reservations eventually produced the movement in his thought toward the more determinist perception of order. It is critical to note that Durkheim's own original theoretical formulations—as compared with his critical commentaries—do not begin until after he has conceptualized this more deterministic approach. Moreover, while his proto-utilitarian understanding of action was crucial for his transition to a more mechanistic position, his first attempts at sociological theorizing rely much more heavily on the concept of habit. These initial "Durkheimian" formulations make morality a reflection of nonmoral collective conditions, although they do not, for that, see action itself as purely efficient.

Durkheim's scientific beginnings, then, are both like and unlike those of Marx. Marx, too, thought that scientific social theory demanded a deterministic and mechanical slant, and like Durkheim he achieved this perspective only after rejecting an earlier and more normative approach. Unlike Durkheim, however, Marx accepted a thoroughly instrumental perspective on action. Where Durkheim employed "habit," Marx referred to "alienation." This turned out to be a crucial choice for the subsequent writings of each: while Durkheim's usage indicates a bad conscience about the mechanistic implications he has embraced, Marx enthusiastically puts instrumental action at the very center of his theory. In this early period, however, the logic of both theories is surprisingly similar, and Durkheim seems as willing to sacrifice voluntarism to achieve order as Marx.

In 1888 Durkheim devoted his opening lecture at the University of Bordeaux to the problem of the sociological study of morality. The structure of his theoretical argument is closely informed by the presuppositional logic just described. He objects, for example, to the focus on such phenomena as religion on the grounds that they insufficiently reveal the sources of constraint. Sociologists must, he insists, study the causes of social phenomena and determine "to what conditions they must conform in order to survive."[171] Much like Marx's base-superstructure model, Durkheim's view is that it is not the symbols but the structures which produce them that should be the subject of sociological analysis. "Institutions," he insists, "result from social life *and merely translate it externally through overt symbols.*"[172] The key process in this non-symbolic generation of social life is "adapt[ation] to the most diverse circumstances of time and place."[173] But these circumstances do not exert themselves on action directly. There is a level of mediation between the forces of necessity and the pattern of belief, and this mediation is habit. Durkheim asserts that "structure is action which has become habit and which has crystallized."[174]

Analyzing the empirical origins of these deterministic conditions, Durkheim turns to the very factor which in his earlier essays he had so forcefully rejected as overly determinist. The purely demographic density or "volume" of social life becomes for him the critical fact.[175] Social control is now conceived only in objective terms, and where Durkheim had earlier tried to reconcile liberty with social constraint, he now argues that freedom can be preserved only in opposition to social life, not through it.

> No doubt the individual is freer than he was formerly, and it is good that it should be so. But . . . though necessary to permit the individual to arrange his *personal* life according to his needs, it extends no further. Beyond this first sphere, there is another far more vast. . . . Here he obviously can no longer assume the initiative of his actions but can only be the recipient or sufferer of them. Individual liberty is, therefore, always and everywhere limited by social constraint, whether this takes the form of custom, mores, laws, or regulations.[176]

Much as Marx reacted against his early formulations, Durkheim seems to have forgotten his own insight into the subjective and social nature of individuality. Like Marx, he ignores an earlier understanding that moral constraint can be seen as the product of individual interaction if only order is conceived in a subjective way.

The lecture with which Durkheim opens his second year at Bordeaux follows a similar line of analysis. Promising his students that he will apply the general definition of sociology established by the lectures of the preceding year, Durkheim devotes himself to a specific institutional area, the sociology of the family. He argues that the basic structure of the family is formed "in those ways of acting which have been consolidated by habit."[177] While common sense views habits as simply customary beliefs, they must, to the contrary, be seen as the true "residue of . . . collective experiences."[178] Familial customs, then, are obligatory; they are habits and for this reason assume an imperative form. Indeed, customs are best distinguished by their reliance on external sanctions like law, which reinforce habits by translating into a concrete form the coercive power of external conditions.[179] It is within this instrumental framework that Durkheim elaborates his sociological history of the family. He argues, once again, that modern social structures have been produced by increases in material density and that institutions become functionally differentiated in order to restore the equilibrium which changes in demographic volume produce.[180]

In the same year that Durkheim published this lecture on the family there appeared the even more empirically specific essay in sociological explanation, "Suicide and the Birth Rate [*Suicide et natalité*]." Though Durkheim applies himself in this work to the level of propositions, he does so, inevitably, within the framework of his general theoretical logic. The result is an attempt to explain this apparently most individualistic of human actions as the mechanical, determined result of external objective force.

At the very beginning of this analysis, Durkheim postulates that every society must be developed in a "regular, harmonious, and proportionate" way.[181] Subsequently, he describes the motor of this social development in completely objective terms, as the increase in numbers signaled by physiological growth (*croît physiologique*). Just as he did in his study of the family, then, Durkheim traces empirical variation to the fact that changes in social volume create a disequilibrium to which individuals and institutions must adapt. All adaptations, however, do not produce pathology. High growth rates actually mean lower rates of suicide, because they strengthen "domestic sentiment." This sentiment depends, Durkheim believes, on men having "the *habit* of domestic solidarity."[182] Since this domestic habit is fixed in an "instinctive and unreflective manner" through repeated interaction, it can be linked directly to the rate of birth. Thus, "the weakening of the birth rate implies a weakening of the domestic spirit."[183] Yet although high birth rates are good, rates that are too high can also disrupt social equilibrium and cause suicide to increase. Durkheim's explanation for pathologically high rates is more directly utilitarian than his discussion of low rates: "In a society where the population multiplies too rapidly, the struggle for existence [*la lutte pour la vie*] becomes too harsh and individuals more readily give up an existence that has become too difficult."[184] This empirical proposition is more mechanical than the explanation that relies on sentiment and habit, but the theoretical logic is the same: external forces have forced the individual to take his own life.[185†]

2.5. CONCLUSION: MECHANICAL ORDER AND DURKHEIM'S RELATION TO THE INSTRUMENTALIST TRADITION

Earlier in this discussion I noted that while Durkheim's critique of economic individualism differed from Marx's by its emphasis on morality, the overall relationship between Durkheim and Marx was not so clear cut. The reason for this is Durkheim's ambiguous explanation of how this morality works. The ambiguity revolves around Durkheim's commitment to reconciling voluntarism and determinism, and it is reflected in his relationship to the different intellectual traditions of his time. While he accepted the organicism of Comte, he rejected Comte's failure to emphasize individualization and free choice. If he applauded Schaeffle's attention to individual interaction, he felt that Schaeffle gave insufficient attention to social control. Finally, this ambivalence can be seen even in Durkheim's relationship to the English tradition itself, for while he was sharply critical of the English economists he always paid a certain qualified deference to the accomplishments of another member of the utilitarian tradition, Herbert Spencer.

I have presented Durkheim's ambiguous analysis of morality in some detail. The first problem is that he posed the order problem in terms of a dichotomous choice. Moral order, for him, is either anti-utilitarian and voluntaristic, or proto-utilitarian and determinist. Eventually, Durkheim's concern to maintain social control and determinism made him draw back from his more voluntaristic approaches to collective order, and he formulated his first sociological investigations in distinctively utilitarian terms. While he accepted the French emphasis on collective morality and the German insistence on the scientific investigation of the relation between morality and concrete institutional life, his initial theorizing about the empirical origins and effects of morality has a distinctly English flavor. The great English sociologist of this time, of course, was Spencer. I will show in this concluding section how closely the general theoretical logic of Durkheim's early sociology resembles Spencer's own.[186†]

Durkheim's most extended confrontation with Spencer in the early writings occurred in his long essay "Studies in Social Science [*Les Etudes de science sociale*]," where he reviewed, along with other French and German works, Spencer's *Ecclesiastical Institutions*.[187] This review appeared in 1886. The fact that it adumbrates, very precisely, the logic employed in the sociological writing Durkheim initiated two years later underscores the autonomy of presuppositional reason in sociological thought. In his search for a satisfactory solution to the problems of order and action Durkheim was driven, ineluctably, toward a certain theoretical position. Durkheim's protests notwithstanding, this position followed in certain crucial respects the utilitarian position Spencer had sketched.

Durkheim begins this review by apparently criticizing the most fundamental elements in Spencer's sociology. He takes issue, first, with Spencer's individualism, arguing that the English sociologist gave actors far too much control over social evolution and acceded to free examination far too great a scope in modern affairs.[188] Durkheim also sharply questions Spencer's rationalist approach to action. "It is far from being true," he writes in reference to one of Spencer's central tenets, "that the place and importance of custom are going to diminish with civilization." To the contrary, "as long as there are men who live together, there will be among these some common faith."[189] When Durkheim turns, however, to his more substantive criticisms of Spencer's sociology, these seemingly clear-cut differences begin to fade.

Spencer's history of religious development, according to Durkheim, rests upon a highly instrumental view of human activity. Religious evolution is the record of actors trying to solve problems posed by their external environment. The notion of spirits, for example, emerged because in this way primitive man was able to "account for the dual, apparently contradictory phenomenon of dream and sleep." Eventually, "to forestall their malevolence and assure himself of their protection," primitive man offered prayers to these spirits. In this manner the first "animistic" religion was born. Spencer believed that "naturism" came about in a less directly calculated way, indeed, almost by accident. Primitive people, out of flattery, called their great leaders by the names which they used to designate the forces of nature. Soon tradition no longer distinguished between these men and the natural forces themselves. This confusion generated a religious orientation that personalized natural forces.

Durkheim's first response to Spencer actually employs Spencer's own theoretical logic to criticize part of his empirical description. Durkheim claims that Spencer has done an injustice to naturism by treating it in an offhand manner as simply the stepchild of animism. Naturism, Durkheim claims, was just as much the result of instrumental problem-solving as animism itself: "One doesn't see why men, once they had formed the concept of a spirit distinct from the body . . . would not have used it in order to render an account of natural phenomena."[190] There is no need, in other words, to refer to such a nebulous factor as tradition.

Far from being derived from animism, naturism would be completely independent of it.[191]

But this critique of Spencer's approach to early religion is not the most important criticism Durkheim had to make, although it clearly indicates his inclination to accept Spencer's calculating conception of action as his own. The "gravest objection" Durkheim raises against this theory of religion is that, in his accounts of later as well as earlier beliefs, Spencer pays insufficient attention to the "complex aggregate of psychic phenomena" that create the "collective being."[192]Arguing for a more collectivist focus, Durkheim in effect makes a case for a much more deterministic and coercive approach to social control. Spencer's individualism, Durkheim believes, led him to focus mainly on the symbols of religion, on the structure of beliefs and their history. For this reason, he gave far too much attention to the role of voluntarism and will in religious development. Thus Durkheim criticizes Spencer because he "attributes to the critical spirit a rather exorbitant role in the development of civilization."[193] A truly collectivist theory, one that emphasizes supra-individual forces, must focus on factors that are far more constraining. What sociologists are interested in, Durkheim asserts, "is not the symbol but what the symbol stands for." Sociology must study "what is thus hidden under this wholly superficial phenomenon [of symbolism]."[194]

Against Spencer's voluntarism Durkheim develops a much more reductionist approach to religious symbols and begins to elaborate the mechanistic approach to order which he will take up in his later sociological investigations. He inclines toward a proto-utilitarianism which is strikingly similar to the theory of religion elaborated by Marx in *The German Ideology*. Symbolic patterns, he argues, stand for social forces which are external to the consciousness of the individual and which affect action through coercive necessity. Symbols play a mediating, utilitarian role between such mechanical conditions and human action, "assur[ing] the adaptation of individuals or of the group to external circumstances."[195] By producing such adaptation, religion, like law and secular morality, assures the "equilibrium of society."[196] Its importance lies, therefore, in its capacity for external control. Durkheim views it not primarily as a vehicle for establishing internal meaning but as a "regulating institution."

The source of religious change cannot be traced to any internal symbolic structures. "If external conditions are no longer the same," according to Durkheim, religion automatically responds to this instability by changing its form. True, this need for religious change is signaled by a feeling of "uneasiness," but the basic cause must be traced to changing external circumstance, not to consciousness itself. This uneasiness serves simply as a warning of disrupted circumstances, a warning to which "consciousness then intervenes ... and acknowledges this dissolution."[197] In direct opposition not only to Spencer and the early Marx but to his own contrasting emphasis on the role of conscience, Durkheim declares that intellectual criticism has no real independent role in religious change.

> Doubtless if the Greco-Latin religion was transformed, it is in part because philosophers had submitted it to criticism. But, if they had submitted it to criticism, the reason is that it could no longer assure the equilibrium of those large communities of men that the Roman conquest had brought into being.[198]

Since external forces have become Durkheim's point of emphasis, the nature of subjective conceptualization no longer interests him; individual volition becomes, in effect, a non-cause. The true sociologist of religion, he insists, should "give little attention to the different ways in which men and peoples have been able to *conceive* the unknown cause and the mysterious foundation of things."[199] If the subjective formulation of perception is not significant, how do objective circumstances affect the patterns of individual religious conduct? Durkheim turns here to the mechanistic substitute for purely instrumental reflection which I discussed earlier. "What makes the force and authority of all discipline," he writes, "is habit." Habits perform a vital religious function. Formed by instinctual responses to shifting events, they supply us with the capacity to act rationally in a complex environment. When Durkheim further argues that habits—in the form of religious or secular "prejudices"—are a necessary part of any complex society, it becomes clear that his earlier critique of Spencer's rationalist attack on the survival of faith is no more than an argument for instrumentalism in a different form. Prejudices are a vital adaptive response to a society in which full knowledge of the environment is impossible.

> Despite the current meaning of the word, a prejudice is not a false judgment, but only a judgment received or regarded as such. It transmits to us, in an abridged form, the results of experience that others have had and that we cannot have for ourselves. Consequently, the vaster the field of knowledge and action becomes, the more things there are that we have to accept on authority.[200]

Prejudices, then, are the result of an external necessity, not the basis or result of collective belief. "A society without prejudices," Durkheim writes, "would resemble an organism without reflexes: it would be a monster incapable of living."[201] Thus, at least two years before he embarked on his own sociological writings, Durkheim had criticized Spencer in a way which allowed him to maintain important aspects of his general theoretical logic.[202†]

Though Durkheim's principal focus in these earliest essays remained the vision of order as moral solidarity, this utilitarian thread was never completely dropped. For example, in his review, the following year, of Guyau's *Irreligion of the Future* (*L'Irreligion de l'avenir*), Durkheim basically reiterates the logic of his Spencer essay. While he reaffirms, against Guyau, that religion or some secular substitute is a permanent part of human existence, he bases this argument, like the earlier retort to Spencer, on instrumental grounds. He explains religion, first of all, in a manner that carefully allows him to maintain an exclusive reference to external conditions: "Men did not begin by *imagining* gods," he insists, and he goes on to argue that if religion is a source of order it is not because of the way it invokes a voluntary commitment: "It is not because they conceived of them [i.e., the gods] in a given fashion that they felt themselves tied to them by social feelings."[203] To the contrary, men "began by linking themselves to the things [*choses*] which they made use of, or which they suffered from," and did so "without reflection, without the least kind of speculation."[204] From this contention, which strikingly recalls Marx's theory of the origins of human life, Durkheim goes on to argue that since the symbolic contents of religion only reflect determinate conditions, it is the condition, not the symbols, which must form the subject of sociological explanation.

> The [religious] theory came only much later [i.e., after the circumstances], in order to explain and make intelligible to these rudimentary minds the habits which had thus been formed. . . .
> In order to study religion, we must [avoid] the representations which are only the symbol and superficial wrapping [*l'enveloppe superficielle*] of these.[205†]

The logic of the argument is somewhat complicated by Durkheim's insistence that the coercive origin of religion complements innate, presocial sentiments. Despite this reference to the earlier position, however, the gist of Durkheim's argument is clear: he means to exclude purely instrumental action only insofar as it assumes complete knowledge of the environment. Once again, he is willing to abide nonrational action only if it is reduced to the status of an instinctual adaptation to external events. Ends are, in Durkheim's theory, effectively reduced to means.

> The end of psychic life is action, the adaptation to the surrounding milieu, be it physical or social, by means of appropriate movements. If involuntary and unreflective adaptation is, in practice, sufficient, intelligence does not intervene, because its intervention is pointless [*inutile*].[206]

While this kind of neo-utilitarian thinking remained a minor current in these first years of Durkheim's writing, by the time of his first sociological investigations they had become its central focus. With these writings Durkheim formulated a theory that finally satisfied his criterion of sociological determinism. In the last published article before he began intensive preparation for his doctoral dissertation, the determinist framework is firmly in place. This article, "The Principles of 1789 and Sociology," reviews a work that criticized conservative attacks on the French Revolution and at the same time rejected the philosophes' theoretical rationalism and individualism. Durkheim endorses this general perspective, but reformulates it in what he believes to be a more sociological form.

He begins by arguing that while the revolutionary slogans of individual liberty and rationality may be incorrect, they must be accepted as moral facts that require explanation. Indeed, Durkheim accords to the famous revolutionary formulae the status of a religious faith, and he proceeds to apply to them the reductionist theory of religion he had worked out in his religious writings. To examine these formulae sociologically one must discover how they "respond[ed] to real and legitimate needs," which means that these symbols must be linked to some extrasymbolic factor.[207] The task, then, is to demonstrate that the symbols "depend not on accidental and local circumstances but on some general change that occurred in the structure of European society."[208] This argument for viewing symbols simply as adaptations to external circumstances rests on the supposition that an individual's reaction to conditions is not mediated by independent moral commitment. Yet, once again, rather than fully reject the instrumentalist position, Durkheim chooses simply to emphasize a more complex environment within which it must operate. People refer to symbol systems, he affirms, not because of their intrinsic attraction but because the "distant causes on which [an event] depends escape us because of their remoteness and their complexity."

> By means of analogies or any other process of reasoning, we must invent reasons for them [the distant events], lacking the real ones which we do not see. . . . These . . . can reflect the underlying reality only in a very inexact way [which is] imperfect and deceptive. . . . They bear no relation to the true cause of the phenomenon.[209]

Durkheim has invoked an instrumental, purely cognitive actor, one whose beliefs reflect no more and no less than the objective, empirical environment which he can see in front of him. This general perspective on symbolism is, of course, directly parallel to the instrumentalist theory of ideology proposed by the mature Marx.

Yet for all the general similarities thus established, Durkheim's nascent sociological theory is neither Marxist, utilitarian, nor Social Darwinian. Each of these specific intellectual traditions involves certain assumptions that Durkheim forcefully rejects. In regard to utilitarianism and Darwinism, his objections pertain to their simplified visions of the actor's environment, which facilitate an unrealistic individualism. For the utilitarian, "collective interest is only a form of personal interest."[210] For the Social Darwinist, "the struggle for life is a product of egoism; it cannot be the basis of disinterested ideals."[211] Regarding the more collectivistic materialism, however, Durkheim, significantly, directs his argument to an assumption at a more specific level of analysis. He rejects not the general structure of action but its specific contents, the notion that "augmentation of [economic] resources, public or private, is a very important fact to most people."[212] Durkheim's objection to materialism, then, is empirical and ideological, not presuppositional. Indeed, his critique of utilitarianism and Social Darwinism recalls Marx's own, extremely qualified, critique of classical economics: Durkheim accepts their definitions of action while rejecting their approach to order. People do make quasi-contracts and they do engage in a struggle that produces a certain kind of survival of the fittest. They do so, however, in circumstances which are not of their own choosing. This combination of critique and acceptance was never more clearly expressed than in the criticism Durkheim directed against utilitarianism in one of his earliest essays.

> If one puts metaphysics aside, a contract is nothing other than a spontaneous adaptation of two or more individuals to one another, *in conditions determined by the social and physical milieu in which they find themselves placed.*[213†]

Durkheim began his early writings with an ideological vision that sought to combine collective control with individual liberty. He realized, moreover, that this reconciliation depended upon recognizing the centrality of morality in social life. Yet the theory with which he concluded his formative period fails his ambition. Durkheim has moved from a conception of collective order as subjective and voluntary to a vision of order as obdurate and coercive. He has accepted a "sociological materialism." The point is not, of course, that he refused to recognize the existence of morality, but that, adopting either directly or indirectly an instrumentalist understanding of action, he explains order "as if" it were purely external. The result is a sociological theory that duplicates the base-superstructure reasoning of Marx and bears a striking resemblance to the utilitarian and Social Darwinian theories which Durkheim originally set out to criticize and overthrow.

Chapter Five

DURKHEIM'S FIRST PHASE (2)

The Division of Labor in Society as the Attempt to Reconcile Collective Order with Freedom

No other work in Durkheim's corpus has received anywhere near as much critical attention as *The Division of Labor in Society*, and perhaps no work in the sociological canon with the exception of Marx's *Capital* has been subject to as much misinterpretation. This book, like *Capital*, has been used to legitimate sharply different kinds of generalized theoretical reasoning. It has been read to justify anticapitalist as well as conservative sociology,[1] to establish materialist as well as normative theories of the modern industrial order.[2] But probably the most striking aspect of this secondary literature is that for nearly all of these readings the claim of Durkheim's utter consistency is advanced. For Filloux and Giddens, the *Division of Labor* lays out the moral basis of industrial society.[3] For Aimard and Cuvillier, Merton, Pope and Traugott, the work is just as consistently an exercise in the application of materialist thought.[4] The exceptions to this claim of consistency—most importantly, the interpretations of Parsons and Nisbet—are few and far between.[5]

One reason for the misinterpretation of this classic work is, of course, the simple fact that interpretive readings are by their very nature exercises in theoretical polemic. "Reading" is an important part of any theoretical strategy, and if the work in question is in any way open to varied interpretation then it certainly will be so interpreted. This last consideration introduces a second reason for the interpretive confusion, for we will see that Durkheim's first book is, indeed, profoundly ambiguous. Given the drive for consistency that motivates most theoretical analysis, it is not surprising that critics of one orientation will focus on a particular strand of Durkheim's argument and consciously or unconsciously ignore the counterarguments he has also proposed. Such selective reading

119

will be especially easy if interpreters are unfamiliar with the early writings which preceded Durkheim's book, as almost always has been the case.

Yet, although each of these factors has contributed to these mistaken ideas about Durkheim's consistency, the most important explanation by far is simply the lack of rigor in theoretical thinking itself. The problem has partly been the failure to separate the presuppositional elements of Durkheim's argument from his ideological perspective and empirical propositions. More profoundly, however, it is a failure to understand the implications of presuppositional logic itself. Critics have often failed to understand what, precisely, are the requisites for instrumental versus normative action or how, exactly, these assumptions about action can be transformed into postulates about individual and collective order.

The Division of Labor in Society is the first work of Durkheim's maturity. In writing it he is engaged in the process of specification—much as Marx was in his writing of *The Communist Manifesto*.[6†] His intent is to place his presuppositional and philosophical assumptions into a more determinate empirical context, and he will do this by strictly adhering to the canons of science. "We must be careful," he warns his readers in his preface to the first edition, "to admit no explanation that does not rest on authentic proofs."[7] In finding an explanatory justification for his presuppositions about order and action, Durkheim will range, as did Marx himself, over the widest possible social canvas. This search for historical and comparative evidence, moreover, will sustain Durkheim's ideological goal as well. Marx's mature writings established the science of political-economic revolution; Durkheim's are intended to create the science of critical morality.[8]

It is not surprising, then, that the *Division of Labor* sets itself the same general task as Durkheim's early writings, the reconciliation of individualism with the need for social control. As Durkheim asks himself in his preface of 1893:

> The question which has been at the origins of this study is that of the relationship between the individual personality and social solidarity. How does it happen that, while becoming more autonomous, the individual depends more completely upon society? How can he be at once more individual and more solidary?[9]

Once again, he insists that individualism and social control can be reconciled. "Contradictory as they appear," these two movements have "develop[ed] in parallel fashion."[10] This was the same answer, of course, that Durkheim offered in his early writings, and it has been seen how ill-prepared he was to conceptualize the actual reconciliation. Doubting the strength of a purely moral order, he had turned increasingly to a deterministic solution that emphasized the conditional constraints on action rather than its voluntary control. Yet by 1893 Durkheim felt he had found a way to reestablish voluntarism within the framework of this material-ism itself. The solution was the division of material labor into differenti-ated, individualized parts. "What resolves this apparent antinomy" be-tween individuality and social control, he announces in the preface, is a "transformation of social solidarity due to the steadily growing develop-ment of the division of labor."[11]

This indeed, is the secret of Durkheim's first great work, and it is one which can be fully understood only within the context of his earlier writ-ings. With the notion of the division of labor Durkheim felt he could es-cape from the stark dilemma he faced at the end of his early period. Since the division of labor is an economic arrangement created by mate-rial conditions, Durkheim can remain true to his earlier rejection of nor-mative action. But since this arrangement seems, at the same time, to rest upon individual choice, this material foundation can, apparently, be rec-onciled with the growth of voluntary will. We will see, however, that this synthesis is a facile one: Durkheim tries to avoid the fundamental the-oretical requisites of a voluntaristic theory by an empirical sleight-of-hand. In fact, Durkheim himself implicitly recognized this weakness of argument, and the manner in which he tried to compensate for it under-mined the logical foundations of his first great work. For the present, however, I wish to investigate the reasoning by which Durkheim first ar-rived at this apparently remarkable theoretical solution. To do so it is necessary to return briefly to the early writings.

1. "MATERIAL INDIVIDUALISM" AS THE ANTIDOTE TO MECHANICAL ORDER: THE DIVISION OF LABOR IN THE EARLY SOCIOLOGICAL ESSAYS

Although Durkheim's earliest sociological articles establish a deter-minism that is mechanical and predictable, they do not totally ignore the question of individual freedom. In fact, it is in these early articles, in the process of establishing an empirical determinism, that the notion of the division of labor first surfaces in Durkheim's work. To understand these earliest references one must recall the confusion about the status of the individual that permeated Durkheim's early writing. Durkheim had once sought to root voluntarism in the innate sociability of individual ac-tors. When he rejected this approach for a more explicitly collective moral order he tentatively proposed a "nonsubstantialist" approach to the individual: individuals could be the carriers of invisible but nonethe-less real collective force. If collective morality could be seen as emerging from voluntary individual interaction, the individual/society dichotomy would be dissolved. As has been seen, however, Durkheim eventually re-coiled from this moral solution to order; at this point in his theoretical development, he could not tolerate such an "analytical," antisubstantialist approach to the individual. If individuals were viewed as the carriers and creators of morality, then this morality must, he believed, itself be irredeemably individualistic. For order to be collective, it must be antithetical to individual control. Driven by this basic theoretical misconception, Durkheim returned to an instrumental approach to action and pursued order in a more coercive way.

We have seen in the preceding chapter how Durkheim's second introductory lecture at Bordeaux, "Introduction to the Sociology of the Family," delivered in 1888, presents a significant empirical specification of this newly established determinism. In this same lecture—and on the basis of the same kind of theoretical logic—Durkheim returns to the problem of individual freedom. The conceptualization he establishes will fundamentally mark his thinking for the next five years. For the first time Durkheim gives a name to the solidarity that orders premodern societies. He calls this "mechanical" solidarity and describes it as a "community of ideas and feelings" which is based on the "intimate contact of members" and on the "similarity of consciousness."[12] The trouble with such a solidarity based on shared ideals, Durkheim believes, is that it is antithetical to liberty, and it is so opposed because social norms intrude upon the absolute individual privacy that must be the basis of true liberty. Mechanical solidarity breaks down the boundaries between individuals, and thus it "unites minds only by fusing them." In this way, the "individual [is] totally absorbed by the group" and the "whole transcends the part."[13]

It is as an alternative to this elimination of autonomy by moral community that Durkheim first introduces the term "organic solidarity."[14†] Organic solidarity rests upon the division of economic labor, and its instrumental, material approach to action assumes the inviolability of individual volition. This preservation of the concrete, "substantialist" barriers between individuals is, indeed, the great advantage of organic solidarity. Because it rests upon the "mutual dependence of *specialized* functions," consciences are not fused: "Everyone has his *own* sphere of action."[15] The parts remain independent of the whole while at the same time they sustain it. Yet the division of labor, Durkheim is careful to point out, is produced by the same objective factors as the modern family, by increases in population volume and ecological density and the disequilibrium which they create.[16] Within the instrumental logic of material necessity, then, Durkheim has found a way of preserving the appearance of voluntarism. It is no wonder that he calls the division of labor the "great innovation which separates contemporary societies from those of the past."[17†]

The same connections between instrumental action, individual separateness, and the division of labor are drawn in the analysis of Montesquieu that Durkheim presented in his Latin dissertation of 1892. The freedom of a modern society, he insists, rests upon the asocial privatization of individual feelings: "In modern society . . . each of us has his own personality, opinions, religion, and way of life; each one draws a profound distinction between himself and society, between his personal concerns and public affairs."[18] If modern solidarity is to preserve this freedom, therefore, it cannot rest upon common, shared commitments to a moral order: "Social solidarity cannot be the same [as in earlier times], nor can it spring from the same source; it results from the division of labor, which makes the citizens and the social orders dependent upon each other."[19] Montesquieu realized, in other words, that only this special kind of economic link could create dependence and cooperation without violating individual autonomy. The way Durkheim presents it, Montesquieu's analysis of the monarchical type of society rests upon the same kind of reasoning. Whereas the members of a republic are sensitive to the needs and interests of the whole society, in a monarchy "each class is concerned only with a limited area of life."

> It sees nothing beyond the function it performs. . . . Each order has only one objective, which is not the common weal but self-aggrandisement. . . . *But this very diversity of the component parts makes for cohesion.* . . . They work *unconsciously* for the common good.[20]

This argument that collective order rests not on conscience but on necessity is amplified in Durkheim's presentation of Montesquieu's ideas about historical causation. In perhaps the most original element in his interpretation, he insists that the kinds of causes Montesquieu emphasizes are efficient ones, and the most important among them is the increase in the volume of society.[21] In his subsequent criticism of Montesquieu's understanding of lawmaking, he tries to turn this argument against the author himself. By suggesting that laws are created by wise men with knowledge of the ends they will help achieve, Montesquieu, Durkheim believes, gives too much emphasis to "final" rather than efficient causes. Instead, laws must be viewed as responding to the same mechanical conditions as the division of labor which they regulate.

> Social life embraces so many phenomena that no mind is capable of reckoning with them all. Hence it is no easy matter to foresee what will be useful and what harmful. Even if such calculation were not, for the most part, beyond the powers of the human mind, it would be so abstruse as hardly to influence men's deliberate actions. Social phenomena are not, as a rule, the product of calculated action. Laws . . . spring most often from causes which engender them by a kind of physical necessity.[22]

The connection of this empirical reasoning to the logic of Durkheim's earlier writings is unmistakable. Although he argues against the importance of calculated action, it is clearly only individual calculation which he rejects. Law develops, like the division of labor itself, from an adaptation to external force which has nothing to do with normative regulation or subjective perception.

In the sociological writings of his early period, then, Durkheim had already moved toward the "division of labor" as an empirical strategy to resolve the theoretical problems he faced. By emphasizing the division of labor as the principal characteristic of modern society, Durkheim could, in effect, historicize the presuppositional orientations between which he was torn. True, individuals had the capacity for shared morality, but such common feelings characterized society only in its earliest stages. As societies moved toward modernity individuals became increasingly instrumental, social structures increasingly reactive vis-à-vis the mechanical pressures of institutional life. This historical compartmentalization of human action, of course, was exactly what Durkheim needed if he were to succeed in emphasizing the individualism of the modern era. If individual actors lost their autonomy by sharing values, only the instrumentalization of modernity would free them from conformity. A similar process of historicization, we may recall, allowed Marx to resolve his presuppositional ambiguity in the first works of his maturity: he could argue—in direct opposition to Durkheim—that while individuals once were subjectively free, the alienation of modern capitalism established mechanical determinism.

2. EMPIRICAL DISCOVERY AND THEORETICAL AMBIVALENCE IN *THE DIVISION OF LABOR IN SOCIETY*

The explicit message of these first sociological writings, therefore, is that Durkheim has resolved the problems produced by trying to combine voluntarism with an instrumental approach to collective force. On closer inspection, however, there is good reason to doubt his success. True, the problem of normative conformity is avoided through historicization, but can the same be said for the issue of determinism? The division of labor apparently institutionalizes free and rational choice, but what of the structure within which it is imbedded? Has Durkheim not described it as determined at every turn by pressures which are completely outside individual volition and control? Has he not described the very laws which institutionalize instrumental individualism as standing completely outside of individual conscience?

This is the problem that Durkheim faces in 1893. Whether or not the "division of labor" could actually maintain voluntarism within the context of instrumental collective order remained very much unresolved, and it is this theoretical challenge that dictates the structure and the empirical argument of his first great book. While he maintains his commitment to the concept of the division of labor, his description of its empirical content shifts back and forth throughout the work. To save the voluntarism which is so imperiled at the end of his early writings, Durkheim shifts peripatetically between the normative and materialist positions he earlier laid out. This vacillation reflects, of course, the conflict in his presuppositional orientation.

The long Introduction to the first edition of *The Division of Labor in Society*—which was omitted from later French editions and which, in the English editions, is largely put into an appendix—is highly revealing.[23] It indicates the same ambiguity about action and the same conflicting approaches to order that informed Durkheim's earliest, most philosophical writings. After reaching the still unsatisfactory solution of his first sociological essays, Durkheim has gone back to the drawing board. If he will not abandon the notion of the division of labor, perhaps he can formulate a different general position within which to articulate it.

The subject of this introduction is morality. In placing the fact of social morality at the very center of his sociological writing, Durkheim has once again demonstrated his difference from Marx. There remains, however, the problem of how this fact of morality shall be explained, and here one finds a familiar ambivalence. Durkheim rejects purely subjective and Kantian approaches as philosophically idealist. He also rejects the utilitarian notion of a morality "based upon individual interest," on the grounds that "nothing comes from nothing."[24] The love of society cannot come from the love of self, the whole from the part. But does this rejection of the utilitarian model extend to instrumental collective order as well? At first it seems that it does, and Durkheim strongly rejects the notion that morality can be viewed simply as a function of social interest.[25] It soon becomes apparent, however, that this is not the case. Durkheim's problem is not with the rationality of motivation but with the simplified conception of its external environment. It turns out that he is actually invoking the "incomplete knowledge" argument which he had earlier used to legitimate a more collectivist instrumentalism.

> Whether or not moral practices are useful to society, surely it is not usually in the light of such a purpose that they are established, for in order for a collective utility to be the spring of moral evolution, it would have to be, in most cases, the object of a rather distinct idea in order to determine moral conduct. Now, these utilitarian calculations, though they be exact, are too intelligently contrived to have had any great effect upon the will; the elements are too many, and the relations uniting them too confused.[26]

Morality is adapted to external repercussions that are wider and more extensive than those located in the actor's immediate environment: "[It is not] sufficient to observe the relatively proximate consequences an action in our restricted personal milieu can produce, but we must measure the repercussions which can result from it in all directions in the social organism."[27] Later, in his discussion of the relativity of moral rules, Durkheim expands on this position by comparing the development of social morality to the results of a scientific experiment; just as a scientist's conclusions are determined by objective conditions, so is the specific morality of any particular society.

> If, then, the ethics of the city-state or of the tribe are so different from our own in certain respects, it is not because these societies were deceived about the destiny of man, but simply that their destiny, as it was determined by the conditions in which they found themselves, would not allow any other ethic. Thus moral rules are moral only in relation to certain experimental conditions; and, consequently, the nature of moral phenomena cannot be understood if the conditions on which they are dependent are not determined.[28]

Shortly after making this point, Durkheim radically alters the ground of his theoretical argument. Instead of affecting action through the external repercussions its violation would produce, morality must be seen as rooted in individual conscience. External sanctions do not indicate the true nature of morality; rather, they are simply the most visible indicators that morality is, indeed, at work. We study sanctions to locate moral rules but we should not confuse these sanctions with their moral source. Instead of sanctions producing states of conscience, the opposite is the case. Nonmoral actions will produce sanctioning repercussions because "it is impossible . . . for the members of a society to recognize a rule of conduct as obligatory without reacting against all those acts violating it; this reaction is so necessary that every normal conscience reproves *even the very thought* of such an act."[29] Collective order rests with the organization of thought, not with conditions. It relies on "public opinion," "disapproval," and on "all the shades of reproach."[30]

Durkheim's Introduction to the *Division of Labor*, then, recapitulates the presuppositional ambiguity of his early writings, and his first empirical references naturally reflect this confusion. Is the division of labor, he asks, "a moral *rule* of human conduct?"[31] If so, then individuals will follow the division of labor because of the moral satisfaction they derive from it. On the other hand, perhaps it is only that the division of labor has moral *consequences;* it may produce beneficent cooperation but effect this through mechanical and nonmoral causes.[32]

Finally, this substantive ambiguity also reflects itself in the model of causality which Durkheim adopts. The great advantage of the functional approach is precisely that it leaves the nature of causes open. Thus, the division of labor could produce morality through purely mechanical means and it could still be described as having a moral "function."

> The term . . . "function" has the great advantage of implying this idea, without prejudicing the question as to how this correspondence is established, whether it results from an intentional and preconceived adaptation or an aftermath adjustment.[33]

Yet even here Durkheim is careful to qualify his argument, to carefully separate his choice of model from his presuppositional commitments as such. While functional causality allows the moral effects of mechanical determinism to be established, it does not necessarily imply that order must in fact be instrumentally based. Even functionally adaptive behavior can become voluntary if it eventually produces rules that are obeyed for intrinsic rather than extrinsic reasons. If this occurs, then the "true function" of the division of labor is "to create in two or more persons a *feeling* of solidarity."[34]

These two vastly different approaches to the morality associated with the division of labor are at war with one another throughout this work. On the one hand, the division of labor produces moral effects through mechanical means. By producing the material context for cooperation and individuality, it lays the basis for harmony and freedom. On the other hand, Durkheim sometimes argues that this labor division is itself the product of moral choice, and it is the latter conception that he emphasizes in the conclusion to his first chapter. He rejects the instrumentalist approach to the division of labor as exchange on the grounds that it creates mutual dependence only "outwardly."[35] He argues, in contrast, that this interconnection is effected by a "whole mechanism of images": "The image of the one who completes us becomes inseparable from ours," an "integral and permanent part of our conscience."[36] Since the image of our partner in the division of labor is internalized, the altruistic desire for the other is the same as the self-interested desire for self.

> We can no longer separate ourselves from it. . . . *That* is why we enjoy the society of the one it represents, since the presence of the object that it expresses, by making us actually perceive it, sets it off more.[37]

The division of labor, then, has an ideal status. It produces cooperation because it transforms independent individuals into potent and attractive symbols whose "vivacity" is voluntarily sought by the members of society.[38] From this perspective, the purpose of Durkheim's work would be to compare this kind of normative solidarity with others in order to show, perhaps, that it is unique to modernity. If law becomes the object of his analysis, it is not because he believes that modern solidarity is produced by these external sanctions but rather because law is a very visible symbol of internal control. "We must substitute for this internal fact which escapes us," Durkheim writes, "an external index which symbolizes it."[39]

2.1. BOOK 1: THE CONFRONTATION BETWEEN INSTRUMENTAL AND NORMATIVE THEORY AS A DEBATE OVER MODERNITY

The main body of Durkheim's *Division of Labor* is divided into three parts, or "books." Durkheim himself offers an empirical rationale for this organization. Book 1 is ostensibly an ahistorical, purely systematic account—hence its title, "The Function of the Division of Labor." Book 2, in contrast, concerns itself with the origins of this social structural type, and Durkheim entitles it "Causes and Conditions." In the third and final Book, "Abnormal Forms," Durkheim apparently considers certain contingent, purely historically-specific characteristics of the division of labor in contemporary Western society. The movement from one book to the next, in other words, is intended to indicate the substantial development of Durkheim's empirical argument. It will be seen, however, that the development it demarcates is hardly one that emerges from shifting empirical concerns alone. It is, much more fundamentally, changes in theoretical perspective that dictate the divisions of Durkheim's first major work, and it is to this shifting orientation toward the most general presuppositional problems that we now turn.

2.1.1. Mechanical and Organic Solidarity as Presuppositional Problems: The Shift Toward Instrumental Individualism

The most crucial theoretical fact in Book 1 is that Durkheim employs the same presuppositional framework to explain "mechanical solidarity" that he has just established—in the Introduction—to explain the solidarity produced by divided labor. The similarity he means to establish between the two modes of explanation is strongly reinforced by what at first appears to be a rather incidental fact: while mechanical solidarity and the repressive legal sanctions which symbolize it are clearly intended to refer to an earlier historical time, Durkheim rarely refers to them in the past tense. Indeed, in the very first paragraph of chapter 2 he sets out to "inquire what crime essentially consists of."[40] Immediately, he rejects an instrumental explanation. "There are many acts," he writes, "which have been *and still are* regarded as criminal without in themselves being harmful to society."[41] Rather, it is sentiments and subjective revulsion that form the basis for social punishment. By way of illustration, Durkheim demonstrates how modern societies punish murder but show no vengeance to the perpetrators of an economic crisis, despite the fact that the latter causes much greater harm in a physical sense. The source of punishment, then, is rooted within the individual rather than without; it is the "collective or common conscience [la conscience collective ou commune]," and Durkheim insists that the "totality of beliefs and sentiments common to average citizens of the same society forms a determinate system."[42] In defining the common conscience, Durkheim clearly applies it to modern society.

> Indeed, it is independent of the particular conditions in which individuals are placed. . . . It is the same in the North and in the South, in great cities and in small, in different professions.[43]

The existence of the collective conscience testifies to the "psychical type of society."[44] In this society even the state enforces its will in a purely moral way: "Its primary and principal function is to create respect for the beliefs, traditions, and collective practices; that is, to defend the common conscience against all enemies within and without. It thus becomes its symbol, its living expression in the eyes of all."[45] If even material sanctions are symbolically based, the enforcement of social order through devices like dishonor and disgrace is even more so. Although these are diffuse rather than specific forms of social punishment, they are firm supports for collective order nonetheless.

Durkheim begins the third section of this chapter by declaring— once again resolutely in the present tense—that "every strong state of conscience is a source of life; *it is an essential factor of our general vitality.*"[46] The threats to this vitality are, correspondingly, normative rather than conditional. The "conflict of sentiments" enfeebles and corrupts us because it produces contrary ideals which, given their subjective status, themselves "become part of our conscience."[47] The antidote to such despair is normative reinforcement, and it is in this context that Durkheim first introduces the concept of "exchange" into the *Division of Labor.*

> Even as contrary states of conscience enfeeble themselves reciprocally, identical states of conscience, in being exchanged, reenforce one another. . . . It contributes to our own idea, superimposes itself, confounds itself with it, communicates to it whatever vitality it has. From this fusion grows a new idea which absorbs its predecessors and which, accordingly, is more vivid than each of those taken separately.[48]

This sort of "exchange" produces public morality, not rational control.

> From all the similar impressions which are exchanged, from all the temper that gets itself expressed, there emerges a unique temper, more or less determinate according to the circumstances, which is everybody's without being anybody's in particular. That is the public temper.[49]

The public temper is a fundamental source of social control in every sphere of social life. It acts in small towns as well as big cities, in patriotic nations as well as in religious communities.[50]

Durkheim has addressed this discussion of mechanical solidarity and collective conscience as much to the present as to the past. This discussion, moreover, is itself congruent with his earlier analysis of the shared symbolic content generated by the division of labor. One would expect, therefore, that his discussion of modern, "organic" solidarity in the chapter following would take much the same path. There are, indeed, certain elements in chapter 3 that emphasize the subjective basis for modern freedom. At an early point in his discussion, Durkheim asserts that organic solidarity must be based on the felt "rights of individuals," and that such recognition cannot be induced simply by the utilitarian desire to avoid war and secure peace.[51] Individuals will pursue peace only if "already united by some tie of sociability."[52] This social unity will recognize individual justice only if human relationships have an altruistic basis.

> In reality, for men to recognize and mutually guarantee rights, they must, first of all, love each other, they must, for some reason, depend upon each other and on the same society of which they are a part. Justice is full of charity. . . . It is the repercussion in the sphere of real rights of social sentiments.[53]

This argument for modern individualism as a manifestation of moral order is, however, short lived. Just as he earlier rejected the normative solution to order as incompatible with individual autonomy, so does he now. Liberty can only be based upon the separation of the individual from society.

> What makes our personality is what distinctive qualities each of us has of our own, what distinguishes us from others. This solidarity can grow, therefore, only in inverse ratio to personality.[54]

Since the very notion of a collective conscience implies the internalization of similar sentiments, modern individuality must imply not simply the changing content of the common conscience but its radical diminution.

> Solidarity which comes from likenesses is at its maximum when the collective conscience completely envelops our whole conscience and coincides in all points with it. But, at that moment our individuality is nil. It can be born only if the community takes smaller toll of us.[55]

The notion that individualism implies a moral altruism is now discarded.

> There are, here, two contrary forces, one centripetal, the other centrifugal, which cannot flourish at the same time. We cannot,

at one and the same time, develop ourselves in two opposite senses. If we have a lively desire to think and act for ourselves, we cannot be strongly inclined to think and act as others do.[56]

Instead of implying a particular type of collective conscience, the order produced by the division of labor is an alternative to it, indeed the "effacement of one is the necessary condition for the appearance of the other."[57] Durkheim has returned to the division of labor as he had presented it in the early sociological essays: "It is in the nature of special tasks to escape the action of the collective conscience."[58†]

Granted, the instrumental nature of the division of labor guarantees the separateness of individual actors; but what of the presuppositional requirement for collective order? We have already seen the answer Durkheim gave in 1888: the "great advantage" of the division of labor is that it can achieve order and voluntarism at the same time. In the context of the present discussion, however, Durkheim's position is a more ambivalent one. He does not at this juncture refer to the long-term collective forces—the growth in volume and density—that he had earlier used to ensure the division of labor's collective status. Instead, particularly in the early part of his discussion, he describes collective order simply as the result of the division of labor rather than its cause. And since he has so stressed the autonomy that divided tasks provide, this discussion leaves the impression that modern order could be the unintended aggregate of individual self-interest. Cooperation, he stresses, reflects the utilitarian sharing of functionally interdependent tasks. At one point, he writes that "society is made up of a system of differentiated parts which mutually complement each other,"[59] and at another simply that the "involvement of one party results either from involvement assumed by the other, or from some service already rendered by the latter."[60†] Order, then, is spontaneous, and it is perfectly represented by contract, for "contracts ... have as their object the adjustment of special, different functions to one another." Durkheim calls contract the "symbol of exchange," and it is clear that exchange assumes here an entirely different, much more conventionally instrumental meaning than in the analysis of mechanical solidarity he so recently concluded.[61†] In organic solidarity, contractual exchange pervades every area previously controlled by collective conscience. Even in the family, the sphere most directly associated with common sentiments and mutual obligations, Durkheim asserts that social order depends on the mutual advantage attained from complementary tasks.

> The history of the family, from its very origins, is only an uninterrupted movement of dissociation in the course of which diverse functions, at first undivided and confounded one with another, have been little by little separated, constituted apart, apportioned among the relatives according to sex, age, relations of de-

pendence, in a way to make each of them *a special functionary of domestic society. Far from being only an accessory and secondary phenomenon, this division of familial labor, on the contrary, dominates the entire development of the family.*[62]

In this quasi-individualistic vein, Durkheim has used the empirical appearance of the division of labor as a crutch. In a superficial sense, labor division certainly seems to emphasize individual decision-making, and insofar as it does it can perform the dual role Durkheim has laid out for it. Yet Durkheim has still spoken only of the results of the division of labor, not of its actual structure. He has yet to consider whether his approach will be able to encase rational action in a more collective frame. In view of his overall theoretical goals, of course, it would be surprising if he did not decide to do so. Indeed, as the reference to contract begins to indicate, Durkheim conceives the division of labor as bound by the legal order, a collective force beyond the immediate context of individual acts. If law remains for Durkheim a symbol of social solidarity and moral sanctions rather than the principal sanction itself—and we will see shortly that this distinction itself becomes very tenuous—he views the legal structure of organic societies as symbolizing their very lack of symbolic integration. Durkheim's theoretical strategy here is to separate completely modern law from punishment. Modern law is restitutive, not repressive. If repressive punishment indicates the violation of strongly held sentiments, restitutive law indicates merely the functional adaptation to external disruption.

Restitutive law is concerned with means, not ends. When the modern judge speaks of damage-interests, for example, he views these legal sanctions as having no penal character: "They are only a means of reviewing the past in order to reinstate it [*C'est seulement un moyen . . . pour le restituer*]."[63] Restitutive law, like the division of labor it regulates, has no relation to subjective belief. "These prescriptions do not correspond to any sentiment in us," Durkheim writes, "they have no roots in the majority of us."[64] Correspondingly, they rarely involve any emotional response.[65] Modern law becomes a purely rational vehicle; it works without reference to notions of social honor or diffuse morality.

> Neglect of these rules is not even punished diffusely. The pleader who has lost in litigation is not disgraced, his honor is not put in question. We can even imagine these rules being other than they are without feeling any repugnance.[66]

With this explicit demonstration of the role he has assigned to external control, Durkheim reveals the determinism that necessarily adheres to the theoretical logic he has adopted. Despite his empirical claim that restitutive law contributes to individuality, the more generalized—and antithetical—implications become at times utterly clear. At one point, for example, he emphasizes that although solidarity is no longer rooted in collective feelings it remains as socially structured as ever before: "Although these rules are more or less outside the collective conscience," he assures the reader, "they are not interested solely in individuals. . . . [To the contrary,] society is far from having no hand in this sphere of judicial life."[67] But if he rejects a normative approach to action and insists, nonetheless, that this action is collectively ordered, Durkheim's only theoretical option for social control is material force. Indeed, he implicitly acknowledges this to be the path he has taken. He insists that the state is the essential source of social control, the state now conceived in mechanical and objective terms. "It is true," Durkheim writes, that generally the state "does not intervene of itself . . . [but] must be solicited by the interested parties." Yet this apparently individualistic fact should not be deceptive: "In being called forth, its [the state's] intervention is none the less *the essential cog in the machine*, since it alone makes it function. It [the state] propounds the law through the organ of its representatives."[68]

When Durkheim had earlier discussed the state in reference to the moral community of mechanical solidarity, he had viewed it as an extension of social ideals, as resting on the voluntary commitment of individuals. His analysis of the state in organic societies could not be more different. The state is a cog in the machine; it is the institutional power that supplies the force to legal sanctions. "The sanctions of juridical rules of all sorts," he now writes, "can be applied only thanks to the interplay of a certain number of functions, of magistrates, of defense counsel, of prosecutors, of jurors, of plaintiffs and defendants, etc."[69] Voluntarism has dropped out of his conception of social control. "The consent of the interested parties," he emphasizes, "suffices neither to create nor to change [the law]."[70] This instrumental law is not merely symbolic, for in an instrumental society coercive legal sanctions are themselves the most effective social controls. Indeed, Durkheim derides moral control as inherently weak. "Suppose that society did not sanction the obligations contracted for," he warns. What would be the result? "They become simply promises which have no more than moral authority."[71]

The state, then, has become the crucial source of social control, and Durkheim's focus on the state becomes more intense as chapter 3 progresses.[72] Still, the reason this control is necessary is not because people are irrational in their calculations. Rather, the environment in which they exercise their rationality is complex. The state issues its laws because people have to act "in diverse combinations of circumstance," in relation to "objects . . . not always present to consciousness."[73] The state, in other words, represents the necessary adaptation to the mechanical and functional equilibrium that Durkheim emphasized in his earlier essays. In a modern society, he maintains, "all that is necessary is that the functions concur in a regular manner. If this regularity is disrupted, it behooves us to re-establish it."[74] The state's function is the "regulation of the different functions of the body in such a way as to make them harmonize." It will adapt to the "repercussions" of a complex world and will issue sanctions to control them.[75]

From the perspective of economic liberalism, the division of labor appeared to embody voluntary action and the individual control of tasks. This empirical perception, however, depended upon more general presuppositions: on the belief that action was rational and that order could be successfully negotiated in an individualistic way. Other presuppositions could produce contrasting evaluations of the division of labor, indeed, could completely reverse the voluntaristic evaluation of classical liberalism. It is this conflict on the presuppositional level that was so central to Durkheim's argument. Surveying his analysis in the conclusion to chapter 3, Durkheim would have us believe that he has demonstrated how labor division successfully resolves the individual/society antinomy: "The individuality of all grows at the same time as that of its parts. . . . Society becomes more capable of collective movement, at the same time that each of its elements has more freedom of movement. . . . The unity of the organism is as great as the individuation of the parts is more marked."[76] As we have seen, however, this intended resolution was hardly a successful one. As Durkheim's perspective on action shifted from normative to instrumental, and from implicitly individual to decisively collective, he subtly but irrevocably transformed the division of labor from a source of voluntaristic order into a vehicle for coercive control. Durkheim is caught in the complex and confusing web that he spun for himself in his earliest sociological efforts. He will make one more effort to extricate himself before surrendering completely to its control.

2.1.2. Modernity as the Differentiated Moral Community: The Last Attempt at Voluntary Order

Durkheim can retain his commitment to voluntarism only by ensuring that collective control has, at least in part, an ideal status. For only normative control can be internalized and can, in this way, become part of the stimulus of individual action itself. In the earlier chapters of Book 1, Durkheim succeeded in this task. Modernity, in his view, continued to support diffuse moral sanctions, and "punishment"—whether material or ideal—still played a major role in contemporary societies. Indeed, the division of labor itself worked according to such a voluntary principle. Although divided and individualized labor depended upon transforming the content of values, in no way did it undermine their very existence. This vision of modernity was, of course, a sociologically idealist one; nonetheless, it provided the basis upon which any more multidimensional perspective would have to build. In the middle chapters of Book 1, however, this voluntaristic orientation dropped away. Much like Marx's historicist approach, Durkheim employed mechanical and organic solidarity to link normative and instrumental presuppositional positions to different historical periods. In the organic solidarity of contemporary society, he now asserted, instrumental action would predominate. The theory remained one-dimensional; it did so, however, in a much more disturbing way, for the period that was supposed to liberate historical individualism was now encased in a deterministic framework. The empirical strategy which Durkheim utilized to articulate this theoretical transformation was simple and direct: the nature of a society's legal sanctions reflects the nature of its solidarity (*a*); legal punishment—penal law—indicates that solidarity has a moral and emotional basis (*b*); modern society has virtually no penal sanctions (*c*); in modern societies, therefore, the collective conscience—the emotional commitment to symbolic resemblances—has ceased to exist (*d*).

In chapter 5 of Book 1, Durkheim makes a final and extraordinary effort to break free from this dichotomizing logic which has forced him to prove exactly the opposite of what he would contend.[77†] He develops an altogether new theory based upon a completely different conception of modernity, one that places individual liberty in a potentially multi-dimensional context. As in the earlier chapters, he accomplishes this by freeing presuppositional orientation from any necessary historical reference. Significantly, the concept "division of labor" is never mentioned in the substance of this argument.

Instead of insisting on the elimination of normative solidarity, Durkheim now talks about radical shifts within it. Indeed, the collective conscience "has not lost anything," it has simply grown more generalized and abstract.[78] The crucial issue for voluntarism becomes the degree to which collective morality is concretely and specifically defined, for "the more defined beliefs and practices are, the less they leave for individual divergencies."[79] What allows modernity to facilitate individual freedom is not the elimination of moral control, therefore, but the fact that "there are fewer quite defined collective representations to enclose in a determined form." As a result, "the collective type loses its background, its forms become more abstract and more indecisive."[80] It is not that individuals can now act without reference to collective belief but rather that the generality of rules forces the individual to creatively apply them to diverse concrete situations. "The more general and indeterminate the rules of conduct and thought are," Durkheim writes, "the more individual reflection must intervene to apply them to particular cases."[81]

Durkheim describes two long-term historical dynamics that have produced this transformation toward individualism and generalized belief. The first concerns the relation between religion and the wider society. While religion defines collective obligations in a concrete and specific way, with historical development this morality becomes increasingly separated from the political power that enforces moral punishment. Durkheim traces the origins of this shift to the Roman Empire, where religious crimes almost totally disappeared: "The State did not lend its authority to religion except in so far as the attacks directed against it also menaced statehood indirectly."[82] In this process of differentiation, of course, the state became much more exclusively instrumental in its orientation—more concerned, in terms of Durkheim's earlier analysis, with the adaptive problems of political equilibrium—but religious beliefs remained, nonetheless, very much part of the actor's general milieu. Religion embraced a smaller and smaller portion of social life, but only in a relative sense. Different spheres, Durkheim writes, could now "constitute themselves apart and take on a more and more acknowledged temporal character."[83] Religion remains important; what has changed is its relation to government. The decline in moral punishment, instead of demonstrating the elimination of the religion, simply indicates the changing position of religion vis-à-vis other institutional parts.

The second and interrelated change Durkheim describes is the transformation of religious belief itself, a shift he connects to the specific nature of the Christianity. This religious development, he believes, pushed the collective conscience toward universalism.

> In becoming spiritual, more general and more abstract, [Christianity] became, at the same time, simplified. . . . Thus, it is made up of articles of faith which are very broad and very general, rather than of particular beliefs and determined practices.[84]

In this more generalized form, Christianity contributed to the same empirical decline of punishment as the earlier differentiation of religion and government: "It no longer demanded repression of infractions of minor importance . . . but only those that menaced some one of its principles."[85] Yet it is even more clear in this case that such a decline of punishment does not indicate in any way the diminishment of moral control. Later in the chapter, Durkheim transforms this analysis of Christianity into a description of religious evolution in general. Evolution in the content of religious symbolism, he emphasizes, is one of the vital sources of increased individual control.

> God, if one can describe the force in this way, who was at first present in all human relations, progressively withdraws from them; he abandons the world to men and their disputes. At least, if he continues to dominate it, it is from on high and at a distance, and the force which he exercises, becoming more general and more indeterminate, leaves more place to the free play of human forces. The individual feels, therefore, that he is really less *acted upon*.[86]

Durkheim makes the same point in his later discussion of the decline of proverbs. Since proverbs are collective sentiments which bring very particular prescriptions to specific situations, they are the opposite of the generalized, abstract collective sentiments which enhance individual autonomy. "These short formulas," Durkheim asserts, become "much too narrow. ... Their unity no longer has any relation to the divergences which are existent."[87]

The collective consciousness, then, has assumed a different structural form in the course of modernization. In what is perhaps the most striking empirical part of his discussion, Durkheim provides a kind of topography of consciousness that portrays these developments in a new and more variegated way. He describes the modern collective conscience as subdivided into specialized parts, or "regions." There is a "central region" that is still strongly defined and which supplies the foundations for penal law.[88] Surrounding this central region are large areas of common morality that are much more general and abstract—for example, the general religious commitments of a Christian society. It is this more abstract region that allows for the proliferation of a whole range of more specific and independent moral spheres. The autonomy of these spheres responds to the particular needs of different institutional complexes, yet that they exist at all guarantees that institutional life will continue to be regulated in a normative way. It is, in fact, this very combination of moral order and institutional autonomy that makes this modern kind of social control voluntaristic.

Durkheim admits, for example, that the regulation of domestic life has almost entirely lost its penal character; yet he insists, nonetheless, that it is still ordered by the moral authority of the family patriarch. The crucial point is that when the father acts to control familial misdeeds, he is acting as a private citizen rather than as a public functionary acting in the name of state law.

> The formation of the patriarchal family has had the effect of taking from public life a host of elements, of constituting a sphere of private activity, a sort of conscience [*une sorte de for intérieure*]. A source of variations is thus opened which until then had not existed. From the day when familial life is taken from the jurisdiction of social action and put into the home, it varies from home to home, and domestic sentiments have lost their uniformity.[89†]

Modern society is filled with such "fors intérieurs." When religious denominations, for example, form moral groupings, their moral diversity is tolerated since no single religion tries to take on the mantle of a publicly sanctioned system of belief.[90] Durkheim also mentions occupational associations, and at a later point in the work he analyzes their peculiarly modern morality in a similar way. "Insofar as labor is divided," he writes, "there arises a multitude of occupational moralities and laws." He insists, however, that this regulation does not contract the sphere of individual action, and in support of this contention he makes two points.

First, freedom is maintained because these new moral spheres refer to only a small and differentiated sphere of society.

> The occupational mind can only have influence on occupational life. Beyond this sphere, the individual enjoys a great liberty. . . . As these rules have their roots only in a small number of consciences, and leave society in its entirety indifferent, they have less authority by consequence of this lesser universality.[91]

These occupational sentiments, moreover, change their character as well. They too become more general and abstract, leaving more space for individual divergences.[92]

If Durkheim has firmly rooted the morality of the division of labor in the "mechanical solidarity" of collective belief, he insists just as strongly that this modern collective conscience must be directly related to more "organic," individuated beliefs. Not only has the topography of the collective conscience changed to include both abstract and concrete segments, but even the still sharply defined central region has undergone significant transformation. This collective core, the source for all penal law and official punishment, has itself become much more abstractly and generally defined. No longer championing any particular kinds of values or reinforcing any particular kind of group, it now defines itself in terms of the "individual."[93] Durkheim emphasizes that even the most primitive societies placed an extraordinary value on the human person, "since men who resemble each other cannot live together without each manifesting to his fellows a sympathy which opposes every act of a kind to make them suffer."[94] With the movement toward modern society these sentiments have grown more intense; their definition of the "person," moreover, has expanded to include the weaker and less privileged members of society. Far from a separated unit performing differentiated tasks, the individual has been transformed in the course of historical development into a transcendent object of religious worship.

> The individual becomes the object of a sort of religion. We have for the dignity of the person a cult which, like every strong cult, already has its superstitions. It is thus, if one wishes, a common faith.[95]

Individuality, then, has a kind of ritual basis. If "religious" intolerance and moral conformity can be exercised to uphold pluralism and freedom, the order that sustains modern life is certainly not the instrumental one Durkheim earlier proposed.

The extent of Durkheim's theoretical ambivalence is now amply demonstrated: in the space of twenty pages he has exploded his own argument that instrumental organic solidarity and divided material labor must provide the basis for modern individuality. Yet this same ambivalence, unfortunately, is also responsible for the fact that as quickly as

Durkheim completes this explosive argument he moves to bracket it. Indeed, he places it within theoretical and empirical parentheses from which it will, henceforth, be unable to escape. As chapter 5 closes, Durkheim seems uncomfortably aware of the radical discontinuity he has created in his theory of modern society. He tries desperately to return to his earlier argument for the centrality of the material division of labor, an argument that is antithetical to the theoretical and empirical breakthroughs he has just so triumphantly achieved.

To navigate this reversal Durkheim pursues three strategies, each designed to neutralize an earlier point and each more artificial and ad hoc than the next. First, he develops a framework for arguing that the topographical and substantive changes in the collective conscience he has described still add up to less—much less—rather than more. In pursuing this point he suggests that there are really three ways to measure the force of the collective conscience: in terms of the relation between the volume of individual and common consciences; in terms of the average intensity of the common conscience; and, finally, in terms of the greater or lesser "determination," or specificity, of the content of common sentiments. It is true, he admits, that the total volume of the common conscience may not have decreased (scale 1); yet the "average intensity" and "mean degree of determination" of the collective conscience (scales 2 and 3) have greatly diminished.[96] The result is that the collective conscience, taken as a whole, must still be seen as fundamentally "enfeebled." But certainly this is an artificial and implausible proof. It would be very difficult indeed to compare the relative strengths of the modern differentiated morality Durkheim described—with its radically different topography and sharply contrasting content—with the much more simply constructed collective conscience of primitive society. In fact, of course, it was the change in quality of the collective conscience rather than the diminution in quantity that was the principal point of his earlier argument.

With his other strategies, Durkheim directly confronts his emphasis on the cult of the individual. At first, he accepts the argument that this segment of the collective conscience has, in fact, grown stronger. Nonetheless, he argues, "there is nothing in these facts which invalidates our conclusion [about the diminution of collective sentiments]."[97] To justify this, however, he must introduce an entirely new criterion for evaluating the growth of collective morality, namely, that it is the novelty of a sentiment rather than its strength or intensity that indicates growth. He can now argue that even if individuals today are strongly protected by this powerful sacred rule, this is due "not to the appearance of a really new penal rule, but to the extension of an old one."[98]

With his third strategic argument, Durkheim disputes the very existence of the cult of individualism itself. Acknowledging that this cult is accepted by the community as a whole, Durkheim contends that it is "individual in its *object*." Thus, it is not to society that the cult attaches us but to ourselves. For this reason, he concludes, "it does not constitute a true social link."[99] Durkheim has seemingly forgotten what he clearly understood in his earlier discussion of the division of labor as a moral community. If individuals attach themselves to a similar object, this is a social link; the content of the symbol—its "object"—simply determines the nature of this common attachment. He has forgotten this possibility because he is once again viewing the individual in a "substantialist" way, as a material monad which can be controlled only from without.[100†]

Durkheim has returned to one-dimensional thinking. "The choice must be made," he insists, between the importance of collective sentiments and the autonomy of the individual.[101] Since he is committed to increased individuation, the choice is clear: he will return to "the tremendous grandeur of the role of the division of labor."

2.1.3. The Surrender to Modern Instrumentalism: Noncontractual Solidarity as Coercive Force

The concluding seventh chapter to Book 1, "Organic Solidarity and Contractual Solidarity," is one of the least understood discussions in classical sociology. Surely it is chapter 5, with its formulation of the differentiated moral community, which should be the object of theoretical veneration, yet chapter 7 is the one which has passed into the annals of sociological history. It has been so elevated because it has been treated as the paradigmatic analysis of nonrational, normative control, and it has been read this way even by those who are aware of contradictory theses elsewhere in the Book. The discussion of the "noncontractual elements of contract" that Durkheim undertakes here is considered the quintessence of his sociology of morality, the first example of his mature sociological reasoning. But if this chapter does, indeed, constitute a crucial turning point in Durkheim's first mature work, it does so for reasons exactly the opposite of the ones that many have supposed.[102†]

Durkheim has, in fact, just given up on his last major attempt at creating a voluntaristic theory of modern society. In the fifth chapter he had made more precise the arguments he first laid out in chapters 1 and 2. Since modernity did not necessarily eliminate normative action, the social control which was such an important part of Durkheim's reformist vision could, therefore, be at least in part a voluntary one. In chapters 3 and 4, however, Durkheim contradicted this theoretical development, returning to an instrumental vision of modern action. The empirical discovery of the division of labor seemed a perfect complement to this instrumental view. Where an instrumental perspective on action has been adopted, individuals are treated as separate and distinct; the division of labor seems to reinforce this separation by defining cooperation as the result of individuals pursuing their self-interest from the vantage point of sharply differentiated tasks. As has been seen, however, this very complementarity raises a vital question: Does the division of labor produce an approach to rational action that is individualistic? If so, then Durkheim has failed to encompass the social control which is so basic a part of his ideological vision. At first it appeared that he was, in fact, making just such a mistake, since he emphasized the contractual, spontaneous, and complementary aspects of the new industrial order. Yet it has been shown that there was a second, much more determinist element to his discussion, and by the end of chapter 3 the danger of individualism has been strongly rejected. Durkheim endorsed the notion of collective structure, first in reference to the binding power of legal rules, second in terms of the power of the instrumental state.

The great weakness of these more instrumentalist middle chapters is that Durkheim never directly confronts the sharp contradiction that exists between two different versions of this argument, between his presentation of the division of labor as the perfect combination of social cooperation and free choice and his much more deterministic understanding of divided labor as controlled by external force. If individuals in complementary positions create social order simply by acting spontaneously in their own rational interests, then the logic of Durkheim's argument differs from the classical economists' only in his concern with coordination rather than wealth. If this division of labor does in fact produce such a "natural identity of interest," then Durkheim has unknowingly adopted the Lockean vision of individualistic order upon which classical economics was built. Social harmony, rational action, and independent individual choice are, in this view, perfectly reconcilable. That Durkheim actually rejected this view is, of course, perfectly clear in chapter 3, particularly in the latter part of this discussion when he shifts away from a focus on the individual and his tone becomes markedly determinist. The classical economic notion, after all, is radically opposed to the critical and reform-minded values that had originally provoked Durkheim to emphasize the need for a strong state. Still, presuppositional logic moves independently from ideological commitment. Nowhere in these middle chapters does Durkheim face directly the conflict between the two positions he has laid out. This is the unfinished business that he takes up in the concluding chapter to Book 1.

The extraordinary fact about this chapter is that Durkheim begins his discussion by attacking Spencer for pursuing the same kind of individualistic instrumentalism that he has himself articulated earlier in Book 1. He ridicules the notion that social solidarity depends on the "spontaneous accord of individual interests," on the "free initiative of the parties," on an exchange relationship of which contracts are the prototypical example.[103] How could it possibly be true, he asks, that individuals "depend upon the group only in proportion to their dependence upon one another" and "only in proportion to conventions privately entered into and freely concluded?"[104†] After stating these apparently ridiculous tenets, Durkheim raises two objections which may appear complementary to one another. Yet when viewed from the perspective of the history of Durkheim's internal theoretical conflict the points surely are irreconcilable; in fact, they would take him along two entirely different paths of sociological analysis. His first objection is that Spencer's view of individual exchange has entirely ignored conscience. For Spencer, he writes, consciences never penetrate each other; they are not, in other words, part of a moral order. Yet this reference is a very brief one, and Durkheim returns to it only rarely in the pages which follow. What is of much greater concern to him, what constitutes by far his greater objection to Spencer's theory, is that it fails to appreciate that the individualistic pursuit of self-interest creates social disequilibrium. Because Spencer simply assumes the "total harmony of interests," he is unable to see that this superficial harmony "conceals a latent or deferred conflict." Indeed, if Spencer were right, if modern societies were actually based only on the division of labor, "we could with justice doubt their stability."[105]†

Under the guise of criticizing Spencer, Durkheim has faced his own individualistic understanding of the division of labor more directly than ever before, and he is now in a position to justify more explicitly his emphasis on collective control. It is vital to understand, however, that if Durkheim has finally pierced the Lockean illusion, he has done so from within the instrumentalist perspective itself. It is Hobbes that puts the lie to Locke, not Comte, and if Hobbes stands behind Locke, so perhaps does Marx, or at least the socialist critique of classical political economy. Harmony is doubtful not because there is moral dissensus but because men are motivated to consider means not ends, and this purely efficient motivation is bound to create conflict. "To be sure," Durkheim acknowledges, "when men unite in a contract, it is because, through the division of labor . . . they need each other."[106] This need, however, has nothing to do with some Lockean instinct for natural association or with internalized morality. It is instrumental: "Each of the contractants, needing the other, seeks to obtain what he needs at the least expense [aux moindres frais]." Each party to the exchange tries to "acquire as many rights as possible in exchange for the smallest possible obligations."[107] Durkheim accepts the Hobbesian understanding of the sources of disequilibrium: "Where interest is the only ruling force, each individual finds himself in a state of war with every other."[108]

If action is instrumental and inherently self-interested, the solution to order must be made from within this framework. No wonder Durkheim quickly discards the notion that cooperation could be achieved if individuals were simply "aware of [qu'ils sentent] the state of mutual dependence in which they find themselves." Rather, the solution must be an external one; it must organize means in such a way that their rational calculation produces unintended harmony. It is, therefore, "the *conditions* of this cooperation [that must] be fixed."[109] Durkheim has rejected the Lockean solution: order can be achieved only by establishing the artificial identity of interests.

It is by this line of instrumentalist reasoning that Durkheim justifies what he had earlier simply asserted as a fact, namely, that the basis of modern social order extends far beyond the division of labor itself. "Exchange is not all there is to contract," he asserts, and this is because there is a need for "the proper harmony of functions occurring."[110] In fact, "wherever contract exists, it is submitted to regulation which is the work of society and not that of individuals."[111] Far from the individual's being more on his own with the advancement of modern society, "the rules determining conduct have multiplied" and "social discipline has not been relaxing."[112] "It is not true," Durkheim asserts, "that it [i.e., society] depends more and more on private initiative." As if to emphasize the instrumental origins of this new and growing discipline, Durkheim employs the reasoning that has become such an important part of his argument for an anti-utilitarian approach to coercive order. Since it is impossible, in his view, for individuals to "predetermine" the conditions which would establish the equilibrium of their interests, the idea of some preconceived plan must be abandoned. To justify this position, he employs the "incomplete knowledge" argument. "We can neither foresee the variety of possible circumstances in which our contract will involve itself, nor fix in advance with the aid of simple mental calculus what will be in each case the rights and duties of each."[113] Collective order, then, can be achieved only by the mechanical adaptation to social equilibrium. Now that he has justified his emphasis on collective order in a systematic and explicit manner, Durkheim is ready to apply the theory to a wide range of institutional areas. In each case he emphasizes the external origins of order. The coercive sanctions which regulate institutional life are necessary, he insists, to restore the equilibrium which has been disrupted by the institution's role in an increasingly differentiated and instrumental society.

In Durkheim's earliest discussions, the family was considered from the perspective of the division of labor, as a system of differentiated and independent tasks and as an exemplar of cooperation produced by individual decisions. At a later point, in chapter 6, Durkheim had reversed this argument. Rather than the antithesis of normative solidarity, the modern family, he claimed, forms an important sphere of private morality that is conducive to individual liberty. In this concluding discussion in chapter 7, the family is neither the result of individual decisions nor the embodiment of normative order; the voluntary element of both these explanations has now disappeared. Durkheim emphasizes, first of all, that the conditions of domestic life are "facts beyond volition," determined by birth and personal status. Once, perhaps, marriage was freely contracted for, but now the "volition of participants" has little to do with cementing this tie. First the church and now the state creates the ties that bind individuals in holy matrimony.[114] Adoption has undergone the same evolution from free contract to regulation by external control. The sources which now control these institutions, Durkheim emphasizes, are not moral beliefs internalized by individuals. They do not produce voluntary adherence, nor are they sustained by individual choice. They are external judicial constraints, formulated by the state, to which rational individuals respond. These judicial rules no longer symbolize the solidarity of society; rather they themselves have become the crucial social sanctions, sanctions which develop in response to disequilibrium. Indeed, the family is subject to this legal control precisely because of the growing complexity of its social environment: any unexpected disruption of family life will have widespread social repercussions.

> Instead of remaining an autonomous society alongside of the great society, it becomes more and more involved in the system of organs. It even becomes one of the organs, charged with special functions, and, accordingly, everything that happens within it is capable of general repercussions. That is what brings it about that the regulative organs of society are forced to intervene.[115]

Rather than social morality, it is the "material conditions of life" that necessitate collective control.[116]

Durkheim applies this same generalized reasoning to economic life. In the earliest sections of his book he had discussed economic life as based upon the moral commitment to individualism, and later had analyzed it in terms of purely individual exchange. His reference now is to external and collective sanctions. Contracts are regulated by contract law, Durkheim emphasizes, and he explains the need for such legal intervention in a purely instrumental way. Contract law "expresses the normal conditions of equilibrium": "What we cannot foresee individually is there provided for, what we cannot regulate is there regulated, and this regulation imposes itself upon us."[117] In an elaborate physiological analogy, Durkheim argues against Spencer that just as the visceral life of an organism must be regulated by the cerebral-spinal system, so must the economic life of a society be controlled by the legal apparatus of the state.[118]

Finally Durkheim explains the growth of the state itself, under the rubric of the expansion of administrative law. This organ, which he had once described as the symbol of the moral community, is now portrayed as the product of "mechanical necessity."[119] Disrupted by individual monads pursuing their own interest, the state must artificially recreate an identity of interests. Every segment of the modern state can be linked to this adaptive task: the tribunals with their specific jurisdictions, the agencies for public health, the departments of transport and communication, the agencies for statistical research, as well as the departments specifically designed for economic regulation.[120] Durkheim still contrasts mechanical, segmented society with modern organic solidarity in explaining the differing rules of primitive and modern states, but his intention now has nothing to do with the different kinds of social morality they embody. What is crucial is that they produce different degrees of disequilibrium. Large political establishments are not necessary in mechanical societies because social conflict can never become widespread.

> When society is made up of segments, whatever is produced in one of the segments has as little chance of re-echoing in the others as the segmental organization is strong. The cellular system naturally lends itself to the localization of social events and their consequences.[121]

In organic societies, in contrast, the interdependence of parts exacerbates conflict rather than contains it.

> As the progress of the division of labor demands a very great concentration of the social mass, there is between the different parts of the same tissue, of the same organ, or the same system, a more intimate contact which makes happenings much more contagious. A movement in one part rapidly communicates itself to others.[122]

Hence the need for the strong modern state. As if to underscore the instrumental nature of this social process, Durkheim illustrates this necessity for intervention with examples drawn from economic life. Whereas the closing of a small shop causes little trouble, the failure of a great industrial company produces massive public upheaval. The same is true for a strike by workers in a modern industrial plant, the effects of which Durkheim explains in a way that parallels Marx.[123] "According to their mutual dependence," Durkheim writes about the workers in a plant, "what strikes one strikes the others, and thus every change, even slightly significant, takes on a general interest."[124]† The result, again, is that the state is "forced to intervene."[125]

In this concluding seventh chapter Durkheim has faced squarely the weaknesses in his individualistic approach to the division of labor. In the process of criticizing this perspective, the voluntary quality of his analysis of modernity has disappeared and a deterministic vision has been formulated to replace it. This was an inevitable development. Individual volition will be eliminated if moral order is denied, for only if the individual is differentiated from his external environment—only if he can control internal resources—can he achieve a more voluntary status. It is revealing, in this regard, that in the last pages of this chapter Durkheim tries to reinstate the centrality of moral order in his theory of modernity. At first he returns to the themes of chapter 5, suggesting that individualistic moral consensus can be built upon the differentiated occupational communities of modern economic life.[126†] Realizing, perhaps, that this suggestion is at variance with the substance of his whole preceding discussion, Durkheim quickly moves to a proposal which he obviously considers more important. Modern morality, he insists, will be built upon the central role of the state and the objective necessity for individual cooperation. But Durkheim's argument here is peculiarly lacking in empirical substance. How would this objective dependence actually produce moral order? After referring to the fact that "the points at which we are in contact with it [the state] multiply" and also that "the individual is not sufficient unto himself, [since] it is from society that he receives everything necessary," Durkheim merely concludes: "Thus is formed a very strong sentiment of the state of dependence in which he finds himself."[127] People will become accustomed to estimating the state at its true moral value, for cooperation somehow has an "intrinsic morality."[128] But this line of reasoning is not tenable. The state does, indeed, occupy a central position in a differentiated society, one upon which individuals are highly dependent in the course of their daily lives. Yet these are the same basic insights which inspired the entirely instrumental analysis that Durkheim has just concluded. If he is to demonstrate that these facts produce a moral community, he must restate them in terms of normative action and internal order. This he cannot do, as the chapter he has just concluded bears eloquent witness.

This first book of the *Division of Labor* has presented an enormously complex argument, as Durkheim has struggled between instrumental and normative approaches to the special conditions of modern life.[129†] In the end, he cannot break through the limitations of his earlier work. Now that these limitations have been reestablished, the remainder of the work becomes a relatively straightforward exercise in instrumentalist analysis.

2.2. BOOK 2: THE INSTRUMENTAL-COLLECTIVE CAUSES OF LABOR DIVISION

In the first chapter of the *Division of Labor*, Durkheim carefully separated "functions" from "causes" on the grounds that the functions of labor division could be moral even if its causes were not. As has been seen, however, even in that opening section of his work Durkheim's analysis showed the function of the division of labor to be more instrumental than normative: if the division of labor contributed to some kind of moral solidarity it did so purely in the utilitarian sense of creating an artificial identity of interest. Since Durkheim's discussion in Book 2 is specifically concerned with the causes rather than the effects of the division of labor, one might suspect—in the light of these earlier methodological scruples—that he would be more directly instrumental in his approach. This, indeed, is precisely the case. The only surprise is that the material causes that he establishes for labor division are far more complementary to its "functions" than he would have earlier predicted.

Durkheim begins this second book by rejecting the utilitarians' notion that the division of labor has increased because of the search for greater happiness. It is not the rationalism of such an explanation that bothers him but rather its naïve individualism, and he discards it on the grounds that it exaggerates the actor's knowledge of the consequences of his actions. The utilitarians do not understand that the more complex the society, the more any action will have "repercussion[s] too remote to be understood by everyone."[130] What creates the division of labor, then, are factors external to the individual actor, and although Durkheim groups these under the rubric "moral or dynamic density" they have nothing to do with moral order properly understood.

In discussing "density," Durkheim points to several different kinds of empirical phenomena, to the growth of population, to urbanization, and to an increase in the means of transportation and communication. If one is going to comprehend the nature of his explanation, however, one must investigate the presuppositions which inform this empirical discussion. It is, in fact, thoroughly informed by the instrumental language of rationalist theory, by the language of "means," "equilibrium," and "adaptation."

Durkheim's analysis proceeds from a Darwinian basis: since action is concerned only with efficient means, it is determined by external conditions. "If work becomes divided more as societies become more voluminous and denser," he writes, "it is not because external circumstances are more varied, but because the struggle for existence [*la lutte pour la vie*] is more acute."[131†] In segmental, mechanical societies the struggle for existence is less intense because community institutions have unchallenged control over the resources they need. As segmental divisions are swept away, however, competition becomes more severe. Institutions formerly insulated from one another must now fight over common resources and for the right to control them.

> Like organs are put into contact, battling and trying to supplant each other.[132]

> The closer functions come to one another, however, the more points of contact they have, the more, consequently, are they exposed to conflict. . . . They inevitably seek to curtail the other's development.[133]

Eventually, one of these functionally overlapping institutions must give way, in the short run because it has insufficient strength, more generally because the new conditions of conflict cannot provide both units with the necessary means of survival: "If some of them present some inferiority, they will necessarily have to yield ground heretofore occupied by them, but in which they cannot be maintained under the new conditions of conflict [*dans les conditions nouvelles ou la lutte s'engage*]."[134] The result of this struggle is that the two institutions divide their former tasks: since they "no longer have any alternative but to disappear or transform," this "transformation must necessarily end in a new specialization."

> The triumphant segmental organ . . . can take care of the vaster task devolving upon it only by a greater division of labor, and, on the other hand, the vanquished can maintain themselves only by concentrating their efforts upon a part of the total function they fulfilled up to then.[135]

Durkheim emphasizes that "everything takes place mechanically."[136] A "break in the equilibrium of the social mass," he explains, "raises conflicts which can be resolved only by a more developed division of labor."[137] Once this division has been produced, once action has adapted to this change in its external environment, equilibrium is restored.[138] The presuppositional perspective Durkheim employs is a thoroughly Hobbesian one, and he has described action as completely determined by external force. He would like to believe, nonetheless, that the division of labor has certain unique empirical qualities. Despite its Hobbesian, determinist causation, the division of labor will effectively abolish the Leviathan; indeed, it will actually encourage individual liberty.

> The division of labor is, then, a result of the struggle for existence, but it is a *mellowed denouement*. Thanks to it, opponents are not obliged to fight to the finish, but can exist one beside the other.[139]

Yet the causes of the division of labor, as has been noted, are not at all so dissimilar from the effects. If the main reason for the survival of the division of labor is that it "furnishes the means of maintenance and survival to a greater number of individuals,"[140] it can hardly provide, at the same time, the internal moral convictions upon which voluntary action must be based.

After completing this self-contained analysis, Durkheim cites certain extenuating conditions that could affect the causal sequence he has outlined. If individuals have more space at their disposal, then increased competition might induce them simply to leave the community and find necessary resources elsewhere, rather than tighten their belts and specialize further.[141] The problem however, in Durkheim's view, is that such extra space would be available more often than not. What would prevent individuals from taking advantage of such opportunities? At this point Durkheim steps entirely outside of the instrumentalist framework which he has constructed. The critical factor, he insists, is subjective loyalty. If loyalty to community exists, then individuals will not impose exile on themselves for the purely utilitarian object of attaining greater resources. "The individuals among whom the struggle [*la lutte*] is waged must already be solidary and feel so."[142] This exploration of normative logic represents Durkheim's only attempt to link his mechanical discussion of the development of the division of labor to his earlier analysis of the mechanical solidarity from which it must be derived. At the same time, this reference remains fundamentally outside the main line of his theoretical argument. If individuals are motivated by such collective sentiments, why do they respond in an entirely utilitarian, Darwinian manner to the economic fact of scarce resources—that is, by engaging only in a competitive struggle? Why is it only the pressure of means that forces them to cooperate through specialization? Durkheim reveals his basic theoretical commitment in the way he discusses the negative case, where the "feeling of solidarity is too feeble to resist the dispersive influence" of worsening economic conditions.[143] The source of this feeble solidarity, he reveals, is itself a result of scarcity and competition, for it occurs mainly "where existence is too difficult because of the extreme density of the population."[144] The residual status of subjective solidarity could not be more clearly illuminated: it is an unexamined category that Durkheim introduced to resolve an immediate explanatory difficulty.

If Durkheim were to make this solidarity more than a residual category in his historical analysis, he would have to make a true connection between mechanical solidarity and the forces that create the division of labor, between change in the nature of the collective conscience and the increasing density that creates new forms of exchange. This seems precisely what he intends to do when he begins the third chapter of Book 2. The pressure created by greater density, he writes, can be "neutralized by a contrary pressure that the common conscience exercises on each particular conscience."[145] Internal commitments, in other words, mediate the search for efficient means. Individual volition, then, becomes a vital part of historical development: Durkheim writes that "the existence of the environment is not sufficient" in itself to determine action, what is also necessary is that "each must be free to adapt himself to it, that is to say, be capable of independent movement even when the whole group does not move with him."[146] Durkheim seems to have taken a radical step beyond his own mechanical framework of historical causation. Adaptation itself is now partly determined by the nature of subjective commitments. In one extraordinary example of this shift, he refers to the crucial role of the "domestic spirit."

Among the Slavs, the Zadruga [tribe] is often increased to such proportions that great misery becomes prevalent. Nevertheless, as domestic spirit is very strong, they generally continue to live together, instead of taking up special occupations such as mariner and merchant outside [of the community].[147]

At another point, he makes an independent variable of the "esteem" in which different occupations are held, an estimation which is determined in his view by public opinion.[148]

After these introductory remarks, however, Durkheim abruptly draws back from such a multidimensional analysis. While ostensibly elaborating this initial position, he effectively reduces collective sentiments to an epiphenomenon. The problem is not in the question he pursues, which is, indeed, the crucial one: how, he asks, can the collective conscience become abstract and diffuse enough to encourage flexible adaptation to new external circumstances? The problem, rather, is in Durkheim's answer, which is that the collective conscience changes because it has to: "It changes its nature as societies become more voluminous."[149] The analysis of independent cultural variation in Book 1, chapter 5, is nowhere to be found. Ideas are portrayed simply as the reflections of material arrangements; they respond to external necessity as the means for adapting to new conditions. If primitive collective conscience is very defined and specific, it is because social conditions have made it so: "The social environment for which they are made is not sufficiently extended."[150] If the collective conscience has become more abstract and diffuse, this too is the product of objective developments. If "societies are spread over a vast surface," Durkheim insists, "the common conscience is itself obliged to rise above all local diversities, to dominate more space, and consequently to become more abstract."[151]

Durkheim's reasoning has become circular. The limitations of his theoretical understanding have prevented him from articulating his crucial empirical insight into the intervening and independent role of changes in consciousness. If collective conscience changes whenever there are changes in action's external environment, then conscience could never itself form an independent barrier to functional specialization. For Durkheim to provide the collective conscience with the independence he had earlier ascribed to it, he would have to return to normative analysis of the kind he essayed in chapter 5, and this he will not do.[152†]

In his concluding chapter to Book 2, Durkheim puts the matter in the most straightforward possible way. Historical development, what he here calls "civilization," is not the result of voluntary, intentional, normatively motivated action. "Civilization appears," he argues, "not as an end which moves people by its attraction for them, not as a good foreseen and desired in advanced."¹⁵³ Rather, it results from the focus on means, "as the effect of a cause," the "necessary resultant" of a given state.¹⁵⁴ The condition that creates these effects is, quite simply, the number of physical bodies, the "numerical factor" ¹⁵⁵ Durkheim returns here to the argument he earlier set forth in such detail. The greater the number of physical bodies in one place, the more difficult it is to live. The division of labor is the product of material necessity.

> It is because there is, for them, no other way of living in the new conditions in which they have been placed. From the time that the numbers of individuals among whom social relations are established begins to increase, they can maintain themselves only by greater specialization, harder work, and intensification of their faculties.¹⁵⁶

> There remains no other variable factor than the number of individuals. . . . The more numerous they are and the more they act upon one another, the more they react with force and rapidity; consequently, the more intense social life becomes. But it is this intensification which constitutes civilization.¹⁵⁷

Durkheim identifies the force of this numerical factor with the forces of nature—he calls it the "law of gravitation in the social world"—and his logic here is precisely parallel to Marx's argument for the determinateness of productive forces.¹⁵⁸ Marx compared the economic forces that created modern society to a battering ram that destroyed the walls of ancient civilizations. Focusing on a different empirical phenomenon, Durkheim's theoretical metaphors have the same presuppositional status.

> The walls which separate different parts [*parties*] of society are torn down *by the force of things* [*la force des choses*], through a sort of natural usury, whose effect can be further enforced by the action of violent causes. The movements of population thus become more numerous and rapid and the passage-lines through which these movements are effected—the means of communication—deepen.¹⁵⁹

The base-superstructure logic of Durkheim's explanation could not be more clearly put. If the "faculty of ideation" has changed, he writes, this is because the "social milieu has [also] changed without interruption."¹⁶⁰ The last sentence of Book 2 simply rewrites the famous aphorism formulated by Marx, that it is not consciousness that determines society, but society that determines consciousness. In Durkheim's words, "society does not find the bases on which it rests fully laid out in consciences; it puts them there itself."[161†] This strange echoing of Marx reaches a crescendo in the third and final section of Durkheim's argument.[162†]

2.3. BOOK 3: THE RESIDUAL CATEGORIES OF DURKHEIM'S CRITICAL MATERIALISM

The third book of the *Division of Labor*—entitled "Abnormal Forms"—has inspired extremely contradictory evaluations. To begin with, it has, for ideological reasons, often been overlooked. For some of Durkheim's liberal interpreters, like Parsons, its critical content challenges the essentially positive approach to modern society which they see as emerging from the earlier sections. For radicals who reject Durkheim, like Friedmann and Zeitlin, the critical quality of this concluding section presents a similarly anomalous quality, challenging the portrait they have drawn of Durkheim as the normatively oriented conservative. Other interpreters, to the contrary, emphasize the importance of Book 3. They place its critical ideological perspective at the center of Durkheim's early sociology; arguing that its materialism is prototypical of this phase of his work, they emphasize the fundamental similarities between the early Durkheim and Marx. For such commentators, of whom Gouldner is probably the best known, Book 3 presents a crucial turning point in Durkheim's development. They argue, in fact, that he later backed away from such an emphasis on pathological forms because in the course of carrying out this analysis he was confronted with the radical ideological implications of this line of reasoning.[163†]

Book 3 is, indeed, a critical part of Durkheim's sociology of modern life. I will contend, however, that the drama of this final section occurs at the most general level of Durkheim's thought. The critical ideological perspective he expresses should certainly be no surprise, since from the beginning of his vocation Durkheim viewed his sociology as providing knowledge for radical social reconstruction. The materialism of this analysis, moreover, is neither prototypical of all of Durkheim's early writings, nor even of the *Division of Labor* itself. Finally, if this concluding discussion brought certain problems home to Durkheim, they were problems with which he had been growing increasingly uncomfortable. Durkheim eventually does discard the logic he employs here, but it is because of presuppositional issues, not ideological ones.

In this final section, Durkheim mounts a surprisingly vigorous attack on the empirical phenomenon which has been at the center of his work, the division of labor in society itself. His ideological orientation is not unexpected: he steers a clear line to the left of French solidarism and to the right of Marxist socialism. What is more interesting is the theoretical framework he develops to articulate these ideological beliefs and the empirical propositions he discovers to justify them.

Durkheim begins Book 3 with an admission that is rather astonishing, at least in the light of earlier parts of the work if not his early writings as a whole. The division of labor, he acknowledges, actually produces less solidarity rather than more. Instead of increasing cooperation there has been disequilibrium and conflict: economic failures, labor/capitalist strife, and, in general, a breakdown of social regulation. What is vital to understand, however, is that these new empirical observations and ideological reservations are expressed in the presuppositional perspective that has evolved in the course of Durkheim's preceding analysis. He traces these "abnormalities," at every point, to material conditions. It is certain peculiarities in the external environment of action, he believes, that have created the disequilibrium of contemporary society.

Durkheim first describes this abnormal development in its "anomic" form. The contemporary division of labor is anomic insofar as the external controls on action have weakened, a situation created by a number of factors. For one thing, the distances between functionally divided institutions are now so great that rational coordination is difficult. The rise of national markets is a good example, for although they place numerous institutions and actors into contact with one another, they do so on a scale that is much too vast and impersonal.[164] This increase in density, moreover, has proceeded in a way that has altered the ratio between concentration and volume, so that certain functional specializations, like big capital and big labor, have developed with much more concentration and social power than others.[165] Increased density has even sometimes resulted in labor that is too divided rather than less so. Though factory tasks are certainly divided and complementary, this division has been achieved at the cost of the work's intrinsic satisfaction.[166] Finally, the speed of functional differentiation has been much too rapid. Overly rapid development has disrupted regulation instead of establishing it, although new and more effective rules will undoubtedly appear after there has been more time for mutual adjustment.[167]

But this state of anomie is only part of the problem, for contemporary society is also beset by a "forced" division of labor which makes some kinds of regulations too strong rather than too weak. Durkheim maintains that external controls over labor can themselves be the source of social conflict if the rewards for labor are distributed "unfairly." By invoking this standard, however, he is not raising the issue of moral justice which he had suggested at an earlier point. In the context of the present discussion, unfairness has a purely instrumental rationale. The issue here is equilibrium, not a symbolic ideal. As Durkheim writes, "the harmony of functions and, accordingly, of existence, is at stake."[168] Rewards are distributed unfairly to the degree that they produce a struggle for increased means and a sense of illegitimate domination. This mal-distribution of means can prevent the mutual adaptation that resolves periods of disequilibrium. Durkheim warns that "if contracts were observed only by force or through fear of force, contractual solidarity would be very precarious,"[169] and this is precisely what he sees as the case in contemporary society. Some persons "receive supplementary energy from some other source [outside the contractual relation]," and this "necessarily results in displacing the point of equilibrium."[170] This, of course, is the fundamental problem of class society, and the analysis Durkheim offers here strikingly resembles the one he first proposed in 1885: "If one class of society is obliged, in order to live, to take any price for its services, while another can abstain from such action thanks to resources at its disposal which, however, are not necessarily due to any social superiority, the second has an unjust advantage over the first at law."[171]

What has created this "forced" division of labor is very clear. It is the "great inequality of the external conditions of the struggle [*la lutte*]" for existence.[172] People find the "conditions under which they live" to be intolerable, but do not have the "*means* to change" them.[173] Social order, then, is enforced only through external constraint; it appears "as if" it were based on purely physical force. If Durkheim started the *Division of Labor* with an empirical emphasis on the achievement of individualism that belied his theoretical determinism, he has concluded it with an empirical analysis that thoroughly supports it. The forced division of labor perfectly expresses the determinism of his presuppositional assumptions.

But if Durkheim's empirical insights are complementary to his more generalized reasoning, they are nonetheless radically discontinuous with the propositions which had up until this time formed the subject matter of his book. His arguments for the abnormal form of the contemporary division of labor either refer to old facts in an entirely unexpected way (as in his discussions of national markets, overly great distances, overconcentration, and overly specialized labor division), or they present factors that are completely new (as in the problem of rapid versus gradual change and the need for equality in external conditions). In Book 3 he has discovered a whole new range of empirical phenomena, and they are crucially important, for they form the critical intervening variables between the fact of divided labor and its effect on contemporary solidarity. My point is not that these variables do not exist—far from it. It is rather that Durkheim fails completely to develop a theory that can account for them.

The factors which form the empirical substance of Book 3 have little connection with Books 1 and 2. It is clear that when Durkheim discovered that his earlier empirical propositions were wrong, he tried to revise his theory in an ad hoc way, for the propositions that form the substance of his new analysis are residual categories. Durkheim has introduced them to resolve anomalous empirical facts; they do not emerge out of a systematic theory of modern society. If the distance between specialized functions is now regarded as an important independent variable, when does it become too great rather than simply great enough to facilitate autonomy? If national markets create too much impersonality, how else could the interdependent institutions of a large differentiated society communicate in a situation of increased density and specialization? Where is the line drawn between the beneficial concentration produced by labor division and the kind of invidious concentrations of power that create anomie? What determines whether the division of labor will produce inequality and class conflict rather than individualization and cooperation? How much time would it "normally" take for the conflicts created by labor division to be reequilibrated and for new regulative institutions to be formed? These are the kinds of questions that Durkheim's new set of intervening variables raises. He can, however, supply no answers, since he has introduced them in a purely ad hoc way.

It is the residual quality of the empirical discussion of Book 3 that makes the normal/pathological distinction Durkheim introduces an abject failure. Normality can be determined only in reference to a particular kind of social system that operates within certain temporal boundaries.[174†] What is the system of reference Durkheim employs in Book 3? For the conflict created by the division of labor to be treated as pathological, his reference must be simply "interdependent" or "functionally specialized" as opposed to segmental, homogeneous societies. Yet in Durkheim's description of such interdependent societies he reaches all the way back to the Roman Empire. His system of reference, then, is extraordinarily general; it covers more than a millenium and includes societies as diverse as patrimonial bureaucracy and Christianized feudalism, class-divided capitalism and decentralized socialism. This reference is too broad; it has no relationship to the factors Durkheim describes in Book 3 as decisive for making societies conflictual or harmonious. If his categorization is to be more productive it must key to the factors which have created the specific disequilibrium he describes. National markets, great concentration, and the inequality of conditions must be seen as part of the "capitalist" system or "industrial" form of differentiated society rather than simply a phase in "interdependent" society itself. But if this is the case, then the "division of labor" drops out as a vital historical cause. Once the system of reference is more historically specific, the conflict Durkheim has described becomes normal rather than pathological.

The *Division of Labor*, then, fails in a double sense. In the first place, the work is a failure empirically: Durkheim can develop no systematic explanation for what in the end are his central propositions. In giving up his voluntaristic perspective from which he began Durkheim was foregoing his most important and original contribution to sociological thought. In the realm of instrumental theory—where he concluded this argument—he had nothing to contribute. It was Marx, not Durkheim, who explored markets, the concentration of power, class conflict and inequality as independent mediators of the division of labor. What can only be residual categories to Durkheim's theory are central to Marx's. Here lies the final irony of Durkheim's return to an instrumentalist sociology. This proponent of a sociology of morality has, in the end, raised questions that are more effectively answered by the founder of historical materialism himself.

It is in terms of this inevitable empirical failure that one can understand why Durkheim has concluded his first great work with such an ad hoc and self-contradictory analysis. The abrupt division between normal and pathological allowed Durkheim to forestall fundamental conflict between his hopes for his division of labor concept and its actual achievement. If contemporary society is assumed to be in perfect equilibrium— the basic assumption he accepts in Books 1 and 2—then Durkheim can effectively ignore the contradiction between the voluntarism he wishfully describes as the result of the division of labor and the deterministic factors which actually regulate it and produce it. He can ignore this contradiction because in a perfectly equilibrated and integrated society actors feel as if their own individual decisions create the structure of their environments. When the members of a society feel dissatisfied, however, this image of voluntary control disappears, and they are more likely to view society as based on domination and conflict; in this situation, the coercive and deterministic elements of the division of labor are visible to all. Only when dissatisfaction is acknowledged, then, does it become painfully apparent that Durkheim has completely failed to resolve the issues he set out to address. It is only natural, therefore, that he would wish to push the "pathological" elements of the division of labor out of his mind, and out of the earlier sections of the book as well. Given his own critical perspective on modernity, it was inevitable that they would return. When they did, they provided an empirical demonstration of Durkheim's inability to transcend the theoretical limitations of his early writings.[175†]

As this last sentence implies, of course, the *Division of Labor* was also a failure in a second and much more important sense, that of theoretical logic itself. Despite his intentions and hopes for the work, Durkheim was unable to develop an approach to order that was at once voluntaristic and collective. He could only look on helplessly as the logic of his argument forced him, inexorably, to eliminate the power of internal moral codes and to locate social structure exclusively in the instrumental state and coercive economic force. The *Division of Labor*, in fact, exactly re-capitulates the theoretical evolution in Durkheim's early writings. Much as he had once hoped to neatly resolve the individual/society dilemma by making collective order the product of some innate individual desire for cooperation, he hoped in this later work that the division of labor would allow individuals to pursue their self-interest and to produce solidarity at the same time. The great advantage of this strategy, like the earlier one, was that Durkheim thought he could preserve the autonomy of the con-crete individual personality—an autonomy which he mistakenly associ-ated with individual freedom—even while individual action was being collectively arranged. Yet in this later work, too, the dangers of such an exaggerated solution to the voluntarism problem soon became apparent: Durkheim was afraid that radical contract theory, like the theory of indi-vidual sentiments, would produce an order that was simply too pre-carious. To prevent this, he turned to a more explicitly collectivist model, and he adopted an instrumental approach to this collective force for much the same reason he had done so earlier: moral order was, he be-lieved, inherently opposed to the individual's freedom of action. Durk-heim had created a deterministic and coercive theory where he had sought a voluntary one. This was the same paradox that haunted his ear-liest writings; indeed, he had first suggested the division of labor as a way out of it. The presuppositions of his sociology, however, were unchanged. No matter what his empirical emphasis, it was inevitable that he would reproduce the final frustration of his earlier work.[176†]

3. CONCLUSION: *THE DIVISION OF LABOR* AS A RETURN TO SPENCER AND MARX

Durkheim finished his first great work much as he had concluded his early writings: with a close relationship to the materialist tradition of so-cial thought. The difference between the two phases of his thought is simply one of level of analysis. With this mature work, Durkheim's the-orizing has become much more empirically specific. His relationship to Spencer and Marx, therefore, now can be traced not only at the presup-positional level but in terms of his treatment of a concrete empirical fact, namely, the division of labor in society.

Durkheim's approach to the problem of action is remarkably similar to Spencer's, not simply in terms of his presuppositions but in the way this epistemological framework structures his understanding of the divi-sion of labor in society. In *First Principles*, published in 1864 and revised in 1875, Spencer conceptualized history as a movement from the homog-enous to the heterogeneous, from simple to complex integration, from functional fusion and segmentation to differentiation and the division of labor.[177] In explaining how this general development takes place,

Spencer refers to the concept of equilibrium and to the need for societies to adapt to its disruption. He makes constant analogy to the physical forces in the natural world and to their mechanical necessity, writing, for example, that homogeneous conditions evolve because of the "changes wrought by external forces."[178] To illustrate how adaptation to instability takes place, Spencer emphasizes the phenomenon of exchange.[179] The division of labor comes about, in his view, because social development takes the path of least resistance: social units "move towards the objects of their desires in the directions which present to them the fewest obstacles."[180] Harmony will be reestablished, in turn, when units have learned to adjust their means to the new external conditions.[181] Population pressure plays a large part in this process. In the first place, it is a crucial factor in creating social instability. "Where there grows up a fixed and multiplying community," Spencer writes, "the functional activity of each specialized person or class [is intensified.]" Because of the increasing pressure on the means of subsistence, "every individual is forced more and more to confine himself to that which he can do best."[182] But population density can itself be adapted to changes in the division of labor, and as it adjusts to the new supply of scarce means it plays a vital role in reestablishing the equilibrium which it had first disrupted.[183]

With the notions of population and external resources Spencer has moved from a purely individualistic rationalism toward a more collectivist position, a transition which, in his haste to separate himself from the English theorist, Durkheim had refused to recognize. Spencer notes, in fact, the growing state regulation which must accompany the increasing division of labor, citing the development of written laws which have passed from "vagueness and irregularity to comparative precision."[184] Yet Spencer's perception of collective order remains relatively underdeveloped and in this respect Durkheim's critique is largely correct. Legal and political regulation are for Spencer residual effects, rarely causes in themselves. He acknowledges the functional necessity for this order, but the structure and process of regulation are never the principal subject of his interest. Indeed, in contemporary society, Spencer writes in this early work, government responds to the "desires of the people," not vice versa.[185†]

If the perception of action which informs Durkheim's analysis of the division of labor strongly recalls Spencer, his perception of how social order regulates that action just as forcefully recalls Marx. The point is not, of course, that Durkheim actually relied on Marx's theories. Rather, as instrumental theorists with a collectivist vision, both thinkers were bound to describe the logic of historical development in fundamentally similar ways. Insofar as they also shared the empirical insight into the individualizing and rationalizing thrust of modernity, this general agreement often expressed itself in their detailed empirical discussions as well. Marx agreed with Durkheim, for example, that the transition from primitive to modern societies could be seen as a shift from the subordination of individual difference to common belief to the emphasis on autonomy through specialized exchange. "The first case," Marx wrote in *The German Ideology,* "presupposes that the individuals are united by some bond: family, tribe, the land itself, etc.; the second, that they are independent of one another and are only held together by exchange."[186] In this earlier writing Marx, too, identifies the division of labor as the efficient cause for the form which this exchange takes.[187] It is the division of labor which allows the egoism of capitalist life to assume a cooperative form.

> Whoever says *egoism,* does he not say common aim? Every egoism operates in society and by the fact of society. Hence it presupposes society, that is to say, common aims, common needs, common means of production.[188]

Like Durkheim, moreover, Marx sees the need for the regulation of this egoistic association by a legal order which is designed to aggregate the misunderstood interests of individuals in a manner that allows exchange to proceed without disruption.[189]

Unlike Durkheim, however, Marx sees that the pathological effects of the division of labor are inextricably tied to these same positive functions. "With the division of labour," he writes, "is given simultaneously the distribution, and indeed the *unequal* distribution, both quantitative and qualitative, of labour and its products."[190] For Marx, the division of labor is inevitably mediated by the forms of property, and if he greatly exaggerates the dependence of the former on the latter at least he is aware of their systematic interconnection.[191] This was, of course, precisely why Marx could dispense with the residual discussion of "abnormality" that so distorted Durkheim's concluding discussion. For Marx, anomic conflict and illegitimate domination were "normal" aspects of certain forms of functionally specialized societies.[192†]

If Marx had no need to qualify and postpone his discussion of the coercive division of labor it was because this empirical condition so directly complemented his more general theoretical logic. Marx was not only aware of this symbiosis, he positively welcomed it. Indeed, he had developed his general perspective on the instrumental quality of modern life with these very historical conditions in mind. Marx believed that capitalist life alienated man from his voluntary powers; he developed his theoretical position more perfectly to express this fact.

For Durkheim, the situation was quite the opposite. He had criticized Spencer's Social Darwinism for ignoring morality and for emphasizing egoistic interest. He had condemned Marx's socialism for describing the state in purely coercive terms and for concentrating on material resources alone. If he concluded his first important work by himself emphasizing the egoism and passivity of man and the mechanical power of material conditions, this was not at all what he had intended.

Marx's later writing merely amplified and refined the first works of his maturity. Since the empirical facts which he had "discovered" largely satisfied his theoretical ambition, he had no need to introduce any fundamental reconceptualization. With Durkheim, however, the very opposite was true. He had not yet found the theoretical means to articulate his general insights into the nature of action and its social arrangement. Only after a fundamental revision of his theoretical system would he be able to discover empirical facts more to his liking.

Part Two

TWO DIFFERENT PATHS TO COLLECTIVE ORDER

Chapter Six

MARX'S LATER WRITINGS
The Elegant Apotheosis of Instrumental Control

If Marx's writings from 1845 to 1848 laid the foundations for the instrumental tradition in sociology, his later writings actually established the structure itself. Marx's instrumentalism was, of course, collective rather than individual. He made the first and what is still perhaps the greatest response to Lockean individualism from within the context of rationalism: the transvaluation of Hobbesian political theory into political economy, the transformation of political economy into the science of society. The price of this purely instrumental response to individualism was the elimination of voluntarism itself, but this was a price Marx was willing to pay. Indeed, this theoretical sacrifice was for him, unlike Durkheim, no real sacrifice at all. His ideological critique of capitalism made him feel that it was morally right, and his empirical insights into capitalism—insofar as they can be separated from their presuppositions—convinced him that it was true.

A coercive approach to the general problem of order, then, fitted with Marx's commitments on the more specific levels of ideology and empirical propositions. It was convergent with his most fundamental methodological commitments as well. Marx developed his presuppositional rationalism, one must remember, in the midst of his transition from philosophy to science. He associated theoretical idealism with a nonempirical methodology, and when he rejected the heights of idealist philosophy's "speculation" for the material realities of everyday life he meant this rejection in both the theoretical and the methodological sense.[1†] Marx identified his new-found materialism with empiricism; he equated the dependence of man on objective nature with the objectivity of the natural scientist. Just as Bacon had argued that true science could be based only on sense perception, Marx believed, so had Hobbes seen that ideas and intellectual representations were nothing but the phantoms of the material world more or less divested of their sensuous form.[2] For Marx this conflation was profound. If man was subject to the same laws as nature, then the focus of historical materialism on the nature-like laws of economic life was surely correct.[3] It was for this reason that the first writings of his maturity describe communist theory as addressing "empirical man" and describe proletarian activity as "empirical action" governed by "empirical interest" rather than by ideas.[4] A revolutionary transformation, he insisted, was not "abstract" action initiated by "spiritual" force, but a "quite material, empirically verifiable act."[5†]

Marx had achieved a striking convergence among crucial dimensions of his theoretical logic. It was no wonder that he never substantially departed from the theory he established in his first mature writings. To a large extent his subsequent work—his "later writings"—must be seen merely as an elegant and far more systematic elaboration of his earlier work. At the same time, this later writing departs and critiques his earlier writing in certain important and revealing ways. To understand these departures one must recall the historical context in which Marx first came to theoretical maturity. The distance between the publication of *The Communist Manifesto* and *Capital* was almost twenty years. During this time, Marx not only witnessed massive historical change, but he observed this change from a new vantage point, from England rather than from Germany and France. As a self-conscious scientist of society, Marx was bound to shape his theory to the new events he observed.

1. HISTORICAL DEVELOPMENT AND THE SLOWNESS OF REVOLUTION

In 1847 there was great economic depression throughout Europe. Although other significant factors were involved, this economic collapse was certainly one of the major reasons why the period from 1848 to 1851 was marked by revolutionary ferment from Austria and Germany to Italy and France. This feverish political activity, however, had no revolutionary issue, and civil strife of such scale and intensity was, in fact, never to reappear in the nineteenth century. It was at the beginning of this brief revolutionary period that Marx and Engels wrote *The Communist Manifesto*, and Marx took the failure of revolution as a personal blow. Marx's correspondence reveals that he was stunned by the quiescent denouement, and his political and journalistic writings demonstrate that he felt compelled to explain it.

In *The Class Struggles in France*, written in the midst of the political upheaval, Marx held that the French proletariat would have to recover from its defeat in June 1848, that it would need time to reconstruct itself as a class and as a political party. Yet he believed this reconstruction had, indeed, taken place in 1849 and the first part of 1850. By the time of *The Eighteenth Brumaire of Louis Bonaparte*, however, Marx had become much more pessimistic. In this work, written as a series of articles after the final defeat of the liberal forces in France, Marx completely reversed his earlier position. The French proletariat, he felt, had never recovered from the initial defeat. To explain this, Marx produced a complex and fragmented argument, and the "backwardness" of the proletariat was often linked to concepts—like the influence of tradition—that stood completely outside his familiar conceptual scheme. I have already referred to the importance of residual categories in Marx's work (ch. 3, sec. 1.3), and will return to the problem at greater length below (ch. 10). What is of interest at this point, however, is the more familiar and self-consistent strand of these postrevolutionary historical writings, in which Marx's response to these new empirical events consisted simply in the elaboration and specification of the materialist theory of revolution he had developed in the *Manifesto*. Although he described at much greater length than before the relationship between class relations and political parties, he continued to argue that the transition from economic to political struggle depended upon the external pressure generated by economic crisis. The trouble, he now concluded, was that economic development had not been sufficiently advanced. If the proletariat had not become a political class-for-itself, this was because the contradictions of capitalism were not yet sufficiently intense. This represented a sharp departure from the *Manifesto*, where Marx had portrayed capitalism as at the breaking point, yet it was, nonetheless, an explanation well within the presuppositional and empirical boundaries of the theory he had there laid out. This theme of disappointment in the slowness of revolution, and the search for new propositions to explain it, characterized the rest of Marx's lifework.[6]

At every point in the ensuing years Marx linked the conservatism and political equilibrium he despised to economic prosperity. In the period immediately following the *Manifesto*, he thought economic collapse was still imminent. In December of 1849 he wrote to Weydemeyer about the "approach of a tremendous industrial, productive and commercial crisis" which would make Europe into a revolutionary continent and drag England along with it.[7] In the final chapter of *The Class Struggles in France*, published the following year, he talked once again about the early renewal of economic crisis as the prelude to revolutionary activity. In the same year, in regard to the English situation, he and Engels wrote in the *Politisch-Oekonomische Revue* that a panic would ensue "at the latest in July or August." Because the tremendous development of the productive forces would soon outstrip even the new markets of the Americas and

Australia, they wrote, this panic "will produce results quite different from all previous ones."[8] A few months later Marx and Engels recognized a slight improvement in the economic situation, but they declared, nonetheless, that the "coincidence of commercial crisis and revolution is becoming ever more unavoidable."[9] In December 1851, Marx was writing that "the crisis, held back by all sorts of chance events . . . must erupt by next autumn at the latest," and in February 1852 he continued to speak of the "ever more imminent crisis in trade whose first signs are already bursting forth on all sides."[10] By the middle of 1852, however, he was becoming slightly more cautious in his predictions. The new markets in California, Australia, and East India, he acknowledged, were "exceptional circumstances" which might postpone the "frightful" crisis at least until the following year.[11] Engels agreed, admitting that "California and Australia are two cases that were not foreseen in the *Manifesto:* the creation of great new markets out of nothing."[12] By 1853, Marx's apocalyptic predictions had subsided, although they by no means disappeared, as shown by his announcement in early 1853 that "the crisis will now become due."[13]

In fact, the frustrating prosperity that Marx held responsible for the defeat of the 1848 revolutions was much more than a temporary aberration, as he himself was beginning to discover. The 1850s and 60s marked a new stage in the industrial revolution, with unprecedented technological advance and a great expansion in material wealth. The new situation was even less propitious for revolutionary activity in England, where Marx had now taken up residence. Indeed, England's exceptional political and economic stability has led one historian to describe the mid-Victorian period of 1852-1867 as the "age of equipoise."[14]

It was no wonder that Marx waited for so long to publish his last great work. Something was clearly going on in the structure of capitalism that he did not fully understand. As his own comments indicate, he found the ad hoc quality of his explanations highly unsatisfying. By 1851, Marx had returned to his historical and economic studies with a vengeance, and in 1853 he embarked on another round of ambitious reading "as if," in the words of a recent German biographer, "he still had much to learn."[15] The problem, once again, was to explain the tardiness of revolution, the failure of the contradictions of capitalism to ripen as they should. This riddle had to be solved, however, without undermining the basic structure to which he had committed himself in his earlier work. The project was interrupted in numerous ways—by the journalism which helped Marx support himself and his family, by the burdens of political organizing and excursions into exile politics, by the publication of potboilers and exotic exercises in diplomatic history. In the early 1850s Marx even did serious reading in subjects rather far removed from the project at hand, not only in the history of technology but also in literary history and in the history of culture and morality.[16] He even hoped, he wrote to a friend at the time, to "be through with the whole economic shit," and, after that, to "throw myself into another science."[17] Yet it was to the economic structure of capitalist society that Marx always returned; it was here that his systematic theory of social order and action lay.

Marx did finally develop new propositions about capitalist development, and they were keyed to the external environment of action, not to the structure of consciousness or to the moral resources for change. He discovered the basic elements of this new theory in an intensely creative period of work in 1857–1858, during which he composed the posthumously published notebooks which have become known as the *Grundrisse der Kritik der politischen Oekonomie* ("Outlines of a Critique of Political Economy").[18] Though some of these ideas were published in 1859 in the short *Critique of Political Economy*, they were significantly expanded and elaborated in the three volumes of *Capital*, which Marx prepared between 1861 and 1867. Only one of these volumes was printed in Marx's lifetime, but he clearly viewed the work, nevertheless, as completing the task of reeducation and understanding he had struggled for so long to achieve. Privately, he described *Capital* as a true example of German science. Publicly, in the Preface to the first edition, he likened his effort to that of the physicist and announced that he had discovered the "natural laws of capitalist production." Armed with a knowledge of these laws, one could "lay bare the economic laws of motion of modern society."[19] These laws, he assured his readers, did indeed establish the inevitability of revolution, for they described tendencies "working with iron necessity towards inevitable results."[20†] With *Capital*, Marx had not simply critiqued political economy but transformed its very foundations, and this transformed political economy became an integral part of his theory of history, class conflict, and alienation. Marx had specified his instrumental and collective presuppositions in a new and significantly more powerful way.

2. ACTION AND ORDER IN *"CAPITAL"*

Capital has been analyzed as flawed or inspired by Marx's ideology, his choice of scientific "model," his methodology, his empirical insights, and by his epistemology in a purely philosophical sense. I will consider it as an exercise in sociological theory, and will demonstrate how Marx's position on the general problems of action and order—which he assumes quite separately from his positions on each of these other more specific issues—determines the overall structure of his work. The picture that Marx provides of capitalist society must be seen as informed by the generalized imperatives of his theoretical logic.

2.1. INSTRUMENTAL ACTION AND THE COMMODITY FORM

Because the wealth of capitalism presents itself as an "immense ac-cumulation of commodities," Marx asserts at the beginning of *Capital*, he must begin his investigation with an analysis of the commodity form it-self.[21] In fact, however, the analysis of commodities upon which he em-barks and which occupies the first major section of his work is not directly concerned with the production of wealth at all. It is a highly for-mal analysis of economic concepts, conducted from a distinctively philo-sophical point of view. We can comprehend this introduction to *Capital* only when we understand that Marx is writing a book about much more than economics. *Capital* is about capitalist society as a whole, a society which because it is capitalist gives economic production the determinate place. Marx begins his analysis with commodities because he finds this form central to capitalist society, not simply to its production of wealth. The commodity form establishes the mode of action in the capitalist pe-riod of history. It defines the relationship between people and material objects and among people themselves. In a society defined by the com-modity form, people must act in certain ways.[22†]

A commodity, Marx informs us, has a split identity, for it has at once a use-value and an exchange-value too. In the course of this discussion Marx develops an economic rationale for this distinction, one which he certainly did not originate. What interests us more is the latent function which this economic distinction serves, for what Marx is doing here is restating his early theory of alienation in the language of political econ-omy itself. The terms "commodity," "use-value," and "exchange-value" carry a double message: they are, at the same time, empirical descrip-tions of the physical world and theoretical descriptions of Marx's pre-suppositional commitments.[23]

Beneath Marx's surface description of the use-value of objects we find the old vision of life-as-praxis. In a "natural" situation, Marx insists, there would be a subjective and emotional relationship between people and their objects.[24†] Precapitalist life was more natural in this special sense. Because of this naturalness, people were concerned with the "qualities" of their objects, hence with their "use." Silk, for example, was appreciated for its beauty and people made silk in order to wear it and display it. Corn was enjoyed because of its taste or for its nutritional qualities, and it was grown to be eaten. If objects are use-values to people, there exists an interpenetration between individuals and the objects they produce, a relationship where activity is praxis. When objects are simply use-values and nothing else, they cannot be commodities.

The opposite kind of situation is the "unnatural" and "artificial" sit-uation of capitalism. People are not concerned with the special qualities of their objects and, therefore, not concerned with their particular use-value at all. Instead, Marx insists, they are concerned with objects only insofar as they can exchange them for others, for their "exchange-value." People care, then, about "quantity," not quality. Silk is grown to sell, not to wear, and corn will be produced only if it brings a good value. In precapitalist society, labor is viewed as labor with a particular aim, a use-value. In capitalism, labor is viewed purely quantitatively, in terms of how much it can produce in a given period of time, in terms, that is, of its exchange-value.[25]

The orientation of capitalist life, then, is an instrumental one. People must abstract from the concrete quality of their experience with the object world in order to calculate their best advantage in exchange. Individuals no longer have a felt, subjective relation to things outside them. Only when exchange has so superceded use as the measure of an object's social value do objects become commodities. "A commodity," Marx writes, "is, in the first place, an object outside of us."[26] The commodity form, therefore, represents alienated praxis, and the goal of Marx's contrast between use-value and exchange-value is to establish the reign of instrumental action. The "commodification of objects" attests to the victory of impersonal and utilitarian calculation over subjectivity and emotion in the relationship between the actor and his situation.

Twentieth-century Marxist interpreters have often argued that this initial discussion of the commodity form represents an attempt by Marx to emphasize the importance of nonrational action in capitalist society. In fact, however, the alienated action to which the commodity form corresponds plays the same role in *Capital* as in Marx's earlier writing. It presents a way of talking about the domination of instrumental action that indicates simultaneously Marx's critique of such rationality, his conviction that it is contrary to the "species" capacity of human nature, and his acceptance of it as an empirical fact. In a subsequent discussion we will observe that far from connecting action in capitalist society to normative order, Marx offers a historical explanation for the commodity form which links it to completely material causes. For now it is necessary only to note that he regards commodities as having completely material effects. The victory of the commodity form means that capitalism is dominated by exchange-value. Any sociology of capitalist life, he reasons, must be conducted within the framework of instrumental action.

The commodity form ensures instrumental action not only because it rationalizes the relationship between people and their products but because it objectifies the relationship among people themselves. Men relate to each other through their products, Marx believes, and because these products take the form of commodities human relations are devoid of subjective feeling. Men treat not only their goods but one another as commodities. For this reason, Marx insists that "in the form of society now under consideration, the behavior of men in the social process is purely atomic" and "the relations to each other assume a material character."[27] He specifies the empirical form of this purely material action in terms of the "dramatis personae" of capitalist and proletarian.[28] The capitalist as Marx describes him has no subjective aim: his "sole motive" is the expansion of exchange value, which is the objective basis of the circulation of his commodities and is determined by the purely efficient calculation of costs and benefits. The capitalist, then, is the "rational miser"; only as exchange value becomes his exclusive concern can he function as a capitalist at all. The capitalist has, in effect, been transformed into a thing, since it is the thing itself, the commodity, which determines his every act. It is, in Marx's words, as if "consciousness" and "will" were now attributes not of human beings but of material commodities.[29] He emphasizes that the proletarian treats himself in exactly the same way as the capitalist; it is simply the empirical content of his action that is different. The laborer too subordinates subjective purpose to external demands. But instead of selling commodities to meet these exigencies he sells himself, or more precisely his labor power. The worker treats his ability to transform the object world not as a source of intrinsic satisfaction but merely as a power to be exchanged. He treats himself as exchange value, and this quantifying orientation ensures that his relation to his fellow men will be an instrumental one.[30]

The historical process which forms this confrontation between instrumental laborer and capitalist is long and complex. For now, I will simply indicate that this very confrontation does, indeed, presuppose that action has been determined by certain historical conditions.[31] In the first place, both actors must own their respective commodities—for the laborer this means control over his labor power, for the capitalist control over his means of production. Such a system of private property, and the competitive system of production and consumption it assumes, means that not only do capitalist and proletarian act in instrumental ways but that there is a direct relation between reward and success: efficiency brings relative advantage. The second important historical condition is that the means at the disposal of these rational actors be radically unequal. The capitalist must be furnished with a surplus means of production and the laborer with no means at all. It is the disproportionate means, not the particularities of ends, that decides the nature of their relationship: capitalist and laborer confront each other as buyer and seller. The latter has no commodities to sell but his own labor power; the former needs only labor power in order to set the process of capitalist production in motion. The capitalist must calculate efficiently in order to maintain a competitive position; the laborer must exercise instrumental rationality in order, quite simply, to exist at all, to replenish the most basic needs of his physical organism.[32]

Laborer and capitalist, the paradigmatic actors in capitalist society,

treat each other, therefore, purely as means, as sources of value in exchange. The crucial social relationship of capitalism is created for
purely instrumental reasons. In Marx's words, "the only force that
brings them together and puts them in relation with each other, is the
selfishness, the gain and the private interests of each."[33] This is the impact of the commodity form in capitalist society. To presuppose this kind
of action is to assume that collective order will have a deterministic cast.

2.2. COERCIVE ORDER AND THE "LAWS" OF CAPITALISM

The order of capitalist society is economic necessity, necessity presented by the market and mediated through diverse hierarchical
institutions. This external domination is produced by the peculiar situation in which capitalist production must occur: only self-interested and
highly efficient action is rewarded, and this efficiency can be obtained
only at the expense of other producers. On the one hand, this constraining situation provides the capitalist with a great opportunity. Faced with
an opponent who must sell his labor power to survive, and possessed of a
surplus in money, the capitalist can turn money into capital and can use
this capital, in turn, to make more money. In Marx's famous formula,
this process is expressed as M-C-M (Money-Commodity-Money).[34†] Yet
this opportunity is, at the same time, a necessity, for if the capitalist cannot complete this process of production, if he cannot act efficiently
enough vis-à-vis external conditions, then he himself cannot survive. It is
relatively easy to convert money into capital (M-C), but it is much more
difficult to complete the second half of this process, to convert this capital into more money (C-M). To do so, the capitalist must produce profit, or
extra value, so that the product of his capital investment will bring more
money than he started out with. But how can an investment produce
more value than the value for which it was exchanged? In an ironic twist
that ties his theory of exploitation back to his perception of alienation,
Marx insists that human labor-power is the only commodity that can so
increase its own value. Labor power has a unique use-value, for it can
provide for its holder more value than he paid for it. Human labor produces surplus value, which is the difference between the money that is
necessary to purchase labor—the money necessary to sustain labor as a
physical force—and the value which this labor creates in the process of
capitalist production.

The external conditions of capitalist production—its privatization
and the unequal distribution of resources—produce the laws of capitalist competition, which operate on the instrumental actions of capitalists
as external force. These exigencies make the capitalist create as much
surplus value as possible. In his search for more surplus value, Marx emphasizes, the capitalist can have no reference to extrarational concerns.

Marx writes of the capitalist's "were-wolf's hunger for surplus-labour," his "vampire thirst for the living blood of labour."[35] The capitalist can stand only on the principle of exchange value, which is of course no principle at all. Like other buyers, he simply "seeks to get the greatest possible benefit out of the use-value of his commodity."[36] The coercive character of this process of exploitation makes the problem of subjective motivation theoretically irrelevant. It is not a question, Marx insists, of the "good or ill will of the individual capitalist." He stresses that the conditions of capitalism eliminate any possibility for voluntary action or self-control: "Free competition brings out the inherent laws of capitalist production, in the shape of external coercive laws having power over every individual capitalist."[37] And, once again, these competitive laws are just as coercive to the worker as to the owner. "Thanks to the development of capitalist product," Marx writes, the worker "is compelled by social conditions, to sell the whole of his active life, his very capacity for work, for the price of the necessaries of life."[38] It is no wonder that Marx believes that the exigencies of capitalist production force the relationship between capitalist and laborer to "assume a material character independent of their control and conscious individual action."[39]

The general law of capitalist competition produces specific laws in different stages of capitalist development. Marx describes the history of this development as a dialectic of conditions and instrumental acts. Each historically-conditioned rational act produces new external conditions, which in turn provide a new context (new economic laws) for the exercise of instrumental efficiency, which produces another change in the economic environment (revised economic laws). The evolution of these specific economic laws, moreover, is mirrored at every step of the way by changes in the organizational context of work. These organizational shifts reflect and concretize the coercive order of economic life. They play a theoretical role parallel to the structures that created Durkheim's organic solidarity. If they are more keyed to economic process than to changes in volume, they are, nonetheless, just as coercive and instrumental.[40†]

During the early centuries of capitalism, the owner increased his surplus value mainly by the strategy of increasing the length of the working day, a strategy Marx calls the production of absolute surplus value. Yet even in this early period surplus value is increased in a relative as well as an absolute way, by increasing the intensity of production in addition to its duration. The capitalist intensifies production through changes in organization. For Marx, such organization has no status as an end in itself, and it in no way relies upon the voluntary participation of its members. Organization is merely the means to the end of greater efficiency, which is, of course, itself a means. Organization is the product of the capitalist's efficient calculation of the broader economic environment and of

the laws of competition it imposes. This product of capitalist action produces, in its turn, the external environment for worker rationality.

The first stage of capitalist production organizes "cooperation,"
where formerly separated and independent craftsmen are brought together under one roof. Capitalists introduced cooperation for purely instrumental reasons, figuring, correctly, that it represented a crucial
"economy in the use of the means of production."[41] Marx emphasizes
cooperation's objective status; it was, he writes, a "revolution in the material [or objective] conditions of the labour-process."[42] As a material force
relegated to the status of means, the result of cooperation must be seen in
a completely physical way. Thus, when Marx describes the "collective
power of [the] masses" that results from cooperation, he refers not to
any psychic or moral results but merely to the fact that "many hands
take part simultaneously in one and the same undivided operation, such
as raising a heavy weight, turning a winch, or removing an obstacle."[43]
Cooperation depends, therefore, not on any moral or intellectual conditions but on situational exigencies, "in the first instance, on the amount of
capital that the individual capitalist can spare for the purchase of labour-power."[44] Cooperation, in other words, is the result of external
force; it is a social phenomenon that has no relation to the internal desires of the people affected. The proletarians' "union into one single productive body and the establishment of a connection between their
individual functions," Marx writes, "are matters foreign and external to
them, are not their own act ..."[45†]

After cooperation has been established, the imperatives of competition force the capitalist to find a new way to intensify the production of
surplus value. One strategy involves increasing supervision over the
work process, a form of coercive control that begins with cooperation
but reaches its most intensive form with the introduction of manufacture and, still later, with the factory system. Marx emphasizes that this
political control of the worker, this crucial manifestation of social authority, is a purely instrumental development. It is only with the "increasing mass of the means of production," he writes, that "the necessity
increases for some effective control over the proper application of those
means."[46] This political task, then, immediately becomes an economic
one: "The work of directing, superintending, and adjusting, becomes one
of the functions of capital."[47] The establishment of hierarchical authority, the "work of direct and constant supervision," becomes simply another form of wage-labor, a job performed by a special class of wage-
laborers. The workers are organized like an industrial army; capitalist
managers play the role of officers, with foremen and overlookers functioning as sergeants.[48]

The division of labor in manufacture presents a horizontal intensification of labor which parallels the vertical pressure of increased super-

vision, and Marx employs the same logic to describe this new extension of organization that he used in his analyses of authority and cooperation. The division of labor, he insists, is in the first place a material fact, one which involves the isolation and disconnection of tasks formerly performed by a single worker. The capitalist introduces this new material process as a response to new economic demands: "An increased quantity of the article has perhaps to be delivered within a given time."[49] It is these "external circumstances," then, which "cause a different use to be made of the concentration of the workmen."[50] The division of labor is neither moral nor, even, political. It is, rather, a "particular method of begetting relative surplus-value, or of augmenting at the expense of the labourer the self-expansion of capital."[51] For accomplishing this task the division of labor is, indeed, an efficient strategy, for the isolation and simplification of tasks allows labor time to be calculated in a purely quantitative way. "It creates a fixed mathematical relation or ratio," Marx writes, "which regulates the quantitative extent of . . . the relative number of labourers, or the relative size of the group of labourers, for each detail operation. It develops . . . a quantitative rule and proportionality for that process."[52] Quantitative calculation, of course, is at the heart of production for exchange rather than use.[53†]

Factory organization, which typifies for Marx the organizational mode of modern capitalism as a whole, is simply the extension of these vertical and horizontal strategies of intensification. Marx sees every aspect of organized factory life as flowing from the economic exigencies of machine production. The impersonality of factory rules, for example, does not refer to any qualitative change in normative order but simply to the fact that "since the motion of the whole system does not proceed from the workman, but from the machinery, a change of persons can take place at any time without an interruption of the work."[54] These unstoppable imperatives of machine production are also completely responsible, in Marx's view, for the increasing severity of hierarchical supervision. He writes that the "technical subordination of the workman to the uniform motion of the instruments of labour. . . give[s] rise to a barrack discipline," that the factory code formulates the capitalist's "autocracy over his workpeople," a system of domination in which the place of the "slave-driver's lash is taken by the overlooker's book of penalties."[55] If the factory is the quintessence, the prototype of social organization in capitalist society, it is because it so starkly presents the coercive exigencies of capitalist production.[56†]

According to Marx's analysis, each of the major forms of organization in capitalist society—cooperation, the division of labor, hierarchical authority and control—has been introduced merely as a means to intensify the production of surplus value. Each is the product of efficient calculation by the capitalist, the rationality of whose decision making may allow him to stay in business despite the laws of economic competition. Yet this increasing productive intensity eventually produces results which are the very opposite of those the capitalist intended, for it is only with the introduction of machinery and factory production that the fundamental contradictions of capitalism finally appear. As the capitalist substitutes machinery for living labor, he alters the "organic composition" of capital. Although this alteration is rational for a capitalist faced with stiff competition, the decision creates a new material environment which places his action under new and more difficult constraints. With the introduction of machinery, variable or living capital decreases relative to the capitalist's investment in the means of production, an investment Marx calls constant capital. The capitalist has become subject to the "law of the progressive increase in constant capital."[57]

The danger of this new specification of the law of competition is that although the capitalist's total profit may well have grown, the greater cost of his initial capital investment actually decreases his profit per item. This is the law of the falling rate of profit, the law that describes the effect on circulation of the productive shift toward constant capital.[58†] This new external circumstance forces the capitalist to extend the working day even further than before, an action which he takes, Marx stresses, without any consciousness of the larger implication of his act.[59] Yet this strategic adaptation to the altered conditions of the falling rate of profit produces simply new and more uncomfortable constraints, for the increased working day is an external condition against which the workers are forced by their objective need for survival to rebel. To keep the labor force from being destroyed, in turn, the bourgeois state responds to the workers' protest and sets limits on the length of the working day. This instrumental action revises still another time the situation within which the capitalist must act. He responds to these new constraints by acting, once again, in an efficient and instrumental way: he continues to alter the organic composition of capital by further centralizing production and concentrating industry.

The stage is now set for the full play of the contradictions of capitalism, for the contradiction between the forces and relations of production to reach a final breaking point. Forces and relations both represent external material constraints, yet while the forces refer to those elements of the industrial apparatus which can transcend the historical organization of capitalist production—to machine production, for example—the relations refer to external constraints specific to the capitalist mode. The relations of production are, in fact, the very same conditions which I have described as vital to the commodity form and which combine with instrumental action to produce the laws of capitalist development: competitive private production and the unequal, class-linked distribution of productive resources. Only when the stage of machine production is reached do these relations of production throw capitalism into a situation of crisis, for only then does the efficient action of the capitalist actually threaten to lower the rate of profit itself.[60†]

The capitalist finds both sides of the surplus-value process more difficult than before. On the one hand, the rising cost of machinery makes it harder to transform money into capital (M-C). To stay competitive, to decrease prices, the capitalist needs ever more sophisticated technology and organization, which includes increasing centralization of production. Yet these productive changes themselves demand increased financial resources. Some capitalists move into areas of low technology where the demands for constant capital are still minimal, but competition ensures that these areas soon become equally focused on constant capital. Eventually these external conditions produce a series of bankruptcies from which the economy can recover only by introducing even more centralization and technology.[61] These innovations, in turn, only hasten the next round of crisis.

This cycle of disruption, induced by the falling rate of profit, Marx calls the production crisis. But even if the capitalist can succeed in purchasing the necessary constant capital and reestablishing himself in production after a major crisis, it becomes increasingly difficult to sell the goods he has produced (C-M). This is the consumption crisis, and it affects the laborer just as strongly as the capitalist, and certainly more deleteriously. The key to the consumption crisis is that desperate competition forces capitalists not simply to introduce more constant capital but to reduce the labor component of their costs as well. Increasing segments of the labor force are thrown out of work. They form an "industrial reserve army" that not only functions as back-up for the wide fluctuations of the capitalist labor market but also serves to lower the wages of those workers still employed.[62] The result of this massive unemployment and generally decreased worker-income is not simply the great difficulty the worker now experiences in maintaining his physical existence. It also becomes much more difficult for the capitalist to turn his capital investment back into money (C-M), to sell to the working class the increased quantity of goods that his new machinery, and the workers themselves, have produced. It is this crisis in consumption that makes the conflict between the forces and relations of production most visible. "The more productiveness develops," Marx writes, "the more it finds itself at variance with the narrow basis on which the conditions of consumption rest."[63]

The crisis of capitalism has not been produced by moral corruption or particularism of any kind. To the contrary, the capitalist, and the proletarian for that matter, has continued to act in a rational, instrumental way. What has changed is the external situation from which such rationality takes its cue. Conditions have been altered in a way that ensures that the action of the capitalist will have disastrous consequences. The lack of any normative reference on the capitalist's part is, in fact, a vital link in this causal chain; without it, the contradictions of capitalism could never occur. Because he can respond only to the external, material exigencies of his situation—because he has no reference to a normative order which transcends his immediate context—the capitalist remains totally "unconscious of this imminent contradiction" between the relations that frame his production and the apparatus of production itself.[64] Indeed, subjective consciousness is so irrelevant to the operation of this fundamental contradiction that the capitalist actually thinks he is lowering the profit rate willingly, "as if [he] adds less profit to the price of the individual commodity of his own free will, and makes up for it through the greater number of commodities he produces."[65] But what the capitalist thinks or feels is irrelevant, for with the intensification of production the economic forces that order capitalist life "assume more and more the form of a natural law working independently of the producer, and become ever more uncontrollable."[66] The contradiction of capitalism is determined by the external environment of action, an environment which is economic and which sets instrumental action on an inevitable course.

> The contradiction of the capitalist mode of production . . . lies precisely in its tendency towards an absolute development of the productive forces, which continually come into conflict with the specific *conditions* of production in which capital moves, and alone can move.[67]

With the law of the falling rate of profit Marx felt he had discovered the secret of capitalism. This law explained, first of all, the relative slowness of revolution. In 1848, for example, the state had only just recently placed limits on the capitalists' strategy of compensating for lowered profit by lengthening the working day. More importantly, however, the law explained why the contradictions of capitalism, when they did ripen, would be impossible to overcome. Marx had first discovered the falling rate during the creative burst of energy that produced the *Grundrisse* in the winter of 1857/58, writing to Engels that he had just "overthrown the whole doctrine of profit as it previously existed."[68] Ten years later, when he described it in the third volume of *Capital*, the law was "a mystery whose solution has been the goal of all political economy since Adam Smith."[69] It was this single proposition, Marx believed, that distinguished his "economics" from all previous political economy.

The reasons for the tremendous importance of this profit law are clear: it supplied empirical proof for Marx's theoretical logic. Since Marx viewed action as instrumentally rational, the impetus for the overthrow of capitalism could come only from external conditions. These external conditions, then, had to make revolution an efficient choice. It was for this theoretical reason, not simply or even primarily for reasons of empirical accuracy, that Marx worried so over the validity of his prediction that the profit rate would in fact fall. In the third volume of *Capital* he spends the better part of two chapters analyzing the "counter-acting influences" that qualify his prediction of imminent economic collapse. The mass of profit could be increased, he admits, by a number of different strategies: through a higher rate of exploitation, through a longer working day, by lowering wages even further, by overpopulation and the exploitation of the industrial reserve army, and by foreign trade.[70] In the twenty years which followed his completion of the first draft of the third volume, Marx filled eleven workbooks in an effort to determine whether these qualifications could, indeed, alter the downward fall of profit itself.[71] Marx worries so, in fact, that he talks about the "law of the *tendency* of the rate of profit to fall."[72] Yet for all of this, Marx simply cannot accept these empirical qualifications as decisive. After examining each in turn, he decides—with more assertion than empirical proof—that none is powerful enough to nullify the general law. "The rate of profit," he declares, "will fall in the long run."[73] The factors that seem to check the fall of profit, he insists, "always hasten its fall in the last analysis."[74†]

The "last analysis" for Marx, here and in the other instances where he invoked this term, is the final imperative created by his own theoretical logic: the rate of profit will fall because it is the only way to verify Marx's presuppositions about order and action. The external conditions of capitalism will create a series of crises which will fundamentally destabilize capitalist society and which will make rebellion an instrumentally rational act.[75†] "Capitalist production," Marx declares in the final pages of volume 1, "begets with the inexorability of a law of nature, its own negation."[76] In the Preface to this volume Marx had already made his general orientation perfectly apparent. "Here individuals are dealt with," he wrote, "only in so far as they are the personifications of economic categories, embodiments of particular class-relations and class-interests." "My standpoint," he continued, "can less than any other make the individual responsible for relations whose creature he socially remains, however much he may subjectively raise himself above them." [77] This general understanding presupposes the propositions Marx later "discovered" about the laws of capitalism and their ultimate effect. It should not be surprising if they describe an order that is as coercive and determinate as nature itself.[78†]

2.3. FALSE CONSCIOUSNESS AND THE REFLECTED SUPERSTRUCTURE

The subtle dialectic composed by the laws of capitalist development creates an explanation for the slowness of revolution which is theoretically self-contained. Given these external conditions, and assuming the technical rationality of action, reference to other kinds of social factors is theoretically unnecessary. Yet *Capital*, I have insisted, is a theory of society as a whole, and alongside these propositions about production and social organization Marx also develops a strikingly original theory of social ideas. Not surprisingly, however, the purpose of this exposition of capitalist ideology is to eliminate any possibility of its independent effect. The cultural commitment of the proletariat to capitalism not only directly enforces instrumental action, but directly reflects the material structure of capitalism itself. Capitalist culture, even viewed in its own terms, is an epiphenomenon.

The only abstract theory of the superstructure that Marx presented in his later writing was his Preface to *The Critique of Political Economy*, the 1859 work in which he first introduced the theoretical ideas developed more fully in *Capital*. It is in this brief but famous programmatic statement that Marx asserts that "it is not the consciousness of men that determines their being, but, on the contrary, their social being that determines their consciousness." Marx clearly establishes here the radical hierarchy of determination which is the essence of instrumental collectivism. "The economic structure of society," he writes, is "the real foundation, on which rises a legal and political superstructure and to which correspond definite forms of social consciousness." Yet, while Marx's intention is perfectly clear, his analysis is not. In fact, he never explains precisely how the base of capitalism will create complementary superstructural forms. His language is vague and imprecise; at different points he describes the base as "corresponding to," "conditioning," and "determining" the superstructure, and he refers to the latter as the "expression" of the base in turn.[79]

Recent analysts have made a great deal of this terminological ambiguity, arguing that the Preface somehow demonstrates Marx's commitment to a multidimensional perspective. McLellan, Marx's most recent biographer, describes the essay as presenting "a series of flexible structural concepts," and Althusser utilizes it to justify a Marxist theory of indeterminate causality.[80] But sociological theory is not simply a linguistic system that can be analyzed independently, as if it had precisely the same status as a literary text. Sociological theory is a system of specialized concepts with a definite explanatory purpose. To resolve Marx's theory of base and superstructure one must look not to language abstracted from theoretical purpose but to theoretical logic itself, at the most general level to the concepts of action and order. Because Marx assumes the complete instrumentality of action, his conception of order cannot be a voluntaristic one, and presuppositional conceptions of order have a clear relationship to models about the relationship between social system parts. Only if there is voluntarism can there be reciprocity or indeterminacy between the ideal and material spheres of social life. The base-superstructure model that Marx employs in his Preface is designed to translate his presuppositional logic into a model of a two-tiered system, with the sole determining power allocated to the bottom level. If Marx's discussion of the translation of material base into superstructural forms remains ambiguous in this highly abbreviated statement of 1859, it is not because he wishes to violate this imperative. Rather than jettison the entire theoretical and analytic system Marx has established, therefore, analysts would do better to simply look elsewhere for a more specific and detailed discussion of superstructural form and material base. It is in *Capital* that such an analysis can be found.

Two approaches to ideas are apparent in Marx's last great work. There is first the simplistic understanding of ideas as direct instruments of class rule that I discussed in the earlier analysis of the third section of the *Manifesto* and of *The German Ideology*. At the end of his first chapter in *Capital*, for example, Marx describes religion as "but the reflex of the real world." Since capitalism forces individuals to reduce their particular private labor to the homogeneous, abstract labor of the commodity exchange, Marx reasons, Protestant Christianity is the most fitting form of capitalist religion, since it too emphasizes the "cultus of abstract man." And after discussing this determinate relation, Marx goes on to relate precapitalist models of production to other religious forms, drawing the connection, for example, from primitive production to nature worship.[81] At another point he talks, in a similar way, about freedom as an idea that originated because the capitalists needed labor-power for which they would not be personally responsible. Only if labor were given its legal freedom, Marx reasons, could capital exploit it without having to pay for that exploitation's human effects.[82]

Through at least the first half of the twentieth century this "vulgar" strand of Marx's theory of ideology was taken, by supporters and critics alike, as the main point of his later treatment.[83] In the 1960s and 1970s, however, there has been a great shift among Marxist interpreters toward a view that superstructural forms actually play a crucial independent role in the theory of *Capital*. The focus has been particularly on the commodity form, and the notion that Marx remains committed to alienation as a pivotal theoretical concept plays a critical role. These interpreters argue that Marx sees commodification as the result of alienation, not its cause. Instead of viewing the commodity form as a material factor ensuring the domination of technical rationality, one which is itself produced by forces of a purely material kind, they view commodification as a form of subjective reification, as a state of mind which distorts the perception of reality much as the consciousness of Hegel's historical actors particularized and contradicted universal reason. In his famous essay "Reification and the Consciousness of the Proletariat," Lukács argued in

1923—long before the subjective approach to Marx gained wide acceptance—that the "stance adopted by men towards [society]" was the crucial focus of Marx's analysis. "The commodity," Lukács argued, "become[s] crucial for the subjugation of men's consciousness" because the reification it produces "assume[s] decisive importance . . . for the objective evolution of society."[84] In a work written almost fifty years later, Ollman simply makes this argument more specific. "The laws of capitalism," he writes in reference to Marx's commodity theory, "become necessary in virtue [*sic*] of everyone *thinking and acting as if they are*." To illustrate what he takes to be this central Marxian point, Ollman produces a series of statements that equate subjective perception with objective constraint: "To *conceive* of machines as needing workers is to accord machines the power to need workers"; "likewise, to *conceive* of money as having the power to buy everything is indeed to have money which has the power to buy everything."[85] Lefebvre has argued in much the same way, describing Marxism as a "sociology of forms" in which commodities function as symbolic "representations" directing thought into patterns that distort reality.[86] The implication of such argument, of course, is that the subjective struggle against alienation represents the main point of *Capital's* directives to the working class, that Marx's primary theoretical emphasis was on consciousness. Social change becomes cultural change. Lefebvre describes the anticapitalist struggle as the task of "acquiring new terms and idioms to supplant obsolete linguistic structures."[87]

This perspective on Marx has permeated the Marxist writing of the late twentieth century, but it is, for all of that, incorrect. The focus on the commodity form does indeed represent the second, and by far the most important, approach to a theory of ideas that Marx offers in *Capital*. Yet the relation between the commodity form and ideas in no way departs from the paradigm of instrumental order I have already laid out. In the earlier discussion I demonstrated how Marx utilized the commodity form to establish the irrelevance of subjective feelings in capitalist society. When we examine the specific relationship between commodities and the superstructure we will see that he is intent on making the same point.

It is true that when Marx talks of the commodity form as ensuring rationality and objectivity he sees it as covering up, or camouflaging, the very alienation which it has produced. The abstraction of commodities hides the "whole mystery of the form of [real] value," Marx writes in reference to the way that the commodity form makes irrelevant the particular kinds of human labor that go into producing goods.[88] With commodities, he writes at another point, "the social character of their [the workers'] labour . . . takes the form of a social relation between the products."[89] It is for this reason, among others, that Marx calls the commodity form an illusion: he insists that alienation, though camouflaged, is real. When he describes this illusory form as a "fetish" that recalls the "mystical" quality of religious life, Marx is simply emphasizing this illusory quality and the fact that he believes it to be contrary to some higher form of human rationality.[90] The crucial point is that the commodity form can carry all of this theoretical baggage without being subjective at all. Marx insists, for example, that the social qualities which commodities hide are "at the same time perceptible and imperceptible by the senses."[91] By this he means that while exchange value indicates that labor is imbedded in a social process, in no way does it reveal the particular and qualitative cooperation that is the real basis of work. This quality would be seen only if labor were considered to have its primary value in use, a fact that is hidden by its commodity status.

The epistemological status of "commodity fetishism" is, indeed, a purely material one. Fetishism, Marx writes, has an "objective appearance."[92] The worker is fooled by it because this appearance is "reflected in his brain"—it imprints itself on his mind with material force.[93] One way to fetishize commodities is to treat human beings and the product of their labor in purely instrumental terms. This mode of action, Marx believes, is established through the objective force of material circumstances. We are back to our fundamental point about the early "Manuscripts": Marx views alienation as a product of material forces; its effect is merely to reinforce coercive order.

The elegance of Marx's superstructure theory lies in the delicacy with which he employs the notion of "commodity form" to fit the norms of capitalist culture to the economic basis of capitalist society. On one level this conjoining is impressionistic. The commodity form, Marx writes at one point, leads the worker to believe in individual rights and liberties, since to function effectively in capitalist society he must treat his own labor-power as a commodity which he can sell in whatever manner he chooses.[94] Equality, too, is a mistaken belief that is created by the commodity form, for goods which contain labor that is incomparable in a qualitative sense are exchanged as equal abstract quantities.[95] But the most systematic mediation that the commodity form establishes between base and superstructure is to be found in Marx's analysis of the wage relationship. This analysis also presents one more differentiation between the earlier and later phases of his mature work.[96†]

Throughout his early economic writings, including those of the transition and the *Manifesto* itself, Marx believed that the capitalist made profit by forcing the laborer to enter an unequal exchange. If the price of goods has to be equal to the labor expended on them, then profit can be obtained only be paying for labor at less than its full cost. But although this theoretical perspective certainly demonstrated the impact of coercive order on the labor process, it had the great theoretical disadvantage of being highly unsystematic. Would one capitalist, for example, be able to get the same amount of surplus value as another? Would the amount vary from one day to another, or from one period to another? Marx was portraying the empirical process of profit taking as unpredictable. If he had continued to do so, he would have been unable to portray economic life as obeying objective laws of capitalist development.

With Marx's discovery in the 1850s that labor takes the commodity form in production—or, more exactly, his discovery of the precise manner in which labor assumes its commodity form—this problem was resolved. There is now a systematic relationship of wages to cost, for it is the cost of reproducing labor power, not some arbitrary strength of the capitalist, that determines wages and the bottom line for profits. The key to this discovery was Marx's insight that labor power is separate from labor itself. In these terms, the worker sells his power and not himself, so the capitalist need reimburse him only for the cost of the power and not for the entire time in which he works. Profit, then, was not made by random exploitation but from surplus value systematically achieved by increasing the intensity of work or by lowering the cost of reproduction.

This insight into the true nature of the profit-making process had yet another great advantage, one relating to the explanation of the superstructure rather than to the base. The fact that the capitalist actually paid the laborer for the full value of his labor power meant that the wage relationship created the objective appearance of equality. In terms of the laws of capitalist society itself, it was, in fact, an equal exchange. When Marx had seen profit making as based upon unequal exchange and random exploitation, it had been hard to understand how anybody could have accepted the capitalist ideology of egalitarianism. Since the world of material order is so blatantly and overtly discriminatory, would there not have to be some kind of invisible moral order, however deceptive, which could hold the worker in his place? With the discovery of the objective equality of the wage relationship, the peculiar tenacity of egalitarian ideas was easier for Marx to explain. It was not a question of the workers being fooled, of them being unable to see their objective situation because of some subjective commitment to a moral order. "Equality" had objective roots in the peculiar nature of the wage relationship, even if such equality belied the true nature of capitalism itself.

> Suppose the working-day consists of 6 hours of necessary labour, and 6 hours of surplus-labour. Then the free labourer gives the capitalist every week 6 × 6 or 36 hours of surplus-labour. It is the same as if he worked 3 days in the week for himself, and 3 days in the week gratis for the capitalist. *But this is not evident on the surface.*[97]

It is not evident on the surface because the nature of the wage system is such that the worker seems to get his wage not for his own reproduction costs—not, that is, for the thirty-six hours—but for his entire labor time, for the entire seventy-two hours in which he worked. Unpaid labor time, which amounts actually to half the time he worked, is now invisible. The wage *"appears* as the value or price of the whole working day," when in fact it "includes 6 hours unpaid for."[98]

The term "appearance" touches the central point in this elegant theory. Marx is describing a two-layered economic world, both layers of which are orders in an external and coercive sense. The true order, the inner layer, is composed of classes with unequal access to the means of production, an inequality that allows one class to enrich itself by buying the labor of the other. The false order, which composes the outer layer and is therefore responsible for the appearance of economic life, is characterized by the wage relationship. The wage relationship mediates between the inner layer of capitalist production relations and the realization of surplus value. Class domination can become operationalized only through this peculiar social relationship of the wage, a fact which gives to capitalist life an illusory equality. *Capital* is shot through with the language of "appearance" versus "reality," of the "phenomenal form" versus the actual or structural form. It is precisely because Marx has pierced the outer layer and gained entrance into the inner that he can become, in his own eyes, the true scientist of capitalism. The outer layer is related to the inner as means to conditions: one material structure is a reflection of the other. The expression "value of labor," Marx writes in contrasting this ideological term with the more accurate one of "labor power," "is an expression as imaginary as the value of the earth."[99] "The relation of exchange subsisting between capitalist and labourer becomes," according to this terminology, a "mere semblance . . . a mere form, foreign to the real nature of the transaction, and only mystifying it."[100] At the same time, Marx stresses that "these imaginary expressions, arise, however, from the relations of production themselves." "They are," he writes, "categories for the phenomenal forms of essential relations."[101] To view the wage form as an indication of true equality is a fetishism produced by commodities, yet it is a fetishism that has a material status, for the wage form makes the more unequal structural relations invisible: "The wage-form thus *extinguishes every trace* of the division of the working-day into necessary labour and surplus-labour, into paid and unpaid labour."[102]

Marx regards the form of the wage relationship as the fundamental basis of capitalist ideology. This economic relationship, which produces effects that are "beyond the cognisance of the ordinary mind," is the source for all the false ideas, the ideological beliefs in equality and liberty, upon which the superstructure of capitalism is built.[103]

This phenomenal form, which makes the actual relation invisible, and, indeed, shows the direct opposite of that relation, forms

the basis of all the juridical notions of both labourer and capitalist, of all the mystifications of the capitalist mode of production,
of all its illusions as to liberty.[104]

The central ideas of capitalism, then, are not really ideas at all. They are,
instead, a peculiar kind of material structure. In terms of his theory of
the base, Marx utilized the commodity form to rationalize action and to
explain the external status of capitalist order. With his superstructure
theory, he used the commodity form to understand the separation of labor from labor power. The commodification of labor power, in turn, allowed him to explain the systematic operation of economic exploitation,
its coercive laws, and the false ideas that made these relationships invisible not just to the laborer but to the capitalist as well.[105] Far from contradicting the purely instrumental quality of action in capitalist society,
Marx's superstructure theory explained why it had to be so.

The final evidence that this theory of commodity forms is directed, in
the first instance, toward the base rather than to the superstructure is
provided by Marx's explanation of its historical origins. The history of
the commodity form is the true subject of *Capital*'s concluding section on
primitive accumulation, a discussion which has usually been read simply as a piece of historical narrative but which actually bears critically
on the most general theoretical points.[106†] If the commodity form were a
truly normative force, one would expect Marx's analysis to follow the
general lines of Durkheim's discussion of the generalization of the collective conscience. Marx might have traced, for example, the origins of the
commodity form in symbolic patterns and cultural movements, or, at
least, he might have established the normative background for this decisive shift in cultural form. In fact, he does nothing of the kind.

When Marx writes that "it is only at a definite historical epoch in a
society's development that ... a product becomes a commodity," he is
talking about development as a phenomenon of instrumental rather than
normative order.[107] Individuals who privately produce goods for exchange
do not engage in commodity relations with their fellow workers; since
they do not sell their labor power it cannot be rationally exploited.[108]
Nor do human relations become commodified in situations like feudalism, slavery, or the corvée, where exploitation is personal and direct and
where the product of the exploited worker is valued for its particular use,
not for its value in exchange.[109] Of course, the development of the commodity form is a long and gradual process, and the commodification of
the products of labor—the development of markets and exchange—is one
important step.[110] Still, only with their separation from the means of production do men treat one another as commodities, and it is upon this process that Marx concentrates the full force of his historical discussion.[111]

Marx's analysis in this concluding section echoes his earlier account of the origins of the proletariat in *The German Ideology* and the *Manifesto:* material conditions are at every point the pivotal factor that initiates change, and it is the search for more effective means to deal with these new conditions that effects the decisive transformations. Marx starts from the fourteenth century, when, he believes, free peasants controlled their own land and basic tools.[112] The rise of Flemish wool manufactures and the corresponding rise in the price of wool in England were the first decisive changes in external conditions. The great feudal lords responded by driving peasants from their land so that they could produce wool themselves.[113] Marx describes a variety of other forcible means to which the king and aristocrats had resort in this transition period, devoting more than thirty pages to the strategies of exploitation in which they engaged and to what he terms the "bloody legislation" they initiated. The end of this process was the intrusion of the commodity form into the human relations of workers and capitalist, not just into the products of their work. A large mass of landless and foodless peasants was created. Capital now had a home market for its goods and a proletariat to produce them. Capitalist life adopted the commodity form because it was forced to do so, and Marx's historical account of that form clearly reinforces his systematic analysis of its contemporary operation.

To read the domination of the commodity form and the "fetishism" it creates as subjective order—which has become conventional wisdom among Marxist interpreters—is fundamentally to misread the true theoretical meaning of Marx's work. These sympathetic critics commit an ironic error, for in exculpating Marx they have ignored the real brilliance of his achievement. Instead of producing some weak and indeterminate theory of the "reciprocity" between superstructure and base, the position that is so diffidently attributed to him, Marx actually created a striking and highly specific theory about the determinate impact of economic structure on symbolic forms.[114†] This theory, moreover, perfectly complemented his explanation of economic development itself.

Descriptions of Marx's superstructure theory as emphasizing irrational factors confuse the ideological level of analysis with the presuppositional, a confusion camouflaged by the multivalent character of the term "rationality."[115†] Certainly Marx considered the commodity form of action to be "irrational," yet this critique of capitalism's purported rationality does not presuppose his sociological analysis in an epistemological sense. It presents, rather, an evaluation of capitalism's moral validity. If Marx is still a Hegelian, he is so only in one sense. He will use a historical standard of rationality to evaluate the putative excellence of contemporary life. He will not, however, allow his own sensitivity to universalistic norms to be incorporated into the judgment of the actors he theoretically describes. Marx's proletarian, indeed his capitalist too, is irrational only in the special Hegelian sense of not knowing his world-historical interest, an ignorance caused by his lack of insight into the inner layer of capitalist production. This is irrationality as "absurdity," to use the term that Marx himself invokes in the third volume of *Capital.* At this same point in the third volume Marx makes his relation to this strand of Hegel's thought explicit. "What Hegel says with reference to certain mathematical formulas," he writes, "applies here: that which seems irrational to ordinary common sense is rational, and that which seems rational is itself irrational."[116] The narrow utilitarian rationality which structures the action of capitalist and worker in the period of commodity production violates reason in a broad normative sense, but Marx departs from Hegelian theory precisely because he will not allow this violation to enter ordinary consciousness. If it did, if critical action could be conceived in a normative way, then Marx's exclusive focus on the external conditions of action would have been at least partly in vain. Concerned with the problems that would later preoccupy Durkheim, Marx would have had to turn from his "economics" to an examination of the structure of the moral order. But this was not necessary, for rather than nonrationality Marx is actually invoking the same kind of "incomplete knowledge" argument that informed Durkheim's earlier phase: Marx's actor is irrational only because he does not have knowledge of a situation that is outside the material context of his action. He cannot have this knowledge because this structure is, in a physical sense, beyond the horizon of his vision. Reality itself imposes his false consciousness, and he will alter his goals and means only when external reality itself is transformed.[117†]

2.4. THE TRUE SOURCES OF OBEDIENCE: THE MATERIAL REPRODUCTION OF LABOR AS THE "INVISIBLE THREAD"

Before we examine more closely the transformation of this external reality, we must analyze in more detail the consequences of Marx's failure to produce a theory of false consciousness as an autonomous force. If subjective commitment does not play a significant role in the worker's commitment to the productive apparatus, what does? The answer, of course, can only be the worker's material dependence. This dependence is a product of the same conditions that created the worker's false belief in equality and freedom: his separation from the means of production and the necessity for him to sell his labor power to maintain his physical existence. It is not, however, the form of the wage relationship that creates obedience but rather its material effects. The famous phrase "wage slave" which has always been associated with Marx's view of the proletariat is not mere hyperbole. Because capitalism forces the worker to receive compensation in the form of a wage, the worker can reproduce himself only by serving at the whim of the capitalist.

By eliminating false consciousness as an independent variable, Marx has dispensed with psychological motivation as a theoretical concern. There is, in fact, only one chapter in *Capital* that deals with the problem of motivation in a systematic way. This short section, entitled "Simple Reproduction," has a dual function. On the one hand it rationalizes Marx's failure to make motivation an integral part of the rest of his theory. On the other hand it systematically organizes an alternative approach to individual commitment.

"Reproduction" refers to action that occurs outside the workplace and outside the immediate exchange of money for labor power, the two typical contexts that preoccupy Marx throughout most of *Capital*.[118†] Reproduction, in other words, concerns what goes on in the worker's private life, the process by which the individual worker creates the "self" which takes on the burden of labor. The point of the theory of reproduction, however, is that Marx makes the link between this private world of the self and the public world of production as tight as it can possibly be. He does so, first, by establishing a crucial qualification; Marx insists, as we have already seen, that what is relevant to the capitalist is not the worker's entire self but only his power to labor. It is only this labor power that is used up during production, and it is only labor power, not the "self" as such, that the capitalist will allow the laborer time and money to reproduce. Since man has been reduced to a mere physical instrument in the productive process, his reproduction will be similarly limited to physical things. Marx emphatically describes labor power as simply an aggregate of physical properties, the "muscles, nerves, bones, and brains of existing labourers."[119] As he writes in the first popular presentation of his late economic theory, *Value, Price, and Profit*, labor power is "the physical force of the labouring man."[120] In capitalism, then, the needs of the self are reduced to conserving the "physical element," and this is the object of the reproduction process. "To maintain and reproduce itself, to perpetuate its physical existence," Marx writes, "the working class must receive the necessaries absolutely indispensable for living and multiplying."[121] Reproduction supplies the "necessary vital functions" of the individual with the "means of subsistence."[122]

In capitalism, therefore, man's reproductive needs can be completely satisfied through the procurement of goods in the marketplace. As material needs, they can be satisfied with material goods alone: there is no theoretical necessity for Marx to discuss the acquisition of subjective properties like psychological maturity or cultural values. It is through consumption and consumption alone that the individual creates his self. Instrumental action triumphs outside production as well as within it. Worker consumption is "confined within the limits of what is strictly necessary" for life itself: food, clothing, shelter, family expense, and the minimum education necessary to make labor power salable.

Marx's reduction of the self to the status of a physical commodity, and the way this reduction is tied to production, could not be more clearly articulated than in the following:

> The labouring power of a man exists only in his living individuality. A certain mass of necessaries must be consumed by man to grow up and maintain his life. But the man, like the machine, will wear out, and must be replaced by another man. Beside the mass of necessaries required for his own maintenance, he wants another amount of necessaries to bring up a certain quota of children that are to replace him on the labour market and to perpetuate the race of labourers. Moreover, to develop his labouring power, and acquire a given skill, another amount of values must be spent.[123]

Marx's theoretical intention is clear: he will convert the potentially nonrational and voluntary arena of private life into one that is subject to forces which are strictly coercive and necessary. In the pursuit of this goal, in fact, Marx goes to the extent of asserting that there is a constant tendency of capitalist production to "force the cost of labour back towards zero," an extreme statement which he modifies in other chapters.[124] "All the capitalist cares for," Marx insists here, "is to reduce the labourer's individual consumption as far as possible to what is strictly necessary, and he is far away from imitating those brutal South Americans, who force their labourers to take the more substantial, rather than the less substantial, kind of food."[125] Marx actually recounts, in this context, some distasteful menus which capitalists suggested "for replacing by some succedaneum the ordinary dear food of the labourer," thereby, to minimize the expense of reproduction.[126]

Marx has demonstrated that private life, although apparently voluntary because it occurs outside the worker's direct contact with the capitalist, actually is controlled by the same social order as working life itself, namely, by the forces of production. Indeed, this is the explanation for the term that is applied to private life, "re-production." "The individual consumption of the labourer," Marx writes, "whether it proceed within the workshop or outside it, whether it be part of the process of production or not, forms therefore a factor of the production and reproduction of capital, just as cleaning machinery does, whether it be done while the machinery is working or while it is standing."[127] The process which provides the model for Marx's theory of reproductive consumption, one can now see, is production itself, the process whereby the worker utilizes raw material to fashion the capitalist's products. Marx draws an exact parallel between this latter process, which he calls "productive consumption," and reproduction, which he calls "individual consumption."

> The labourer consumes in a two-fold way. While producing he
> consumes by his labour the means of production, and converts
> them into products with a higher value than that of the capital
> advanced. This is his productive consumption. . . . On the other
> hand, the labourer turns the money paid to him for his labour-
> power, into means of subsistence: this is his individual consump-
> tion.[128]

As if to emphasize the similarity of motivation in economic production
and private reproduction, Marx notes, further, that reproductive consumption occasionally takes place right on the assembly line.

> The labourer is often compelled to make his individual con-
> sumption a mere incident of production. In such a case he sup-
> plies himself with necessaries in order to maintain his labour-
> power, just as coal and water are supplied to the steam-engine
> and oil to the wheel. His means of consumption, in that case, are
> the mere means of consumption required by means of produc-
> tion; his individual consumption is *directly* productive consump-
> tion. This, however, appears to be an abuse not essentially
> appertaining to capitalist production.[129]

The reproduction theory supplies an empirically specific explanation for the motivation to work which makes motivation itself an irrelevant analytic category. The worker's volition—whether he chooses
certain kinds of reproductive activities, or even whether he enjoys them
at all—is not an issue. Tied to production, reproduction is an objective
necessity that will continue whether the worker likes it or not.

> The fact that the labourer consumes his means of subsistence for
> his own purposes, and not to please the capitalist, has no bearing
> on the matter. The consumption of food by a beast of burden is
> nonetheless a necessary factor in the processes of production,
> because the beast enjoys what it eats.[130]

Individual will, the intentional choice of means in the service of valued ends, has disappeared. The capitalist system of production has created a worker without the means to produce his own subsistence. He can
acquire these only by allowing himself to be exploited by the capitalist.
After this exploitation has been completed, he must expend his income to
purchase the necessities he has produced. Yet in this very act he has reduced himself to a subsistenceless state and he must, for that, return to
work once again. "From a social point of view," Marx writes, "the working class, even when not directly engaged in the labour-process, is just as
much an appendage of capital as the dead instruments of labour."[131] It is
the material effects of private reproduction that tie workers to the labor

process: "Individual consumption provides, on the one hand, the means for their maintenance and reproduction: on the other hand, it secures by the annihilation of the necessaries of life, the continued re-appearance of the workman in the labour-market."[132] Reproduction ensures that the entire history of primitive accumulation—the process by which the worker was separated from his means of production and turned into a commodity—will be recapitulated day after day in the life of the contemporary workingman. "The process of production," Marx writes, "takes good care to prevent these self-conscious instruments [i.e., the workers] from leaving it in the lurch, for it removes their product, as fast as it is made."[133]

> Capitalist production, therefore, of itself reproduces the separation between labour-power and the means of labour. It thereby reproduces and perpetuates the condition for exploiting the labourer. It incessantly forces him to sell his labour-power in order to live, and enables the capitalist to purchase labour-power in order that he may enrich himself. It is no longer a mere accident, that capitalist and labourer confront each other in the market as buyer and seller.[134]

Reproduction makes capitalism into a self-perpetuating, thoroughly mechanical system.

> The capitalist system pre-supposes the complete separation of the labourers from all property in the means by which they can realize their labor. As soon as capitalist production is once on its legs, it not only maintains this separation, but reproduces it on a continually extending scale.[135] . . . The organization of the capitalist process of production, once fully developed, breaks down all resistance. . . . In the ordinary run of things, the labourer can be left to the "natural laws of production," i.e., to his dependence on capital, a dependence springing from, and guaranteed in perpetuity by, the conditions of production themselves.[136]

The process of reproduction, in other words, is one more hidden reason for the successful domination of worker by capitalist. Reproduction presents crucial verification for Marx's presupposition that collective order is purely external and coercive. Instrumental domination may not be as visible in private life as in production, but it is just as real: "The Roman slave was held by fetters: the wage-labourer is bound to his owner by invisible threads."[137]† This elegant specification of Marx's general logic demonstrates in yet another way that it is not false consciousness that maintains obedience and order in the capitalist system, but rather the crushing exigences of the material world itself. The contradictions of capitalism, therefore, can manifest themselves only as crises of material reproduction. There will be disloyalty and rebellion only if the worker's ability to reproduce himself fails.

2.5. TRUE CONSCIOUSNESS: THE INSTRUMENTAL RATIONALITY OF CLASS STRUGGLE AND REVOLUTION

The paradox of Marx's theory of class struggle and revolutionary action is that it seems, at first glance, to describe association according to theoretical principles quite antithetical to those which have been considered thus far. Marx invokes "consciousness" as a pivotal element in the class struggle; he writes about the intentions and purposes of the workers and of their ability to oppose external conditions. At first sight, therefore, he seems to be limiting his instrumental-collectivist orientation to the early, non-class-conscious period of capitalism alone. The society of isolated, rationally related, competitive individuals apparently becomes a first phase of capitalism, one that gives way to a second period in which there emerges an island of growing order and moral community, the organized proletariat. Marx's utilization of such antitheses as "individual versus class interest," "false consciousness versus class consciousness," and "class-in-itself versus class-for-itself" seems, indeed, to attribute to the revolutionary class a moral integration and internal reciprocity similar to the qualities that Durkheim ascribed to solidarity. Perhaps instrumental action gives way to altruistic and moral behavior. If this were true, Marx's theory of class struggle would represent, at the minimum, a significant inconsistency, and would cast serious doubt on the validity of the interpretation I have presented thus far.

The argument that Marx's theory of class consciousness constitutes a normative counterweight to other, more economistic sections of his work has been a major premise of the most important twentieth-century interpretation. Although this reading is surely the implicit point of Lenin's argument for the vanguard party in *What Is to Be Done?* (1904), it only becomes self-conscious and explicit with Lukács' *History and Class Consciousness* (1924). Ever since that time, the notion that Marx sees class consciousness as based on an independent process of solidary integration has been an integral part of the readings which emphasize the analytical independence in his work of the concepts of alienation and commodity fetishism. This association has occurred for a very clear theoretical reason: if the orientation of the falsely conscious proletarian is assumed to have an autonomous normative element—e.g., if it is distorted by quasi-religious "fetishism"—then any change in consciousness toward class militancy or revolution must also be conceived as involving independent changes in normative order.[138†]

The most important analysis of class struggle in the later writings occurs in *Capital*. Although the normative interpretation of that work has a surface plausibility, it actually misreads this analysis in a serious way.[139†] Recent interpreters, it seems, have inadvertently revised Marx's analysis rather than articulated it. They have seen what they would like to see, what they have hoped Marx would say rather than what he actually said. To establish the truth of the matter we must scrutinize the presuppositions by which Marx's account is informed. What is the conception of action he employs, and the conception of order upon which it is based? We will find that Marx describes class consciousness as occurring completely within the commodity form, and that he links the instrumental action this implies to the coercive order of capitalist production. The organization of the working class responds to the same kinds of contradictions as capitalism itself. But this should not be surprising, for if false consciousness is established by the imprint of material conditions then true consciousness must wait for these conditions to change.

The argument that Marx develops a voluntaristic theory of class consciousness usually points to his emphasis on working-class struggle as an independent catalyst of events. The most substantial and systematic discussion Marx ever wrote about such struggle is his discussion in *Capital* of the fight for limiting the working day. In one sense, Marx does give to this conflict an independent role, for he describes the limitation of the working day as the outcome of a battle between two class forces. "In the history of capitalist production," he writes, "the determination of what is a working-day, presents itself as the result of a struggle, a struggle between collective capital, *i.e.*, the class of capitalists, and collective labour, *i.e.*, the working class."[140] In these terms it could be argued that the limited working day is won through the will power and determination of the working class. At one point, for example, Marx alludes to the capitalists as the class "from whom the legal limitation and regulation had been wrung step by step after a civil war of half a century."[141]

In view, however, of the inverse relationship I have established between instrumental order and individual freedom, one might justifiably doubt whether this purely class-oriented struggle—which Marx himself describes as a conflict in which "force decides"—can be a truly voluntary one.[142] Doubts increase when one realizes that Marx goes out of his way to emphasize that the motives involved on both sides are purely rational ones. The ends of the actors focus on control over state legislation, legislation that Marx defines as itself merely instrumental for the achievement of the parties' economic goals. Before the greatly increased exploitation that marked the introduction of machinery—Marx generalizes here from the English case—the state was directed against working-class interests in a ruthless way. Acting as the representative of the bourgeoisie, Parliament had passed laws which limited the working day but it had not voted a penny for carrying them out.[143] Even if these laws were violated, moreover, the lawbreaking capitalist would never have been successfully prosecuted, for as the originators and implementers of the legal system capitalists merely sat in judgment on themselves.[144] After machinery was introduced, however, and the working day considerably lengthened, state action toward the working class became more conciliatory. Yet it became so, Marx insists, because the self-interest of the capitalists demanded it. The greater working day had provoked tremendous conflict, and equilibrium could be restored only by state action. "The Factory Inspectors," Marx writes, "urgently warned the Government that the antagonism of classes had arrived at an incredible tension."[145] Support for new legislation was also provided by more specific kinds of upper-class interests. In the early 1840s, for example, the bourgeoisie hoped to enlist the proletariat in its Anti-Corn Law struggle against the landowning aristocracy, and it gave qualified support to limiting the working day as a quid pro quo. And in the late 40s, after the repeal of the Corn Laws, the defeated Tories helped further regulation in order to gain political revenge against the free-trading bourgeoisie.[146] Extensions of the law were also supported by manufacturers whose competitive position was endangered by its uneven application.[147†]

Given this description of action as based upon rational calculation alone, it should not be surprising to find that Marx actually subjects this apparently independent class struggle to the most stringent and determinate kinds of conditions. After all, in relation to what will the workers and capitalists calculate their interests? Since reference cannot be made to solidarity or morality, the calculation must be determined by the material environment. The class struggle proceeds because of the crisis of reproduction, a crisis, we have seen, that systematically relates general economic laws to the private and apparently voluntary activity of the worker himself.

On one side, class struggle is bounded by the physical limits of biology. When the working day is extended too far, Marx writes, it "leads to a reaction on the part of society," the "very sources of whose life are threatened."[148] This threat to life naturally produces a reaction by the proletariat, whose "instinct for self-preservation" leads it to protest the longer working day. But, the biological danger also produces regulatory action by the capitalists themselves. Although Marx makes reference to moral concerns in passing, his focus clearly is on the capitalists' fear for their profits: if labor power cannot be reproduced then the owners' capital investment will be lost. He insists that the working day eventually became so long that capitalist production was killing its very source of wealth. "In its blind unrestrainable passion," Marx writes, "capital oversteps not only the moral, but even the merely physical maximum bounds of the working-day."[149] The same biological reinforcement for the workers' natural moral indignation is cited time and time again. "All bounds of morals and nature, age and sex, day and night, were broken down," Marx writes at the beginning of his famous section on the struggle for the normal working day.[150] And in a later chapter on the introduction of machinery: "Lengthening the working-day beyond all bounds set by human nature [met] with certain natural obstructions in the weak bodies and the strong wills of its human attendants."[151] The real problem, then, the problem that provoked the protective reaction, was that the capitalists had tried to transcend the material boundaries of nature itself. The lengthening of the working day had produced a frightening physical degeneration of the proletariat.

> They were ordinary men, not Cyclops. At a certain point their labour-power failed. Torpor seized them. Their brain ceased to think, their eyes to see.[152]

The purely instrumental calculation of the capitalists had brought them up against an external condition which they could not deny: "The same blind eagerness for plunder that in the one case exhausted the soil, had, in the other, torn up by the roots the living force of the nation."[153] Indeed, the physical degeneration of the proletariat is simply the living embodiment of the economic contradictions of capitalism, for it is created by the fact that capitalists can stay in business only by increasing surplus value and cutting costs.

> The capitalist mode of production . . . produces thus, with the extension of the working-day, not only the deterioration of human labour-power by robbing it of its normal, moral and physical, conditions of development and function. It produces also the premature exhaustion and death of this labour-power itself.[154]

Faced with this biological limit, capitalists supported the limitation of the working day as an efficient strategy of material interest: "It would seem therefore that the interest of capital itself points in the direction of a normal working-day."[155]

The physical world, then, sets one of the boundaries for class struggle, a boundary that is permeable neither to moral indignation nor voluntary choice. The other boundary is a social one, yet in terms of its relationship to action this boundary functions "as if" it were also a natural one. Marx carefully emphasizes that the physical threat to labor and the struggle it provokes must be linked at every point to overarching economic laws. In effect, he encapsulates the biologically based response within this social one; in this way, the apparently voluntary struggle between classes will more clearly be seen for what it is: a necessary reflection of external conditions. Marx has linked the object of his ideological interest—the activism of the proletariat—to the collective order that has been the major object of his analytic effort. If it is the change in the organic composition of labor toward constant, or machine-based, capital that first lengthens the working day in such an extreme way, it is this same "law of the progressive increase in constant capital" that produces the opportunity to shorten it.

> The changes in the material mode of production, and the corresponding changes in the social relations of the producers gave rise first to an extravagance beyond all bounds, and then in opposition to this called forth a control on the part of Society which legally limits, regulates, and makes uniform the working-day and its pauses.[156]

It is the natural and irreversible laws of capitalism, not voluntary will or self-conscious intention, that produce the sequence of class struggle, state action, and bureaucratic regulation that eventually limited the working day.

> It has been seen that these minutiae, which with military uniformity, regulate by stroke of the clock the times, limits, pauses of the work, were not at all the products of Parliamentary fancy. They developed gradually out of circumstances as natural laws of the modern mode of production. Their formulation, official recognition, and proclamation by the State, were the result of a long struggle of classes.[157]

So much does Marx view the proletarian revolt against the working day as a predictable response to economic laws that he makes the success of this revolt an integral part of his larger economic theory of capitalist development. The result of this rational action by the proletariat to protect its life was the creation of new external conditions for the capitalist. The limitation of the working day—which, of course, was stimulated by the capitalist's self-interest as well—created a new external condition for capitalist production. The shorter working day forced production to emphasize relative surplus value.

> Extension of the working-day and intensity of the labour mutually exclude one another, in such a way that lengthening of the working-day becomes compatible only with a lower degree of intensity, and a higher degree of intensity, only with a shortening of the working-day. So soon as the gradually surging revolt of the working-class compelled the state to shorten compulsorily the hours of labour, and to begin by imposing a normal working-day on factories proper, so soon consequently as an increased production of surplus-value by the prolongation of the working-day was once for all put a stop to, from that moment capitalism threw itself with its might into the production of relative sur-

plus-value, by hastening on the further improvement of machinery.[158]

It was, we recall, this very law of capitalist development, the rule of relative surplus value with its intensification of labor and its vast unemployment, which, Marx believed, would create the conditions for the revolutionary overthrow of capitalism itself. New external conditions, the introduction of machines, had created reformist class struggle. This rational action, in turn, produced a new external condition, the shorter working day. Under this new condition the class struggle would have to become much more radical if it were efficiently to achieve its goal.

In his earlier writings—in *The German Ideology*, *The Poverty of Philosophy*, and *The Communist Manifesto*—Marx had employed a similarly instrumental approach to class conflict. Yet in that earlier phase he had seen this struggle as almost purely revolutionary: his "economics" had all but neglected the reformist effort to limit the working day. In *Capital*, by contrast, these reform struggles became the center of Marx's attention, and those of the revolutionary period of proletarian activity were significantly less prominent. When Marx did speak of revolutionary activity in his later writings, however, his logic was precisely the same.

It is only in the period of relative surplus value, Marx believed, that the revolutionary upheaval by the proletariat can occur. Revolution, in other words, corresponds to the factory stage of capitalism. This is not, however, because of the greater chances for cooperation and solidarity that the factory provides; rather it is because factory organization, as we have seen, has a crucial effect on the laws governing economic life. Mass unemployment and impoverishment are produced by the law of the falling rate of profit. Revolution will occur insofar as the counteracting tendencies on the profit law fail to modify these central effects—a failure, it will be recalled, which Marx considered inevitable. The working class will overthrow capitalism, therefore, not because the workers have seen through the ideological structure of the wage relationship or because they have developed an alternative moral order, but because they are forced to act by the same external conditions of production that create the commodity form itself. Once again, Marx's empirical analysis specifies this presuppositional logic by describing the action of labor as limited by two insurmountable barriers. On one side, the falling rate of profit acts as a nature-like power, locking labor-capitalist relations on a collision course. On the other side, the physical-biological conditions of the workers' life become entirely untenable. Marx neatly combines these two boundaries when he writes that "the higher the development of labor productivity, the more precarious the existence."[159]†

Socialist revolution and the organization to support it are designed to reverse the relations of production. Once these external conditions have changed—once there is public property and a more equal distribution of the means of production—the efficient calculations by producers will result in the full utilization of the technological forces of industrial production. The results of these decisions will be more ample food, clothing, and shelter for the working population, a new set of external conditions in which any further revolt would be an irrational, inefficient act. Revolution, then, is an objective necessity: it must occur if the workers' lives are to be sustained. Marx expressed this idea clearly in *The Civil War in France*, in 1871, when he wrote that the workers "have no ideals to realize" and act merely to "set free the elements of the new society with which the old collapsing bourgeois society itself is pregnant."[160] He describes the same logic of revolutionary revolt in *Capital*. The final expropriation of the capitalists, he writes in the concluding pages, "is accomplished by the action of the imminent laws of capitalist production itself."[161] Revolution is produced by capitalist production "with the inexorability of a law of nature."[162]†

Marx's description of the first phase of postrevolutionary communism, a period later Marxists described as socialism, further reflects the instrumental character of this struggle. Here, too, his concentration on the relations of production reduces the ends of revolution to a struggle over means. Although it was Engels who wrote the pamphlet *Socialism: Utopian or Scientific*, Marx believed just as strongly that "ideological nonsense" about the morality and the altruism of the new society was out of place in a serious workers' movement intent on changing external conditions.[163] It is in *The Critique of the Gotha Programme*, the response he made to a German socialist program in 1875, that Marx laid out his systematic justification for this contempt. He argued that communism would have to be divided in two phases, and only in the second could action be ordered by the altruistic morality of "from each according to his abilities, to each according to his needs." The stage of communism that immediately succeeds the revolution will be a society still governed by exchange value and the law of commodities. Action will be just as instrumental as before: it will be more cooperative only because of the restructured external conditions to which it is oriented. Marx insists that "the same principle prevails" in this first phase of communism "as that which regulates the exchange of ... commodity-equivalents: a given amount of labour in one form is exchanged for an equal amount of labour in another form." The only difference is that in the communist case the exchange of labor for money no longer results in the extraction of surplus value: "The individual producer receives back from society— after the deductions have been made [for the reproduction of capital]— exactly what he gives to it."[164] The order of the new society is thoroughly instrumental and economic; the transition to it cannot be governed by an antithetical, normative logic.

3. THE EMPIRICAL STATUS OF THE LATER WRITINGS

The focus of this chapter, thus far, has been the presuppositional logic of Marx's later writings. Marx presented this logic more consistently and specified it more systematically than any instrumentalist theorist before or since. In a later chapter I will discuss the rare departures he made from this powerful theoretical position. There were, indeed, certain empirical anomalies and political-ideological exigencies which forced him to introduce elements of anti-instrumentalist thinking, elements which have since become the focus of great controversy. The present discussion, however, will limit itself to considering those empirical and ideological problems which did not, in fact, force Marx to change his fundamental framework. Empirical problems did challenge Marx's predictions about capitalist development, and moral difficulties arose from the ethical framework that he provided, or failed to provide, for the class struggle. Per se, however, such problems do not force the abandonment of a general theoretical position: by refining and revising his theory on more specific and less consequential levels of analysis, Marx could incorporate apparently contradictory tendencies or find ways to ignore the problematic issues they implied.

The problems that beset Marx's empirical theory are not hard to see. His point in the later writings has been to specify his most general commitments, presuppositional and ideological, in a way that makes them empirically persuasive. In order to accomplish this he made some very precise empirical commitments: the capitalist economy must produce an extreme form of alienation; it must be powerful enough to dominate the other spheres of society; it must produce the kind of unstable and impoverishing development that can create proletarian revolution. The heart of this empirical theory is the falling rate of profit, a proposition which despite certain ambiguities is admirably specific and direct. Anything that would undermine the falling profit rate is potentially disastrous not only for Marx's empirical theory but for his presuppositional and ideological commitments as well.

In fact, if a small number of specific propositions are invalidated, the necessity of general and irreversible economic crisis that Marx predicted can, at least in the narrow sense, easily be disproved. The critical question is whether capitalist accumulation could, after all, negotiate the crucial transition toward capital-intensive production without necessarily creating massive unemployment and merely subsistence wages. As various critics from within and without the Marxist tradition have long attested, the successful negotiation of this transition is certainly within the realm of possibility. Cut-throat competition can be broken by government intervention or by monopolization; capital-intensive production may not, after a certain period, involve reducing the contribution of labor in relation to machinery. In either case, accumulation could proceed without the incessant pressure to lower labor costs in an extreme way.[165]

Marx himself was not unaware of such theoretically dangerous possibilities. Indeed, as his discussion of the counteracting tendencies to the falling profit rate indicates, much of his empirical discussion is structured with these questions in mind.[166†] There is only one place in the later writings, however, where Marx confronts the fundamental question of the successful transition to capital-intensive production directly, and this is in the notebooks known as the *Grundrisse*, which he composed in 1857–1858. Discovered in the early 1920s, published in German editions in Moscow, 1939–1941, and in Berlin, 1953, and translated into English only in the 1970s, the *Grundrisse* manuscript has been hailed by most recent Marxist scholars as an equal and independent counterpart to *Capital*. In the continuing effort to revise Marx from within, critics have "read" the *Grundrisse* as a mature specification of Marx's early Hegelian theorizing, as the proof that Marx never held an objectivist social theory. The *Grundrisse* has also been viewed as providing a counter-theory of capitalism's actual development, one which allows that growing affluence and technological change can occur within the capitalist framework.[167] Neither line of interpretation is correct. Taken by itself, the *Grundrisse* is an overrated manuscript. Of course, as a first draft that reveals the process by which Marx discovered the conceptualization for *Capital*, the *Grundrisse* is a fascinating document. Yet its status as a working draft is precisely the point, for in most essentials the *Grundrisse* differs hardly at all from the later work. For readers of *Capital*, the major points of the *Grundrisse* are familiar ones: the distinction between labor and labor-power, the falling rate of profit, and the historical description of alienation as created and destroyed by the material relations of property. The major departure from Marx's future analysis is his brief discussion, in the manuscript's seventh and final notebook, of the way in which the capitalist's introduction of machinery threatens to make human labor time an irrelevant measure of economic value. Since such a development would strike at the heart of Marx's theory of exchange value and commodity production, his response to this empirical possibility is worth some more consideration.

In this seventh notebook of the *Grundrisse*, written in early 1858, Marx approaches the possibility that technological advancement could continue under capitalism without generating the economic contradictions which his theory of revolution assumes. "To the degree that large industry develops," he writes, "the creation of real wealth comes to depend less on labour time and on the amount of labour employed than on the power of the agencies set in motion during labour time, whose 'powerful effectiveness' is itself in turn out of all proportion to the direct labour time spent on their production."[168] In this situation, "direct labour [is] reduced to a mere moment of this [production] process."[169]

Although these formulations may appear simply to anticipate Marx's later insistence on the changing organic composition of capital, his explication suggests that more contradictory possibilities may be involved.

First, this reliance on machines rather than labor time gives to technology an apparently independent role. Marx speaks, for example, of the "tendency of capital to give production a scientific character," and he argues that the "entire production process appears as not subsumed under the direct skillfulness of the worker, but rather as the technological application of science."[170] The theoretical danger in this proposition is revealed by the last phrase: technology is based upon science, but science is precisely the kind of ideational complex that belongs to the superstructure rather than the base. If science has become the new determinant of the real value of commodities, then consciousness rather than necessity rules production, and cultural change rather than external law would direct economic growth. Marx seems indeed to be heading in precisely this direction when he writes that in the transformation of the organic composition of capital it is the producer's "*understanding* of nature and his mastery over it . . . which appears as the great foundation-stone of production and of wealth."[171] Since "the degree [of] general social knowledge has become a *direct force of production*," he writes at another point, "the conditions of the process of social life itself have come under the control of the general intellect and been transformed in accordance with it."[172]

In this discussion of the scientific sources of technology, Marx's inversion of his own base-superstructure analysis of capitalist production could not be more explicit. His apparent separation of labor time from "real wealth" has implications that are equally profound for the transformation of capitalism itself. Indeed, Marx seems to suggest that workers will become aware of this discrepancy between their labor time and the wealth they produce, and, further, that this consciousness of future abundance and increased leisure will produce a voluntaristic movement toward revolution. "The theft of alien labour time, on which the present wealth is based," Marx writes, "appears a miserable foundation in face of this new one, created by large-scale industry itself." Once labor has ceased to be the major source of wealth, "labour time ceases and must cease to be its measure, and hence exchange value [must cease to be the measure] of use value." Once "production based on exchange value breaks down, and the direct, material production process is stripped of the form of penury and antithesis," the liberating results of the introduction of machinery become explicit and visible. This utopian vision includes, in Marx's words, "the free development of individualities, and hence not the reduction of necessary labour time so as to posit surplus labour, but rather the general reduction of the necessary labour of society to a minimum, which then corresponds to the artistic, scientific, etc. development of the individuals in the time set free."[173]

Nowhere in this discussion does Marx specify the relationship between the new objective possibilities for free development and the actual process of revolution. Production for exchange "must cease," he tells us, but he never actually links this cessation to the proletariat's imagined vision of the liberating society. This omission turns out to be absolutely crucial, for if this section of the *Grundrisse* is read carefully one cannot be persuaded that Marx actually has developed a new, anti-instrumentalist form of reasoning. The contradiction between potential free time and the necessary work time of capitalism, it turns out, is expressed by purely economic pressures. The increasing capacity to create leisure time is actually the same decreasing capacity to utilize human labor that Marx describes as producing the falling rate of profit. The reason is simple: the capacity for free time which comes with increased technological capacity must be converted into increased surplus labor if the capitalist is to survive. When it cannot be so converted, when capital cannot increase its profits and reproduce its technological base, economic crisis results. It is this objective crisis, not the imagined utopia of the free development of individuality, that motivates revolutionary action against technologically advanced capitalism.

> Despite itself, [capital is] instrumental in creating the means of ... disposable time, in order to reduce labour time for the whole society to a diminishing minimum, and thus to free everyone's time for their own development. But its tendency always, on the one side, [is] *to create disposable time, on the other, to convert it into surplus labour.* If it succeeds too well at the first, then it suffers from surplus production, and then necessary labour is interrupted, because *no surplus labour can be realized by capital.* The more this contradiction develops, the more does it become evident that the growth of the forces of production can no longer be bound up with the appropriation of alien labour, but that the mass of workers must themselves appropriate their own surplus labour. Once they have done so—and *disposable* time thereby ceases to have an *antithetical* existence—then ... *disposable time* will grow for all.[174]

Only after the seizure of power and the economic reconstruction of capitalism, in other words, will labor time actually cease to be the measure of value and will exchange relations be dissipated.[175]

Despite his utopian explorations and his critical description of capitalism's moral bankruptcy, Marx has not developed a theory that transcends the limitations of utilitarian thought. He has described the broader human ramifications of the laws of capitalism but not denied in any way their causal efficacy. Capitalist squandering of potentially free labor time must cease because it is inefficient and ultimately self-destructive: the drive for technological intensification is impeded by the instrumental "relations" of capitalist production. This orthodoxy is reinforced by the way that Marx neutralizes his discussion of the autonomy of scientific technology. The technological intensity of advanced industry, he writes, occurs only after "all the sciences have been pressed into the service of capital." The reliance on technology does not, therefore, indicate the autonomy of consciousness, since scientific invention itself has become a business, "and the application of science to direct production itself becomes a prospect which determines and solicits it."[176†] Marx declares that "science too [is] among [the] productive forces" of capitalism. He has, thus, completely encapsulated his analysis of advanced capitalist development within the instrumental formulation of "forces versus relations of production."[177] The farsighted empirical speculations of the *Grundrisse* now fit perfectly within the confines of Marx's presuppositional logic.[178†]

4. THE ETHICAL STATUS OF THE LATER WRITINGS

Because Marx was committed to an instrumental perspective on action, his collectivist solution to order had to maintain a strict dichotomy between subject and object. Marx's individual actor incorporates, or internalizes, none of the society of other individuals. He does not interpenetrate with the social institutions around him. He is not in any sense a "part" of his society. Since action does not involve intentionality, it does not depend upon the structure of the self. The actor does not regulate himself, a fact which Marx implicitly recognizes by developing no independent conceptualization of human motivation. "Constraint," therefore, operates in one dimension only; it does not acquire theoretical differentiation. There is no middle ground between coercion, which is the total limitation of individual action by external circumstance, and freedom, which can be defined only as the complete absence of constraint.

This portrait of the actor in society raises crucial ethical questions for Marx's theory of class struggle in capitalism. Can there be any rules by which parties to the class struggle are bound, rules which transcend their immediate instrumental interest? In terms of Marx's strict analytic logic, there cannot. Marxism is, in this sense, a historicism that relativizes all morality.[179†] Because Marx's actors have roots only in their particular situations, they have no commitments to more universal moral codes which transcend their situation and bind their immediate interest. Superstructural logic cuts both ways, for if ideas are mere reflections of material interests, morals cannot be less so. Morality becomes merely an instrument in the class struggle, divided, in Trotsky's famous phrase, into "their morals and ours."[180] This radical relativism obviates the individual's moral responsibility for his actions, and the stage is set intellectually for some future conjoining of "humanism and terror," the logical conclusion drawn by Merleau-Ponty in his famous apology for Stalinism.[181]

The cruel irony, of course, is that Marx himself would have been horrified at these intellectual consequences, no matter how logically drawn and analytically correct. For this reason, those who have accused the later Marx of being antihumanistic—for example, Bell and Althusser—are both right and wrong. In terms of his value commitments, in terms of the ideological dimension of his work, Marx remains committed to the humanist ideal of returning the world to man. He would have heartily endorsed the Renaissance declaration of Pico della Mirandola, in his "Oration on the Dignity of Man," that man is, "by the acuteness of his senses, by the discernment of his reason, and by the light of his intelligence the interpreter of nature." *Capital*, indeed, is a work of moral denunciation in this humanist tradition, and it calls for the return to man of his rightful powers. Nonetheless, *Capital* does not produce a theory that is humanistic in the theoretical sense. Its explanatory laws are postulated upon an assumption of the destruction of species-being and the mechanical instrumentality of action. Every one of Marx's major works is self-described as a "critique," yet he does not, for that, incorporate the capacity for critique into his conception of the order that binds social actors. What has changed from the early to the later Marx, then, is not his ideological humanism but the presuppositions of his scientific theory. These presuppositions will not allow to Marx's actors the moral intensity of Marx himself. Ethics are reduced to instrumental interest not just in the realm of general ideology but in terms of the rules that guide class conflict itself. This is a morally dangerous situation, one to which Marx himself never directed his attention. His lack of interest, of course, is precisely the point. To pretend that ethics have an autonomy in Marx's thought is to ignore the most distinctive analytic achievement of his later work.[182†]

Marx's presuppositional position raises difficult questions for his theory of communism as well. Because constraint has no theoretical differentiation, the postrevolutionary society must be an either-or proposition. Early communism, with its continuation of exchange relations and instrumental order, provides an analytical justification for the "dictatorship of the proletariat" that Marx periodically prescribed for the period of transition between the revolution and the utopian society. Although he justified this period of extrademocratic force on grounds of strategic necessity—that it would be necessary to subdue and disarm the rebellious members of the old ruling classes—the rule of Marx's post-revolutionary state would have to be conceived as coercive on theoretical grounds as well: if exchange value dominates social relations there is no basis for independent moral commitment and the rule of universalistic law.[183†]

This problem is no more successfully resolved in the implicit theory that Marx offers for the later period of true communism. Why do Marx's references to this future society remain so sketchy and undeveloped? His defenders, quite rightly, have suggested that his dialectical conception of history made Marx less inclined to develop abstract schemas of the future, that he believed communism could only grow organically out of the struggle against capitalism.[184] Yet this cannot be the only reason. In describing a future society unconstrained by economic necessity Marx would have had to abandon the theoretical framework within which he had established Marxism itself. Within Marxism, the abolition of economic and coercive constraint means the abolition of constraint in general, indeed, of supra-individual order itself. In fact, the cooperation which characterizes late communist society—the society in which "the springs of cooperative wealth flow more abundantly"—is theorized by Marx in terms of the inherent rationality of species-being, not in terms of a voluntaristic moral order in a sociological sense.[185] "Free, conscious activity," he declared in the 1844 "Economic and Philosophical Manuscripts," "is the species-character of human beings."[186] In the third volume of *Capital* he writes simply of the realm of "freedom" that will emerge after economic "necessity" has been abolished.[187] Ironically, when Marx speaks about the future of mankind he returns to a theoretical position that is antithetical to the one he has employed for capitalism and its prehistory. Armed with the faith in natural man's inherent rationality, Marx takes up the theory of the natural identity of interests that inspired Locke and Rousseau, each of course in a different way. Marx's theory of true communism, in other words, is theoretically naïve. It is an individualistic theory, denying the dimension of collective order that Marx so carefully established in his sociology of capitalism. With the achievement of true socialism, therefore, Marx's sociology ends.[188]†

5. "SOCIAL" DETERMINISM: THE CONFLATION OF ACTION AND ORDER AND MARX'S PROBLEM WITH THE "INDIVIDUAL"

The brilliance of Marx's analytical achievement made his work the prototype for every subsequent theorist in the rationalist tradition who was not satisfied with an individualistic orientation. As I pointed out in the final pages of chapter 3, moreover, Marx was himself fully aware of his unique position in the rationalist tradition. No doubt he did not perceive the ethical implications of his collectivist instrumentalism; nonetheless, he was quite willing to accept the deterministic consequences in terms of its theoretical and empirical effects. Yet like all innovative theorists Marx sought to "naturalize" his achievement, to make his conclusions appear common-sensical and empirically inevitable. He did so by

resorting to a theoretical strategy which I earlier described as fundamental to one-dimensional theorizing: he conflated order and action. The
only possible alternative to individual order, he insisted throughout his
career, was collectivism of a rationalist and materialist sort. He maintained that the other alternative, the one which emphasized normative
order, was simply individualism in disguise. This conflationary strategy
is the source for the famous aphorism that appears in various forms
throughout Marx's work: it is not the individual who determines society,
but society that determines the individual. Marx tried to usurp the "social" for his own purposes, to limit the collectivist position to his own
special approach to it. Henceforth, any discussions of "social origins," or
of "social history," would carry a special kind of meaning, for they would
be weighted down with order in a purely materialist sense.

It is significant that this fundamentally misguided theoretical logic
was first established in the crucial writings of Marx's transitional period,
between 1845 and 1847. In Marx's attack on his old philosophical comrades in *The German Ideology*, he relies heavily on this conflationary
strategy, insisting that idealism cannot articulate a collective order and
equating it at every point with a purely individualistic position. Rather
than relating ideas themselves to supra-individual control, Marx argues
that they derive purely from the actions of individual actors. "According
to their fantasy," he writes about the Young Hegelians, "the relationships
of men, all their doings, their chains and their limitations are products of
their consciousness." According to idealists, then, there is nothing beyond the individual which must be challenged if social order is to be
transformed: "The Young Hegelians have to fight only against these illusions of consciousness." Political struggle takes the form of individual
argument: "The Young Hegelians logically put to men the moral postulate of exchanging their present consciousness for human, critical or
egoistic consciousness, and thus removing their limitations." Marx insists, quite rightly, that such a logic cannot conceptualize real change, for

while the individual's orientation may be altered the social components of existence remain the same. "This demand to change consciousness amounts to a demand [only] to interpret reality in another way, *i.e.*, to recognize it by means of another interpretation."[189] Idealist thinkers, in other words, subscribe to a theory that is voluntaristic in a radically individualistic way; they can see no external constraints on history. Hence Marx's description of the Young Hegelians on the 1842–1845 period in German history: "Principles ousted one another, heroes of the mind overthrew each other with unheard of rapidity," and "the absolute spirit . . . decompose[d], entered into new combinations and formed new substances."[190] Marx can conclude that if social control is given an internal rather than external status, its supra-individual, "social" claim is completely undercut. The following passage is from *The Holy Family*.

> *Absolute Criticism* has at least learned from Hegel's *Phenomenology* the art of transforming *real*, *objective* chains existing *outside me* into *merely ideal*, merely *subjective* chains existing *in me*, and hence the art of transforming all *external* sensuous struggles into mere struggles of thought.[191]

Marx repeats this conflationary error throughout his later writings. The logic is most starkly expressed in his aphorisms, like the famous juxtaposition of "consciousness" and the "social" in his Preface to *The Critique of Political Economy:* "It is not the consciousness of men that determines their being, but, on the contrary, their social being that determines their consciousness."[192] In the *Grundrisse*, however, the reduction is carried out in a more elaborate way. In this work, which is as much notes to himself as it is formal theorizing, Marx reflects at various points on the relationship between the individual and society. At one point, for example, he seems to adopt a simple collectivist position. "Society does not consist of individuals," he writes, rather it "expresses the sum of interrelations, the relations within which these individuals stand."

> It is as if one chose to say: From the standpoint of society, there are no slaves and no citizens: both are human beings. On the contrary, they are that [i.e., merely human beings] outside society. To be slave or citizen is a social designation.[193]

At another point, however, Marx's reductionistic understanding of this collective order becomes apparent. His "social" determination can be exercised only through its organization of instrumental means: "Socially determined interest . . . can be achieved only within the conditions laid down by society and with the means provided by society." Hence the "reciprocal and all-sided dependence of individuals," he insists, is a "social bond" that is "expressed in *exchange value*."

The power which each individual exercises over the activity of others or over social wealth exists in him as the owner of *exchange values,* of *money.* The individual carries his social power, as well as his bond with society, in his pocket.[194]

This conflation of order and action is an independent theoretical error of major proportions, but in the rationalist tradition it is always accompanied by a fundamental error of another kind, namely, the inability to perceive the individual in an analytical rather than a concrete way. In his analysis of capitalism, Marx can perceive the individual only concretely, only as a material thing. If order is to be social and supra-individual, therefore, it must be external in an ontological sense. Ironically, Marx utilizes this confusion about the individual to present the collectivist position on order as if, in contrast with idealism, it were voluntaristic. Idealism, he insists, does not deal with the real individual but rather with some abstract phantom. He himself will be different, Marx argues, because he will recognize the real person. As he writes in *The German Ideology:*

> The premises from which *we* begin are not arbitrary ones, not dogmas, but real premises from which abstraction can only be made in the imagination. They [our premises] are the real individuals, their activity. . . . The first premise of all history is, of course, the existence of living human individuals.[195]

Such a promise to rely on real individuals is unarguable, and could presage a real voluntaristic position. But this general statement is immediately specified in a much more questionable way. Marx objects to idealism not on the grounds that it ignores the individual per se but because it ignores the individual in a materialist, economic sense.

> The social structure and the State are continually evolving out of the life-process of definite individuals, but of individuals, not as they may appear in their own or other people's imaginations, but as they really are; i.e., as they are active under certain material conditions and assumptions independent of their will.[196]

But if the individual can be defined only in a material way, and if collective order must be supra-individual, then what is "social" can share nothing with the individual. The social is completely external, completely outside the actor. We can now see that the concrete approach to the individual is the complementary error, indeed the inevitable consequence, of an exclusively instrumental approach to action. Marx's approach to individuals, then, is not only "concrete" but also coercive. Marx expresses this interconnection in an early analysis of the nature of social life before the division of labor. "Conceiving, thinking, the mental intercourse of men," he writes, "appear at this stage as the direct efflux of their material behavior." Yet he proceeds to relate this determinate image to an insistence on individual actors as the source of his theorizing: "Men are the producers of their conceptions, ideas, etc." How can this apparent incongruity be resolved? The answer is that Marx does mean to refer to "real, active men," but only "as they are conditioned by a definite development of their productive forces."[197]

Marx has developed an intricate theoretical strategy that at once reflects the errors in his most generalized logic and rationalizes them. On the one hand, he can deny the influence of any noneconomic, subjective factors by claiming that they are individualistic rather than social. At the same time, he can argue that only a materialistic explanation can take the real rather than abstract individual truly into account. Upon this apparently voluntary yet nonetheless determinist basis, he can produce a position that is anti-individualistic and coercive. This is precisely the procedure Marx employs in his famous attack on Proudhon in *The Poverty of Philosophy*. Marx begins by likening Proudhon to Hegel, that is, to an idealist who views society as the product of individual actors.

> The philosophy of history [for Hegel] is nothing but the history of philosophy, of his own philosophy. There is no longer a "history according to the order in time," there is only "the sequence of ideas in the understanding." He thinks he is constructing the world by the movement of thought.[198]

Once the ghost of Hegel has been invoked to reduce normative currents to individual desires, Marx contrasts Proudhon's neo-Hegelian emphasis on ideals and principles with his own emphasis on "social" factors.

> Each principle [for Proudhon] has its own century in which to manifest itself. The principle of authority, for example, had the eleventh century, just as the principle of individualism had the eighteenth. In logical sequence, it was the century that belonged to the principle, and the principle that belonged to the century. In other words, it was the principle that made the history and not the history that made the principle.[199]

As an alternative, Marx proposes that he will be at once more social and more respectful of the true individual. To avoid Proudhon's error, one must concentrate on real historical actors, on "men as the actors and authors of their own history." In fact, however, these are men only as they are defined by their economic needs.

> We are necessarily forced to examine minutely what men were like in the eleventh century, what they were like in the eighteenth, what were their respective needs, their productive

forces, their mode of production, the raw materials of their production.[200]

This consideration of the needs of real individuals, then, leads ineluctably to an understanding that individual acts are determined by external conditons.

> Truly, one must be destitute of all historical knowledge not to know that it is the sovereigns who in all ages have been subject to economic conditions, but they have never dictated laws to them. Legislation, whether political or civil, never does more than proclaim, express in words, the will of economic conditions. Was it the sovereign who took possession of gold and silver to make them the universal agents of exchange by affixing his seal to them? Or was it not, rather, these universal agents of exchange which took possession of the sovereign and forced him to affix his seal to them and thus give them a political consecration?[201]

The logic by which Marx proceeds, of course, makes sense only if one presupposes the same narrowly instrumental outlook as he has himself. Once one steps outside this framework it can be seen that instead of maintaining a respect for the individual actor, Marx has actually eliminated individual intention from his theoretical scheme.[202†] It will be recalled that Durkheim, after his earliest writings, made much the same mistake. Order can be established, Durkheim believed, only by placing society outside of individual control. Anything that goes on inside the concrete individual (in Durkheim's early vocabulary the "substantialist" individual) cannot, therefore, be the object of sociological concern. We have seen that Marx continued to accept precisely the same position throughout the writings of his maturity. In the following chapter we will see how Durkheim came eventually to reject it.

Chapter Seven

DURKHEIM'S LATER WRITINGS (1)

The Transition to Morality as a Spiritual Force

When *The Division of Labor in Society* appeared in France in 1893 it was a major intellectual event. This recognition came to Durkheim's first mature work not primarily for his empirical or theoretical achievement, though each was considerable, but rather for his aggressive application of the methods of positive science to a major social issue of the day. But if Durkheim's book was considered an intellectual landmark, there was still wide disagreement about its implications. Some thought it would lead down the road to scientific progress and perhaps even social unity, others that it presaged merely scientism and the despiritualized objectivism of industrial life. On the point of controversy, however, all were agreed: Durkheim had made more ambitious claims for this new science than any before him.[1†]

Durkheim could only have been heartened by this response, for it was precisely his ambition to create a science of society purged of subjectivity and presupposition. He had early expressed his conviction that sociology could be built purely upon facts alone. "A science has for its point of departure facts, not hypotheses," he stated in his opening lecture on sociology at Bordeaux.[2] "There is only one manner to arrive at the general," he declared, and "it is to observe the particulars, not only superficially and in general, but minutely and by detail."[3] In his essay on the social sciences in Germany he insisted that empirical reality could be approached only through observation, no matter what its particular content: "It is necessary with morality as with other fields," he wrote, "to begin by observing."[4] In the Latin dissertation he wrote that experimentation would never be subordinated to deduction, for, as he noted in the essay on German social science, sociological analysis must proceed with "perfect impartiality."[5]

Throughout these early writings, indeed, Durkheim had insisted that theoretical errors were created by inadequate methodological positions, positions which did not allow their authors sufficient closeness to observable fact. The classical economists had erred because they had tried to deduce their descriptions of market behavior from a priori assumptions.[6] The utilitarians were guilty of a similar error, for they had not "induced this general proposition [of utility] from methodical observation."[7] Spencer was more a philosopher than a scientist, which explained his misdirected focus on the isolated individual.[8] French individualistic thinkers made exactly the same "methodological error" when they refused to engage in real experiments.[9] Yet Comte himself was hardly better. Despite his knowledge of biology, he had failed to recognize the variegated quality of human evolution. This could only be because he too had engaged more in "philosophical meditation" than true scientific study.[10]

This very conflation of presuppositions with methodology is what gave Durkheim confidence that he would be more successful in his theoretical effort than his predecessors had been in theirs. It was by this logic that he promoted sociology in his opening lecture at Bordeaux. Because they had not had recourse to the scientific method, Durkheim argued, thinkers before the nineteenth century had been misled into supposing that society was purely an individual creation rather than an organization that operated with "natural necessity."[11] Nineteenth-century economists, because of their scientific method, had at least been the first to see that social behavior is as subject to law as objects in the natural world.[12] Sociology had only to extend this insight to other kinds of social facts. As the first sociologist, Comte had realized that even human liberty cannot escape the laws of natural necessity.[13] Later, in his Latin dissertation, Durkheim claimed Montesquieu as the first real scientist of society by virtue of the objectivity of his method. The "moralists" of Montesquieu's time—those who disdained science—had conceived social institutions as emerging from individual will.[14] Montesquieu had realized, to the contrary, that "the subject matter of science can consist only of things that have a stability of their own and are able to resist the human will."[15]

Durkheim was arguing that if social thought were objective and scientific it would yield a collectivist understanding of social order. It is not surprising, therefore, that in his Preface to *The Division of Labor in Society* Durkheim claimed the book to be a model of objective analysis. "In the search for causes," he wrote, he had "put aside all that too readily lends itself to personal judgments and subjective appreciations." The results, he insisted, were all that he had hoped for: he had discovered "certain rather profound facts of the social structure, capable of being objects of judgment, and consequently, of science."[16] Through this new social science, Durkheim announced, the "apparent antinomy" between individual autonomy and social determinism had been resolved: social solidarity would be transformed in a manner beneficial to both individual and society, and this would occur because of the "steadily growing development of the division of labor."[17]

Beneath this veneer of self-confidence, however, Durkheim must have had profound misgivings, conscious or not, about the sociological theory he was proposing. The detailed analysis of the *Division of Labor* undertaken earlier (ch. 5) has shown it to be a deeply ambivalent and self-contradictory statement about the nature of modern society and the presuppositions which must inform its study. Durkheim's claim that he has resolved the antinomy of individual and society is, therefore, a hollow one. Indeed, he concluded his work by demonstrating that far from resolving this tension, the "steadily growing development of the division of labor" actually leads to the oppression of the individual by society. Marx would have been satisfied with a theory that demonstrated the elimination of freedom in capitalist society, but Durkheim certainly could not be. He had rejected the emphasis of Marxian socialism on coercive order as a pathway to liberation and had dedicated himself to finding a way to restructure society without sacrificing freedom. Empirically this meant, in his view, an emphasis on morality. In more generalized terms, it meant that social order had to be constructed from the interactions and intentions of individuals.

We have seen, in chapters 4 and 5, how in the pursuit of this goal Durkheim had struggled with a succession of theoretical strategies. At the beginning of his career he had emphasized the "sympathetic instincts" that were inherent in every human being. Since these natural sentiments led to associations, Durkheim thought he had discovered a way that moral order could be social and individual at the same time. Yet eventually he rejected this solution as too precarious. Such independently motivated individuals, he believed, would develop no sense of the social whole outside of their own selves. Even if they were enmeshed in society, they would not feel any subjective connection. As an alternative to this vision, Durkheim considered the position that morality was in some way external to the individual and could, therefore, more powerfully control him. Yet he worried then about the status of voluntarism, and to resolve this worry he postulated that such a moral order could grow out of individual action itself. Following Wundt, he portrayed the individual as permeable and "anti-substantialist," so order could be internal and external at the same time. Yet this flirtation with Wundt turned out to be brief, for, once again, Durkheim worried that if individual volition was involved social order was bound to be unstable.

Order, then, would have to be really external, external in the ontological sense. Durkheim turned inevitably to a materialist position. He had always had a latent model of the actor as an adaptive and rationalizing force. This model now became manifest, and Durkheim drew upon it to resolve his theoretical stalemate. The adaptive actor was endowed with egoistic motives and was portrayed as responding to material conditions. At first Durkheim thought that this transformation would finally accomplish his goal. He suggested that modern life was organized by the division of labor, a device that allowed free choice and the spontaneous ordering of interests at once. But he had committed himself to an instrumentalist perspective, and if he wanted order to be collective he would eventually have to accept the consequences. The idealized division of labor soon gave way to a division of labor regulated by the coercive state and by unequal material conditions. It became the product of the struggle for existence, which itself was produced by the increasing volume and density of population which occurred when groups lost control over scarce resources. Durkheim had discovered the "law of gravitation of the social world," one which operated with unstoppable mechanical force.

The actual publication of the *Division of Labor* seemed to break this spell. I will later speculate about what some of the extratheoretical reasons might have been for this change of mind and heart, but for now will limit myself to insisting that first and foremost the transformation was theoretically motivated. Durkheim was dissatisfied intellectually, and it was intellectual inspiration that allowed him to change. It was not that he abandoned the model of objective science. He continued to posit an unreconstructed positivism for the rest of his life; indeed, this veil of objectivity has made it difficult for many interpreters to see the movement toward subjectivity upon which he had actually embarked. But those who would tie the levels of methodology and presupposition to one another are mistaken. Durkheim transformed his science, but he did not do so through any new observation of the empirical world.[18†]

1. REFUTING *THE DIVISION OF LABOR IN SOCIETY*: THE MIDDLE YEARS AND DURKHEIM'S INITIAL RECONCEPTUALIZATION OF MORAL ORDER

In two brief essays which appeared immediately after the publication of *The Division of Labor in Society*, Durkheim implicitly refuted the empirical and theoretical foundations of that first great work. The earlier of these pieces was a review of Gaston Richard's *Essai sur l'origine de L'idée de droit* ("Essay on the Origin of the Idea of Law"), which Durkheim began with an observation that seemed to put the objectivism of his *Division of Labor* into some perspective. "It seems," he writes, "that from the moment that one practices the method of observation, one is necessarily condemned to deny the reality of duty and that of disinterest, that is to say to make of the one and the other pure illusions." What Richard shows us, Durkheim continues, is that such a "prejudice" is unfounded.[19†]

Durkheim reads Richard's book as a statement about the nature of modern law and the kind of order it represents. Richard believes, as does Durkheim in the *Division of Labor*, that modern law is distinguished by its emphasis on guarantees of reparation, or restitution, as against simple punishment. But what ensures these reparations to the victim? Many philosophers have thought that law could be maintained only by an apparatus of external coercion like the state, that such a calculus of interest might teach humanity to prefer the unpleasantness of obedience and discipline to interminable war. This belief is unfounded, Durkheim now believes, and he approvingly writes of Richard's belief that "it is inside the conscience and not outside, it is in the sympathetic and altruistic dispositions and not in the sentiments of interest that it is necessary to go to look for the solution to the problem." It is these feelings that will create the kind of emotional solidarity with the victim that guarantees justice, for only "completely interior sentiments" can be relied upon. The sanctions of an organized state, then, are not necessary: "It is sufficient that the individuals who compose it [i.e., the state] feel *solidary* in the struggle [*la lutte*] for existence."[20] On these grounds, Richard argues that reparation and punishment—the two legal systems that Durkheim sharply separated in the *Division of Labor*—are not really very distinct, since both depend upon the organization of emotional feelings. Durkheim now agrees with Richard, emphasizing that every modern system must have both.[21] In sharp contrast to his earlier rejection of the relevance of collective conscience to modern society, Durkheim asserts that a modern society can guarantee reparation only if the law is founded upon sentiments of charity, if justice is based on the mutual limitations of man's natural powers which can emerge only from a "spirit of entente and harmony."[22]

In "Note sur la définition du socialisme," written toward the end of the same year, Durkheim follows the same path of implicit disavowal of key elements in his earlier work. He describes the problems of capitalism as moral rather than instrumental. Whereas in the third Book of the *Division of Labor* it was the lack of material interaction that he cited as the principal cause of anomie, he now insists that the problem does not derive from the lack of "material contiguity." Businesses may well have material relations with one another, "acting and reacting" among themselves. Workers too may well pursue their own interests alongside their fellows. The strain, Durkheim now suggests, arises because these material contiguities do not guarantee that the businesses or the workers "have ends which are common to them"; in fact, they do not form among themselves any "moral community" at all. If problems are posed in this manner, what can the "socialist" solution be? In the *Division of Labor*, Durkheim had emphasized structural reorganization and the redistribution of wealth. Although he certainly would not dispense with such material changes, they no longer seem to him the most significant reform. The "social question" is not one of salaries, he writes, adding that "we are, to the contrary, among those who think that it is above all a moral question." Neither is the political control of economic organization sufficient, for "one understands now that such a revolution could not occur without a profound moral transformation."[23]

Durkheim has revised radically his approach to two of the fundamental questions that preoccupied him in the *Division of Labor*, the nature of modern law and socialist regulation. What he has revised, most fundamentally, is his conception about the nature of the order they represent; rather than the instrumental form he had attributed to them, they now take on a subjective and voluntary hue. In terms of the abstract logic of theoretical thought, such a revision in order could occur only if action were also reconceptualized. This, in fact, is precisely the case. Durkheim makes his new position on action most explicit in the Richard review. In each individual conscience, he now argues, there exist two states of consciousness. One is social, the spirit of "mutual protection." The other is physical, "the sentiment of the struggle [*la lutte engagée*] between the individual appetites of the members of the same group." It is the first, the "sympathetic sentiments," that prevents conflicts from degenerating into open war, pushing warring parties into arbitration and moving the arbiter himself to intervene.[24†] Though at this point rather diffuse and unthought-out, such a dualistic understanding of the nature of action has tremendous theoretical significance, for it presents a radical reversal of the perspective proposed in the *Division of Labor*. There, it was the instrumental action motivating struggle—"*la lutte*"—that eventually produced the collective order regulating society. Now, however, this self-interested sentiment of struggle leads to continued individualism and conflict. Collective order can emerge only from the altruism and sociability embodied in the sentiments of sympathy.

At first glance the presuppositional position of these early essays does not seem like an important departure. We recall that Durkheim talked about innately sociable sentiments in his earlier writings, and about the capacity of morality to regulate individual needs as well. The difference, and this is the major point, is that Durkheim had earlier seen both these approaches to order as precarious. To overcome this problem, without resorting to material externality as he had done in his earlier work, Durkheim would have to find a way to portray moral order as powerful and external while linking it simultaneously to individual sentiments and intentions. The essays of 1893 indicate that Durkheim has begun to discover this crucial relation between internal volition and external constraint. He sees that certain sentiments, without constituting order in themselves, are essential to producing the kind of interaction that can. Upon such interaction, perhaps, social institutions can be emotionally suasive, externally compelling, and individually rooted at the same time. This is precisely what Durkheim sets out to prove in *The Rules of Sociological Method*.

1.1. THE RULES OF SOCIOLOGICAL METHOD *AS THEORETICAL CRITIQUE*

Although *The Rules of Sociological Method* appeared as a monograph in 1895, its individual chapters were published as a series of articles in 1894, the year immediately following the publication of the two essays discussed above. In his Preface to the book, Durkheim claims he is merely making explicit the methodological position that was implied in the *Division of Labor:* "We wish here to expound the results of our work in applied sociology in their entirety and to submit them for discussion."[25] This, however, is hardly the case.

Everything of importance in the *Rules* can be found in the short first chapter, innocuously titled "What Is a Social Fact." Durkheim apparently sets out in a positivistic way simply to define the proper object of sociological science. A fact, he writes, is distinguished by its "objectivity" and by its coercive and external status vis-à-vis the individual. Apparently, then, a sociological fact must have a collective status.[26] But the very first substantive paragraph of the chapter, where Durkheim begins to define such facts, immediately gives one pause.

> When I fulfill my obligations [or] when I execute my contracts, I perform duties which are defined, externally by myself and my acts, in law and in custom. Even if they conform to my own sentiments and I feel their reality subjectively, such reality is still objective, for I did not create them; I merely inherited them through my education.[27]

Conforming to sentiments? Feeling reality subjectively? Inheriting through education? We heard nothing like this in the developing line of Durkheim's early sociology. He proceeds to define sociological facts in a startling way. They are, he writes, "ways of acting, thinking, and feeling" [*les manières d'agir, penser, et sentir*], a phrase which he often reduces to the shorthand "beliefs and practices" [*les croyances et les practiques*].[28] But can such subjective facts be the basis of social order in modern life? We seem to be back on familiar ground when Durkheim writes that such facts must always be grounded in a substratum of which they are simply expressions. When he identifies this substratum as the "social organization" produced by association—two materialist concepts so important in the *Division of Labor*—this familiarity seems confirmed. Yet when Durkheim defines this substratum in more detail, we find that his subjective definition of facts has permeated even the substratum that defines them. It consists, Durkheim writes at one point, of "religious denominations, political, literary, and occupational associations," and at another he refers to "legal and moral regulations, religious faiths, financial systems."[29] Religious faith, of course, did not play a principal role in Durkheim's earlier analysis of modern society; apparently, he has returned to the anomalous position of the fifth chapter of the *Division of Labor.* Yet Durkheim goes beyond merely stating the role of subjective order in modernity: he explores the bases of such a substratum in a radically different way. The "actions and reactions" which create social organization are completely emotionalized. They refer to the "special energy" created when individual consciousnesses interact, and their product is "collective sentiment."[30]

This transformation of association into an emotional rather than an instrumental interaction marks Durkheim's crucial break with his past. Working with his new understanding of the nature of action, he has found a way to maintain the externality of his earlier focus on "organization" while linking it to internal constraint. In his earlier writings, altruistic sentiments marked an approach to "order" in themselves; here they constitute merely a mode of "action." This, it turns out, is a crucial development. In themselves, as the inherent properties of individuals, they were too precarious to order the acts which they also motivated. Seen more properly as action, however, the sentiment of sociability becomes crucial, for in motivating association of an emotional kind it can lead to the formation of an order that is independent of individuals but subjective nonetheless.

Upon this presuppositional change, Durkheim constructs a radically different theory of the structure that association creates. Collective facts, he now insists, can be composed only of more or less crystallized emotion. When emotion is still close to the liquid form of pure association, it creates volatile phenomena like "transitory outbursts" or "great movements of enthusiasm."[31] Eventually, however, emotion acquires a certain "rigidity"; it develops "a body, a tangible form" that is more sharply differentiated from the individuals which first produced it.[32] Social order, then, is simply "currents of opinion" more or less solidified, currents which reflect the state of the collective "soul," or "spirit" [*l'âme*], at different times.[33†] Social structure is a continuum stretching between rigidified and liquid emotion. Legal regulations, for example, are no less structural than architectural forms, but they are less rigidified. Moral maxims are still more "malleable" than regulations, though less so, Durkheim believes, than professional customs or fashion. The critical point is that each of these examples of structure has the same ontological status. Each is subjectively formed, constructed from the stuff of human emotions.

> There is thus a whole series of degrees without a break in continuity between the facts of the most articulated structure and those free currents of social life which are not yet definitely molded. The differences between them are, therefore, only differences in the degree of consolidation they present.[34]

The most rigid and the most liquid specimens of structure share the same subjective status: "Both are simply life, more or less crystallized."[35†]

Now that Durkheim has found a way of giving supra-individual forms a subjective status he can achieve his long-sought-after goal of a voluntary order. It is a strange fact, he notes, that even when constraint is at its strongest it is often "felt only slightly" and sometimes not at all.[36] Structure that has its ontological status in the emotions can only be approached by actors through an equally subjective epistemology. Actors know order not through its material constraint but through their subjective connection with its emotional essense. If it was the emotional association of altruistic actors that first produced these structures, it follows that these social arrangements would come to be "invested with a particular authority" which actors "recognize and respect."[37] Collective order structures action through voluntary adherence, through the actor's ability to see and feel in institutions something familiar and desirable.

But if structure is necessarily subjective, the emotions which compose it are not necessarily our own. In fact, this is rather unlikely, since crystallized emotions assume an autonomy vis-à-vis individual actors, creating institutions that survive not only the immediate association but often the actors' lives and generation. How then is the felt relation to structure established? This is the task of education, the "continuous effort to impose on the child ways of seeing, feeling, and acting which he could not have arrived at spontaneously."[38] If education is successful, if motivation is fitted to the emotional core of the crystallized structure, then constraint is no longer experienced as such. Education, Durkheim writes, creates "internal tendencies that render [explicit] constraint unnecessary."[39] If individual motivation begins to disengage from the more crystallized, social structuring of emotion later in life, order will be reestablished through indirect means like social ridicule and isolation.[40]

It is only fitting that Durkheim concludes this first, revolutionary chapter of *Rules* by inverting his early discussion of morphology, his main explanatory variable in *Division of Labor.* Population density and the movement of population toward urban concentration, he writes, "is due to a trend of public opinion, a collective drive that imposes this concentration on individuals." It is "channels of communication" that "prescribe the direction of internal migrations and commerce." "No doubt," he writes, "it may be of some advantage to reserve the term 'morphological' for those facts which concern the social substratum, *but only on condition of not overlooking the fact that they are of the same nature as the others.*" "Ways of existing," Durkheim writes in reference to morphological facts, are only crystallized "ways of acting."[41]

The rest of *Rules* occupies itself with ground that is familiar from the *Division of Labor*, and Durkheim assiduously affirms much of what he said in that earlier work. All this, however, is epilogue, for despite his affirmations to the contrary Durkheim has repudiated that work's central tenets—insofar, at least, as they were instrumental in their presuppositions.[42†] He admits to this incongruity only once, and this in an indirect and obfuscatory way. The determinants of association, he writes, are the number of individuals, which he calls "size," and their degree of concentration, which he calls "density." Size may be a material variable, but density is not, for it is "the function of the number of individuals who are actually having not only commercial but also social relations, i.e., who not only exchange services or compete with one another but also live a common life."[43] A more fundamental departure from the gist of the *Division of Labor* could not be found, and it is perhaps for this reason that Durkheim feels compelled on the next page to add the following note:

> We made the mistake, in our *Division of Labor*, of presenting material density too much as the exact expression of dynamic density. Nevertheless, the substitution of the former for the latter is absolutely legitimate for whatever concerns the economic effects of the latter, e.g., the division of labor as a purely economic fact.[44]

If this "confession" were true, then the *Division* could be saved insofar as it concerned the division of labor as an economic fact. But this, one must recall, was actually the opposite of Durkheim's earlier intention, which was precisely to explain its moral significance. More to the point, the confession itself is falsely conceived, for Durkheim implies here that his present definition of "dynamic intensity" as a specifically moral and emotional fact applied to the *Division* as well. This was emphatically not the case, however, for Durkheim had treated moral and material density as synonymous, offering the same demographic and economic causes for the first as for the second. Whether he will admit to it or not, Durkheim has effectively reversed the logic of his earlier work. In doing so he has resolved the critical challenge toward which his attention was always directed, but he has also opened himself up to problems of a totally different kind. Durkheim has embarked upon an idealist path.

1.2. SOCIALISM *AND* SUICIDE: *EXCHANGE AND ASSOCIATION AS MORALITY AND AFFECT*

The trajectory of Durkheim's early career had been similar to Marx's: he had given up on the independent normative status of morality in order to pursue, in *Division*, a more materialist path. Now Durkheim has reversed the momentum that led him to this initial, flawed work of his maturity, and he has taken the opposite road to the one followed by the mature Marx. Marx had earlier held the notion that man's "praxis" infused his social environment with recognizable meaning and emotion, and his portrayal of social institutions as manifestations of human spirit closely resembled the one that Durkheim now assumes. However, as Marx moved toward an appreciation and then an overappreciation of the economic elements in collective order, he argued that in capitalism this praxis could not provide the infusion of meaning and emotion that he had earlier supposed. Praxis, which in Hegel's terms could be seen as a continuous process by which internal emotion is "reified" to form external structure, was now viewed as alienated, its subjective components essentially negated. With the transition back to an altruistic and emotional conception of action, Durkheim is asserting that praxis does not assume such an alienated form. He rejects the historicization of presuppositional logic that Marx assumes in his later writings, and which Durkheim himself proposed in the *Division of Labor.* Action still has an emotional element, and social structure therefore retains its connection to the actor's meaning and intention. Although Hegel is not the source for this development, Hegelian notions recur throughout Durkheim's later work, and we find—in terms of presuppositional commitments, at least—the younger spiritualized Marx in sociological form.

But if Marx falsely reduced reification to alienation, Durkheim makes the opposite kind of mistake. Although Durkheim acknowledges the autonomy of crystallized structure from immediate individual control, he is confident that the sense of "former praxis," as it were, can be reconstructed. Where in the *Division of Labor* Durkheim assumes that structure in modern society almost always assumes a materialist form, in his subsequent writings he will rarely admit that it ever does so. Praxis may be reified, but it is never alienated to the point that it becomes an inhuman, purely objective structure that operates without any reference to the wishes of individuals. This is a serious error, and it will prevent Durkheim's later theorizing from presenting a completely satisfactory theory of the society as a whole. Yet for all of that, Durkheim has made, in this critique of his former materialism, a tremendous breakthrough, one which would have to inform any theory that would not abandon the voluntaristic element of social life. In the two years following the initial publication of *Rules*, in the last two works of what might be called the "middle period" of 1894–1896, he makes this breakthrough more empirically specific, and it is to the consideration of these works that I now turn.

In the years 1894–1895, Durkheim offered a series of lectures on a subject in which he had been interested before he had ever taken up sociology, namely, the problem of socialism. Since Durkheim's initial theoretical formulations had been stimulated by an ideological commitment to socialism, it was only natural that after the cataclysmic theoretical reformulation of the previous year he would wish to return to this normative issue for further reflection. It is true that in the course of these lectures, published posthumously as *Le Socialisme* and in English as *Socialism and Saint-Simon*, Durkheim never denies the existence of economic classes and material inequality. Yet his explanations of how this inequality was created, why it produces social unhappiness, and how it will be overcome are radically different not only from the theories of Marx's maturity but also from Durkheim's own positions in the *Division of Labor*. It is as if Durkheim has wrapped *Capital* in a gauze, bracketing the economic laws in a way that makes them irrelevant to the very problems of which Marx tried to make them a reflection.

The theme of Durkheim's lectures is the role of the state, for he defines socialism as the regulation of the economy by a centralized polity. Yet this political discussion is imbedded in an implicit general theory of modern society as a whole. Durkheim views society as the product of moral exchange and symbolic communication, and the state, which he describes as the "directing and conscious center," assumes its directing role only as it is imbedded in these processes. This state does not fix the environment of action by producing the organizational and material arrangements for an artificial identity of interests; it gains its effectiveness, rather, through intelligence and insight, by regulating the moral exchange and symbolic communication that occurs between diverse social groupings. Durkheim makes an analogy with the brain:

> Everything that occurs in the various administrations, in local deliberating assemblies, in public education, in the army, etc., is susceptible of reaching the "social brain," by paths specially destined to assure these communications, so that the state is kept up to date without the surrounding portions of society being notified. Further, there are other paths of the same kind, by which the state sends back its action to the secondary centers. Between them there are continuing and diversified exchanges.[45]

It is on the basis of this general theory that Durkheim analyzes the problems of capitalism—or, as he calls it, "early industrial society"—and the means by which socialism can resolve them.

Durkheim always believed that socialism would be viable only if it could achieve regulation in a voluntary way. Schaeffle had shown him that this middle road could be achieved only if socialist regulation was conceived as a kind of spontaneous occurrence, the result of a reciprocal interaction among different social parts. This notion disappeared, however, after Durkheim moved toward a more instrumental orientation. Armed with his newly clarified theoretical understanding, Durkheim returns to Schaeffle's schematic proposal. First, he redefines the problem of capitalism in a strikingly anti-instrumental way. Capitalism is inadequate because it excludes economic life from the process of communication by which the state regulates the rest of social life; in capitalism, the economy can "activate" this directing center only "feebly and intermittently."[46] But it is particularly the laboring class which suffers from this exclusion, for without any wider communication it cannot make the state and public opinion conscious of the inequities of its position. "By wedging himself between worker and society," Durkheim writes, "[the capitalist] prevents labor from being properly appreciated and rewarded according to its social value."[47] The solution to this moral exclusion can be overcome only by placing the working class into communication with the other centers of society, to reestablish the "connection of all economic functions . . . to the directing and conscious centers of society."[48] Socialism equalizes moral exchange, in other words, by creating "constant communication" between the economy and society. This new communication, Durkheim insists, involves the "rapport" between economic and political functions, not the "subordination" of the former to the latter. Coercion is not necessary, since renewed "contact" will create moral understanding and social reform.[49]

But if moral regulation is the only path by which effective structural reform can occur, it is also needed to reformulate the motives of the economic actors themselves. Because the really significant stimulus to action is internal, dissatisfaction can be ameliorated only if reform affects the actor's motivation as well as his environment. "Appetites cannot be appeased unless they are limited," Durkheim writes, "and they cannot be limited except by something other than themselves."[50] The new access to moral communication, then, will serve a double purpose. It will lead not only to structural reform but to new self-control and internal commitments among the formerly excluded actors. Durkheim now insists that the crucial solutions in the third book of his *Division of Labor*, reorganization and redistribution, will be ineffective unless the "state of our morality" is also reformed.[51] In reference to the former proposal, Durkheim warns that "in any social organization, however skillfully ordered, economic functions cannot co-operate harmoniously nor be maintained in a state of equilibrium unless subject to moral forces which surpass, contain, and regulate them."[52] His critique of the redistributive solution is even more direct. "Picture," he invites the reader, "the most productive economic organization possible and a distribution of wealth which assures abundance to even the humblest." What would be the result? "Perhaps," Durkheim admits, "such a transformation, at the very moment it was constituted, would produce an instant of gratification." "But this gratification," he insists, "could only be temporary," for desires, "though calmed for an instant, will quickly acquire new exigencies."[53]

> What is needed if social order is to reign is that the mass of men be content with their lot. But what is needed for them to be content, is not that they have more or less but that they be convinced they have no right to more. And for this, it is absolutely essential that there be an authority whose superiority they acknowledge and which tells them what is right.[54†]

If the strains in capitalism are normative, and the solutions that Durkheim proposes are moral as well, it is only logical that he should describe the movement to establish socialism as motivated by considerations of a similar kind. The long-term reason for the birth of socialism is the growth in the ideal of equality. "This new inclination," Durkheim writes, "is the feeling—stronger and more generalized—of social justice; it is the belief that the position of citizens in societies and the remuneration of their services should vary exactly with their social value."[55] Only after the sentiment of equality has become widespread do men react against material inequality, for only then does it violate their inner sense of what social order should be. "If inequality is thought of as unnatural, it is because men's consciences have rejected the idea of it."[56] Durkheim invokes here, one should note, the very same social process that he had once relegated primarily to "mechanical societies": the unthinking, automatic outcry against any act that violates the collective conscience. Yet if this deep-seated indignation against the "crime" of inequality is the fundamental basis for the movement for socialism, it is not its most efficient cause. For this revulsion to create institutional reform it must be translated into the political regulation of economic activity. This can only come about, Durkheim believes, through the moral redefinition of the relation between economic and political life. Such a shift in the public conscience occurred in France only after the Revolution of 1789, inspired in good part by the growth of statist values: "The political transformations of the revolutionary epoch brought about the extention to the economic order of the ideas and tendencies of which they themselves were the result."[57]

Once the sentiment of equality has been established and the means for its specification has come into being, the socialist transformation depends upon the movement among workers themselves. Committed to

ideas of equality and armed with the knowledge that the state can intervene, workers respond to their excluded situation with the "cry of grief"
that is socialism.[58] Socialism is an "idea" and it gains "inspiration" and
"fervor" from the association of the workers who believe in it.[59] The goal
of this association is to broaden its scope, indeed, to abolish the narrow
grounds of its existence: the workers want to be included in the wider
interaction of the society as a whole, to be part of the dominant moral
order even as they effectively transform it.

> What they desire . . . when they demand better treatment, is to be
> no longer kept at a distance from the centers presiding over col-
> lective life but be bound to them more or less intimately. The
> changes they hope for are only one form and result of this more
> complete integration.[60†]

Durkheim's lectures on socialism have rarely been the object of theoretical analysis, and on the occasions when they have provided a focus
they usually have been taken as an indication of Durkheim's early continuity with Marxism and materialism rather than as an announcement
of his opposition.[61†] The attitude toward his famous work on suicide,
completed in 1896 and published the following year, has, of course, been
far different. *Suicide* has received enormous critical attention. Still, this
secondary analysis has more often been aimed at Durkheim's propositions and method than at his more generalized concerns. When general
issues have become the point of focus, moreover, *Suicide* has been
treated in isolation. First, it has not been related to the lectures on socialism, which were given during the period of Durkheim's most intense
work on the book. Second, it has been viewed as a break with the positivism and purported rationalism of *Rules*.[62†] I will demonstrate, to the contrary, that *Suicide* merely specifies the theoretical revolution that *Rules*
initiated. If *Le Socialisme* can be viewed as polemically directed against
the third Book of the *Division of Labor*, *Suicide* can be seen as directed
primarily against the second book, where Durkheim formulated his instrumental theory of association and material density as the crucial factors of group formation.

Suicide gives the lie to Durkheim's claim that *Rules* is a retrospective
explication of the method and substance of the *Division of Labor*. *Suicide*
reveals that *Rules* is actually prospective, that it looks ahead to the formation of a new kind of empirical analysis. Despite its apparently empirical purpose, its careful attention to method and factual proposition,
Suicide closely follows the theoretical prolegomena that Durkheim laid
out in 1894. Its object of investigation is a "social fact," the propensity to
suicide which Durkheim attributes to "suicidogenic currents" and defines as a "collective force of a definite amount of energy."[63] As this definition indicates, the inclination to suicide, like other social facts, has a

collective status, and I will analyze how it orders individual actions shortly. To understand fully this discussion of "pathology," however, it is crucial to establish the broader framework that Durkheim provides.

As Durkheim indicated in *Rules*, social facts have a base, and in *Suicide* he defines this "substratum" the same way as in that earlier work. What constitutes society, Durkheim writes, is a certain number of "beliefs and practices." The more "numerous and strong" these beliefs and practices are—the greater their density in a specifically moral sense—the stronger the integration of the society of which they are a part.[64] Indeed, here Durkheim makes the strongest statement yet of his transvaluation of the substratum concept. Society, he argues, has a "psychical existence."[65]

But it is in the analysis of the formation of this "psychical" substratum that *Suicide* presents the real advance over Durkheim's two earlier works, for Durkheim now shows precisely how the natural sentiments for altruistic action are linked to association and hence to group structure. Once again, he emphasizes the dualistic nature of man, part of whose nature concerns physical existence and individual concerns, while another part, composed of "sentiments of sympathy and solidarity," directs itself to "transcendental purposes." It is by these sentiments, Durkheim writes, that we are drawn toward others.[66] When persons are in contact with one another, this instinct for sociability creates association. During the course of association, individuals transfer some of their individual psychic energy to the sentiments that circulate in the group. Sentiments which are most common, or most strongly held, receive the greatest energy. "Where collective sentiments are strong," Durkheim writes, "it is because the force with which they affect each individual conscience is echoed in all the others, and reciprocally."[67] The dominant ideas and opinions that result are examples of the crystallized emotion that Durkheim described in *Rules*. This newly crystallized form, infused with the energy from group interaction, helps integrate the group. Its energy reinvigorates the affective and moral exchange upon which it was based.

> There is, in short, in a cohesive and animated society a constant interchange of ideas and feelings from all to each and each to all, something like a mutual moral support, which instead of throwing the individual on his own resources, leads him to share in the collective energy and supports his own when exhausted.[68]

The social order that results from this association of nonrational actors is adhered to in a voluntary way, not simply because the dominant ideas are attractive to those who helped produce them but, more profoundly, because these ideas are part of the actors themselves. When Durkheim speaks of "society itself incarnated and individualized in each one of us" he has broken completely with the "substantialist" conception of the individual—what I have called the "concrete" individual—which provided such a roadblock in his earlier work.[69†] Because order can be located inside the actor, adherence to order can become part of individual desire itself. Order can be located within because it is a psychical, nonmaterial entity: it can cross the physical boundaries of the individual body and enter into the imagination. Its status is psychical because it results from interchanges of emotion and remains forever no more than the crystallization of affect more or less formed. This interchange, finally, can occur only because men are motivated by feelings of sympathy that lead them to solidary association with others whenever possible. For these reasons, then, insofar as people are not acting in a nonsocial, completely individualistic way, they yield to the authority of society "spontaneously."[70] Force and violence, Durkheim insists, have no place in the establishment of collective order.

> When we say that an authority is necessary to impose this order on individuals, we certainly do not mean that violence is the only means of establishing it. Since this regulation is meant to restrain individual passions, it must come from a power which dominates individuals; but this power must also be obeyed through respect, not fear.[71]

The overtly empirical point of Durkheim's book, the explanation of suicide, can now be addressed. The social fact under consideration, suicidogenic currents, is the result of social disequilibrium, but this is not the kind of material or physical maladjustment that was the point of Durkheim's account in the *Division of Labor*.[72] It is rather the "moral constitution of society" that "establishes the contingent of voluntary deaths."[73] Hence it can be understood that the empirical subject of this book, suicide, really has a double meaning, for it is employed to demonstrate a theoretical as well as an empirical fact. Suicide is self-inflicted punishment, but Durkheim's theoretical explanation makes it paradigmatic of self-motivated action in general. What Durkheim tries to demonstrate is that this isolated human act actually represents the voluntary adherence to a pathological form of collective order, an order of "moral individualism."[74] The structures that control it, of course, are primarily invisible, "currents of egoism, altruism or anomie" which express themselves through the highly subjective emotions of individuals, through the "tendencies to languorous melancholy, active renunciation or exasperated weariness derivative from these currents."[75] For all his polemic against individualistic explanations, it is, in the end, these highly personal *feelings* of self-destruction that Durkheim emphasizes in his description of egoism and anomie. The individual's low estimation of the value of existence leads to egoistic suicide: it is because "we *feel* detached from society" that we actually become so. When Durkheim describes the "currents of depression and disillusionment" that can create such detachment, he uses the technique of the inner voice, presenting the internal dialogue which the depressed egoist has with himself.

> For what purpose do these rules of morality, these precepts of law binding us to all sorts of sacrifices, these restrictive dogmas exist, if there is no being outside us whom they serve and in whom we participate? What is the purpose of science itself? . . . What is the end of suffering, above all? . . . The more the believer doubts . . . the more does he become a mystery to himself, unable to escape the exasperating and agonizing question: to what purpose?[76]

Egoistic currents, quite clearly, produce their effects because the egoist cannot answer satisfactorily these internal questions. Anomie operates in a similar manner. Its substance is an "article of faith," the belief that the race belongs only to the ruthless and the swift. Once again, Durkheim refers to the anomic actor's inner thoughts to demonstrate the volition upon which this external current depends.

> Greed is aroused without knowing where to find ultimate foothold. Nothing can calm it, since its goal is far beyond all it can attain. Reality seems valueless by comparison with the dreams of fevered imaginations. . . . Nothing remains behind or ahead of [the greedy] to fix his gaze upon. Weariness alone, moreover, is enough to bring disillusionment, for he cannot in the end escape the futility of endless pursuit.[77]

There are times in Durkheim's analysis of anomie when he refers to changes in objective conditions, to the shift in collective revenues, to economic depressions and booms. But he emphasizes at every point that these changes can have a deleterious effect only if there is, at the same time, "moral declassification." It is changes in the public conscience, not the objective inability for functional adaptation, that lead to the kind of voluntary action with which Durkheim is concerned.[78] Indeed, in *Suicide* Durkheim conducts a thinly veiled polemic against any material explanation at all. To what, he asks, do the effects of economic crisis on suicide owe their influence? "Is it because they increase poverty by causing public wealth to fluctuate? Is life more readily renounced as it becomes more difficult?" Durkheim dismisses with barely concealed contempt such "seductively simple proposals."[79] Such statements, of course, can be taken as mere empirical commentaries asserting the falsity of specific propositions about the concrete case at hand. But, in fact, they have a much more general ring, and it seems that Durkheim is, once again, using suicide as a paradigmatic case for theoretical logic. Is it simply empirical considerations that lead Durkheim to insist, so broadly, that "economic distress does not have the aggravating influence so often attributed to it" and to argue that the "material comfort of workers," the "growth in [their] glory and power," leads often to further unhappiness?[80] His underlying point is clearly not empirical but theoretical, namely, that the most significant forces of order are not material and that internal resources, not external ones, are the crucial predictors of action.

Durkheim's concluding discussion of how the pathological rate of suicide can be ameliorated contains an even more direct refutation of his earlier position. What must be created, he argues, is a "new sort of moral discipline." This can only be the product, in turn, of much more intense association between workers and capitalists and among workers themselves. Within these new occupational groupings, "when the relations between themselves and the group to which they belong are thus close and continuous, sentiments of solidarity as yet almost unknown will spring up, and the present cold moral temperature of this occupational environment, still so external to its members, would necessarily rise." It is not the material but the moral environment of men that must be reformed, and once this new affective association occurs it will create a moral discipline far stronger than that of any material force or self-interested group.

> Standing above its own members, it [this new moral discipline] would have all necessary authority to demand indispensable sacrifices and concessions and impose order upon them. By forcing the strongest to use their strength with moderation, by preventing the weakest from endlessly multiplying their protests, by recalling both to the sense of their reciprocal duties and the general interest, and by regulating production in certain cases so that it does not degenerate into a morbid fever, it would moderate one set of passions by another, and permit their appeasement by assigning them limits.[81†]

A number of critics, particularly recent English and American ones, have misunderstood the status of interaction and association in this middle phase of Durkheim's development. They have called Durkheim's emphasis a "structural" one, making analogy to Marx's theory of the power of society over consciousness and to the determination of the economic base over the cultural superstructure. Perhaps these analysts have taken Durkheim's rhetoric as accurately reflecting theoretical reality, but it is likely that they have also made a much more important error, one that concerns basic questions of the nature of theoretical logic. They have, it seems, failed to distinguish the difference between sociological idealism and materialism, and they have done so because they have failed to distinguish the question of action from that of order. Durkheim emphasizes the collective, extra-individual status of social sanctions, and in this his theorizing appears similar to Marx's own. But the fact that there are social "structures" of interaction does not in any way indicate a materialist intention, for it is the nature of this collective order that is crucial, not simply its existence.[82†] Order is specifically defined only when we understand the nature of the action that informs it. For Durkheim, this action is anti-instrumental, motivated by feelings of solidarity and sentiments of altruism. The order therefore is subjective. It resides inside the actor and cannot present him with impersonal, ineluctable alternatives from without. Durkheim's order is the structuring of ends, not means; it cannot encompass "scarcity" or the external coercion that organizes scarce means to dominate and control. Durkheim can no more do this than Marx could encompass the inner springs of order that Durkheim has begun to lay out. Durkheim is not an idealist in the philosophical sense; he recognizes objects which are external to the actor ontologically: hence his very emphasis on association. The crucial issue, however, is how these social objects become activated. For Durkheim, the arrangement of social objects in the world represents the social distribution of affect and morality. Durkheim's interest cannot be described as socially structured sentiment; it is, rather, sentimentally structured society. He has created a *sociological* idealism, and it is in this creation that his greatest achievement lies.

There are, of course, a number of critics who have recognized the nonobjective nature of Durkheim's theorizing. Yet even here there is usually a certain confusion about the precise status of this achievement. Some would view this theorizing as sufficient in itself, refusing to recognize the one-sidedness of the new position that Durkheim has so brilliantly articulated. Others argue that Durkheim had maintained such an exclusively normative position all along—that, in fact, the writings of the middle period merely expand and amplify the *Division of Labor* and his earliest writings as well.[83†] My own position has been that Durkheim's middle-period work presents an extraordinary accomplishment that is radically antithetical to the momentum of his earlier work. From the latter part of 1893 through 1896, Durkheim rewrote the central theses of his first sociological theory. The period began after Durkheim's assertion in the *Division of Labor* that the collective utilitarian model was basically correct, an admission that had reduced his historical theory to an impoverished version of Marxist analysis. By the period's conclusion, he had overthrown the utilitarian model and begun a theory that instead of mimicking Marxism would present its most challenging alternative.

1.3. THE THEORETICAL STATUS AND CAUSES OF DURKHEIM'S INNOVATION

It is impossible to explain this break in Durkheim's work without reference to the most generalized level of his thought. Durkheim could only have been severely dissatisfied with his theoretical position in the *Divi-*

sion of Labor, a dissatisfaction which is amply evidenced by that work's extraordinary ambivalence. I have demonstrated, moreover, how this presuppositional ambivalence, this constant back-and-forth movement between aggressive assertion and just as aggressive denial, colored Durkheim's writings from the very beginning of his career. Only such long-standing theoretical dissatisfaction could explain how Durkheim could have written two essays that implicitly refuted the *Division*—and which essentially returned to positions earlier laid out—in the very shadow of its publication. Certainly no shifts in the political environment could have reversed Durkheim's development if he had not already been so inclined, nor could critical scholarly reaction have moved him to such anger and dismay, and ultimately to internal revision, if his original position had not been so insecure. To the contrary, it was precisely because Durkheim himself had such profound misgivings about his stance in the *Division* that these other developments had such an effect.

The early 1890s marked the renewal of Marxism in French society. This was stimulated in part by increased class conflict in the political and economic realms, as indicated, for instance, by the election in 1893 of fifty socialists—by no means all of the Marxian variety—to the French parliament and by the great upsurge in strikes and worker protests that characterized this period.[84] These social developments were certainly not primarily stimulated by Marxian ideology, but they constituted, nonetheless, important reasons for the growing attention that French intellectuals paid to Marxist theory.[85] Leading journals like the *Revue de métaphysique et de morale* and the *Revue philosophique*, where Durkheim had published most of his important early work, published ongoing discussions of socialist theory and reviewed numerous works by Marx and Engels and their followers. The first exclusively sociological journal in France, the *Revue internationale de sociologie*, also devoted considerable space to articles on socialism and Marx, and in the first issue of the *Annales de l'Institut international de sociologie* historical materialism became the focus of a number of the authors. This new enthusiasm for Marxism spread even to Durkheim's inner circle. "Some of the most brilliant among his own students," writes Durkheim's nephew and collaborator Marcel Mauss, "were converted to socialism, especially Marxism." Mauss adds that "in one 'Social Study' circle, some examined *Capital* as they elsewhere considered Spinoza."[86]

This contextual information allows Durkheim's predicament in the early 1890s to be hypothetically reconstructed. He had just concluded his first major work, a treatment which he had already begun to regret and which he concluded he had better revise. Yet he was in the midst of the revival in popularity of a system of thought that seemed closely to resemble the one he had just published, not only in its ideological commitment to socialism and science, but in its presuppositions and its empirical analysis of modern society. He must have wished very much to distinguish his new ideas from those of Marxism, without indicating, of course, that they differed in any way from those he had previously held. When he realized that his French audience viewed him as a confirmed materialist very much in the Marxist mode, if not a Marxist himself, his sense of frustration may be easily imagined.[87†]

Almost without exception, the reviews that Durkheim received in the four years following publication of the *Division of Labor* presented his subsequent writing—as he himself had asked for it to be read—merely as the extension of that first work. They were in universal agreement, moreover, that the *Division* had been one-sidedly materialist in its orientation.[88†] Durkheim never acknowledged even the partial validity of these critical reviews, and he carried a bitter resentment against them throughout the rest of his life. In the Preface to the first edition of *Rules* in 1895 he protests against "what critics have called our 'positivism'," objecting that although his method "will perhaps be judged crude and will possibly be termed 'materialistic'," it is actually nothing of the kind.[89] In the second Preface, in 1901, Durkheim appears even more frustrated, since "on the very points on which we had expressed ourselves most explicitly, views were freely attributed to us which had nothing in common with our own; and opponents held that they were refuting us in refuting these mistaken ideas."[90†] A year after his first protest, in 1896, Durkheim sent off a fiery letter protesting the views of another critic.[91†] In 1898, Durkheim's younger follower Célèstin Bouglé wrote a long critical essay refuting still another "misinterpretation" of Durkheimian sociology, and Durkheim complained in a private letter to Bouglé that he had "never dreamt of saying that one could do sociology without any psychological background, or that sociology is anything other than a form of psychology."[92†] In the year preceding, Durkheim had written in the concluding section of *Suicide:* "We do not expect to be reproached further, after this explanation, with wishing to substitute the exterior for the interior in sociology."[93] Fifteen years later he is making the same complaint, protesting in *The Elementary Forms of Religious Life* against the materialist label which has been attached to his work and offering the "hope that this analysis and those which follow will put an end to [such] an inexact interpretation of our thought, from which more than one misunderstanding has resulted."[94] Yet it was the criticism of the early period which stung Durkheim most sharply, for at that time he was not the famous *maître* that he had become in his later years. Mauss recounts Durkheim's belief that the attacks on him as materialist had kept him from receiving the professorships in Paris which he so ardently sought and which he surely deserved.[95†] This practical consideration could only have exacerbated the enormous frustration that Durkheim already felt.

The social and intellectual climate which Durkheim faced, then, underlined the urgency of his theoretical task: he had to find a way to articulate collective order in a manner that left the autonomy of the individual actor in no doubt. To achieve this articulation, he had to break with some of the central themes of his earlier work. He had already begun this task in 1893; the hostile reception he received from his critics, and his fears about his isolation from the center of French intellectual life, caused him to redouble his efforts to clarify and specify the position he had newly proposed. He broke with the *Division of Labor* for theoretical reasons and for ideological ones, for careerist motives and because of pedagogical ambition. Durkheim wanted to clear his good name, for his own conscience and for the good opinion of others. We have seen the first results of this effort in the works of 1894–1896. The effort at theoretical self-clarification continues in the years following, and with extraordinary results.

2. SPIRITUALIZING MORALITY: RELIGION AS THE MODEL OF VOLUNTARY ORDER

Durkheim never abandoned the general model he established in his middle period, the subjectification of collective order that Filloux calls the theory of "expressive causality."[96] The dual nature of man was a recurrent theme in Durkheim's work for the rest of his life. The most self-conscious statement of this position came in 1914, in one of the last essays he ever wrote. Here Durkheim criticizes utilitarian theorists for their belief that "man is one," and that "moral activity is only another aspect of self-interested activity."[97] By contrast, Durkheim emphasizes that duality is "one of the most characteristic peculiarities of our nature."[98] He acknowledges that in one part of our nature, we are concerned with "sensations and sensory tendencies" like hunger or thirst. But such appetites, he insists, can be only egoistic: "They have our individuality and it alone as their object." Another part of our nature, however, is concerned with "conceptual thought and moral activity," a capacity which is "distinguished by the fact that the rules of conduct to which they conform can be universalized." By definition, therefore, this part of human nature "pursue[s] impersonal ends," for "morality begins with disinterest, with attachment to something other than ourselves."[99] But the richest and most expressive statements about man's dual nature occur in Durkheim's more casual discussions. In his 1902 Preface to the *Division of Labor*, for example, he writes that individuals associate simply "to have the pleasure of communing [*le plaisir de communier*], to make one out of many."[100†] In that same year, in his lectures on professional ethics, Durkheim makes the same point in a more ample way.

When individuals who share the same interests come together, their purpose is not simply to safeguard those interests or to secure their development in face of rival associations. It is, rather, *just to associate, for the sole pleasure of mixing with their fellows and of no longer feeling lost in the midst of adversaries, as well as for the pleasure of communing together,* that is, in short, of being able to lead their lives with the same moral aim.[101]

This innate desire to live together continues to be the analytic basis for Durkheim's subjective approach to collective order, for it is this desire that leads individuals to deep, nonutilitarian association with others whenever the possibility arises. Durkheim never puts this connection between action and order more explicitly than in one of the lectures comprising the posthumously published *Moral Education.*

> It might be said that since altruistic drives, when they are satisfied, give us satisfaction, they are selfish like any other drives. But there is always this considerable difference: that in the one case we find our satisfaction in the pursuit of objects personal to ourselves; whereas in the other case we find satisfaction in the pursuit of objects that, although they penetrate our consciousness symbolically, are nevertheless not distinctive elements of our personality.[102]

Once initiated, this association with others liberates and circulates affect, the energy that Durkheim at various points describes as a free current, a liquid, a fluid.[103] But association also crystallizes this liquid emotion, for once it is removed from its origin in the individual it can become reshaped in a variety of different forms and degrees of concreteness. Sometimes this energy is "so far materialized as to become an element of the external world," but even in these cases collective order retains its subjective character, for it is merely human affect "fixed on material supports."[104]

Yet Durkheim still was far from being completely satisfied with the theorizing of these middle years. If he never abandoned this model of association at its most general level, he was, nonetheless, unhappy with its failure to specify the voluntaristic order he had in mind. "We must confess," he wrote in *Suicide,* "that we have only a vague idea of . . . the complex process whence come collective sentiments."

> We know little as yet how and according to what laws mental states of even the single individual combine; much less do we know of the mechanism of the far more complicated combinations produced by group-existence. Our explanations are often mere metaphors.[105]

Although Durkheim never indicated explicitly what his reservations were, once his theoretical ambition is understood they are not difficult to see. Durkheim's model of how social facts affect individuals still retains a certain mechanistic quality. In *Suicide*, for example, despite his sensitivity to internal volition as the expression of order, he often presents the causes of suicide in a very different manner. Suicidogenic currents, he insists, cause death by striking "the individual's weak points, where the outside current bearing the impulse to self-destruction most easily finds introduction."[106] The deterministic, quasi-materialist quality of such an empirical statement clearly contradicts Durkheim's theoretical intent.[107†] He would have to learn still more about the "complex process" by which collective sentiments were formed, about the "laws of mental states," before his theoretical ambition could be fulfilled.

2.1. THE "REVELATION": DURKHEIM'S ENCOUNTER WITH THE SACRED

At a later and more secure point in his intellectual career, Durkheim talked about the "revelation" that had allowed him to resolve the difficulties of this middle period. "It was not until 1895," he wrote, "that I achieved a clear sense of the essential role played by religion in social life."

> It was in that year that, for the first time, I found the means of tackling the study of religion sociologically. This was a revelation to me. That course of 1895 marks a dividing line in the development of my thought, to such an extent that all my previous researches had to be taken up afresh in order to be made to harmonize with these new insights. . . . [This reorientation was due] entirely to the studies of religious history which I had just undertaken, and notably to the reading of the works of Robertson Smith and his school.[108†]

Durkheim refers here to the course on religion which he first offered at Bordeaux in the school year of 1894/95, and we will see shortly that the discovery, or rediscovery, of the significance of religion did in fact have an enormous impact on his sociological work. Indeed, by the time *Suicide* appeared in print, Durkheim had already embarked upon a new phase of theoretical development, one which emphasized the "spiritual" aspects of social life. No more than halfway through the transitional "middle period," therefore, Durkheim had begun significantly to rethink the very model of social life and association which had itself constituted a major innovation and break with his intellectual development. This rethinking was, as Durkheim himself recounts, stimulated and guided by his encounter with religion. While it would seem to be less revolutionary than Durkheim would have us believe, the encounter was, nevertheless, far more profound than his interpreters have yet recognized.

In 1895 Durkheim faced the same kind of dilemma which I earlier described as having stimulated his initial movement away from an instrumentalist theory. On the one hand, as has just been seen, he was not completely satisfied with this new phase of his theoretical development, particularly because it did not fully articulate the voluntary order that he was striving to achieve. At the same time, moreover, he had strong evidence before him that his critics did not recognize the theoretical departure that *Rules* represented. Almost without exception, the reviewers treated *Rules*—as Durkheim himself explicitly advised—simply as the extension of the materialist method of his earlier work. For both these reasons, then, Durkheim must have felt compelled to search for a way of making his revolutionary subjectification of social order at once more explicit and more refined. It was in this context that he gave his course on religion and encountered the new anthropological writings of Smith and his followers. Soon after, he gave to his model of secular society a directly religious cast. With this, he made the voluntaristic quality of his theoretical system as forthright and unmistakable as it could possibly be.[109†]

By the time Durkheim encountered Smith, he already shared Smith's emphasis on the human practice, or association, that underlined any commitment to ideal beliefs;[110†] the difference was simply that Smith applied this thinking about the relation between beliefs and practices to religious activity, not to social action in general. Durkheim could have been so attracted to Smith only because he himself had already embarked on a similar path. It is perplexing, therefore, that Durkheim's public statement insists that his encounter with Smith initiated a much more radical break, one that forced him completely to rethink all his previous work. One must recall, however, that Durkheim never publicly admitted, and may himself never consciously have been aware, that his writing had already taken a dramatic turn with the earlier publication of *Rules*. Unfortunately, those Durkheim interpreters who acknowledge the discontinuity of his work have also accepted Durkheim's own account of the singular impact of his encounter with religion. These critics do not, however, have the excuse of Durkheim's understandable lack of self-consciousness; they have simply taken Durkheim at his word, marking the encounter with religion as an epistemological break sui generis. But one should not fully accept Durkheim's own account, for he did not, in fact, really abandon all of his pre-1895 sociology. Indeed, it was the momentum created by his earlier shift that led him to find in the anthropology of religion the more voluntaristic vocabulary he so urgently sought. The subjective model of association was already in place by early 1894. When Durkheim encounters religion later that year, or in 1895, there is more of a convergence than a radical break. Rather than a call to start anew, Durkheim sees in this writing on religion a means of finally completing his own theoretical development. He reads this theory of religion in a way that meshes perfectly with his own developing theory of association.

Thus, rather than his taking over a model of religion and merely applying it to secular society, there was a constant interplay between his theorizing about the sacred and secular worlds. One can find no better example of this interrelationship than Durkheim's first major article on religion, published in 1899, which is clearly influenced by the sociology of the middle period while going beyond it in certain fundamental ways.

Although Durkheim had written on primitive religion already in the previous year, it is only in this essay, "De la définition des phénomènes religieux" (On the definition of religious phenomena), that he articulates his new thinking in a general way. Religion, Durkheim insists, is composed not only of beliefs but of practices as well.[111] At first he establishes this point by criticizing the notion that religion is somehow produced by the conception of a divine being.[112] The divine, he says, is only an example of sacred things. More importantly, however, he argues that no religious ideas can exist without reference to rites, or cults.[113] The rite, in fact, is nothing other than a certain kind of practice, or "defined ways of acting," and this underlying action is of a "sympathetic" kind.[114]

But Durkheim notes, quite rightly in terms of his earlier association theory, that this definition of actions and beliefs fails to differentiate religion from other kinds of secular activities like morality and law. The difference, he argues, is that religion "is an ensemble of practices which concern *sacred things.*"[115] The crucial quality of religious phenomena, then, resides in the sacred, which Durkheim defines as presenting a single distinctive particularity, namely, that "the society which professes them does not permit its members to deny them."[116] Sacred beliefs, above all, are defined by this quality of denying "interdiction," but this interdiction is not always sanctioned by punishments in the traditional sense of the term, nor is the transgression always called a crime. Nevertheless, sacred beliefs impose themselves in an obligatory way: their force simply comes more from respect than from fear of retribution.[117] Only after defining the role of ritual and the nature of the sacred can one understand Durkheim's final definition of divinity. It is, he writes, an individualistic formulation of the sacred that concentrates and concretizes collective sentiments.[118] It is a principle that groups and unifies society by giving to collective sentiments a material form.[119]

The parallels between this definition of religious phenomena and the theoretical model of Durkheim's middle period could not be more explicit. Like the social phenomena that he had defined earlier, religion is composed of practices and beliefs. The practices are based upon sympathetic sentiments that inspire association, and this association produces objects that present emotions in a more or less materialized form. In fact, by the final pages of his 1899 article Durkheim has completely reversed the very point that had allowed him to maintain the distinction between religious and secular things, for he now admits that secular phenomena can also partake of the sacred. He begins by admitting that "it is true that between science and religious faith there exist intermediaries; these are common beliefs of every sort connected to objects that are secular in appearance, such as the flag, one's country, some form of political organization, certain heroes or historical events." Indeed, he concludes, "they are, in a certain measure, indistinguishable from beliefs that are properly religious." The identification is now complete. The "motherland, the French Revolution, Joan of Arc," Durkheim concludes, "are for us sacred things." As such, they are invested with the same sanctions against interdiction as properly religious facts: "We do not permit them to be touched." "Public opinion," Durkheim writes, "does not willingly allow one to contest the moral superiority of democracy, the reality of progress, [or] the idea of equality, just as the Christian does not allow his fundamental dogmas to be questioned."[120] It is still possible to distinguish religious from secular beliefs, but the quality of sacredness is no longer the point of distinction. It is not the fact of sacredness but its particular content; sacred beliefs are religious only if they explicitly embrace the reality of another world, if they are cosmological.[121] But it is impossible for any collective beliefs to escape the rubric of the sacred itself. Just as we sense things under the form of color, Durkheim writes, "society represents to itself its life and that of the objects with which it is in relation under the form of sacred things. . . . It colors them with religiosity."[122]† Sacred beliefs, then, cover everything "for which society itself has elaborated the representation." These elements "are combined according to the appropriate laws of the social mentality."[123]

With this shift in his definition of the sacred, it becomes evident why Durkheim was so eager to apply to religion the sociological form of his middle-period work. If religion is basically social in its form, the social can also be said to be basically religious. Durkheim began by writing an article about religious phenomena, but he ended by writing about the religious society. What he really wanted to demonstrate, it turns out, is that secular processes actually have a sacred form. Now he will be able to discover the "laws of mental life" that only two years earlier—in the concluding pages of *Suicide*—he had professed such difficulty in seeing. He will find them, it is clear, by making analogies to religious life.

Before indicating how Durkheim's encounter with religion altered his theory of secular life, I must mention an important fact that is rarely understood: in its essentials, Durkheim's sociology of religion never changed after 1898. It is true that fourteen years later he published what is perhaps his most monumental work, *The Elementary Forms of Religious Life*, on exactly the same subject. His theory is more differentiated and nuanced in the *Elementary Forms*, his empirical reference more vast, and his propositions are much more complex and systematic. It is even true, as he maintains in a footnote to his opening theoretical discussion, that he is in 1912 much more concerned with the actual content of sacred beliefs and not just their form. All of this is true, but the *Elementary Forms* still does not deviate from the earlier essay in its model of the religious process.

Durkheim's principal point, once again, is to criticize the notion that religion can be defined by its reference to a deity, and he does so in much the same way, by drawing a portrait of religion that emphasizes the dialectic between association and the ideas it helps to produce.

> These two elements of the religious life are too closely connected with each other to allow for any radical separation. In principle, the cult is derived from the beliefs, yet it reacts upon them; the myth is frequently modelled after the rite in order to account for it, especially when its sense is no longer apparent. . . . So these two parts of our analysis cannot fail to overlap.[124]

Although Durkheim's reference now is to totemic figures rather than personalized divinities, his point about the social or group reference of these ideas is the same, and refers just as much as his 1898 essay did to the associational theory of the middle-period work. The totem, he writes, is the "outward and visible form" of the god, but "it is also the symbol of the determined society called the clan." "If it is at once the symbol of the god and of the society," Durkheim asks, "is that not because the god and the society are only one?" "The totemic principle," he concludes, "can therefore be nothing else than the clan itself, personified and represented to the imagination under the visible form of the animal or vegetable which serves as totem."[125] Durkheim's language here is more precise than before; he uses the word "representation" to denote the specific process by which the group gets transmogrified into symbols as well as to indicate the nature of the symbol itself. Yet his essential point is not different from what it was before. And he insists, once again, that even though these symbols have a social basis they are in themselves fundamental sources of social order. "The clan," he writes, "could not exist . . . without the totem.[126] The totem is the "very type of sacred thing," and it is the subjective acceptance of the same sacred things that creates the group.[127]

> For the members of single clan are not united to each other either by a common habitat or by common blood, as they are not necessarily consanguineous and are frequently scattered over different parts of the tribal territory. Their unity comes solely from their having the same name and the same emblem, their *believing* that they have the same relations with the same categories of things.[128]

The *Elementary Forms* provides a detailed discussion of both sides of this dialectic, the practice and the symbol. While Durkheim understands more clearly than before the transition from practice to symbol, his general theoretical logic is the same. The starting point of the "social organization" that ritual practice represents is a psychic force which he calls, in the language of anthropology, "mana." Mana is diffuse energy, an "anonymous and impersonal force" that "animates" human association.[129] Ritual, then, is the prototype of the association that is necessary for this psychic energy to be released and intensified.

> The very fact of the concentration [in a ritual] acts as an exceptionally powerful stimulant. When they [clan members] are once come together, a sort of electricity is formed by their collective exaltation. Every sentiment expressed finds a place without resistance in all the minds, which are very open to outside impressions; each re-echoes the others, and is re-echoed by the others. The initial impulse thus proceeds, growing as it goes, as an avalanche grows in its advance.[130]

In the middle-period writing, this reinforced sentiment was regarded, in itself, as the new collective sentiment of the group. Now, however, with the model of religious process in mind, Durkheim understands more clearly that there is some distance between a strong group sentiment and a collective idea, and that this gap can only be filled by the same kind of creative, transformative process which is the heart of religious symbolization. "What the totem really consists in," he writes, "is only the material form under which imagination represents this immaterial substance [i.e., mana], this energy diffused through all sorts of heterogeneous things, which alone is the real object of the cult."[131] At the height of ritualized association, when emotional "effervescence" has reached a fever pitch, individuals are moved to "represent" dominant sentiments in a totemic form. "These material manoeuvres" then, Durkheim writes in reference to the rituals, "are only the external envelope under which the mental operations are hidden."[132]†

The sacredness of totemic symbols derives from the powerful energy which they embody. "The sentiments experienced fix themselves upon it," Durkheim writes, "for it is the only concrete object upon which they can fix themselves."[133] This material form enables the collective energy to be effective beyond the actual interaction itself: "The totem is the means by which an individual is put into relations with this source of energy."[134]

> It continues to bring them [collective sentiments] to mind and to evoke them even after the assembly has dissolved, for it survives the assembly, being carved upon the instruments of the cult, upon the sides of rocks, upon buckles, etc. By it, the emotions experienced are perpetually sustained and revived. Everything happens just as if they [the sentiments] inspired them directly.[135]

Because the sacred is built from human emotions, it has a highly liquid form, and because of this liquidness, the sacred flows easily into other things. Durkheim describes this as the sacred's "extraordinary contagiousness"; "even the most superficial or roundabout contact," he writes, "is sufficient to enable it to spread from one object to another."[136] Once again, in other words, the emotional source of sacred things—the kind of action that is believed to inform collective structure—explains their ordering power, for not only is the sacred itself powerful by virtue of its connection to diffuse energy but it can, merely by contact, make other things powerful as well. Precautions must be taken to prevent objects that are not idealized from touching sacred things, and this imperative structures a whole series of ritual practices that Durkheim calls negative rites or taboos. Taboos "confine themselves to forbidding certain ways of acting," and they inspire in the faithful a fear of the sacred thing.[137] Positive cults, by contrast, are inspired by an opposite attitude toward the sacred's contagious liquid: the desired contact with the sacred is actually encouraged to take place, and order is achieved by directing the flow of energy in certain distinct directions.[138]

Ritual association, then, creates sacred beliefs. These beliefs, in turn, order association itself. But while sacredness materializes emotion and gives it power beyond the action from which it was derived, the sacred will lose its power unless it is periodically reinvigorated by the emotions of association. These are rites of creation and renewal. In the latter case, "the rite ... can serve only to sustain the vitality of these beliefs, to keep them from being effaced from memory and, in sum, to revivify the most essential elements of the collective consciousness."

> Through [the rite], the group periodically renews the sentiment which it has of itself and of its unity. ... The glorious souvenirs which are made to live again before their [the group's] eyes, and with which they feel that they have a kinship, give them a feeling of strength and confidence.[139] ... By this means, they mutually show one another that they are all members of the same moral community and they become conscious of the kinship uniting them. The rite does not limit itself to expressing this kinship; it makes it or remakes it.[140]

The structure of Durkheim's explanation in 1912, therefore, closely resembles the model already proposed in 1898. In the later work as in the earlier, Durkheim has brought the model of nonrational association to bear on religious order. As he described his intention in the later work shortly after its publication: "We attempted ... to show that sacred things are simply collective ideals that have fixed themselves on material objects. ... And the particular virtues that we attribute to these ideals are not due to any mysterious action of an external agency; they are simply

the effects of that singularly creative and fertile psychic operation—
which is scientifically analyzable—by which a plurality of individual
consciousnesses enter into a communion and are fused into a common
consciousness."[141] This understanding of the close parallel between the
early essay and the later book is of crucial importance. In the first place,
it puts into an entirely different perspective the diverse writings that
Durkheim published between 1898 and 1912. As the following chapter
will demonstrate in some detail, instead of seeing the religious theory in
Elementary Forms as a departure from the "social" concerns of the preceding writings, as most critics do, we can now understand that the opposite is actually the case. If Durkheim already had developed a mature
theory of religious behavior by 1898, then his subsequent writings were
surely informed by it, and the conventional notions about these later
writings must be radically revised.

Yet the similarity between the earlier and later religious statements
is also significant for the light this sheds on the theoretical reasons for
Durkheim's initial turn toward religion. I suggested earlier that Durkheim did not study religion merely to validate the theory of his middle
period but, in fact, to transcend it. As he had already made abundantly
clear in his article of 1898, his insight into the social nature of the religious sensitized him to the religious nature of the social. His theory of
religion had not simply reaffirmed the social basis of ideas. It had provided a more subtle and more activist understanding of the way ideas are
produced from emotion and of how the order produced by the carriers
of this emotion depends on commitments of a spiritual kind. The more
elaborated religious theory of *Elementary Forms* makes this even more
plain to see: Durkheim's study of religion provided a still more voluntaristic picture of the order produced by nonrational association. His encounter with religion, in other words, allowed him to clarify and
consolidate his new, anti-utilitarian theory of society. When Durkheim
began *Elementary Forms*, he wrote that he had taken primitive religion as
his subject not because of its intrinsic interest but "because it has seemed
to us better adapted than any other to lead to an understanding of the
religious nature of man."[142] It was this understanding of man's essentially "religious nature" that allowed him to move beyond his middle-period work.

2.2. THE IMPACT OF DURKHEIM'S RELIGIOUS SOCIOLOGY
ON HIS MIDDLE-PERIOD WORK

Although it is not known whether Durkheim began his reading in the
anthropology of religion specifically to resolve the problems of his middle period, he was certainly aware that this was the result. His understanding of religion had allowed him to perceive the religious basis of

society, and he set up the analogy between these two domains in a direct and explicit way. He wrote, for example, about the "characteristic of the sacred in morality," about the "sacred character which marks and has always marked moral things."[143] Without a "religious character," he insisted, "no [moral] ethic has ever existed."[144] He offered, at the same time, historical reasons for this close relationship between religion and secular morality. "For centuries," he wrote, "morals and religion have been intimately linked and even completely fused." "It is apparent," he concluded, "that moral life has not been, and never will be, able to shed all the characteristics that it holds in common with religion."

> When two orders of fact have been so closely linked, when there has been between them so close a relationship for so long a time, it is impossible for them to be dissociated and become distinct. For this to happen they would have to undergo a complete transformation and so change their nature.[145]

But his reasoning was analytic and theoretical as well as evolutionary and historical. "It is very difficult to understand moral life," he writes, "if we do not relate it to religious life": "There must . . . be morality in religion and elements of the religious in morality." "In fact," he concludes, "present moral life abounds in the religious."[146]

Morality, then, works in a religious way. To find out how morality functions, it is necessary only to secularize religious process. This is precisely what Durkheim set out to do.

> Sacredness, can be expressed, I believe—and I feel bound to express it—in secular terms. *That is, in fact, the distinctive mark of my attitude.* Instead of joining with the utilitarians in misunderstanding and denying the religious element in morality, or hypostatizing with theology a transcendent Being, *I feel it necessary to translate it in rational language without thereby destroying any of its peculiar characteristics.*[147]

When morality and religion are fused, Durkheim writes at another point, morality is clearly derived from a transcendent being and its sacred status is clear to all. The task is more difficult now that morality has assumed a secular form. To continue to understand its sacredness, we must understand that even though it is now attached to a purely empirical reality, this is the same reality "of which the idea of God [was itself] only the symbolic expression."[148†] This demonstration, of course, was precisely the point of Durkheim's sociological analysis of religion. Sacred ideas are the product of the same social and psychological forces as collective sentiments. This insight, inversely, allows one to understand that even secularized morality has a sacred form. With this "rational language," Durkheim can apply the concept of the sacred to secular life without destroying any of its "peculiar characteristics." It is to the exposition of these that I now turn.

There are three central concepts that Durkheim imported from religion into his theory of secular life. Each allows him to define with more security the "laws" that govern mental life, and each allows him to articulate the operation of these "laws" in a way that demonstrates the extraordinary voluntarism that, he has come to believe, characterizes social order as a whole. These concepts are ritual, authority, and representation.

In the revolutionary breakthrough that initiated his middle-period theorizing, Durkheim perceived association as having an emotional rather than instrumental basis. Yet this portrayal was flawed by mechanistic residues, by the picture of atoms interacting and giving off quasi-electrical energy. By adopting religious ritual as an analogy for this association, Durkheim could finally shed the mechanistic and covertly antivoluntaristic elements of his explanation. Rituals present association that is prototypically emotional and voluntary, where actors are motivated to participate solely by fervent adherence to their god and to one another. The model of ritual, therefore, allowed Durkheim to emphasize, much more strongly than before, the emotional practice that is the foundation of belief. The depth of his analogy is demonstrated, indeed, by his frequent substitution, in the later work, of the concepts of "rite" and "creed" for the earlier terms of practice and belief.

In his analysis of religion, Durkheim had established that rituals are creative and ceremonial. He now applied these terms to secular life, and he extended the ritual concept to embrace, still further, the everyday, often mundane practices which "religious" beliefs inform and by which, he now believed, they must be seen as reinvigorated in turn. "In the present day just as much as in the past," he wrote, "we see society constantly creating sacred things out of ordinary ones."[149] These creative episodes arise because association can, on certain occasions, impart to everyday life a transcendent status.

> From the actions and reactions between its individuals arises an entirely new mental life which lifts our minds into a world of which we could have not the faintest idea had we lived in isolation. This we observe best at those signal epochs of crisis when some great collective movement seizes us, lifts us above ourselves, and transfigures us.[150]

As with periods of religious creativity, these secular episodes occur because of the "influence of some great collective shock." The shock draws men together, and their interaction creates a new emotional intensity that allows for the revolutionary transformation of their internal states.

> Social interactions ... become much more frequent and active.
> Men look for each other and assemble together more than ever.
> That general effervescence results which is characteristic of rev-
> olutionary or creative epochs. Now this greater activity results in
> a general stimulation of individual forces. Men see more and dif-
> ferently now than in normal times. Changes are not merely of
> shades and degrees; men become different.[151]

This kind of secular, revolutionary ritual, Durkheim now believes, has
been the source of the great historical transformations that have created
modern civilization.

> It is, in fact, at such moments of collective ferment that are born
> the great ideals upon which civilizations rest. ... Such was the
> great crisis of Christendom, the movement of collective enthusi-
> asm which, in the twelfth and thirteenth centuries, bringing to-
> gether in Paris the scholars of Europe, gave birth to Scholasti-
> cism. Such were the Reformation and Renaissance, the revolu-
> tionary epoch and the Socialist upheavals of the nineteenth
> century. At such times the ideal tends to become one with the
> real, and for this reason men have the impression that the time is
> close when the ideal will in fact be realized and the Kingdom of
> God established on earth.[152]

It is these spiritual upheavals that have set Western societies on a certain course. What will assure that they maintain it? Their direction will
be maintained through collective force; this force, however, will be voluntarily conceived: it will be associational in its form. In conceptualizing
such reaffirming association, Durkheim turns again to the model of ritual behavior. If order was first created by spontaneous spiritual renewal,
it will be affirmed by it as well. Because men feel the need to reenact the
association that originally created them, revivifying ritual is a natural response to weakened commitments. "All parties," Durkheim insists, "political, economic or confessional, are careful to have periodical reunions
where their members may revivify their common faith by manifesting it
in common."[153]

> There can be no society which does not feel the need of uphold-
> ing and reaffirming at regular intervals the collective sentiments
> and the collective ideas which make its unity and its personality.
> Now this moral remaking cannot be achieved except by the
> means of reunions, assemblies and meetings where the indi-
> viduals, being closely united to one another, reaffirm in common
> their common sentiments; *hence come ceremonies which do not
> differ from regular religious ceremonies, either in their object, the*

*results which they produce, or the processes employed to attain
these results.*[154]

Finally, Durkheim insists that even the association of everyday life may
be seen as a kind of superannuated ritual experience, "for there is not, so
to speak, a moment in our lives when some current of energy does not
come to us from without."

> The man who has done his duty finds, in the manifestations of
> every sort expressing the sympathy, esteem or affection which
> his fellows have for him, a feeling of comfort, of which he does
> not ordinarily take account, but which sustains him, none the
> less. The sentiments which society has for him raise the senti-
> ments which he has for himself. Because he is in moral harmony
> with his comrades, he has more confidence, courage and bold-
> ness in action, just like the believer who thinks that he feels the
> regard of his god turned graciously towards him.[155]

Religious ritual has now become the model for all social practice and
association: it explains the revolutionary creation of a new order as well
as its sustenance in organized activity and everyday life. Durkheim has
discovered a much more supple and systematic way of talking about the
activity that he first identified in his middle-period work;[156†] yet by this
very act of theoretical refinement he has even further idealized it. By
spiritualizing his model of emotional association and moral exchange, he
has drawn the contrast that much more sharply between his later presuppositional stance and its instrumental or multidimensional alternative. Society is not sustained by politics or economics in Durkheim's
emerging theory; there is only ritual in its secular form. Yet for all of its
exaggerated voluntarism, Durkheim has discovered a model that relates
individual effort to social structure in a brilliant and highly innovative
way.

If the action that sustains order has become in Durkheim's later writing a secular ritual, then order must itself have changed its form. Although Durkheim knew in his middle-period work that order had a
moral quality and that it was activated voluntarily, his emphasis on its
coercive and external quality partly obscured this insight. After he discovered how order worked in religious society, he could express this theoretical intent much more clearly. As he related secular action to ritual,
he analogized secular order to the sacred; for the implication—no matter how unintended—of coercion and power he substituted the notions
of voluntary adherence and sacred authority.

Durkheim notes that there is a peculiar, self-contradictory quality
about sacred things: they inspire respect and fear, but at the same time
they are objects of love and desire.[157] These are precisely the qualities he

now assigns to collective order in general. Moral rules, he insists, are both obligatory and desirable. They are obeyed because they must be—their power leaves the individual no choice—yet they are followed also because they are believed in, *"simply because* they command."[158] Sacred rules are obeyed because they are believed to emanate from a divine source; moral rules share this same quality. "The domain of morality," Durkheim writes, "is as if surrounded by a mysterious barrier which keeps violators at arm's length, just as the religious domain is protected from the reach of the profane. . . . It is a sacred domain."[159] Like religious rules, then, morality presents a "system of commandments";[160] and the special position conferred by virtue of its sacred status Durkheim calls "moral authority."[161] The "spiritual power" that identifies moral authority—and which accrues to it because it is the object of ritual behavior—means that it achieves control purely through voluntary acquiescence.[162]

> It commands those acts which will realize it, and it does so, not by a material coercion or by the perspective of something of this sort, but by the simple radiation of the mental energy which it contains. It has an efficacy coming solely from its psychical properties, and it is just by this sign that moral authority is recognized.[163]

Durkheim insists that in comparison with moral authority, utilitarian sanctions are ineffective, and he poses the issue as a choice of either one form of order or the other. If order is really to be powerful, the "useful consequences" of behavior—for example, whether disobedience will produce "harmful results"—can be of no consequence.[164] Moral authority is effective only because it consists of "interior and wholly spiritual pressure" rather than material force.[165] It is because of the moral, the authoritative basis of social order that Durkheim can conclude that it is "in spiritual ways that society gets us to act."

The third crucial element that Durkheim draws from his secularization of religious theory concerns the precise means by which ritual action is transformed into sacred order, the mediation between internal emotion and external object which he terms "representation." It is important to understand that Durkheim had always accepted the notion of representation in the strict psychological sense in which it was invoked in the nineteenth century and has been in our own as well. In this psychological sense, representation refers to the debate between sensationalists and rationalists over the status of mental perception. From his earliest writings on moral science in Germany, to his discussions in the *Division of Labor*, through his analysis in the middle-period works, *Rules* and *Suicide*, Durkheim demonstrated a clear understanding that perception is not merely the reflection of the material world, that it involves an independent intellectual "representation," and that it is this "reasoned" representation, not immediate sense data, that is codified in the neurons of the brain as memory. This insight by Durkheim certainly had a polemical point, for with it he could oppose Tarde's description of social behavior as automatic imitation. Yet the commitment was still deeper than that: it meant that even when Durkheim pursued materialism in a sociological sense he was never a materialist in terms of his actual epistemology.[166†]

But Marx too shared an antimaterialist epistemology, so it could not have been this early acceptance of the fact of psychological representation that helped make Durkheim's later theory unique. Representation became important to Durkheim only after his encounter with religion. He now makes a double analogy: first, between psychological, or individual, representation and the formulation of collective ideas that occurs in the midst of religious rituals; second, between this process of religious representation of sacred things and the formulation of ideas in secular life.[167] This new understanding, in fact, can be located rather precisely; it derives from Durkheim's rethinking the place of "deities" in his sociology of religion. Rather than a powerful entity in itself, he has argued, a divinity is powerful because it is related to the energy of the community which believes in it. Divinities, then, are merely ways that individuals "represent" to themselves the ordering force of their own society. In so rethinking the role of gods in religion, however, Durkheim has not relegated the representational process to an epiphenomenal status. The process must be important in itself, for, as will be recalled, it is by noting the contribution of individual conceptualization to religious life that Durkheim's later theorizing avoids the earlier implication that moral forces coerce the actor from without. Representation, then, provides the crucial mediation between individual interaction and group force, or social order. It is the means by which subjectivity is transferred from immediate association to the ideational order that will govern future acts. Indeed, Durkheim thinks such an individually-mediated order might itself be said to consist of "collective representations."[168†]

Like sacred order, therefore, secular order is composed of representations, and with this understanding Durkheim can still more firmly articulate the voluntary nature of collective life. The fact of representation allows us to understand more clearly how social structures are simply the externalization of human emotion and, at the same time, why every structure outside of us must be internalized as well. It is the process of representation, in other words, that explains the dialectic of externalization and internalization upon which Durkheim's mature sociological theory rests.

Representation is the subjective imputation of form to emotion. If all social facts are representations, then such facts must be the product of the externalization of emotion and, indeed, emotional themselves. Representations are often material things, but this is simply because materiality often offers a more convenient way of representing emotions than abstract concepts.[169] In fact, since representations merely give form to sentiment, they are all—whether religious, legal, moral, political, or economic "facts"—tinged with the same "spirituality" that the faithful have called divine.[170] The very representation of any external element, moreover, whether a material thing or a moral concept, makes that element part of our internal being. To represent something, after all, is to give to a thing an internal idea.

> We cannot become attached to an external thing, whatever its nature, without representing it to ourselves, without having an idea of it, a sentiment about it. . . . *By virtue of this fact alone—that we do represent an external object to ourselves—it becomes in certain respects internal.* It exists in us in the form of the representation that expresses it.[171]

Representation, then, is the process by which human practice breaks down the rigid dichotomy between subject and object upon which sociological materialism is based. Because of representation, "things, beings from the outside, penetrate into our consciousness, mingle intimately in our inner lives, become intertwined in our existence, and, conversely, we merge our existence with theirs." Because of representation, there is already "something of us in the objects that become assimilated, or that we assimilate, into our lives."[172] The material world is subjectified and, at the same time, the subjective world is objectified. "Our whole social environment seems to us to be filled with forces which really exist only in our minds. . . . Yet the powers conferred, though purely ideal, act as though they were real; they determine the conduct of men with the same degree of necessity as physical forces."[173] When Durkheim says that because of representation "we have egoism embedded in altruism" and "altruism in egoism," the parallel to Marx's early discussion of praxis and species-being could not be more direct.[174†]

It is eminently clear that Durkheim has used the concept of representation to further separate himself from the kind of materialist theory that Marx presented in his later writing. It is only fitting, therefore, that Durkheim should conclude his first essay on representations, published in 1898, by insisting that its discovery would finally put an end to the misdirected criticisms that had dogged his work. "Nothing is wider of the mark," he writes, "than the mistaken accusation of materialism which has been levelled against us." "Quite the contrary," he argues, "from the point of view of our position, if one is to call the distinctive property of the individual representational life *spirituality*, one should say that social life is defined by its hyper-spirituality."[175] Only after he had discovered the true nature of religious life could Durkheim define the distinctive property of individual representations as "spirituality." Only after he had discovered religion did he feel that he could finally lay the accusations of materialism to rest.[176†]

2.3. CONSOLIDATING THE NEW THEORY: DURKHEIM'S REFUTATION OF MARXISM AND THE ESTABLISHMENT OF L'ANNÉE SOCIOLOGIQUE

With his new understanding of religion, Durkheim had found a way to fulfill his long-standing ambition to reconcile order and voluntarism. The problem was that he had solved it too well. Like Marx's critique of idealist thought, Durkheim's attempt to qualify sociological materialism became paradigmatic of an approach to social structure that denied it any status at all. From the time of its initial conception to the present day, it has represented for sociological thought the theoretical antithesis to the structuralism of Marx.

Durkheim himself was thoroughly aware of the opportunity that his breakthrough to symbolic order provided: he could now create a theoretical alternative to Marxism which could match its generality and scope. This new theory would be just as collectivist as Marxism but would be resolutely anti-instrumental. It would not be unfair to say that ever since his first days as a sociologist it had been Durkheim's goal to create such an alternative. In 1886, it will be recalled, he had agreed with Schaeffle that the internal contradictions of socialism could be overcome only if Marxism were renounced in its "fundamentals." In his early work, however, Durkheim was quite unable to do so. After his encounter with religion, his break with materialist thought could be much more decisive.

In 1897, the year in which his first explicitly "religious" writings appeared, Durkheim initiated debate with two of the leading Marxists of the day. One of these Marxists, Paul Lafargue, the son-in-law of Marx himself, was engaged only indirectly.[177] Lafargue had reviewed a book on Marxist socialism by Gaston Richard, at the time a member of Durkheim's circle and the author of the book on law which had earlier been the occasion of Durkheim's first break with the *Division of Labor.* Lafargue denounced Richard's work on socialism as anti-Marxist and idealist. Durkheim chose to reply to Lafargue with a review of his own. For the most part, this review consisted in a complimentary summary of Richard's sharp rejection of Marx's ideas. Toward the end of the review, however, Durkheim took Lafargue directly to task. "We . . . find at once surprising and regrettable," he wrote, "the attacks to which he [Richard] has been subject on the part of the authorized representatives of socialist doctrine."[178] After this rebuke, Durkheim stresses that his own position on socialism is similar to Richard's. Socialism has no valid-ity as a scientific theory, he writes. It must, rather, be viewed as a collec-tive representation: "Socialism is, above all, the way in which certain strata of society which have been tested by collective suffering represent the latter to themselves."[179] The popularity or persuasiveness of social-ism must not be viewed, in other words, as evidence for the validity of Marx's theory about the coercive and external nature of social order. To the contrary, socialism itself was a "religious" force; its power, therefore, only demonstrated the representational character of social life. Social-ism could be understood, Durkheim concludes, only by penetrating the underlying moral reality that produced it. This brief review makes more subtle and decisive the position that Durkheim had outlined in his lec-tures on socialism in 1895. It was Durkheim's new ability to define social-ism specifically as a "representation" that evidently gave him the confidence to make the challenge to Marx much more direct.

More important, however, is Durkheim's challenge to Antonio La-briola, in a review that directly engages Marxism as a theoretical system. Labriola's *Essays in the Materialist Conception of History* had just been translated into French, and Georges Sorel, in an introduction to the work, had hailed its publication as a "landmark in the history of social-ism."[180] Labriola was one of the premier Marxist philosophers of his time, and he presented his master's theory in anything but a vulgar light. In making his review, therefore, Durkheim could publicly confront the major alternative to his nascent sociological theory in its most respected form. Two years earlier, Sorel had reviewed Durkheim's own work and found it to be seriously wanting in contrast to Marx's (see n. 86, above). Only now, after Durkheim had significantly refined the theory of his mid-dle-period work, could he finally respond to the gauntlet Sorel had thrown down.

Durkheim organized his response to illuminate the differences be-tween his theory and Marx's at the most general, presuppositional level. After a balanced presentation of Labriola's argument, he approvingly discusses the anti-individualistic position of historical materialism. In-stead of focusing on pure ideas, or on isolated individuals, historical ma-terialism concentrates on a much more fundamental level, on "the artificial milieu which the work of associated men has created of whole cloth and then superimposed on nature."[181] Durkheim insists, however, that this kind of collective emphasis is not exclusive to Marx.[182] What is peculiar is that his collectivist theory emphasizes the primacy of mate-rial factors. "Just as it seems true to us," Durkheim writes, "that the causes of social phenomena must be sought outside individual represen-tations, it seems to that same degree false that they can be reduced, in the final analysis, to the state of industrial technology, and that the economic factor is the mainspring of progress."[183] It is the nature of action, in other words, not the position on order that distinguishes his theory from Marx's. Durkheim then demonstrates this Marxist error by discussing his own newly discovered view of the importance of religion. In opposition to historical materialism, he claims that "historians tend more and more to meet in the confirmation that religion is the most primitive of all social phenomena." "Everything," he insists, "is religious in principle." Is it not probable, he asks, "that the economy depends on religion much more than the second on the first?"[184] Durkheim's interpreters have often mistakenly read his religious theory as a kind of deracinated materialism. Others, when they have recognized the seriousness of the break, usually insist on seeing in the theory that results from it an alternative that subsumes Marx's by being much more multidimensional in scope.[185†] Durkheim's confrontation with Marxism in 1897 demonstrates that both views are incorrect.[186†]

In the years following the publication of the *Division of Labor* Durkheim had attracted a number of talented students and followers. After the revelation that allowed him to resolve the outstanding theoretical problems of that earlier work, he moved quickly to discover an organizational form to express this new spirit. With his followers and students, he founded the *L'Année sociologique*, a journal that certainly constituted one of the premier collaborative efforts in the history of social thought, and one which created an *école* that left a permanent mark on the disciplines of anthropology and sociology. Most significantly, from our perspective, Durkheim clearly understood *L'Année* as a vehicle to specify in more propositional form the radically voluntaristic orientation of his later work. Two organizational features of the journal strikingly demonstrate this intention and, in addition, the success with which Durkheim carried it out.

The first feature is the leading position that Durkheim gave in every issue to religious phenomena. "This year, as well as last," he wrote in his important "Preface" to the second volume of *L'Année*, "our analyses are headed by those concerning the sociology of religion." He acknowledges that the "according of the first rank to this sort of phenomenon has produced some astonishment," but he defends this decision on grounds which clearly derive from his recent theoretical insights.[187†] "It is these [religious] phenomena," he writes, "which are the germ from which all others—or at least almost all others—are derived." Durkheim asserts that "religion contains in itself from the very beginning, even if in an indistinct state, all the elements which in dissociating themselves from it, articulating themselves, and combining with one another in a thousand ways, have given rise to the various manifestations of collective life." Evidently he had already transformed this general insight into a specific evolutionary theory of the relation between religious and secular phenomena: "From myths and legends have issued forth science and poetry;

from religious ornamentations and cult ceremonials have come the plastic arts; from ritual practice are born law and morals. One cannot understand our perception of the world, our philosophical conceptions of the soul, or immortality, of life, if one does not know the religious beliefs which are their primordial forms." *L'Année* would concentrate on demonstrating exactly these historical connections and, by implication, Durkheim's analytic point as well. For Durkheim concludes this defense of his organizational format by emphasizing that religion is not important only from an historical perspective; it is equally crucial in terms of the general theoretical framework that it provides. "A great number of problems change their aspects completely," he writes, "as soon as their connections with the sociology of religion are recognized." He concludes by insisting that "our efforts must therefore be aimed at tracing these connections."[188†]

The second striking feature about *L'Année* was not unconnected with the primary emphasis given to religion: the new, much more subjectivistic approach to morphology. In a step which must have been just as astonishing to certain followers of Durkheim as the leading position he now assigned to religion, the first volume of *L'Année* did not devote an independent section to morphology, the subject which only four years before had been perhaps the most prominent feature in Durkheim's work. By the second volume—the same in which Durkheim felt compelled to defend the journal's deference to religion—morphology had a section of its own. But in introducing this section to his readers, Durkheim placed it in a theoretical context that demonstrated the great shift in his thinking since his morphological analyses in the *Division of Labor.* He continues to call morphological variables the "substratum" of society, yet by virtue of his radically different treatment this term becomes almost a parody of its former self. Morphology identifies the same demographic and ecological phenomena as Durkheim had earlier discussed, "the mass of individuals who comprise the society, the manner in which they are disposed upon the earth, and the nature and configuration of objects of all sorts which affect collective relations."[189] His analysis of their causal role is, however, entirely different. These "material forms of society" are now conceived as an external milieu that—while they have an effect on action—are in no sense constitutive of it. Durkheim makes an analogy here to the role of the physical tissue in psychological perception, a reference which carries particular interest because at about the same time this analogy was also basic to the double analogy by which he established the fundamental role of representations in secular life. Social phenomena must relate to morphology, he writes, just as perceptions must have a neurological element; but social forms can no more reflect morphology than can perceptions be merely the reflection of neural matter. Morphology is not "constitutive" of society, and for this reason the sociological study of morphology should concentrate much more on the social processes that create it than on its less important effects. Sociology should observe morphology "in the process of creation."

> It must investigate the conditions which *cause* variations in the political territory of different peoples, the nature and aspect of their borders, and the unequal density of the population. It must ask *how* urban agglomerations are born, what the laws of their evolution are, *how* they are recruited, what their role might be.[190]

The source of this causal analysis could, of course, only be the emotional and spiritual association that has now become the focus of Durkheim's sociology. Beneath the morphological "substratum," in other words, there is a subjective one from which it is derived.[191†]

The effect of Durkheim's morphological analysis in *L'Année*, therefore, is to subjectify this formerly objective determinant in order to make it consistent with the radically voluntaristic theory he is trying now to formalize. The reviews that occupy him in this new section of *L'Année*'s second volume carry out this mandate. Durkheim considers a wide cross-section of work on demography and urban history in Germany and France, and his evaluations effectively refute the main lines of his argument in Book 2 of the *Division of Labor*. He argues that the deprivation of material resources cannot be the source of increased emigration to cities or of the increased concentration that results from it. This emigration, rather, is only one part of a much larger and more general process of concentration that is not necessarily economic in nature.[192] In contrast to such materialist explanations for the growth of cities, Durkheim argues that it is the "exceptional intensity of life" that creates such movement.[193] Cities start from markets and fairs, but these are not simply the natural expansion of the division of labor; they indicate, rather, the "moral and juridical unity of the population."[194] This subjectification of morphological concerns continues in subsequent issues. In volume 3, for example, Durkheim attacks the objective status of population growth, the variable which had been at the very center of his discussion in *Division*. "The insufficiency of our birthrate," he writes, "is the result particularly of moral causes and . . . the principal among these consists in a certain development of the spirit of individuation."[195]

Durkheim's contributions to subsequent volumes of *L'Année* continued in this vein. Most were reviews, of which Durkheim usually contributed more than thirty and sometimes sixty or more. A few were much more substantial: a reevaluation of legal evolution in 1901, technical discussions on the anthropology of primitive societies in 1902 and 1905, an essay on primitive thought in 1903, a definition of the concept of "civilization" in 1913.[196†] Above all, Durkheim continued in subsequent volumes to amplify the role of the "spiritual" and moral elements in social life. Matrilinearity did not occur because of the shift to agriculture but because it was the female line that carried the totemic symbol;[197] legal evolution was produced by moral concentration;[198] criminal statistics were classified with moral ones because they were only two aspects, the negative and the positive, of the same collective morality;[199] primitive thinking evidenced the same polarizing and dichotomizing thinking as religion itself;[200] civilizations demonstrated the autonomy of the universal spirit from social structure.[201] These were the kinds of propositions for which *L'Année* had first been invented.

3. CONCLUSION: DURKHEIM'S CONFESSION "MALGRÉ LUI"

With the single exception of the brief reply to a critic which we have noted above, Durkheim never admitted the extent to which his encounter with religion had transformed his sociology. Indeed, he never admitted to any radical break in his work at all. He never disclaimed the presuppositions of the *Division of Labor*, nor did he ever acknowledge that *Rules* was not a codification of the theory employed in this earlier work, but rather a blueprint of things to come. Needless to say, if the middle-period writing was not accorded its revolutionary status, the religious encounter that transformed his later work could hardly be accorded its due. This silence about the true inner development of his work is perhaps the major reason for the gross misinterpretation to which it has been subject, not just among so many contemporary critics but among observers in his own time and even among his own students. Like all the great sociological theorists, Durkheim desperately wanted to present his work as a consistent whole. To do anything else, to acknowledge, for example, that an encounter with religion could cause major theoretical upheaval, would imply that the great body of work was not completely "scientific," that it was not, in other words, derived simply from acute insight into the structure of the empirical world.

We are denied, therefore, Durkheim's own reflection on the abrupt transitions that transpired in the years 1894–1897. Ironically, however, Durkheim did concern himself publicly with an intellectual shift in the thought of one of his most important predecessors, a shift that closely resembled the one on which he himself had embarked. In the school year immediately following his crucial lectures on religion, Durkheim delivered the lectures on socialism which I discussed earlier. The heart of this course was Durkheim's analysis of the thought of Saint-Simon, whose ideas about the restructuring of industrial society had clearly inspired the analysis in the *Division of Labor.* For the most part, Durkheim's course was devoted to this latter concern, to Saint-Simon's understand-

ing of the shift in power and authority which demarcated industrial society and of the economic and political reforms that would be necessary to
ensure its equilibrium. In the last part of his lectures, however, Durkheim begins to speak about the radical shift in emphasis on new "spiritual bonds" that characterized Saint-Simon's last work.[202] At first
Durkheim tries to maintain that this emphasis was not in any way inconsistent with Saint-Simon's earlier writing; later he equivocates, and finally he acknowledges the rupture in Saint-Simon's thought and seeks
out a rational explanation. One cannot help but think that in talking
about Saint-Simon Durkheim is talking about himself as well, about the
rupture that he is consciously or unconsciously in the process of making
but which is still, at that time, completely unknown to those outside his
immediate circle.

In his initial response to this discontinuity in Saint-Simon's work,
Durkheim says that "when one hears . . . the founder of positive philosophy call for the establishment of a new religion, one is tempted to believe
that along the way some revolution has occurred in his thinking, and that
he has become unfaithful to his principles." Durkheim seeks to assure
his audience that this was surely not the case. "Nothing," he says, "is less
accurate than this interpretation." He insists that Saint-Simon had always been sensitive to religious facts even though he previously had not
emphasized them.

> There is no doubt that religious preoccupations were very in-
> tense in Saint-Simon in all periods of his intellectual develop-
> ment. . . . At all times he had a very high regard for the role
> Christianity had played in the world. . . . Thus Saint-Simon never
> conceived positive and scientific philosophy as excluding all re-
> ligious systems.[203]

In fact, Durkheim tells his listeners, Saint-Simon was clearly of the opinion that the positive philosophy led naturally to religious considerations.
This philosophy was designed to end all intellectual particularism, and
Saint-Simon knew that religion was dedicated to the same end. If a new
religion was necessary, therefore, it was only "because—since Christianity has lost its influence—men no longer have a common faith from
whose breath they draw the feeling of solidarity." Once this solidarity
disappeared, men returned to particularistic, individual pursuits, and it
was "against this tendency toward dispersion that religion must react."
The new religion would retain the universalism of Christianity by forging a spiritual unity more appropriate to secular society.

> It has a role no different [from] that of philosophy. Religion does
> not require a celestial image opposed to the earthly ones. Its true
> mission is not to turn humankind away from temporal reality in

order to bind it to some supra-experimental object, but simply to emphasize the unity of reality. And that is precisely what causes it to be summoned to furnish the spiritual bond which should unite the members of human society with one another.[204]

Yet, Durkheim's own contention to the contrary notwithstanding, how could this new spiritual emphasis not have constituted a radical break with Saint-Simon's earlier work? Equally to the point, how could Durkheim's new appreciation of religion not help but rupture the continuity of his own early work? No matter how secular and this worldly the religion Saint-Simon proposed, it provided an order radically opposed to that of a purely industrial kind. Just as Durkheim himself would be forced publicly to admit this discontinuity more than a decade later, he acknowledges at a later point in these lectures that there had, in fact, been a rupture in the thought of Saint-Simon. "Towards the end of his life," Durkheim admits, Saint-Simon "had become aware of the inadequacy of his system on this point and had accentuated its religion."[205] "Even if no about-face occurred in his thinking," Durkheim says, "and although he never went from an irreligious or a-religious rationalism to a mysticism scornful of science, there is nevertheless a difference between the early and later forms of this system." In fact, he now finds this change to be "unquestionable." Just as Durkheim himself had begun to understand the importance of religious phenomena only after the new emphasis on moral order in the middle-period work, so he attributes this shift in Saint-Simon's views to the fact that "he was led to attribute a more and more important role to purely moral sentiments." Saint-Simon developed this new appreciation of morality, Durkheim thinks, because he no longer believed that instrumental interest, no matter how well organized, could furnish the basis of social order. "As long as he believed egoism capable of insuring the progress of societies—provided that these were well organized—[there] was no need to specially urge individuals to play their social role, since their natural penchant towards egoism brought this about voluntarily." Durkheim describes here, of course, precisely the wistful solution to the order problem that he himself had attempted in the *Division of Labor*. When he says that Saint-Simon eventually realized the fallacy of this belief, he could just as well be describing his own realization: "But this [belief in self-interest] was no longer enough once Saint-Simon recognized that without charity, mutual obligation, and philanthropy, the social order—and still more the human order—was impossible." Order could be achieved only if human beings shared internal commitments. "To have an active reason to fraternize," Saint-Simon realized, "they had to feel a positive bond among them, a community of nature, a unique kinship which made them brothers." This moral bond, moreover, could be brought about only if it had a certain transcendent quality. Men "had to feel it is the same life's blood which circulates in all bodies, the same spirit which animates all minds."[206]†

By the concluding lectures of his course, Durkheim had come to realize that his most original insight into the thought of Saint-Simon actually lay in his analysis of its discontinuity. He criticizes Saint-Simon, in fact, for his lack of self-consciousness about this new theoretical direction, and argues that his inability to formulate a satisfactory theory of modern society was due to the lack of analytic differentiation between his new theory and his older one. Saint-Simon recognized that modern society could be integrated only by a new religion, but he believed that his faith could be founded completely upon the "industrial principle," upon a faith in economic progress and in the importance of material well-being. Saint-Simon's religion would have "science for theology and industry for creed," and it would have for its goal the distribution of jobs according to ability and of income according to services. But to reduce religious principles to such utilitarian considerations, Durkheim now insists, amounts to a contradiction in terms, for this religion will be unable to address the moral and spiritual issues which are the true source of conflict and unhappiness.[207]

Durkheim takes the failure of Saint-Simon's understanding of religion very much to heart. In the parting words of his final lecture, he urges that Saint-Simon's "undertaking must be renewed and [pushed further] in the same direction," and he suggests that the history of Saint-Simon's intellectual development "can serve to show us the way." "What caused the failure of Saint-Simonianism," he concludes, "is that Saint-Simon and his disciples wanted to get the most from the least, the superior from the inferior, moral rule from economic matter."[208] Durkheim is determined that this mistake will not happen to him. In 1893, he had confessed that "we do not actually possess a scientific notion of what religion really is."[209] By the lectures of 1895, he seemed not only to know what it was, and to be able to criticize Saint-Simon for offering a vulgarized version of it, but to believe that the correct scientific understanding of religion held the key to any understanding of society as a whole. We have seen that in the years immediately following these lectures Durkheim firmly established the analytic independence of religion from economic and political force. In the substantive sociology that is informed by this insight, he will use the independence of religious belief to establish a new explanation for the origins and sustenance of social institutions.

Chapter Eight

DURKHEIM'S LATER WRITINGS (2)

The Religious Model and the Idealist Theory of Society

In 1901, Paul Fauconnet and Marcel Mauss, two of Durkheim's closest collaborators, wrote an article for *La Grande Encyclopédie* in which they defined sociology as the "science of institutions."[1] A year later, in his second Preface to *The Rules of Sociological Method*, Durkheim accepted this definition as his own.[2] This acceptance marked the routinization of Durkheimian sociology after the revolutionary transformations of the preceding decade, and it was during this phase of routinization that most of the important contributions to the idealist theory of society were accomplished. Fauconnet and Mauss had, of course, been faithful to Durkheim's preceding theorization. They defined institutions as given beliefs and actions, and they were careful to note that despite their orderly status institutions were "incessantly changing" and were never exactly the same from moment to moment.[3] Even so, these brilliant followers had not lived through the same revolution as Durkheim himself: it is not clear they were even aware it had occurred. Certainly they did not make the profound connection between the subjective history of the spirit and materialized form that was so crucial to Durkheim himself, the insight which he had won only after concerted theoretical struggle.

"Institution" is a dry word. One must place this concept against the background of the theoretical revolution which preceded it if the true nature of Durkheim's substantive sociology is to be understood. In accepting the definition by Fauconnet and Mauss, indeed, Durkheim reveals much more clearly its relation to his revolutionary past. Institutions, Durkheim writes, are a product of joint activity and association, the effect of which is to "fix," to "institute" outside us certain initially subjective and individual ways of acting and judging.[†4] Institutions, then, are the "crystallizations" of Durkheim's earlier writing. Sociology must focus on the dialectic between institutions and the practices which produce them. In terms of the special vocabulary of this later period, sociology is the study of sacred forms and the rituals upon which they are based. As Durkheim writes in *The Elementary Forms of Religious Life*, "The problem of sociology ... consists in seeking, among the different forms of external constraint, the different sorts of moral authority corresponding to them and in discovering the causes which have determined these latter."[5] Durkheim had emphasized in his transitionary period that despite their subjective origins, representations, "once they are constituted," are "autonomous and capable of being causes in turn."[6] Architecture, roads, machines, and tools start with actual practice; legal precepts and even economic laws were once part of individual emotions and sentiments. As soon as such representations become "autonomous realities," however, they become forces in themselves. They represent the various "orders" of social life.[7]

To study these sacred orders, then, it is necessary to move back and forth between their fixed form and the practice that sustains them. This involves analysis on three different levels. First, it is necessary to describe the congealed meaning of the institution in its present form, the ends to which it corresponds.[8] In Durkheim's new vocabulary, this level concerns the definition of moral authority and the everyday "ritual" practices that continually revivify sacred ideals. The second object of analysis is the long-term practice that first created this fixed form. In order to root objectivity even more firmly in subjectivity, one must study objective forms historically. These fixed forms have their origins, as Durkheim asserted in *L'Année*, in the history of the sacred; contemporary institutions, in fact, are merely recently differentiated parts of older religious forms. As he wrote in a later programmatic essay in 1909, it is "not enough to consider the institution in its completed and recent form": the basic problem of sociology is to study the historical process of institutional development, the "association" of the various elements over time. In the end, "to explain an institution is to account for the various elements which served in its formation."[9] Finally, and this is the third level of analysis, sociology must study the episodic "renaissances" which revive practices as they lose their original emotional meaning. "A Renaissance," Durkheim writes, "is a portion of social life which, after being, so to speak, deposited in material things and remain[ing] long latent there, suddenly reawakens and alters the intellectual and moral orientation of peoples who had had no share in its construction."[10]

The study of institutions proposed by Durkheimian sociology, then, is deeply imbedded in the theoretical revolution Durkheim completed in the latter 1890s. He will analyze the "religious status" of institutions by focusing on the ritual practice, sacred moral authority, and processes of representation that sustain them; he will trace each back to its primitive religious form; and he will discuss the periodic episodes of intense association that, along with everyday practice, sustain it in the present day. Durkheim developed this sociology of modern life primarily between 1897 and 1906, although certain earlier and later articles were important as well.[11†] In these years, he rewrote his theory of society for a final time. In the first work of his maturity he had argued for the irrelevance of religion to modernity. In this later theory, he argues that modernity itself is a religious phenomenon. These later views were occasionally published as essays, but they were much more often public speeches and lectures. It is to the consideration of this effort that we now turn.

1. NORMATIVE SOCIETY: THE HIERARCHY OF INSTITUTIONS

Durkheim began to outline his final theory of modern society during the famous struggle over Captain Dreyfus's right to a fair trial, a cause which was supported by the "progressive" intellectuals, liberals, and socialists leading the movement for social change and opposed by "traditionalists" who sought stability through renewed deference to authority and religious belief. Durkheim's position in this struggle was on the left; he was a committed Dreyfusard. His emphatically "spiritual" portrayal of social order, therefore, was initiated at the very time that he expressed his fervent public support for the prototypically "modern" social structure of individual rights and equal opportunity. In his own mind there was no contradiction between these two commitments, one presuppositional, the other ideological. In fact, he felt that the only way to protect modernity from the attack of traditionalist conservatives was to demonstrate that such modernity would change the content of religious society but not its form. Durkheim's later theory of modernity, in other words, emerges from chapter 5 of *The Division of Labor in Society*. It is refined enormously and rests upon a much surer theoretical base, but the ideological vision is much the same. Modern society has the same kind of "collective conscience" as "mechanical" society, but it retains the individual and social differentiation of a more "organic" form. It is governed by a religious order, but it is not a religious society in the traditionalistic sense.[12†]

Durkheim pictures modern society as composed of a series of continuums (which I have tried to present in the accompanying diagram— see fig. 2): from the individual to the group, from unformed to formed sentiments, from amoral to moral forces, from particularism to universalism. Most powerfully, society is a hierarchy.[13] The individual is at the bottom of this hierarchy. Immediately above him are unformed collective currents, and above those are crystallized institutions. The latter, in-

Figure 2
Durkheim's Map of the Modern World

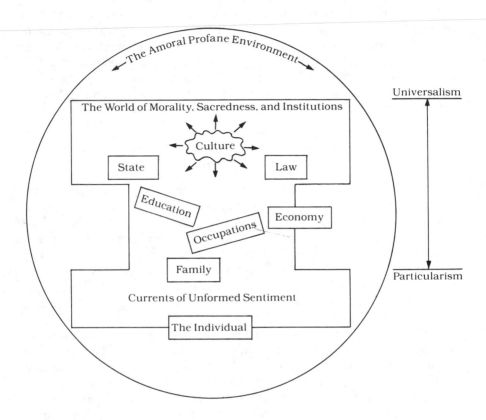

stitutionalized world is the same as the sacred world of secular morality.
Some life still exists outside of this moral sphere; it is the Hobbesian
world of instrumental coercion, that partly characterizes, for example,
economic activity. The institutions that create the world of morality
range from particularistic to universalistic forms. At the top is culture,
which is without any necessary referent to individual and group circumstances or interests.[14] Culture constitutes the most "general milieu" of
action, the element that informs everything else; below it is ranged a series of increasingly more particularistic "special milieus," at the bottom
of which is the family.[15] The schools are more universalistic and therefore "above" the family, yet they are partly mediated by the occupational

milieu and are, therefore, certainly less independent of particular circumstances and interests than the state and the law. Occupational milieus are less universalistic still; far removed from the world of the state and the law, they mediate the abstractions of culture with the very particular demands and interests of the workaday world. Finally, the state and the law present forces closest to the potential universalism of culture itself; they particularize culture but at the same time they regulate in a relatively more universalistic way the interests of families, schools, and occupations. In Durkheim's final portrait of modern society, then, the sacred has become differentiated into a set of specialized spheres.

2. CULTURE AND THE SACRED INDIVIDUAL

It is their status as sacred things that gives to representations their autonomy, indeed their central and determining power, in the society. Though themselves products of association, as representations of collective sentiments ideas gain autonomy from association and sentiments in turn. If ideas were not representations, in other words, there could be no culture at all. "The emblem is not merely a convenient process for clarifying the sentiment society has of itself: it also serves to create this sentiment; it is one of its constituent elements."[16] In fact, association could not even occur without shared symbols, for it is these shared representations that allow communication to occur. "Individual minds cannot come into contact and communicate with each other except by coming out of themselves," Durkheim writes, and "they can communicate only by means of signs which express their internal states."[17] In a very real sense, therefore, symbolic representations are the center of society, the strongest determination of its institutional forms: "The ideal type which each society demands that its members realize is the keystone of the whole social system and gives it its unity."[18]

Durkheim identifies three different kinds of cultural representations—the cognitive, the moral, and the aesthetic—but it is only the first two that receive any substantial attention. Today, only moral representations continue to have a truly religious status: they produce the kind of powerful commitment that repels all individual argument and rational contestation. The cognitive representation of truth, in contrast, is now given over completely to rational debate. In the realm of truth, Durkheim affirms, modern society will always choose individual reflection over sacred dogma.[19] He insists that religion has given up its "ancient ambition" to subordinate intellectual speculation to sacred morality, that religion no longer constitutes a "cosmology."[20] But although truth is pursued without deference to dogma, the perception of nature upon which this pursuit is based retains a religious quality; the "logic" of empirical, ra-

tional analysis rests upon certain beliefs whose normative status is un-
questioned. The modern *capacity* for cognition, in other words, has a
sacred base; it supplies to the undogmatic search for truth the general
categories of thought itself, notions like identity, contradiction, causation, and force. It should not be entirely surprising, therefore, that Durkheim's finest analysis of the sacred origins of culture actually is a history
of the religious origins of rational logic.

Durkheim begins with the assumption that cognitive categories are
basic to communication and, therefore, an essential element in social
order itself.[21] "Society could not abandon the categories to the free
choice of the individual without abandoning itself."[22] While primitive
man had a natural desire to speculate about his surroundings, the models for his explanations could be developed only by his analogizing from
the structure of collective sentiments to the objects to be explained. For
primitive man, Durkheim writes, "a species of things [i.e., a primitive
form of cognitive classification] is not a simple object of knowledge but
corresponds above all to a certain sentimental attitude": "There are sentimental affinities between things as between individuals, and they are
classed according to these affinities." It was, therefore, states of the collective "soul" that gave rise to the first primitive kinds of intellectual
groupings. Since religious classifications were at the center of the primitive "soul," it was derivations of spiritual thinking and action that structured primitive logic and classifications. The most obvious example is the
logical tendency to classify things into dichotomous categories, a cognitive capacity which derives directly from religious thought. For primitive man, Durkheim writes, "things are above all sacred or profane, pure
or impure, friends or enemies, favourable or unfavourable; i.e., their
most fundamental characteristics are only expressions of the way in
which they affect social sensibility."[23] Cognitive classifications, then, began as sacred collective representations. Once they were formulated in
primitive association, they gained an autonomy which they have had
ever since. Because they had retained the energy of their original association, they had the power to structure the material world; they continue to be so empowered today.[24†]

Cognitive representations, then, do have at least a residually sacred
status in modern life. But the principal elements that continue to organize social life by virtue of their sacred power are moral ones. In modern
societies, Durkheim believes, moral life is overwhelmingly organized
around a single kind of belief, the belief in individualism. There are occasions in his later work when he offers an explanation for this modern
individualism that closely resembles the materialist analysis of his earlier work.[25] For the most part, however, Durkheim's clear intention is to
break with that early historicism. He does not deny that changes in material structure facilitate a more individualistic society, but he now argues

that this individualism must not be confused with the "utilitarian egoism of Spencer and the economists."[26] Time and time again, Durkheim insists that modernization has not brought any epistemological change. Action and order still have a spiritual status; the only difference is that with modernity the object of divinization has shifted from heaven to earth: modernization means that society is "coming to be held by individuals, in its own right and in its wholly secular form, in sufficient esteem for its needs and interests—even the purely temporal ones—to appear as preeminently respectable and sacred."[27] Other-worldly gods have been divested of their sacred power; the earthly "individual" now assumes their sacred role. The content of religious symbolism has changed, but not its form. The "individual," Durkheim assures us, has everything that is necessary to make it the focus of religious sentiments. It is an ideal, one which "so far surpasses the level of utilitarian goals that it seems to those minds who aspire to it to be completely stamped with religiosity."[28]

> On the one hand, it inspires us with a religious respect that keeps us at some distance. Any encroachment upon the legitimate sphere of action of our fellow beings we regard as a sacrilege. It is, as it were, sacrosanct and thus apart. But at the same time human personality is the outstanding object of our sympathy and we endeavour to develop it. It is an ideal to be realized in ourselves as completely as possible.[29]

Nothing could be further removed from the "concrete" or "substantialist" approach to the individual that blocked Durkheim's earlier understanding of the complementary relationship between order and freedom. After his encounter with the spiritual order of religion, he can describe individualism—the very quintessence of modern freedom—as produced by normative order itself. Individualism does not separate the person from social control but actually simply links him to collective order of a different kind, one in which the human person, as "the touchstone which distinguishes good from evil," is considered "sacred in the ritual sense." "The respect which is given it," Durkheim writes in reference to the idea of the individual, "comes precisely from this [religious] source."[30] This socialization has developed because the individual has become the new organizing focus of collective sentiments, he is "an autonomous center of activity, an impressive system of personal forces whose energy can no more be destroyed than that of . . . cosmic forces."[31] As the carrier of such energy, the individual "partakes of the transcendent majesty that churches of all time lend to their gods; [he] is conceived of as being invested with that mysterious property which creates a void about sacred things, which removes them from vulgar contacts and withdraws them from common circulation."[32] Durkheim had earlier ar-

gued that the contemporary order takes on a religious form because it
has itself evolved from earlier, less differentiated religious facts. He
makes exactly this point about modern individualism. Where the ancient
religion of the city-state rested upon acts of external, ritualistic piety,
Christianity emphasized the personal conviction of the individual. "It is
therefore a singular error," he insists, "to present the individualistic
ethic as the antagonist of Christian morality." Quite the contrary, "the
former derived from the latter." "By attaching ourselves to the first," he
insists, "we do not deny our past; we only continue it."[33] The presuppositional, antihistoricist continuity between past and present means that the
modern belief in individualism inherently assumes a religious form.

Since morality provides the order of society, and since individualism
is the central tenet of modern morality, then individualism must be maintained if social order is to be preserved. All of society's more concrete,
task-oriented institutions must be devoted to preserving this sacred end.
Durkheim argues, for example, that the state, as "an organ of public
life," is "only an instrument, a means," to this moral end.[34] It is moral
authority, after all, not material power, that is the crucial organizer of
collective life. Individualism has "penetrated our institutions," Durkheim observes, and if "we had to give it up, we would have to recast our
whole moral organization at the same stroke."[35]

Like all moral authority, individualism imposes itself because the
emotional energy already invested in it allows it to direct other psychic
energy along a similar path. The violation of individualism is felt to be
sacrilegious because it threatens internal, emotional commitments.
"Every enterprise directed against the rights of an individual," Durkheim writes, "weaken[s] the feelings it transgresses against"; and "since
these feelings are the only ones we hold in common, they cannot be
weakened without disturbing the cohesion of society." The voluntary expression of individual self-interest can, for this reason, become a means
of upholding the supra-individual normative order: "The individual who
defends the rights of the individual defends at the same time the vital
interests of society, for he prevents the criminal impoverishment of that
last reserve of collective ideas and feelings which is the very soul of the
nation."[36] "Individualism thus extended is the glorification not of the self
but of the individual in general. It springs not from egoism but from sympathy."[37] To explain the fundamental basis of modern order, Durkheim
has invoked here the kind of penal retribution that he earlier relegated to
primitive, "mechanical" society. He now believes, however, that modern
"respect for authority" is compatible with reason and freedom. "This
cult of man," he writes, "has as its primary dogma the autonomy of reason and as its primary rite the doctrine of free inquiry." Authority, therefore, will be respected only if it is "rationally grounded," for if it is not,
then authority itself is profaned. Durkheim is distinguishing here between presuppositional and ideological rationality. To be fully consistent

with sacred authority—to be accepted on the nonrational level—modern institutions, he insists, must be fully rational and "competent"; they must be based upon the most effective and humane means to achieve the ends which individuals themselves have proposed. Given the nature of the modern faith, in other words, the only way to sacralize modern authority is to humanize it.[38]

The individualism which so sustains the modern moral order is, clearly, a radically cosmopolitan representation. It is an "impersonal and anonymous" force, one which "pass[es] beyond the political frontiers" of any nation state and which "develop[s] over periods of time that exceed the history of a single society."[39] Durkheim calls this kind of cosmopolitan ideal civilizational, for a civilization "constitutes a kind of moral milieu encompassing a certain number of nations, each national culture being only a particular form of the whole." The ideas that create civilizations create "symbolic frontiers [*frontières idéales*]" which "dominate and develop the collective life of each people."[40] Durkheim acknowledges that any national culture also contains representational currents of a more particularistic sort. He refers on occasion to various "myths" and "religious or moral legends" that still play a role in modern life;[41] he speaks about the continuing influence of nationalistic, patriotic sentiments;[42] and he recognizes that most citizens still accept traditional religion, with its other-worldly beliefs and membership in a particularistic church.[43] Yet while he admits that "religious ideas . . . still remain the preeminent form of public and private thought for the vast majority of men," he maintains that even for the faithful religion no longer provides an explanation of the world in cognitive terms.[44] Modern religion is a more "disciplined morality" than traditional faith.[45] Only by understanding this self-limiting quality, Durkheim contends, can one comprehend contemporary "indifference" to separation of church and state. This indifference, he argues, "seems to give strong evidence that [traditional] religious beliefs are linked to consciences only by rather weak roots."[46] Durkheim makes the same kinds of qualifications for the other kinds of beliefs he has mentioned. Legends and myths may still exist, but they no longer have a significant moral or cognitive role. Nationalism is a fact of life, but it is overshadowed by a dominant humanitarianism. He insists that it is "individualism" that is the dominant modern faith, and it is to this sacred representation that he related every other, more particularistic institution.

3. FAMILIES AND OCCUPATIONS: TWO SPHERES OF PARTICULARISTIC SPIRIT

In the *Division of Labor* Durkheim had talked about the modern family as functionally interdependent, and as facilitating individual freedom precisely for this material reason. His later writings, in contrast, carefully emphasize that the institution of the family, whether ancient or modern, has, rather, a moral and spiritual status. In his revisionist second Preface to the *Division of Labor*, he talks about the family as "a school of devotion, of abnegation, the place *par excellence* of morality," and he explains that while this collective order does develop because of "concentration," this concentration is of a moral rather than instrumental type: it concerns the "mutual adaptation of consciences."[47] In public lectures given at about the same time, he talked about the family in terms of the "sentiment of solidarity" that is aroused "by intimate and constant contact of all the associated minds and by a mutual interpenetration of their lives."[48] This subjective interaction, he concludes in an article in *L'Année*, produces a certain kind of religious cohesion, "the spirit of the family." It is this spirit that is crucial for the "domestic order."[49]

The spirit of the family has changed enormously in the course of historical development. In ancient society, family religion was at one with the public faith. The family was relatively independent of society, or, more accurately, was "society" itself, for its members were able to perform most important social functions for themselves.[50] This public form and explicitly social function gave to the family an "abstract personality," one which did not recognize the individuality of its members.[51] The first change in this situation occurred with patriarchy, which significantly privatized family life by allowing a single member, the father, to monopolize the relations between the family and the outside world.[52] Later, with the development of the faith in the "individual personality," families decrease further in size and withdraw completely from the public world; only in this way can the parents fulfill their desires to treat their children and one another as true individuals.[53] The domestic order produced by this new, "conjugal" family is much more intense than ever before, for in this smaller unit the members "have been brought more directly and constantly into contact." Familial order is still religious, but the nature and context of family interaction makes it a religion of a different type. It is a private, domestic religion that Durkheim has in mind, and he writes, in classical Victorian fashion, about "the religious respect which the hearth inspires" in modern times.[54]

The new religion of the hearth is much too particularistic to be the source of public morality and social control. Of course, the family still produces altruistic sentiments and the "first feelings of solidarity."[55] The problem, however, is that this altruism takes the form of an emotional and privatistic sentimentality, one in which the "spontaneous sentiments of the heart" dominate group interaction and where "impersonal" and "lofty" regulation is virtually nonexistent.[56] The circle of familial interests is extremely restricted; the family tries to enclose its members in limited loyalties, "swallowing them up" in its religion of private sentimentalism.[57] Because the religion of individualism still informs this institution, in the special hothouse of domestic life it takes on a hue very different from the universalism that sustains its general promise. Any modern nation that is serious about such universalism must subordinate familial religion to forces outside it.[58]

Though connected to the state and certainly outside the family, occupational groups, which present another specialized milieu in Durkheim's theory, remain just as particularistic. They are also as "religious" in the way that this order is maintained. The premise of Durkheim's analysis of occupations, once again, is an implicit critique of the main thrust of his treatment in the *Division of Labor*, in this case his contention that the divided labor creates integration through interdependent functions. He continues to recognize that economic life must, indeed, be characterized by the fact of its specialized, functional status, but he now insists that what is crucial is not the actual performance of the function but the ethic that "governs" them.[59] Specialized functions are "occupations" or "professions"; they require "particular aptitudes and specialized knowledge." These internalized orientations are sustained by certain practices. Interrelating abstract beliefs and practical association, occupations constitute, in this way, a milieu that is formally parallel to the religious one. In each occupation, Durkheim writes, "certain ideas, certain practices, certain modes of viewing this, prevail."[60]

The members of a similar economic niche, or profession, become integrated through exchange, but this is an exchange of sentiments, not matériel. As the embodiments of these sentiments, professional ethics regulate economic actors by virtue of the moral authority with which they are invested.

> Each branch of professional ethics being the product of the professional group, its nature will be that of the group. . . . The greater the strength of the group structure, the more numerous are the moral rules appropriate to it and the greater the authority they have over their members. For the more closely the group coheres, the closer and more frequent the contact of the individuals, and, the more frequent and intimate these contacts and the more exchange there is of ideas and sentiments, the more does a public opinion spread to cover a greater number of things.[61]

Durkheim's language is clearly that of religious activities, of rites and creeds. Members of the same occupation "feel a mutual attraction, they seek out one another, they enter into relations with one another and form compacts and so, by degrees, become a limited group with recognizable features." Once this group is formed, Durkheim insists, "nothing can hinder an appropriate moral life from evolving, a life that will carry the mark of the special conditions that brought it into being." Just as ritual produces creeds, so economic association produces its regulatory rules. "The sense of this whole becomes acute, and then, as it is applied to affairs of communal life—the most ordinary as well as the most important—it is translated into formulas, some more defined than others."[62] Some of these formulas come to be administered by specialized agencies, and in this way occupational ethics become attached to the universalism of the state.[63]

But if emotional association creates certain creeds, Durkheim is careful to emphasize that, just as the representations sacralized by ritual assume a powerful life of their own, occupational morality regulates the very practice from which it was derived. Individuals engage in specialized economic activity because it is a "calling"; like the religious virtuoso "called" to serve God, their specialized labor has a sacred meaning to which they are emotionally attached.[64] The teacher is inspired by the faith that his task is vital to the sacred center of society.[65] In scientific activity, motivation is, in a similar way, merely the other side of the regulating ethic. "However great the role of individuals may be in it," Durkheim insists, "science is something pre-eminently social." As social action, it is morally regulated: "Its methods and techniques are the work of tradition, and they constrain the person with an authority comparable to that of rules of law or morals."[66] The scientist's sense of his own calling, however, ensures that this regulation is enthusiastically accepted. "The mental process involved in the self-sacrifice of the scientist impassioned by his work," Durkheim writes, "resembles [so] closely those involved in true moral self-sacrifice that it must to a certain extent participate in the feelings which the latter inspire."[67]

As in his analysis of the family, Durkheim insists on linking this analytic demonstration of the "religious" order of occupational life to an account of its historical association with traditional religious phenomena. In Rome, occupational guilds were overtly religious. Durkheim talks about the "spiritual kinship" that united them and discusses in detail the ritualistic feasts, festivals, and ceremonies that created their unity.[68] Later, guilds took their inspiration from Christianity. They established themselves in a local parish, placed themselves under the protection of a patron saint, and attended en masse various religious activities that consecrated their sacred identity.[69] The twelfth century marked the height of such guild formation. Durkheim discusses in detail, for example, the intimate relationship between Christianity and education that allowed the development of the first guilds for college professors, as well as the intricate set of rituals that sustained it.[70]

Subsequent historical development secularized this religious integration, for economic specialization now occurred within a cultural context that was ruled by the cult of individualism. These secular occupational orders have a special character. It is not that they have become more material in their integration, but rather that the symbols which unify them have taken on a different form. Like the family, occupations in modern society perform specialized tasks; they are, therefore, relatively isolated from the public faith. Occupations are internally integrated by ethical concerns, but because their specialized practice isolates them from the wider society this ethic is relatively unintegrated with the concerns of the broader public. The "public conscience," Durkheim writes, regards it with indifference. "There are no moral rules whose infringement, in general at least, is looked on with so much indulgence by public opinion."[71] Professional ethics, then, "find their right place between the family morals . . . and civic morals."[72] Certainly they are less spontaneous and sentimental than the spirit that regulates family life. But for all their impersonality and rigidity, they are still particularistic. The association which produces them is wider than a single family, but it is separated in a similar manner from the association of society as a whole. Only the state can institutionalize sentiments that represent association on such a mammoth scale.

4. THE STATE AND THE LAW AS TRANSCENDENT REPRESENTATIONS

Durkheim has discussed two segments of society which despite their moral foundations are distinctively particularistic in their content. The state, he believes, functions to modify this particularism. The state in the *Division of Labor*, we may recall, functioned in much the same way, as the coordinator of different segments, the neo-utilitarian articulator of the general interest. There is, however, a radical difference between the early and later visions, and this concerns the manner in which the state accomplishes this task. How does it become more "general" in its perception of interests than the segments which it regulates, and how is this regulation effected? In the *Division of Labor*, this generality of vision was achieved and effected mechanically. The state had an interest in stability, both for itself and as the instrument of those it governed; if the parties to an exchange produced conflict, this interest would be threatened. The result would be state intervention to change these noncontractual aspects of contract. In Durkheim's later writings, this empirical explanation is radically revised to fit with the shift in Durkheim's generalized orientation. He sharply distinguishes the administrative executive organs of government from the "state" itself. These organs, which have the power to act, were precisely the object of his analysis in his earlier work.[73] But Durkheim now rejects this identification of the state with a "cog in a machine."[74] The true function of the state is to think, not to act, and its heart is deliberation, discussion, and research.[75]

The new model for Durkheim's theory of the state is religion, particularly the relationship between association, collective energy, and representation. Political society, Durkheim now believes, is a field for psychological and moral association. What makes the association political is that it occurs not simply among the masses themselves but between them and a differentiated organ, the state. As in religious ritual, the contact between state and society releases energy: "Parliament and the government are in touch with the masses of the nation and the various impressions released by this contact."[76] In ritual, this energy becomes focused through a general process of group representation. In political society, in contrast, the representational process has become specialized: it is carried on by the state. The state "represents" the society to itself by "canalizing" and "concentrating" the energy produced by the contact between it and the public at large.[77] These representations are political decisions, and they affect society by feeding a new idea back into the "ritual" association: "The vaguely diffused sentiments that float about the whole expanse of society affect the decisions made by the State, and conversely, those decisions made by the State, the ideas expounded in the Chamber, the speeches made there and the measures agreed upon by the ministries, all have an echo in the whole of the society and modify the ideas strewn there."[78]

The point, of course, is that this new idea is not simply another representation like any other. The organizational autonomy of the state and its access to a wide range of social contact means that its representations are particularly clarifying and rational. "The debates in the assemblies," Durkheim claims, are "a process analogous to thought in the individual." They have the "precise object of keeping minds very clear and forcing them to become aware of the motives that sway them this way or that and to account for what they are doing." Only with this kind of representation before it, Durkheim believes, can a collectivity avoid "action that is unconsidered or automatic or blind."[79] The consciousness of the state, compared with the general consciousness of the society, is "higher" and "clearer," and has a "more vivid sense of itself."[80] As a result, the upshot of the state's deliberations, discussions, and statistics is to provide "the starting point of a new mental life."[81] But if the state's representations allow more clarity and self-reflection, they are not always democratic. Democracy depends not on the differentiated quality of government consciousness but on its "range." Only if the state can interact with the affectivity and morality of a wide spectrum of social forces will its representations be "representative" in the democratic rather than simply religious sense of the term.[82]

Once again, Durkheim supports this analytic argument for the "religious" quality of modern political society with evidence about its historical development. In the *Division of Labor* he had conceded that the state could play a moral role, but in general he limited this moral connection to primitive, mechanical societies. In this primitive period, other-worldly religion and civic values were fused, and it was only for this reason, only because there was literally a political religion, that the state took on spiritual functions as the "authorized interpreter of collective sentiments," the institution that "maintain[s] the common conscience itself."[83] Once this fusion of religion and state had disappeared, the state assumed its modern function of rational arbiter of the collective interest. In his later writings, however, Durkheim's understanding of secularization has been transformed. Modern society is still imbedded in religious sentiments; they are simply sentiments that sacralize the individual rather than God himself. The modern state, therefore, continues to play the same kind of spiritual and moral role as the ancient one; the difference is in the nature of the religious sentiments that inform it. "It is just as simple," Durkheim writes, "for men to draw together to work for the greatness of man as it is to work for the glory of Zeus or Jehovah or Athena."[84] Other-worldly religion has become strictly segmented from the rest of society, so the state is now executor of the cult of the individual.

> The whole difference of this religion, as it affects the individual, is that the god of its devotion is closer to his worshippers. But although not far removed, he does nevertheless still transcend them, and the role of the State in this respect is what it was formerly. It rests with it, shall we say, to organize the cult, to be the head of it and to ensure its regular working and development.[85]

The state still represents the collective conscience, but it is now the defender, not the enemy, of individual freedom and independence.[86] "The institution of these rights," Durkheim says, "is in fact precisely the task of the State."[87]

This historical analysis of the state's sacred origins not only adds strength to Durkheim's analytic argument but allows him to specify it in an important way. The state, one now sees, is not engaged only with the diffuse sentiments of different social segments, for when it acts to represent such "collective particularism" it is already informed by the religion of individualism, the universalistic creed that informs the basic roots of society itself.[88] Just as ritualistic representation is necessarily informed by the religious tradition within which it occurs, so is the political representation of particularistic sentiments informed by the broad commitment to individual rights. The state, therefore, is in conflict with particular segments even while it tries to represent them; it tries to reflect back to them their "better self," not simply the empirical self with which it interacted. The state "remind[s] these partial societies," Durkheim writes, "that they are not alone and that there is a right that stands above their own rights." "Wherever these particular collective forces exist, there the power of the State must be, to neutralize them: for if they were left alone and to their own devices, they would draw the individual within their exclusive domination."[89] The state is effective only if it can "persevere in calling the individual to a moral way of life."[90]

Yet no matter how universalistically the state acts, it still retains an element of particularism, for its reference is to a particular nation rather than to mankind in general. In this sense, political morality is not different from that which governs the worlds of family and occupations; all three refer to the "duties that men have towards one another because they belong to a certain definite social group." The law, in Durkheim's view, is different, for legal duties are "independent of any particular grouping." Even when other actors are not part of one's family, nation, or geographic or ethnic group, one must respect their life, property, and honor. Legal rules, therefore, order action in a significantly more universalistic way than the other institutions Durkheim has considered, although they are still more concrete and specific than the institution of culture itself.[91]

In the *Division of Labor*, Durkheim had historicized his analysis of law in order to make his picture of modernity consistent with his instrumental presuppositions. In primitive societies, he wrote, law was directly connected to the collective conscience; in modern societies, it was formulated as an adaptive response to social conflict and disequilibrium. Since modern law was separated from the collective conscience, anger and indignation were not the primary responses to its violation. Precisely this lack of strong emotional undergirding, Durkheim believed, allowed modern law to be so closely responsive to individual rights, for instead of focusing on punishment it could direct its energy simply to restitution.

The revolution of Durkheim's middle period, and his later encounter with religion, changed all this. In his Preface to the second edition of the *Division of Labor*, published in 1902, he decisively rejects the historicization of his earlier theorizing and the empirical analysis of law which it informs. Juridical regulations, he now insists, reflect "a state of opinion." Laws reflect ways of acting that have become "consecrated" by public opinion and hence given special authority.[92] Later he makes this analogy between religious and legal regulations even more direct. The sociology of law, he writes, must focus on the moral "spirit of the law." Taking as his model the relation between ritual spirit and totem, he writes that the legal code gains its authority because it "incarnates" the spirit of the law, "translat[ing] it into definite formulations."[93] The control of action by specific rules, he writes at still another point, does no more than define public opinion with greater precision; "it translates into precepts ideas and sentiments felt by all." To define law only by its material sanctions and specific prohibitions is a mistake, he warns, for this would be to "regard its outer aspect and grasp the letter of it alone." Like the totem or representation, the rigidity of the law's outer wrapping is merely the expression of "the spirit that animates it."[94] In view of this emphasis on the internal spiritual commitment that makes the law, it is not surprising that Durkheim makes an analogy, in yet another essay, between "the horror which crime inspires" and the feeling "with which a believer reacts to sacrilege."[95] Laws are obeyed, not from fear of material retaliation, but rather out of the same feeling of voluntary, internal deference that is inspired by sacred things: "We refrain from performing the acts they forbid simply because they are forbidden."[96] The material sanctions threatened by the law, in fact, are no more significant than the material objects which are often the bases for sacred representations. Not important in themselves, they are simply the "outward sign" by which actors recognize the moral and spiritual order to which they are subordinate.[97]

Durkheim supports this subjectification of the law with an elaborate evolutionary analysis of the law's sacred history. This history, which constitutes a major portion of the lectures on ethics given during the 1902/3 school year, drastically revises the genealogy he presented in the *Division of Labor* ten years before. Legal evolution does not proceed as a result of the movement from collective conscience and collective sentiment to rational state and utilitarian restitution. What changes, rather, is the content of collective sentiments, not the fact of their existence. The object of religious action has shifted, but it is religious all the same.

Durkheim begins by considering the crimes of murder and theft. The first of these was considered a nonrepresentative modern crime in the *Division of Labor*; the second was considered in a utilitarian way. Both are now taken as central to modernity, and both are related to the demands of collective sentiments. Durkheim emphasizes, in fact, that murder has come to be considered heinous only in modern times. In primitive societies, the group rather than the individual was the object of sacred honor; the murder of an individual, therefore, was treated with relative indifference.[98] With modernity, however, there has been a transformation in "collective sensibility." Only after "our more highly developed altruism is repulsed by the idea of making another suffer," only "when the sympathetic sentiments of man for man were affirmed and developed," did murder become a sacrilege and, hence, a crime.[99]

Durkheim treats laws against theft in a similar way. How are we to explain, he asks, the respect that the property of others inspires in modern times, a respect that the law endorses by means of penal sanctions? "How does it happen that things should attach so closely to the person that they share his inviolability?"[100] The reasons for this shift in respect, the reason for the connection between things and people, can be discovered only if we understand the religious aspects of social life. Property can become individualized, first of all, only because the individual has become the object of religious sentiments: "Private property came into existence because the individual turned to his own benefit . . . the respect inspired by the society."[101] Objects become invested with the new respect accorded to individuals because the liquid quality of sacred respect makes it highly contagious; composed of psychic energy, sacredness will spread to everything it touches.[102] If the individual is sacred, then, eventually, so will his property be. "It is inevitable," Durkheim believes, "that this sacred virtue which invests the individual should be extended to the things he is closely . . . connected with." "The sentiments of respect for him," Durkheim continues, "cannot be limited to the physical person alone; the objects considered as his own must certainly have a share in them."[103] Private property has become law, in other words, because it shares the religious authority of the individual who possesses it; "Property is property only if it is respected, that is to say, held sacred."[104]

Durkheim begins his more detailed consideration of the origins of sacred property by reaffirming this religious model. The very concept of property, he points out, means that an object is distinguished from objects in common use. This feature is also shared by all religious and sacred things. "Whenever we have a religious ritual, the world over, the feature that distinguishes the sacred entities is that they are withdrawn from general circulation; they are separate and set apart."[105] Or, again, he notes that property means that "all about us there are objects which are forbidden to us," and that this has a directly religious parallel in the case of "taboo." Since the same kind of behavior is mandated for law as for religion, he argues, it is extremely likely that "they will be of the same nature."[106] In fact, Durkheim insists, the very idea of property first developed when men surrounded their newly cultivated fields with a protective boundary of sacred significance. On this strip of land they made religious sacrifices and conducted seasonal rituals. The first boundary markers were blocks of wood that played an intimate part in these religious ceremonies.[107] This familial property first became individualized after one of the members of the family group had been raised in rank. As the representative of the group, this outstanding individual now became the object of the ties that had previously bound things to the group as a whole. "Since this individual embodied in himself the whole group, men and things, he was in fact invested with an authority that placed things as well as men under his dominance, and thus an individual property came into existence."[108]†

From this history of the laws of landed property, Durkheim proceeds to an analysis of the history of contract, the very center of his utilitarian discussion in the *Division of Labor.* "New institutions," he writes, "begin as a rule by taking the old as their model," and contract is no exception. Durkheim closely relates the origins of contract to the sacred ties that bound members of the same family, or clan, to one another. Contracts are means to bind strangers. Prototypically, a stranger is a person outside one's own family. It follows, therefore, "that when men felt the need to create ties other than those of their own family status, that is, ties which they willed, they conceived them as a matter of course in the likeness of the only ties familiar to them."[109] Strangers formed an artificial community by the symbolic sharing of blood, which was achieved through various kinds of ritual acts. Working from the proposition that food makes blood and blood makes life, "contracts" were accomplished through rites of communion, like the breaking of bread and the sharing of wine. The ritual of handshaking, Durkheim believes, began in a similar way, as a symbolic procedure through which the blood of strangers could take on the sacred familial form.[110]

These early forms of sacralizing the relationship between strangers gradually assumed more modern forms, and exchange was guaranteed in a more specific way. The first stage of this development, the "real contract," ensured the equality of exchange by giving to material goods the importance which had earlier been assigned simply to the individuals themselves. Property took on the sacredness of its owners, so if property was given, the recipients felt honor bound to offer an equal part of their own wealth in exchange.[111] In the oath-bound contract, the form that followed, words rather than goods took on the sacred form. "There is something in words," Durkheim writes, "that is real, natural and living and they can be endowed with a sacred force, thanks to which they compel and bind those who pronounce them."[112] Contracts are compelling only if an oath is pronounced in its ritual form and under ritual conditions. Under these conditions, the obligatory words are now more powerful than the individuals who pronounce them, for "the oath . . . is a means of communicating to words . . . the kind of transcendence we see in all moral things."[113] The formal legal contract follows naturally from this oath-taking form, for it is merely the further crystallization, the further "exteriorizing," of the same kinds of internal psychic commitment: "The juridical formula is only a substitute for sacred formalities and rites."[114] At the same time that the formal legal contract emerges, there develops also the notion of the consensual contract, by which guarantees of reciprocity are established without any formalization at all. What is important here is simply that the parties to an exchange have followed certain legitimate procedures, such as, for example, declaring their intention to engage in reciprocal exchange. With the emergence of this consensual exchange, contractual obligations become almost completely a matter of conscience. Yet Durkheim insists that the very recognition that informal procedures could guarantee reciprocity was the product of the earlier religious forms. The consciousness about procedure derived from ritual participation and liturgy. Eventually, this consciousness was "detached from the cause that originally produced it and linked to another cause—of which the useful effects are preserved, although they are reached by a different procedure."[115]

The final, most highly evolved relationship of exchange is governed by the just contract, which ensures that all transactions—for example, the exchange of services for money in the contract for labor—must not only be formally but substantively equal. This new form of contract institutionalizes more fully than ever before the cult of the individual; it comes into being only as the faith in this cult is deepened. The just contract, Durkheim writes, is the "sequel in law of . . . the sympathy that man has for man," a sentiment that "tends to eliminate or strip away from all social sanctions every kind of physical and material inequality."[116] Insofar as individuals adhere to a just contract, it is because their "consciences rebel" against any inequality of exchange.[117] By linking this most modern of social controls to the emotional and moral response that prevents sacrilege in religious life, Durkheim has concluded this radical revision of his earlier writing on contract in an ironic, if fully appropriate, way.

Durkheim's later analysis of modern law has established that it shares the same religious basis as its primitive counterpart. At the same time, however, he has insisted on the great divergence in the law's content. If the motivation to punish is the same, the acts which induce punishment are often entirely different. So, Durkheim demonstrated in an early article in L'Année, is the nature of punishment itself. With the development of cultural notions about the importance of the individual, repression shifts from physical dismemberment and capital punishment to the simple deprivation of freedom. In the course of the same development, kinship and corporate groups gradually lose their control over individual action. Because individuals can then avoid punishment by fleeing, the development of prisons becomes crucial to the new form of more individualistic punishment.[118]

But this social need for equilibrium does not, in Durkheim's later thinking, produce necessary institutional change, and here Durkheim returns to the revisionist theory of his later work. If prisons are to develop, what is needed is the "idea of a prison." Prisons, like any other material structure, are representations of the social spirit; they can develop, therefore, only if the proper spirit, the right idea, is there to be concretized. But ideas are produced by moral concentration, and in earlier societies this concentration was not of a sufficient magnitude. Durkheim's analysis is directly derived from his understanding of religious ritual and the requisites for sacred representation. In earlier societies, he writes, "public life is very meager, very intermittent," and because of this there is no need for architectural forms that could represent public sentiment in a grandiose way. But when public life becomes more intense, the material form of representing it is simultaneously transformed: "As collective life, instead of being dispersed into a vast number of minor foci," is "concentrated about a more restricted number of points . . . and becomes more intense and continuous," the "dwellings of those who are in charge are transformed." Authority grows in stature as the sentiments it represents are intensified, and as authority becomes grand so must its material embodiments. The relationship between material form and spiritual substance is substantial and elaborate.

> The more the authority of those who live in them grows, the more those dwellings are singularized and distinguished from the rest. They take on a grandiose air; they are sheltered by higher walls and deeper moats in such a way as to denote visibly the line of demarcation which thenceforth separates the holders of power and the mass of their subordinates.[119]

Once public buildings had taken on this differentiated and imposing quality, "the preconditions of prisons [had] come into being."[120] The nature of punishments has changed, therefore, but the social order upon which it is based remains decisively normative and emotional.

5. EDUCATION: THE RELIGIOUS NATURE AND HISTORY OF A CONTEMPORARY INSTITUTION

Because education serves as an introduction to the wider social order, theories of education are crucially determined by the understanding of its social environment. Identifying the ultimate source of order with the world of occupations and markets, Marx viewed education as a means by which labor could be funneled into these particularistic spheres. Education was "reproduction," and the children of the working classes were supplied only with the minimum of specific skills necessary to fulfill their later obligations to the capitalist. Durkheim acknowledges that workers receive specialized education, but he argues that this education, like the education of other groups, rests upon a cultural base that is shared by the whole society. It imparts the "ideas, sentiments, and practices" common to all. This communication of common values represents the "true education" that every member of society receives.[121]

For Durkheim, then, as for Marx, education is a transitional institution, but for him it mediates between family and culture, not family and occupation. Durkheim views education not as part of an instrument of material coercion, but as a link between two kinds of moralities, the affective morality of family life and the more rigorous, impersonal faith that controls civic society.[122] The challenge of education is to impart the civic "spirit," to communicate the "ideal of man" that each society sets up for itself.[123] In modern society, education must create the "individual" in accordance with the cult that consecrates him. Through its authority, in other words, it creates liberty.[124] It does so by training the individual to recognize the demands of his own conscience, to be his own master by using reason on the world.[125] Through a rational moral education, the child develops the ability for criticism and reflection that is fundamental to the modern faith.[126] In this way, education is a means of reproduction, but it reproduces universalistic culture rather than particularistic economic relations. By transmitting the general and abstract ends of the collectivity, society "perpetually recreates the conditions of its very existence." Education provides for the "socialization of the younger generation" by "fixing . . . in the mind of the child, the essential similarities that collective life presupposes."[127] As a result of this socialization, the transformation of himself into a social being, the child will learn to be moral before he faces the material demands of later life. Because of education, he will be able to act in later life for moral rather than physical reasons.[128]

This socialization will be accomplished through educators who are not servants of the state or of capital, but who represent the moral whole. It is public "opinion" that makes teachers act in appropriate ways. It is opinion, Durkheim tells the teachers-in-training at the Sorbonne, that "exert[s] on us . . . a moral pressure so that we may thus understand our duties as educators."[129] The state plays neither an ideological nor a coercive role; it presents simply a more specific form of moral pressure, for its extensive organization allows it to "remind the teacher constantly of the ideas, the sentiments that must be impressed upon the child."[130] This opinion which directs the state, and education in turn, is not of an economic origin but it is indomitable nonetheless, for "opinion is a moral force whose constraining power is not less than that of physical forces."[131]

Durkheim's more specific analyses of the process of education closely follow his model of religious order. When it is effective, he writes, education retains the "quasi-religious character of morality."[132] This religious character is vital, for example, in understanding the proper role of the teacher. It is the feeling of transmitting something sacred that gives the teacher authority. Because he feels himself to be in touch with sacred morality, he feels himself "speaking in the name of a superior reality."[133] The teacher pursues his calling, therefore, with an "inner faith";[134] Durkheim speaks of his "ministry," and draws an elaborate comparison between the teacher's role and that of the priest.

> It is the priest's lofty conception of his mission that gives him the authority that so readily colors his language and bearing. For he speaks in the name of a God, whom he feels in himself. . . . So, the lay teacher can and should have something of this same feeling.

He also is an instrument of a great moral reality. . . . Just as the priest is the interpreter of God, he is the interpreter of the great moral ideas of his time and country. Whatever is linked with these ideas, whatever the significance and authority attributed to them, necessarily spreads to him and everything coming from him since he expresses these things and embodies them in the eyes of children.[135]

The sacred is contagious. The teacher is invested with "extra energy" by his contact with the moral order, and this contact gives him the warmth that is necessary to stir the heart of his students.[136] Moreover, the teacher's respect for authority, the sacred energy which has infected him, spills over to his students. Because of this contagious effect, the teacher exerts order not through violence or repression but through his "moral authority."[137] Students obey his authority because of its "prestige" and "energy"; they view it as "sacred and inviolable."[138] Like the authority of religious representations, the teacher's power is sustained through a process of association and interaction which is "like an echo from all the little minds with which he deals" and which "rebounds toward him enlarged by all these repercussions."[139] The classroom, after all, is not different from any other social group; Durkheim describes it as a field of "collective psychology" dominated by "phenomena of contagion" like "over-excitement" and "effervescence."[140] No more than religious representations can the teacher's authority submit readily to violation if it expects to survive. "Everything that might induce children to believe that it is not really inviolable," Durkheim writes, "can scarcely fail to strike discipline at its very source," for "a sacred thing profaned no longer seems sacred."[141] The problem of profanation is exacerbated because school children have not yet internalized the rule which they are expected to obey. They themselves, therefore, cannot feel the moral outrage which is the principal source for voluntary order in the adult world. It is for this reason, Durkheim believes, that strict discipline and punishment must play such an important role in school life. Only the teacher's strong disapproval can identify a student's action as immoral, or sacrilegious. The form of punishment follows the nature of the order it is trying to instill: it seeks to create in students the religious reaction that would have occurred if they had known that the sacred was being violated. Thus, "the principal form of punishment has always consisted in putting the guilty on the *index*, holding him at a distance, ostracizing him, making a void around him, and separating him from decent people."[142†] The guilty student is treated, in other words, as the carrier of the sacred in its negative form; the teacher can thus graphically illustrate the underlying religious meaning.

As with his analyses of other institutions, Durkheim supplements this argument for the "spiritual" order of educational life with a demonstration of its historical evolution from explicitly religious forms. In this case, however, his historical analysis far overshadows his contemporary one. In 1904/5, Durkheim devoted an entire course of lectures to the "History of Education in France," lectures posthumously published as *L'Evolution pédagogique en France* and in English as *The Evolution of Educational Thought*. Durkheim concerned himself in these lectures with two fundamental questions: first, how the institution of the school itself came to be formed; second, how these schools came to be differentiated from the church. The answers he offers present a model of "institutional" history. They are the most sustained historical effort that Durkheim attempted after 1893, and they represent the theoretical alternative to the historical sociology he essayed in *The Division of Labor in Society*.

Institutional history, Durkheim insists, is equivalent to the "history of ideas," if we understand ideas not as sui generis forms but as collective representations for changes in collective sentiment. This definition of institutional history is, of course, in keeping with his position in the later work that it is sentiments and ideals that are at the heart of any institution. French educational institutions are certainly no different. "The French educational ideal," Durkheim believes, "articulates" itself in various pedagogical doctrines, and "realizes" itself in academic institutions.[143] To study the history of French education, therefore, one must "trace the genesis of the institution [from] the moral forces" which produced it and from "the animating spirit which determined [its] orientation."[144] The subject of such history is "mental evolution," for "it is the depths of ... the social conscience from which everything else derives."[145]

The religious model, therefore, is omnipresent in this institutional history, which is very much the history of the transition from spirit to "tangible forms" and "visible consequences."[146] In one sense, the work can be understood as the study of one extended ritual experience. Durkheim begins with the "pure spirit of Christianity" in the Middle Ages, and he characterizes this as the "germinative cell" from which all later structures emerge. Because the Greeks and Romans who preceded Christianity had either a utilitarian or an aesthetic approach to education, they did not conceive of it as an intense emotional experience. They did not, for this reason, concentrate education in a single "school," but chose, rather, to spread it over different points. Christianity presented a radical alternative to this idea and to its institutional form, for Christians believed that education must be directed to the "soul," toward creating a "general disposition of morality and will."[147] In order to provide for such an intense educational experience, the church established institutions that could concentrate education in a single place. In the early Middle Ages, then, tiny "schools," closely attached to individual churches, were scattered all over Christendom. Durkheim describes as a sort of long and extended ritual the movement of spiritual intensification that brought these scattered schools into the large, much more concentrated structures that are the educational institutions of the modern day.

> Certain points of light gathered here and there: they are these humble schools which survive in the cloisters and in the cathedrals. . . . These feeble glimmers of light gradually came to revitalize themselves, to grow little by little in strength and brilliance; then, instead of remaining in isolation somewhere or other, coming closer together, amalgamating, mutually reinforcing one another as a result of this concentration until they became, as colleges and universities, powerful centres of brightness.[148]

In another sense, however, Durkheim's history is an account of many different rituals, not just one extended gathering of forces. The long process of concentration is composed of episodic movements of similar ritual structure. Durkheim describes successive "renaissances," periods of "general effervescence" where the "superfluity of energy," the "accumulation of vitality" was so great that it could find an outlet only in new institutional forms.[149] Early ritual episodes created new structures, which, in turn, were reenergized and reformed by "religious" episodes at a later time.

The deep structure of Durkheim's history is an account of "movement," of human association motivated by moral hopes and by shifts in spiritual order. The surface structure relies heavily on political developments, on organizational developments by men and groups and nations. But in keeping with his earlier analysis of the state, Durkheim spiritualizes this "political" history. The political movements are either themselves promoted by moral effervescence, or they are immediately accompanied by them.

The first revitalizing renaissance occurred as a result of the migration of Benedictine monks to England. The Benedictines had tremendous energy, but their conception of education was relatively undeveloped. In England, they encountered the Irish monks, who, while not as energetic and evangelical, had managed to continue to uphold a much higher sense of true Christian education. The Benedictines subdued the Irish, but the significant result was cultural not political: through absorption of Irish influence, Christian educational ideals were reinvigorated, and the Benedictines proceeded to expand these reinvigorated monastic schools all over the Continent.[150] This energy subsided, however, and before larger educational institutions could develop there would have to be another renaissance of moral life. This opportunity was initiated by the political centralization of Charlemagne, but

Durkheim emphasizes that Charlemagne performed merely as the collective representation for a feeling of potential unity that was already widespread. "All the peoples of Christendom," he writes, "had a vague feeling of belonging to a single whole"; Charlemagne simply found the means to "express" and "organize" it: "This idea of the unity of Christendom, which had been slumbering in a state of semiconsciousness, was given substance by him and became a historical reality." As the symbolic expression of this unification, Charlemagne "was naturally inclined to concentrate all the intellectual forces" of Christendom into one cultural and intellectual center. This was the Ecole de Paris, or University of Paris, headed by the famous scholar and administrator Alcuin.[151]

With Charlemagne's death, the Carolingian renaissance declined and so did the vitality of educational institutions. Further change awaited a new "vital charge," another "new and forceful mind" to "set in motion the public intellect." The last days of Charlemagne's empire had involved tremendous social upheaval, and in the period of comparative tranquility that marked the following century the "moral energy" which had been generated in political struggle was "set free and rendered available" for other tasks. There followed a period of great "general effervescence," of nomadicism and movement, of which the Crusades were only one manifestation. Not surprisingly, this new energy affected education; men traveled all over Europe to seek out the best "schools." This movement resulted in the establishment of scholarly chairs throughout Europe, the great moral authority of which further contributed to the concentration of education and the enlargement of the schools.[152]

Once again, political centralization played a crucial role in carrying this movement of moral concentration further, in this case the beginnings of the French state that the Capetian monarchy initiated in the early part of the twelfth century. As the emerging center of French national life, the principal representation of national sentiment, the monarchy acquired tremendous prestige, and by the process of contagion that is common to all sacred things it shared this energy with the University of Paris. The energy of the latter, in turn, was now such that it soon attracted young scholars away from all the other chairs in Europe.[153] This vigorous association brought even more new energy in its stead. As a consequence, the twelfth century in Paris became "one of the periods of the greatest effervescence of the human mind," one in which most of the institutional reforms associated with the modern university were fathered.[154] Abelard, the university's most brilliant scholar and teacher, became a figure as famous as the royalty of the day. Adding the power of representation to the sentiments that produced him, Abelard's reputation further enhanced the university's great attraction.

The University of Paris became a spiritual magnet, bringing together students and scholars from all over Europe. The influx was so great, in fact, that the traditional church schools comprising the university could not handle it. To handle the overflow, schools were forced to establish themselves outside of the church. With these new bases of association, Durkheim believes, it was inevitable that new ideas about education would result.[155] Teachers formed independent solidary associations, and to protect their independence as well as to express their solidary feeling they developed an intense corporative life, replete with rituals of initiation like the *inceptio*. It was "by a kind of spontaneous evolution from the practice of the *inceptio*"—by, in other words, a spontaneous crystallization of the ritual spirit—that the first professional code for teachers was created.[156] This new code, however, came into immediate conflict with the church's own authority to set standards and grant degrees. The "secularists" won this moral battle and set up the first university outside of church control, but this institution was hardly secular in anything other than a formal sense. It was, in fact, merely the same Christian spirit in a different material form. Composed of "laymen who had to some extent retained the appearance of clerics," the new university was "a magnificent expression of the system of ideas which was its soul."[157]

What remains for Durkheim's institutional history is to trace the further rationalization of this new educational form. Again, he points to the effects of political centralization, the final nationalization of the French political structure in the fifteenth century. This political movement had a major effect, but once again this effect was a moral one. The monarchy was integrated around a highly rationalized "spirit of order," and by a process of moral association this spirit penetrated the university and changed its material form in a significant way. "It was not surprising," Durkheim writes, "that this vast corporation which was the university, being in frequent and direct contact with the state and with roots that reached down to the very interiors of medieval society, should have been animated with the spirit of orderliness, of organization, or regimentation which imbued all the institutions of the era."[158] Yet although significantly rationalized, the university still rested upon the corporate, solidary spirit from which it had first derived. The first degrees and examinations, for example, were simply secular derivatives of early corporate rituals.[159] With changes like these, and the more individualized instruction later promoted by the Jesuits, the form of the modern educational institution was complete.[160]

Further developments in education involved mainly its content rather than its form. Although Durkheim devoted a great deal of time to the discussion of the relative value of different educational ideas per se, his sociological analysis of the evolution of this educational content is less systematic and developed than his history of educational structure. Still, his general perspective remains the same. The seed of development is to be found in Christianity. Christianity was antiritualistic, insisting that its God must be "believed in" and "thought about," rather than simply experienced. In Christian civilization it was mind rather than matter that became the focus of intellectual speculation. It is consciousness and the disciplining of consciousness, therefore, that becomes the sacred task of education.[161] Pedagogical ideas have always carried one specification or another of this Christian emphasis on abstraction. Evolution has occurred when there was a "contradiction" between abstraction in its traditional form and new developments in the public mind.[162] Such spiritual conflicts have produced the movement from grammar as the subject of instruction to the dialectical emphasis of the Scholastics, from the dialectic to the classical learning of the Renaissance, and from the Renaissance to the "revolutionary spirit" of realism that marked the nineteenth century.

The history of Western educational thought has for the most part been a history of formalism. Naturalistic religions emphasized the concrete; Christianity, combined with the emphasis on logic that it inherited from the ancients, emphasized form and abstraction. The grammar and dialectic of the later Middle Ages were symbolic techniques of formal manipulation, examples of "ascetic rationalism" whose antinaturalistic biases enraged Durkheim's realistic conscience. At first glance, the Renaissance appears to depart from this tendency. In Durkheim's analysis of the Renaissance, economics takes the place of politics as an "external milieu" that impinges upon moral life, but here, more than at any other place in his lectures, this instrumental milieu becomes integrated in a multidimensional way. Durkheim recounts how new inventions and new routes of trade created the expansion in material security that produced an aristocratic upper bourgeoisie. This class, he believes, demanded a form of education that was less rigid than Scholasticism. Additional pressure for new forms also emerged from more purely cultural sources. The Scholastics themselves had "taught reason to be self-confident," and this confidence was reinforced because the movement to the disciplining of consciousness, therefore, that becomes the sacred task of education.[161] Pedagogical ideas have always carried one specification or another of this Christian emphasis on abstraction. Evolution has occurred when there was a "contradiction" between abstraction in its traditional form and new developments in the public mind.[162] Such spiritual conflicts have produced the movement from grammar as the subject of instruction to the dialectical emphasis of the Scholastics, from the dialectic to the classical learning of the Renaissance, and from the Renaissance to the "revolutionary spirit" of realism that marked the nineteenth century.

Although political and economic forces played a role in pushing the pedagogical spirit to take a more "realistic" form, Protestantism was the most significant factor.[165] The effect of these social changes was to shift the focus of spiritual concern back from heaven to earth. Only then could society itself become the sacred object of veneration. "It is only towards the middle of the eighteenth century," Durkheim told his students, "that we French began to respond to this sentiment."

> This was the moment when French society was becoming directly aware of itself, was learning to think about itself from outside the framework of all religious symbolism. It was coming to be held by individuals, in its own right and in its wholly secular form, in sufficient esteem for its needs and interests—even the purely temporal ones—to appear as pre-eminently respectable and sacred.[166]

The "revolutionary spirit" and "effervescence" of the Revolution marked the most decisive shift in this spiritual orientation.[167] The long mental development of rationalism that Christianity had sponsored could now be applied to nature and society. Naturalism and positivism became important pedagogical doctrines. The nineteenth century was a battleground between these newer, more realistic forms of the educational spirit and the more idealist, more "humanistic" ones that usually took on a traditionally religious form.[168] Durkheim, of course, played a critical role in the struggle for secular realism. The practical lesson which he drew from his historical analysis reveals in an extremely interesting way one connection between his later "spiritual" theorizing and his modernist ideology. If secular, rational education was to succeed, he argued, it must resolutely maintain its "religious" form. As a secularist, Durkheim maintains that "the human mind cannot concede that there exists in us a supernatural guiding principle which is an emanation from the divine." As the sociologist of his later writings, he argues, nevertheless, that "it remains true— and empirically true at that—that the *human conscience* is still the single most important fact about the world, that which gives it incomparable value." This conscience must remain the sacred center of any rational education. "Our secondary school curriculum," Durkheim acknowledges, "just like our primary school curriculum, is secular nowadays. . . . But if it is to take the place of the religiously orientated curriculum, which it has a rightful claim to replace, then it must still be able to provide the same services."[169]†

6. MORAL ECONOMICS AND THE DISADVANTAGES OF IDEALISM

In this institutional analysis of education, Durkheim successfully specified the theoretical breakthrough that resolved the outstanding problem of his middle-period work. I will place this accomplishment in its fullest perspective in section 7, but here I would like to call attention, once again, to its peculiar one-sidedness. For Durkheim, the challenge, above all others, was to articulate a voluntaristic order, to show the reconcilability of organization and freedom. When he finally met this challenge, however, he significantly changed its form. He insisted not simply that order was reconcilable with freedom, but that it is always so. He had overreacted to the dilemma he had created for himself at the end of *The Division of Labor in Society*. Immediately after publishing this work, he had realized, to his obvious dismay, that the material order upon which he had relied was the very antithesis of the one he had sought. But instead of rejecting material order as the *exclusive* regulator of the division of labor, he now neglected it altogether. He could no longer find any instrumental interest at all in occupational groups, any coercive power or "artificial identity" in the state, any rationalizing purpose in the law, any ideology in education.

This society of "institutions" operated purely and simply along religious lines. The point was not that this society was therefore good and right—far from it. Durkheim readily recognized the particularistic and anomic shortcomings of many spiritually organized groups, as his discussions of families, occupations, and individualism reveal. The point, rather, is that these shortcomings, insofar as they could be sociologically described, had to lie within the religious realm itself. The model of religion had allowed Durkheim to articulate the relation of order and action as he had always hoped but had never been able to achieve. It had been a "revelation" to him, and he took the model much more seriously than has generally been realized.

Is it possible, Durkheim asks himself at one point, that the legal guarantees of private property were promoted only by self-interest, that their publicly religious form was more of an "expedient" than a sincerely held belief? "The owners," he reasons hypothetically, "might have made use of religious beliefs to keep intruders at distance." No sooner than he raises it, he dismisses the idea out of hand. Why? Because religion would lose its very meaning if it were instrumentally defined. "A religion," he writes, "does not descend to the level of expediency, unless the beliefs it inspired are no longer a very living thing."[170] Law cannot be instrumental because religion cannot; law, then, is either religious or it is nothing at all. The same is true for the state. In the essay in *L'Année* in which he revised his earlier thinking about legal evolution, Durkheim acknowledges that the relative repressiveness of the state is a variable that affects legal development independently of changes in religious ideals. Yet this variable is treated in a completely residual way: Durkheim offers nothing to explain the growth of a repressive state apparatus. For all intents and purposes, such political repression operates completely independently of the evolutionary process of differentiation that constitutes his main historical explanation.[171] Durkheim is confident of the state's good intentions and of its moral integration. He suggests, at one point, that individuals can "become instruments of the State" without any worry, for the state's interest will always be their own.[172] The state may grow too large, it may be able to articulate national values in only an attenuated way, but it will never be a bureaucracy that responds as much to interest and force as to the moral commitments of the nation. In a similar vein, Durkheim admits in his discussion of education that the society offers a specialized education for the working classes. His argument that such education shares a common cultural basis with the education of other social classes is certainly not an implausible one. What is one-sided is the fact that he shows no interest at all in the nature of this "specialized" education or in the kind of circumstances that would create its necessity.[173†]

There is no sphere of Durkheim's institutional analysis where this idealist underpinning is more striking than his analysis of economic life. It will be seen in section 7 that Durkheim sometimes excludes the economic dimension from sociology altogether; there is, indeed, no record of any publication or lecture that he devoted specifically to the economic sphere as such. There is, nevertheless, an orientation to economic facts that permeates Durkheim's later writing; this is the consideration of economic facts as moral things.

The only occasion on which Durkheim offered a general rationale for his reduction of economic force to morality was in a debate on the relationship between political economy and social science that appeared in 1908 in the *Bulletin de la Société d'économie politique*. Though the debate was designed as a discussion between two different disciplines, and conducted by the other participants as a topic for empirical argument, Durkheim himself viewed the question of the relationship between the disciplines as a question of the most general relevance, in fact as an argument over the substance of collective order itself. The crucial question, for him, is the nature of economic facts—in my terms, their presuppositional status. At first glance, he admits, political economy and social science seem to have as their object facts of a completely different nature. The objects of social science, like legal and moral rules, are created by public opinion; they are composed of ideas. The object of political economy, on the other hand, is wealth, which appears to be essentially objective and independent of any opinion. But if this formulation of the presuppositional status of economic and noneconomic objects is true, Durkheim warns, then the apparently greater objectivity of economic phenomena will allow them a determinate power over moral facts, and if this is allowed economic materialism will have triumphed over (Durkheim's) sociology.

What, then, could be the relationship between two kinds of facts that are so heterogeneous? The only conceivable one is that the external realities the economist studies, so objective and almost physical, will be considered as the base and as the support of all the others. What results from this is the theory of economic materialism which makes economic life the substructure of all social life.[174]

Faced with these extremely general ramifications—"economic science would exercise on the milieux of other sociological disciplines a veritable hegemony"—Durkheim argues that, in fact, economics and social science do not necessarily deal with facts that are of a different nature. "Economic facts may be considered under another aspect," and this aspect, not surprisingly, is that of public opinion. Durkheim documents how changes in taste and in wage levels have been created by changes in public morality and, more daringly, he claims that changes in the mode of production itself sometimes rest upon prior cultural shifts.[175]

These economic references cover a broad territory, and Durkheim only pursued one of them up with any fidelity. This is the problem of wages. The assertion that the value of labor is a product of opinion rather than supply and demand—let alone, labor's objective exchange value—runs like a red thread through Durkheim's later work. He announces it first in *Suicide*, mentions it again in the 1898 article on collective representations, and reaffirms it in his later analyses of sociological methods, primitive religion, and occupational groups.[176] The most extensive discussion appears in the latter, the 1900 lectures on the history of contract. Durkheim's approach here is particularly interesting because he examines the topic of labor value from an ideological and empirical perspective that would have been very congenial to Marx's own: the evolution of wages from the period of unfair compensation to one of the fair exchange of wage for service to, finally, a period of financial compensation according to need alone.[177†] In Marx's terms, this is the transition from capitalism to socialism to communism, a movement produced by changes in the infrastructure of society. But while Durkheim agrees with Marx about the ideological desirability of such change, he disagrees completely about the social forces that will produce it. Durkheim begins with a situation he had twice described in his earlier writings, the fact that one class of persons, in order to live, must make its services available whatever the cost. Yet the explanation that Durkheim now offers for this domination is moral rather than material in nature. This forced, unequal compensation occurs because public opinion does not equally value the contributions of different classes; there is, in other words, a class bias to morality.

We are still inclined, under the influence of all kinds of prejudices inherited from the past, not to consider men of different classes from the same point of view. We are more sensitive to the distresses and undeserved hardships that a man of superior class may undergo, who has important duties, than to the distress and burdens of those given up to humbler duties and labours.[178]

The movement away from this situation toward fairer payments for labor must replace this perspective with a more universalistic morality. It is not, as Marx believed, a reorganization of production, effected either through the changing organic composition of capital or the introduction of socialism itself. To the contrary, this economic change will occur, Durkheim writes, when "the misfortunes of one class will no longer seem more deplorable than the distresses of the other," and when "we shall consider them both as equally painful."[179] It is the "growing revolt of men's consciences" that will overthrow economic injustice and institute a true meritocracy. The value of labor, he insists, is not a matter of the labor time required for producing something, but of how socially valuable society judges this labor to be.[180] When society has moved to the point of considering all human activity equally important, the inequality of wages will be impossible morally to defend. Yet even in such an egalitarian society, Durkheim writes, there will still be unfairness, for the difference in natural abilities will allow some workers to receive better pay. This, of course, was the very recognition that led Marx to propose that the socialist distribution of "to each according to his ability" must evolve into the more altruistic communist stand of "to each according to his needs." Marx himself could never outline how such a transition would occur, for it seemed inherently to involve a major cultural shift. He did insist, however, that the movement would occur only after material "scarcity" had already been abolished. Durkheim takes an opposite tact. Because he views the shift as part of the same change in public opinion that created the original movement away from inequality, he can outline the process that Marx could not. The movement beyond meritocratic equality will occur with the deepening of the religion that already guides modern life, when the religion of individualism moves from the espousal of merit to the support of charity.

> For if it is man as a human being that we love and should love and regard, not man as a scholar of genius or as an able man of business, [then] are not these inequalities of merit fortuitous, too? For these all men are born with—by temperament, and it seems hardly just to make them bear responsibility for them. To us it does not seem equitable that a man should be better treated as a social being because he was born of parentage that is rich or of high social rank. But is it any more equitable that he should be better treated because he was born of a father of higher intelligence or in a more favorable milieu? It is here that the domain

of charity begins. Charity is the feeling of human sympathy that we see becoming clear even of these last remaining traces of inequality. It ignores and denies any special merit in gifts or mental capacity acquired by heredity. This, then, is the acme of justice.[181†]

7. CONCLUSION. THE DECEPTIVENESS OF "SOCIAL" FACTS: SOCIOLOGICAL IDEALISM AS THE CONFLATION OF ACTION AND ORDER

In moving beyond the instrumentalism of the *Division of Labor*, Durkheim adopted an exclusively normative and emotional understanding of action. For this reason he could conceive order only as a moral force, and he produced a theory that was neither nominalist nor phenomenalist in a strictly philosophical sense but was, nonetheless, voluntaristic and idealistic in the theoretical terms of sociology.

In terms of the basic logic of sociological theorizing, the presuppositional questions of action and order must be regarded as separate issues that vary in a completely independent way. Only if we understand this autonomy can we encompass the full range of theoretical options that the history of sociology reveals; all the different combinations that can logically be constructed by matching individualistic or collective ideas about order and instrumental or normative understandings of action have, in fact, been proposed as legitimate and correct. Only in this way, moreover, can we understand the possibilities for a truly multidimensional theory, for only if these presuppositional questions are seen as independent can we understand that collective order is not necessarily tied to either instrumental or normative action per se, but can encompass both. Insofar as a theorist departs from multidimensionality, he will try to obscure the independence of these theoretical questions. To make his own choice as persuasive as possible, he will try, consciously or unconsciously, to obscure the fact that a choice could even have been made. He will argue, for example, that a certain position on order inherently demands the adoption of a certain position on action. Hence, any truly "sociological" or "social" explanations must, by their very nature, be voluntaristic or determinist. For Marx this strategy was a principal means of defending his later materialism. In defense of an entirely opposite theoretical position, Durkheim's strategy is exactly the same.

In the latter part of his career, in a general methodological essay on sociology, Durkheim made a point that is particularly revealing in these strategic terms. Until recently, he claims, thinkers believed that social change was an arbitrary and individualistic thing, that powerful men, like legislators and kings, "could . . . at their pleasure change the aspect of societies, make them change from one type to another." But such be-

liefs, Durkheim writes, were illusory, for social life changes only according to collective, not individual forces, and these forces can be
understood in terms of immutable "laws."[182] This point could have come
from Marx's pen; it closely resembles the position he staked out in his
critique of Proudhon in *The Poverty of Philosophy*. Both men decry explanations that are individualistic, and both stake their own hegemonic theoretical claims on the fact of their collectivism alone. Marx moved from
his critique to the "logical" point that kings were ruled not by themselves
but by economic forces. For Durkheim, the "obvious" reason for the
great superiority of collective facts is their moral nature.

The roots of Durkheim's conflation of action and order lay in the very
dualistic understanding of human nature that allowed him to transcend
the materialism of the *Division of Labor*, for he argues in this theory not
only that cooperative moral sentiments can be linked to collective facts
but that they alone can be. The "sensual and sensory tendencies" in
human nature, the ones that "satisfy our hunger, our thirst, and so on,"
simply cannot be social; they "are necessarily egoistic: they have our individuality and it alone as their subject." The other part of human nature, "conceptual thought and moral activity" is, in contrast, social "by
definition."[183]

> No doubt, there are egoistic desires that do not have material
> things as their objects, but the sensory appetites are the type *par
> excellence* of egoistic tendencies. We believe that desires for ob-
> jects of a different kind imply . . . a movement out of ourselves
> which surpasses pure egoism.[184]

This conflation of presuppositional questions can be made only because
Durkheim will no longer accept coercive, material order as a viable theoretical option. Certainly egoistic desires can provide the basis for structures that transcend the individual; indeed, this was the very reason why
Durkheim had first been so attracted to the division of labor as an order-
creating device. Individualism, then, could not be Durkheim's true objection. In truth, his objection is to the fact that the order that results from
such egoistic motives will not be transcendent in the religious sense: it
will not allow collective arrangements to be articulated in a voluntary
way. Rather than argue this position in a straightforward manner—justifying it as a means of preserving voluntarism at all costs—Durkheim
would present the situation as if it were embedded in the nature of the
empirical world. In this way, potential criticism of his position will be
more difficult: many would agree about the desirability of collective
order even if they disagree about its moral form.

This strategic conflation provides theoretical camouflage for Durkheim in every major work in the middle and later period. To justify the
exclusively moral emphasis of *Suicide*, for example, he argues that the

social functions that are "indispensable for physical life," that are designed to "repair organic exhaustion," are forces that "concern only the
individual."[185] The collective "bond" that man accepts, is "not physical,
but moral; that is, social." Man "is governed not by a material environment brutally imposed on him, but by a conscience superior to his own,
the superiority of which he *feels*."[186] Financial upheavals are not crises
simply because they are "disturbances in the collective order"; since the
forces exterior to an individual "can only be moral," financial upheavals
create crisis only if they affect moral society.[187] Later, in his revisionist
Preface to the second edition of the *Division of Labor*, Durkheim acknowledges that, "to be sure, individuals working at the same trade have
relations with one another because of their similar occupation." But this
kind of organization—the cohesion that results from the division of economic labor—rests upon physical and material needs, and these relations, Durkheim now concludes, can "have nothing ordered about
them."[188] In the lectures on professional ethics and civic morals he
makes the same point. Without "moral discipline," he argues in his introduction, "there would be no reason why he [the individual] should not
make his way or, at the very least, try to make his way, regardless of
everyone in his path."[189] He later justifies his sociology of education on
precisely the same grounds. Education concerns itself exclusively with
morality because morality is the only force that can order individual life.
"To the egoistic and asocial being that has just been born," Durkheim
writes, society "must, as rapidly as possible, add another, capable of
leading a social and moral life." "Such," he adds, "is the work of education, and you can readily see its great importance."[190]

   As this wide application of Durkheim's strategic reduction of the social to the moral indicates, the elimination of instrumental order that it
rationalizes affects every sphere of his institutional analysis. By far its
most important application, however, is to economic life. As has been
seen, Durkheim consistently tried to moralize his explanations of economic facts, but there were also many occasions when he recognized
their relative intractability to moral concerns. In these situations, where
the moralization of economic life was impossible, Durkheim argued that
economic facts simply were not social, and that they were, for this reason, "inexplicable" in sociological terms.[191] The paradigmatic example
of this two-pronged strategy toward economics occurs in Durkheim's
analysis of religion itself. There is, it turns out, a crucial ambiguity in his
treatment of the "profane," the element in the religious model to which
the economy corresponds. He argues, on the one hand, that the profane
is directly defined by the sacred; in this case, the profane is a cultural
phenomenon, part of the symbolic order of religion. It is this approach
that provides the basis for the moralization of economic facts in Durkheim's later work. Durkheim also argues, however, that the profane op-

erates on a plane orthogonal to the sacred. In this usage, he equates the profane with the physical, the material, and the individualistic. In his first essay on religion, for example, Durkheim describes profane things as "quite naked individual impressions" and emphasizes that only sacred facts are collectively conceived.[192] In his later writings, while he sometimes defines the profane as symbolic, he also identifies it with "sensations coming from the physical world," "vulgar things that interest only our physical individualities."[193]

If religion is the model of social explanation in the later work, insofar as economic facts are areligious they are excluded from any explanation. Economic life, Durkheim writes time and time again, is simply unregulated, and he does not mean this only in the ideological sense of his critique of laissez-faire. In his lectures on socialism, the middle-period work where he intimates his recent "revelation" about religion through his defense of Saint-Simon, Durkheim announces that economic life is entirely outside of the collective conscience.[194] In the later lectures on professions, he maintains that business has no professional ethics and that the practice of business is subject to no regulation whatsoever by public opinion. And in *The Elementary Forms of Religious Life*, the economic life of aboriginal tribes is the prototype of the dispersed, individualistic existence that attenuates the collective energy generated by ritual association. The social life of the aborigines, indeed, is composed of "two phases."

> Sometimes the population is broken up into little groups who wander about independently of one another, in their various occupations; each family lives by itself, hunting and fishing, and in a word, trying to procure its indispensable food by all the means in its power. Sometimes, on the contrary, the population concentrates and gathers at determined points for a length of time varying from several days to several months. This concentration takes place when a clan or a part of the tribe is summoned to the gathering, and on this occasion they celebrate a religious ceremony.[195]

Yet even if Durkheim had been inclined to describe the independent impact of economic forces on social action, it seems doubtful that he would have been able to do so: Durkheim not only ignored the profane economic domain, he seemed not to have understood it. In a debate in 1906 about the relative patriotism and internationalism of different social classes, Durkheim argued that economic interest could not explain the internationalism of the working classes because the bosses were exposed to as much "economic restraint" as the workers and yet did not share their attitude. He could not, in other words, differentiate this restraint in terms of different material environments and different structures of instrumental interest; it was only the workers' moral environment, in his view, which facilitated their more rebellious attitude toward conventional patriotic ideas.[196] In a 1910 review of a work on the Indian caste system, he exhibits a similar inability to understand any relationship between classes and material forms. Occupational specialization, he insists, has little effect on caste divisions, even though it is true, he acknowledges, that in every economic division of labor there is the germ of the hierarchy about which the caste system is organized. Castes must rather be considered as the translation of certain hierarchical collective sentiments; in fact, they form a kind of religious institution themselves.[197] At one point in the 1906 exchange on the relative patriotism of different classes, one of Durkheim's opponents asserted that "it is very natural that the worker, in the face of war, does not have the same attitude as the boss," adding that "the moral effect produced on the worker is different, since the economic conditions are different." Durkheim responded by asking, rather naïvely, "What could the worker really lose from the war?" At this point in the transcription of the debate, we find the following entry: "Several speak at once: Life!" Durkheim did not really understand; he replied weakly, "The boss, too."[198]

By the later part of his career, then, Durkheim had completely reversed the materialism that had characterized his earlier sociology. And his theoretical development, taken as a whole, was even more complex than this transition would make it appear. At first, he had held out some possibility for an individualistic moral theory, and he had also considered in his earliest writings a theory of collective moral sentiments. Before producing a theory of his own, however, he had given up these positions, and he defined sociology primarily as a materialistic enterprise, one which would show, to be sure, the moral consequences of material organization. When this orientation produced an order that was too deterministic, Durkheim shifted his position, without any explicit notification to his critics or supporters, back toward his earlier emphasis on the importance of ideal forms, a position which he could now accept because he better understood the relationship between individual subjectivity and collective structure. Durkheim left a tortuous path for his followers and sympathizers. Indeed, we will see in the chapter following that neither Durkheim's followers, nor sometimes even Durkheim himself, proved willing or able to follow this shifting theoretical path to its final conclusions.

Part Three

ONE-DIMENSIONAL THEORY AND ITS DISCONTENTS

Chapter Nine

EQUIVOCATION AND REVISION IN THE CLASSICAL THEORY OF SOCIOLOGICAL IDEALISM
Durkheim and "Durkheimianism"

Durkheim and Marx created magisterial theories of social explanation that have provided the polar alternatives for sociological discourse throughout the present century and will, undoubtedly, continue to do so in the century to follow. The paths to their mature statements of voluntarism and determinism were complex and involved substantial change, yet each theorist, in his maturity, produced a theory of remarkable consistency and scope. The problem is that neither is more than partly convincing; in fact, each presents an extraordinarily one-sided portrait of social order and the action which informs it.

This theoretical dissatisfaction brings us face to face with the question of how scientific theories change. I have spoken about this issue at some length in my introductory discussion; it can now be discussed in a more concrete context. Theories do not change simply because they are wrong. The relationship to empirical "reality" is not such that a general proposition can either be factually verified or unequivocally disproved. This is not to say, of course, that the empirical dimension is unimportant. Kuhn, in fact, has provided a sophisticated way of approaching the impact of empirical problems in his analysis of "anomalies."[1] When new "facts" become inexplicable within a given framework, theories, instead of being refuted by these anomalous facts, become elaborated in a manner that encompasses them. Whether the theoretical framework is objectively true or not is irrelevant. A successful theory, in other words, is one that will become sufficiently supple and complex to explain these new inputs from the empirical world. In my own understanding of theoretical change, I will accept such "emergent inexplicability" as one prime mover in the elaboration of theoretical tradition. Social theories are historically rooted. With historical change, theories that once seemed adequate may no longer seem so. Durkheim and Marx both were subject to precisely this kind of pressure from the empirical world, and their followers faced it to an even higher degree. Confronted with such pressure, Marxism and Durkheimianism could succeed only if they changed enough to explain these new developments.

Theories are vulnerable not only to historical and empirical "pressure," but to a very different source of strain as well. They change partly because of internal strains that are generated purely on the conceptual level itself. If his presuppositional position is one-sided, or only weakly multidimensional, the theorist may feel uneasy, and he will experience the need to introduce certain qualifications. If ideological assumptions are unresolved, they may produce new or implicitly contradictory propositions. New assumptions about empirical equilibrium, or assumptions ambivalently held, can in turn produce new formulations at more general levels, as can shifts or strains in a theorist's perception of appropriate models. Finally, of course, understandings about the relationship between the different levels of science can produce enormous theoretical strain. The drive to conflate one level of analysis with another can produce tremendous theoretical inconsistency, for the theorist tries repeatedly to utilize one kind of formula to resolve problems of a very different type.

If these theoretical strains are acknowledged, and if the theoretical revisions are self-consciously made, a theorist's work will undergo a transition that is obvious for all to see. Change is explicit, and it will usually be acknowledged to the intellectual world by the theorist himself. After this break, a new consistency will emerge. On the other hand, theoretical strains are often unacknowledged by the theorist, unrecognized by even his closest students, and certainly invisible to the intellectual community at large. Yet they are privately experienced by the theorist nonetheless, and as he confronts theoretical criticisms of his work he may implicitly alter his commitments at different levels of the scientific continuum. The problem is that these revisions are ad hoc. Made implicitly rather than explicitly, they are camouflaged by the formal structure of theoretical work. They occur inconsistently, and usually in the theoretical interstices. As a result, the categories they introduce will be merely residual to the main line of theoretical argument, and the writings of the theorist, while consistent on the level of formal argument, will be contradictory when considered as a whole. These internal contradictions are evidence of the strains in the original argument. They are the very same strains, of course, that inspire covert revision in the works of the students that form the theorist's school. In the name of defending and clarifying the work of their fathers, the best students will offer revisions to better defend themselves against their own intellectual peers.

Not only the residual categories of Marx's and Durkheim's original writings, then, but the histories of "Marxism" and "Durkheimianism" as well should follow the fault lines which we have discovered in the explicit theoretical statements.[2†]

1. DURKHEIM'S "SECOND THOUGHTS": THEORETICAL CONFLATION AND RESIDUAL UTILITARIANISM

Durkheim, like Marx, was vitally concerned with the moral and political problems of his day, with psychological anxiety, with inequality and conflict, and particularly with the lack of social integration and community. This concern spanned his entire career, and at various stages, as has been seen, he developed different theoretical orientations with which to understand the "pathology" that characterized his time. These problems, Durkheim came to believe, were of a primarily moral nature, and he devoted himself to describing the conflicts between traditional and modern culture, between particularistic and universalistic moral codes, and between egoistic and altruistic symbols that created the often depressing situation of modern industrial society. It is particularly the latter conflict, between egoistic and altruistic moralities, that is interesting here. One of the crowning achievements of Durkheim's late development was the proposition that the egoism that threatened modern social integration was of a moral rather than utilitarian cast. He rejected his early understanding of the "substantialist" individual; he understood that every individual was the product of social, that is, moral forces. All this is true. Why, then, does one find throughout Durkheim's later writings the periodic insistence that the instability of modern life can be traced back to the complete isolation of the individual from social control, to an egoism that is just as self-interested as that suggested by the most fervent utilitarian? The answer is complex. This ambivalent revision of Durkheim's theory can be traced back, first of all, to certain equivocations in his ideology. It also involves the attempt to conflate this ideological ambivalence with commitments that Durkheim made at other levels of the scientific continuum.

Durkheim was ideologically committed to "individualism," but this value held for him, as it did for most nineteenth-century intellectuals, complicated and even contradictory meanings. It is important to understand that "individualism" first emerged as a term of opprobrium, a term which French intellectuals developed in reaction against the French Revolution. Even when it was taken over by left-wing thinkers like the Saint-Simonians, "individualism" continued to embody, particularly in France, the fear of social disintegration that reflected the often exaggerated anxieties about individual isolation produced by institutional differentiation and cultural secularization. By the middle of the

302   The Antinomies of Classical Thought

nineteenth century, there emerged a tradition in French liberal thought that emphasized the positive side of individualism along with the negative. Blanqui, Fourier, Proudhon, and later Juaréz wrote about the emancipatory aspects of individualism, the acquisition of political and economic rights that it implied.[3] Durkheim certainly was part of this tradition of liberal thought, yet he shared, nonetheless, some of the misgivings about individualism that produced the antagonism to it among more traditional and more radical thinkers. In one part of his mind, Durkheim always felt that individualism meant the utter disregard for the community and the denigration of the self to a merely utilitarian ego. "Individualism," he wrote in *Suicide*, "is of course not necessarily egoism, but it comes close to it."[4] If individualism implied such a social egoism, then equilibrium could be maintained only by anti-individualistic controls or the invocation of traditional authority. There are times in Durkheim's writing where he seems in accord with precisely such sentiment. "The present malaise," he wrote in 1901, "derives essentially from a dissolution of our moral beliefs. The ends to which our fathers were attached have lost their authority and their appeal, without our seeing clearly, or at least with the necessary unanimity, where to find those that must be pursued in the future."[5] But, if individualism is itself a form of moral belief—the point which Durkheim's later work usually insists upon—then how can the malaise created by it indicate "moral dissolution"? If we adopt such a morality of individualism, moreover, how can there ever be "unanimity" about the actual directions society should pursue? There is, in other words, a strain in Durkheim's writing, unacknowledged and certainly uncharacteristic of his general position, that employs "individualism" to evoke the traditionalistic anxiety about merely utilitarian individualism and to urge the reimposition of authority that it implies. Durkheim urges his compatriots, for example, not to liberalize the divorce law, for society could not exist without some form of group control. The mere fact of increased divorce, of course, would in the sophisticated terms of Durkheim's later work in no way indicate the existence of asocial or utilitarian behavior. But this, nonetheless, is what Durkheim implies.[6†]

Our concern here, however, is not with Durkheim's ideological commitments per se, but with his presuppositional orientation and his theoretical explanation as a whole. Yet, while ideology does not have any direct effect on presuppositional commitment, it can have a very powerful effect on the manner in which these general commitments become articulated in the overall theoretical ensemble. This is particularly true if a theorist employs his presuppositional orientation in a conflationary manner, that is, if he tries to make it appear that his ideological commitments derive directly from his presuppositions. Durkheim is certainly a case in point. An unabashed positivist, he was convinced that objective explanation would produce correct judgments about political values, that "there is a state of moral health which science alone is able to determine competently."[7†] What Durkheim's science "discovered," of course, was the importance of the very social facts his theory presupposed, namely, the importance of morality. This positivism, in other words, led him to "derive" ideological evaluations from his assumptions about action and order: collective morality must be socially beneficial. This initial conflation is combined with a second, which I discussed at some length in chapter 4 (in the third part of section 2.3.2). On the specific level of propositions, Durkheim was committed to certain assumptions about the crucial importance, and empirical prevalence, of social equilibrium and cooperation. He conflated these propositional assumptions, moreover, with the most general presuppositions of his theory. The result is the equation that permeates much of his work: collective moral order will produce empirical equilibrium. The obverse of this statement is that the existence of social conflict implies the lack of morality. It should be clear that this conflation with propositional commitments is complementary to the conflation with ideological ones: moral commitments produce social harmony, and both produce the good society. The lack of moral commitment—the emergence of instrumental action and purely individualistic order—produces social conflict, and must be *evaluated* in a negative way.

To understand fully the impact of these two equations on the internal structure of Durkheim's theory, we must recall the content of the presuppositions with which these empirical propositions and ideological commitments are conflated. Durkheim's presuppositions are idealistic; they reduce material force and instrumental action to an asocial, residual status. These presuppositions, then, strongly reinforce his ideological and empirical conflation. When Durkheim observed conflictual or apparently instrumental activity, his presuppositional idealism allowed him two logical options. He could subjectify these empirical phenomena by showing how they really were manifestations of moral forces, or he could, on the other hand, allow them a material status but leave this status largely unexplained, defining them simply as manifestations of an asocial, purely individualistic force. We have seen above (ch. 8, sec. 6) that Durkheim often resorted to the second strategy to deal with certain aspects of economic life; in fact, such an ad hoc and residual explanatory strategy appears in every segment of his sociological analysis. It does so because his presuppositional problems are exacerbated by the conflationary tendencies just described. Because of the ambiguities in the empirical and ideological levels of his work, whenever Durkheim saw conflict and individualism there was one part of him which was strongly inclined to explain them as the manifestation of a material rather than an ideal force, and as the result of individual rather than social patterns of order. Occasionally, but persistently, he gave in to this inclination, and for this reason there is a strain in his work that presents modern life in a utilitarian way. If modern life is marred by selfishness and individualism, if it is racked by conflict, and if it is obviously ripe for social reform, then perhaps this is because individuals have been allowed to run amok without moral control, subject only to material force.

This vision of material subjection and personal anarchy runs completely contrary to the theory of Durkheim's middle and later work: it denies the major theoretical accomplishments for which he is justly famous. Yet, this resort to residual category, ironically, also allows Durkheim to escape from the limitations of this later theorizing, albeit in an ad hoc way. If he cannot explain material facts in a positive manner, at least he can acknowledge them and account for them in a negative way—that is, by what they are not.[8†] He tries to resolve the presuppositional limitations of his work, in other words, by "explaining" material force while, at the same time, never giving up for a moment his overreaching idealism. That this "explanation" is camouflaged and contradictory is, one may infer, a price that Durkheim was more than willing to pay in order to assuage his theoretical "bad conscience."

There is no segment of Durkheim's mature sociology that escapes this contradiction, no area of his sociology of modern life where Durkheim does not at some point paradoxically and continually affirm the asocial and amoral character of modern life. In *The Division of Labor in Society*, whose ambivalent utilitarianism could more effectively sustain such an imprecation of modern egoism, Durkheim ends with the prophetic warning that "our faith has been troubled" and "tradition has lost sway," and he concludes from this breakdown of traditional authority not that a more individuated morality has emerged but, more starkly, that "individual judgment has been freed from collective judgment," that there is simply no more collective control at all.[9] Yet even in *Suicide*, where Durkheim's theoretical orientation has become resolutely anti-utilitarian, he suggests at different points the same theme. Contradicting his major insight, and principal proposition, that suicide is a voluntary, willed act inspired by commitment to a certain kind of moral order, Durkheim describes it as the action of an individual freed from all collective control.[10] "All regulation is lacking," he writes about the modern period, and it is because "there is no restraint" that "appetites, not being controlled by a public opinion, become disoriented."[11] Because individuals are "without mutual relationships," they can only "tumble over one another like so many liquid molecules, encountering no central energy to retain, fix and organize them." There simply is no collective order: "For most of their lives, nothing draws them out of themselves and imposes restraint on them."[12] In *Professional Ethics and Civic Morals* and also in *Moral Education*, Durkheim denies, at certain points, the very existence in contemporary society of the secondary associations which, in these same lectures, he spent so much time describing.[13] In his writing on the family, he argues, on certain occasions, that the family, instead of providing a bulwark against individualism, actually reinforces it.[14] In a later essay on the economy, he laments that because of the predominance of commerce and industry there is a "multitude of individuals" for whom "the greatest part of their existence takes place outside the moral sphere."[15] And when he is discussing the state, he contradicts, in a passage of several pages, his argument about the regulatory role of modern politics by asserting that "the State is incapable of bringing a moderating influence to bear" on individuals. Noting the "chaos seen in certain democracies, their constant flux and instability," he writes that "it is almost impossible for . . . votes to be inspired by anything except personal and egoistic motives."[16] Even in *The Elementary Forms of Religious Life*, the book where Durkheim articulates most brilliantly the sacred basis of secular life, this despair about the utilitarian nature of secularism is not entirely absent: "The old gods are growing old or already dead, and others are not yet born."[17]

It is this residual negation of the ability of modern life to exert collective order that explains the unrealistic, highly utopian proposal for reorganization that crops up throughout Durkheim's career, the "occupational group."[18] This modern-day guild structure would be at once family and workplace, polity and school, effervescent church and rationalizer of public debate. It would combine workers and employers in a harmonious representation of the public interest, and it would produce the opportunity for decentralized community while maintaining the national scope of the modern nation. It would be socialist without the need for revolution, and it would end the isolation of the individual without sacrificing individual liberty. Nowhere in his analysis of the development of modern society does Durkheim offer any evidence that such guild organization is on the historical agenda. Nowhere in his systematic analysis of the workings of modern institutions does he indicate that such radical reorganization is necessary to reconcile individual and community. Nowhere, that is, except in his discussions on modern life as a society undermined by egoistic, instrumental individualism. Durkheim's proposal for the occupational group is related not to the main body of his work but to his residual utilitarianism. Just as Durkheim's ideological ambivalence led him periodically to view all conflict and individualism as inspired by instrumental, material force, it also occasionally brought him to believe that modern life can be reformed only if differentiation and individualization are completely reversed. The occupational group is a magical formula for accomplishing this, one whose political implications or actual historical possibility are never explored.

In his first lecture on sociology at Bordeaux, Durkheim demonstrated to his students the weaknesses of utilitarian theory by noting that, for the utilitarians, "nothing is left but the sad portrait of an isolated egoist."[19] Ironically, it is precisely this sad portrait that Durkheim occasionally offers in his own mature work. Without acknowledging the partial validity of utilitarian theory—without, indeed, any acceptance of materialist explanation at all—this occasional reference can only be a residual category. Certain liberal and Marxist commentators on Durkheim's work have never seen this strand of utilitarianism, the first because it would seem to make Durkheim more of a traditionalist than a defender of liberal society, the second because it would make him seem more like a radical critic of bourgeois society than its principal ideologue.[20] Others have not only recognized this reference but disproportionately emphasized its importance, arguing that it represents the major tendency in Durkheim's analysis and implying that with it he achieved a multidimensional theory as sensitive to material facts as Marx.[21†] Neither approach is correct. The liberal and Marxist critics are wrong because the reference to egoistic instrumentalism certainly does exist. Yet the second group of critics distorts Durkheim's thought more seriously, for they ignore the enormous incongruity between this utilitarian strand and the main body of his work.

There are certain occasions where Durkheim's ideological ambivalence, his tendency toward conflation, and the one-sided character of his most general presuppositions come together in a manner that makes it difficult for Durkheim to say what he really means. The result is his resort to a residual category that mars his theoretical achievement. This residual reference, then, represents a limitation of his thought, not its fulfillment or highest expression. To avoid it, Durkheim would have needed a surer ideological critique of industrial society, a firmer sense of the independence of this critique from the theoretical commitments he was making at other levels, and, perhaps most important of all, a less one-sidedly normative understanding of the nature of collective order. We will see that this is precisely what his most effective students tried to achieve.

2. "DURKHEIMIANISM" AS PARADIGM REVISION: MAKING IDEALISM INSTRUMENTAL

Durkheim's major students, all of whom were gathered around him at *L'Année sociologique*, have usually been considered an extraordinarily loyal and unified group of disciples, presented as such by outside observers and by themselves as well."[22] When their sociology is examined more closely, however, it becomes clear that they were often sharply divided among themselves and, covertly to be sure, distanced from Durkheim as well. One could examine these divisions institutionally, focusing on the hierarchical division of power among them, which was certainly un-equal, or on the unevenness of their participation in *L'Année*, which re-sulted, for example, in different degrees of intimacy with the master.[23] One could also look at the differences among them, and between them and Durkheim, in terms of their ideological disagreements, of which there were certainly many. I will, however, choose neither of these as foci of primary interest. Instead I will focus, as throughout this work, on the disagreement and theoretical revision that occurred at the most general level of analysis, the presuppositional one. The efforts to revise Durk-heim's theorizing on this level are certainly affected by disagreement along these other axes, but they do not in any instance exactly corre-spond to them.

Earlier discussion, in this and preceding chapters, has demonstrated that contradictory currents emerged within Durkheim's own theoretical corpus. Stimulated by ideological as well as theoretical ambivalence, they represented, in part, an effort to overcome the one-sided character of his presuppositional orientation. It is this effort that also defines the history of "Durkheimianism." Operating within the context of Durk-heim's theoretical program, his most distinguished students went back to the most general questions that motivated his work—the presupposi-tional questions about voluntarism and determinism, idealism and mate-rialism, and the relationship between individual and society—and tried to restructure them in a manner that would resolve the strains in Durk-heim's original theory. They did all this, of course, without ever question-ing the original program in an overt way. Covert questioning and overt fealty were combined by a strategy which we will see employed also by the students of Marx: phases of the master's theoretical development which he himself had considered incompatible were brought together in a manner that enabled his students to make a presuppositional challenge that would appear as a merely more faithful rendering of the master's work.[24†]

In terms of their explicit relationship to Durkheim's theory, his major students seemed aware of his idealist tendency and appeared publicly to accept it. They appeared completely unaware, moreover, of any conflict between the earlier and later phases of his work. In his 1938 Introduc-tion to *The Evolution of Educational Thought*, for example, Maurice Halbwachs approvingly noted Durkheim's insistence in that work on the spiritual essence of education, on the historical movement from ideal effervescence to material form, and on the necessity to study institutions in terms of their initial, spiritual formation.[25] Marcel Mauss's introduc-tion to *Socialism and Saint-Simon* appears to indicate a similar accep-tance of Durkheim's exclusively moral orientation to social change.[26] Yet the implicit response of Durkheim's students to their knowledge of his idealist strain was not, in fact, nearly so accepting, at least as this response informed their efforts at creating "Durkheimian" sociology. Some did, of course, continue to espouse a sociology that faithfully re-flected Durkheim's original approach. Georges Davy's *La Foi jurée* (The Legal Faith, 1922) and Paul Fauconnet's *La Responsabilité*(1920) both emphasized the primordial importance of solidarity and sentiment in ways that echoed the work of Durkheim's middle period.[27] The writing of other students, particularly R. Hertz's symbolic studies of death and hand usage and Marcel Granet's analysis of Chinese thought, similarly reflected Durkheim's concentration on exclusively ideal forms, though they derived more from the later religiously-inspired writing than from the middle-period work.[28] Other students, however, and these were cer-tainly the most important in terms of their sustained contributions to so-ciological thought, produced sociologies that were, implicitly, much more critical of Durkheim's middle and later work.

Those who took this more critical path were severely hampered by the fact that they felt compelled to do so without violating, in any way, the given framework of Durkheim's thought. They tried to achieve a more multidimensional perspective than Durkheim, therefore, by work-ing exclusively within his corpus, combining the later emphasis on nor-mative order with the morphological determinism of the *Division of Labor*. But the relationship between these phases of his work was one Durkheim himself had merely finessed; his students, though more insis-tent on the need to combine them, could hardly do better. They interre-lated the two explanatory schemes, but the results remained mixtures instead of becoming true compounds; because of this fact, their so-ciological products were almost always partly contradictory, for the ma-terialism of one strand of their explanation directly opposed the idealism of the other. To truly overcome these strains, Durkheim's students would have had to develop a new, overreaching conceptual scheme, and this they were neither willing nor able to do. If they opposed Durkheim, it was by insisting on the validity of both phases of his work, yet these were phases that Durkheim himself had seen as clearly antithetical.

The contradictory results characteristic of such combinations is manifest in Davy's Introduction to *Professional Ethics and Civic Morals*, in 1950, the first publication of the lectures which epitomized Durk-heim's thinking in the later period. Quite appropriately, Davy tries to re-late these lectures to the methodology Durkheim set forth in *The Rules of Sociological Method*. He reads that emphasis on the exteriority of social facts as an argument for their material status; yet he cautions the reader, at the same time, that such materiality does not in any way mean that social facts cannot be also ideal: "The fact being given as a thing in no way excludes its also, or at the same time, being an idea, a belief, a senti-ment, a habit or behavior, which are, no less than matter, realities, exist-ing and having effect and therefore capable of being observed."[29] The problem here is that, in his search for Durkheim's multidimensionality, Davy has confused Durkheim's methodological insistence on the facticity of social phenomena with a presuppositional emphasis on material force. He continues to misread Durkheim in this wishful way as reconciling idealism and materialism by asserting that the *Division of Labor*—above all, an instrumental analysis—actually illustrates Durkheim's understanding of symbolism.[30] Yet it would be difficult indeed to demonstrate the compatibility of the later interest in symbolism with the *Division of Labor*, and, as was earlier noted, even Davy does not do so, preferring to model his own work on the sociology of the middle period.

A more complex and elaborate attempt to maintain Durkheim's framework while shifting it implicitly toward multidimensionality can be seen in the article on sociology that Mauss and Fauconnet wrote for the *Grande Encyclopédie* published in 1901. They argued that sociology has three modes of investigation: it explains collective representations by other collective representations, collective representations by social structure, and social structures by collective representation.[31] Sociology, in other words, employs both idealistic and materialistic forms of explanation. Mauss and Fauconnet assert, quite rightly, that although this general logic may seem contradictory, it is a multidimensionality that is inherent in the nature of reality itself.

> It might seem, it is true, that such explanations turn in a circle, since the forms of the group are presented in such versions now as effects and now as causes of the collective representations. But this circle, which is real, does not imply any begging of the question. It is the rhythm of the things themselves. Nothing is more vain than to ask whether ideas have produced societies, or whether societies, once formed, have given birth to collective ideas. They are inseparable phenomena, between which there is no place for the establishment of a primacy, either logical or chronological.[32]

Yet in the very same essay, Mauss and Fauconnet do, in fact, idealize sociology, and they do so by faithfully following the understanding of institutions that Durkheim presented as the rationale for his later work. Spirit and culture, they insist, are at the heart of economic institutions;[33] more or less diffuse opinion is the cause that changes all social rules;[34] and social life consists entirely of collective representations.[35]

In a more detailed analysis of the contradictory nature of such attempts at theoretical revision, I will concentrate on the four students of Durkheim who were considered to be most significant by their contemporaries: Marcel Mauss, Célèstin Bouglé, Maurice Halbwachs, and François Simiand.[36†] These students varied in their ideological orientations. Though never Marxist, Mauss, Halbwachs, and Simiand were more critical and militant in their socialism than Durkheim, while Bouglé, though he supported socialist movements, was more liberal. Mauss follows Durkheim's negative perception of the egoistic instrumentalism implied by modern individualism, the others do not. Yet, while each thinker more or less conflates his ideological commitments with his theoretical and empirical positions, none is inclined to use this conflation to justify covertly a more multidimensional perspective. To the contrary, each attempted to include material references in an explicit way. Although I do not know how self-conscious they were, each moved to overcome the split that Durkheim initiated between external conditional and normative understandings of order, and each did so by a similar strategy: the combination of the framework of the *Division of Labor* with that of the later work. If Durkheim himself never fully acknowledged the radical split between these two phases of his work, these students did not acknowledge it at all. Yet by bringing the framework of *Division* into the later writings, they forcefully acknowledged the weaknesses in his middle and later theorizing, even if in only an implicit way.

In addition to this presuppositional level, at least three of these students addressed the problem of voluntarism and determinism at another level. They tried to undo the unfortunate conflation of positivist method and collectivist presupposition that sometimes gave even to Durkheim's later theory an antivoluntarist cast. In his study of suicide, for example, Halbwachs specifically brought individual motives into consideration, and he emphasized that their inclusion did not threaten a sociological understanding.[37] Influenced by Bergson, he also never hesitated in his later writing to apply "scientific" sociology to the explorations of inner thoughts and feelings.[38] Mauss, similarly, was more open than Durkheim to the sociological significance of psychological studies; he maintained a responsiveness to psychological and psychoanalytic theories to which Durkheim would have been resolutely opposed.[39] Bouglé, for his part, was strongly influenced by Simmel, and his explanations for modern solidarity often referred to individual perceptions and interests in a way that was entirely absent from Durkheim's work.[40†]

Mauss's famous essay *The Gift* (1925) has usually been regarded, and evidently was so regarded by Mauss himself, primarily as a critique of the utilitarian approach to economic life. Mauss merely carries out, in this sense, Durkheim's own theoretical critique of instrumental action and individualistic order by demonstrating in great empirical detail the noneconomic elements of exchange in primitive and archaic societies. It is this moral emphasis, one should note, which allows Mauss also to follow Durkheim's ideological point by contrasting the communal ethics and emotions that regulated primitive economics with the "cold and calculating" and "brutal" world of capitalist economics, the critique which underlay his strong plea for socialism.[41]

Yet, *The Gift* must also be regarded in another way, for with its description of primitive exchange it adds a significant emphasis on self-interest to Durkheim's ritualistic approach to primitive societies. In his own account, Durkheim had clearly wanted to replace ideas about self-interest and negotiation with a vision of primitive order as emerging from the purely spontaneous authority generated by the sacred. He assumed that if primitive gifts had a moral and religious status, then their exchange would be based simply on mutually reinforcing altruism. Mauss tries to show that, on the contrary, the communal and moral status of primitive material things can be viewed as supplying a common denominator for the manipulation of self-interest and for the acquisition of authority and wealth.[42] Actors strive for an exchange that benefits themselves, but because the media they manipulate are religiously and morally defined, these apparently self-interested exchanges will end up reinforcing solidarity. Where Durkheim talks about "mana" as the sacred heart of primitive ritual, Mauss writes about it as the center of an interest struggle.[43] Where Durkheim writes about ritual effervescence as producing moral exchange, Mauss is fascinated by the way that effervescence leads to material exchange.[44] Mauss brings interest, bargaining, and the concrete individual back into Durkheimian theory even as he develops an argument that relativizes their importance. He does so, in part, by bringing the notion of material exchange that permeated Durkheim's *Division of Labor* to bear on the sacred things that Durkheim described in his later work. Because his analysis in *The Gift* is resolutely empirical, Mauss can avoid confronting the theoretical problems raised by this awkward welding. His short essay is devoted almost entirely to describing how different exchange systems actually work; it introduces few generalizations and never tries to link these interactions to a theory of primitive social structure.

The latent confusion in Mauss's revision comes through more directly in his earlier pioneering monograph on Eskimo society, *Seasonal Variations of the Eskimo*, which first appeared in *L'Année sociologique* (1906). Mauss presents himself as following Durkheim's theory about the interrelationship of morphology and collective representations, yet he ignores the fact that Durkheim's morphological theory had changed drastically before the notion of collective representations was ever systematically introduced. Thus, more than ten years after Durkheim himself had forcefully rejected a purely material approach to morphology, it is precisely a materialist morphology that informs the major thrust of Mauss's essay. For Mauss, the major determinant of Eskimo life is the seasonal change in climate which forces the Eskimo groups to make drastic alterations of their demographic and ecological form. Mauss insists that he is not advocating geographical determinism, that geography and climate must be mediated by "social" facts. But the social fact he points to most frequently is technology, so while avoiding one kind of instrumental analysis, his theory simply reproduces another form, one that is, in fact, much like that employed by Marx.[45] Mauss writes about "how the material form of human groups—the very nature and composition of their substratum—affects different modes of collective activity."[46] He emphasizes the "implacable physical laws" that in winter keep Eskimos close to starvation and force their clan societies to follow the same migration patterns as the animals they hunt.[47] Conversely, in the altered food conditions of summer life, a different demographic density results that allows a completely different kind of social life.[48]

Mauss himself would not accept this materialist interpretation of his work. He insists, for example, that affective contagion, arising from material interaction, is an intervening variable between physical form and social organization.[49] Yet, contrary to Durkheim, this contagion is rarely treated as a cause in itself.[50] In fact, despite his great empirical insight and his good theoretical intentions, Mauss is confused about the mode of analysis he is employing. This confusion arises because while on the one hand he is unaware of the break in Durkheim's theorizing, he is trying, nonetheless, to revise it, to force the categories of the middle and later period to interrelate with the materialist morphology of Durkheim's early sociology. Mauss cites as his guides in this effort not only the *Division of Labor* but also the *Rules of Sociological Method* and Durkheim's 1899 introduction to the new morphology section of *L'Année*. Yet, in each of the latter two instances Durkheim produced analyses quite antithetical to his work in 1893.[51] Similarly, *Suicide* is cited by Mauss as the model for his analysis of emotional contagion, when actually his treatment is radically different from Durkheim's own.[52†] But the confusion in Mauss's essay can also be demonstrated directly from the argument itself. In an early section, he insists that he is not selectively emphasizing material factors: "It is insufficient simply to assert that the climate or a configuration of the land draws them [the Eskimos] together; their moral, legal and religious organization must also allow a concentrated way of life."[53] Yet, at the end of the essay, he makes the following assertion: "We have proposed, as a methodological rule, that social life in all its forms—moral, religious, and legal—is dependent on its material substratum and that it varies with this substratum, namely with the mass, density, form and composition of human groups."[54] In the concluding pages he notes also that men feel the "need to reunite in the same place" at certain periods every year, and he suggests that this subjective need has been a major reference in his preceding analysis.[55] In fact, however, the essay is almost entirely devoted to describing how Eskimo solidarity, collective representations, laws of property, familial organization, and architecture must be seen as merely the "effects" of geographical, ecological, and technological arrangements.[56]

It should be clear, then, that Mauss, Durkheim's closest collaborator and a blood relative, sought to bury Durkheim's normative theory as much as to praise it. Mauss would not have wanted to admit this, and his own theorizing remains confused and unresolved as a result; but his attempt at revision remains a fact all the same, and it is a fact that testifies to the deep and unsatisfying strains that weaken Durkheim's original work. Indeed, some observers, in Mauss's time and our own, have enthusiastically taken his essays as an empirically acute, ideologically undogmatic form of Marxism. The Hungarian sociologist Oscar Jaszi called the work on Eskimo society an "inductive vindication of historical materialism" and concluded from its materialist morphology that "the Durkheimian postulate . . . *is* historical materialism itself."[57] The same sentiments are echoed, this time in regard to Mauss's entire oeuvre, in a recent French retrospective on his work.[58] Certainly these observers are wrong if their claims are taken literally, but it is not at all difficult to see how they could have been moved to make them. The student of a thinker whose work created classical sociology's alternative to Marx, Mauss implicitly tried to close the distance between the two.

Like Mauss, Bouglé either was unaware of the transition that occurred in Durkheim's thought or else chose not to recognize it publicly. An active political intellectual in the Third Republic, he was intent on forging a coalition between individualistic, liberal Republicanism and more working-class oriented socialism. Partly for these political reasons, but also for purely theoretical ones, Bouglé persistently rejected the extremes of Durkheim's thought, seeking a more multidimensional position that was neither positivist nor antiscientific, neither idealist nor completely insensitive to normative order.[59] Yet, he accomplished this more by blurring the lines of Durkheimian theory than by articulating an alternative theoretical model.

Durkheim's *Division of Labor* always remained for Bouglé the starting point of his analysis—long after Durkheim himself had rejected the presuppositional position it implied. Very much in keeping with this early Durkheimian instrumentalism, Bouglé asserted the theoretical, though not ideological, commonality between Durkheimianism and Marxism. For example, in the following passage from his 1907 work *Qu'est-ce que la sociologie?* (What Is Sociology?) he implicitly elides the Durkheimian emphasis on morphology and material density with the Marxian emphasis on the productive forces.

> The effort of men to produce riches exercises a thousand pressures on the constitution of societies. Social density depends closely on modes of economic production; one form of collective property tends to augment it, whereas some forms of property tend to diminish it. . . . Doesn't the development of an industrial

regime, by insisting on ever-increasing specialization, augment
the heterogeneity of social forms?[60]

Yet, despite this apparent endorsement, Bouglé never completely embraced such materialism, and he always made an effort to recognize,
without any attempt at theoretical precision, the parallel significance of
cultural forms. Thus, he added, several pages after the passage just
quoted, that "at other times" religious beliefs have also had a significant
effect on social development.[61] Part of this sensitivity to values reflected
Bouglé's reservations about the positivism that led Durkheim to present
historical forces as impervious to individual will. Durkheim himself recognized this reservation, criticizing Bouglé's tolerance for Tarde and
Simmel.[62] Yet, despite Bouglé's admonitions that externality must be
considered only as an analytical argument for the collective status of social facts rather than as an empirical argument for determinate social
laws—a position he shared with a critic of Durkheim, Elie Halévy, who
was also one of his closest friends—he characteristically failed to make
this criticism very precise.[63†] He demurred from positivistic determinateness, but he endorsed, all the same, the long-term causal structure of the *Division of Labor*. He championed Simmel's emphasis on
individuality as emerging from *"la complication,"* the criss-crossing web
of group affiliation and interest that induced individuals to adopt more
libertarian outlooks, yet much like Simmel himself he placed this argument for the wider scope of individual perception within a materialistic
historical framework.[64]

Bouglé's substantive sociology concerned the possibility of maintaining equality in a differentiated society that could also sustain individual
freedom. In part, this concern was reflected in his investigation into the
growth and acceptance of "egalitarian ideas," published as his doctoral
dissertation in 1899. Though Bouglé had already, implicitly, criticized
Durkheim's exclusively instrumental focus (in his review in 1896 of a book
by the German idealist critic Paul Barth), he still devotes this work, *Les
Idées égalitaires*, primarily to material, morphological developments, arguing that egalitarian ideas will develop to the degree there is greater
number, density, mobility, and heterogeneity of behavioral interactions.[65†]
More sensitive to the role of political force in social integration than
Durkheim, he also departs from the empirical content of the early Durkheim by following Simmel in discussing the impact of social differentiation in terms of the choices that confront the concrete individual.[66]
Neither of these emphases, however, departs from the more general instrumental framework of Durkheim's early work. Much as Durkheim
did in 1893, Bouglé notes how a more generalized conception of man
emerges with the division of labor, but he treats it, much like Durkheim,
as an effect rather than a cause in itself. Still, Bouglé does not see himself

as offering a completely materialist revision of Durkheim's later work. In the concluding pages of his book, he argues that "the idea of equality is active and powerful," indeed, that it is "the soul of the greatest modern revolutions."[67] Immediately after this admission, however, he reasserts his earlier position that "social," not ideational, changes are the key to the growth of egalitarian ideas.[68]

In his early work, then, Bouglé conducted a covert revision of Durkheim's emerging normative emphasis, even while he recognized the need to bring ideational elements into a more independent position. In his later writing he was more able to achieve such a balance. In the 1907 introduction to sociology, for example, he insists that the division of labor by itself is incapable of producing equality and cooperation, that there must also be a "whole ensemble of pre-existing feelings" and a "certain moral atmosphere."[69] This is, of course, much like the critique Durkheim himself made of his earlier material emphasis, and there can be little doubt that Bouglé is, in part, simply restating here the shift which appeared in Durkheim's work more than ten years before. Yet, this later recognition of the significance of moral beliefs never eclipsed Bouglé's earlier emphasis on instrumental facts. The difference is only that he could now make his argument for multidimensionality more explicit and clear. Thus, in *Essais sur le régime des castes*, published in 1908, where he tries to explain the origins of the Indian caste system, Bouglé continues to acknowledge the significant pressure for equality exerted by labor division; but his major interest has now shifted to the factors that prevent this purely economic pressure from having its expected egalitarian effect. In part, this investigation merely leads him to elaborate the political instrumentalism of his earlier work: he analyzes the political dominance of the Brahmin elite, stressing its drive for power and how the Brahmins reinforced their position through the manipulation of law.[70] At the same time, however, Bouglé insists on the significance of Hindu religion, whose hierarchical conception of the sacred independently reinforces the extraordinary economic and political inequality of Indian society. Indeed, he now judges religion to be so important that he writes at one point: "Caste is essentially a religious affair." Yet, he finds Hinduism so politicized that "rather than one of its fruits," one could say that "caste is the very seed of Hindu religion."[71] Indeed, the problem for Indian development was the unparalleled "interpenetration of the sacred and the social," a fusion that forced Indian society to resist economic pressure toward the kind of "bourgeois and profane" law upon which Western developments like the bourgeois city depended.[72]

No critic has made the mistake of identifying Bouglé as a Marxist, the fate suffered by some other Durkheimians. He was much too outspokenly anti-Marxist ideologically and too obviously devoted to liberal Republican morality for that. His work manifests, nevertheless, a distinct movement away from the exclusively normative emphasis of Durkheim's middle and later period. If Bouglé's work begins, at a middle point in his own development, to notice the autonomy of religious elements, he completely rejects the kind of completely anti-instrumental model that constituted the great innovation of Durkheim's later work. This antipathy to what he perceived as the idealist strain in Durkheimianism is clearly brought out in the consultations that ensued before Bouglé published his *Essais sur le régime des castes.* On the advice of Durkheim, he submitted his manuscript to Mauss for a prepublication reading. Mauss was quite evidently displeased with the work, writing back to Bouglé that he had completely ignored the most important fact, namely, "the religious character of caste."[73] It was no doubt after this harsh critique that Bouglé produced his final manuscript, where caste's religious character is firmly in place. In private, however, he fumed over the incident, writing derisively to his friend Halévy that he had been gored by the "taboo-totem clan" of the "united sociological party."[74] Nothing could demonstrate more acutely the ambivalence with which Bouglé approached his multidimensional revision, or the splits among Durkheim's students over the manner in which such revision should be conducted. He himself had publicly endorsed the independent importance of religious sentiment before the book on caste ever appeared. Yet, despite these proclamations, his interest clearly was focused more on political and legal phenomena. Even in the final, revised version of his book on caste, Bouglé's emphasis on religion's importance was partly neutralized by his failure to accord it a systematic place. He had not chosen, after all, to completely rewrite the manuscript, and this only partial accession to Mauss's critique is obliquely acknowledged in a small footnote to his central discussion. "If we are not consecrating a special chapter to religious phenomena," Bouglé writes, "it is because, in each of our chapters, whether it is a question of law, of economics, or of literature, we shall never stop seeing [religious] beliefs and scruples at work."[75] He would have us believe, in other words, that his relative neglect actually comes from his perception of Hinduism's importance, rather than, as was in fact the case, from his initial inability to give it much importance at all. Such statements of public fealty and private reservations are the very stuff of which paradigm revision is made.[76†]

The same kind of public affirmation and implicit revision marks the work of Halbwachs, perhaps the most empirically creative and original of Durkheim's students. When Halbwachs published, in 1930, the results of his own research into the phenomenon of suicide, Mauss wrote in his preface that though the later study altered "this or that thesis" of Durkheim's original work, by far the greater part reaffirmed Durkheim's earlier interpretation.[77] The two works, he assured his readers, "are two moments of the same research, conducted in the same spirit." This un-

questioned loyalty, however, is open to doubt. No more than Mauss himself had strictly followed Durkheim's line did Halbwachs do so in his
turn. Mauss asserts that a new book on suicide was necessary because
historical development since Durkheim's original publication had produced "new facts." Originally, he admits, the intention had been simply
to add a supplementary chapter or a new introduction to the original
text. "Little by little," however, Halbwachs "felt himself forced" to write
an entirely new book. New facts, I would suggest, were hardly the only
issue. Like his compatriots before him, Halbwachs was undertaking, under the cover of mere empirical elaboration, a revision of the most general assumptions that formed Durkheim's middle and later work.

There are, to be sure, extremely important similarities between the
two approaches to suicide. Halbwachs accepts Durkheim's intuition that
the psychological motivation which produces suicide is a sense of isolation from the warmth of the social world. Durkheim's sociological ex-
trapolation from this motive, the importance of solidary integration, is a
basic factor in Halbwachs' analysis of family-related suicides.[78] Yet this
reiteration of Durkheim's middle-period theme should not be deceiving,
for in most other respects Halbwachs' *Les Causes du suicide* represents,
like the work of Mauss and Bouglé, a compromise between the formulas
of this normative Durkheimianism and the orientation of the earlier *Division of Labor.* Halbwachs' own empirical contributions shift attention
away from the causal efficacy of subjectively integrating factors like solidarity and religion to more mechanical causes like geography and economic development. Although he does not specifically alter his
conception of action, Halbwachs describes the significance of such morphological factors in an unmistakably utilitarian way; they offer, he
writes, increased "opportunities" for suicide. Halbwachs is particularly
sensitive to the differentiation and conflict induced by urban social structure, and he argues that the frequency of interaction in urban as opposed
to rural life is the factor that creates higher rates of suicide. He employs
here the very concept that Durkheim used in such a strikingly affective
and moral way—frequency of interaction—as an indicator of the very
upsurge in suicides that Durkheim thought it reduced. The difference, of
course, is that Halbwachs employs "interaction" in a purely behavioral
way; it implies for him external "opportunities" rather than solidary
commitments.

In specifying the contents that provide such opportunities, Halbwachs seems to align his thought with Durkheim's by utilizing the same
general term, "social milieu"; yet, once again, he employs the term in a
decidedly more instrumental way. For example, neither family nor religious group are truly effective milieus; they must be related to "more
comprehensive" circumstances.[79] These turn out to be, as they were in
Mauss's investigations, circumstances of geography, ecology, and econ-

omy. Geographical factors are at the base because they closely inform residence patterns and the kind of labor performed. Custom and beliefs, Halbwachs believes, are only the translation of these more comprehensive facts.[80] Because Durkheim took as his primary reference subjective sentiments of solidarity, he viewed the decline of suicides in wartime as produced by the intensification of emotions. With his contrary emphasis on more instrumental order, Halbwachs reads the same statistical trend as evidence of the fewer opportunities that wartime allows. "It is less the rhythm of sentiments and collective passions," he writes, "than the decreasing degree of the complexity of life and the growing simplicity of social structure."[81] Finally, once again following the example of Mauss, Halbwachs brackets and minimizes the "moral contagion" which was the crucial discovery of Durkheim's middle period, arguing that it is important not as a factor in itself but only as a factor that creates homogeneity among suicide rates within a given geographical area. Halbwachs similarly discounts the independent importance of religious facts, the principal focus of Durkheim's later work. "There is no reason," he writes, "to look at complex groups only from a religious point of view."[82] Rather than religion, it is "social structure" that usually explains group cohesion, e.g., the fact that Catholics come from rural areas and Protestants from urban ones.

Yet, *Les Causes du suicide* is not an attempt to develop a consistently materialist revision. Halbwachs never specifically instrumentalizes individual motivation, and he talks about the independence of affective solidarity in his sections on the family. It would be more accurate to say that this work is contradictory, that it refers to both material and ideal factors on the empirical and propositional level without providing a general framework to articulate their relative position and interrelationship. Why, for example, would integration be so important in a family group but so unimportant in a nation at war?

Indeed, far from being committed to a completely instrumental vision of order, Halbwachs engages in other kinds of research where he approaches social morphology in a markedly normative way. The book on suicide appeared in 1930. By that time, Durkheim's students had certainly had ample time to absorb the shifting currents of his later work. Halbwachs' analysis gives little evidence of his having done so, or, more accurately perhaps, demonstrates a strong reluctance to follow Durkheim's lead. Less than a decade later, however, in 1938, Halbwachs returned to the problem of morphology in a more systematic way. This later book, *Morphologie sociale*, provides a radically different perspective on the same kind of ecological factors. Halbwachs' understanding of spatial arrangements is highly subjectified: exterior forms now express interior facts. "There is no society," he writes, "that does not organize its place in the spatial milieu, and which does not have at once a wide expanse and material support. . . . Every collective activity supposes an adaptation by the group to physical conditions."[83] Instead of reducing religion to ecological facts, Halbwachs analyzes the morphological forms produced by religious and political life. In a similar way, he devotes a later monograph to demonstrating that the historical location of Christian religious shrines has followed the path of intense religious feeling.[84] And in a posthumously published work on collective memory he shows how spatial relationships can be motivated by the desire to represent and sustain the social sentiments of earlier times.[85] When considered as a whole, therefore, Halbwachs' work on morphology is equivocal. At times he adopts an extremely antinormative perspective, and his critical revision of Durkheim is very clear. At other times, however, his morphology builds upon the most central tenets of Durkheim's later work. Halbwachs can avoid confronting the contradictions in his perspective only because—once again, much like Mauss—he resolutely eschews any attempt at general conceptualization, confining himself to detailed empirical description and specific propositions.

Halbwachs' research on social classes has been described as subjectivist by some Marxist observers, yet in terms of the theoretical tradition within which he wrote it is quite the opposite, an attempt to revise Durkheimianism in a materialist direction.[86†] Whereas his work on suicide drew on Durkheim's early material morphology, his writing on class takes the propositions of historical materialism itself as the empirical specification of his more instrumental presuppositions. At the center of Halbwachs' analysis of the nature and consciousness of contemporary social class are the material circumstances of economic production. It is from the perspective of this productive position that he judges the degree to which the members of different classes are able to interact with the symbolic and material centers of collective life, an interaction that he feels is essential for the full integration of social groups.[87] Only the upper classes, he believes, are able to work directly with people and with their prestigious symbols. Manual workers deal only with things, middle-class workers with people who are treated as things.[88] By this combination of material and ideal considerations, Halbwachs sketches what is, in effect, a continuum of alienation.[89] The relative alienation of each class from the center of society determines its rewards, but, more significantly for Halbwachs, it also determines family expenditures as well. The consumption of each class, in his view, is a collective representation of its social position, motivated first by the nature of its labor and subsequently by the understanding of the relationship between this labor and the broader society.[90] Halbwachs explains the consistently lower proportion of income that manual workers spend on housing, for example, by arguing that the materiality of manual labor alienates the worker from his family.[91] Because the needs of an economic class become collective representations with a life of their own, Halbwachs can explain, further, manual workers' "economically irrational" resistance to any wage reduction, their desire to direct any lowered compensation to areas other than wages related to consumption. In the same way, he can explain why class needs seem to be infinitely expandable: they have a representative rather than material function.[92]

Far from being idealist, it could be argued, in fact, that Halbwachs' extremely interesting class analysis is often overly determined by the physical situation of work, and that it lacks sufficient reference to the more solidary and moral aspects of class situations. This weakness, however, is not an argument against the plainly multidimensional ambition that inspired these studies. It testifies, rather, to the schematic and often vague character of Halbwachs' general conceptual scheme. Once again, Halbwachs has sharply limited himself to the barest features of the empirical world. He incorporates an important Marxian point, but he makes no reference at all to Marx's broader historical analysis or to his theory of social classes. He utilizes part of Durkheim's theory about collective representations, but he offers no explanation for the manner in which he substitutes material structures for the sacred values and ritualized reproduction that Durkheim's original theory of representations entailed. If Halbwachs had tried to make some of these broader connections, of course, he would have had to confront his revisions of Durkheim's theory; since he remained merely at the empirical level, the contradictory nature of his work could remain unexposed. One French commentator on Halbwachs has called his work a "spontaneous materialism" that "announces a new materialist sociology."[93] Certainly Halbwachs intended nothing of the kind. He was a Durkheimian, indeed one of the greatest among them. If the implications of his sociology are difficult to understand, it is only because his revision of Durkheim was forced to take such a subterranean form.

The economic sociology of François Simiand gives evidence of the same covert revision as the work of Durkheim's other students. His general statements seem, at first, to follow the path Durkheim laid out. Economic problems cannot be solved, he insists, without rejecting the abstractness of traditional economic theory for the "positive" method of sociology. Classical economics' assumptions about the inherent and unchanging rationality of the actor must be altered, and the individualistic "economic man" must be placed within a wider context. Yet, under the guise of these apparently Durkheimian directives, Simiand's work actually comes closer to Marx than that of any of his fellow students.

Simiand's sociology may be regarded as directed toward an empirical dilemma he finds at the center of classical economics. "How does one know," he asks in a 1912 work, *La Méthode positive dans la science économique* (The positive method in economic science), "if economic man, when he is faced with a choice between two considerations, would estimate that his greatest interest is in augmenting his capital even at a risk or, to the contrary, that it is better to conserve his capital, even without a gain?"[94] In 1902, in one of his major empirical studies, the essay on the price of coal, he puts the same question in a more specific way. If demand grows, will price necessarily go up, or will the capitalist increase his production and lower his price?[95] Classical economics, he believes, cannot answer such questions because it considers only "economic man" in the abstract. A more truly scientific economics would have to consider the actual "social psychology" of the economic actor, his "experiences" in the real world.[96] It is people who make prices, so prices are matters of human estimation and opinion.[97] Supply and demand, then, are not the results of an automatic calculus, but the products of a particular social situation.[98] In terms of his general statements, then, Simiand's work seems to echo the later Durkheim's theory about the moral basis of economics. Yet it is evident that at least in his more technical economic analysis his "social psychology" remains an instrumental one. He departs from classical economics only by taking the actual content of economic motivation as variable, and he relates this variation to changes in action's external environment: "Actions and passions differ and change for the same cases, according to the societies, according to the epochs, according to the milieus, according to the classes and social groups."[99]

The principal question that Simiand asks in his essay on the price of coal is this: What will happen as the demand for coal increases? What will happen, he argues, depends upon particular empirical circumstances, on the rational knowledge that the actor has of his situation, and on the structure of the situation itself—on legal, technological, political, and scientific factors as well as on purely economic ones.[100] Prices will be lowered, for example, only if the producer is certain that he can increase his supply and his economy of scale, possibilities that depend on the natural resources available in different geographical regions and on the state of industrial technology.[101] If the capitalist is convinced that demand is unstable, as when, for example, rights of importation have recently been granted to a competitor, assurances about the security of resources and technology will be ignored.[102] The stability of demand is also affected by the producer's perception of other markets; if neighboring markets have crashed, he will be more likely to adjust to increased demand by keeping output steady and raising his price.[103] Simiand also considers the case of falling demand, and concludes in much the same way that, "contrary to appearance, it is not necessarily inevitable that prices will drop."[104] Once again, only a concrete examination of actual empirical circumstances can determine what decisions will be made. Simiand does, in fact, take "the psychology of the social class" as his point of departure, but it is a Benthamite psychology devoted to the relative balance of costs and rewards.[105] He wants to critique "natural identity" theory not by showing how cooperation depends upon normative agreement but rather by demonstrating that an "artificial identity" of interest is preserved by unequal social force.

> [Economic] results are inexplicable by the hypothesis according to which economic persons, acting according to their interest rightly understood ... have equal freedom in making an exchange. It would seem, on the contrary, that the observed phenomenon becomes intelligible only if it is understood that such "interest rightly understood" is "understood" in a very different fashion by different categories of persons and if the inequality among parties is the rule rather than the exception.[106]

It would be wrong, however, to conclude from the examination of these two works that Simiand has simply opted for an instrumental sociology. If this were the case, he would be an opponent of Durkheim rather than a creative, revisionist student. In his general declaratory statements, Simiand adheres to Durkheim's collective understanding of order, and while in his studies of market behavior he usually accepts action as instrumental, in work on other aspects of economic life he often pushes collective order along a path that more closely resembles Durkheim's later work. For example, in his well-known essay "Money, A Social Reality" (1934) Simiand argues for the importance of the noncontractual elements of economic interaction in a symbolic rather than an instrumental sense. Even the most rational economic actors, he observes, have much the same attitude toward money as believers have toward religion, treating it as an irrational "representation" of the world which must, nonetheless, be accepted as a collective fact.[107] Making the same kind of evolutionary argument as Durkheim in his later work, Simiand argues that this contemporary similarity between money and religion has a historical root. When it first appeared in primitive society, money made use of the same ornaments as religion, utilizing their "divine and sacred nature" to inspire solidarity and trust in exchange relations.[108] Although social circumstances have greatly changed, Simiand asserts that money still retains for modern economic man some of this "magical-religious superstition."[109] Because the base of money is a "social belief," even a "social faith," contemporary economic interaction continues to depend upon an element of nonrational normative order, namely on "trust."[110]

In important respects, therefore, Simiand's work resembles that of Halbwachs. There are significant strains of instrumental analysis where his criticism of Durkheim's later work is blatantly clear, yet these are combined with other instances of a directly normative character. Taken as the sum of its parts, then, Simiand's writing is multidimensional, revealing an implicit attempt to alter the Durkheimian theory in a manner that focuses it on the collective forces of the material as well as the ideal world. Yet the "whole" of Simiand's work, as opposed to simply this "sum," presents not a multidimensional theory but, rather, a series of potentially contradictory statements. He avoids the necessity of reconciling these currents, and of criticizing Durkheim directly, because his work, like that of the other Durkheimians with whom he worked and studied, remains extremely specific. It is directed toward concrete empirical problems and to discrete theoretical questions. It partakes here of the Marxist critique of classical economics—where the instrumentality of action is preserved, and there of the Durkheimian critique—where action itself becomes the object of contention. Since Simiand remained a loyal Durkheimian, how he would have reconciled these positions must remain an unanswered question.

Although the theoretical logic of this second generation of Durkheimians was often highly contradictory, theoretical inconsistency or weakness has never been the only reason for the decline in influence of a major scientific school. For the mechanism that triggered the denouement of Durkheimianism we must look also to more social forces. By the 1930s, the moral and political coalition which had provided the social base and audience for Durkheimian ideas was in serious disrepair. The liberal thought of the French middle classes was becoming increasingly conservative and individualistic, the socialist ideology of the working-class movement increasingly sectarian and radical.[111†] As the interwar period progressed, therefore, the Third Republic appeared less able to resolve the problems of its social and political extremes. Yet this was precisely the same period which witnessed the movement of Durkheim's major students to the center of the French sociological establishment. Their persistent call for the moral integration of society and their analysis of the necessarily intimate relationship between social institutions and the sacred seemed, in this context, more like a call for the "sanctification" of a troubled society than a theory that would provide the means to change it.[112]

The 1930s in continental Europe was a time where the center did not hold, a period of violence and revolution that confronted the conscientious individual with the demand for effective political action and the necessity to choose between radically different values. It was, in short, a period more conducive to Hegelianism, existentialism, and Marxism than to the kind of liberal neo-Kantianism that Durkheim represented. It was precisely to the former intellectual currents that the younger generation of French intellectuals turned as they tried to resolve, in Sartre's words, the critical problems "of the end and the means, of the legitimacy of violence, of the consequences of action, the relationship between the

individual and the group, between individual initiative and historical in-
variables."[113] Raymond Aron, who also came of age in the 1930s, was a
protégé of Bouglé, and in certain respects his career is symbolic of his
intellectual generation as a whole. Rather than follow his teacher's
Durkheimianism, Aron turned to German thought and to Max Weber, interpreting this tradition in a highly existentialist way. Aron viewed Durkheim's thought as particularly irrelevant to the political and intellectual
questions of the day; he was, from the beginning, one of Durkheim's
harshest critics. In 1937, Bouglé edited a book on the state of social science in France, and Aron, his collaborator in this project, wrote the chapter on sociology. He attacked Durkheimianism for its conflation of social
and moral authority, a judgment that certainly is a more accurate reflection of the ideology of the time than of Durkheim's work. Durkheim's
sociology is as much philosophy, Aron asserts, as a science of social facts.
The very separation of sociology from philosophy, and of social structure
from morality, is rendered difficult because of "the way in which Durkheim puts in the service of a prophetic ardor the dialectic of a philosophy
that dreams about restoring an imperative and positive morality."[114]
French sociology can revive itself, Aron concludes, only if it can become
much more "attentive to the questions that the present poses to the man
of action."[115]†

The 1930s in France, therefore, were not very hospitable to Durkheimian theory. Durkheim's students would have had to revise it drastically if it was to survive, and the younger generation of French
intellectuals upon whom this challenge would naturally have devolved
were in no mood to take it up. Durkheimian theory died as a coherent
"paradigm," as an "exemplar" for research carried by a coherent group
of scholars. It did not die, however, as a more general and less compact
theoretical tradition, continuing to exert a powerful influence on Western social science, particularly on anthropology and functionalist sociology. What is most interesting, from the viewpoint of the present study, is
that those who were influenced by this tradition continued to be polarized by the presuppositional strains in the original work. Durkheim's
ideas were taken up by anthropologists and sociologists, but they were
taken up only partially. The most powerful thinkers who did research
and theorizing in his name were always, implicitly, trying to push his
thought in a more materialist or idealist, more determinist or voluntarist
direction.

The anthropology of Radcliffe-Brown, for example, can be described
as an attempt to explain the symbolic and religious analysis of Durkheim's later work within the functionalist and utilitarian logic of his earlier *Division of Labor*. Radcliffe-Brown was not consciously influenced by
Durkheim until after he had already conducted important research
within the English rationalist tradition, and it is clear that his later writ-

ing "Spencerizes" Durkheim as much as it operationalizes him. Raising the banner of anthropology as a positivistic science, Radcliffe-Brown employed this methodological orientation, much like the early Durkheim, as a rationale for concentrating on the objective, material, physical elements of the social world. He studied institutions from a mechanical perspective, in terms of their equilibrium, and although solidarity was important for him he viewed it as the effect of shifts in mechanical equilibrium rather than as an independent factor in the process of symbolic representation.[116] Although he identified his work with Durkheim's, the problem of cultural symbols that took up the greater part of Durkheim's later career seemed to make no impression on him. Reducing culture to social structure, he asserted, much as Durkheim himself had done in his earliest sociological writings, that culture is merely the formation that habits produce after repeated interaction.

> A social usage . . . is the name for a certain collection of acts of behavior of different human individuals. . . . While they [such usages] characterize a certain number of individuals, they are the product in those individuals of the action upon them of other individuals within a specific social system. That, I think, is what Durkheim had in the back of his mind when he seemed to want to say that the social usage is a thing. . . . You cannot have a science of culture [because] you can study culture only as a characteristic of a social system. Therefore, if you are going to have a science, it must be a science of social systems.[117]

It was this reductionistic understanding of culture that informed all of Radcliffe-Brown's writing on religious ritual, which he analyzed only as it related to the stability of the social system, never to the problems of meaning engendered by the problem of the sacred per se.[118]

A contrary strain in modern anthropology has been developed by Evans-Pritchard, who takes up Durkheimian theory at a different point in its development. Though he began his career as a functionalist in the mode of Radcliffe-Brown, by the 1930s his thought had shifted toward the symbolic concern of Durkheim's later work, to the study of "societies as moral systems and not as natural systems."[119] Rejecting positivism as well, his work reflects a presuppositional commitment to maintaining voluntarism without sacrificing an understanding of collective control. In his classic *Nuer Religion*, for example, Evans-Pritchard understands the collective processes of "ideation" in a manner that accepts the centrality Durkheim assigned to them in his crucial transition to religious sociology. "The view is taken," he writes in his preface, "that religion is a subject of study *sui generis*."[120] And his analysis of the Nuer conception of spirit is self-consciously directed against the reduction of representation to material group-interest that characterized Durkheim's earlier approach, and Radcliffe-Brown's as well.

> It is not that the members of a group see themselves as a group through a totemic class of objects which are then further conceptualized collectively as a spirit of the class, but rather that the conception of Spirit, which is in itself quite independent of the social structure, is broken up along the lines of segmentation within the structure.[121]

The cultural "structuralism" of Lévi-Strauss represents the third strand of "Durkheimian" thinking in modern anthropology, and it seeks to resolve the strains of the original theory in still a different way. Lévi-Strauss has usually disguised his debt to Durkheim's thought by elevating Mauss to the status of *maître*, praising Mauss for his empirical perspicacity, his exemplary "modernity," and his recognition of the autonomous status of primitive mental life.[122] His brief references to Durkheim are extraordinarily ambivalent, although they are an accurate reflection of the ambiguities of the original theorist himself. In 1945, in his famous survey of French sociology, Lévi-Strauss condemns Durkheim as a social reductionist: "Instead of showing how the appearance of symbolic thought makes social life altogether possible and necessary, Durkheim tries the reverse, i.e., to make symbolism grow out of society."[123] In 1962, in his essay on totemism, he reverses this judgment, at least in part. For "Durkheim at his best," Lévi-Strauss now admits, "all social life, even the elementary, presupposes an intellectual activity in man of which the formal properties, consequently, cannot be a reflection of the concrete organization of the society."[124] Yet that same year, in *The Savage Mind*, he talks once again about the "Durkheimian thesis of the social origin of logical thought," and argues that his own work derives from a "dialectical relation between the social structure and systems of categories" that is antithetical to Durkheim's conception.[125] Although Lévi-Strauss could indeed have been reacting against the social determinism of Durkheim's early thought, particularly against its incarnation in the anthropology of Radcliffe-Brown, it seems undeniable that he was deeply and formatively affected by Durkheim's later, more idealist formulations about the collective processes of ideation. Lévi-Strauss's "structuralism" takes the later Durkheim and radicalizes it. Generalizing from Durkheim's dichotomous divisions of the sacred and profane, he makes antithesis the major organizing principle in all of cultural life.[126†] With little attention to affect or personality and no systematic reference to the intervening affects of social institutions, Lévi-Strauss has brilliantly reproduced the advantages and disadvantages of the idealism that marked Durkheim's later work.

If empirical anthropology continues to reproduce the strains that undermined Durkheim's original theoretical vision, a sociological theorist, Talcott Parsons, has responded to Durkheim by trying to resolve them.[127†] Parsons possessed the creative analytical abilities that were lacking in Durkheim's immediate students and his anthropological followers. Addressing the voluntarism problem, Parsons firmly separated the essence of Durkheim's general theorizing from any necessary relation to its positivist method. By explicitly articulating both the interdependence and relative autonomy of the personality and cultural codes, an articulation he achieved by combining Durkheim with Freud, he was able to talk about "socialized" individuals in a much less reified way.[128] Sensitive to the problem of Durkheim's idealism, Parsons tried to integrate the Durkheimian understanding of normative order with elements from Weber's theory of institutional, coercive force. The theory that resulted from this effort, which revolved around the analytical independence of culture and social system, pursued the redolent meanings of Durkheimian "society" in a way that helped to resolve the central dilemmas of Durkheimian thought.[129†] Yet, as will be seen in the fourth volume of the present work, Parsons' thought is itself riven by the tensions that weakened Durkheim's theory. His synthetic and integrating ambition was undermined by his ambivalent tendency to reduce collective order to affectively rooted culture. Even with the clarifying legacy of Parsons' work, therefore, the strains in Durkheim's original legacy have never been completely resolved.[130†]

Chapter Ten

EQUIVOCATION AND REVISION IN THE CLASSICAL THEORY OF SOCIOLOGICAL MATERIALISM

Marx and "Marxism"

The movement from Marx to Marxism begins with the implicit revisions initiated by Marx and Engels themselves. While basic theoretical revision derives from errors or irresolutions in the fundamental presuppositions of the founding theory, it is often the tension between different levels of this theory that creates the actual movement toward theoretical revision itself. This was certainly the case for the revision of Durkheim's theory. It is true for the revision of Marx's theory as well: to analyze the revision of this classical tradition one must begin with the conflict between the ideological and presuppositional levels in Marx's thought.

As I have emphasized in my earlier discussions, what Marx wants in a normative and ideological sense is not what he sees around him empirically or presupposes theoretically. Marx wants a society that is collectively ordered but which achieves this order through voluntary, rational consensus of its members, a society that promotes affective solidarity and sanctions individual deviation only by the application of moral standards which the actors themselves know to be right. What he sees before him, however, is a society ordered coercively by economic force, where individuals act instrumentally without reference to internalized moral standards. It is this empirical vision, of course, that "allows" Marx to share political economy's presuppositions about instrumental action; because he does so, he can make his revolutionary thought into a propositional science.

Marx resolves the potential conflict between his ideological vision and his theoretical and empirical commitments by utilizing "alienation" in a very specific way. If the economic forces of capitalism cause alienation, if they are responsible for separating the instrumental side of action from the affective morality of "species being," then the laws of a revised political economy can hold for this historical period without the need for Marx to surrender any of his revolutionary moral ideas about human potential. This society is coercively ordered, but it need not always be so. Economic laws, predictable on the basis of a critical political economy, create revolutionary movement. On the basis of the force exerted by a certain arrangement of economic laws, the pursuit of self-interest by the working classes will move ineluctably in a revolutionary way. Revolution occurs because there is no other "means" of preserving instrumental self-interest in the context of capitalism's collective order. Only after the revolution, and after the first stage of communism as well, can scarcity be defeated. With the productive forces of late communism, society will finally be open to voluntary behavior and to its restructuring by a moral order rationally understood.

This forms Marx's explicit social "science," the body of models, general propositions, laws, and detailed predictions that form the tightly organized conceptual scheme of which he was justly proud. This science represents the positivistic sublimation of Marx's revolutionary, prophetic fervor. Yet, while it is a highly successful example of social scientific thought, it has certain grave disadvantages for Marx himself, for it clearly implies the necessity for Marx and other revolutionaries to wait until the objective contradictions of capitalism have fully ripened. This, of course, was exactly the backdrop against which Marx composed his mature work: *Capital* was an attempt to understand and explain the slowness of revolution after the tantalizing and ultimately severely disappointing upheavals of 1848. But Marx was an impatient man. Science could not, in fact, completely sublimate his inner desire for critical action. It was all right, perhaps, publicly to portray the revolution as an "old mole" that was gradually but surely "grubbing" its way to the surface of society, but Marx preferred to see himself as a steam-driven shovel or an air hammer rather than a plodding, if forward-moving, beast.[1]

Marx's self-conscious science, in which the instrumental actor was envisioned as responding only to external conditions, was violated in his own conduct of life. He was inclined to the prophetic mode, employing moral denunciation and moral judgments as weapons in the political struggle. He carried out his life's work against all pressures and sanctions from the external world, and he persistently called on others to do the same. Marx never sat around waiting for history. He was a dedicated and indefatigable organizer of everything from letters-to-the-editor to full-fledged newspapers and political parties. It was inevitable that this activistic and moralistic ideology would seep into his published work, even if its appearance must contradict the propositions and presuppositions of his formal science.

1. MARX'S "SECOND THOUGHTS": REVOLUTION AS THE PRODUCT OF MORAL SOLIDARITY AND VOLUNTARY ACTION

Unlike Durkheim, Marx usually kept this ideological "seepage" from invading the strand of his writing which was resolutely and systematically scientific. On the few occasions where it does appear, however, it creates residual categories that stand out awkwardly from the main course of his argument. In earlier chapters, I have discussed some of these residual categories in the writings between 1845 and 1848. Similar ad hoc references occur in *Capital*. At several points, for example, Marx refers to the operations of the state in a manner which relates it directly to social values and to personality rather than to instrumental, objective actions. In the preface to the first German edition, he refers to the universalistic impartiality of the investigators appointed by the British Parliament. "We should [also] be appalled by the state of things at home," he writes to his German readers, "if, as in England, our governments and parliaments appointed periodically commissions of inquiry into economic conditions; if these commissions were armed with the same plenary powers to get at the truth; if it was possible to find for this purpose men as competent, as free from partisanship and respect for persons, as are [England's] factory inspectors, her medical reporters on public health, her commissioners of inquiry into the exploitation of women and children, into housing and food."[2] At several points in the main body of the work, Marx acknowledges noneconomic dimensions of the state in a different way. When he describes the enclosure movement of the fifteenth and sixteenth centuries, he writes that the now landless peasants could not "suddenly adapt themselves to the discipline of their condition" as proletarians. They could assume the regular hours of methodical labor only after they had acquired a certain "education, tradition, [and] habit." It was the state's function, he writes, to provide this discipline, for the simple existence of the capitalist productive apparatus is not enough to compel men to work. Thus, the newly landless peasants of the fifteenth and sixteenth centuries became beggars, robbers, and vagabonds, and only the brutal penal legislation of the absolutist state produced the discipline that, eventually, transformed them into a docile proletariat.[3]

These residual references contain two implicitly contradictory views of the state. For example, if in a certain period of crisis the state's representatives appoint fair and objective observers to produce documents critical of the capitalist system, why should they in another instance necessarily act only in a brutal way, with regard only for the purely particularistic interests of the capitalist ruling class? More importantly, however, these views contradict major arguments upon which *Capital* is based. If the so-called representatives of the upper classes can achieve such universalistic objectivity, why are economic struggle and political force the only means of creating political reform? Why, indeed, are the representatives of the upper and lower classes destined, inevitably, to be in constant struggle with one another? Finally, if the English inspectors could achieve such objectivity, their ideas could not, in fact, be the result of their class position alone. From what source independent of class, then, do their ideas come?

The statement about the need for the state to discipline workers has an equally disruptive potential. If workers must be disciplined, the separation of the worker from the means of production could not have been the only source for the workers' participation in capitalist development. The purely objective constraints on lower-class behavior that Marx usually describes are insufficient; his reproduction theory, which focuses only on material consumption and objective conditions, would have to be radically revised. If workers must be psychologically adapted to the mode of production, problems of legitimacy and moral authority would have to be brought into a central position in Marx's critical analysis.

An equally important residual category is introduced when Marx tries to account for an empirical anomaly that relates to wages: the wages of workers in different countries does not vary strictly according to the cost of their physical reproduction.[4] For the most part, this anomaly is completely ignored, for in Marx's formal theory the wage relation is the product of a purely instrumental exchange. Its very instrumentality, indeed, forms one of the pivotal points of his theoretical apparatus. In at least two instances, however, Marx tries to construct an ad hoc explanation that will both acknowledge this anomaly and incorporate its explanation into his general theory. The material wants of the worker to which wages correspond, Marx writes at one point, depend "to a great extent on the degree of civilization of a country," and "on the habits and degree of comfort" in which its "class of free labourers has been formed."[5] At another point, Marx links the worker's compensation to the "general state of culture [*Kulturzustand*]."[6†] Yet, far from incorporating national wage differences into his systematic theory, these explanations actually imply theories that are contradictory to it. With factors like "civilization" and "habits" Marx is subjectifying his understanding of cost; in doing so, he challenges the instrumental and exclusively "means" orientation of exchange. The logic of commodities will not hold if the costs of labor power depend partly on the mutual consensus among workers themselves about their moral worth and on the implicit agreement about this estimation by capitalists. If this were true, the workers could hardly be only objects to themselves, or merely objects to the owners. The determination of such moral consensus, moreover, would have to be linked to something other than the mode of production in a material sense; it would have to be connected to a nonrational order like "civilization" or "culture". These are not aspects of social life that Marx would have liked to explore.[7†]

Despite these occasional lapses, however, in the writings that he regarded as his scientific work Marx usually exercised extraordinary restraint, for they are consistently organized around his instrumental-collective presuppositions. When we enter the world of his more informal writings, on the other hand, the picture is strikingly different. In his letters and speeches, journalistic articles and pamphlets, Marx introduces, alongside the references to the determinate force of economic production and class, a consistently voluntaristic and moralistic strain. In these more political writings, Marx is addressing himself directly to political actors, and he is speaking as one activist to another. Even when he is analyzing the failure of a particular movement, his analysis is tied to political practice in a way his scientific work is not. In this "practical" writing, Marx relies more on his tacit knowledge of political life than on his formal theoretical assumptions and models. If he cannot admit it as a scientific theorist, as a political activist he knows that political organization is vital, that it is the product of self-motivated coordination and not simply the reflection of economic conditions. He understands also that felt solidarity is the core of such organization, that political organization depends upon voluntary acquiescence to intellectual and moral ideas. Because of such tacit knowledge, Marx knows that it is much harder to separate means from ends than his scientific writing allows; the immediate economic and political issues of the day are inextricably intertwined, for the struggling worker, with the ideals that will regulate his communist future. To be sure, the tacit knowledge that informed Marx's political practice is never put into the form of an explicit analytical theory. It is clear, indeed, that Marx was never really conscious that this tacit theory existed. Yet this is precisely the point: given the nature of his activist and critical ideological commitment, Marx was forced to introduce notions that were completely residual to his systematic theoretical work.

These letters, speeches, and pamphlets make it clear that Marx began with the assumption that must inform any effort at political organization: subjective orientations can vary widely in any single situation. Throughout his life, Marx was frustrated by the proletariat's inability to understand its interests in a sufficiently radical way, in the way, that is, that he did himself. Nationalist feelings, prejudices, moral deference to authority—all of these "attitudes" were keeping the proletariat in chains. A case study in this insight is Marx's disillusionment with the English working class. He expressed this disappointment in a series of letters in 1869 and 1870 that took as its background certain comparisons between the political situations of the English and the Irish. The English workers could not overthrow their landed aristocracy by themselves,

Marx was certain, and they could not do so because they regarded this ruling class as the "traditional dignitaries and representatives of the nation."[8] The English ruling class, in other words, commanded from its proletariat a certain respect and admiration by virtue of simple national feeling. This same ruling class, however, could be overthrown in Ireland, because in that country their class domination was threatened by the workers' national sentiments rather than preserved by them. To the Irish proletariat, the landlords were their "mortally hated oppressors."[9] The overthrow of the English landed aristocracy in Ireland, moreover, not only would weaken its material hold over the English working classes, but would undermine its "moral strength" as well, and this subjective confidence was, along with the national deference of the workers, one of the vital means by which the landed aristocracy maintained its domination in England itself.[10] The English proletarian revolution, then, would have to begin in Ireland. There were, besides the national issue, differences in national temperament between Irish and English workers that would make an initial revolution in Ireland more likely. Marx believed that Irish proletarians were "more passionate and revolutionary in character than the English."[11] Finally, an initial English revolution was unlikely because the English working class was weakened by the ethnic antipathy that divided it from the Irish part of the proletariat. The English worker feared the Irish as a threat to his standard of living, but there was an internal and voluntary component as well, for the English worker "cherished religious, social, and national prejudices against the Irish worker."[12]†

The task of the revolutionary must be directed toward changing the conservative consciousness of the working classes, which he can clarify only through his nonrational "influence" rather than his instrumental power. Marx expressed this understanding at a political meeting during the German uprising of 1848: "We must turn to the people and influence them with all the means at our disposal, through the press, placards and public meetings."[13] When he spoke to the Central Committee of the Communist League in 1850, he made this strategy more specific. The workers can achieve victory only "by clarifying their minds as to what their class interests are" and "by taking up their position as an independent party."[14] Revolution involves a theoretical strategy and a political one. Workers' decisions are voluntary, made with reference to a theoretical understanding of the world. Yet the simple writing of good theory is not sufficient. Activists can further influence the working class and its leaders by institutionalizing these theories in a political organization. Guided by this tacit knowledge, Marx dedicated his efforts to keeping "idiots," "adventurers," and incompetent "theoreticians" out of positions of power in the organizations of the working classes.[15] If they assumed power despite his efforts, he issued moral denunciations and theoretical exposés that would purge such "bad lines" from the workers' parties.[16] In 1870, Marx thought that his work with the German workers had borne fruit, and he boasted to Engels that "the German working-class is theoretically and organisationally superior to the French."[17] Less than ten years later, he was more pessimistic. Once again, he explained the situation in terms of political and moral factors, not economic ones. As the result of a political compromise by working-class leaders, certain incompetent theorists had been allowed to write in the party journal. They had filled the workers' heads with erroneous ideas and now "a rotten spirit is making itself felt in our Party in Germany."[18]

The most important and ambitious step Marx ever took as an activist was his effort to construct the Working Men's International Association. His inaugural address in 1864 focused on why the English workers had so far been defeated in their revolutionary efforts and why a new political party would provide the necessary antidote. This public statement is noteworthy for the way it departs from the analysis that informed Marx's scientific theory. The defeat of the 1848 revolutions, Marx told his listeners, had had a profound and depressing moral effect on the entire proletarian movement, for it had replaced the "dreams of emancipation" with an epoch marked by "industrial fever, moral morasme [sic], and political reaction."[19] The impact of this defeat on the English working class was moral and psychological. Not only had it "unmanned the English working classes, and broken their faith in their own cause," but it had also "restored to the landlord and the money-lord their somewhat shaken confidence."[20] The faith of the working classes was partly restored, and the confidence of the ruling classes correspondingly weakened, by the passage of the Ten Hours' Bill, which had "immense physical, moral, and intellectual benefits."[21] Marx stresses particularly its intellectual impact, asserting that the successful functioning of the English economy after the limitation of working hours indicated the "victory of a principle," for "it was the first time that in broad daylight the political economy of the middle class succumbed to the political economy of the working class."[22] One "practical upshot of [these] theories" of socialist economics was experimentation in worker-initiated and -directed factory cooperatives.[23] Yet these cooperative experiments, Marx insists, were motivated by socialist theories of the wrong kind. If socialism were going to triumph, it would have to be through a national rather than a local movement, and it would have to achieve political power. To accomplish this, the revolutionary movement needed correct theoretical knowledge, a large number of adherents, and absolute political unity. Warning against the dangers to socialism of international war, Marx especially emphasized the need for international unity among the working classes of different countries. A strong "bond of brotherhood" was necessary if workers were to be inspired to resist the chauvinist pressures of their national bourgeoisies. It was this "thought," Marx says, that "prompted the working men of different countries . . . to found the International Association."[24] One of the first actions of this international group, he concludes, should be the establishment of a working-class-oriented foreign policy, which in the face of bourgeois-inspired war could "combine in simultaneous denunciations . . . to vindicate the simple laws of morals and justice, which ought to govern the relations of private individuals, as the rules paramount of the intercourse of nations."[25]

In 1871 the International formally adopted rules that closely adhered to the provisional rules drawn up by Marx in 1864.[26†] The preamble to the rules asserts that the workingmen's movement must be subordinated to a strongly felt end, and that this end must be economic: "The economic emancipation of the working classes is therefore the great end to which every political movement ought to be subordinate . . ."[27] Workers had thus far not been able to attain this end because they had not established sufficiently strong moral and affective ties: "All efforts aiming at that great end have hitherto failed from the want of solidarity between the manifold divisions of labour in each country and from the absence of a fraternal bond of union between the working classes of different countries." If "disconnected movements" were to be brought together and a new solidarity established, an association must be organized that would allow increased communication. The first rule, therefore, is that "this association is established to afford a central medium of communication and cooperation between Working Men's Societies," the second records the name of the society under which this communication will occur, and the third mandates an annual meeting where "the Congress will have to proclaim the common aspirations of the working class."[28] The fourth rule asserts that the meetings must occur each year at a formally established time and place, the fifth that each meeting must consist of delegates from different countries, and the sixth that an international agency must be formed so that this communication among parties will not be only periodic: "The working men in one country [must] be constantly informed of the movements of their class in every other country."[29] The seventh rule urges workers "to combine [their] disconnected working men's societies" so that they can be "represented by central national organs," and the eighth guarantees each society the right to appoint a secretary to correspond with the national council; the ninth states that any person who "defends the principles of the International Working Men's Association is eligible to become a member"; the tenth promises that "each member of the International Association, on removing his domicile from one country to another, will receive the fraternal support of the Associated Working Men." In the eleventh rule, the International assures the national societies that by joining the Association they do not lose their individuality: "The working men's societies joining the International Association will preserve their existent organizations intact."[30]

A more Durkheimian understanding of the basis for association could not be found. Marx argues here that organization is merely the structural location for symbolic exchange, that periodic reunions of this group must occur, and that between these "ritual" occasions of renewal communication should occur as frequently and as continuously as possible. If such interaction occurs, a moral solidarity will form upon which each member of the group can draw; yet this group force, because it is moral and not instrumental, will not limit the individuality of any of its members. The strategy, as Marx sums it up in a letter to Engels, could not have been better articulated by Durkheim himself: "The community of action, which the International Workers' Association calls to life, the exchange of ideas through the different organs of the sections in all countries, finally the direct debates in the general Congresses, will gradually create a common theoretical program for the international workers' movement."[31]

Thus far we have examined primarily Marx's letters and speeches, documents that were written for directly political consumption. It is in his journalistic pamphlets, however, that Marx's political writing more closely approaches self-consciously analytical argument. Designed as documents of short-term political persuasion, they were, at the same time, essays that Marx knew would reach an intellectual public as well as a popular one, essays which he knew he might have to answer for in a more scholarly way. The greatest of these is *The Eighteenth Brumaire of Louis Bonaparte*, published in 1852.[32†] Marx develops in this essay two strategies of explanation which never occur in his "scientific" work. In the first, he retains his instrumental assumptions about action and order, but he specifies them in terms of a different model of society: political structures order action without economic determination, subject only to the forces of individual and organizational skill. The second explanatory strategy marks an even more radical deviation, for Marx reverses here not only the institutional model of historical materialism but its presuppositions as well. For my purposes, the latter strategy is the most interesting, but a full understanding of the essay also demands reference to the first, for at many points the two *ad hoc* explanations are intricately intertwined.

The *Eighteenth Brumaire* is about a revolution that failed, a period of little more than three years in which French society moved from a new republic strongly influenced by the working classes to a dictatorship favored by the high aristocracy. The most strikingly anti-instrumental explanation Marx offers for this failure is a voluntaristic model that views revolution as depending upon psychological capacity regulated by moral order. Revolutions can only be successful, Marx believes, if there is heroism and sacrifice. Revolutionaries can perform in this outstanding way only if they have "the spirit of revolution," for only with this spirit can men "keep their enthusiasm on the high plane." Such spirit is difficult to maintain, however, because of the "anxiety" men feel when they are faced with the task of rebellion, and when they must create something completely new. In earlier revolutions, men resolved these anxieties by turning back to the past. By adopting the "austere traditions" of preceding revolutions, they steeled themselves by magnifying the present task, and their selves, in their "imagination."[33] Modern revolutionaries, however, cannot rely on past tradition to fortify themselves and to create the proper spirit; instead, they must have resource to "an intellectual consciousness in which all traditional ideas have been dissolved."[34] For modern revolutionaries, then, "the tradition of all the dead generations weighs like a nightmare on the brain of the living."[35]

The revolutionary process of 1848-1851 ended in failure and reaction, Marx believes, because its leaders proved incapable of heroism; they were "cowardly," "broken-spirited," and "meally-mouthed."[36] They lacked the requisite psychological strength, in turn, because they could not escape their memories of past revolutions. The most important actors on the political stage, the Bourgeois Republicans, were hampered because even when they acted positively they were driven to do so by "memories of the old republic" of 1830.[37] The proletariat, for its part, was incapable of providing aid to these Republicans at crucial times because it suffered from the "recollections of June 1848," the period when the Republicans had turned on the working classes to gain power for themselves.[38] The peasants, despite their objective interest in revolution, were also undermined by the force of subjective recollection, memories which reflected their own "superstition" and "prejudice." "Historical tradition," Marx writes, "gave rise to the belief of the French peasants in the miracle that a man named Napoleon would bring all the glory back to them." This internalized expectation is what produced the revolution's final defeat: "The fixed idea of the Nephew [the new emperor Napoleon III] was realised, because it coincided with the fixed idea of the most numerous class of the French people."[39]

Alongside of this moral and psychological framework, Marx tries to mount an explanation that relies on his more familiar concepts of productive forces and economic relations. He wants, therefore, to portray classes as the principal actors in the revolutionary process. The problem, however, is that he focuses in this essay primarily on parliamentary struggles in the French state, and the actors in this drama are political parties. Marx must refer, then, to parties, but in doing so he tries to associate each party with the needs of a particular class. In the revolutionary party, for example, there are the "Bourgeois" Republicans, and, in the

Party of Order, there are two different classes commingled, "haute bourgeois" Orleanists and "aristocratic" Legitimists. Despite this clear intention, Marx acknowledges in a tacit way throughout his account that
there is usually substantial distance between the actions of the party and
the interests of the class which, he maintains, it represents. In fact, the
two most important political setbacks of the revolutionary period involved party actions guided more by references to normative order than
any economic interest.

The defeat of the revolution can be viewed as the history of the decline and eventual disintegration of the largely middle-class Republican
party, which Marx often identifies as the "Republican faction of the bourgeoisie." It was this party's initial defeat in the Constituent Assembly that
paved the way for the revolution's general collapse, and until the very
end of the revolutionary process it continued to play a pivotal role.[40] Yet
this vitally important party, Marx acknowledges in one crucial passage,
was not, in fact, a faction of the bourgeoisie at all. "It was not," he admits, "held together by great common interest and marked off by specific
conditions of production."[41] Rather, the party represented a "clique,"
not a class, an informal group of middle-class writers, lawyers, military
officers, and officials. Evidently bothered by the problem of the composition of this democratic party, Marx returns to the issue at a later point.
Yet his conclusions are much the same. What makes the leaders of this
party "representative" of the lower bourgeoisie is not their instrumental
needs but simply the kinds of ideals they uphold. Because "in their *minds*
they do not get beyond the limits which the latter [the petty bourgeoisie]
do not get beyond in life . . . they are consequently driven, *theoretically*, to
the same problems and solutions to which material interest and social
position drive the latter practically."[42]

The later process that undermined any chance for a continued parliamentary republic was the internal dissension and eventual dissolution
of its more conservative supporters, the political grouping Marx calls the
"Party of Order." Whereas with the Bourgeois Republicans Marx defined
the separation between party and class at the outset of his analysis, for
this more conservative group he describes the split as if it appears only in
the context of the crisis itself. The Party of Order dissolved because there
developed a split between the bourgeois inside parliament and the bourgeois outside parliament.[43] To explain this political division between representatives of the same class, Marx introduces the distinction between a
party's "ideologists" and "literary representatives," and the class itself.[44]
As French political life became increasingly unstable, the representatives of the class outside parliament—that is, the "class itself"—came to
feel that their interests could be served only by a strong government, yet
this was exactly what the ideological representatives inside parliament
were unable to provide.[45] The reason, Marx believes, is that these inside

leaders became committed to a peculiar normative outlook, "parliamentary cretinism." This ideology, "which holds those infected by it fast in an imaginary world and robs them of all sense, all memory, all understanding of the rude external world," caused the bourgeois politicians to be more interested in electoral formalities than in the true economic interest of their bourgeois brethren.[46] Misguided by this internal orientation, the parliamentarians soon lost the support of the ministry, the army, the people, and public opinion.[47] Faced with a weak and ineffectual parliamentary group, the bourgeois outside parliament deserted democratic formalism altogether, throwing their support to Bonaparte. At this point, a crucial number of class representatives inside parliament also deserted, but if they did so it was not for reasons of class solidarity: "A squad of representatives . . . deserted from [the Bourgeois] camp, out of fanaticism for conciliation, out of fear of the struggle, out of lassitude, out of family regard for the state salaries so near and dear to them, [and] out of sheer egoism."[48]

Marx produces a similar analysis of the relationship between political and economic interest in the two classes that are less central to his account, the proletariat and the peasantry. Despite the fact that its economic interest should have led it to struggle actively for the Republic, after strong initial support the French proletariat demonstrated nothing of the kind. Marx's judgment against the workers is severe, and he refers to the "stupidity of the masses" who allowed themselves to be seduced by the false "dreams" of clever bourgeois politicians.[49] Their passive stupidity he attributes to political and cultural factors. Most immediately, the more sophisticated leaders of the proletarians' party were arrested early in the revolutionary struggle.[50] The proletariat also lacked the necessary organs of communication, like an effective party press, which would have allowed them to maintain integration and direction even without strong leadership. More generally, the French workers simply did not have the education to understand the true meaning of unfolding events.[51] As for the peasants, who, Marx maintains, also had an objective interest in the revolution's success, this class was split into politically radical and conservative camps. Marx offers explanations only for the triumph of conservatism: the peasants were divided and could communicate only if they had a single individual to "represent" them, a function well filled by Bonaparte,[52] the peasants were "demoralized" by political repression and by the arrest of their leaders;[53] the "peasant religion" embodied the myth of the Napoleonic savior.[54] Each of these explanations, of course, involves important normative components which do not spring from economic interest in the familiar sense. None of them, moreover, explains how the significant strain of peasant radicalism could ever have developed.

Marx has indicated that political parties rely on factors other than common class interest, that members are motivated by reasons of shared belief and an interest in immediate power. But what structures the actions of such parties once they are formed? While Marx's explanations are ad hoc and conceptually unintegrated, they present a decidedly multidimensional picture. In describing the actions of the bourgeois Republicans, for example, he argues that they were effective because they appealed to general values, to "personal antipathy to Louis-Philippe" (the prerevolutionary monarch), to "memories of the old republic," to Republican "faith," and, above all, to "French nationalism."[55] But party action is also structured by more specifically political factors. Most of all, it is influenced by what Marx refers to time and time again as the "public." By invoking this notion, Marx appears to accept the existence of an enormously influential group that crosses class boundaries, a group defined simply by the political fact that it is outside parliament. Marx's public is the creation of parliamentary institutions, for the institutional autonomy of the parliament, Marx believes, allows a government to present political ideas to citizens in a rational and unprejudiced way. The process of open parliamentary discussion strips interests of explicit class bias; they are "transformed into general ideas, debated *as* ideas."[56] The process by which such abstraction and neutralization is achieved is complex. It involves continuous communication and the exchange of ideas: "The struggle of the orators on the platform evokes the struggle of the scribblers of the press; the debating club in parliament is necessarily supplemented by debating clubs in the salons and the pothouses; the representatives, who constantly appeal to public opinion, give public opinion the right to speak its real mind in petitions."[57]†

Public opinion, then, is a classless pressure group based upon communication and facilitated by the structural independence of the bourgeois state. The history of the 1848 revolution can be viewed as the failure of successive groups to convince the public of the normative justice of its position. The Bourgeois Republicans, who had earlier become popular by their puritanical attacks on aristocratic ostentation, failed to maintain this popularity after they came to power.[58] Yet the conservatives, too, ended up "without public opinion."[59] They could have saved parliamentary institutions only if they had allowed public opinion to continue to operate in an unfettered way, but their narrow class interest forced them instead to "wage an uninterrupted war against public opinion and mistrustfully mutilate [and] cripple the independent organs of the social movement."[60] Their failure to be aggressive in the struggle against Bonaparte left the public cheated of its legitimate expectations, and their fateful undermining of the Constituent Assembly cost them the "last remnant of respect in the eyes of the public."[61] When Bonaparte finally showed his hand and assumed his dictatorship, the public was so "blasé" about parliamentary groups that it could no longer feel indignation.[62] Besides, by this time it had embraced Bonaparte as the very embodiment of its public will.

Because publics are united by emotional and moral bonds, universal suffrage can be viewed as a process which confers moral authority on the victorious party. The Party of Order, for example, became important only after it was "morally strengthened by the [early] general elections, which made its rule appear as the will of the people."[63] Later, an electoral victory by the Bourgeois Republicans created a brief "moment of popular enthusiasm" and a "favourable mood" in the army, but the Republicans allowed the "revolutionary energy [to] satiate itself" and the opportunity to restore revolutionary momentum passed them by once again.[64] In the end, however, the conservatives themselves lost out to Bonaparte, and the latter's moral authority was an important reason. A single person elected by the entire body of the French people, he became the "incarnation" of the "national spirit."[65]

Finally, party actions are dictated simply by the independent structure of the parliamentary state. The democratic nature of parliamentary rule, for example, allowed parties with conflicting material interests to compromise and rule conjointly.[66] The democratic constitution also regulated party action in more specific ways. Its mandated separation of powers, for example, forced every struggle of economic interests to take the form of a conflict between parliament and president, a form that gave a would-be dictator like Bonaparte an enormous strategic advantage in the struggle for public opinion.[67] Even the specific rules for parliamentary voting had tremendous repercussions. Because the French constitution required three-quarters rather than a simple majority in parliament to pass amendments, if a clever politician gained majority support he could oppose the rules of the constitution in the name of the people. It was precisely in this way, Marx believed, that Bonaparte gained legitimacy for the overthrow of the constitution that ushered in his dictatorship.[68]

Marx has detailed the separation of party from class; the determinants of party success by solidarity, by values, by authority, and by information; the significance of the independent structures of the parliamentary regime. There is, finally, the autonomous power of the state bureaucracy itself. The French state had begun as a strategic vehicle for transforming feudalism, but, once formed, it became sui generis, a powerful instrument that had to be conquered if any revolutionary group was to remain in power.[69] The gigantic apparatus made every class and group helpless by comparison, yet its very independence allowed it to appear to each class also as a potentially important ally.[70†] To the army, the state meant increased prestige; to the peasants, release from debt; to the bourgeois, restoration of monarchy; to the proletariat, revenge against the upper classes.[71] Because their material support

342 The Antinomics of Classical Thought

came in the form of direct state funds, the French army had a tradition
of intervening to ensure political continuity, and, as nominal head of the
army, Bonaparte manipulated this tradition in his successful coup d'-
état.[72] More important than this strategic weapon, however, was the nature of Bonaparte's popularity. Every class thought him to be its personal
savior, and because he was all things to all people he was the perfect can-
didate to represent and control the independent bureaucratic state. He
gained this popularity, moreover, not because he was promoted by any
particular class but because of his "unrecognized genius" for political
bribery and corruption, which "a long life of adventurous vagabondage
had endowed him with."[73]

Marx has engaged an awesome array of explanatory strategies. Most
are plausible, some are brilliant. He makes no attempt at conceptual integration, and if he had done so he would have found it an incredible task.
Not only do many of the explanations implicitly contradict one another,
but taken together they undermine the central tenets of his scientific
work. On the one hand, Marx seems sublimely unaware of his theoretical
danger, asserting periodically that his account actually demonstrates the
determinate power of objective conditions.[74] At other points, however,
Marx seems conscious of the apparently contradictory nature of his approach. About a third of the way through his account, for example, he
brings himself up short. "Before we pursue parliamentary history further," he writes, "some remarks are necessary to avoid common miscon-
ceptions regarding the whole character of the epoch that lies before
us."[75] To be sure, Marx warns his readers, parties appear "at first sight"
to be unrelated to productive forces, to be guided by "principles," led by
"lawyers, professors, and smooth-tongued orators," and dependent for
their success upon "confession[s] of faith."[76] He assures his readers,
however, that nothing could be further from the truth: "If one looks at
the situation and the parties more closely . . . this superficial appearance,
which veils the *class struggle* and the peculiar physiognomy of this period, disappears." Parties are kept apart not by any "so-called principles," but by "their material conditions of existence, [i.e., by] two different kinds of property."[77] Marx would now have us believe that the Republican party is simply petty bourgeois, though he has elsewhere demonstrated quite the opposite; that the loyalist Party of Order is divided
only by class interest, though he has shown it rent by political conflict;
that Bonaparte was the peasant's man, though he has shown him the
leader and misleader of every class and faction; that, finally, the constitution was merely a piece of paper continually reinterpreted by the strongest class, when he has clearly demonstrated its powerful independent
effects.[78] But it was Marx himself who first suggested that parties were
composed of lawyers, demagogues, and other noneconomic actors, that
they were united by principles and theories rather than class interest,
and that they depended upon faith for their political success.

Marx's ambivalence is revealed in an extraordinary way in the very same paragraph where he offers his description of the "true" physiognomy of the time. Immediately following his attempt to reassert a purely class analysis of the Party of Order, we find the following sentence: "That *at the same time* old memories, personal enmities, fears and hopes, prejudices and illusions, sympathies and antipathies, convictions, articles of faith and principles bound them to one or the other royal house, who is there that denies this?"[79] In the more considered moments of his scientific work, Marx himself would have been the first to do so. He had struggled long and hard to develop a consistent empirical theory of instrumental order and action, one which linked productive force directly to political struggle and subjective belief. Armed with this scientific theory, he had explained how revolutionary action would result from the instrumental calculation of interest. As a political activist, however, he realized that this could not be so, and the residual categories of his political writing demonstrate the strains and one-sided character of his theoretical work.[80†]

2. "MARXISM" AS PARADIGM REVISION: MAKING "MATERIALISM" NORMATIVE

The anomalies that history has produced for Marx's scientific theory are clear. The theory predicted revolutions in Western capitalist societies, and none have occurred. There were, instead, a series of new empirical developments that Marx had not foreseen. In the first place, socialist reformism created parties dedicated to the working classes which gained some degree of institutionalization in Western societies. Citizenship became defined more broadly, as a social rather than as a merely political or legal category, and the welfare state allowed reforms which had once been considered inherently socialist to come into being in what were still apparently capitalist societies. The second development was the emergence of Fascism and Nazism. Although no socialist revolutions occurred in Western societies, there was a series of barbaric revolutions from the right. Third, when left-wing revolutions did occur, they were located in underdeveloped countries rather than in developed, capitalist ones, and they produced a kind of totalitarian proletarianism that Marx had never foreseen. Finally, alongside the relative though still unfinished incorporation of the working classes, new sources of systematic strain developed in Western capitalist societies. Subjective problems of boredom, anxiety, and frustration became central foci for ideological debate, and they created new sources of instability, not only among students and young people but in the factory and middle class as well.

Marxist theory responded to these empirical challenges as any general theory tends to do, by revision rather than falsification. In effect, Marxists made the kind of dramatic revisions that Durkheim's students in the 1930s were unable to make. Yet the revisions of these Marxists had, nevertheless, certain commonalities with the changes that Durkheim's students had initiated earlier: they occurred along the fault lines of the original theory. If Durkheim's students implicitly revised him in a materialist direction, Marx's followers tried, in an equally covert way, to revise him in an idealist and voluntaristic one. The inadequacies and strains of the general theory, in other words, determined the course of the "empirical" revisions.[81†] The immediate stimulus for these revisions was often, although by no means always, the confrontations that occurred between Marxists and other theorists as Marxism became increasingly central to Western intellectual life. Marxism often responded to its critics by incorporating parts of rival systems. The result was a series of hyphenated Marxisms: Hegelian-Marxism, Freudian-Marxism, existential-Marxism, structural-Marxism. By this kind of incorporation, Marx was found by such followers to have maintained a consistently voluntaristic and multidimensional stance. Yet in making such findings, I will argue, they have mixed arguments from Marx's political writings with his explicitly scientific work, and they have obscured issues in theoretical logic about which Marx himself was perfectly clear.

These interpreters of Marx's work have often been brilliant and original theorists themselves, but they have chosen, for political and ideological as well as cognitive reasons, to present their innovations as simply more accurate readings of Marx himself. They have relied particularly on two strategies to legitimate their presentations. They have resorted, first of all, to the myth of "vulgar Marxism." First systematically set out in the early 1920s by Karl Korsch in *Marxism and Philosophy*, the myth places responsibility for the instrumental and deterministic quality of historical materialism on certain followers of Marx rather than on Marx himself—in Korsch's words, on "the extraordinarily banal and rudimentary vulgar-Marxism of the epigones."[82] It was the mechanistic positivism of the late nineteenth century that perverted the praxis-oriented philosophy of Marx, the Kautskys and Plekhanovs that were instrumentalist rather than Marx himself.[83†] The second mode of legitimation, which provides further support for the myth of vulgar Marxism, was made possible by the discovery in the early twentieth century of the unpublished manuscripts of Marx's early works. Important strains in this early writing are Hegelian and idealist. By arguing for its direct continuity with the mature Marx—an argument that depends, as I have tried to demonstrate earlier, on certain misleading theoretical manipulations—his followers have used the early writings to rationalize their own, more voluntaristic departures as truthful to a now Hegelianized Marx.

Each major revisionist effort has identified itself as orthodox Marxism; indeed, most present their version of Marxism in the guise of an elaborate interpretation of Marx's ideas. Yet Marx's mature theory did not make room for these deviations, any more than Durkheim's later theory made room for the materialist assertions of his ostensibly loyal followers. Just as Durkheimianism introduced significant residual categories into Durkheim's original theory, so Marxism has affected the theory of Marx: insofar as Marxism includes a voluntary and multidimensional strain, it introduces into its own conceptual structure inconsistencies and contradictions. Every major revision of Marx's thought moves back and forth between the two equally unacceptable horns of the "Marxian dilemma." On the one hand, if it is to converge with the original theory, the revision must reintroduce determinism "in the last instance." This, of course, can only be achieved by partly neutralizing the revisions themselves. On the other hand, if the theorists will not neutralize their contributions, and if, at the same time, they wish to avoid the direct opposition to Marx's theory that would place them outside the Marxist tradition, there is only one option available: they must leave their revisions largely unspecified and, in the process, open up their theories to serious indeterminacy. A theoretical revision of Marx can resolve this choice between indeterminacy and the last instance only if it takes neither option; to that degree, it moves beyond the boundaries of Marxism itself.

In 1891, Karl Kautsky published *The Class Struggle*, a work which restated the central theses of Marx's positivistic and deterministic science with special reference to recent empirical developments like the growth of the state and the continued resilience of the peasant class in industrialized capitalism. Kautsky explained these new developments by changes in the mode of capitalist production. He reassured his readers that the peasants would disappear, as would the middle class; that there would be steadily increasing economic misery; that science was the essential vehicle for discovering the objective laws that would in time overthrow the capitalist system.[84] Yet even as Kautsky published this orthodoxy, the "internal breakdown" of Marx's original theory had already begun, and it was initiated by Marx's closest collaborator and most faithful disciple, Engels himself.

Though in his own scientific work Engels had generally followed the determinism of Marx's scientific theory, at the end of his life he deviated sharply from Marx's logic in a letter to Bloch, dated September 1890.[85] The letter has become famous, and it deserves to be, for in it Engels first articulated the dilemma that would occupy Marx's disciples thenceforth. Asked by Bloch to define what Marx precisely meant by the materialist conception of history, Engels qualifies the "determinate" power of the base in a number of ways. The superstructure, he insists, is not without effect. In fact, the "various elements of the superstructure"—and here he refers to constitutions, political and philosophical theories, religious views, and traditions—"play a part" in history. The base is the "*ultimately* determining element," but superstructural elements "exercise their influence" on events and institutions. They do so "in many cases by [being] preponderate in determining their form." With these qualifications, Engels has undermined the clarity of Marx's theory and replaced it with a studied indeterminacy. What can be the difference between causal "influence" and "determination"? When is an event "ultimately" determined as compared with simply "determined"? If this is a temporal statement, it is misleading, for it is always possible to take history back one step further. If it is an ontological assertion, then the importance of the factor creating "simple" determinism is null and void. What, finally, is the distinction between form and substance? If institutions have a different form, will their substance remain the same? If so, when does formal change become substantive? But if Engels has caved in to the strains of Marx's theory by moving to indeterminacy, he tries, nonetheless, to maintain his theoretical allegiance. His message in the letter, therefore, is also permeated by the residual category of "the last instance." There may be institutional interaction, but "the economic movement finally asserts itself as necessary." Superstructures may have determinate power, but productive forces are "ultimately" determining. But the very notion of a "last instance" is logically impossible. Is there some historical instance after which there can never be another?[86†]

The Marxist generation that followed Engels likewise felt themselves compelled to introduce covert qualifications into the original theory.[87†] The social-democratic alternative was less creative theoretically than the revolutionary one, yet it often responded more accurately to the empirical tendencies of Western capitalist society. In *Evolutionary Socialism*, published in 1899, Bernstein operated mainly within the presuppositional framework that Marx had set out, but he altered his more specific propositions to explain what the more faithful Kautsky could not: the growth of the middle classes and the fragmentation of class hierarchy, the growing income of the working classes and the evening-out of capitalist crises, the possibility that political democracy could be institutionalized within capitalism rather than outside of it.[88] Bernstein's most generalized departure from Marx was to suggest that ethics had an independent status in the class struggle, a Kantian position he never elaborated in a systematic way. If he had done so, his empirical deviation would have taken on an even more heretical hue, and he would not have been able so easily to make the claim that, despite certain departures, he was still loyal to Marx's method.

A much more radical theoretical departure within the social-democratic tradition, though one with lesser political repercussions, was initiated by Bauer in his independent analysis of nationality. In determining nationality, Bauer stepped completely outside the instrumental frame-work. Nationality is determined by "common history," because it is only shared history that produces "common morals and customs, common laws, and a common religion, and hence . . . a common cultural tradi-tion."[89] Because a national grouping is a "community of character," Bauer insists, it must be distinguished sharply from the concept of class. Rather than seek to eliminate national identities, therefore, socialist movements must make an accommodation with them, and socialism might well be conceived as a multinational society.[90] Bauer completely avoids the last instance argument, but his radical break introduces wide indeterminacy into the more general theory. He has defined ethnicity as an independent problem, yet in the rest of his writing he reproduced ar-guments for the determinacy of the economic base; the specific relation-ship between ethnicity and class is never directly confronted.

The revolutionary generation that emerged around the turn of the century is generally of more theoretical interest, since its radical ideolog-ical voluntarism was more strongly in tension with Marx's commitment to determination by external conditions. If Marx himself, as a revolution-ary actor, was pushed to introduce voluntaristic arguments, these later revolutionaries felt the strain in an even stronger way. The contradic-tions in their work are, for this reason, that much more striking.

Lenin presents the theoretical voluntarism of the revolutionary revi-sion of Marx in its most clear-cut form, and *What Is to Be Done* (1902) is his paradigmatic statement. In a preceding work he had written at great length about the significance of capitalist development in Russia. In 1902, engaged in the concrete labor of political organization, he adopts a tacit theory that is much different. What imprisons the Russian pro-letariat is the lack of will, not its objective condition but its subjective con-sciousness. "The strength of the modern movement lies in the awakening of the mass," he writes, and "its weakness lies in the lack of consciousness and initiative among the revolutionary leaders."[91] The problem was created by the "economists," leaders who believed that mere economic conditions determined political events. Lenin will have nothing to do with such an essentially passive presupposition: "We Revo-lutionary Social-Democrats, on the contrary, are dissatisfied with this submission to elemental forces, i.e., bowing to what is 'at the present time.' "[92] Lenin's famous solution, of course, was to organize a vanguard party, a group of professional revolutionaries dedicated to transforming proletarian consciousness. The Leninist party would be independent of economic constraint, a product of revolutionary will and determination. Yet this voluntary commitment, Lenin knew, depended upon the struc-ture of internal ideational commitments. The vanguard party would have to be guided by the right kind of theory, for "without a revolutionary theory there can be no revolutionary movement." Indeed, "the role of vanguard can be fulfilled only by a party that is guided by an advanced theory."[93]

A manual for the modern revolutionary prince, Lenin's pamphlet provides a luminous array of empirical strategies by which the vanguard party can radicalize class consciousness. The problem, however, is that he has stepped outside the elaborate framework of Marx's scientific work. Lenin never generalizes from his political recipes to a conceptual theory of politics, for if he had done so he would have overturned historical materialism itself. The result is an indeterminate political theory, one that allows politics an undefined freedom in shaping economic and cultural events. For Lenin, the last instance never comes; he moves toward a voluntarism that the scientific Marx would have abhorred.

While in certain respects, Trotsky's *History of the Russian Revolution* (1930) partakes of the achievements and weaknesses of Lenin's voluntarism, it remains, much more solidly than Lenin's work, within the orthodox program of historical materialism. In one strand of his writing, Trotsky maintains Marx's general presuppositions, and his principal contribution is to make more elaborate and subtle the propositions about economic development in backward countries.[94] It is this theory of "uneven and combined development" that earns Trotsky's work its well-deserved accolade as a masterpiece of Marxist history. Yet alongside this new articulation of external conditions, there is a strand in Trotsky's analysis that follows the radical voluntarism of Lenin. He asserts that without the Communist Party, and particularly without the brilliant leadership of Lenin, the contradictions of Russia would have been without issue.[95] Trotsky's revolutionary history, therefore, embodies the Marxian dilemma in an extraordinary way. On the one hand, the revolution is described as completely dependent on the unpredictable will of the party and the intuitive resourcefulness of a single leader—this is the pole of indeterminacy. On the other hand, time after time Trotsky insists that the victory of the revolution was inevitable, an act that proceeded with the natural force of Greek tragedy—here he refers to the polar alternative, the residual category of the last instance.[96] If Trotsky never confronts this contradiction, the logical reasons for his reluctance are clear enough: he sees himself as the last great carrier of the true Marxist tradition. It is no accident, however, that when he invokes Marx it is almost always the Marx of the political pamphlets rather than the theorist of the "scientific" work.

Trotsky's analysis of the origins of Stalinism in *The Revolution Betrayed* (1937) is even more empirically creative and theoretically revisionist, and to that degree it is even more internally contradictory. On the one hand, he maintains his commitment to Marx's insistence that political force is determined by class position and relation to the means of production. On these grounds, he insists that the Soviet Union is a proletarian state. Simultaneously, however, he refers to a political force that has no class or economic base at all, the Soviet bureaucracy. "In no other regime," he writes, "has a bureaucracy ever achieved such a degree of independence from the dominating class."[97] The bureaucracy has its own interests and goals; indeed, this purely political power has successfully "expropriated the proletariat politically."[98] Classes, then, are not completely characterized by their relation to the means of production; and the state can hardly be called proletarian if the proletariat itself has been expropriated by its bureaucratic directors. Tacitly acknowledging this contradiction, Trotsky argues that history itself has created this indeterminacy, not the theory which he employs to analyze it. The domination of social by political forms, he insists, is a "new and hitherto unknown relation."[99] One way out of this dilemma would be to acknowledge the intervening factors of Russian culture and tradition, but Trotsky insists, formally at least, that his analysis is purely objectivist, that it demonstrates how "being determines consciousness."[100] In the interstices of his argument, however, subjective factors can be seen as playing a pivotal role. It is because the Soviet proletariat "has no tradition of dominion or command" that the bureaucracy so easily defeated it, and if any hope for proletarian socialism remains, it is only because, among other things, the revolution still exists "in the consciousness of the toiling masses."[101] Yet Trotsky would rather leave his contradictory statements in an indeterminate relation than confront the weaknesses of Marx's theory directly. The confusion that arises he attributes, once again, to the fact that he is studying "dynamic social formations which have had no precedent and have no analogies."[102]

Trotsky and Lenin present the response of Marxist theory to the empirical anomalies of revolution in the East and the revolution of the right. Neither was specifically concerned with the particular problem of left-wing revolution in Western societies. The latter becomes the concern of revisionists promoting a form of theorizing which has been called "Western Marxism," and I will treat such theorizing shortly. Before doing so, I must briefly consider the work of the last great theorist of "Eastern Marxism," Mao Tse-tung. Mao's writing is regarded as atheoretical and unscientific by more orthodox critics, and if he fails to bring his generalizations about political practice into an integrated conceptual scheme, it is certainly because he has no immediate scientific ambition. There is, however, another more basic reason, one he shares with all important "Marxists": to do so, he would have to directly oppose the theory under which he legitimates and identifies his work. Indeed, the very closeness between Mao's theory and his political practice allows his work to reveal the strains in orthodox theory in a particularly revealing way.

Like Trotsky, Mao made important contributions to orthodox Marxist theory by applying the instrumental theory of classes to a new situation, in his case the role of the peasantry in an unevenly developing nation.[103] Yet he also advanced a theory of history that overturned the very presuppositions upon which such orthodox class theory is based. In his famous essay "On Contradiction" (1937), Mao moves back and forth between the poles of the Marxian dilemma. On the one hand, he is determined to move beyond the structuring of action by external conditions, defined either as economic or political organization. To do so, he introduces the notion that every historical situation contains a plurality of contradictions, and that it is the "particularity of contradictions" in any specific instance that determines the course of the historical process.[104] The "basic" contradiction is an economic one, but other "big and small contradictions" may be subject only to its "influence," and they themselves can consist of any combination of cultural or political forms.[105] At the same time, however, Mao wishes to identify himself with the determinacy of the scientific Marx. To do so, he must introduce the residual category of the last instance. He stresses, therefore, that productive forces and economic foundations "generally manifest themselves in the principal and decisive role," and he acknowledges that "we recognize that in the development of history as a whole it is material things that determine spiritual things and social existence that determines social consciousness."[106] Yet even while asserting such determination by the "basic" contradiction, he forcefully denies it. "Under certain conditions," he argues, "the relations of production, theory and the superstructure in turn manifest themselves in the principal and decisive role; this must be admitted."[107] In specifying these conditions, moreover, he moves toward radical voluntarism and strong indeterminacy. He insists that whenever a willed political or cultural end is opposed by the forces of economic constraint, the internal commitment will triumph over external conditions.

> When the productive forces cannot be developed unless the relations of production are changed, the change in the *relations of production* plays the principal and decisive role. When, as Lenin put it, "Without a revolutionary theory, there can be no revolutionary movement," the creation and advocacy of the revolutionary *theory* plays the principal and decisive role. When a certain job . . . is to be done but there is as yet no *directive* . . . defining how to do it, the directive . . . is the principal and decisive factor. When the superstructure . . . hinders the development of the economic foundations, *political and cultural reforms* become the principal decisive factors.[108]

In his postrevolutionary theorizing, Mao utilized the voluntaristic and indeterminate strain of his theory to justify an emphasis on the strategic importance of moral and cultural persuasion over instrumental coercion.

Contradictions in socialist society, he declared, are nonantagonistic.[109] The members of a socialist society must "start off with a desire for unity," for "without this subjective desire for unity . . . the struggle . . . is liable to get out of hand."[110] Once this internal motivation is firmly established, and, indeed, as part of the effort to establish it, communists should rely on the methods of "persuasion and education" rather than on "commandism or coercion."[111]

Though greatly influenced by Leninist thought, the theoretical revision called "Western Marxism" dates from the appearance of Georg Lukács' *History and Class Consciousness* in 1923. Writing in the wake of the successful Eastern revolution which had failed to materialize in the West, Lukács strives to maintain Marx's historical optimism and theoretical orthodoxy, yet his originality derives from his failure to do so. He introduces into the Marxist tradition of revolutionary thought an extraordinary idealism that is profoundly pessimistic. Moving back and forth between orthodoxy and deviation, Lukács recapitulates the Marxian dilemma.

In the subjective strain of his analysis, Lukács takes as his starting point "the stance adopted by men," the way in which social phenomena are "perceived."[112] From this point of view, the capitalist nature of modern society is rooted in the structure of consciousness. True, Lukács defines the content of this consciousness in much the same way as Marx himself: it is the instrumentality and individualism associated with commodity relations. Yet it is the mental processes themselves which are Lukács' concern, not the fact that instrumentality allows rational economic exchange. He writes, therefore, about the contents of the "reified mind."[113] Because consciousness is alienated, "the *principle* of rationalization" structures every sphere of modern interaction.[114] Law, science, bureaucracy, philosophy, art, even time and space—all are degraded to mere calculable form.[115] The result is that "the structure of reification progressively sinks more deeply, more fatefully and more definitively into the consciousness of man."[116] The proletariat can be no exception, for the importance of differences in economic position has been undermined by Lukács' emphasis on principles of normative order: "The proletariat shares with the bourgeoisie the reification of every aspect of its life."[117]

Because the degradation of the capitalist and the subjection of the proletariat are normatively produced, external crisis does not necessarily lead to a revolutionary result. The normative chains must be addressed directly, by a normative critique. The most important source of change, then, is correct theory. "The dialectical method," Lukács insists, "destroys the [bourgeois] fiction of the immortality of the [reified] categories," and for that reason "it also destroys their reified character."[118] Such a critical intellectual orientation can be carried to the masses only from without, by a revolutionary party. Lukács praises Rosa Luxemburg, for example, because she understood that "the Party is assigned the sublime role of *bearer of the class consciousness of the proletariat and the conscience of its historical vocation.*"[119] The party will be effective because of nonrational, subjective facts. Correct theory gives it legitimacy, and the proletariat will turn to it to find meaning for what at first is a purely economic rebellion. "The true strength of the party is moral," Lukács writes. "It is fed by the trust of the spontaneously revolutionary masses whom economic conditions have forced into revolt."[120] Once the party has infused a new orientation into the working class, the revolution will proceed in a voluntary way. "Class consciousness," he asserts, "is the 'ethics' of the proletariat," and "the moral strength conferred by the correct class consciousness will bear fruit in terms of practical politics."[121]

This proto-theory is as Hegelian as it is Marxist. But if Lukács has introduced notions that are different from those of the mature Marx, he has left them in a rather indeterminate state. Where, for example, do these antireifying ideas come from? What about the revolutionary party? By whom is it composed and by what means can it institutionalize its theory? Without further specification, these factors have merely the role of a deus ex machina; as Lukács himself acknowledges, they simply operate "outside" the process of reification. To make them more concrete, Lukács would have to make a historical analysis of the relation between culture and society, and in this analysis cultural forms would have had to achieve a firmly independent place. Faced with such a danger, Lukács leaves this normative analysis in schematic form, and, confined by the theoretical limits of the Marxist dilemma, he proposes as an alternative a new form of the last instance argument. Reified consciousness, he claims, must be seen simply as the reflection of the economic form of capitalist commodity exchange.[122] It actually is not the "principle" of reification that orders different institutional parts, but the needs of an expanding capital. "The real framework of every rational calculation," he writes, "presupposes the strict ordering of all that happens."[123] Following the argument of the later Marx, he now insists that "the atomization of the individual is . . . only the reflex in consciousness of the fact that the 'natural laws' of capitalist production have been extended to cover every manifestation of life in society; that—for the first time in history—the whole of society is subjected . . . to a unified economic process, and that the fate of every member of society is determined by unified laws."[124] Lukács now argues, for example, that in the legal sphere, "the real basis for the development of law" is merely "a change in the power relations between the classes."[125]

This orthodox line of analysis implies the return to an instrumental understanding of a "final" capitalist crisis. One can find no reference to such a crisis, however, anywhere in Lukács' book. Insofar as he rejects this possibility, he seems to be announcing that he will not completely neutralize his voluntarism by returning to the full determination of the "last instance." Yet if he rejects this option, and wishes, nonetheless, to remain loyal to Marx, he is faced with a fundamental problem. Within the context of his more materialist argument, if he abandons the reference to economic crisis he cannot explain what will cause proletarian revolution. If consciousness is caused by material position, and the commodity form produces reification, it would seem that the proletariat is chained to external conditions in a completely helpless way. At one point, Lukács appears to recognize just such an implication: "As labour is progressively rationalised and mechanised his [the laborer's] lack of will is reinforced by the way in which his activity becomes less and less active and more and more . . . [a] contemplative stance adopted towards a process mechanically conforming to fixed laws [and] impervious to human intervention."[126] Lukács will not, however, be so disloyal to Marx, or so violate his own ideological commitments, that he will allow revolution to disappear. But if revolution can be motivated neither by material crisis nor by normative intervention, how can it come about? Lukács can only return to the pole of indeterminacy. The proletariat will rebel because of a purely logical postulate; every negation will produce its own negation. The very fact of the absolute depravity of the proletariat's position, its reduction to complete "objectivity," guarantees that it will recapture its subjectivity. The working class, then, is "the identical subject-object of the social and historical processes of evolution."[127] Because its labor time is completely quantified, the "dialectical antithesis" will be produced which "mediates" the worker's objectivity.[128] Thus, "the quantitative differences in exploitation . . . must appear to the worker as the decisive, qualitative categories of his whole physical, mental, and moral existence."[129]

Assured by this purely logical mediation of the proletariat's objectified passivity, Lukács resolves the potential danger of his materialist strain without referring to any "outside," ideal forces: "The category of mediation is a lever with which to overcome the mere immediacy of the empirical world and as such it is not something (subjective) foisted on to the objects from outside."[130] To the contrary, the workers' revolutionary activism has now become *"the manifestation of their authentic objective structure."*[131] Rejecting the normative references of his idealist analysis, Lukács can return to Marx's original emphasis on objectively different class position. If "the bourgeoisie is held fast in the mire of immediacy from which the proletariat is able to extricate itself," this can only imply that "the distance between these two theoretical positions is an expression of the differences between the social existence of the two classes."[132]

But if Lukács has succeeded in neutralizing the notion of critical theory as instigator of revolution without giving up his opposition to the emphasis on economic crisis, he has done so only at the cost of tremendous indeterminacy. He never offers the slightest evidence for his proletariat's "negation of the negation," nor does he conceptualize any empirical tendencies which would explain how this could come about. Such a capacity for negation is opposed by the overwhelming evidence of economic rationalization he himself has presented. Indeed, if the proletariat's material position does not change there seems no reason, according to this materialist strain, to believe that its consciousness would either. The "identical subject-object" is merely a logical trick, a residual category that allows Lukács not to confront the radical theoretical revisions he has so brilliantly introduced.

As the great founder of "Western Marxism," Lukács, with his culturally-conscious rationale for the instrumentalism of modern capitalism, set one major strategy for the Marxism of the postwar period, an investigation of "alienation" and "technical reason" formalized by the "Frankfurt school" and confirmed by the discovery of Marx's early writings, writings which exhibited the same profound internal contradictions as his original work. The writings of the Frankfurt school will be considered shortly. First, however, the other pillar upon which postwar Marxism rests must be considered: the theorizing of the great Italian Marxist Antonio Gramsci. The atmosphere in which Gramsci composed his version of Marxian thought—in the 1920s and 1930s in Italy—was even more redolent with the empirical anomalies produced by twentieth-century history than the environment within which Lukács composed his work. Gramsci was still inspired by the revolutionary voluntarism of revolution in the East, yet he lived in the very midst of the Fascist upheavals and directly experienced the frustration of instigating worker opposition to them. Gramsci certainly did not fully escape the dilemma of Marxist revision, yet more than any other communist intellectual of his time he developed a revision that stepped outside the boundaries established by Marx.

If Marx wrestled his socialist radicalism into the presuppositions of political economy, Gramsci's project can be seen as bringing the empirical and ideological commitments of revolutionary communism into line with presuppositions derived from an understanding of religious faith. In his analysis of European capitalism, at least, Gramsci sharply rejected an instrumental approach to action. Individuals are motivated by "feelings, wishes, real passions," and they have the need to organize these emotions in terms of some kind of intellectual position.[133] "A man of the people," he writes, forms "opinions, convictions, criteria of discrimination, standards of conduct."[134] Given this understanding of action, Gramsci cannot avoid explaining collective order in a similar way. "A standard of conduct," he writes, "is undoubtedly one whose character is determined not by reason but by faith."[135] Gramsci insists, in fact, that the opposite understanding, the notion that action is ordered by a purely nonsubjective external world, must itself be understood as the product of some kind of belief. "The public 'believes,' " he writes, "that the external world is objectively real, but it is precisely here that the question arises: what is the origin of this 'belief' . . . ?"[136] He suggests that to understand exactly the full significance of this belief, it is necessary to realize that many notions "do not cease to be 'objectively real' even though analysis shows them to be no more than a conventional, that is 'historico-cultural construction.' "[137] "World view" becomes the center of Gramsci's analysis of order. It is "theoretical consciousness," he believes, that "holds together a specific social group" and "influences moral conduct and the direction of will."[138] Finally, because Gramsci can visualize order in this normative way, he takes a voluntaristic approach to the individual: "Any conception of the world, any philosophy which has become a cultural movement, a 'religion', a 'faith' . . . has produced a form of practical activity or will."[139] Once again, he inverts the contradictory notion of anti-voluntaristic determinism by polemically encompassing it within a normative framework. "Mechanical determinism," he suggests, is simply an intellectual commitment in which "real will takes on the garments of an act of faith in a certain rationality of history." Indeed, because such determinism "appears in the role of a substitute for the Predestination or Providence of confessional religions," it can itself become "a tremendous force of moral resistance," inspiring the voluntarism that it formally denies.[140]

These presuppositions lead Gramsci to specify Marx's model and empirical propositions in a strikingly different way. His point of reference remains the "ruling" economic class, but his understanding of its hierarchical position is multidimensional. Alongside instrumental "domination," there is "intellectual and moral leadership."[141] The position of a class is, therefore, dependent upon its cultural "hegemony," on the "intellectual subordination and submission" of the lower classes that occurs when they are forced to explain the world in terms of a world view that is not their own.[142] Rather than obedience based upon their separation from the means of production, a separation that in Marx's view tied the proletariat to capital by the "invisible threads" of material need, Gramsci sees the typical situation as " 'spontaneous' consent given by the great masses of the population to the general direction imposed on social life by the dominant fundamental group; this consent is 'historically' caused by the 'prestige' (and consequent confidence) which the dominant group enjoys."[143] The corollary to the importance of such cultural esteem is the "complex structure" which Gramsci would substitute for Marx's base-superstructure model, the "ensemble of relations" among which there is no apparent last instance.[144]

This complex structure held together by consent is relatively invulnerable to the kind of objective economic crisis that Marx made the centerpiece of his analysis. Since order is significantly normative, even in a catastrophic depression "the defenders [of an order] are not demoralized, nor do they abandon their positions, even among the ruins, nor do they lose faith in their own strength or their own future."[145] Lukács, one will remember, rejected economic crisis in much the same way, but his ambivalent commitment to materialism led him to assert that the proletariat's objective conditions would still be the mainspring of revolt. Gramsci has no need to follow Lukács into such indeterminacy. For him, not economic crisis but the "crisis of authority" is primary, the "content [of which] is the crisis of the ruling class's hegemony."[146] This crisis is created when political authority creates expectations that are frustrated by subsequent events—when, for example, "the ruling class has failed in some major political undertaking for which it has requested, or forcibly extracted, the consent of the broad masses." In such a situation, the power of upper-class institutions and groups is separated from the "fluctuations of public opinion," and the most important basis of control has disappeared.[147] "If the ruling class has lost its consensus, i.e. is no longer 'leading' but only 'dominant,' exercising coercive force alone, this means precisely that the great masses have become detached from their traditional ideologies, and no longer believe what they used to believe previously."[148]

Only in this situation can revolutionary struggle succeed, and it is toward such a situation that a revolutionary movement must build. The main tasks of Marxism, therefore, are cultural and educational.[149] Gramsci believes a vanguard party to be the most effective strategy, but it is a party that "must be and cannot but be the proclaimer and organiser of an intellectual and moral reform," one directed to creating a "collective will" rather than simply turning an economic crisis to best advantage.[150] His model for the party is the Catholic church. A successful party directs itself to "men's consciences," where it "takes the place of the divinity or the categorical imperative, and becomes the basis for a modern laicism and for a complete laicisation of all aspects of life and of all customary relations."[151] Such a comprehension of the normative order upon which the vanguard party rests allows Gramsci, finally, to sketch the strategic importance of a social group that every other Marxist theorist ignored, the intellectuals. "There is no organization without intellectuals," he insists, "that is, without organisers and leaders, without the theoretical aspect of the theory-practice nexus being distinguished concretely by the existence of a group who 'specialised' in conceptual and philosophical elaboration of ideas."[152]

Gramsci has presented an orientation opposed to the scientific Marx in almost every important respect. Yet Gramsci's attitude toward Marx was complex. Writing for the Italian socialist newspaper *Avanti*, he hailed the Russian Revolution of 1917 as a "revolution against *Capital*," and this theme reappears at various points throughout his work.[153] Yet, at the same time, he preferred to characterize his ideas as faithful to the true essence of Marx's thought—to the "philosophy of praxis," as he called Marxism in the purposefully camouflaged language of his prison writings. His explicit and caustic attacks on mechanical determinism and instrumental explanations are reserved for "vulgar" Marxists like Bukharin, even though his ridicule of the "search for essential causes" could be just as fairly directed against Marx himself.[154] This faithfulness to Marx, moreover, does not stem only from ideological loyalty, for close examination of Gramsci's writing reveals that even he has not fully escaped from the Marxian dilemma. Despite his conscious rejection of the last instance, a residue of the purely instrumental manipulation of culture permeates much of his work. While he grants that intellectuals are oriented to a world view and are a specialized stratum, he insists, at the same time, that they are always tied to the interests of a class. "Intellectuals," he writes at one point, "are the dominant group's 'deputies' exercising subaltern functions," and he insists that the distribution of class power "determine[s] or give[s] form to the production of various branches of intellectual specialization."[155] Thus Croce, for instance, "feels himself closely linked to Aristotle and Plato [but] does not conceal . . . his links with senators Agnelli and Benni [who represent certain class interests], and it is precisely here that one can discern the most significant character of Croce's philosophy."[156] And while Gramsci is insightful about the independent effects of Catholicism and Protestantism, he usually ties the sources of these movements directly to the needs of particular social classes.[157]

This contradictory strain toward instrumentalism is nowhere more clearly demonstrated than in Gramsci's analyses of American society, which he considers the prototype of a pure capitalism, one in which feudal elements do not exist to mar the capitalist-proletarian relation.[158] The culture of early twentieth-century American life, which Gramsci calls "Americanism" and "Fordism," is treated in a purely epiphenomenal way, as deriving from an "inherent necessity to achieve the organization of a planned economy."[159] The "Puritanism" of American culture, which accounts for such a movement as Prohibition, has developed simply to "give an external form of persuasion and consent to the intrinsic use of force," and has "simply the purpose of preserving, outside of work, a certain psycho-physical equilibrium which prevents the physical collapse of the worker, exhausted by the new method of production."[160] Even Gramsci, it seems, was not immune to the seduction of the last instance. If he turned, at crucial points, to the omnipresent power of social class, it was not only because of empirical considerations; it was as much because he never completely understood the full implications of his eclectic and diverse writing. This failure to provide conceptual integration imparts to Gramsci's theorizing a certain indeterminacy. In part, this was the result of the barbaric circumstances in which he worked—most of his important writing was composed during the years of his imprisonment by Mussolini's Fascist government—yet it was also the result of his desire not to directly take issue with Marx. Because of this failure, Gramsci's revision of Marx remained partial and covert. He was imprisoned not just by external reality, but, in part, by the Marxian dilemma as well.

For Western Marxism after the Second World War, historical development appeared even more anomalous. The relative passivity of the working classes vis-à-vis Fascism, the barbarism of Russian communism, the decline of revolutionary antagonism in the most advanced capitalist countries—these problems set the challenge for postwar Marxist theory. In trying to incorporate and explain these trends, the three great traditions of latter-day Western Marxism—existential Marxism, structural Marxism, and the "critical" Marxism of the Frankfurt school—achieved the most creative conceptual innovations in the history of the Marxist school. At the same time, their work reveals the strains of the Marxist dilemma in their starkest form. In each tradition, the theorists set out radically to revise Marx's presuppositions. For each, the theoretical logic of instrumental Marxism set boundaries they were unable, or unwilling, fully to transcend.

At the most general level of his thought, primarily in *Search for a Method* (1960), Sartre sets out a framework of explanation that is completely outside of the scientific framework Marx laid out. His early existentialism makes him particularly sensitive to the epistemological conditions for voluntarism, and he is insistent that an instrumental perception of action must be completely overthrown. In mechanical Marxism, he writes, "ends have disappeared." The goals of men are either set by forces beyond their control or "reduced to the diffusion of a physical movement across an inert milieu."[161] Ignoring what is, in fact, "the whole life of men," "Marxism becomes an 'inhumanism.' "[162] In opposition to this instrumental actor, man must be seen as a "signifying" one, representing his environment through symbols that express his passions and needs.[163] Only upon this basis can order become multidimensional, symbolic as well as material, and only in this way can a truly voluntaristic understanding be achieved. "What we call freedom," Sartre insists, "is the irreducibility of the cultural order to the natural order."[164] Upon this revision of the most general presuppositions of revolutionary theory, Sartre tries to reconstruct the rest of Marx's theoretical continuum. Rather than the base-superstructure model, he describes a complex model where a "hierarchy of mediations" allows relative autonomy to noneconomic "milieux."[165] The superstructure, in this view, must be seen as obdurate and irreducible.[166] On the level of method, Sartre rejects a focus on "laws" for the analysis of particular "experience" and unique "events," a focus that involves close attention to the "movement of ideas."[167] Empirically, propositions must not neglect the external world, but they should regard it primarily as the reference point for the crucial process of "internalization." The so-called objective world, in turn, must be seen, in part, as the field for fantasied projections, or "externalizations" of the actor's internal world.[168]

If Sartre's general framework seems much more closely to resemble Durkheim's than Marx's, this impression can only be strengthened by his major substantive work, *Critique of Dialectical Reason*.[169] Sartre's preoccupation is the creation and destruction of community, a process he closely ties to internal need and material contiguity. In periods of "dispersal," the inhospitable environment acts upon peoples' feelings: they internalize the isolation and, in turn, externalize their wounded passions in violent and oppressive acts.[170] In this situation, actors form a "series" rather than a true "group," an association formed by compassionate reciprocity and felt solidarity. It is the collective order of the series that underpins most Marxist analysis of capitalist economic life, and Sartre implicitly argues that such theorizing must be fundamentally revised to bring into account the role that internal projections play in sustaining this social order. For Sartre, fetishism is not simply a way to characterize the inhuman operation of purely economic interest; rather, it indicates a situation that is genuinely based upon human externalization and self-contempt. Classes interiorize their situation; they re-create their objective constraints according to a prior internal image.[171†] If they go beyond purely empirical and material constraints, moreover, it is a transcendence that usually corresponds to their interior need. Nineteenth-century capitalists, for example, must not be viewed as introducing exploitation simply by virtue of their obedience to blind laws. Having interiorized an inhumane situation, they created a brutalized proletariat through intentional violence, a projective repression that corresponded to their serialized need to transform an unstable condition.[172]

Yet to recognize the internal needs of human beings is to acknowledge that they have a latent desire to overcome this serialized separation, and, indeed, there is a "constant effort to establish lived bonds of solidarity between . . . members" of different groups.[173] Certain conditions allow them to do so, and it is because of such occasions that there occurs in human history the "constant metamorphosis of [serialized] gatherings into groups and of groups into gatherings."[174] As an example of such a turning point, Sartre discusses the siege of the Bastille in June of 1789. Because the citizens thought that Paris was surrounded by enemy soldiers, they became a "confined crowd." Their anger at this third party transformed it from a purely external object to a mutually confirming symbol. By orienting themselves similarly to a common enemy, they could see themselves as indivisible, each actor the "incarnation" of the whole. Thus, while they felt themselves to be acting as individuals, they actually exhibited "common behavior." They were "fused" into one group, and the expression of their anger released tremendous social "energy." This energy became the basis for "contagion." Symbols circulated rapidly throughout the crowd, and orders were obeyed because they were "common *praxis*" rather than because they came from an external force.[175] In the storming of the Bastille, this energy of solidary fusion was *directed* by the material environment—the roads, the buildings, the threatening enemy guns—but its *source* was the internal, group-structured passion and need.[176]

All fused groups, Sartre insists, eventually return to serialization, and it is in the understanding of this process that we comprehend the structure and meaning of institutional life. After the passionate event is completed, groups face the "chances of dispersion."[177] Because the group "desires permanence," every outside development comes to be viewed as a "danger to the group."[178] It is in this "struggle against dispersal" that the differentiation of functions develops, that leadership and sovereignty come into being, that terror and violence are initiated, and that bureaucracies emerge.[179] These developments present "degraded forms of community," distorted projections of the need for security and fusion.[180] Power and domination, then, emerge not from economic interests but from the psychological passivity that overwhelms individuals in their isolated, serialized state.[181]

Sartre has constructed a radicalized approach to subjective order and community life, one that combines a sensitivity—inspired by Freud and by the Durkheimian problematic as well—to the problems of voluntarism with a critical understanding of the "alienation" that stirred the early Marx.[182]† Yet for all of this, he has not escaped the theoretical boundaries of the Marxian dilemma. We are first alerted to this failure by the extraordinary indeterminacy of his sociological model. The dialectic from seriality to fusion and back again is frustratingly abstract, exhibiting a rigidly logical rather than empirical quality. There is, for example, no reference to the impact of differential historical context. Is seriality simply the same in feudal and capitalist societies? Is development circular without any accumulating effects of economic or social development? Is there no way at all that a "partial" community could be stabilized? Institutional effects are similarly ignored. Does the state simply have a "serializing" effect? Does it matter not at all if its regulations are personal and ad hoc or impersonal and rationalized? Precisely in what institutional contexts does a transition to fusion come about? It could not depend simply upon external threat, for of these there is certainly a continuous supply. Even the relationship between group development and individual freedom, the major theme of the work, is only vaguely ascertained. Sartre, the advocate of self-consciousness and individual responsibility, often appears, incongruously, to endorse the notion that freedom is synonymous with spontaneous emotional expression. His commitment to the abstract notion of the "negation" of alienated seriality makes him unable to consider that fused groups could as easily be repressive as liberating. He would have to specify in more detail the diverse circumstances of fusion if he were to make this a viable theory, but to do this, of course, he would have to step outside the purely "dialectical" logic of Marx.

If Sartre's theoretical departure from Marx is fundamentally indeterminate, it can be only because he has refused to take the final and decisive step beyond Marx's work. Sartre cannot escape the Marxist dilemma because he secretly maintains an awed respect for the very orthodoxy he has overtly rejected. In fact, Sartre periodically affirms that the determinacy of material facts still holds for the last instance. Though he is critical of "Marxism," he almost never criticizes Marx himself: it is the figures like Engels and Plekhanov and the "Stalinist deviation" from Marxism that draw his explicit ire.[183] His new "method," he paradoxically insists, never threatens the boundaries of Marx's scientific theory of history: it simply transforms its approach to individual acts. "Historical materialism furnish[es] the only valid interpretation of history and ... existentialism remain[s] the only concrete approach to reality."[184] The mode of production still "is the infrastructure of every society in human history,"[185] so there is "no need to add to it [i.e. to Marxism] any other factor."[186] Sartre has articulated a theory of the nonrational, one in which the search for community is the motor of historical development. But he wishes to assert, at the same time, that, somehow, an antithetical order of instrumental force still holds. Society may be a hierarchy of mediations, but at the bottom of this hierarchy there is an economic base which the higher levels "can never get outside."[187]

Sartre tries to "resolve" the paradox created by his insistence on the last instance by equating serialized groups with material scarcity. Instead of being treated simply as a condition created by differentiated human society, by the exigencies of everyday life and the vicissitudes of war and conflict, the "serializing" pressures that undermine the possibility of stable fused solidarity are traced to the economic exigencies of precommunist scarcity. "It is certainly true," Sartre admits, "that the economic motive is not always essential, and is even sometimes, not to be found at all," yet the pervasiveness of the economic can still be seen if one understands that it simply appears in another form, as "the man of scarcity in the form of the anti-human."[188] What produces seriality is the "material practico-inert," the economically based "alienation" Marx described in *Capital*.[189] But in this rationale for the last instance, material order becomes so powerful that individual freedom becomes merely formal. The external order becomes, implicitly, immutable: it "comes to him [the actor] from outside," and "he *has* to interiorise it and realize it practically."[190] Even economic determinism, the very theory against which Sartre has resolutely set himself, raises its ugly head. He insists, at one point, that the bond between men "changes with the type of machine."[191] Such a narrowed focus is revealed in the fact that it is only revolutionary struggles against the ruling class which Sartre examines as actions creative of community, and he professes to believe that communist economic organization will break the seriality-fusion continuum altogether.

Sartre produced a theory of freedom and normative order, but he would insist, nonetheless, that Marx's materialist strictures still hold firm. His indecision, and the contradictoriness of his theory, are nowhere more clearly revealed than in his insistence, near the conclusion of *Critique of Dialectical Reason*, that a single group action can be both normative and instrumental, free and determined, at the same time: "The group is both the most effective *means* of controlling the surrounding materiality in the context of scarcity and *the absolute end* as pure freedom liberating men from alterity [i.e., seriality]."[192] The ambivalence of this statement recalls Lukács' insistence that the proletariat is, simultaneously, the "subject-object" of historical development.[193†] It indicates, with equal force, the limitations that loyalty to instrumental presuppositions, even the most faint-hearted loyalty, place on theoretical logic.

The Frankfurt school of Marxism was inspired by German Idealism, by psychoanalysis, and by the cultural sociology of Weber and Simmel. Yet the drama of this "critical theory" is the peripatetic movement between its creative attempt to resuscitate a critical multidimensional theory and its conservative invocation of the last instance. Each non-Marxist discipline expands critical theory's analytical repertoire, bringing into its framework another "relatively autonomous" theoretical "moment," yet each discipline and each moment is eventually manipulated in a manner that allows "capital" to be the ultimate determinate and Marx to remain the real theoretical master.[194†]

Marcuse sets forth the Marxian dilemma in its prototypical form in his classic work *Reason and Revolution* (1941). Learning from the pioneering statements of Horkheimer and Adorno, Marcuse condemns capitalism because it violates classical reason, because it denigrates the universalistic capacities of the human mind. The implication of this critique, one that Marcuse makes the real political point of his book, is that critical thinking must be restored if humanistic socialism is to be saved. At the same time, however, Marcuse claims that this normative theory of revolution conflicts in no way with Marx's own, and he develops a last instance argument that explains the roots and effects of the denigration of critical thinking in a traditional way. Capitalism alone, not any cultural movement, has produced this contemporary impoverishment, which Marcuse, along with Horkheimer and Adorno, calls "technical reason." Produced by capitalism, this positivistic mentality allows the "laws" of Marx's economics to remain effectively determinate. Marcuse can argue, then, that socialism will be the product of a blind economic unfolding while at the same time he argues the case for the necessary revival of critical reason.

Marcuse follows the same contradictory path in his two other major works. In *Eros and Civilization* (1955), he radicalizes Freud by arguing that neurosis is historically specific to "scarce" economies, and that psychological repression and sexual genitality are not historical absolutes. Because actors' unconscious minds reflect their social structure, the implication of this radical Freudianism is that the continued success of capitalism rests upon psychological foundations, and that its destruction depends, in turn, upon psychic renewal. Yet Marcuse hesitates before such a conclusion. He argues that unrepressive psychological action can occur only after economic transformation has been achieved. "Surplus repression" becomes epiphenomenal. The effect of economic mechanisms, it can be changed only as the after-effect of mechanical development. Mind itself is not an active variable, and, as a result, the nature of the transition to socialism is clouded in indeterminacy. Marcuse makes the same paradoxical argument in *One Dimensional Man* (1963). Modern capitalism has created a purely technical civilization, one in which impoverished culture creates no independent leverage for critical reason. Through advertising and other forms of propaganda, the proletariat and middle classes "introject" their own domination, projecting a passive dependency that makes rebellion subjectively impossible. Yet, once again, in explaining the roots of this situation Marcuse claims the "ultimate" causes are located simply in economic exigencies. Since the economic base of capitalism will not change, this one-way determinism makes any comprehension of the path out of this degenerate condition completely impossible.

Despite this pessimism, Marcuse remains committed to revolution, and in his later writings he searches for critical rebellion in "outsiders," like students and minorities, and in aesthetic impulses that capitalism has failed fully to repress.[195] Yet he has insisted that the personality in capitalism represses all of its contentious id impulses, and students and exploited minorities should be no exceptions. Moreover, if "technical reason" is, in fact, the cultural code of capitalism itself, upon what basis could aestheticism become a formidable opponent? Confined by the instrumental limitations of Marx's theory even while he tries to negate it, Marcuse moves back and forth between indeterminacy and the last instance.

The work of Jürgen Habermas, the leading contemporary representative of the Frankfurt school, is even more finely stretched between these two poles. The importance of Habermas derives from his partly successful effort to open critical theorizing to a fully multidimensional model. Sharply critical of Marx's tendency to define action instrumentally, he is extraordinarily sensitive to the repercussions that such reduction has for a theory that tries to make order permeable to voluntary, critical opposition. The problem with Marx, Habermas writes, is his "reduction of the self-generative act of the human species to labor," a rationalization that makes Marx's scientific theory inattentive to the symbolic and traditional realms.[196] But if "social production can be viewed according to the model of instrumental action," then order is "social practice [reduced] to one of its ... elements."[197] Habermas purposely sets out to avoid these pitfalls. Action is instrumental, but it is also interpretive and affective. Order has an economic component, but society must be conceived as composed of interacting subsystems, each with a distinctive causal specificity.[198] "Work" and "interaction" both matter, and the importance of the latter means that "cultural tradition," "symbols," and "norms" are crucial to domination and to liberation as well.[199]

Yet Habermas, these explicit statements to the contrary, will not really assent to the notion that Marx's original theory differs markedly from his own. "Certainly," he writes, "Marx understood the dialectical method well enough not to misuse it crudely."[200] It was Engels who did so, and who produced the basis for an instrumental Marxism. In fact, Habermas asserts, Marx's sociology constantly refers to the active, subject side of action,[201] and "Marx always takes account of social practice that encompasses both work and interaction."[202] Marx, like Habermas, describes revolution as arising from "the felt disruption of a moral totality,"[203] and he views the communist party in primarily an interpretive role, as the emancipating "therapist" vis-à-vis the proletarian "patient."[204] Yet the thinness of this normative reading is revealed by Habermas' inability to cite textual evidence for his claim. In the end, he tries to resolve his ambivalence by arguing that this duality really exists in Marx himself, although it is a duality preponderantly weighted to the normative side. The "philosophical self-understanding" of Marx's inquiry is limited and instrumental, but in his "practice of inquiry" in his "empirical analyses," Marx's work is fully multidimensional.[205]

This generalized ambivalence is strikingly demonstrated in the two concrete analyses Habermas offers of the structure and process of capitalist life. In each case, he sets out a normative or multidimensional explanation that stands, to some degree, as an independent explanatory tool. In each case, however, he strives to qualify his revolutionary departure by invoking the last instance and by allowing a substantial indeterminacy.

In one strand of his later work, Habermas introduces a cultural explanation for the stasis and irrationality of capitalism.[206] The problem here is "distorted communication," a linguistic fact making the true causes of capitalist suffering unrecognizable to the very people whom it affects. By excluding some members from discourse altogether, and by constructing opaque ideological norms that mediate and impair the communication that does occur, capitalism deprives its members of the will and intelligence for rational, critical acts. The invocation of norms opens this analysis to the influence of tradition and culture, but Habermas tries, at the same time, to narrow it to the resources of orthodox Marxism itself. The source of communicative distortion, he argues, is commodity fetishism, the phenomenon that derives, according to Marx, from the economic structure of the wage relationship. Fetishism makes people unable to see the unequal material distribution that underlies their apparent freedom. But if Habermas completely accepted this explanation, he would have to follow Marx in assigning objective transformation the task of liberation, a passivity that he has already explicitly rejected in general and, more specifically, in the work of Marx himself. It is because of the unacceptability of this logical conclusion that Habermas moves from this "last instance" argument to theoretical indeterminacy. He rarely specifies the partners in "distorted communication" in any precise empirical way, nor does he indicate by what processes, other than economic transformation, such distortion could be remedied. He suggests the model of psychoanalytic therapy, but the relationship of this model to the empirical processes of capitalist society remains vague and undefined.[207]

The much more concrete account of capitalist contradiction in *Legitimation Crisis* (1973) ultimately suffers from similar difficulties. On the one hand, Habermas draws upon phenomenology, symbolic interactionism, and Parsonian systems theory to develop a critical analysis of an interdependent system in which contradictions develop in different and relatively independent institutional spheres. There is not simply "economic crisis," but "political crisis," "motivational crisis," and, ultimately, a general "legitimation crisis" that permeates and destabilizes the society as a whole. Though linked to specific structural deficits, the contradictory quality of these strains develops because the outputs of the subsystems in capitalist society can never be reconciled with the universalistic expectations generated by its cultural traditions. At the same time, Habermas cross-cuts this multidimensional picture with the argument that each independent crisis is really the result of the development of the capitalist economy. He makes the contradictions and crises chronological rather than simultaneous, temporally rather than analytically differentiated. Western history begins with a nineteenth-century capitalism that is completely technical and instrumental. Only as this economy grows more complex do political, moral, and psychological "deficits" develop, and each is linked ultimately to an economic cause. "In the final analysis," Habermas insists, the capitalist "class structure is the source of the legitimation deficit" that undermines modern society.[208]

This attempt to remain faithful to the scientific Marx creates irresolvable tensions in Habermas' argument, for while he makes the discovery of capitalism's contradictions dependent on certain structures of mind and patterns of tradition, he insists, nonetheless, that they are also objectively based. This last instance strategy leads Habermas, ineluctably, to the other pole of the Marxian dilemma, to the problem of indeterminacy. Why, for example, given the plasticity of symbolic constructions, are the strains in capitalist society "ultimate contradictions" in the Marxian sense? While he expresses his faith that the capitalist economy will always manifest a particularizing tendency, Habermas never specifies why such particularistic frustration will ever produce the kind of concerted and radically antagonistic rebellion that would stop the capitalist system entirely. If the contradiction is simply objectively determined, Habermas could demonstrate this stasis as Marx does, in an economic way. Yet he insists that capitalism rests upon certain internal orientations as well, and he never demonstrates why the conflict between universalistic expectations and conditional restraints should produce anything more than the continual frustration of limited reform, the oscillation between progress and backlash that can create amelioration but never revolution. He never identifies, in other words, the strain in capitalism which is ultimately irresolvable, some inherent contradiction which can lead only to socialist transformation.[209]

In all of postwar Western Marxism, the French structuralists are the most self-conscious about their relationship to the original theory and the innovations they intend to produce. Despite this knowledge, however, their theorizing involves a basic self-deception. Althusser, the originator of this structuralism, professes to absolute loyalty, while he implicitly introduces a series of fundamental departures. It is because of the effort to contain innovations within the strict limits of Marx's original thought that structuralism remains mired in the Marxian dilemma.

Althusser sees himself as the heir of Engels, Lenin, Mao, and Gramsci, as the ultimate interpreter of the anomalies of the Russian Revolution, Stalinism, and right-wing revolution. Focusing on the nature of order rather than action, he makes his fundamental revision in his assertion that the ideological and political "instances" or "elements" of society are "relatively autonomous" and are "isolated" from the economic base. At any given empirical moment, Althusser insists, any one of the three instances—ideological, political, economic—may assume "structured dominance."[210] As he writes in *Reading "Capital"* (1970), there is "a certain type of *complexity*" of "what can be called levels or instances which are distinct and 'relatively autonomous' [and which are] articulated with one another according to specific determination."[211] Although these determinations can never be reduced to a single element, they do form a "structured whole," a "synchronicity" or "totality."[212] This totalization, however, must never be viewed as produced by the base alone. "From the first element to the last," Althusser insists in one of his most elegant formulations, "the lonely hour of the 'last instance' never comes."[213]

This open, interdependent conception of the social system is laid out in abstract terms without concrete specification about the mode of subsystem interrelationship in any historical instance. As such, the theory suffers from a fundamental indeterminacy, and it raises the possibility— just as bad, from Althusser's perspective—of its convergence with functionalist modes of non-Marxist thought.[214] It is no doubt because he was aware of these distasteful possibilities that Althusser resolutely embraced the other pole of the Marxian dilemma, the orthodoxy of the last instance. Despite his insistence on complex determination, his massive effort at modeling an abstract interdependence, and his explicit disavowal of every form of reductionist thought, like every other great Marxist of the twentieth century Althusser makes the crucial qualification that the nature of every totality is "fixed in the last instance by the level or instance of the economy."[215] Only the economic level, he paradoxically asserts, can determine the relative dominance of the noneconomic dimensions of social order. When he explains his reasoning, this fear of indeterminacy is apparent, as is his desire to avoid any confusion between his theory and "empiricist," bourgeois functionalism.

> This "determination in the last instance" is an absolute precondition for the necessity and intelligibility of the . . . displacement of "dominance" between the structured levels of the whole. . . . Only this "determination in the last instance" makes it possible to escape the arbitrary relativism of observable displacements by giving these displacements the necessity of a function.[216]

Instead of outlining a truly independent form of order, then, Althusser has reverted to the approach to superstructural elements that Marx perfected in his theory of fetishism (see ch. 6, sec. 2.3, above). Superstructural forms appear independent, but they are, in fact, simply covers for arrangements in the productive sphere. True, there are times when one can study production only by decoding these superstructures, but they are epiphenomenal all the same.

> The economic is *never clearly visible*, does not coincide with the "given" [of] the capitalist mode of production in that we know that the latter is the mode of production in which *fetishism* affects the economic region *par excellence*. . . . Precisely because of

the "massive" character of this fetishized "obviousness," the only way to the essence of the economic is to . . . reveal the articulation of this region with other regions.[217]

This strategy of the last instance permeates the more empirical analyses that Althusser and his associates attempt. Balibar, for example, considers the reproduction of labor power to be prototypical of the way that apparently independent instances actually are rooted in the economic. Like Marx himself, Balibar emphasizes that in social reproduction there is created the appearance of "a private act which takes place outside the sphere of circulation itself." Contrary to this appearance, however, "the analysis of reproduction shows that these moments have no relative autonomy or laws of their own, but are . . . predetermined in the nature and quantity of the means of consumption produced by the total social capital." That this linkage undermines the possibility for voluntarism Balibar is well aware. In fact, in his eyes, it is one of his central accomplishments that, once reduced, reproduction "ceases to appear as a contingent factual state."[218] With this analysis, the determination of the last, economic instance is proved beyond doubt. "Moments [which] seem to belong to a different sphere from that of production" have been reconnected: "The analysis of reproduction seems genuinely . . . to articulate together levels which have hitherto been isolated."[219†] In the only major empirical essay that Althusser himself attempts, "Ideology and Ideological State Apparatuses," this mediated reduction is documented in just as assertive a way, and with just as deterministic results. He is trying to explain apparently independent public education and the "rules of morality, civic and professional conscience" that were the object of so much of Durkheim's thought.[220] Although education and other Ideological State Apparatuses "present themselves to the immediate observer in the form of distinct and specialized institutions," Althusser rejects their autonomy out of hand. Explanation can only be found in the economic base.[221] The "rules" that are the object of education, for example, are simply "the attitudes that should be observed by every agent in the division of labour, according to the job he is 'destined' for," and are, hence, nothing more than the "rules of respect for the socio-technical division of labour and ultimately the rules of the order established by class domination."[222]

Structuralism has been attacked by more voluntaristic Marxists as a particularly deterministic strand of postwar Marxist theory, one that must be distinguished on these grounds from the traditions of Sartre and the Frankfurt school. That Althusser moves more quickly to the last instance is probably true, although his abstract model of the interdependent social system is as antireductionist as any other. That other traditions do not also embrace the determinate last instance, however, is certainly incorrect. Confined by the logical poles of the Marxian dilemma, Western Marxism moves back and forth between indeterminacy and economic reduction. No variant has yet broken completely free of the constraints set by Marx's instrumental thought.

The history of the covert theoretical revision that is Marxism demonstrates in the most effective possible way the fallacies of so much of contemporary theoretical debate. In the name of more radical theorizing, critics have argued for a focus on "conflict" rather than "order," arguing that this relatively specific theoretical commitment has decisive political consequences. Yet within the school of conflict par excellence, in the revolutionary theoretical tradition of Marxism itself, the crucial theoretical debate has concerned an entirely different issue. It has revolved around the presuppositional issues of action and order. The most creative theorists have tried to push Marxism, haltingly and equivocally, toward the embrace of a more normative position. These Marxists have not been afraid that such an anti-instrumental position would produce a bias toward stability and social order; indeed, they have usually argued that the comprehension of struggle and revolution depends precisely upon disengaging Marxism from its instrumental form. Contemporary "conflict theorists," then, are blind to the central theoretical issues within the history of Marxism itself. Falsely equating an angry Hobbesianism with sophisticated revolutionary theory, they have deprived themselves of the lessons of an entire theoretical tradition.

In fact, if one searches for a single biographical factor that has separated the most innovative and creative Marxist intellectuals from their more traditional theoretical comrades, it will be found in their strong exposure to idealist theorizing before their conversion to Marxism. Bernstein and Bauer were forcefully affected by the renewal of Kantianism in late nineteenth century Germany. Lukács had once been an adherent of German Idealism, and had looked to Weber and Simmel along with Hegel as his masters. Gramsci was a student and follower of the influential Italian idealist Croce. Mao's intellectual history was formed by the Kantianism that affected important philosophers in late nineteenth-century China, and by the revival of a voluntaristic and activistic neo-Confucianism. Sartre was an existentialist before becoming a Marxist, strongly influenced by Freud as well as by Hegel and later phenomenology. Marcuse was first a phenomenologist and Hegelian, and later brought psychoanalytic and aesthetic thought into his Marxist framework. Habermas was also inspired by Hegel, yet he has learned from American pragmatism and from "normative" functionalism as well.[223†] Althusser himself, though a resolute critic of Hegel, has absorbed important lessons from Mao and Gramsci, along with crucial conceptions from Parsonian theory.[224†]

The problem that these thinkers faced, indeed, was that none ever succeeded in fully reconciling his idealist predilection with his commitment to Marxist thought. Each confused the espousal of a revolutionary theory of equality and community with loyalty to Marx's instrumental presuppositions. It is from this failure, of course, that the problems of the Marxian dilemma derive. It is because of the barriers this dilemma presents that Marxism still has not developed a theory of the superstructure of society. There are discussions about the "crisis" of Marxist theory, firm assertions about the importance of giving the normative element its due, and even warnings that to develop a theory of the superstructure Marxists may have to give up on Marx altogether. Yet Marxism, it seems, is always starting this effort over from scratch.[225†]

3. CONCLUSION: THE INSTABILITY OF ONE-DIMENSIONAL THEORY AND THE NEED FOR ITS TRANSCENDENCE

What Marxism needs, but what it will not allow itself to have, is the kind of unhesitating and systematic approach to the relation of culture and society that was the crowning glory of Durkheim's theoretical career. The most important students of Marx, indeed, can be seen as moving toward "Durkheimian" propositions at every turn. Durkheim's students, it will be recalled, moved in exactly the opposite direction. They embraced, partially and inconsistently to be sure, the kind of materialist notions associated with Marxist thought. This history of equivocation and revision in the idealist and materialist traditions of classical sociology—the traditions to which I have devoted the present volume—demonstrates persuasively that one-dimensional theorizing is unstable and, ultimately, unsatisfying. Durkheim and Marx laid out two parallel but fundamentally opposed lines of analysis. Certainly, each must be preserved in certain important respects. We would do well, however, to seek a theoretical mode that starts from a multidimensional premise. Only such a more inclusive theory, it would seem, can produce a truly satisfactory explanation of the complexity of social life. The classical proponent of this effort at integration was Max Weber. If students of Marx and Durkheim were ever to meet, it would surely be on the site that Weber marked out. It is to Max Weber, and his ambiguous effort to resolve the antinomies of classical thought, that I devote the third volume of this work.

Notes

CHAPTER ONE

1. A clear and succinct argument for this erroneous understanding can be found in Arthur L. Stinchcombe's *Constructing Social Theories* (New York, 1968). In his first pages, Stinchcombe describes Marx, Durkheim, and Weber as "those great empirical analysts . . . who did not work mainly at what we now call theory." Instead of "theory," he insists, these classical thinkers "worked out *explanations* of the growth of capitalism, or of class conflict, or of primitive religion," and in doing so, he concludes, "they used a wide variety of theoretical *methods*." (P. 3, italics added.) This argument for treating classical works solely as exemplars for research is continued in Stinchcombe's *Theoretical Methods in Social History* (New York, 1978). For a critical review of the latter, see Jeffrey C. Alexander, "Looking for Theory: 'Facts' and 'Values' as the Intellectual Legacy of the 1970's," *Theory and Society,* 10 (1981): 279–292.

2. Merton, "On the History and Systematics of Sociological Theory," pp. 1–38 in his *On Theoretical Sociology* (New York, 1967).

3. Ibid., pp. 28, 30.

4. Ibid., pp. 36–37.

5. Ibid., p. 35.

6. Herbert Butterfield provides an interesting description of just such a use of history in his account of the origins of modern physics:

> If the orthodox doctrine of the middle ages had been based on Aristotle, however, it has to be noted that, both then and during the Renaissance (as well as later still), the attacks on Aristotle—the theory of impetus included—would themselves be based on some ancient thinker. Here we

touch on one of the generative factors, not only in the formation of the
modern world, but also in the development of the scientific revolution—
namely, the discovery of the fact that even Aristotle had not reigned unchallenged in the ancient days. All this produced a healthy friction, resulting in the emergence of important problems which the middle ages
had to make up their own minds about, so that men were driven to some
kind of examination of the workings of nature themselves, even if only
because they had to decide between Aristotle and some rival teacher.
(*The Origins of Modern Science* [New York, (1957) 1965], p. 21.)

7. John Rex and Ralf Dahrendorf reread Weber and Parsons to establish conflict theory, which also gained support through Lewis A. Coser's
rereadings of Simmel, Freud, and Parsons (Rex, *Key Problems in Sociological Theory* [London, 1961]; Dahrendorf, *Class and Class Conflict in
Industrial Society* [Stanford, Calif., 1959]; Coser, *The Functions of Social
Conflict* [New York, 1956]). George C. Homans reread Smelser and Parsons, and Alvin W. Gouldner reread Parsons in their arguments against
systems theory (Homans, "Bringing Men Back in," *American Sociological Review* 29 [1964]: 809–818; Gouldner, *The Coming Crisis of Western
Sociology* [New York, 1970]). C. Wright Mills reread Parsons, as did
Gouldner and Robert J. Friedrichs in their arguments for ideological reduction (Mills, *The Sociological Imagination* [New York, 1959]; Gouldner,
Coming Crisis; Friedrichs, *A Sociology of Sociology* [New York, 1970]). For
empiricism as rereadings, see Merton (n. 1) and Stinchcombe (n. 1, both
works).

Stinchcombe, who argues that all efforts at interpretation should be
replaced by efforts to build theory simply through empirical explanation, himself builds this argument through a series of interpretations of
classical works! Merton's middle-range theorizing and arguments for
middle-range strategies also usually rely upon persuasion about the true
nature of classical work (as mentioned in vol. 1, ch. 1). M. J. Mulkay, in
fact, actually criticizes Merton's sociology for not being sufficiently inductive on the grounds that he has relied too heavily on the older theories
of Durkheim and Weber for his scientific concepts (pp. 104–112 in
Mulkay, *Functionalism, Exchange, and Theoretical Strategy* [New York,
1971]). A good recent example of how readings can assume major importance for current controversy is Peter P. Ekeh's *Social Exchange Theory:
The Two Traditions* (Cambridge, Mass., 1974). Ekeh traces the major disagreements and inadequacies of contemporary exchange theory to the
conceptions of exchange propounded by Frazer, Mauss, and Malinowski,
and finds compelling solutions to these problems in the more recent classic work of Lévi-Strauss. Ekeh's rationale for this strategy is worth quoting here. "Try as they might," he writes, "sociologists cannot brush aside
their intellectual forefathers. This is partly because the forefathers do
not belong to all of us." (P. 218.)

I should not be interpreted, however, as saying that theoretical argument *must* proceed through rereadings. This is a fundamental form of theorizing, but is far from being the only one. Theorizing can proceed through directly philosophical argument and it can proceed by building new theories of the empirical world or through empirically referenced critiques of other theories.

8. Friedrichs, *A Sociology of Sociology*, p. xix.

9. Gouldner, *Coming Crisis*, passim. One should note, however, the much more dialectical treatment in Gouldner's later *The Two Marxisms* (New York, 1980), which develops many of the same understandings of scientific development articulated here.

10. Giddens, *Capitalism and Modern Social Theory* (London, 1972), p. vii. The anti-Parsonian referent of this reading, however, explicitly emerges only in Giddens' argument that "order" is not a central problem of social theory.

11. The classical convergence argument was put by Parsons in *The Structure of Social Action* (New York, [1937] 1968) and his notion permeated sociological theory until the 1970s. It also informs the influential history by Robert A. Nisbet, *The Sociological Tradition* (New York, 1966), and more recently the important work by Dick Atkinson, *Orthodox Consensus and Radical Alternative* (New York, 1972). For a salutary response to this tradition, see S. N. Eisenstadt and M. Curelaru, *The Forms of Sociology: Paradigms and Crises* (New York, 1976). The best theoretical argument about the misleading and whiggish quality of most theoretical "histories" is Robert Alun Jones, "On Understanding Sociological Classics," *American Journal of Sociology* 82 (1977): 279–319. I disagree strongly with Jones, however, in his historicist assumption that the "true" history of theoretical creation can actually be discovered in an objective empirical way, and therefore with his postulate that a break between history and theory is possible.

12. Parsons, *Structure*; Nisbet, *Sociological Tradition*; Hughes, *Consciousness and Society* (New York, 1958). Thus, by reading instrumental theorizing out of the "modern" convergence of the 1890s, Parsons uses "history" to justify the sociological idealism described in vol. 1, ch. 3.

13. Elie Halévy, *The Growth of Philosophic Radicalism* (1901–1904; New York, 1972; Max Horkheimer, *Critical Theory* [New York, 1972]).

14. The fact that this is as true of natural as of social science underscores the fact that even relatively greater accumulation on the propositional level does not mean resolution in terms of more general commitments. As the historian of science Gerald Holton points out:

Thematic questions do not get solved and disposed of. Nineteenth century atomism triumphs over the ether vortices of Kelvin—but then field theories rise which deal with material particles again as singularities, now in a twentieth century continuum. The modern version of the cosmological theory based on the theme of a life cycle . . . may seem to triumph on experimental grounds over the rival theory based on a theme of continuous existence, and throw it out the window—but we can be sure that it will come in again through the back door. For contrary to the physical theories in which they find embodiment in x-y [i.e., positivist] terms, themata are not proved or disproved. (*The Thematic Origins of Science from Kepler to Einstein* [Cambridge, Mass., 1973], p. 62.)

15. Friedrichs and Gouldner, the preeminent crisis theorists of the post-1960s period, self-consciously associated themselves with the ideological-political polarization of the 1960s and linked their theoretical analyses to the particular groups involved (see references to Friedrichs' and Gouldner's work above). T. B. Bottomore's "The Crisis in Sociology" (pp. 44–54 in his *Sociology as Social Criticism* [New York, 1974]), similarly posits a fundamental social crisis that explains and predicts the intellectual conflicts he describes (pp. 47–48). For an approach to theoretical crisis that avoids the conflation of social and cognitive elements, and which links crisis mainly to difficulties in the latter, see Norman Birnbaum's "The Crisis of Marxist Sociology" (pp. 95–129 in his *Toward a Critical Sociology* [London, 1971]). My notion of crisis as superimposition can also be found in the discussions by Eisenstadt and Curelaru (n. 11 above) and in Joseph Ben-David, "The State of Sociological Theory and the Sociological Community: A Review Article," *Comparative Studies in Society and History* 15 (1978): 448–472.

16. Such perfectly helpful tools are sometimes employed as "camouflage" even by the most serious theoretical reinterpreters. Giddens, e.g., in the Preface to his *Capitalism and Modern Social Theory* (n. 10 above), indicates that his reading actually rests upon "recent scholarship" and on the discoveries of new Marx texts. Guenther Roth partly rests his rereading of Weber on the until-recently untranslated sections of *Economy and Society* (see his Introduction in Max Weber, *Economy and Society*, ed. Guenther Roth and Claus Wittich [Berkeley and Los Angeles, 1978], pp. xxxiii–cx). Arthur Mitzman argues that his rereading of Weber proceeds from the discovery of new biographical material (*The Iron Cage* [New York, 1970]).

17. I recognize, of course, that this interpretive exercise does not proceed simply upon the basis of the logic of social thought alone, but that it also involves particular techniques and modes of interpretive, or hermeneutical, practice per se. In this sense, theoretical interpretation is simply a genre of general interpretation—it is a parallel to literary criticism. Although it would be impossible to outline in any detail the interpretive perspective in this broader sense which pertains here, I venture a few very brief statements.

As works of the imagination, theoretical texts have an underlying logic and construction of which their authors are not by any means always aware. Influenced, therefore, by the now venerable "New Criticism" and ultimately by the historical hermeneutical tradition itself—and on this point contemporary structuralist critics would certainly agree—I have sought, above all, to consider theoretical texts in a sui generis way, to see them as standing on their own. I have sought, therefore, to describe the "structures" that permeate them and give them meaning apart from the author's conscious intention. In this context, I have not hesitated to record ambiguities and contradictions in a theoretical text of which the author was unaware and of which he would certainly not have approved if he had known of their existence. It is naïve and unnecessarily self-limiting to operate within what might be called the "consistency assumption" when analyzing a great theorist's work. Yet this is precisely the assumption which has usually been taken up. Analysts understandably feel deferential when faced with the brilliance of a great mind; they also assume that a theory's "scientific" quality gives to it a halo of logic and consistency. Most great theory, however, is enormously conflictual, for it is written by ordinary human beings who have not completely resolved their feelings about their ideas. Theorists, in other words, often feel ambivalence, albeit in an unconscious way. The ambivalence of the theorist often leads to extraordinary ambiguities in the text, ambiguities which the logical and deductive qualities of analytic argument are designed to camouflage. The ambiguities and contradictions, therefore, may be sucessfully shunted off into categories that are actually residual to a consistent line of scientific argument, or they may assume a central if unrecognized role in the very heart of the work.

As William Empson, one of the earliest and most profound New Critics, pointed out more than fifty years ago, such debilitating ambiguities can be of several different types. An author may be discovering a new idea in the course of a single piece of work and, not being able to hold two ideas simultaneously, he may use the same concept or word in radically different ways (*Seven Types of Ambiguity* [London, (1930) 1953], ch. 5; we will see exactly this problem in Marx's writings of 1843–1845 and in Durkheim's book of 1893 and his writings of 1894–1895). Other ambiguities may have a more radically atemporal quality: an author is quite simply of two minds. Empson explains this with reference to the psychoanalytic notion that "what you want involves the notion that you must not take it" (p. 193 and ch. 7, passim; we will find such ambiguity in Durkheim's earliest writings, of 1885–1893, and particularly in Weber's and Parsons' work). With all such cases of unresolved contradiction, Empson emphasizes, the reader is forced to invent interpretations of the author's meaning or intention (ch. 6). Critics, however, should not be simply enthusiastic readers. They are critical readers and they must see the actual structure of the text, not be hoodwinked by its camouflage or by the wishful desire for meaningful consistency.

All of this is not to say that in the following pages I will be uninterested in the historical or social context of theoretical creation or in the nature of the author's actual conscious intention. I do not hold to either a pure New Criticism or a structuralist program. To the contrary, contextual data will be actively sought out, and with the help of such context I will strive to construct a hypothetical "state of mind" for the theorist which can account for the tensions discovered in the text. I will, however, always start with the text itself, for a knowledge of the environment or intention of an author is never sufficient for the understanding of his creative product.

CHAPTER TWO

1. See, e.g., Karl Kautsky's *The Class Struggle*, (New York, 1971), published in 1891 as a popularization of the Erfurt Program of the German Social Democratic party, a program which, with Engels' help, Kautsky had closely fashioned around Marx's theses in his "Critique of the Gotha Program." In this work, particularly in chs. 1–3, Kautsky presents Marx's findings as completely empirical and continually makes analogies to modern physical science (see, e.g., pp. 8–9). Engels' testimonies to Marx as an empirical scientist are well known. See, for example, Engels' introduction to the English edition of his *Socialism: Utopian and Scientific*, written in 1892, where he quotes Marx's laudatory descriptions of the emergence of British materialistic empiricism and compares Marx's scientific discoveries to those of Darwin (Karl Marx and Frederick Engels, *Selected Works* [Moscow, 1962], 2:93–115).

2. Korsch, *Karl Marx* (London, [1938] 1963), passim. E.g.: "Marx and Engels never considered their new principle of economic and social research as more than a new scientific approach to a strictly empirical investigation of the historical development of the modern capitalist mode of production" (p. 167). This later work by Korsch is, however, much less valuable than his earlier, more critical writings.

3. Bernstein, *Evolutionary Socialism* (1899), passim.

4. Michels, *Political Parties* (1911).

5. Mallet, *La Nouvelle Classe ouvrière* (Paris, 1963); Goldthorpe and Lockwood, "Affluence and the British Class Structure," *Sociological Review* 11, no. 2 (1963): 133–163; André Gorz, *Strategy for Labor* (Boston, 1967).

6. Bottomore, *Sociology as Social Criticism* (New York, 1974), particularly pt. 2, "Classes and Elites," and pt. 3, "Social Movements and Political Action." For a discussion of these aspects of Bottomore's work, and his positivist approach to resolving the theoretical problems in Marx's work, see my review in *American Journal of Sociology* 81 (1976): 1120–1123.

7. Coser, "Marxist Thought in the First One-Quarter of the Twentieth

Century," in *Varieties of Political Expression in Sociology* (Chicago, 1972), pp. 173–201.

8. Giddens, *Capitalism and Modern Social Theory* (Cambridge, 1971), pp. xi–xv, 185–190.

9. Nisbet, *The Sociological Tradition* (New York, 1966), pp. 132–141.

10. Robert C. Tucker, *Philosophy and Myth in Karl Marx* (Cambridge, 1961). It must be emphasized, however, that though Tucker describes Marx's work as a mythical projection of Marx's fantasy, he does not offer this interpretation in a pejorative manner.

11. Lichtheim, *Marxism* (New York, 1961), particularly pt. 5, pp. 203–354; Avineri, *The Social and Political Thought of Karl Marx* (Cambridge, 1968), passim, but particularly the Introduction, pp. 1–7; Habermas, "Between Philosophy and Science: Marxism as Critique," in his *Theory and Practice* (Boston, 1973), pp. 195–252.

12. Dahrendorf, *Class and Class Conflict in Industrial Society* (Stanford, Calif., 1959). See also Randall Collins, *Conflict Sociology* (New York, 1975).

13. Piotr Sztompka, *System and Function* (New York, 1974).

14. Louis Althusser, "On the Materialist Dialectic," pp. 161–218 in his *For Marx* (London, 1969).

15. Jürgen Habermas, *Knowledge and Human Interests* (Boston, 1971), esp. "The Idea of the Theory of Knowledge as Social Theory," pp. 43–63; Wellmer, *Critical Theory of Society* (New York, 1974).

16. Jean-Paul Sartre, *Search for a Method* (New York, 1963), passim; Dick Atkinson, *Orthodox Consensus and Radical Alternative* (New York, 1972), pp. 34–65.

17. Giddens (n. 8 above), p. xv.

18. Ollman, *Alienation: Marx's Conception of Man in Capitalist Society* (Cambridge, 1971), p. 204.

19. Friedrich Hegel, "Introduction" to *The Philosophy of History* (New York, 1900), esp. pp. 29–34. Cf. Herbert Marcuse, *Reason and Revolution* (Boston, [1941] 1960), pp. 169–223.

20. Marx, "On a Proposed Divorce Law" (*Rheinische Zeitung*, December 19, 1842), in Loyd D. Easton and Kurt H. Guddat, eds., *Writings of the Young Marx on Philosophy and Society* (New York, 1967), p. 139, italics added.

21. Ibid., p. 140, italics in original. In subsequent references to Marx's writings, I add the pages in *Marx-Engels Werke* (Berlin, 1962; hereafter cited as *MEW*) when I have made changes in the cited English translation.

22. Marx, "Comments on the Latest Prussian Censorship Instruction" (completed in January 1842 for the *Deutsche Jahrbücher*, first published in *Anekdota*, February 1843), in Easton and Guddat, p. 78.

23. Ibid.

24. For the distinction between these two conceptions of rationality and the importance of distinguishing between them in my analysis of theoretical logic, see vol. 1, ch. 3, sec. 2.3.

25. Marx, "Preparatory Notes" to "The Difference between the Democritean and Epicurean Philosophy of Nature" (doctoral diss., University of Jena, April 15, 1841), ibid., p. 52.

26. Marx, "Religion, Free Press, and Philosophy" (lead article, *Kölnische Zeitung*, no. 179, July, 1842), ibid., p. 118.

27. Marx, "Preparatory Notes," ibid., p. 52.

28. Ibid., p. 54, italics added; Marx, "Comments on the Latest Prussian Censorship Instruction," ibid., p. 81 (*MEW*, supp. 1:15).

29. "Preparatory Notes," ibid., p. 61, italics in original (*MEW*, supp. 1:327).

30. Ibid., pp. 61–62, italics in original.

31. "Religion, Free Press, and Philosophy," ibid., p. 122.

32. "Comments on the Latest Prussian Censorship Instruction," ibid., p. 69, italics added.

33. Ibid., p. 68.

34. "Religion, Free Press, and Philosophy," ibid., p. 125.

35. Marx, "Communism and the Augsburg *Allgemeine Zeitung*," ibid., p. 135, italics added (*MEW*, 1:108).

36. Ibid.

37. "Comments on the Latest Prussian Censorship Instruction," ibid., p. 82, italics in original.

38. Marx, "The Philosophical Manifesto of the Historical School of Law" (*Rheinische Zeitung*, April or May 1842), ibid., p. 98, italics altered.

39. "Religion, Free Press, and Philosophy," ibid., p. 120.

40. For these biographical factors, see David McLellan, *Karl Marx* (New York, 1973), pp. 189–225.

41. See excerpts from this article in McLellan's *Marx before Marxism* (New York, 1970), pp. 95–97.

42. Marx, "Defense of the Moselle Correspondent: Economic Distress and Freedom of the Press" (*Rheinische Zeitung*, early weeks of 1843), in Easton and Guddat (n. 20 above), p. 144, italics altered.

43. Ibid., italics added.

44. Ibid., italics in original.

45. McLellan, *Karl Marx*, p. 57.

46. Marx, "Defense of the Moselle Correspondent," in Easton and Guddat, p. 145, italics deleted (*MEW*, 1:189).

47. For the influence of this work on Marx, see McLellan, *Karl Marx*, pp. 66–70, and Tucker (n. 10 above), pp. 124–125.

48. For an informative discussion of the political and intellectual atmosphere of Paris at the time of Marx's arrival, and of the social network in which Marx lived and traveled, see Boris Nicolaievsky and Otto

Maenchen-Helfen, "The Communist Artisans of Paris," pp. 81–91 in their *Karl Marx: Man and Fighter* (London, [1933] 1973).

49. Marx, "On the Jewish Question," in T. B. Bottomore, ed., *Karl Marx: Early Writings* (New York, 1963), p. 14.

50. Ibid., p. 13 (*MEW*, 1:354–355). *Bürgerliche Gesellschaft* is a critical phrase for the comparison I will make later between Marx and Weber. The translation of *Bürger* can imply the independent legal fact of the possession of legal rights, as in "citizen," or simply an economic or geographical position, as in "burgher," "city dweller," or "member of the middle class." In his earliest writing, Marx often used *Bürger* in the first, much more normative sense, as in his "Defense of the Moselle Correspondent," written in January 1843, where he employs *bürgerlichen* to indicate the "civic" heart which is not compromised by private, capitalist interests (see n. 46 above). But as Marx's writing moves into its materialist phase, it is the second, more instrumental use of *Bürger* which is the truer translation, for Marx now clearly identifies civic society with material life itself. Thus, in the ninth "Thesis on Feuerbach," written in 1845, Marx discusses "the perception of the single individuals in the civil [*bürgerlich*] society" (Nathan Rotenstreich, *Basic Problems of Marx's Philosophy* [Indianapolis, 1965], p. 82), and in the later writings *bürgerliche Gesellschaft* becomes synonymous with purely instrumental bourgeois capitalism. See, e.g., Marx's "Afterword" to the second German edition of *Capital*, vol. 1, where he writes about "the development . . . of modern bourgeois society [*bürgerliche Gesellschaft*]" (Moscow, n.d., p. 13 [*MEW*, 23:18]). In Weber's work, in contrast, one finds the first, much more normative meaning of *Bürger* consistently employed. Whereas Marx can be described as following more faithfully Hegel's conception of civil society, Weber was more influenced by Hegel's understanding of the normative role of the state as a mediator of purely individualistic, material interests.

51. Marx, "On the Jewish Question" (n. 49 above), p. 24.

52. Ibid., p. 13.

53. Ibid., p. 15.

54. Ibid., p. 24.

55. Ibid., p. 26, italics added.

56. Ibid., p. 13, italics added.

57. Ibid.

58. Ibid., p. 55.

59. Marx, "Contribution to the Critique of Hegel's *Philosophy of Right*," pp. 41–60 in Bottomore (n. 49 above), pp. 58–59.

60. Ibid., p. 43, italics added.

61. Ibid., p. 44.

62. Ibid., p. 43, italics added.

63. Ibid., p. 44.

64. Ibid., p. 52.

65. Ibid., p. 53.

66. Ibid., p. 52, italics in original (*MEW*, 1:385).

67. Ibid., p. 53.

68. Ibid., p. 47.

69. Ibid., italics in original.

70. Ibid., p. 53, italics in original.

71. Marx, "Kreuznach, in September 1843" (letter to Arnold Ruge, originally published in *Deutsch-Französische Jahrbücher*, February 1844), in Easton and Guddat as "An Exchange of Letters," pp. 211–215, quoting p. 212.

72. Ibid., p. 23, italics added (*MEW*, 1:344).

73. Marx, "Cologne, in May 1843" (letter to Ruge, as in n. 71), ibid., pp. 205–211, quoting p. 206, italics added (*MEW*, 1:338).

74. Marx, "Kreuznach, in September 1843," ibid., p. 212, italics in original.

75. Ibid., p. 213.

76. Ibid., p. 215.

77. Indeed, I have utilized Marx's definition of praxis (along with Parsons' definition of action) to illustrate the dialectical, or multidimensional, understanding of epistemology in vol. 1, ch. 3, sec. 1.

78. Marx, "First Thesis: Old and New Materialism," in Rotenstreich (n. 50 above), p. 27, italics in original but fewer than Marx's in *MEW*, 4:5.

79. Marx, "Third Thesis: Man and Circumstances," ibid., p. 54.

80. "First Thesis," ibid., p. 27, italics in original.

81. "Third Thesis," ibid., p. 54. Engels first published the "Theses on Feuerbach" in 1888 with a few editorial alterations of the 1844 original, which he described as "hurriedly written down, absolutely not intended for publication, but invaluable as the first document in which the ingenious germ of the new world-view is put down" (*MEW*, 3:547, n. 1). One of Engels' editorial deletions is the term "self-changing," which Marx notes as equivalent to "human activity" in the Third Thesis. Both versions are in *MEW*.

82. "First Thesis," p. 27.

83. Marx, "Alienated Labour," pp. 120–134 in "Economic and Philosophical Manuscripts" (Bottomore [n. 49 above]), p. 127.

84. Ibid., p. 126, (*MEW*, supp. I, p. 515).

85. Ibid., p. 127.

86. Marx, "Private Property and Communism" pp. 152–167 in "Economic and Philosophical Manuscripts," p. 158, italics in original.

87. Ibid.

88. Ibid., italics deleted.

89. Ibid., p. 157, italics altered.

90. Ibid., p. 158.

91. Ibid., p. 159, italics in original.

92. "Alienated Labour," p. 127, italics altered.

93. "Private Property and Communism," p. 159, italics altered.

94. "Alienated Labour," p. 128, italics added.

95. Ibid., p. 127.

96. Ibid., p. 129.

97. Ibid., pp. 122–123, italics in original.

98. Ibid., p. 122.

99. Ibid., p. 128.

100. Ibid., p. 125, italics in original.

101. Marx, "Wages of Labour," pp. 69–84 in "Economic and Philosophical Manuscripts," p. 72.

102. "Alienated Labour," pp. 123, 124.

103. Ibid., p. 125, italics added.

104. There is also, I must add, a tilt toward instrumentalism even in the concept of praxis itself. In the second Thesis, Marx argues for the identification of theory and practice, asserting that objectivity is not a question of abstract theoretical standards but, rather, a matter of whether this theory can be utilized successfully vis-à-vis the material world. Theory only becomes real, he argues, in practical action: "The dispute over the reality or non-reality of his [man's] thinking isolated from practice is a purely *scholastic* question" (Rotenstreich's translation [n. 78 above], p. 47, italics in original). Taken literally, this position eliminates the true independence of intentionality and purpose, since it argues that the subjective side—in Marx's terms, the reference to theoretical reason—is not forceful as an independent activity, as purely mental or philosophical argument. This position indicates how far Marx has moved by 1845 from his earlier writings, where critical philosophical activity was viewed as forceful in itself. It also helps to explain the more one-sided character of Marx's critiques of Feuerbach in the Fourth through Seventh Theses. Rotenstreich articulates this tension in Marx's praxis concept very precisely when he notes that with the definition of action as practice "a question is raised about historical materialism itself":

> If theory exists without actualization in the identity between theory and practice, the position that theory is entirely determined by the historical process cannot be maintained. The force of theory is independent, and as such it requires the acknowledgment of historical reflection. . . . The complete historicity of consciousness and of reason are not possible, and hence [the] analyses of the concept of "praxis" leads to a conclusion directed against the extravagance of historical materialism. (Pp. 43–44.)

105. Marx's "Economic and Philosophical Manuscripts" actually takes the form of long quotations and notations from the writings of French and English political economists and Marx's commentaries upon them.

As to these empirical laws, this is not to say that Marx accepted them wholly, for he certainly did not. His critical attitude toward political economy will be explored shortly.

106. "Alienated Labour," p. 132.

107. Ibid., p. 120.

108. Marx, "Needs, Production, and Division of Labour," pp. 168–188 in "Economic and Philosophical Manuscripts," pp. 173–174.

109. Marx, "The Relationship of Private Property," pp. 137–144 in "Economic and Philosophical Manuscripts," p. 138.

110. "Wages of Labour," p. 79.

111. Ibid., p. 76.

112. Ibid.

113. Marx, "Rent of Land," pp. 103–119 in "Economic and Philosophical Manuscripts," p. 105.

114. "Alienated Labour," p. 127.

115. Ibid., p. 121, italics deleted.

116. Ibid., pp. 121–122, italics added.

117. Ibid., p. 123, italics added. Although there are significant points of disagreement between my position and Louis Dumont's important argument in *From Mandeville to Marx* (Chicago, 1977), on this fundamental point we completely agree. Dumont writes:

> Marx turns to the economy as to something pertinent to his categorical imperative, to his revolutionary faith. What does he find? He finds a discipline that, in order to constitute itself as an independent science, has had not only to neglect moral issues but to proclaim that they are irrelevant within its precincts, where the facts will deliver the norms. . . . It is not to be wondered at that Marx found economic theory indispensable as affording a scientific demonstration of what had hitherto been an ethical norm. (P. 147.)

More than any other contemporary interpreter, Dumont has emphasized the close continuity between Marx's conception of action and that of the classical economists of his day.

The only other critique of which I am aware emerges from the ostensibly "Marxist" polemic of the British historian E. P. Thompson, whose understanding of the limitations of political economy follows from his critical commitment to a more voluntaristic political praxis (a correspondence I will develop at some length in ch. 10, below). Thompson's criticism is worth quoting at some length, for it invokes the same general logic that I have offered here even while it is launched from otherwise very different premises.

> From the outside, in the 1840's it [political economy] appeared to Marx as ideology, or, worse, apologetics. He entered within it in order to overthrow it. But, once inside, however many of its categories he fractured

(and how many times), the structure remained. For the premises supposed that it was possible to isolate economic activities in this way, and to develop these as a first-order science *of society*. It is more accurate to say that Marx . . . did not so much remain within the structure of "Political Economy" as develop an *anti*-structure, but within its premises. The postulates ceased to be the self-interest of men and became the logic and forms of capital, to which men were subordinated; capital was disclosed, not as the benign donor of benefits, but as the appropriator of surplus labour; factional "interests" were disclosed as antagonistic classes; and contradiction displaced the sum progress. But what we have at the end, is not the overthrow of "Political Economy" but *another* "Political Economy." [Thus,] Marxism was marked, at a critical stage in its development, by the categories of Political Economy: the chief of which was the notion *of* the "economic ," as a first-order activity, capable of isolation in this way, as the object of a science giving rise to laws whose operation would override second-order activities. . . . Marx has moved across an invisible conceptual line from *Capital* (an abstraction of Political Economy, which is his proper concern) to *capitalism* ("the complicated bourgeois system"), that is, the whole society. . . . But the whole society comprises many activities and relations (of power, of consciousness, sexual, cultural, normative) which are not the concern of Political Economy, and for which it has no terms. . . . Political Economy, including Marx's "anti" structure, had no terms—had deliberately, and for the purposes of its analytical science, *excluded* the terms—which become, immediately, essential if we are to comprehend societies and histories. Political Economy has terms for use-value, for exchange-value, for monetary, and for surplus-value, but not for normative value. (*The Poverty of Theory and Other Essays* [London, 1978], pp. 252–256, 356, italics in original.)

118. "Rent of Land," p. 120.

119. Ibid., p. 124. It should be clear, then, that I am not arguing here that Marx accepted a utilitarian understanding of human nature. Nothing could be further from my point. Marx was a radical humanist, in ideological terms, because he envisioned a mode of relationship far different from the utilitarian. He was a rationalist-collectivist in presuppositional terms, on the other hand, precisely because he believed that, in capitalist society, the alienation of this human potential made people subject to the coercion of economic laws. In a later discussion of the founder of the utilitarian school, Jeremy Bentham, Marx emphasizes his *historical* approach to the relation between human nature and the presuppositions of social action.

He that would criticize all human acts, movements, relations, etc., by the principle of utility, must first deal with human nature in general, and then with human nature as modified in each historical epoch. Bentham makes short work of it. With the dryest naïveté he takes the modern shopkeeper, especially the English shopkeeper, as the normal man. Whatever is useful to this queer normal man, and to his world, is absolutely useful. This yard-measure, then, he applies to past, present, and future. (*Capital*, vol. 1 [1867; Moscow, 1962], p. 609, n. 2.)

In accepting part of the logic of political economy, Marx accepts utilitarian action for the present, but he will not follow Bentham in applying this narrow standard to the past or to the future. Nor will he argue that this kind of action presents a valid epistemological position *per se*, in any historical period. (As noted earlier [vol. 1, ch. 3, sec, 2.1], Bentham's utilitarianism is only one variant of an instrumental approach to action. Marx does not have to accept the pleasure-pain principle to adopt what is nonetheless a completely rationalist approach to capitalist action.)

Dumont (n. 117 above), in his otherwise penetrating discussion of Marx's approach to individual rationality, fails to emphasize sufficiently this distinction between Marx's understanding of the species potential of human nature and its alienated degeneration in the modern world. As a result, he gives the incorrect impression that because Marx incorporated utilitarian presuppositions into his social theory he accepted the amoral quality of political economy itself. This problem in Dumont's analysis ultimately is related to his failure to distinguish questions of action from questions of order, and I will discuss it further in the conclusion to ch. 3.

120. Ibid., p. 121.

121. Ibid., p. 120, italics added.

122. Marx, "Profit of Capital," pp. 85–102 in "Economic and Philosophical Manuscripts," p. 98.

123. Ibid., p. 102.

124. "Wages of Labour," p. 83, italics in original.

125. Ibid., p. 70.

126. "Rent of Land," pp. 109–111.

127. "Wages of Labour," p. 70.

128. Ibid., p. 75.

129. "Profit of Capital," p. 85, italics added.

130. I distinguish social epistemology from epistemology in general to indicate that while a theorist may well acknowledge the importance of subjectivity in his abstract approach to knowledge, it is the specific relation between means and ends—whether action is defined as completely efficient or as more or less normative—that produces the consequential epistemology for social theory. For an extended discussion of this issue, see vol. 1, ch. 3, sec. 1.

131. "Private Property and Communism," p. 156.

132. "Alienated Labour," p. 131.

133. Ibid., italics added.

134. Ibid., emphasis deleted.

135. Ibid., p. 126.

136. "Private Property and Communism," p. 159, italics altered.

137. "Alienated Labour," p. 125, italics added.

138. Ibid., p. 131.

139. This early discussion by Marx of the capitalist-proletarian relationship suggests precisely the kind of theoretical reasoning involved in Hegel's famous analysis of the master-slave relationship, which is also rooted in a symbiotic and, in presuppositional terms, voluntaristic emotional relationship. Hegel writes: "What is done by the bondsman is properly an action on the part of the master. . . . What the master does to the other he should also do to himself, and what the bondsman does to himself he should do to the other also." (G. W. F. Hegel, *The Phenomenology of Mind* [1807; London, 1967], p. 236.)

140. "Alienated Labour," p. 131.

141. Ibid., p. 132.

142. Ibid.

143. "Private Property and Communism," p. 159, italics added.

144. Ibid., p. 160. Italics in original.

145. "Alienated Labour," p. 132.

146. "Private Property and Communism," p. 153.

147. Ibid., p. 159.

148. Ibid., p. 161.

149. Ibid., p. 160.

150. E.g., David McLellan, Marx's recent biographer, writes about this discussion: "Marx . . . described in a few tightly written and pregnant pages his own idea of communism" (*Karl Marx* [n. 40 above], p. 118).

151. "Needs, Production, and the Division of Labour," p. 176, italics added.

152. Ibid., italics added.

153. Althusser (n. 14 above), pp. 32–34, 37–39, 153–160, 167–168.

CHAPTER THREE

1. Marx and Engels first met in Paris in September 1844. *The Holy Family* was finished by December of that year and published in February 1845. It was written principally by Marx, with only limited collaboration by Engels. In the spring of 1845, Marx went to Brussels, where he spent several months reading heavily in the French literature on economic and social history. When Engels arrived in April, Marx had already worked out the main lines of his economic interpretation of history. According to Engels' later recollection: "When I again met Marx at Brussels . . . he had it [the new theory] already worked out, and put it before me, in terms almost as clear as those in which I have stated it here" ("Preface to the English Edition of the Communist Manifesto of 1888," Marx and Engels,

Selected Works [Moscow, 1962], 1:29). During the summer of 1845, Marx and Engels took a six-week trip to England which they spent in Manchester reading English political economy, both radical and liberal. *The German Ideology* was written collaboratively between September 1845 and August 1846. It responded, first, to continuing criticism from the German socialists and particularly to their negative responses to *The Holy Family*, and, second, to the need Marx and Engels felt to systematize their new social and economic knowledge and to formalize the perspective which Marx had already established. By the time Marx began writing his reply to Proudhon in 1847, published in that year as *The Poverty of Philosophy*, he had already begun actively meeting and collaborating with communist workers' organizations and politically committed intellectuals. It is clear not only from Engels' statements but from the historical evidence that Marx can justifiably be referred to as the principal author in their collaborative work, and I will consider him as such. See David McLellan, *Karl Marx* (New York, 1973), pp. 137–188. This is not to say, of course, that Engels did not play an indispensable role.

2. Marx and Engels, *The German Ideology* (1847; New York, 1970), p. 105.

3. Ibid., pp. 65–66.

4. Ibid., p. 64.

5. Ibid., p. 105. In his conclusion to *The Holy Family* (in Loyd D. Easton and Kurt H. Guddat, eds., *Writings of the Young Marx on Philosophy and Society* [New York, 1967], pp. 361–398), Marx approvingly quotes from Bentham's *Théories des peines et des récompenses* (3d ed.; Paris, 1826), in which Bentham, in Marx's words, "opposes the 'general interest in the political sense' " (p. 398). It is revealing to compare Bentham's classical utilitarian argument with Marx's theory of the state in *The German Ideology*, which I have just presented in sec. 1.1. This is the passage from Bentham which Marx quoted:

> The interest of individuals . . . should give way to the public interest. But . . . what does this mean? Is not each individual part of the public as much as any other? The public interest you personify is only an *abstract* term: it represents only the mass of individual interests. . . . Individual interests are the only *real* interests. (Ibid., italics added.)

Marx has clearly followed the same logic as Bentham, rejecting the general interest as a nonreal entity because it exists only in thought and arguing that only concrete, material interests actually exist. Of course, for Bentham's emphasis on the individual, Marx has substituted the empirical focus on class, although at other points Bentham himself takes a more anti-individualist approach.

6. Marx, *The German Ideology*, p. 54.

7. Ibid.

8. Ibid., italics in original.

9. Ibid., p. 80.

10. Ibid., pp. 79–80.

11. Ibid., p. 80.

12. Ibid, italics in original.

13. Ibid., p. 106.

14. Ibid., p. 57.

15. Ibid., p. 52, italics in original.

16. Ibid., p. 99, italics in original.

17. Ibid., p. 108.

18. Ibid., p. 42, italics in original. This is not to say, however, that Marx has now accepted a simple materialist epistemology. He still views "man" as purposive, but it is now clear that from the origins of human society this purposiveness has been distorted by a forced focus on subsistence and means. This raises the question of whether "alienation" is actually as historically specific to capitalism as Marx at other points contends. I will investigate this problem further below.

19. Ibid., p. 42.

20. Ibid.

21. Ibid., p. 50.

22. Ibid., p. 42.

23. Ibid., p. 50.

24. Ibid., p. 54.

25. Ibid.

26. Marx, "Letter to P. V. Annenkov," Brussels, December 28, 1846, in appendixes to Marx, *The Poverty of Philosophy* (New York, 1963), p. 180.

27. See, e.g., *The German Ideology*, pp. 68–78 and *The Poverty of Philosophy*, pp. 135–144.

28. Marx and Engels, *The Holy Family* (1845), pp. 361–398 in Easton and Guddat, *op. cit.*, p. 379, (n. 5 above), italics in original. For the same reversal of Marx's earlier "chains" metaphor, see *The German Ideology*, p. 41.

29. *The Holy Family*, p. 379.

30. *The Holy Family* (Moscow, 1956), p. 160 (*Marx-Engels Werke* [Berlin, 1962], 2:126).

31. *The Holy Family*, in Easton and Guddat, p. 382, italics in original.

32. *The German Ideology*, pp. 58–59.

33. Ibid., p. 61.

34. *The Holy Family*, pp. 364–365.

35. *The Poverty of Philosophy*, p. 125.

36. *The Holy Family*, p. 375.

37. Ibid., pp. 377–378.

38. Ibid., p. 383.

39. *The German Ideology*, p. 37. To prevent any misunderstanding

about my purpose here, I should emphasize that to criticize Marx's attack on these critical German idealists is not to accept the idealists' own theory as necessarily a valid one. While the idealists' arguments which I have produced here were, for the most part, legitimate in themselves, they usually were part of a general theoretical framework that was altogether one-sided in its emphasis. Marx's criticisms of these arguments, however, were also incorrect, because he allowed no autonomy to the normative components of action and order, rejecting positions he himself had once forcefully promoted. Insofar as Marx was now more sensitive to an exaggerated antimaterialist theory, he could have criticized the German moralists from a multidimensional perspective.

40. *The Holy Family*, p. 367, italics added.

41. *The German Ideology*, p. 53. There is clearly a contradiction between this kind of historical approach to alienation, where the nature of specifically capitalist life is used to justify a completely naturalistic, materialist theory, and the vision of human life, presented elsewhere in *The German Ideology*, as always having been oriented primarily to tool use and to acquiring the means of subsistence. It is conceivable that Marx now believes that alienation begins with human history itself, in which case this dilemma would be resolved. There are, however, several reasons to argue against this possibility. First, tool-using and concentration on the means of subsistence characterized even the pre-surplus period of primitive communism, which for both Marx and Engels is often pointed to as a kind of adumbration of communist "species" life and nonalienated existence. Second, although Marx does acknowledge that alienation develops simultaneously with the division of labor itself, tool using and subsistence orientation precede any division of labor properly so called. Third, at various points Marx argues that even feudal society is relatively nonalienated, more personalistic and praxis-informed than capitalist society, and that because the latter is the only historical period to produce an economy oriented entirely to impersonal exchange it is the only one to produce completely instrumental, means-oriented action. Although it is possible that this dilemma could be resolved by formulating different kinds and degrees of alienation, Marx himself never does so. The very existence of this deep ambiguity in Marx's work indicates how far he has moved from a multidimensional sociological orientation, for it raises the specter if not the reality of human history as exclusively means-oriented and instrumental. It is the existence of this kind of retrospective historicizing that helps to explain why interpreters have been able to ignore completely the alienation concept in Marx's later works, for if consciousness was never subjectively informed there certainly is no need to understand the processes by which it became transformed into its present form of technical-instrumentalism.

42. *The Holy Family*, p. 390.

43. *The Poverty of Philosophy*, p. 51.

44. See, e.g., *The Holy Family*, p. 362; *The Poverty of Philosophy*, p. 81; and "Letter to P. V. Annenkov" (n. 26 above), p. 186.

45. *The Holy Family*, p. 363.

46. *The Poverty of Philosophy*, pp. 65, 69.

47. Ibid., pp. 166–168.

48. Ibid., pp. 41–42. The elements of Marx's theoretical strategy presented in this paragraph will be examined in much greater detail in my later discussion of *Capital.*

49. *The Holy Family*, p. 363.

50. Ibid.

51. *The German Ideology*, p. 53.

52. Ibid.

53. Ibid., p. 93; cf. pp. 56, 86.

54. *The Holy Family*, p. 370. It would be wrong, in other words, to view the exclusively economic vision of communism outlined in these writings, or later in *The Communist Manifesto* for that matter, as an indication that Marx has given up completely on his humanistic commitment to species being and to the spiritual transformation of the self. This is clarified at a much later point in Marx's career in his "Critique of the Gotha Program" (1875), which I will discuss at some length later in this volume. When Marx writes in this later document that the early phase of communism is still characterized by the distributive standard *"to each according to his abilities,"* he indicates that material incentives, exchange relationships, and utilitarian calculation will still be central to the social order of the first period of postrevolutionary society; they will simply occur within a more egalitarian framework. Only the distributive standard of the later phase—*"from each according to his abilities, to each according to his needs"*—indicates a nonalienated social environment, where altruism and morality rather than utilitarian calculation would form the basis for work and social organization.

Although this later analysis by Marx offers a more accurate view of his continuing humanism, it in no way alters the objectivism of his understanding of the early phases of the struggle for socialism, both within capitalism and in the postrevolutionary society itself. To the contrary, it reaffirms that the shift I have described in Marx's theory of the transition to communism has indeed occurred.

55. Ibid., p. 368, italics in original.

56. *The German Ideology*, p. 56, italics in original.

57. Ibid., p. 92, italics added.

58. *The Holy Family*, p. 368, italics in original.

59. *The German Ideology*, pp. 56–57, italics altered.

60. Ibid., p. 82.

61. Ibid., p. 70.

62. Ibid., p. 46; cf. pp. 69–70.

63. Ibid., p. 70.

64. Ibid., p. 82, italics added.

65. *The Poverty of Philosophy*, p. 172.

66. Ibid., italics added.

67. Ibid.

68. Ibid.

69. Ibid., p. 173.

70. Ibid., p. 175. Marx is quoting here from George Sand, *Jean Ziska:* "Le combat ou la mort; la lutte sanguinaire ou le néant. C'est ainsi que la question est invinciblement posée."

71. For an interpretive effort that emphasizes the tight logical systematicity of Marx's theorizing, see Neil J. Smelser's introductory essay to his selection of writings by Marx, *Karl Marx on Society and Social Change* (Chicago, 1973), pp. vii–xxxvii.

72. The best discussion of the nature and function of residual categories in social theory is to be found in Talcott Parsons, *The Structure of Social Action* (New York [1937], 1968), pp. 16 ff.

73. *The German Ideology*, p. 77.

74. Ibid.

75. Ibid., p. 71.

76. Ibid., pp. 87–88.

77. As Marx and Engels wrote in their preface to the 1872 German edition of the *Manifesto:* "However much the state of things may have altered during the last twenty-five years, the general principles laid down in this Manifesto are, on the whole, as correct today as ever" (in *Selected Works* [n. 1 above], 1:21).

I should perhaps mention once again that Engels himself affirmed that the framework of the *Manifesto* must be considered to be Marx's own. As Engels wrote in the preface to the German edition of 1883, "the basic thought running through the Manifesto . . . belongs solely and exclusively to Marx" (ibid., pp. 24–25). And in the preface to the English edition of 1888, he writes: "The 'Manifesto' being our joint production, I consider myself bound to state that the fundamental proposition, which forms its nucleus, belongs to Marx" (ibid., p. 28).

78. Marx and Engels, *Manifesto of the Communist Party* (1848), in *Selected Works* (n. 1 above), 1:34–65, quoting 36.

79. Ibid., p. 37.

80. Ibid., p. 36.

81. Ibid.

82. Ibid., p. 44.

83. Ibid., p. 36.

84. Ibid.

85. Ibid., p. 34. Marx and Engels, *Manifest der Kommunistischen Par-*

tei (Munich, 1969), p. 48; hereafter cited as *MKP.* Where I have altered the English translation, I will note the German original.

The full sentence is informed by the preceding clause, "In earlier epochs of history . . ." In other words, Marx intends here both the presuppositional point I am emphasizing—that society is bound by a collective order that is instrumental in form—but also a more propositional point as well. He is arguing about how order is formed in precapitalist as against capitalist societies: in earlier precapitalist societies, this hierarchical and collective order was a more finely graded one.

86. Marx and Engels, *Manifesto* (n. 78 above), p. 34.

87. Ibid., p. 41.

88. Ibid.

89. Ibid., p. 37.

90. Ibid., p. 41.

91. Ibid., p. 36 (*MKP*, p. 50).

92. Ibid., p. 35.

93. Ibid.

94. This tight relationship between Marx's conception of action, or volition, and his concrete theory of history was forcefully articulated by Henri de Man in 1927, in some passages which are worth reproducing:

> Every categorical interpretation of history is the intellectual auxiliary construction of a volition which raises to the rank of final cause, the phenomena on which its primary aim is to act. If Marxism selects the economic category as the cause of social evolution, this means no more than that Marxists consider that their main task must be to set economic motives at work, in order thus to realize their vision of the future. The aim of the will decides the form of knowledge. A reputedly objective cognition of causes is only a mirage of the subjective valuation of motives. . . . A belief in economic *causation* is, fundamentally, a belief in economic *motive.* Volition is the starting-point of the theory. . . . If we regard economic causation as a first cause, this only means . . . that the motive of economic interest is the ultimate determinant of the will of human beings who live in society. (*The Psychology of Socialism* [New York, (1926) 1928], pp. 357, 362, italics in original.)

I would disagree with de Man only in his assessment of the ahistorical character of this commitment to economic motive. Some Marxists may have been economic hedonists, but Marx himself was not, and the causal connection between instrumental action and the objective history which de Man so forcefully describes holds only for the historical period during which alienation itself holds sway.

95. Marx and Engels, *Manifesto*, p. 35.

96. Ibid., italics added.

97. Ibid.

98. Ibid.

99. Ibid., p. 37.
100. Ibid., p. 40.
101. Ibid.
102. Ibid., p. 39.
103. Ibid., p. 45.
104. Ibid.
105. Ibid.
106. Ibid., p. 42.
107. Ibid., italics added.
108. Ibid., p. 54 (*MKP*, 70). The English translator's addition of "compelled *by the force of circumstances*" (my italics) adds an unnecessary but telling phrase to the deterministic quality of the original text.
109. Ibid., p. 42.
110. Ibid., pp. 43, 45.
111. Ibid., p. 45.
112. Ibid., p. 44; cf. p. 54.
113. Ibid., p. 48.
114. Ibid., p. 55, italics added.
115. Ibid., p. 56–57. *MKP*, p. 74.
116. Ibid., p. 60, italics added.
117. Ibid., p. 58.
118. Ibid., p. 62.
119. Ibid., p. 44.
120. Ibid., p. 43.
121. Ibid., p. 46.
122. This argument is made, for example, by Daniel Bell, "In Search of Marxist Humanism," *Survey*, no. 32 (April–June 1960), pp. 21–31.
123. *Manifesto*, p. 36.
124. Ibid., p. 40.
125. Ibid., pp. 40, 49.
126. Ibid., p. 54.
127. Ibid., p. 47.
128. Ibid., pp. 53–54. Nowhere in Marx's later readings do we find an elaboration of the kinds of social processes which the creation of such altruistic free association would involve. Even in the "Critique of the Gotha Program," where the division between utilitarian and non-utilitarian phases of communism is made completely explicit, this discussion does not occur. One reason for this absence must be that any such analysis would have involved Marx in the elaboration of an anti-instrumentalist sociological theory, a step which would have returned him to the so-called idealist theorizing of his early writing.
129. Anthony Giddens, *Capitalism and Modern Social Theory* (Cambridge, 1971), pp. xi–xv, 185–190.

130. Dick Atkinson, *Orthodox Consensus and Radical Alternative* (New York, 1972), p. 41, italics added.

131. Bertell Ollman, *Alienation: Marx's Conception of Man in Capitalist Society* (Cambridge, 1971), p. 202, italics added.

132. Shlomo Avineri, *The Social and Political Thought of Karl Marx* (Cambridge, 1968), p. 42.

133. Ollman has listed three criteria for proving that the theory of the later Marx constitutes a radical departure from the earlier:

> First, one must show that Marx was aware of such a break, that he actually and clearly refers to his earlier views as incorrect. Second, one must show that what Marx either approves or disapproves of in his first works is treated in a contrary manner later on. And third, one must show that a significant number of early concepts do not enter into later works at all. (*Alienation*, p. xiii.)

Ollman believes that none of these criteria can, in fact, be met. I would contend, to the contrary, that my preceding analysis has demonstrated each of these points to be true.

134. For a general discussion of this issue, see vol. 1, ch. 3, secs. 1 and 2.1. (For my use of the term "sociological epistemology," below, see vol. 1, ch. 3, n. 133.)

135. Giddens (n. 129 above), p. 21, italics added.

136. Ibid., p. 13.

137. Avineri, pp. 38–39.

138. Ibid., p. 39.

139. Ollman, p. 114.

140. Giddens, pp. 24–34.

141. Ibid., p. 16.

142. Ibid., p. 19.

143. Avineri, p. 69.

144. Ibid., p. 81.

145. Ibid., p. 256. I must admit here to a certain "reading in." Avineri simply distinguishes between Marx's "philosophical system," on the one hand, and the "more concrete predictions" which Marx "could not relate to his philosophical premises," on the other. The concrete predictions, he suggests, simply "grew out of his [Marx's] ordinary socio-political intuition." (Ibid., p. 256.) This discussion indicates once again Avineri's general failure to distinguish philosophical from sociological reasoning. In between philosophical and purely concrete intuitive thought, there is surely sociological theory, which is at once more empirical than philosophy and more analytical and systematic than intuition.

146. Ollman, p. 239.

147. Ibid., pp. 240–241.

148. Ibid., p. 242.

149. It is interesting to note that Atkinson is forced to make reference to the same kind of residual categories as Ollman. Atkinson, as noted above, claims that Marx sees subjective projections as the source of material power. In order to understand, however, why the proletariat has not made a revolution, he cannot actually utilize the alienation theory, since Marx has already moved by late 1844 to an entirely instrumentalist theory of empirical conflict and association. Instead, Atkinson turns to Marcuse's Freud-inspired analysis of false consciousness and internalization, arguing that Marcuse "attempt[ed] to expand the body of his [Marx's] work in much the way we might have expected from Marx himself if he had not died before Freud made his singular contribution to social thought" (Atkinson [n. 130 above], pp. 36–37; cf. pp. 37–40, 60–65, 115–126). But the very fact that Atkinson must turn to Freudian ideas indicates that Marx's theory of false consciousness was, in fact, quite antithetical to the Freudian one which Marcuse created.

150. Bell (n. 122 above), p. 26.

151. At one point, Bell acknowledges that the later Marx still conceived of the abolition of the division of labor (and, hence, alienation) as possible, but he dismisses this continued reference as "utopian," given Marx's overwhelming emphasis on the nationalization of property as the key to the creating of communism. Yet this, of course, is precisely the point. Marx's proposal now appears to be utopian because while he remains ideologically committed to ending alienation, the instrumentalism of his description of the communist transformation has made ending alienation a mere epiphenomenon of material change. Like the interpreters inspired by the New Left, Bell conflates Marx's presuppositional reasoning with his ideology, although with opposite intent. The recent analysts have tried to argue from Marx's ideological humanism to voluntaristic presuppositions, while Bell tried to argue from Marx's instrumentalist presuppositions to an antihumanistic ideology.

152. Louis Althusser, "Marxism and Humanism," pp. 219–247 in his *For Marx* (London, 1969), p. 230, italics altered.

153. Ibid.

154. Ibid., p. 230, n. 7.

155. For Althusser's discussions of the epistemological break, see ibid., pp. 32–34, 37–39, 153–160, 167–168.

156. Setting 1845 as the date for this supposed break merely illustrates further the arbitrary character of Althusser's judgment. Marx had begun to accept an instrumentalist perspective on action—a *theoretical antihumanism*" in Althusser's sense (ibid., p. 230)—as early as 1842. This emerging perspective was in continual conflict with his more voluntaristic theory throughout the rest of the early writings. The year 1845 does, however, finally mark the end of Marx's theoretical ambivalence.

157. Herbert Marcuse, *Reason and Revolution* (Boston, [1941] 1960), pp. 273–274.

158. Ibid., p. 304.

159. Ibid., p. 302.

160. Jürgen Habermas, "The Idea of the Theory of Knowledge as Social Theory," pp. 43–63 in his *Knowledge and Human Interests* (1968; Boston, 1971), p. 43.

161. Ibid., p. 44.

162. Ibid., p. 53.

163. The ambiguity of Habermas' interpretation of Marx is demonstrated even in his criticism of Marx's instrumentalism, for to claim that Marx's identification of praxis with labor is the cause of Marx's instrumentalism is to argue simply metaphorically. On the one hand, Marx did not think that *precapitalist* labor was necessarily instrumental, for he believed that such labor allowed subjectivity some intrusion into the creation of the object. On the other hand, Marx did not confine instrumental action simply to labor in capitalist society, but extended it to all forms of action and association in that period. The point, then, is not that Marx adopts an instrumental, technical perspective because he identifies practice with labor, but that he identified praxis with the labor of capitalist society because he accepted action in general as instrumental and alienated.

164. For a general discussion of the nature of this "utilitarian dilemma," which was first formulated in this systematic form by Parsons, see my earlier discussion in vol. 1, ch. 3, sec. 3. As I made clear there, the "rationalist tradition" to which I am referring here is not that invoked in the rationalist-empiricist debate, where the "rationalist" position indicates aprioristic reasoning. By rationalism I am referring to the tradition of social theory which assumes action to be an instrumental and purely efficient exercise.

165. The following reading of intellectual history has been most informed by the interpretive works of Elie Halévy, *The Growth of Philosophic Radicalism* (1901–1903; New York, 1972); Talcott Parsons, *The Structure of Social Action* (n. 12 above); H. Stuart Hughes, *Consciousness and Society* (New York, 1958); and Noel Annan, *The Curious Strength of Positivism in English Political Thought* (London, 1959). I depart from these works, however, in significant ways.

166. In order to avoid confusion on this too often ambiguous point, I should reaffirm here—in line with the earlier discussion in vol. 1—that for Hobbes the "order problem" involves two questions that are, in fact, analytically differentiated: the problem of social harmony and equilibrium and the problem of patterned versus atomistic social arrangements. Since Locke also made the same conflation, for the purposes of this discussion I do not insist on separating the two issues. Hobbes took a

collectivist position on presuppositional order; he also posited equilibrium as impossible without such a collective force. It was because Locke believed that equilibrium could be obtained without collective order that he tried to maintain an individualist position on the order problem in a presuppositional sense, i.e., in the sense of order as patterning. Although these distinctions seem rather superfluous at this point, they have had enormous repercussions in contemporary sociological theory, where, e.g., a Marxist solution to order is associated with the exclusive emphasis on social conflict. (See vol. 1, ch. 3.)

167. John Locke, *The Second Treatise of Government* (1690; Indianapolis, 1952), p. 6.

168. Thomas Hobbes, *Leviathan* (1651; New York, 1962), p. 98.

169. Although the association of Marx with the rationalist tradition should be amply demonstrated by the argument of this chapter, there is Marx's personal testimony as well.

In coming to terms with German idealism in the transitional years 1844–1847, Marx warmly embraced the French and English materialist traditions. In *The German Ideology*, while he is ostensibly tracing the impact of the industrial revolution on the social theories that emphasized rational action and exploitative order, there can be little doubt that he is, in fact, tracing the lineage of his own intellectual position.

> The advances made by the theory of utility and exploitation, its various phases, are closely connected with the various periods of development of the bourgeoisie. . . . Hobbes and Locke had before their eyes both the earlier development of the Dutch bourgeoisie (both of them had lived for some time in Holland) and the first political actions by which the English theory and the preceding development of the Dutch and English bourgeoisie emerged. . . . In the case of Helvétius and Holbach, the actual content of the theory . . . reflected not so much the actual fact but rather the desire to reduce all relations to the relation of exploitation, and to explain the intercourse of people from material needs and the ways of satisfying them. . . . Helvétius and Holbach were confronted not only by English theory and the preceding development of the Dutch and English bourgeoisie, but also by the French bourgeoisie which was still struggling for its free development. . . . These premises [among others] gave the theory of Helvétius and Holbach its peculiar universal colouring, but at the same time deprived it of the positive economic content that was still to be found among the English. The theory which for the English still was simply the registration of a fact becomes for the French, a philosophical system. This generality devoid of positive content, such as we find it in Helvétius and Holbach, is essentially different from the substantial comprehensive view which is first found in Bentham and Mill.
>
> The content of the theory of exploitation that was neglected by Helvétius and Holbach was developed and systematized by the Phys-

iocrats—who worked at the same time as Holbach; but . . . they remained in thrall to the feudal outlook insofar as they declared landownership and land cultivation to be that which determines the whole structure of society.

The theory of exploitation owes its further development in England to Godwin, and especially to Bentham, who gradually re-incorporated the economic content which the French had neglected. . . . The complete union of the theory of utility with political economy is to be found, finally, in Mill. (Marx and Engels, *The German Ideology*, [n. 2 above], pp. 111–112).

When we recall that Marx produced this intellectual history at the same time that he first articulated a theory which explained individual interaction "from material needs and the ways of satisfying them" and which gave to the general theory of exploitation an extremely specific economic content, it is clear that Marx is discussing those whom he considers his crucial intellectual forebears. At one point in this same discussion, he acknowledges that the anti-individualist strand of utilitarian theory supplied him with his general orientation: "The idea had already been stated in political economy that the chief relations of exploitation are determined by production by and large, independently of the will of individuals who find them already in existence" (ibid., p. 113). At the same time, he argues that even this Benthamite utilitarianism was blinded to crucial empirical facts because of its ideological commitment to the status quo.

> Prejudiced in favor of the conditions of the bourgeoisie, it could criticize only those relations which had been handed down from a past epoch and were an obstacle to the development of the bourgeoisie. Hence, although the utility theory does expound the connection of all existing relations with economic relations it does so only in a restricted way. (Ibid.)

Marx's own position in the intellectual history of this tradition is now clear: because of his connection with the rising proletariat, Marx would be able to make "the connection to all existing relations with economic relations" in an unrestricted and hence more empirically accurate way.

In *The Holy Family*, Marx particularly emphasizes his connection with eighteenth-century French materialism, asserting that "the followers of Babeuf were crude, uncivilized materialists" but "even mature communism comes *directly* from *French materialism*" (Easton and Guddat [n. 28 above], p. 395, italics in original).

> The latter returned to its mother-country, England, in the form Helvétius had given it. Bentham founded his system of enlightened interest on the morality of Helvétius, just as Owen, proceeding from Bentham's system, founded English communism. (Ibid., italics deleted.)

In fact, Marx concluded this book by reproducing central passages in

Helvétius, Holbach, and Bentham to the effect that collectivist theories inherently produce critical and reformist ideologies (ibid., pp. 396–398).

In *The Poverty of Philosophy*, Marx's attitude toward the radical wing of English, Benthamite political economy is elegiac, and as an antidote to Proudhon's errors he reproduces a six-page quotation from J. F. Bray's "remarkable work," *Labour's Wrongs and Labour's Remedy* (1839). This long excerpt is preceded by these words:

> Anyone who is in any way familiar with the trend of political economy in England cannot fail to know that almost all the socialists in that country have, at different periods, proposed the equalitarian application of the Ricardian theory. We could quote for M. Proudhon: Hodgskin, *Political Economy*, 1827; William Thompson, *An Inquiry into the Principles of the Distribution of Wealth Most Conducive to Human Happiness*, 1824; T. R. Edmonds, *Practical Moral and Political Economy*, 1828, etc., etc., and four pages more of etc. We shall content ourselves with listening to an English Communist, Mr. Bray. (*The Poverty of Philosophy* [n. 26 above], p. 69, italics deleted.)

Three intellectual traditions have usually been associated with Marx's intellectual history: French socialism, English political economy, and German idealism. Only the first two, I believe, were decisive for Marx's presuppositional orientation in his sociology of capitalism. The influence of Hegel is, rather, responsible for Marx's departure from a simplistic application of this orientation in either its French or English form. This departure is clear, first of all, in Marx's historical perspective on his own theory of capitalism. Because he adopts the notion of species-being and alienation from German Romanticism, he can take a more historicist approach to his theory, arguing that its instrumental logic is appropriate only for a limited period of time.

> Hegel has already proved in his *Phänomenologie* how this theory of mutual exploitation, which Bentham expounded *ad nauseum*, could already at the beginning of the present century have been considered a phase of the previous one. . . . The apparent stupidity of merging all the manifold relationships of people in the *one* relation of usefulness, this apparently metaphysical abstraction arises from the fact that, in modern bourgeois society, all relations *are* subordinated in practice to the one abstract monetary-commercial relation. . . . The utility relation [means] that I derive benefit for myself by doing harm to someone else (exploitation de l'homme par l'homme); further . . . the use that I derive from some relation is in general alien to this relation, just as . . . from each ability a product alien to it was demanded, a relation determined by social relations—and this is precisely the relation of utility. *All this is actually the case with the bourgeois.* (*The German Ideology*, pp. 109–110, italics added.)

Hegel also decisively turned Marx against the linearity of materialist theories, convincing him that historical development and social strains followed the dialectical path of thesis, antithesis, synthesis. Thus, Marx describes even the most negative empirical consequences as producing—"behind their backs"—the forces for their positive transformation.

The contemporary subjectification of Marx has been achieved by overemphasizing Hegel's influence and neglecting the impact on him of the rationalist tradition. Ironically, this interpretive strategy can be viewed as a "theoretical subterfuge" that follows, in certain interesting ways, Locke's revision of Hobbes, for it attempts to soften the consequences of Marx's instrumental rationality without explicitly altering his central theoretical tenets. The real casualty of this exercise is not "radical thought," for the direction taken by this camouflaged transformation of Marx is, according to the standards that inform the present discussion, a movement toward a better social theory. The casualty is rather the quality of theoretical reasoning itself. It is theoretical thinking itself which has been seriously weakened by the interpretive developments of recent years, for the wish to transform Marx's thought has seemingly led the interpreters to distort the logic of his actual theory.

There are a few contemporary interpreters who have, however, accurately perceived the instrumentalism of Marx's position, although even they equivocate in certain crucial ways. The Polish theorist Piotr Sztompka emphasizes the rationalism of Marx's theory and his rejection of voluntarism, but he reconciles too easily Marx's emphasis on political activism and creative practice with his emphasis on purely external, economic causation (*System and Function*, [New York, 1974], p. 176). More than any other contemporary analyst, Louis Dumont has perceived the close link between Marx's theorizing and the thinking of classical political economy, and how Marx's vision of rationality produces an individual actor isolated from community (*From Mandeville to Marx* [Chicago, 1977], pp. 111–185). But while Dumont is certainly right to see Marx's work as marking the triumph, not the defeat, of economic man and as constituting a major reason for the continued vitality of instrumental reasoning in modern social thought, he insufficiently recognizes the historicist nature of Marx's vision. By not making it explicit that noninstrumental forms of action characterize Marx's description of both precapitalist and postcapitalist societies, Dumont ignores the crucial function of alienation in Marx's thought. Dumont also overemphasizes the individualistic action of Marx's vision of capitalist man, ignoring the anti-individualist critique of laissez-faire that Marx launched from within the rationalist tradition itself. Because he fails to differentiate the questions of action and order, he does not recognize the innovations that Marx could produce in the approach to order even though he remained wedded to the rationalist approach to action. The uniqueness of Marx's sociology of collectivist rationality, the connection between Marx and Hobbes which truly differentiated Marx from his intellectual predecessors, is much more clearly emphasized by Gianfranco Poggi, who tries to argue, nonetheless, that Marx can be placed in the voluntaristic tradition of social theory as well, a point the preceding argument demonstrates to be false (*Images of Society* [Stanford, Calif., 1972], pp. 148–151; for support of the position I have taken on this last point, see the argument by Percy Cohen in his *Modern Social Theory* [London, 1968], pp. 79–81).

CHAPTER FOUR

1. Robert K. Merton, "On Sociological Theories of the Middle Range," pp. 59–60 in his *On Theoretical Sociology* (New York, 1967); cf., ibid., p. 152, n. 23.

2. Arthur L. Stinchcombe, *Constructing Social Theories* (Baltimore, 1968), p. 25; Whitney Pope, *Durkheim's "Suicide"* (Chicago, 1976). Pope's book is certainly the most elaborate reduction of this sort. Pope defines "theory" in the most resolutely positivistic manner, as concerned solely with specific correlations and propositions. "A theory is, above all, an explanation," he writes, insisting that "if it cannot explain fluctuations in its dependent variable, it is unsuccessful" (p. 146). Pope argues that Durkheim's statistical analysis ignored the independent effects of age, sex, and region, and on the narrow grounds he has articulated he concludes that the theory is unsuccessful. Yet Pope acknowledges that, confronted with these new independent variables, "Durkheim *could* have constructed an adequate theory" and that "to reject that possibility may be to underestimate his skill as a theorist" (ibid., italics added). But the only grounds upon which Durkheim could have so reconstructed his specific explanation are the more generalized and not so empirically contingent assumptions and models which Pope seeks to dismiss as untheoretical! It is not surprising, then, that Pope judges as irrelevant one of the principal theoretical issues which did, in fact, motivate Durkheim's empirical work, i.e., the significance of the social as opposed to the individual approach to order: "The debate over emergence promises to continue," but "whatever the ultimate outcome," it "will probably have little impact upon sociology" (ibid., p. 202).

3. E.E. Evans-Pritchard, *Theories of Primitive Religion* (London, 1965), pp. 48–77.

4. For a direct critique of such positivist analyses, see, e.g., Anthony Giddens' evaluation of the nineteenth-century French literature on suicide and its relation to Durkheim's work, in which he concludes:

> The originality and vitality of Durkheim's work did not lie in the empirical correlations contained in *Suicide:* all of these had been previously documented by other writers. . . . Where Durkheim's work differed decisively was in the attempt to explain previous findings in terms of a coherent sociological theory. . . . No writers before Durkheim had presented a consistent framework of sociological theory which could

bring together the major empirical correlations which had already been established. ("The Suicide Problem in French Sociology," pp. 322–332 in Giddens, *Studies in Social and Political Theory* [New York, 1977], pp. 323–324.)

The same antipositivist point is made in the probing examination of *Suicide* by Toby E. Huff, "Discovery and Interpretation in Sociology: Durkheim on Suicide," *Philosophy of Social Science* 5 (1975):241–257. See also Hanan C. Selvin's careful methodological appreciation of *Suicide*, where an evaluation of the sophistication of Durkheim's statistical methodology is carefully intertwined with an emphasis on the crucial intervening role of more general theoretical insights ("Durkheim's *Suicide:* Further Thoughts on a Methodological Classic" [1958], pp. 113–136 in Robert A. Nisbet, ed., *Emile Durkheim* [Englewood Cliffs, N.J., 1965]).

5. Nizan, *Les Chiens de garde* (Paris, 1932), pp. 191–192.

6. Kagan, "Durkheim et Marx," *Revue d'histoire économique et sociale* 24, no. 3 (1938): 233–244, quoting p. 243.

7. E. Benoît-Smullyan, "The Sociologism of Emile Durkheim and His School," in H. E. Barnes, ed., *An Introduction to the History of Sociology* (Chicago, 1948) , p. 518.

8. Zeitlin, *Ideology and the Development of Sociological Theory* (Englewood Cliffs, N.J., 1968), p. 235.

9. Lewis A. Coser, "Durkheim's Conservatism and Its Implications for His Sociological Theory," pp. 211–232 in Kurt H. Wolff, ed., *Emile Durkheim et al.: Essays on Sociology and Philosophy* (New York, 1960).

10. A.R. Radcliffe-Brown, "The Sociological Theory of Totemism" (ch. 6), "Religion and Society" (ch. 8), and "On the Concept of Function in Social Science" (ch. 9) in *Structure and Function in Primitive Society* (New York, 1965); Harry Alpert, "Durkheim's Functional Theory of Ritual" (1938), in Nisbet (n. 4 above), pp. 137–141; Albert Pierce, "Durkheim and Functionalism," pp. 154–169 in Wolff (n. 9 above); Whitney Pope, "Durkheim as a Functionalist," *Sociological Quarterly* 16 (1975):361–379.

11. For critiques of Durkheim along these lines, see Randall Collins, "Reassessments of Sociological History: The Empirical Validity of the Conflict Tradition," *Theory and Society* 1 (1975):147–178, and Reinhard Bendix, "Two Sociological Traditions," in idem and Guenther Roth, *Scholarship and Partisanship* (Berkeley and Los Angeles, 1971), pp. 282–298. For a defense of Durkheim in terms of this narrow "conflict" issue, see Mohamed Cherkaoui, "Consensus or Conflict? Return to Durkheim's Proteiform Theory," *Theory and Society* 10 (1981):127–138, and idem, "Socialisation et conflit: Les Systèmes éducatifs et leur histoire selon Durkheim," *Revue française de sociologie*, 1976, pp. 197–212. For a good criticism of the conflict issue as an approach to the interpretation of Durkheim, see Anthony Giddens, "Four Myths in the History of Social Thought," *Economy and Society* 1 (1972):357–385, esp. 368–372.

12. Anthony Giddens, "Introduction," pp. 1–50 in Giddens, ed., *Emile Durkheim: Selected Writings* (London, 1972), p. 41; cf. his "Four Myths," pp. 358–361, for a similar misunderstanding of the order problem in Durkheim's thought.

13. David McCloskey, "On Durkheim, Anomie, and the Modern Crisis," *American Journal of Sociology* 81 (1976):1481–1488; Stephen R. Marks takes the same position in "Durkheim's Theory of Anomie," ibid., 80 (1974):329–363; Pope (n. 10 above) conflates all three of the levels I have mentioned: functional model, presuppositional order, and empirical equilibrium.

14. Nisbet, "Introduction" (n. 4 above), pp. 1–102, quoting p. 28.

15. Talcott Parsons, *The Structure of Social Action* (New York, [1937] 1968), pp. 313, 346–347.

16. Pope (n. 10 above), pp. 369–374; Pitirim Sorokin, *Contemporary Sociological Theories* (New York, 1928), pp. 465–466; Don Martindale takes the same position on Durkheim in *The Nature and Types of Sociological Theory* (Boston, 1960), pp. 86–92, as does Georges Gurvitch in "Le Problème de la conscience collective dans la sociologie de Durkheim," pp. 351–408 in his *La Vocation actuelle de la sociologie* (Paris, 1950).

17. Peter M. Blau, "Structural Effects," *American Sociological Review* 25, no. 2 (1960):178–193, quoting 180.

18. Blau, "Objectives of Sociology," in Robert Bierstadt, ed., *A Design for Sociology* (Philadelphia,1969), pp. 43–71.

19. Raymond Aron, *Main Currents in Sociological Thought* (New York, 1970), 2:11–118.

20. Mark Traugott, "Introduction," pp. 1–42 in Traugott, ed., *Emile Durkheim on Institutional Analysis* (Chicago, 1978), n. 60. Marks (n. 13 above) takes the same position on the basic convergence of Marx and Durkheim, as does Anthony Giddens in *Capitalism and Modern Social Theory* (London, 1971).

21. Parsons, *The Structure of Social Action* (n. 15 above); Jean-Claude Filloux, *Durkheim et le socialisme* (Geneva, 1977); Robert N. Bellah, "Introduction," in Bellah, ed., *Emile Durkheim on Morality and Society* (Chicago, 1973), pp. ix–lv; Steven J. Lukes, *Emile Durkheim: His Life and Work* (New York, 1972); Dominick LaCapra, *Emile Durkheim: Sociologist and Philosopher* (Ithaca, N.Y., 1972); Giddens, *Capitalism and Modern Social Theory* (n. 20 above). Although these works will come in for their share of criticism in the pages which follow, each of them is an important contribution to our understanding of Durkheim's thought. I have greatly benefited from their insights—along with those of Nisbet, Coser, and Marks—in my own reading of Durkheim.

22. See, e.g., Anthony Giddens, "The 'Individual' in the Writings of Emile Durkheim," pp. 273–291 in his *Studies in Social and Political Theory* (n. 4 above), esp. p. 290; Bellah (n. 21 above), p. xix.

23. E.g., Lukes, LaCapra, and Parsons simply cite the role Durkheim assigns to social institutions and to individual interaction as evidence that he has transcended sociological idealism. Lukes' position is qualified, however, by his later criticism of the idealist element in Durkheim's thought.

24. For the group mind argument, see Pope (n. 10 above); for the consistency of Durkheim's multidimensional position, see Bellah (n. 21 above); Giddens argues for the continuity of Durkheim's structuralist approach throughout his interpretive writings (see the citations to Giddens' writings on Durkheim above).

In the generation of earlier Durkheim interpreters, Parsons is the exception to this tendency to give Durkheim's work a false continuity. In *The Structure of Social Action* (1937), his acute sensitivity to the shifts in Durkheim's thought—though in some ways seriously flawed—can be favorably compared in this respect with the contemporaneous work by Harry H. Alpert, *Emile Durkheim and His Sociology* (1939), which reads Durkheim's work as if it exhibited fundamental continuity. In his important introductory essay to *Emile Durkheim* (n. 4 above, pp. 1–102), Nisbet essentially follows Parsons' lead. Among the later generation of critics, Lukes (n. 21 above) is the only major interpreter to emphasize the discontinuity of Durkheim's theoretical development. Without acknowledging the influence of Parson's work, Lukes nonetheless follows the general lines of that earlier interpretation, though his discussion of the discontinuity is ambiguous in certain crucial respects. My own interpretation of the developmental tensions of Durkheim's work differs in fundamental ways from each of these authors.

25. Between 1885 and 1890, Durkheim published sixteen pieces—essays, reviews, and lectures. (In addition to these relatively mature works, there also survives the prize lecture Durkheim gave in 1883 on the role of great men in history, "Discours aux lycéens de sens," *Cahiers internationaux de sociologie* 43 [1967]:25–32, reprinted in Bellah [n. 21 above], pp. 25–33). Although these writings have rarely been the subject of theoretical commentary, they remain singularly important to any overall understanding of Durkheim's intellectual development. They do not reveal a wholly unimagined strand of Durkheimian thought, as did the discovery of Marx's early writings. Nevertheless, the insights they provide into Durkheim's thinking in the eight productive years before the publication of what has usually been taken to be his earliest important work, *The Division of Labor in Society* (1893), demonstrate the necessity for revising previous conceptions of Durkheim's intellectual development. The early writings place the *Division of Labor* as well as the writings of the immediately subsequent period into an entirely new light. On the one hand, the thematic similarity of much of the early writing to the later invalidates the kind of "epistemological break" that writers like Parsons and, to some degree, Lukes have portrayed as occurring in 1897. On the

other, the often startlingly disjunctive ideas within this early period just as clearly invalidate arguments for the consistency and unilarity of Durkheim's theoretical development. Only with the understanding of these early writings can one see why Durkheim turned so forcefully to the division of labor in his doctoral dissertation of 1893, and only on this basis can one appreciate the long history of theoretical speculation which provided him with the resources for the decisive shifts which immediately followed its publication.

All of this is not to say, however, that I am presenting here a *historical* argument about Durkheim's theory and taking authority for it from some new piece of empirical data (i.e., the early writings). These early texts do not interpret themselves, any more than do Marx's famous manuscripts. In an article of 1970 on these early writings, "Durkheim as a Review Critic" (*Sociological Review*, 18:171–196), Giddens concludes that they demonstrate complete consistency with Durkheim's mature theory: "The review writings reveal very clearly the continuity of Durkheim's basic perspective upon sociology, both in terms of the main problems which occupied him in his life's work, and in terms of the direction in which he sought the solution of those problems" (pp. 189–190). Wallwork, in the only other sustained treatment to appear in English, reaches the same basic conclusion though in a more elaborated way (*Emile Durkheim: Morality and Milieu* [Cambridge, Mass., 1972], pp. 27–46; see, e.g., pp. 40–41, n. 44). In what follows, I will argue that these interpretations seriously distort the nature of these early writings and their place in Durkheim's thought.

Some French writers have begun to examine the early works with greater sensitivity to their autonomous status. Jean-Claude Filloux, however, in the crucial section of his *Durkheim et le socialisme* (n. 21 above) entitled "Un Engagement" (pp. 22–34), still essentially sees these writings as mere adumbrations of the later works. Bernard Lacroix's "La Vocation originelle d'Emile Durkheim" (*Revue française de sociologie* 17, no. 2 [April-June 1976]) and Paul-Laurent Assoun's "Durkheim et le socialisme de la chaire" (*Revue française de science politique* 26, no. 5 [October 1976]) are valuable correctives to this reading. Assoun, however, takes the conflationary position that Durkheim's incorporation of parts of the German historical school made him a conservative supporter of capitalism and even a critic of democracy, and "explains" these (never held) positions with reference to Durkheim's social environment. Such conflation of ideology and presuppositions obscures the relative independence of Durkheim's general theoretical logic. Lacroix's treatment of the relation between environment and theory is much more revealing than Assoun's, focusing on the early Durkheim's political theory. I will discuss these interpretations at greater length below.

26. For a particularly vivid recounting of these conditions and their

relation to Durkheim's early theoretical development, see Lacroix, pp. 219–220; also Filloux, pp. 9–14.

27. Durkheim, "Les Etudes de science sociale," *Revue philosophique* 22 (1886):61–80, quoting 76. (Translation mine, as elsewhere unless otherwise indicated.) This essay reviews H. Spencer, *Ecclesiastical Institutions* (pt. 6 of *Principles of Sociology*); A. Regnard, *L'Etat: Ses origines, sa nature et son but;* A. Coste, Aug. Burdeau et L. Arreat, *Les Questions sociales contemporaines;* and A. Schaeffle, *Die Quintessenz des Socialismus.*

28. Durkheim, "A. Fouillée, *La Propriété sociale et la démocratie,*" *Revue philosophique* 19 (1885):446–453, quoting 450.

29. Durkheim, "La Science positive de la morale en Allemagne," *Revue philosophique* 24 (1887):33–58, 113–142, 275–284, esp. 54. This essay included reviews of Wagner, Schmoller, Schaeffle, Ihering, and Post.

30. Ibid., p. 54. For an insightful discussion of the role of such cosmological thinking in Comte and of its critique by Durkheim, see Part Three of Steven Seidman's *Liberalism and the Origins of European Social Theory* (Berkeley and Los Angeles, 1983).

31. Durkheim, "La Science positive," p. 54.

32. Ibid. Durkheim's dilemma was certainly not a new one. The Republican tradition in France had always been characterized by such an uneasy attempt at reconciliation. Renouvier, the Republicans' great theoretician whose work spans much of the nineteenth century, was strongly committed to individualism, egalitarianism, and criticism. At the same time, however, one finds in Renouvier's work a strong if diffuse religious feeling, an emphasis on the importance of emotional feelings of solidarity, and the recognition that if individualism is to survive it must become an ethos strongly rooted in an independent moral sphere. In his *Science of Morals* (1869), Renouvier writes, e.g., that "no society can be moral which does not recognize as the basis of all moral order the individual's conscience, his right, his reason; any other assumption leads to an arbitrary arrangement of society and of the whole universe according to the fancy or passions of philosopher or priest; there is no longer any guarantee of justice" (quoted in Roger Soltau, *French Political Thought in the Nineteenth Century* [New Haven, Conn., 1931], p. 307).

For discussions of Renouvier, see John A. Scott, *Republican Ideas and the Liberal Tradition in France, 1870–1914* (New York, 1951), pp. 52–86, and Soltau, pp. 306–321. Renouvier was strongly influenced by Saint-Simon's egalitarianism, on the one side, and by Fourier's associationalism and emphasis on solidarity, on the other.

It is this unique character of the Republican tradition in France that undermines Nisbet's claim (n. 4 above) that Durkheim's sensitivity to the organic and nonrational qualities of social life makes him a "philosophical conservative" (p. 28). It would be much more accurate to say, with Melvin Richter, that Durkheim's work presents a "sociological restatement of liberalism," especially if one notes that this liberalism was of the French, not the Anglo-Saxon variety ("Durkheim's Politics and Political Theory," in Wolff [n. 9 above], esp. p. 179; cf. Giddens, "Four Myths" [n. 11 above], pp. 376 ff.). For Durkheim's links to the progressive, Saint-Simonian tradition of French thought, as shown in his lectures on socialism, see Alvin W. Gouldner's introductory essay to *Socialism and Saint-Simon* (1928; Yellow Springs, Ohio, 1958), pp. x–xv. Nisbet, in his enthusiasm for separating Durkheim from ideological liberalism, ignores the historical specificity of the French as compared with the Anglo-Saxon liberal tradition.

33. Durkheim, "La Science positive," p. 54.

34. For a good background discussion of the place of Marxism and socialism in fin-de-siècle France, see W. Paul Vogt, "The Confrontation of Socialists and Sociologists in Prewar France, 1890–1914," in Western Society for French History, *Proceedings* 4 (1976):313–320.

35. Marcel Mauss, "Introduction" to Durkheim, *Socialism and Saint-Simon* (n. 32 above), pp. 1–4. This important statement first appeared as the introduction to the posthumous French publication of Durkheim's lectures in 1928.

36. Durkheim, "Review of Schaeffle, *Bau und Leben des Sozialen Korpers, Erster Band*," pp. 93–114 in Traugott (n. 20 above), p. 108. First published in *Revue philosophique* 19 (1885):84–101; reprinted in *Emile Durkheim: Textes* (Paris, 1975), 1:355–377, hereafter cited as *Textes*.

37. Durkheim, "La Science sociale selon De Greef," in *Textes* 1:37–43, quoting 37; first published in *Revue philosophique* 22 (1886):658–663.

38. In 1928, Mauss (n. 35 above, p. 3) wrote that Durkheim was introduced to Marx's work in 1885 in Germany. Filloux thinks it probable that Durkheim knew it much earlier, indeed from his days at the Ecole Normale Supérieure between 1879 and 1881, by which time the Ecole had already ceased to be simply a reclusive island of scholarship. Filloux speaks of the student's growing interest in socialism and the "workers' question." A number of Marx's works were available in French by the time Durkheim entered the Ecole: *The Poverty of Philosophy* had, of course, been written by Marx in French in 1847, and the first volume of *Capital* was translated between 1872 and 1875. In 1882, the year Durkheim left, *The Communist Manifesto* was published in the well-known socialist magazine *L'Egalité,* and in 1883 an abridgment of *Capital* appeared under Marx's auspices. (Filloux [n. 21 above], pp. 9–11, 125–126.) Whether or not such an intimate and direct acquaintance occurred, it is clear that Durkheim was familiar with various currents of socialist thought, and that he felt sufficiently secure about his knowledge to identify the distinctive aspects of Marxian socialism. (For other discussions of the degree and nature of his acquaintance with Marxian and socialist thought, see Vogt [n. 34 above] and Joseph R. Llobera, "Durkheim, the

Durkheimians, and Their Collective Misrepresentation of Marx," paper presented to the Ninth World Congress of Sociology, Uppsala, Sweden, August 10–18, 1978.) At this point, however, my discussion remains purely at the ideological, not the presuppositional level, and I am treating Durkheim's evaluation of socialism purely as a political judgment. This judgment indicates how the stress on individual volition always accompanied and, in effect, qualified Durkheim's stress on the collective and regulative aspects of socialism. I will indicate below how his rejection of Marxian socialism was also emphatically theoretical.

39. For a discussion of these shifts in the tentative title and orientation of Durkheim's doctoral dissertation, see Mauss (n. 35 above).

40. Durkheim, "Review of Schaeffle," in Traugott (n. 20 above), p. 108 (*Textes*, p. 371).

41. Ibid.

42. Durkheim, "La Programme économique de M. Schaeffle," in *Textes*, 1:377–383, quoting 379; first published in *Revue d'économie politique* 11 (1888):3–7.

43. For an excellent discussion of the German historical school in the late nineteenth century and its internal divisions, see Fritz Ringer, *The Decline of the German Mandarins, 1890–1914* (Cambridge, Mass., 1969), pp. 143–162. For a contrast to Schaeffle's emphasis on democratic participation in a reformed industrial order, see Schmoller's rejection of democracy and endorsement of aristocratic governance in his "Social Relations and Progress" (1875), in Eugene N. Anderson, Stanley J. Pincetl, Jr., and Donald J. Ziegler, eds., *Europe in the Nineteenth Century, 1870–1914* (Indianapolis, 1971), pp. 49–77. It should be noted, perhaps, that Durkheim was wrong to include Brentano in the quasi-authoritarian group.

44. Durkheim, "Les Etudes de science sociale" (n. 27 above), p. 77. In the 1888 review of Schaeffle (n. 42 above), he makes virtually an identical statement in defending Schaeffle against critics who accuse him of being too collectivistic (p. 378).

45. Ibid., p. 379.

46. Ibid.

47. Alfred Fouillée's most influential book on solidarism was *Science sociale contemporaine* (1880). For background on the role that Fouillée and solidarism in general played in French Republican thought, see Scott (n. 32 above), pp. 157–186. For a more specific discussion of the differences between Durkheim and the solidarists, see J. E. S. Hayward, "Solidarist Syndicalism: Durkheim and Duguit," *Sociological Review* 2d ser., 8 (1960):17–36.

48. Durkheim, "Fouillée" (n. 28 above), p. 449.

49. "La Science positive" (n. 29 above), p. 54.

50. Filloux (n. 21 above) is particularly illuminating on the relation

between Durkheim's social and scientific commitments; see the section "Le Sentiment de mission" (pp. 8–22) and, more generally, his entire first chapter, "Naissance d'un projet" (pp. 5–42). This connection between Durkheim's scientific ambition and his ideological commitment to the restructuring of France is revealed by the kind of prophetic quality that he evidently brought to his work, by his belief that his science was intimately related to larger issues of social practice. In an important biographical account written shortly after Durkheim's death, Georges Davy recalls that, for Durkheim, teaching meant "to teach a doctrine, to have disciples and not only students, to play a role in the social reconstruction of France battered by defeat" (p. 183 in "Emile Durkheim: L'Homme," *Revue de metaphysique et de morale* 26, [1919]:171–198). Durkheim himself made the same kind of connection between his science and the history of political conflict which he had experienced in his early years. Writing in 1900 in *La Revue bleue*, he described the period following 1871 as a "reawakening":

> The organization, or rather the façade, which constituted the imperial system had just collapsed; it was a question of re-making another, or rather of making one which could survive other than by administrative artifice—that is, one which was truly grounded in the nature of things [*la nature des choses*] ("La Sociologie en France au XIXᵉ siecle," *La Revue bleue*, 4th ser., 12:609–613, 647–652, reprinted in Bellah, [n. 21 above] as "Sociology in France in the Nineteenth Century," pp. 3–22, quoting p. 12).

51. Durkheim, "Course in Sociology: Opening Lecture," pp. 43–70 in Traugott (n. 20 above), p. 46. First published as "Cours de science sociale: Lécon d'ouverture," *Revue internationale de l'enseignement* 15 (1888): 23–42.

52. "Les Etudes de science sociale" (n. 27 above), pp. 73 ff.

53. "Course in Sociology: Opening Lecture," p. 47.

54. "La Science positive" (n. 29 above), p. 37.

55. "Course in Sociology: Opening Lecture," p. 47.

56. "La Science positive," p. 37.

57. Ibid.

58. Ibid.

59. "Les Etudes de science sociale," p. 73.

60. Ibid.

61. E.g., after attacking the classical economists for accepting at face value the surface reality of individual rights in capitalist society, Marx suggests that if one substitutes "classes" for "individuals" the true hierarchical ordering of capitalist society will be exposed:

> On leaving this sphere of . . . the "Free-trader Vulgaris" with his views and ideas, and with the standard by which he judges a society based on

capital and wages, we think we can perceive a change in the physiognomy of our dramatis personae. He, who before was the money-owner, now strides in front as capitalist; the possessor of labour-power follows as his labourer. The one with an air of importance, smirking, intent on business; the other, timid and holding back, like one who is bringing his own hide to market and has nothing to expect but—a hiding. (*Capital*, Vol. 1 [1867; Moscow, n.d.], p. 176.)

62. Durkheim, "La Science positive," p. 39.

63. "Course in Sociology: Opening Lecture," p. 60.

64. "La Science positive," p. 34.

65. Ibid., p. 38.

66. "Les Etudes de science sociale," pp. 75, 71.

67. Ibid., p. 73.

68. For Durkheim's reasons for his rejection of Kantianism in its pure form, see his essay, "La Philosophie dans les universités allemandes," in *Textes*, 3:437–486, esp. 465 ff. (first published in *Revue internationale de l'enseignement* 23 [1887]:313–338, 423–440). For discussions of the influence on Durkheim of Renouvier and Boutroux, see Wallwork, *Durkheim: Morality and Milieu* (n. 25 above), pp. 5–17; Lukes (n. 21 above), pp. 54–58; Henri Peyre, "Durkheim: The Man, His Time, and His Intellectual Background," in Wolff (n. 9 above), pp. 3–32.

69. For these elements in Comte's work, see *The Positive Philosophy*, vol. 2, ch. 3; for Durkheim's positive comments on this aspect of Comte, see, e.g., "Course in Sociology: Opening Lecture," pp. 50–52.

70. Durkheim, "The Principles of 1789 and Sociology," pp. 34–42 in Bellah (n. 21 above), p. 38. Durkheim is characterizing here the thinking of Ferneuil, in a review which was published originally as "Les Principes de 1789 et la sociologie" in *Revue internationale de l'enseignement* 19 (1890):450–456.

71. Alfred Espinas, *Les Sociétés animales*, (1877).

72. Durkheim, "La Science positive," p. 118.

73. Ibid.

74. "Review of Schaeffle" (n. 36 above), pp. 102–103. For an endorsement of Schaeffle's realism, see ibid., p. 93.

75. Ibid., p. 103. Cf. Durkheim's comments on Regnard in "Les Etudes de science sociale," pp. 70–71.

76. "Course in Sociology: Opening Lecture," pp. 54–57.

77. "Fouillée" (n. 28 above), p. 452.

78. "La Science positive," p. 37.

79. Ibid., p. 45.

80. Ibid., p. 37.

81. Ibid.

82. Durkheim, "Guyau, *L'Irreligion de l'avenir: Etude de sociologie*," *Revue philosophique* 23 (1887):299–311, quoting 307.

83. "La Science positive," p. 37.

84. "The Principles of 1789 and Sociology" (n. 70 above), p. 38.

85. Ibid.

86. "La Science sociale selon De Greef" (n. 37 above), p. 43.

87. Ibid.

88. "La Science positive," p. 145.

89. This statement occurs in the second paragraph of Marx's *The Eighteenth Brumaire of Louis Bonaparte*, written in 1852. The same very limited kind of correction of individualistic rationalism continues, of course, today, as pointed out in my discussion in vol. 1, ch. 3. See, e.g., the kind of collectivist transformation that James S. Coleman tries to effect in Homans' individualistic exchange theory, in "Foundations for a Theory of Collective Decisions," *American Journal of Sociology* 71 (1966): 615–627.

90. Durkheim, "La Science positive," p. 45, 48.

91. Ibid., p. 118.

92. E.g., in one of his most influential works, *Science sociale contemporaine*, the solidarist leader Fouillée begins by asking "for what end do individuals make contracts and pledge themselves to observe common laws?" (3d ed., 1880; p. 32). He contends, in fact, that men conceive more or less clearly the type of social organism they wish to form, and that when they unite effectively it is under the conscious guidance of this conception. "The notion of a social duty," he maintains, "when it is examined closely, is only a sort of deus ex machina that intervenes every time one is unable to find in individuals and their common situation the real explanation of such duty" (p. 28).

93. Durkheim, "Review of Schaeffle" (n. 36 above), p. 109.

94. Ibid.

95. In logical terms, of course, the solution to order must be bound by the conception of action, since collective order, no matter how it is formulated, is simply the aggregation of individual acts. In this sense, we could say that Durkheim's search for a solution to the order problem is limited by his profound ambivalence about action. In biographical terms, however, action and order may be more or less simultaneously conceived and their conceptualizations mutually reinforcing. In Durkheim's case this was particularly true, since, as has been seen, his discussion of action is greatly affected by an implicit argument against individualistic order. It is not surprising, then, that Durkheim's discussion of order occurs against a background that is highly critical of utilitarian motivation but insists, at the same time, on qualifying this criticism in certain crucial respects.

96. "La Science positive," p. 32.

97. Ibid., p. 276; cf. "La Philosophie" (n. 68 above), p. 465.

98. "La Science positive," p. 46.

99. "Les Etudes de science sociale" (n. 27 above), p. 71.

100. "Review of Schaeffle" (n. 36 above), p. 114.
101. "Guyau" (n. 82 above), p. 309.
102. "Review of Schaeffle," p. 114, italics added.
103. Durkheim, "La Sociologie selon Gumplowicz," in *Textes*, 1:344–354, quoting 349. First published as "Gumplowicz, Ludwig: *Grundriss der Soziologie,*" *Revue philosophique* 20 (1885): 627–634.
104. "La Science positive," p. 133.
105. "Les Etudes de science sociale," p. 79.
106. "Review of Schaeffle," p. 114; cf. "La Science positive," p. 121.
107. "Review of Schaeffle," p. 107, italics added.
108. "Guyau," p. 309. Most commentators have ignored this early emphasis by Durkheim on natural social sentiments, despite the fact that he indicates his positive appreciation for this position in at least five of his first eight essays (the 1885 reviews of Schaeffle, Fouillée, and Gumplowicz; the 1886 essay, "Les Etudes de science sociale"; and the 1887 work, "La Science positive de la morale en Allemagne"). Lukes, e.g., notes Durkheim's relation to Espinas, but sees in it only what the later Durkheim viewed the results of this relationship to be: an appreciation for the objective status of collective life and representations (*Emile Durkheim* [n. 21 above], pp. 79, 84). Because these commentaries assume that Durkheim's later emphasis on man's natural egoism—or, at least, his dualism—extends back into his earliest writing, they underemphasize the kind of theoretical transformations involved in his later movement to a consistently collectivist position (see, e.g., La Capra, *Emile Durkheim* [n. 21 above], p. 225; the same kind of error is made by Parsons and Nisbet). Wallwork, on the other hand, the only interpreter to notice this early tendency in Durkheim, fails to appreciate the limitations of this approach, the tensions with Durkheim's other proposed solutions to order, and the way Durkheim turns against this perspective in his later work (*Durkheim* [n. 25 above], pp. 29–30).
109. Espinas, *Les Sociétés animales* (n. 71 above), p. 424.
110. Ibid., p. 415.
111. Ibid., pp. 411 ff., 437.
112. Durkheim, "Review of Schaeffle," p. 114, italics added.
113. Ibid.
114. "Fouillée (n. 28 above), p. 453.
115. "La Science positive," p. 134.
116. Ibid.
117. "Fouillée," p. 450.
118. "La Philosophie" (n. 68 above), p. 465.
119. "La Science positive," passim; see, e.g., the passage on p. 46.
120. "Les Etudes de science sociale," p. 79.
121. "La Science positive," p. 52.
122. Ibid.

123. "La Sociologie selon Gumplowicz" (n. 103 above), p. 350.

124. "La Science positive," p. 52.

125. Ibid., p. 53.

126. Ibid.

127. "La Sociologie selon Gumplowicz," p. 350.

128. "La Philosophie," p. 465.

129. "Les Etudes de science sociale," p. 79.

130. "La Science positive," p. 36.

131. Ibid., pp. 239–240.

132. "Review of Schaeffle" (n. 36 above), p. 96.

133. "La Sociologie selon Gumplowicz," p. 352.

134. "La Science positive," p. 44.

135. Ibid., pp. 123–124.

136. "La Sociologie selon Gumplowicz," p. 352, italics added.

137. Ibid.

138. "La Science positive," p. 46.

139. "Review of Schaeffle," p. 103, italics added. For a similar statement, see "Course in Sociology: Opening Lecture" (n. 51 above), p. 60.

140. "La Science positive," pp. 113–142.

141. For a full discussion of the terminology employed here, contrasting the more satisfactory "analytic" approach to the individual with the "concrete" approach, see vol. 1, ch. 3, secs. 3.2–3.4.

142. "La Science positive," p. 128.

143. "Les Etudes de science sociale," p. 76.

144. "La Science positive," p. 46.

145. "Review of Schaeffle," p. 105.

146. Ibid.

147. Ibid., p. 106.

148. Ibid., p. 97.

149. "La Science positive," p. 138.

150. Ibid., p. 139.

151. "Course in Sociology: Opening Lecture," pp. 63–64.

152. "La Science positive," p. 40.

153. In speaking of this "radical shift" in Durkheim's work, I do not want to imply that there is a completely linear sequence to the three different approaches to order I have identified. All three, in fact, were simultaneously present throughout the bulk of the early writings, and this is, in itself, important evidence of Durkheim's theoretical uncertainty. Particularly in the middle years of the early period, Durkheim shifts back and forth between the solutions, sometimes within the same paragraph, often within the same essay, and always within the same chronological period of time. For example, in the long review essay of 1887, "La Science positive de la morale en Allemagne," all three notions are explicated and taken up in some detail at various points in Durkheim's argu-

ment. Still, one can discern a loose chronological sequence in these order proposals. The notion of innate individual sentiments occurs more frequently in the writings of 1885–1887, and it is virtually, although not completely, eliminated from the later essays. The conception of collective moral order as resting upon voluntary, nonrational action also appears most frequently in the writings of 1885–1887, although it remains an important part of Durkheim's review of Schaeffle, "Le Programme économique de M. Schaeffle" (n. 40 above), published in 1888. The more instrumentalist notion of moral order which is dealt with in the present section dominates the writings from 1888 to 1890. This division into "early" versus "late" approaches must, however, be qualified by two facts: (1) the essay on Spencer which appears in 1886 as part of "Les Etudes de science sociale" ("Studies in Social Science") represents one of the most important rationales for the instrumentalist approach which only appears in full flower two years later (the 1887 review of Guyau also contains similar elements); (2) the elements I am about to identify as the crucial theoretical resources for this later instrumentalist model were already present in Durkheim's very first publications, although they did not at that time combine to form the instrumentalist perspective.

It is true that as Durkheim moved closer to formulating his own sociological theory he moved increasingly toward a consistent instrumentalist solution, and I will show how this preoccupied his sociological thinking from 1888 through 1893. Yet it would be a mistake to believe that the alternative, anti-instrumental approach was altogether eliminated even in this period. It remained, rather, in the background, both as a negative example of something to avoid and as an ambiguous reference to include. It also remained as a clear alternative, one that waited only upon a more satisfactory formulation to transcend the problems that undermined its appropriateness in the earlier work. While it is impossible, then, to understand Durkheim's development without linking his theoretical solutions to some sense of chronological development, it is just as impossible to tie his theoretical shifts to temporal sequence in an absolutely linear way.

This overemphasis on a linear temporal sequence is one of the problematic points in Lacroix's very interesting and often penetrating effort to present the evolution of Durkheim's early thought (1885–1887) through a detailed reading of the texts ("La Vocation originelle d'Emile Durkheim" [n. 25 above]). Lacroix identifies the same conflict in Durkheim's theorizing as I have emphasized here, the conflict between a Hobbesian vision of instrumental order like the one presented by Gumplowicz and the more normative vision of Schaeffle. He argues, however, that Durkheim developed his position on this issue by concentrating mainly on the role of the state in society, and, moreover, that his thinking evolved from an early emphasis on the direct control of society by normative political authority to a more pluralized vision of state/society differentiation, where political authority is more the product of society's moral cohesion than its cause. I would make three objections to this treatment. First, although the state is a significant reference point for the early Durkheim, this occurs from the beginning within a broader concern for social cohesion and morality per se and, more generally still, within an independent context of generalized "epistemological" concerns as defined here. Second, in terms of the specific political issues, Durkheim was already conscious of the differentiation of authority and society in 1885, as his qualified support of Fouillée's emphasis on the individual makes clear. On this issue, indeed, there is not a great difference between Durkheim's reviews of Schaeffle in 1885 and 1889. Third, in terms of the presuppositions that Durkheim employs in this political writing, the case for his consistent emphasis on moral order simply cannot be made. Lacroix believes that Durkheim had articulated his mature vision of society as based on moral solidarity by 1887. We will see, to the contrary, that by 1888 Durkheim had actually moved toward a more instrumental position, which manifested itself in a vision of the state not so different from Gumplowicz's own.

The other important recent French discussion of these early writings, that of Filloux (n. 21 above), makes the same kind of claim for Durkheim's normative consistency, although Filloux focuses more on Durkheim's social psychology than on his political sociology and sees the mature vision as solidified already in 1885 rather than in 1886 or 1887. Although Filloux describes Durkheim's position in the early writings as more "doctrine" than "theory," he argues that all of the later concepts are already present: the dominance of internal, subjective concerns; the notion of the collective conscience and the centrality of collective psychology; the allegiance to laws through social communion; the dominance of religious concerns (pp. 22–34). We will see that the status of these ideas was far more tenuous than Filloux believes.

154. For a discussion of this conflationary problem in contemporary theoretical debate, see vol. 1, ch. 2.

155. Durkheim, "Fouillée" (n. 28 above), p. 450.

156. Ibid., p. 451; cf. p. 453.

157. This discussion should put into a new perspective the evaluation of Durkheim qua "functionalist." In the first place, this commitment does not in any sense describe Durkheim's theory considered as a whole, since it refers to only one element in his work, namely, his commitment to a certain kind of model. This model commitment, moreover, is nowhere nearly as ramifying as the problems Durkheim addresses at the presuppositional level of analysis. The functional model he employs can only come into play insofar as it relates to Durkheim's broader conception of order and action. In other words, functional models are not necessarily

reductionist and mechanical (as in materialist functionalism), nor are they necessarily voluntary and moral (purely normative functionalism), as Durkheim's own ambivalence amply attests. Finally, to employ the equilibrium aspect of functional models as a reference point does not mean that a theory ignores conflict in any way. It is only insofar as the theory conflates the achievement of empirical order with certain kinds of presuppositional order that the commitment to an equilibrium model begins to pose serious theoretical problems. This general problem will be much more fully explored in my discussion of Talcott Parsons in vol. 4.

158. "La Science positive," p. 47.

159. "Review of Schaeffle," p. 104.

160. "La Science positive," p. 138.

161. Ibid., p. 38.

162. Ibid., p. 122.

163. "Les Etudes de science sociale," p. 76.

164. "La Science positive," p. 35.

165. Ibid., p. 55.

166. Ibid., p. 51.

167. Ibid., p. 52.

168. Ibid., p. 40, italics added.

169. Ibid., p. 52.

170. Wallwork (n. 25 above) has also discussed Durkheim's emphasis on "habit" in the early writings, but he regards this as complementary with his emphasis on nonrational action and moral order (pp. 39–40). In contrast to the position taken here, Wallwork—despite his often perceptive examination of the early writings—takes Durkheim's continuous emphasis on morality as an indication that his theoretical explanation of morality remained constant. He does not examine, therefore, the kind of coercive and antivoluntaristic solution toward which Durkheim is increasingly drawn, nor the important role which "habit" plays in establishing this early posture.

171. Durkheim, "Course in Sociology: Opening Lecture" (n. 51 above), p. 67.

172. Ibid., p. 66, italics added.

173. Ibid., p. 65.

174. Ibid., p. 66; cf. p. 51 for a statement in which Durkheim emphasizes that habit is a collective rather than individualistic phenomenon.

175. Ibid., p. 58.

176. Ibid., italics added.

177. Durkheim, "Introduction to the Sociology of the Family," pp. 205–228 in Traugott (n. 20 above), p. 214. First published as "Introduction à la sociologie de la famille," *Annales de la faculté de Bordeaux* 10 (1888):257–281.

178. Ibid., p. 214.

179. Ibid., pp. 214–215.

180. Ibid., pp. 206–207.

181. Durkheim, "Suicide et natalité: Etude de statistique morale," in *Textes*, 2:216–236, quoting 217. First published in *Revue philosophique* 26 (1888):446–463.

182. Ibid., p. 235, italics added.

183. Ibid.

184. Ibid., p. 232.

185. It should be noted that Durkheim also includes in his explanation an account that relies on the more individualistic "innate sociability" theory which I have discussed as Durkheim's first approach to the order problem. In this strand of his analysis, Durkheim asserts that the need for "family life is in the nature of the organism at least as it has evolved" ("Suicide et natalité" [n. 181 above], p. 235). On this basis, he can argue that "*as he is actually constituted*, man is *made* to be united with his fellows in a community more binding than everyday life or simple friendship" (ibid., italics added). It follows from this that a falling birth rate will induce suicide, since smaller families violate an innate psychological-cum-biological need. Durkheim's reference to this kind of explanation at this relatively late date demonstrates how despite the general chronological sequence that can be drawn, the different conceptualizations of order have a certain independent life throughout the period of the early writings.

In relation to this issue of the relative independence of theoretical elements, it is interesting to note that at about the same time that Durkheim was formulating this self-consciously scientific approach to suicide, he was offering, in another context, a much more personal, ad hoc analysis, one that violated every one of the theoretical tenets he expressed in this scientific work. In the funeral eulogy of his close friend Victor Hommay, delivered in 1887, Durkheim searched in an informal way to find some sociological reasons for Hommay's tragic, self-inflicted death ("Notice biographique sur Victor Hommay," in *Textes*, 1:418–424; reprinted from *L'Annuaire de l'association des anciens élèves de l'Ecole normale supérieure*, January 9, 1887, pp. 51–55). Almost nowhere in this strongly felt address does Durkheim subordinate the subjective perceptions and feelings of Hommay to the objective conditions in which he lived. Instead of establishing the nature of Hommay's environment, he identifies the external world only in terms of Hommay's own perceptions of it. Thus, while solidarity is an important referent in Durkheim's proto-utilitarian scientific analysis, only in this informal account does he radically separate Hommay's feelings of solidarity from the actual density of the groups in which he spent his life. It was the closeness and intimacy of Hommay's contacts that mattered, and small groups and individual friendships were more important than large groups and public relationships. Throughout, Durkheim describes Hommay as feeling free to the degree that he was part of a solidary community, another sharp departure from the more individualistic and limited approach to freedom which appears in the scientific discussion.

The contrast between these two treatments indicates the relatively autonomous dimension in which presuppositional reasoning occurs vis-à-vis the realms of empirical observation and value judgment. It also demonstrates how the limitations in Durkheim's early presuppositional logic made him unable to express his actual insight into the social world. In his later account of suicide, his ability to make this translation substantially increases.

186. Rather than directly consider Spencer's work, I make this comparison, instead, on the basis of the internal contrasts Durkheim himself reveals in a long review of Spencer's work, and on the relationship between Durkheim's theoretical logic there and the kind of thinking he has elsewhere described as characteristic of utilitarian and Social Darwinian thought. I focus, as well, on the relationship between this logic and the proto-utilitarian and neo-Darwinian elements of his thinking which have already been examined. (I discuss Spencer's work in more detail in the analysis of Durkheim's *The Division of Labor in Society* in ch. 5 below.)

187. This book is pt. 6 of Spencer's *Principles of Sociology*. My subsequent citations refer to the translation by Robert Alun Jones, which appeared as "Durkheim's Critique of Spencer's *Ecclesiastical Institutions*," *Sociological Inquiry* 44, no. 3 (1974):205-214. This English selection translates pp. 60-69 of Durkheim's "Les Etudes de science sociale" (n. 27 above).

188. Ibid., 212-213.

189. Ibid., p. 213.

190. Ibid., p. 211.

191. Ibid.

192. Ibid., p. 212.

193. Ibid.

194. Ibid.

195. Ibid., pp. 212-213.

196. Ibid., p. 212.

197. Ibid., p. 213.

198. Ibid.

199. Ibid., italics added.

200. Ibid. I have slightly changed Jones' translation here.

201. Ibid.

202. To clarify briefly an issue I will discuss below, Durkheim has criticized Spencer's approach to order as too individualistic while generally accepting his understanding of action. In my discussion of the *Divi-*

sion of Labor (ch. 5) it will be seen that to a certain extent Durkheim has
overemphasized Spencer's individualism.

The elements of resemblance between Durkheim's and Spencer's
ideas is not anomalous in historical terms. Spencer's ideas permeated
French intellectual circles in the 1870s, and two of the thinkers who influenced Durkheim most, Espinas and Schaeffle, were themselves highly
influenced by Social Darwinian ideas (see, e.g., Scott [n. 32 above], p.
161). The relationship between Durkheim and Spencer has, of course,
been the subject of great controversy (see below, ch. 5, n. 185). The main
point of confusion has been the refusal to differentiate the most generalized elements in their respective theories and to define the issues which
are involved on this level in purely analytic terms. In ch. 5, I will indicate,
however, that the similarities between the early Durkheim and Spencer
extend to important empirical aspects of their work as well.

203. "Guyau" (n. 82 above), pp. 308–309.

204. Ibid., p. 309.

205. Ibid. The English version prepared by Giddens translates "les
habitudes" as "modes of behavior." For my purpose, the more literal
meaning better communicates the connection of this passage with the
mechanical explanation Durkheim has adopted for the nonrational aspect of human motivation. Giddens has also rendered "l'enveloppe superficielle" as "surface expression." I would prefer "superficial
wrapping," since it seems more expressive of the kind of base-superstructure logic Durkheim is employing here. For Giddens' translation,
see p. 219 in his *Emile Durkheim: Selected Writings* (n. 12 above).

206. "Guyau," p. 308.

207. "The Principles of 1789 and Sociology" (n. 70 above), p. 37.

208. Ibid., p. 41.

209. Ibid., p. 36.

210. "La Science positive" (n. 29 above), p. 38.

211. Ibid., p. 127.

212. "Suicide et natalité" (n. 181 above), p. 217.

213. "La Science sociale selon De Greef" (n. 37 above), pp. 41–42, italics added. Durkheim's extremely complex relationship to these three different versions of the instrumentalist tradition, combined with the fact
that only in his latest essays was he committed to a thoroughgoing rationalism of his own, helps explain the great interpretive difficulties presented by some of his early writings. In the 1885 essay on Gumplowicz (n.
103 above), e.g., one is tempted to read Durkheim's diatribe against
Gumplowicz's instrumentalism as a general rejection of any instrumentalist theory, yet this temptation should be resisted. Despite his admonitions against collective force, Durkheim develops this critique in
reference only to Gumplowicz's Social Darwinism. By doing so, he has
limited his warning to a very particular kind of collectivist coercion: that

which is imposed by groups of individuals who act in a self-conscious and fully reflective way. While Social Darwinism refers to group coercion and control, it basically conceives groups as voluntary individuals writ large. A coercive approach to order, in other words, could still be considered by Durkheim to be a legitimate theoretical strategy if it were conceived of as imposed in a more indirect and less than fully conscious way. Thus, despite the obvious parallels between elements in Gumplowicz's theory and Marx's, Durkheim carefully avoids at this very early stage of his development any final rejection of the kind of generalized reasoning employed by Marx.

CHAPTER FIVE

1. For the anticapitalist argument, see, e.g., Alvin W. Gouldner, "Introduction," in Emile Durkheim, *Socialism and Saint-Simon* (Yellow Springs, Ohio, 1958), pp. x–xv, and Anthony Giddens, "Four Myths in the History of Social Thought," *Economy and Society* 1 (1972):357–385. For the conservative argument, see Robert A. Nisbet, "Introduction," in Nisbet, ed., *Emile Durkheim* (Englewood Cliffs, N.J., 1965), pp. 1–102.

2. For the materialist justification, see Guy Aimard, *Durkheim et la science économique* (Paris, 1962); Armand Cuvillier, "Durkheim et Marx," *Cahiers internationaux de sociologie* 4 (1948):75–97; Leo F. Schnore, "Social Morphology and Human Ecology," *American Journal of Sociology* 62 (1958): 620–634; Mark Traugott, "Introduction," in Traugott, ed., *Emile Durkheim on Institutional Analysis* (Chicago, 1978), pp. 1–42. For the normative justification, see Talcott Parsons, *The Structure of Social Action* (New York, [1937] 1968), and Robert N. Bellah, "Introduction," in Bellah, ed., *Emile Durkheim on Morality and Society* (Chicago, 1973), pp. ix–lv.

3. Giddens, "Four Myths"; idem, "Introduction," in Giddens, ed., *Emile Durkheim: Selected Writings* (London, 1972); and idem, "Durkheim as a Review Critic," *Sociological Review* 18 (1970): 171–196. See also Jean-Claude Filloux, *Durkheim et le socialisme* (Geneva, 1977), esp. pp. 64–98.

4. Aimard (n. 2 above); Cuvillier (n. 2 above); Whitney Pope, "Classic on Classic: Parsons' Interpretation of Durkheim," *American Sociological Review* 38 (1973):399–415; Robert K. Merton, "Durkheim's 'Division of Labor in Society,' " in Nisbet (n. 1 above), pp. 105–112; Traugott (n. 2 above).

5. Parsons, *Structure of Social Action*, and Nisbet (n. 1 above).

6. Although there is not an exact parallel, Durkheim's earliest sociological essays, from 1888 to 1892, on the nature of sociology, on the family, and on Montesquieu's social theory, seem to have played much the same role for him as the works published from 1845 to 1847, *The Holy*

Family, The German Ideology, and *The Poverty of Philosophy*, played for Marx. Both sets of early scientific writings were much more empirically specific and propositional than the earliest, more generalized works, yet they did not represent the systematic sociological statements contained in *The Division of Labor in Society* and *The Communist Manifesto*.

7. Durkheim, *The Division of Labor in Society* (New York, [1933] 1964), p. 36; hereafter cited as *DLS*. This book was first published in 1893 as *De la division du travail social*; hereafter cited as *DTS*. When comparison of the original French and the published English translation warrants it, I have made alterations in the translation and have indicated this by adding the French reference (3d ed.; Paris, 1911), in parentheses.

8. *DLS*, p. 32.

9. Ibid., p. 37 (*DTS*, p. xliii).

10. Ibid.

11. Ibid.

12. Durkheim, "Introduction to the Sociology of the Family," in Traugott (n. 2 above), p. 206.

13. Ibid.

14. The question of where Durkheim derived the term "organic solidarity" has been debated at some length in the interpretive literature. The question generated such discussion because "organic" seems to imply an antimechanistic perspective that is, as I will show, often at odds with what seems to be a major line of Durkheim's analysis. Traugott (n. 2 above), e.g., notes the term's appearance in Durkheim's 1889 review of Tönnies' *Gemeinschaft und Gesellschaft* in the *Revue philosophique*; he speculates that the term may have originated from Durkheim's criticism of the kind of mechanistic and coercive approach to modern collective control that Tönnies and others advanced (pp. 12–13; for the translation of Durkheim's review of Tönnies, see pp. 115–122, particularly pp. 121–122). The problem with this viewpoint is that it obscures the instrumental presuppositional framework within which "organic solidarity" is itself imbedded. Although I have found no independent corroboration for this from Durkheim's own writing, it seems very likely that he actually derived the term from Espinas's *Les Sociétés animales*, which was first published in 1877 and which Durkheim knew very well. One of the most important French popularizers of Spencer's Social Darwinism, Espinas introduced the term "organic solidarity" to describe the coordination that results from the relationship between functionally differentiated organs in animal life. Since this was probably the source for Durkheim's own usage, the relevant passage from Espinas is worth quoting at length.

> It is not possible that a great number of individuals, partaking themselves of diverse functions, fulfill each of these functions equally. To one or several among them must devolve the preponderate, essential, and dominant function. The more it fulfills this function, the better it will

have to acquit itself of it; and thus it will withdraw from the furthest regions of the social organism in order to fix itself at the center. In this way, even without the deliberate intention of the other individuals or groups of individuals, an individual or a central group of individuals will become preponderant and will subordinate all the others to itself. From then on it will represent in itself the entire social body, the life of which will be as if summarized [resumé] in it. The destinies of all will be attached to its own destiny, and by virtue of organic solidarity, it will receive the echo of all the changes created by other parties, even as the parties will receive the reactions created by it; what is more, if it so reacts, it will be the center of movement as it is the center of impressions. Thus the highest degree of cooperation is achieved. (Alfred Espinas, Les Sociétés animales 3d ed. [Paris, 1924], p. 416.)

This passage indicates how Durkheim's criticism of Tönnies' "mechanistic" approach referred to the artificial quality he gave to the modern state, not to the fact of mechanical, "physiological" control per se. Espinas's vision emphasizes the spontaneity of collective order, and this was the very combination that Durkheim was striving to achieve.

15. Durkheim, "Introduction to the Sociology of the Family" (n. 12 above, p. 206, italics added).

16. Ibid., p. 207.

17. Ibid. This same general perspective on a sociological theory of modern society—that it should be able to combine individual autonomy and collective coordination—is the main point of Durkheim's criticism of Tönnies in 1889. He argues that Tönnies is wrong to believe that the "dispersive effects" of modern individualism "can be prevented only for a time and [only] through artificial means by the action of its state" ("Review of Ferdinand Tönnies, Gemeinschaft und Gesellschaft," in Traugott [n. 12 above], p. 121; originally printed in Revue philosophique 27 (1889):416-422. Durkheim maintains, to the contrary, that there is a means of ordering modern life that is every bit as collective as Tönnies' state but is much more natural and spontaneous. He does not discuss here what this alternative is. "We would," he writes at the time, "need an entire book to prove this" (p. 121). It seems clear that The Division of Labor in Society was the book he had in mind.

18. Durkheim, "Montesquieu's Contribution to the Rise of Social Science," pp. 1–64 in Durkheim, Montesquieu and Rousseau (Ann Arbor, Mich., 1960), pp. 33–34, italics added. This work was originally published as Durkheim's Latin dissertation in 1892 and in French as "Montesquieu: Sa part dans la fondation des sciences politiques et de la science des sociétés" in 1937.

19. Ibid., p. 34.

20. Ibid., p. 30, italics added.

21. Ibid., p. 37.

22. Ibid., pp. 42–43.

23. *DLS*, pp. 411–435. In terms of the first French edition, this material would have begun after the sixth paragraph of the Introduction; in the English edition, the excerpt from the original Introduction has been made after p. 40.

24. Ibid., p. 415.

25. Ibid., p. 416.

26. Ibid., p. 417.

27. Ibid., p. 418.

28. Ibid., p. 423; cf. p. 33.

29. Ibid., p. 425, italics added.

30. Ibid., p. 427.

31. Ibid., p. 41, italics added.

32. Ibid., p. 39.

33. Ibid., p. 49.

34. Ibid., p. 96, italics added.

35. Ibid., pp. 61–62.

36. Ibid., p. 61.

37. Ibid., p. 62, italics added.

38. Ibid.

39. Ibid., p. 64.

40. Ibid., p. 70.

41. Ibid., p. 72, italics added.

42. Ibid., p. 79 (*DTS*, p. 46).

43. Ibid., p. 80 (*DTS*, p. 46).

44. Ibid.

45. Ibid., p. 84.

46. Ibid., p. 96, italics added.

47. Ibid., p. 97.

48. Ibid., p. 99 (*DTS*, p. 67).

49. *DLS*, p. 102.

50. Ibid.

51. Ibid., p. 120.

52. Ibid., p. 121.

53. Ibid., pp. 121–122.

54. Ibid., p. 129 (*DTS*, p. 99). This translation of the French original makes the contrast between these two approaches to historical development more stark.

55. Ibid., p. 130.

56. Ibid.

57. Ibid., p. 137; cf. p. 148.

58. Ibid., p. 127. In his recent and very interesting discussion of the moral basis of Durkheim's sociological theory, Filloux (n. 3 above) also emphasizes the fact that Durkheim's initial discussion of mechanical so-

cieties occurs in the present tense and makes significant reference to aspects of contemporary life (p. 76). ("In much the same way," Filloux also notes, "one picks up the frequent uses of the phenomenological-projective 'we' when, in *The Elementary Forms of Religious Life*, Durkheim tries to reconstruct the sentiments of primitives living in the moments of creative effervescence" [ibid.].) But Filloux argues that primitive, mechanical society is for Durkheim only a "formalized social ideal," never an ethnological or historical reality. This interpretation misses Durkheim's great ambivalence over the status of modernity and its relationship to presuppositional context. If at first Durkheim did identify both primitive and modern society with normative order, he later reversed himself and completely historicized this theoretical emphasis. Primitive society came to have a very real historical reference, and this fact must be understood if one is to understand the great tension in Durkheim's discussion of modern society.

59. *DLS*, p. 151 (*DTS*, p. 124).

60. Ibid., p. 124 (*DTS*, p. 93). Although in terms of the presuppositional framework within which they are articulated these two phrases define the same kind of action and order, they refer to contrasting theoretical traditions in a way that underscores Durkheim's ambivalence. In the first clause, the phrase "a system of differentiated parts (*un système de parties différenciées*)" refers to the functional language of biology, to the organic solidarity of the body. The French *la partie* implies a part of a whole, in contrast to another synonym for the English "part"— *la part*—which has much more the connotation of "share" or "portion," as in "to share an interest in the profits," or "to share in the profits" *(avoir une part dans les bénéfices).* It is significant, then, that Durkheim chooses the former usage, *la partie.* Yet in the second clause—the phrase "some service already rendered *(un service déja rendu)"*—Durkheim has chosen a phrase which directly implies monetary transaction or exchange. Indeed, in the footnote to this clause, Durkheim writes, "for example, in the case of a loan with interest." This reference to instrumental action as rooted in the exchange simply between individuals or in exchange between parts of a greater whole was the same double reference—to economic laissez-faire and to biological organicism— embodied in Spencer's work. (The same contrasting uses of "parts" occurs in Durkheim's early writings as well. While he often employed *les parties*, he also referred to *les intéressées* and *les composants*, both of which, while similarly translated as "parts," have a more mechanical meaning.)

61. Ibid., pp. 124–125. Recent discussions of "exchange" in Durkheim's work often assume that Durkheim uses the notion consistently in either an instrumental or normative way. For instance, Traugott (n. 2 above, passim), emphasizing the materialism of the *Division of Labor*, as-

sumes that the later discussions of morphological position follow a similar presuppositional path. As I have noted, however, Durkheim himself employs a much more subjectivist approach to exchange even in these earlier writings, as in his review of Wundt's work on collective beliefs. In a more extensive discussion of "exchange" in Durkheim's work, Filloux (n. 3 above) takes the opposite approach, arguing that Durkheim always means by exchange the interaction of individual consciences (p. 67). He argues that throughout the *Division of Labor* Durkheim describes the "moral likenesses" of individuals as the basis of modern solidarity, giving to societies a "mechanical solidarity in order to understand both the constitution of modern societies and their development" (p. 76). But this analysis completely obscures the materialism of Durkheim's early work and the fact that at this point Durkheim himself came to the conclusion that moral exchange initiated by individuals could not supply the collective order he thought society needed.

62. *DLS*, p. 123, italics added.

63. Ibid., p. 111 (*DTS*, p. 79).

64. Ibid., p. 112.

65. Ibid., pp. 127–128.

66. Ibid., p. 112.

67. Ibid., p. 113.

68. Ibid.

69. Ibid., p. 126.

70. Ibid., p. 114.

71. Ibid.

72. Ibid., pp. 125 ff.

73. Ibid., p. 128 (*DTS*, p. 97). Here the more cognitive translation of *conscience* seems appropriate.

74. Ibid.

75. Ibid.; cf. p. 115.

76. Ibid., p. 131.

77. There are four major chapters in Bk. 1 of the *Division of Labor*. Ch. 2, "Mechanical Solidarity through Likeness," presents the argument for the presuppositional continuity of traditional and modern societies. Ch. 3, "Organic Solidarity Due to the Division of Labor," breaks with this position and historicizes Durkheim's theoretical position. Ch. 5, "Progressive Preponderance of Organic Solidarity: Its Consequences," tries to reassert moral order through a theory of a differentiated moral community. Ch. 7, "Organic Solidarity and Contractual Solidarity," which I will consider shortly, moves back sharply to an instrumentalist perspective. Chs. 1, 4, and 6 are less important. In ch. 1, Durkheim tries to justify his choice of a functional model, with the ambiguous results discussed earlier. Ch. 4, "Further Proof of the Preceding," amplifies the instrumentalist analysis of the important preceding chapter, although it also con-

tains some discussion of structural differentiation. (This instrumentalist phase of Durkheim's discussion actually extends into the introduction to ch. 5 as well, so it includes pp. 111–152 in the English edition.) Ch. 6, in contrast, marks a return to the strong instrumentalist emphasis that Durkheim will amplify in the concluding chapter to Bk. 1.

78. Ibid., p. 152.

79. Ibid.

80. Ibid., p. 71; cf. p. 172.

81. Ibid., p. 152.

82. *DLS*, p. 161, italics added (*DTS*, pp. 143–144).

83. Ibid., p. 169.

84. Ibid., p. 163.

85. Ibid.

86. Ibid., p. 169, italics in original.

87. Ibid., pp. 170–171.

88. Ibid., pp. 152–153.

89. *DLS*, p. 157, n. 20 (*DTS*, p. 130, n. 4). "For intérieure" is a particularly strong term for "conscience"; thus, "en son for intérieure" could be translated as "in his heart of hearts."

90. Ibid., p. 281.

91. Ibid., pp. 302–303.

92. Ibid.

93. Ibid., p. 172.

94. Ibid., p. 166.

95. Ibid., p. 172 (*DTS*, p. 147).

96. Ibid., pp. 152–153, 167.

97. Ibid., p. 166.

98. Ibid., p. 289.

99. Ibid., p. 172, italics added.

100. At a later point in his discussion, Durkheim neutralizes this argument that the cult of the individual produces moral solidarity in much the same manner as he does here (see p. 400).

101. Ibid., p. 173 (*DTS*, p. 147).

102. I will discuss some of the interpretive literature on this issue in the conclusion to my discussion of this chapter. See n. 129 below.

103. Ibid., p. 203.

104. Ibid. It is possible to read these rhetorical questions as containing a certain qualification of the very collectivist critique that Durkheim is introducing, namely, can "individuals depend upon the group *only* in proportion to their dependence upon one another" and "*only* in proportion to conventions privately entered into?" (ibid., italics added). These qualifications, if they are such, indicate, once again, Durkheim's wish to be able to emphasize collectivism without giving up individual freedom.

105. Ibid. In fact, of course, Durkheim does doubt their stability. He

does so because he, unlike Spencer, can appreciate the power of supra-individual coercive forces. He has slipped into this proposition about social stability because his discussion of social pathology and the instability of contemporary society is relegated to an entirely separate part of his discussion, namely, to Bk. 3. By separating these discussions, he can continue to maintain the fiction that the division of labor resolves the individualism/collectivism dichotomy throughout the major part of his argument. I will discuss this further below.

106. Ibid., p. 212.

107. Ibid., p. 213 (*DTS*, p. 191).

108. Ibid., pp. 203–204.

109. Ibid., p. 212 (*DTS*, p. 190), italics added.

110. Ibid., p. 217.

111. Ibid., p. 211.

112. Ibid., p. 205.

113. Ibid., p. 213.

114. Ibid., p. 207 (*DTS*, p. 185).

115. Ibid., p. 213.

116. Ibid.

117. Ibid., p. 214.

118. Ibid., pp. 217–218.

119. Ibid., p. 223.

120. Ibid., pp. 221–222.

121. Ibid., p. 223.

122. Ibid., p. 224.

123. Ibid.

124. Ibid., p. 223. Traugott (n. 2 above, pp. 255–256), who gives Durkheim a "structuralist" reading, notes the strong similarities between this approach to cohesion and the explanation Marx offers for class consciousness in his famous discussion of peasants versus workers in *The Eighteenth Brumaire of Louis Bonaparte*. There is indeed a strong resemblance between this instrumentalist phase of Durkheim's thinking and Marx's mature work, as I have emphasized here and will demonstrate further below. This strand of analysis, however, does not exhaust the theoretical resources of Durkheim's thinking in either the early or the later writings.

125. *DLS*, p. 224.

126. Ibid., p. 227. There is actually another paragraph at a much earlier point in this chapter where Durkheim refers to this possibility for a moral community based on occupational association (see p. 215). This reference, however, is completely isolated from the instrumental argument Durkheim is making at the time. I should mention that although I have tried to construct a reading of Bk. 1 that stays as close as possible to the actual texts of Durkheim's argument, there are several passages, like

the one just noted, which contradict my interpretation of the direction in which Durkheim is taking his argument. Such passages, in my opinion, are anomalous; indeed, they seem to attest to some relatively unconsciousness premonition on Durkheim's part that he has embarked on an inconsistent and contradictory path.

127. Ibid., pp. 227–228.

128. Ibid., p. 218.

129. The very pronounced ambivalence of Durkheim's analysis in Bk. 1 makes the emphasis in the recent secondary literature on Durkheim's consistency hard to understand. Giddens, e.g., believes that Durkheim has presented a successful theoretical argument for the moral basis of modern society. "The most important substantive conclusion which Durkheim reached in *The Division of Labor*," Giddens writes, "is that organic solidarity presupposes *moral* individualism" ("Durkheim's Political Sociology," pp. 235–272 in his *Studies in Social and Political Theory* [New York, 1977], p. 238, italics in original). As this judgment would imply, Giddens believes that Durkheim successfully resolved the individual/society dilemma as well. "The main thesis of *The Division of Labour*," he insists, "is that while individuation is a necessary concomitant of the dissolution of traditional society, it implies, not the complete eradication of the *conscience collective* but its transmutation in the form of the development of new moral ideals: those comprised in the 'cult of the individual' " (Giddens [n. 3 above], p. 6; cf., Giddens, "Four Myths" [n. 1 above], p. 360). Filloux's work (n. 3 above) makes a similar, and equally untenable, argument for Durkheim's consistently normative position, as I have indicated above.

The argument for the consistency of Durkheim's argument has, ironically, also been recently made from a completely opposite perspective—e.g., Traugott's argument (n. 2 above, p. 29) that the *Division of Labor* "is by all odds the clearest illustration of Durkheim's own variety of materialist analysis." Much earlier, Merton (n. 4 above, pp. 109–110) argued in a similar manner when he claimed that "in affirming the preponderance of organic solidarity in modern societies, Durkheim tends to depreciate unduly the persistent factor of community of interests." Merton concluded that "the fact that such forms of mechanical solidarity still subsist suggests additional grounds for rejecting Durkheim's argument of unilinear development."

Parsons' early treatment in *The Structure of Social Action* (n. 2 above, pp. 301–342) much more accurately emphasized the unresolved character of Durkheim's account. Even Parsons' discussion suffers, however, from an attempt to moralize Durkheim's dominant theme, and from the drastic misreading of certain crucial chapters upon which this moralization rests. Parsons claims that the "non-contractual element of contract" emphasized by Durkheim in Bk. 1, ch. 7, was, in fact, the "original problem" (pp. 319, 310) that occupied Durkheim throughout the *Division of Labor.* Parsons claims, moreover, that these noncontractual elements were for Durkheim synonymous with moral rules, and that his approach here was completely antithetical to the "dualism of state versus the nexus of individual interests which characterized the whole utilitarian tradition" (p. 315).

One reason for this misreading is, perhaps, that Parsons virtually ignored Durkheim's development before 1893. He argues that Durkheim develops in a linear manner from an early rationalistic positivism to a more subjective and normative position, and he identifies the former position simply on the basis of Durkheim's discussion in 1893. As has been seen, however, the writings before 1893 demonstrate that Durkheim was torn between antithetical theoretical frameworks from the very beginning of his career. (The extent of Parsons' misjudgment of this early period can be seen from his acceptance of Durkheim's claim that his one-year stay in Germany in 1886/87 had no significant effect on his thinking [p. 307]. Parsons believes Durkheim was too involved in positivism at that time to be affected by German idealist thought.) In fact, the direction of Durkheim's theorizing prior to 1893 was toward an instrumentalist position, and the major, if highly ambivalent, thrust of the *Division of Labor* was to try to resolve the voluntarism/collectivism problem within this general framework. In this context, it becomes clear that the "noncontractual" focus of ch. 7 is about the nature of the instrumental legal order and coercive state control rather than about normative order. Indeed, it is ch. 5, not ch. 7, that constitutes Durkheim's most important contribution to a theory of modern moral order. Interestingly, it is this very theme of moral differentiation, which was the focus of ch. 5, that Parsons focuses on in his brilliant later analysis of Durkheim's theory, "Durkheim's Contribution to the Theory of the Integration of Social Systems" (in Kurt H. Wolff, ed., *Essays on Sociology and Philosophy by Emile Durkheim et al.,* [New York, 1960], pp. 118–153); yet even here Parsons never refers to ch. 5. (For another important treatment of the theme of structural and moral differentiation in Durkheim's work, see Bellah, "Durkheim and History," in Nisbet [n. 1 above], pp. 153–176.)

For these reasons, although Parsons correctly sees Durkheim's early discussion of collective conscience and mechanical solidarity as being directed to basic theoretical issues as much as to historical ones, he can offer no real explanation as to why this emphasis progressively disappears in the course of the book's development. In fact, he sometimes argues that it was Durkheim's ad hoc decision to focus on law as an indicator of morality that led him to the historicist dichotomization he expressed as repressive versus restitutive law (*Structure of Social Action,* p. 318). In this connection, we will see that Parsons treats Bk. 2 of the *Division of Labor* as an anomalous part of Durkheim's analysis (p. 323), when in fact it could much more accurately be described as the main line of argument. It is not surprising, therefore, that Parsons never even discusses the contents of Bk. 3, which is still more consistently instrumentalist than Bks. 1 and 2. Though Bellah (n. 2 above) shares Parsons' basic perception that Bk. 1, ch. 7, is concerned with normative order and sounds the keynote of the whole work, he is more sensitive than Parsons to the "ambiguity and ambivalence" in Durkheim's treatment of such issues as the cult of the individual and social justice ("Introduction," pp. xxiv–xxvi).

130. *DLS*, pp. 233–234.

131. Ibid., p. 226 (*DTS*, p. 248). Durkheim's emphasis throughout Bk. 2 on *la lutte* as the crucial determinant of historical progress—translated as "struggle" and connected by him either to *la vie* ("existence") or *la domination* ("domination")—offers an opportunity to make a direct linguistic comparison between his conceptualization of theoretical logic and Marx's. Marx, we recall, concludes *The Poverty of Philosophy* (1847; New York, 1963, p. 175), his only book written directly in French, with a quotation from George Sand's *Jean Ziska* which he believes sums up what "the last word of social science will always be" under the capitalist system: "Le combat ou la mort; la lutte sanguinaire ou le néant. C'est ainsi que la question est invinciblement posée [Combat or death: bloody struggle or extinction. It is thus that the question is inexorably put]." Such similar invocations of *la lutte* cannot, of course, provide proof for the convergence of presuppositional perspective. It is, nonetheless, highly suggestive that Durkheim employs this same term time and time again in his analysis of the historical causes of labor division.

132. Ibid., p. 269.

133. Ibid., p. 267.

134. Ibid., p. 269 (*DTS*, p. 251).

135. Ibid.

136. Ibid., p. 270.

137. Ibid.

138. Ibid., p. 268.

139. Ibid., p. 270.

140. Ibid.

141. Ibid., pp. 275–276.

142. Ibid., p. 276 (*DTS*, p. 260).

143. Ibid.

144. Ibid.

145. Ibid., p. 283.

146. Ibid., p. 284.

147. Ibid.

148. Ibid., pp. 284–285.

149. Ibid., p. 287.

150. Ibid., p. 290.

151. Ibid., p. 287; cf. p. 290.

152. The case for making the generalization of collective morality a truly independent variable can, in fact, be found in Durkheim's own discussion of German social theory in 1887. Durkheim refers there to the increase in social volume as having primarily a moral effect rather than a material one, and he sees the more generalized collective conscience as an independent, indeed as the prime agent in history. Of course, Durkheim himself reverses this position in his subsequent early writings. Indeed, this reversal in *Division of Labor* simply echoes the early reversal. On this parallel in terms of Durkheim's specific reversals, see n. 176 below.

153. Ibid., p. 337.

154. Ibid., p. 336.

155. Ibid., p. 337.

156. Ibid., p. 336.

157. Ibid., p. 339.

158. Ibid.

159. Ibid., italics added (*DTS*, p. 330 n. 1).

160. Ibid., p. 348.

161. Ibid., p. 350. As if further evidence of his base-superstructure reasoning were needed, Durkheim refers in this final page of Bk. 2 to the reductionistic analysis of religious beliefs as reflections of demographic change which he made in his 1886 review of Spencer's *Ecclesiastical Institutions*. (I have examined this treatment at some length in the preceding chapter.)

162. Recent interpreters of Bk. 2 have shown an unfortunate tendency to take Durkheim's own perspective on his discussion. That is, they accept his equivalence of moral and demographic density and see Bk. 2, therefore, as perfectly consistent with the elements of normative order Durkheim emphasized in Bk. 1. Pope, for example, views Durkheim's emphasis on population expansion and exchange as simply another example of the "social realism" that dominates the entire work ("Classic on Classic: Parsons' Interpretation of Durkheim" [n. 4 above]). This perspective, however, conflates the problem of order with that of action, failing to distinguish the radically different approaches to action which are possible even when a collectivist, social-realist position is accepted. Though much more nuanced and generally more accurate than Pope's account, Lukes' discussion similarly fails to distinguish the tremendous differences between moral and material density in Durkheim's discussion (*Emile Durkheim: His Life and Work* [New York, 1972], pp. 154, 169). In his discussion of Bk. 2, Lukes often simply reproduces the vagueness and contradictory elements of Durkheim's original analysis (pp. 168–172). While he accuses Durkheim of technological determinism

and of being inconclusive about the basic details of the social change he describes (p. 164), these charges are never systematically documented. One reason for this failure is Lukes' argument for the close continuity of the *Division of Labor* with Durkheim's earlier writings. In fact, he views the whole of Durkheim's writings from 1885 to 1893 as comprising a series of theoretical clarifications and empirical specifications rather than as embodying any intrinsically opposed theoretical logics.

Filloux adopts an even more sanguine attitude toward this second book, accepting the complementarity between Durkheim's discussion of the instrumental causes of the division of labor and of moral evolution. He does so by taking Durkheim's statement about the necessary mediation of morphological factors by the collective conscience as the centerpiece of his historical discussion (*Durkheim et le socialisme* [n. 3 above], pp. 74–78). On this basis he can argue that Durkheim's historical analysis has nothing in common with that of Marx. I have shown, to the contrary, that Durkheim's insistence on such mediation is very short-lived and represents no more than a residual category in terms of his historical analysis taken as a whole. It is interesting that Nisbet—despite his very real insight into the tension between instrumental and normative perspectives that marks the *Division of Labor*—also seizes upon this brief emphasis on the normative mediation of demographic change. This passage, he claims, represents the crucial transition from Durkheim's utilitarian to his normative arguments, "the point at which the secondary argument [i.e., the normative one] begins to overshadow the initial [utilitarian] thesis" (*Emile Durkheim* [n. 1 above], pp. 36–37). Not only is this an incorrect interpretation of the significance of this passage, but it misreads the preceding and following arguments as well. Durkheim was certainly far from being unequivocally committed to contract theory earlier in the work, and after this section he continued to maintain a strongly instrumentalist discussion in Bk. 3.

Within the English-language tradition, the instrumental character of Bk. 2 was much more clearly recognized by functionalist theorists in arguments that long preceded these more recent interpretations. In 1934, Merton—strongly influenced by Parsons—discussed this section of Durkheim's work as clearly informed by Social Darwinian notions of the struggle for existence (n. 4 above, p. 106), though his discussion wrongly takes this as prototypical of the entire work. In 1937, Parsons himself discussed the Darwinian component of Durkheim's argument in *The Structure of Social Action* (n. 2 above), emphasizing particularly its biologistic emphasis on reproduction and survival, although in contrast with Merton he viewed this as diverging from the main part of Durkheim's argument.

In the French tradition, in contrast, it is particularly those interpreters with an economistic or Marxist orientation that have perceived this instrumentalist logic. Guy Aimard, in *Durkheim et la science économique* (n. 2 above, pp. 217–218), writes about the "determinist and materialist character" of Durkheim's argument, paraphrasing it in distinctly Marxist language. "When these conditions are realized," he writes in reference to Durkheim's discussion of the growth of volume and density, "the division of labor and organic solidarity, with the juridical forms and the corresponding collective representations, result from it necessarily." According to Durkheim, he argues, "a rupture of equilibrium in the social mass following its growth and condensation necessarily entails conflicts with the social organization resting on the principle of similar juxtaposed organisms"—i.e., on mechanical solidarity. Aimard, however, wrongly conceives this approach as descriptive of the *Division of Labor* taken in its totality. Armand Cuvillier, in his well-known article "Durkheim et Marx" (n. 2 above) makes this link between Durkheim's discussion in Bk. 2 and Marxism even more directly. Citing Durkheim's explanation of the human psyche as "in the last analysis [created] by purely mechanical variations in volume and density," he asks whether one must not admit that Durkheim has described subjective ideals as a "simple epiphenomenon of morphological variations" (p. 83). Georges Kagan, more outspokenly Marxist, notes the "striking analogies" between Marx's and Durkheim's reductionist theories of ideas, juxtaposing the two men's statements about the social determination of beliefs ("Durkheim et Marx," *Revue d'histoire économique et sociale* 24, no. 3 [1938]: 233–244).

163. Durkheim's argument in Bk. 3—precisely because of the empirical peculiarities I will discuss below—played an interesting role in postwar sociological theory, indicating, once again, how interpretive readings are crucial strategic elements in sociological theorizing. Critical theorists like Gouldner and David Lockwood utilized the instrumentalist emphasis of this purportedly normative thinker to challenge the dominance of what they viewed as the normative functionalism espoused by Parsons and postwar American functionalism. Gouldner's introductory essay to Durkheim's *Socialism and Saint-Simon* (n. 1 above, pp. v–xxvii), which strongly emphasizes Durkheim's discussion of the crucial role of unequal wealth and property relations, explicitly challenges Parsons' assertion that Durkheim emerges from the Comtean tradition. In a similar manner, Lockwood invokes the instrumental elements of this part of Durkheim's analysis at crucial strategic junctures in his influential antifunctionalist essays "Some Remarks on 'The Social System'" (*British Journal of Sociology* 5 [1956]: 134–145) and "Social Integration and System Integration" (in George K. Zollschan and Walter Hirsch, eds., *Explorations in Social Change* [Boston, 1964], pp. 244–257). Despite their insight into the antinormative elements in Bk. 3, however, both these critical theorists fundamentally misread it, first, as a highly successful mul-

tidimensional analysis (when in fact it is a one-dimensional and antivoluntarist), and, second, as prototypical of Durkheim's early work. Still, these exaggerated readings of Bk. 3 are more accurate than those of some of Durkheim's other radical interpreters, like Georges Friedmann, whose critique of Durkheim's theory of the division of labor simply fails to take his discussion of "pathology" seriously (*The Anatomy of Work*, [New York, 1961], pp. 68–81; cf. Irving Zeitlin, *Ideology and the Development of Sociological Theory* [Englewood Cliffs, N.J., 1968] pp. 242–252). From the other side, the liberal one, Parsons' neglect of Bk. 3 is equally indefensible. In *The Structure of Social Action*, e.g., Parsons writes that "in the *Division of Labor* Durkheim, while questioning the Spencerian explanation of the stability of contractual society, did not doubt the fact," referring in passing to the "relatively slight reservations contained in his [Durkheim's] discussion of the 'abnormal' forms of the division of labor" (p. 338, n. 1). As will be seen shortly, however, these reservations were not at all slight, and we have already seen that if Durkheim doubted Spencer's explanation it was in part because he perceived the instability of contemporary society in a way Spencer did not.

164. *DLS*, p. 370.

165. Ibid., p. 354.

166. Ibid., p. 356.

167. Ibid., pp. 369–370.

168. Ibid., p. 388.

169. Ibid., p. 382.

170. Ibid., p. 384.

171. Ibid.

172. Ibid., p. 370 n. 26 (*DTS*, p. 362 n. 1).

173. Ibid., p. 356, italics added.

174. The theoretical and empirical prerequisites for the normal/pathological distinction are implicit in Bk. 3. They are spelled out more explicitly in the final chapter to Durkheim's *Suicide* and in *Rules of Sociological Method*, ch. 3. Lukes (n. 162 above, pp. 172–178) also makes a strong critique of this distinction.

175. This last point should provide some perspective on the argument that the *Division of Labor* is consistent with, rather than discontinuous with, Durkheim's later writing and, indeed, with his earlier writings as well. Giddens, e.g., claims the work provides "a definitive perspective upon the emergence of the modern form of society which Durkheim never abandoned and which constitutes the lasting ground of all his later works" ("Durkheim as a Review Critic" [n. 3 above], p. 190). I have shown that, in both presuppositional and empirical terms, this is certainly false. Durkheim's extraordinary theoretical ambivalence and his ultimate failure to resolve the voluntarism/determinism issue in the way he had intended made him unable to construct a consistent empiri-

cal theory of the roots of modern instability and conflict. This assertion
about Durkheim's consistency is true, however, for one level of Durkheim's argument in the *Division of Labor*, and this is the ideological one.
Here as in all the rest of his work Durkheim emphasized the uniqueness
of modernity, its antithetical position vis-à-vis traditional, more cosmological systems, and its distinctive features of individualism and
equality. In this sense, the distinction between mechanical and organic
kinds of solidarities does remain central to Durkheim's later writings
after all, even if he later chooses to abandon these terms because they are
associated with presuppositional and empirical positions he eventually
rejects. What changes in the later writings, in other words, is the presuppositional and empirical commitments Durkheim employs to express
this ideological commitment to the restructuring of traditional society.
This is the sense in which Giddens is right about the consistency of Durkheim's development and Nisbet wrong about the drastic shift, for the latter argues that Durkheim adopted a "conservative philosophical"
perspective in his later work and, in fact, that this conservatism played
an increasing role in the *Division of Labor* itself (*Emile Durkheim* [n. 1
above], p. 28). Still, both Giddens' and Nisbet's arguments for the continuity or discontinuity of this first important work fail because they conflate the ideological, empirical, and presuppositional levels of
Durkheim's thought.

176. Given this parallelism on the general level, it is not surprising
that specific, concrete points of reversal are also the same in *Division of
Labor* and the early writings. (1) As has been seen in the later work, Durkheim's confusion about the bases of individual freedom—whether it
must be rooted in the "substantialist" individual or whether it can be
produced by morality itself—is revealed in the way he immediately contradicts his discussion of the "cult of the individual" as a source of social
control. This same reversal occurs in the early writings in the crucial essay on Wundt, where Durkheim rejects the substantialist approach for
an emphasis on the symbolic individual, only to return, almost immediately, to an emphasis on individual will as separated from society. (2) In
the early writings, Durkheim argues at first that the purely economic
emphasis on physical needs is inadequate because it ignores the necessary reference to uniquely human needs like honor and *esprit*, yet he
later asserts that population growth *(le croît physiologique)* must be considered the sole cause of any changes in the moral life, e.g., his analysis of
changes in *l'esprit domestique* in the 1888 article on suicide. This is precisely the same reversal that occurs in the later work in Durkheim's shift
from honor and moral indignation as the basis of legal control, where
law is connected with the collective conscience, to his emphasis on restitutive law as initiated by disequilibrium and the necessity for adaptation to external threat. Thus, in the later writings of the early period—

particularly the first sociological essays—as in the later chapters of *Division of Labor*, Durkheim continually emphasizes the struggle for existence (*la lutte pour la vie* and *la lutte pour domination*). (3) In his earliest essays Durkheim warns against viewing the state simply as a vast machine to forcefully repress unsocial behavior, and this is echoed in his analysis of the intimate relationship between the state and the collective conscience in his later discussion of mechanical solidarity. Once again, in the later essays of the early period and in the later chapters of *Division of Labor* (as well as in the chapters on organic solidarity), Durkheim reverses himself and explicitly embraces the mechanistic approach to the modern state. (4) Finally, in the early writings Durkheim criticizes political economy for equating social forces with natural ones, with, for example, the law of gravity. Yet in Bk. 2 of *Division of Labor*, and in the later writings of the early period as well, this is exactly what he recommends, defining the law of increasing numbers as the law of gravity of the social world. It is interesting that in this recapitulation of his earlier theoretical logic Durkheim does not feel the need to camouflage his commitment to coercive order through the reference to "habit" which was so crucial to his early work. Certainly this would have continued to be an effective conceptual device and would have modified, to a certain extent, the kind of abrupt ruptures that characterize the argument he develops. One can only speculate that with the discovery of the division of labor Durkheim felt he had no need for this kind of empirical compromise.

177. Herbert Spencer, *First Principles*, 6th ed. (New York, 1903), pp. 289–290, 314–318.

178. Ibid., p. 388; cf. p. 390.

179. Ibid., pp. 222–223.

180. Ibid., p. 222.

181. Ibid., pp. 446–466.

182. Ibid., pp. 417–418.

183. Ibid., p. 466.

184. Ibid., pp. 365–366.

185. Ibid., pp. 469–470. The opinion widely shared in contemporary sociological theory, first strongly argued in 1937 by Parsons in *The Structure of Social Action*, follows Durkheim's own insistence on the vast disparities between his theory and Spencer's. A historian of social theory, Robert Alun Jones, has recently reiterated this position, presenting Durkheim's differences with Spencer in *DLS* by elaborating the references that Durkheim makes in his own work ("Durkheim's Response to Spencer: An Essay toward Historicism in the Historiography of Sociology," *Sociological Quarterly* 15 [1975]: 341–358). Like most historicist reconstructions, however, Jones' essay is insufficiently clear about certain vital analytical distinctions, particularly the presuppositional distinction between the questions of action and order in Spencer's and Durkheim's

theory. He correctly stresses the fundamental individualism of Spencer's as compared with Durkheim's work, particularly the way Spencer takes the individual as existing prior to social organization and the way he radically underemphasizes the role of the state in industrial societies. Although these differences on the order question—as I have pointed out above—are in themselves somewhat exaggerated, the more important weakness in this argument is Jones' neglect of the way that Durkheim tended to share Spencer's perspectives on the instrumental nature of action in his discussion of historical development and in his analysis of societies with divided labor. In response to Jones, Perrin rightly emphasizes the similarities between Spencer and Durkheim (see Robert G. Perrin, "Durkheim's Misrepresentation of Spencer: A Reply to Jones' 'Durkheim's Response to Spencer,'" *Sociological Quarterly* 16 [1975]: 544–550; for a much more detailed discussion, see Perrin's "Herbert Spencer's Four Theories of Social Evolution," *American Journal of Sociology* 81 [1976]: 1339–1359). At the same time, however, Perrin's revisionist reading of Spencer underestimates the individualistic strand of Spencer's theorizing, which despite the modifications he introduced in some of his later writings maintains a distinctly laissez-faire perspective. Although it is true that Spencer described free actors as capable of altruistic motivation, his continued emphasis on the spontaneous "natural identity of interests" allowed him to maintain that this altruism was identical with economic self-interest as structured by the market and by the division of labor. This identification of instrumental interest with social reciprocity was, of course, precisely what Durkheim had attacked in his theory of the supra-individual elements of contract.

186. Marx and Engels, *The German Ideology* (1846; New York, 1970), p. 68.

187. Ibid., p. 43.

188. Marx, *The Poverty of Philosophy* (n. 131 above), p. 149, italics in original.

189. Marx and Engels, *The German Ideology*, p. 106.

190. Ibid., p. 52, italics altered.

191. Ibid., pp. 52–53.

192. Cuvillier, who quite correctly sees the materialist elements of Durkheim's analysis, argues, in effect, that Durkheim has offered a rather vulgar and mechanistic kind of Marxist analysis. The differences, in his opinion, are not so much in the two theorists' analyses of the problems of capitalist society but in their schemas for accomplishing its reconstruction. He rightly emphasizes that Durkheim presents a less dialectical approach because his systematic morphological theory focuses on the social whole rather than on the conflict between its parts. ("Durkheim et Marx" [n. 2 above], pp. 77–81.) In a similar vein, Aimard (n. 2 above) argues that the two analyses differ primarily in that Marx's is

more historically specific in his discussion of the effects of the division of labor in society. If the particulars of Durkheim's later empirical argument are taken seriously, he insists, "one would not know how, from this point of view, to consider it [the anomic conflict of capitalism] as 'abnormal' " (p. 227). Kagan (n. 162 above) makes basically the same point, as does the American Marxist James O'Connor ("The Division of Labor in Society," *Insurgent Sociologist* 10, no. 1 [1980]: 60–68). Once again, I would disagree with these French and American Marxist critics only in their argument that this materialism constitutes the entirety of Durkheim's first great work. I would also dispute, of course, their implicit contention that any purely instrumental argument, Marxist or otherwise, can in itself present a satisfactory general orientation for social analysis.

CHAPTER SIX

1. For Marx's critique of the role of intervening concepts, see *The Holy Family* (1845), pp. 361–398 in Loyd D. Easton and Kurt H. Guddat, eds., *Writings of the Young Marx on Philosophy and Society* (New York, 1967), p. 370, and Marx and Engels, *The German Ideology* (1846; New York, 1970), p. 48. Marx insists that premises can be verified only through purely empirical investigation (*The German Ideology*, pp. 42, 46, 47). He argues that an emphasis on the "speculative" component of science, its abstract element, would make it resemble idealist philosophy (*The Holy Family*, p. 372; *The German Ideology*, p. 103); that the scientist must adopt an either/or position on the determination of empirical investigation by the factual or metaphysical worlds (ibid.); and that there is not any role for philosophical orientations in science (ibid., pp. 48, 62).

2. *The Holy Family*, pp. 391–392.

3. Ibid., p. 392.

4. Ibid., pp. 377, 378.

5. *The German Ideology*, p. 58. Within the Marxist tradition only the philosophers of the Frankfurt school have been able to perceive the relation between the problems in Marx's theory and his method. Herbert Marcuse, in his early *Reason and Revolution* (Boston, [1941] 1960), drew the relationship between Marx's insistence on the omnipresence of alienation and his reliance on abstract scientific laws of explanation for capitalist society. "Marx's dialectical method," he wrote, "still reflects the sway of blind economic forces over the course of society."

> The dialectical analysis of social reality in terms of its inherent contradictions and their resolution shows this reality to be overpowered by objective mechanisms that operate with the necessity of "natural" (physical) laws—only thus can the contradictions be the ultimate force that keeps society moving. The movement is dialectical in itself in-

asmuch as it is not yet piloted by the self-conscious activity of freely associated individuals. (P. 316.)

But Marcuse has avoided drawing the obvious conclusion: he avoids criticizing Marx's methodology as undialectical only by expanding the dialectic to include a capitalism which denies self-consciousness to its
actors. In this way, Marcuse never confronts the tensions which such an
objectivist methodology creates for Marx's substantive theory.

Among the later generation of theorists, Albrecht Wellmer is the
most sensitive to these problems. "The union of historical materialism
and the criticism of political economy in Marx's social theory," he writes
in *Critical Theory of Society* (New York, 1974), "is inherently
contradictory."

> In particular, the basic assumptions of Marx's interpretation of history
> suggest, in contrast to the ideology-critical approach of the theory, an
> "objectivistic" concept of revolution in a twofold sense: on the one hand,
> they determine the revolutionary *function* of critical theory as that of a
> post-ideological, "positive" science, whereas on the other hand they lead
> to the camouflaging of the distinction between the *inevitable* and the
> practically necessary transformation of capitalist society, thus allowing
> the transition to the classless society to appear as the enforced result of
> the solution of problems proper to the capitalist system (p. 74, italics in
> original; cf. pp. 104–105).

My evaluation of Marx's scientific method does not, however, necessarily imply positivism in the technical sense of total dependence upon
observation without intervention of concepts. In this technical sense,
Marx's self-conscious method should be called empiricist, since he felt
that he used his empirical generalizations in an analytic way. The best
example of this self-consciousness can be seen in his "Introduction" to
the *Grundrisse*, particularly in the section entitled "The Method of Political Economy." There Marx remarks that "it seems to be correct to begin
with the real and the concrete," but "on closer examination this proves to
be false." It is better, he writes, to begin with "abstract determinations
[which] lead towards a reproduction of the concrete by way of thought."
(Karl Marx, *The Grundrisse: Foundations of the Critique of Political Economy* [New York, 1974], pp. 100–101.) The problem, however, is that Marx
never acknowledged the relation between these "abstract determinations" and nonempirical determinants like intellectual tradition or ideology. He described his science as revolving only around the empirical
pole, rather than as constituting a true two-directional continuum. Marx
would insist throughout his career that his work be taken as science in
the purely empirical sense. He concluded his 1859 Preface to *The Critique of Political Economy*, e.g., in the following way:

> This sketch of the course of my studies in the sphere of political econ-
> omy is intended only to show that my views, however they may be

judged and however little they coincide with interested prejudices of the ruling classes, are the result of conscientious empirical research lasting many years (*Marx-Engels Werke* [Berlin, 1962], 13:11).

The same kind of self-conception is reflected in his Preface to the first German edition of *Capital*, vol. 1. Marx takes the physicist as his model, declaring that the physicist "either observes physical phenomena where they occur in their most typical form and most free from disturbing influence, or, wherever possible, he makes experiments under conditions that assure the occurrence of the phenomenon in its normality" (1867; English trans., Moscow, n.d., p. 8). These are the words that Marx uses to justify to the German working class his exclusive reliance on the English case, the "typical" or "normal" capitalist country.

6. Marx, *The Eighteenth Brumaire of Louis Bonaparte*, in Marx and Engels, *Selected Works* (Moscow, 1962), 1:247–344 (hereafter cited as *MESW*), and *Class Struggles in France*, ibid., 1:247–344, 139–242. My understanding of the contrast between these two works was sharpened greatly by Jerrold Siegel's discussion in *Marx's Fate: The Shape of a Life* (Princeton, N.J., 1978), pp. 206–213.

7. Quoted in David McLellan, *Karl Marx* (New York, 1973), p. 281.

8. Ibid.

9. Ibid., p. 242.

10. Ibid., p. 281.

11. Ibid.

12. Quoted in Siegel (n. 6 above), p. 223.

13. Ibid., p. 303.

14. On the general intensification of industrialization throughout Europe see, e.g., David Landes, *Prometheus Unbound* (London, 1969, pp. 193–230). For the English case, see W. L. Burn, *The Age of Equipoise* (New York, 1964), passim.

15. Maximilien Rubel, *Marx-Chronik: Daten zu Leben und Werk* (Munich, 1968, p. 42), quoted in Siegel, p. 301. This discussion of the difficulty Marx had in understanding the slowness of revolution in the post-1851 period and the relationship of this difficulty to the empirical innovations Marx finally achieved in his later economic writing is indebted to Siegel (chs. 10 and 11).

16. Marx's notebooks from this period are preserved at the library of the International Institute for Social History, Amsterdam. See Siegel, p. 431, n. 25.

17. Quoted in McLellan, (n. 7 above), p. 283.

18. For English edition, see n. 5 above.

19. Marx, *Capital* (n. 5, above), 1:8, 10.

20. Ibid., p. 8. In the "Afterword" to the second German edition, Marx lauds a reviewer who offers a completely positivist account of his work (p. 18).

21. Ibid., p. 35.

22. The point that *Capital* presents a theory of the whole society rather than simply a theory of the economy has been correctly emphasized by the same twentieth-century interpreters who have tried—quite wrongly, in my opinion—to establish in this work the independent status of alienation. This extra-economic emphasis began with the fundamental reinterpretation by Georg Lukács in *History and Class Consciousness* (1924; Cambridge, Mass., 1971), where he wrote:

> The internal organization of a factory could not possibly have such an effect [e.g., an alienating one]—even within the factory itself—were it not for the fact that it contained in concentrated form the whole structure of capitalist society. The fate of the worker becomes the fate of society as a whole; indeed, this fate must become universal as otherwise industrialism could not develop in this direction. (Pp. 90–91.)

Yet even the interpreters before Lukács who had viewed *Capital* more exclusively as a theory of the economy still equated the work with an explanation of capitalist society as a whole. This reductionist equation was later articulated by Karl Korsch, the distinguished Marxist scholar and theorist who himself had once shared Lukács' view:

> Marx's new science is . . . above all, economic research. . . . It proceeds methodically from the view that when we have examined the bourgeois mode of production and its historical changes we have thereby examined everything of the structure and development of present-day society which can be the subject-matter of a strictly empirical science. In this sense, Marx's materialistic social science is not sociology, but economics. (*Karl Marx* [New York, (1938) 1963] p. 234.)

23. In the following, I am drawing generally upon the entire discussion in *Capital*, vol. 1, pt. 1, "Commodities and Money."

24. To avoid any confusion, it should be noted that whereas Marx talks about use-value as a more "natural" relationship in *Capital*, and exchange-value as artificial, in his early writings this distinction between a praxis-supporting economic order and an alienating one was spoken of as involving a contrast between "species man" and "natural man" (see ch. 2, sec. 2.2). The concept of "natural," then, is used in opposite ways in the two periods, though the theoretical and empirical meaning is precisely the same.

25. Ibid., p. 195; cf. pp. 508–509.

26. Ibid., p. 35.

27. Ibid., pp. 92–93.

28. Ibid., p. 176.

29. Ibid., pp. 152–153.

30. Ibid., pp. 167–168.

31. Ibid., 713–714.

32. Ibid., p. 171.

33. Ibid., p. 176.

34. Marx actually uses *C* to indicate simply commodities in general, since capital can refer to money as well as to technology—it is, in other words, a functional definition. I have altered this definition by narrowing it to refer to commodities of a specific kind: the means of production and labor which are used to produce money.

35. Ibid., pp. 243, 256.

36. Ibid., p. 233.

37. Ibid., p. 270.

38. Ibid., p. 271.

39. Ibid., p. 93.

40. The following discussion of organization is, in a technical sense, an analysis of an important segment of Marx's theory of the superstructure, for despite its concrete location in the economic world Marx considers any kind of political organization superstructural. I will continue this analysis of the political component of Marx's superstructure theory in my discussion of the struggle over the working day immediately below and in section 2.5. A more systematic analysis of the superstructure theory, with special reference to the role of "ideas," follows in the next section.

41. Ibid., p. 325.

42. Ibid., p. 324 (as before, when I have changed the cited English translation, I will cite also the original in *Marx-Engels Werke* [Berlin, 1962], abbreviated as *MEW*; in the present instance, see *MEW*, 23: 343).

43. Ibid., pp. 325–326.

44. Ibid., p. 330.

45. Ibid., p. 331. Marx is concerned, in other words, with the effects of cooperation rather than with its actual content. This is revealed in an interesting way by examining the eight different efficient causes which Marx offers for cooperation "in a given case." All but one of them are actually economic in content—e.g., the fact that cooperation allows the working mass to perform different functions simultaneously. (These causes are evidently assumed to operate through feedback mechanisms.) One cause, however, is not economic or material in the concrete precise sense. Cooperation, Marx writes, "excites emulation between individuals and raises their animal spirits" (ibid., p. 329). Even this quasi-subjective factor, however, is portrayed as a habit that automatically affects workers qua animals. It functions, in other words, much like "habit" in Durkheim's early writings.

46. Ibid., p. 331.

47. Ibid., p. 332.

48. Ibid.; cf. p. 360 for a parallel description of authority in the period of manufacture.

49. Ibid., p. 337.

50. Ibid.

51. Ibid., p. 364.

52. Ibid., p. 346.

53. It is in this discussion of the division of labor that Marx's specifically empirical theory of historical development comes closest to Durkheim's. Compare, for example, the following passage from *Capital* with Durkheim's discussion in Bk. 2 of *The Division of Labor in Society.*

> The exchange of products springs up at the points where different families, tribes, communities, come in contact; for, in the beginning of civilization, it is not private individuals but families, tribes, &c., that meet on an independent footing. Different communities find different means of production, and different means of subsistence in their natural environment. . . . It is this spontaneously developed difference which, when different communities come in contact, calls forth the mutual exchange of products. . . . The social division of labour arises from the exchange between spheres of production, that are originally distinct and independent of one another. In the former, where the physiological division of labour is the starting-point, the particular organs of a compact whole grow looser, break off, principally owing to the exchange of commodities, with foreign communities, and then isolate themselves so far, that the sole bond, still connecting the various kinds of work, is the exchange of the products as commodities. In the one case, it is the making dependent what was before independent; in the other case, the making independent what was before dependent. (*Capital*, 1: 351–352.)

54. Ibid., p. 421.

55. Ibid., pp. 423–424.

56. It was, of course, the factory that Lukács referred to in the argument, mentioned above, that Marx's theory included the entire society and not just economic life. In my analysis of the reproduction of labor power, which follows in a later section, this point will be made even more strongly.

57. Ibid., p. 622.

58. Marx, *Capital*, vol. 3 (1894; English trans., Moscow, 1966), p. 226. Marx never specifically names the falling rate of profit in vol. 1, although he is actually discussing it in many places.

59. *Capital*, 1:407.

60. Those interpreters who place subjective alienation at the center of Marx's theorizing regard "relations of production" as Marx's representation of the universalistic cultural tradition of Western society (see, e.g., Shlomo Avineri's *The Social and Political Thought of Karl Marx* (London, 1969), passim, and Bertell Ollman, *Alienation* (London, 1971), particularly ch. 6). If this subjectivity is granted, the entire movement of Marx's theory beyond his early Hegelian emphasis on critique is in-

comprehensible. On this issue, as in so many others in the interpretation of Marx's later works, the French structuralists are correct in the narrow sense. As Maurice Godelier writes in his important article "System, Structure, and Contradiction in 'Capital' ":

> Marx is . . . drawing attention *to aspects of reality which cannot be referred to any consciousness* nor explained by consciousness. . . . This basic, unintentional, non-original contradiction is not the opaque involuntary residue of intersubjective action. It is unintentional and without teleology. . . . These limits are "immanent" to capitalist relations of production and cannot be "overcome." (*The Socialist Register*, Ralph Miliband and John Saville, eds. [New York, 1967], p. 105, italics in original.)

The problem with the structuralist interpretation—and it is a fundamental flaw—is that it remains perfectly satisfied with this loss of theoretical voluntarism, seeing the reduction, much as Marx himself does, as a necessary correlate not only to capitalism but to science as such. The relationship between Hegelian and structuralist interpretation is an ironic one. The former correctly views voluntarism as theoretically necessary but misreads Marx's work as actually containing it; the latter wishes for an antivoluntaristic theory and, more correctly, sees Marx as successfully maintaining one. Once again, Marcuse is one of the few Hegelian-inspired interpreters who understand that Marx's emphasis on objective necessity is the corollary of capitalist alienation. "The law of value" which creates social contradictions, Marcuse writes in *Reason and Revolution* (n. 5 above), "has the force of natural necessity." After stating the law, he adds: "The results are of the same blind sort [as those of the laws of nature]. The falling rate of profit inherent in the capitalist mechanism undermines the very foundations of the system and builds the wall beyond which capitalist production cannot advance." (P. 312.)

61. Marx, *Capital*, 1:626.

62. Ibid., pp. 628, 632.

63. Ibid., 3: 245.

64. Ibid., 1:407.

65. Ibid., 3:230.

66. Ibid., p. 245.

67. Ibid., p. 257, italics in original.

68. Quoted in Siegel, (n. 6 above), p. 312.

69. *Capital*, 3:213.

70. Ibid., pp. 232–266.

71. These workbooks are discussed in Siegel, p. 346.

72. *Capital*, 3:211, italics added. This, of course, is the title of pt. 3 of vol. 3.

73. Ibid., p. 230.

74. Ibid., p. 233. Marx's emphatic assertion that the qualifying ten-

dencies do not, in the end, counteract the course of the falling profit rate is actually somewhat softened by the way Engels reedited vol. 3 of *Capital*, as Jerrold Seigel has recently discovered from extensive historical research (*Marx's Fate* [n. 6 above], pp. 336–351). Marx himself provided no chapter headings for the third volume. Instead, he supplied only the broad division into seven parts. Engels faithfully reproduced these, and the third part is "The Law of the Tendency of the Rate of Profit to Fall." In editing this third part into three chapters, however, Engels introduced his own opinion about the fate of the profit law, which was (as he makes very clear in his "Supplement" to vol. 3) that the law was false. These chapters (13–15) are entitled "The Law as Such," "Counteracting Influences," and "Exposition of the Internal Contradictions of the Law." The titles give a false impression of Marx's public intentions, although they more accurately reflect his underlying hesitancy. The misrepresentations created by Engels' editorial revisions are clear from an examination of the actual contents of ch. 15, where it is evident that Marx never talks about internal contradictions in the law but rather about the internal contradictions in capitalist society which are caused by the law. But Engels' editorial changes are much more drastic than simply reinterpreting chapter headings; he actually rearranged the sequence of Marx's manuscript. In Engels' published version, the final pages of ch. 13, which state the law, conclude with a six-page argument for the ultimate validity of the law in the face of any counteracting tendencies (pp. 225–231 in the Moscow edition). The chapter in the public version is then followed with the chapter devoted to the counteracting influences themselves (pp. 233–240). The final chapter in the section (ch. 15) exposes the ill effects of the law on society. In the original manuscript there is one fundamental difference from this published version: the six summarizing pages (pp. 225–231) that apparently conclude ch. 13 actually were placed by Marx at the end of the chapter on counteracting influences. In the original, in other words, Marx's commitment to the ultimate validity of the falling profit rate is much more clearly and assertively stated than in Engels's partly unfaithful reproduction.

This extremely interesting historical evidence throws some doubt, as Siegel emphasizes, on the conventional view that Engels was more committed to a positivistic and rationalistic theoretical system than Marx himself. (For further expressions of doubt, see Alvin W. Gouldner, *The Two Marxisms* [New York, 1980], ch. 9, and E. P. Thompson, *The Poverty of Theory and Other Essays* [London, 1978], "The Poverty of Theory," passim).

In the end, of course, this issue can be decided only by a theoretical analysis of Marx's actual writing, a task to which the present treatment is devoted.

75. The language of instability, functional disequilibrium, etc., is Marx's. The analysis in vol. 3 leaves little doubt that Marx employed a working model of society as a functioning system, in which institutions either challenged or contributed positively to the stability which was necessary for the system to continue. The best analysis of the functioning of this model in Marx's work is Neil J. Smelser's "Introduction" to his compilation, *Karl Marx on Society and Social Change* (Chicago, 1973), pp. vii–xxxviii.

76. *Capital*, 1:763.

77. Ibid., p. 10.

78. This reference to "nature" should be taken precisely in the rhetorical sense of a simile and not as a direct equation of social and natural laws. This is, indeed, precisely the relationship which I would wish to draw between Marx and Engels in terms of their treatment of nature and materialism in general. There can be no doubt that the later Engels articulated an approach to explanation that, no matter how subtle, gave to matter a role unmediated by human activity. This is most clearly stated in his *Dialectics of Nature* (completed in 1882 but published for the first time in its entirety in 1925), but it is also clear, e.g., in his *Ludwig Feuerbach and the Outcome of Classical German Philosophy* (New York, 1941), where he describes the materialist conception of history as "simply conceiving nature just as it exists without any foreign admixture" (p. 68 [*MEW*, 20: 469]; this passage is actually omitted from Engels' original publication of *Ludwig Feuerbach*, though the section in which it occurs was part of the original manuscript; it appears in *MEW*, 20:466–471, as an appendix to the *Dialectics of Nature* and in English in the 1941 book as "an omitted fragment from 'Ludwig Feuerbach,' " pp. 65–69). Engels expressed the same kind of thinking in his letter to Conrad Schmidt, where he claims that Marxism's distinction vis-à-vis Hegelianism is its realization that the "dialectic in our heads is in reality the reflection of the actual development going on in the world of nature and of human history in obedience to dialectical forms" (November 1, 1891, in *Karl Marx and Frederick Engels: Selected Correspondence* [Moscow, n.d.], p. 520).

Marx, it should be clear, never shared this kind of materialistic, unreflective epistemology; for him, nature and conceptions of nature were always mediated by human reflection. Nonetheless, as I argued at some length in ch. 2, above, and also in vol. 1, ch. 3, one must draw a distinction between Marx's epistemology in the purely philosophical sense and his "sociological epistemology," which derives from the conception of action and order he employs in his sociological analysis. These presuppositions, it should be just as clear, do in fact assume that within the period of capitalism and exchange value man assumes a passive position vis-à-vis nature and that social laws have the appearance of natural laws. Yet this holds true—and here Marx remains faithful to his reflexive epistemology—because of a social condition: the alienation of man from his species-being.

The problem with the critical attack on Engels' materialism is that it tries to shift onto Engels' shoulders the mechanical elements in Marx's own work. This attempt, of course, is intimately tied up with the failure of contemporary criticism correctly to understand the role that alienation plays in Marx's theory, and the failure to differentiate between his philosophical and sociological epistemology. E.g., in *The Concept of Nature in Marx* (London, [1962] 1971), Alfred Schmidt presents Marx's theory as "subjectively" informed without considering the impact of alienation on his specific sociology of capitalism. The ambiguity which such a position creates can be seen in Avineri's important analysis of the Marx-Engels relationship and of the subjectivity of Marx's thought in general. Although Avineri insists on the epistemological distinction between the two, he actually acknowledges that Marx might have neglected intentionality in his analysis of contemporary society. As a result, Avineri has great difficulty in making his argument for subjectivity in a fully consistent way.

> Marx's epistemology thus conceals an internal tension. It *tries* to solve the traditional epistemological problems, but it *tacitly* holds that human consciousness could operate according to the new epistemology [i.e., the anti-objectivist, dialectical one] *only if the obstacles in its way in present society were eliminated.* Hence Marx's epistemology is *sometimes* divided against itself: it is *both* a description of consciousness and a vision of the future. Consequently Marx *never fully denies* the validity of traditional mechanistic materialist modes of consciousness as expressions of alienated life in existing society. These *imperfect* modes of consciousness will exist as long as bourgeois society continues to exist. (*Social and Political Thought of Karl Marx* [n. 60 above], p. 69, italics added.)

Marx's epistemology is, however, *always*, not just sometimes, divided against itself, for it is a systematic characteristic of his sociological theory of history. It is revealing that in the concluding chapter of his work Avineri disclaims any intention of having discussed Marx's "socio-political intuition," and insists, instead, that he has considered only Marx's "philosophical system" (p. 256). Avineri has not in fact confronted the manner in which Marx's philosophical ideas become specified in the shape of a historical theory of society.

As for Engels, the epistemological and ontological materialism which he espoused in his later writing did not necessarily mean that he approved of mechanistic economism in his sociological and historical work. He was careful, for instance, to give to each level of material organization an independent reality, an insistence, as Schmidt rightly points out, that differentiated him from vulgar materialism. It is clear from the "qualifying" letters that Engels wrote about historical materialism after Marx's death (which I will discuss in ch. 10, below), as well as from his ultimate rejection of the law of the falling rate of profit, that Engels expressed some hesitation, despite his epistemological materialism, about an overemphasis on the economic sphere of society. Given his generalized position, however, he was incapable of translating this self-conscious concern into an alternative theory of society. Of course, as one can see from Marx's own residual categories, which I will also discuss further in ch. 10, he too sometimes hesitated when he was confronted with the full implications of his general theory.

79. *MESW*, 1:363.

80. McLellan, (n. 7 above), p. 40. For the Althusserian reading see, e.g., Louis Althusser and Etienne Balibar, *Reading "Capital"* (London, 1970), pp. 201–208.

81. *Capital*, 1:79.

82. Ibid., p. 176.

83. See, e.g., the treatment by Isaiah Berlin in his *Karl Marx* (New York, [1939] 1963), p. 139.

84. Lukács (n. 22 above), p. 86.

85. Ollman, *Alienation* (n. 60 above), p. 202, italics added.

86. Henri Lefebvre, *The Sociology of Marx* (New York, 1968), pp. 60, 62.

87. Ibid., p. 73.

88. *Capital*, 1:48.

89. Ibid., p. 72.

90. Ibid., p. 71.

91. Ibid., p. 72.

92. Ibid., p. 82.

93. Ibid., p. 73.

94. Ibid., p. 168.

95. Ibid., pp. 74, 37.

96. The first and most interesting discussion of this transition in Marx's empirical economic theory is Engels' "Introduction" to the revised edition of *Wage-Labour and Capital*, a pamphlet that appeared first in 1849 and later, in the revised form, in 1891. As I emphasize, however, this revision does not alter the generalized logic that informs Marx's work. For a discussion of this earlier theory in the context of Marx's general logic, see ch. 3 above, secs. 1.2 and 2.

97. *Capital*, 1:236, italics added.

98. Ibid., p. 539, italics added.

99. Ibid., p. 537.

100. Ibid., p. 583.

101. Ibid., p. 537.

102. Ibid., p. 539, italics added.

103. Ibid., p. 541.

104. Ibid., p. 540.

105. Ibid., p. 310.

106. For instance, Marx's recent English biographer, McLellan, calls the section on primitive accumulation "the finest chapter in the book," the finale to the "masterly historical account of the genesis of capitalism" that occupies Marx in the last three-quarters of *Capital* (*Karl Marx* [n. 7 above], pp. 348, 347). The debate over the status of this last section is part of the larger debate between the historicist-Hegelian and structuralist readings of *Capital*. As the present analysis makes clear, a purely historicist reading, which views Marx's account of contemporary capitalism as the outcome only of particular past events, is incorrect. Such a reading refuses to recognize the sui generis theoretical logic around which Marx's discussion is constructed. Godelier's brief article (n. 60 above) provides an excellent example of the "structuralist" reading which is in certain important respects complementary to the one taken here. (Godelier's parallel between Marx and Lévi-Strauss's structuralist method, however, is largely gratuitous; any nonhistoricist, functional method would be similarly parallel.) Yet the structuralists misunderstand the analytic sources of the logic which they often recognize—attributing it to the acuteness of Marx's "science" or to the correctness of his ideological views. For this reason, they usually ignore the drawbacks and alternatives to his approach; their own theorizing, in fact, indicates the same conflation of methodological positivism and presuppositional instrumentalism as Marx's own.

107. *Capital*, 1:61.

108. Ibid., pp. 72–73.

109. Ibid., p. 77.

110. Ibid., pp. 87, 88, 89.

111. Ibid., p. 169, and, for the most important statement of this, p. 713.

112. Ibid., p. 717.

113. Ibid., p. 718.

114. A good example of the kind of weak interpretations of Marx's superstructure theory to which sympathetic critics have been reduced is Giddens' statement that, for Marx, "the productive activity of individuals, in inter-relationship with one another and with nature, involves a continual and reciprocal interaction between social behavior and consciousness." Giddens writes as if Marx had explained the origins of ideas by pointing simply to the interaction between individuals, social structure, and nature. The specificity of Marx's explanation, in his view, comes into play only *after* these ideas are produced, in that their relative success is affected by the disproportionate resources of class society: "The ideas which are thus generated are conditioned in their diffusion or accep-

tance by the structure of class domination." (Anthony Giddens, *Capitalism and Modern Social Theory* [London, 1971], pp. 42–43; cf. pp. 209–211.)

Another strategy that has recently been employed to distinguish Marx's superstructure theory from a mechanistic theory is to focus on the residual categories to which his analysis, like any other, is periodically subject. The great equivocation that must accompany any such attempt is clear in the following passage from Gianfranco Poggi's discussion of Marx's superstructure theory:

> Marx's statements, for all appearances to the contrary, are compatible with a nondeterministic interpretation. . . . Many of Marx's statements are not as unequivocally deterministic as they are claimed to be. . . . Many of the deterministic-sounding statements appear to me rather less programmatic and rather more ambiguous than they have seemed to many readers. (*Images of Society* [Stanford, Calif., 1972], pp. 113–114.)

A similar attempt to focus on the exceptional passages by Marx is made by McLellan (n. 7 above, pp. 292–293). E.g., McLellan emphasizes the importance of Marx's analysis of Greek art in the *Grundrisse* (n. 5 above, pp. 110–111). Yet this discussion, in fact, was completely ad hoc. Marx wonders why Greek art should remain so universally esteemed if the material basis for its creation has long been surpassed. His answer is that although its conditions of production were primitive, the product itself was not, and that the charm of the art can still be enjoyed much as childhood memories may be enjoyed by adults. But if this argument were taken seriously it would completely undermine the empirical analysis of superstructure Marx presented in *Capital* and almost everywhere else, for the continued attractiveness of superstructural forms, their relevance as normative standards of evaluation, would then be related to their intrinsic qualities rather than to the conditions of their material production.

Jürgen Habermas has often argued that Marx's reductionistic approach to the superstructure is exclusively a matter of abstract theory—one belied by his actual empirical practice. But the utter consistency and empirical specificity with which Marx develops his theory of the superstructure in *Capital* effectively refutes this view. I have been unable to find in Marx's "practice of inquiry" the attention to "the structure of symbolic interaction and the role of cultural tradition" to which Habermas attests (*Knowledge and Human Interests*, [Boston, 1971], p. 42).

115. See the earlier discussion of the different approaches to the term "rationality" in vol. 1, ch. 3. This confusion over the meaning of Marx's use of "rationality" indicates the tremendous theoretical and, ultimately, empirical ramifications that assumptions about the rationality of action acquire in sociological argument.

116. *Capital*, 3: 799.

117. Cf. Godelier (n. 60 above): "In the practice of the capitalist system everything occurs *as if* the wage were paid for the worker's labour, and as if the capital had of itself the property of automatic growth and of rendering a profit to its owner. In day to day practice there is no *direct* proof that capitalist profit is unpaid workers' labour, no *immediate* experience of the exploitation of the worker by the capitalist." (P. 92, italics in original.)

118. Marx has also used the concept of simple reproduction in *Capital* to refer to the reconstruction and refurbishment of the machines and nonliving capital involved in production. In the present discussion, however, I refer not to his description of the simple reproduction of this constant capital but rather to his analysis of the reproduction of variable capital, which concerns, in his words, the "reproduction of the value of social labour-power" (*Capital*, 2: 345). Outside of vol. 1, Marx also discusses the simple reproduction of labor power in ch. 20 of vol. 2.

119. *Capital*, 1: 572.

120. Marx, *Value, Price, and Profit* (1865; New York, 1935), p. 57.

121. Ibid., p. 57.

122. *Capital*, 1: 572.

123. *Value, Price, and Profit*, p. 39.

124. *Capital*, 1: 600.

125. Ibid., p. 572.

126. Ibid., p. 601; more generally, pp. 599–603.

127. Ibid., p. 572.

128. Ibid., p. 571.

129. Ibid., italics added.

130. Ibid., p. 572.

131. Ibid., p. 573 (*MEW*, 23: 598).

132. Ibid., pp. 573–574.

133. Ibid., p. 573.

134. Ibid., p. 577.

135. Ibid., p. 714.

136. Ibid., p. 737.

137. Ibid., p. 574. On a few occasions, it should be noted, Marx does talk about the price of wages, and hence the cost of reproduction, as having a moral as well as an economic basis. In each of these instances, however, this morality is used as a residual category. Marx never explicates the nature of this purported moral factor, not does he integrate it in any way with his systematic theory. The reasons for such an ad hoc treatment should be clear. If Marx had integrated it, he would have had to invoke normative order and to explain how the moral aspect of wages can affect individual action. I discuss this particular residual category at greater length in the analysis of the struggles for the working day in sec.

5 of the present chapter, as well as in the concluding chapter to this volume, "Equivocation and Revision in the Classical Theory of Sociological Materialism: Marx and 'Marxism.' "

138. This interpretation of Marx's theory of class conflict has involved two different but often concurrent themes. One formulation has emphasized the emergence of a class-for-itself and views the new normative order of the working class as a reaction against alienation which reinstitutes the solidarity of "species-being." (See, e.g., Avineri [n. 60 above], pp. 141–163, and Lukács [n. 22 above], p. 178.) The second approach emphasizes the formulation false-versus-true class consciousness and describes the normative element as an intellectual construction which is brought to the working class from a source outside the immediate productive apparatus. (For this, see Lukács, pp. 326–327, and Lefebvre, *The Sociology of Marx* [n. 86 above], p. 73.)

139. Marx's other major discussions of class struggle occur in *The Eighteenth Brumaire of Louis Bonaparte, The Class Struggles in France, The Civil War in France, The Communist Manifesto, The German Ideology,* and *The Poverty of Philosophy.* I have referred to the arguments in each of these works at earlier points in the argument (see ch. 3. above), and will return to them, particularly to *The Eighteenth Brumaire,* in the concluding chapter to this volume.

140. *Capital,* 1: 235.

141. Ibid., pp. 295–296.

142. Ibid., p. 235.

143. Ibid., pp. 278–279.

144. Ibid., p. 289.

145. Ibid., p. 292.

146. Ibid., pp. 381–383.

147. Ibid., p. 292. It is hard to reconcile this hard-headed view of the state as an instrumental reward in the struggle for economic power with the view that Marx understands the state as resting upon alienation and psychological projection, which has been proposed by recent interpreters. Ollman, e.g., describes Marx's view of the state in the following terms:

> As with commodities, man's political products, through their appropriation under conditions of alienation, have acquired a life and movement of their own, a metamorphosis which carries them into and out of various forms independent of man's will. In this way . . . parliaments, laws and the rest have assumed the guise of quasi-supreme beings to which their own creators are asked to pay obeisance. . . . Regard how constitutions manipulate the very people who drafted them, to say nothing of those who looked on, because they treat these rules as holy writ. (*Alienation* [n. 60 above], p. 216.)

148. *Capital,* 1: 409.

149. Ibid., p. 265.
150. Ibid., p. 278.
151. Ibid., p. 403.
152. Ibid., p. 253.
153. Ibid., p. 239.
154. Ibid., p. 265.
155. Ibid., p. 266.
156. Ibid., p. 298.
157. Ibid., p. 283.
158. Ibid., p. 409 (*MEW*, 23: 432).

159. Ibid., p. 645. In this same discussion Marx graphically elaborates the relationship between the conditions of the worker's life and the laws of relative surplus value in a manner which also sheds further light on the status of alienation in his later work:

> We saw ... when analyzing the production of relative surplus value: within the capitalist system all methods for raising the social productiveness of labour are brought about at the cost of the individual labourer; all means for the development of production transform themselves into means of domination over, and exploitation of, the producers; they mutilate the labourer into a fragment of a man, degrade him to the level of an appendage of a machine, destroy every remnant of charm in his work and turn it into a hated toil; they estrange from him the intellectual potentialities of the labour-process in the same proportion as science is incorporated in it as an independent power; they distort the conditions under which he works, subject him during the labour-process to a despotism the more hateful for its meanness; they transform his life-time into working-time, and drag his wife and child beneath the wheels of the Juggernaut of capital. ... The law ... that always equilibrates the relative surplus-population, or industrial reserve army, to the extent and energy of accumulation, this law rivets the labourer to capital more firmly than the wedges of Vulcan did Prometheus to the rock. ... Accumulation of wealth at one pole is, therefore, at the same time accumulation of misery, agony of toil, slavery, ignorance, brutality, mental degradation, at the opposite pole. (Ibid.)

The language of inversion—the inverse relation between an intentional activity (the increased productiveness of labor) and its actual result (the degradation of the laborer)—presents a formal parallel to the social-psychological process of the alienation or reification of mental powers that occurs in the early Marx and in Hegel. Yet here Marx concentrates exclusively on the physical impoverishment of the worker and relates it directly to economic law, which reveals the completely different presuppositional status of the later writings.

160. *MESW*, 1: 523.
161. *Capital*, 1: 763.

162. Ibid., p. 763. I say "concluding" pages because the chapter on colonialism that actually completes *Capital* was probably added by Marx as a gesture to conciliate the political fears of his publisher.

It is now clear how much my view of Marx's class struggle theory differs from that of recent interpreters who, having emphasized normative elements in Marx's theory of capitalist domination, must similarly emphasize the role of solidarity and voluntarism in his theory of revolution. Dick Atkinson, for example, claims that Marx developed an "extended view of normative structure beyond that contained in the 'objective' class situation," that he discussed "those cultural traditions and standards, the myths and fantasies, which prevented rational understanding and action." On this basis, Atkinson goes on to argue that Marx's understanding of class consciousness has a strong voluntary strain. (*Orthodox Consensus and Radical Alternative* [New York, 1972], pp. 62, 112.) Avineri makes the reading even more directly subjective. "The activist and practical elements of this consciousness," he writes in reference to Marx's theory of class struggle, "imply that circumstances will change with the self-change of the proletariat." Revolutionary praxis, he insists, "is the self-change the proletariat achieves by its self-discovery through organization." (*Social and Political Thought* [n. 60 above], pp. 144, 143.)

Earlier generations of Marxist interpreters had, I believe, a more accurate perception of the theoretical logic that defines the relationship Marx described between revolutionary will and external conditions. Henri de Man, in *The Psychology of Socialism* (New York, 1927), wrote that "Marx should not be regarded (as he is so often regarded) as a fatalist in the sense that he denied the influence of human will upon the historical process." "Nevertheless," he adds, "it is true that he regarded the will as itself determined."

> In the Marxist view, social evolution is regulated by laws; this evolution is achieved by means of the class struggle; the struggle is itself the inevitable result of the economic evolution which creates a conflict of interests; its essence and its conclusion are determined by a specific objective, which is nothing else than a knowledge of the laws of social evolution. ... In becoming aware of this end, Marxist socialism realizes an action determined by the natural laws of social evolution. ... According to such a view, the will of the human beings who realize this historical destiny is predetermined by the laws of economic evolution. (Pp. 391, 392, 385.)

Sidney Hook offered a similar understanding of what he called "Marx's conception of purpose" in his important interpretation which appeared in 1938, *From Hegel to Marx: Studies in the Intellectual Development of Karl Marx* (reprinted, Ann Arbor, Mich., 1962).

454   Notes to Page 198

> The process of social development has no ends to realize which are not
> the ends willed by men. But those ends are not realized merely because
> they are willed by men. *What* is willed must be continuous with a situa-
> tion which is not willed but accepted. *When* it is willed must be deter-
> mined by objective possibilities in the situation. Only when these
> conditions are fulfilled, can the ends willed by men be realized. (P. 58,
> italics in original.)

Despite their differing subjective evaluations of Marx's position, both of
these writers have seen the presuppositional logic he employed very
clearly: although Marx endows his revolutionary workers with a will, his
insistence in the rationality of their perception makes it appear *as if* this
will has no independent status vis-à-vis external conditions. In this way,
the exercise of revolutionary will always realizes the possibilities established by external conditions. (For a parallel account of Marx's analysis
of the relationship between voluntarism and determinism, see Karl
Kautsky's chapter on the revolutionary will in *The Road to Power*
[Chicago, 1909], particularly pp. 36, 39, 40–41.)

Wellmer's critical assessment stands out among recent interpreters'
for its similarity to these earlier views. "[In] Marx's interpretation of history," Wellmer writes, "technical progress, the abrogation of 'dysfunc-
tional' social repression and the dissolution of false consciousness are so
indissolubly joined, that the irresistible advance of technical progress,
which starts with the capitalist mode of production, has to be interpreted
as the irresistible advance toward the commonwealth of freedom" (*Critical Theory* [n. 5 above], p. 73).

The empirical corollary to this theoretical debate, its traditional empirical specification, is the debate over the relevance of economic impoverishment to Marxist struggles in the contemporary world of
advanced capitalism. (For the orthodox position on the continuing
pauperization of the working class, see Roger Garaudy, *Karl Marx: The
Evolution of his Thought*, [New York, 1967], pp. 156–158. For the challenge to Garaudy's thesis from the more subjectivist New Left position—
also written from within the French left—see André Gorz, *Strategy for
Labor* [Boston, 1967], pp. 20–22.) If I have correctly presented Marx's
general logic, it is absolutely necessary to uphold the pauperization thesis if the precision and elegance of Marx's sociological theory is to be up-
held. The theory can, of course, be revised "upward" in the terms of my
presentation of the scientific continuum, in which case "Marxism" remains while some of its central empirical propositions are modified. I
will explore some of these more empirical challenges to Marx's theory in
the following section.

163. Marx, *Critique of the Gotha Programme*, in *MESW*, 2: 18–37,
quoting p. 25.

164. Ibid., p. 23.

165. For the effects of monopolization and state intervention from a Marxist point of view, see, e.g., Paul M. Sweezy, *The Theory of Capitalist Development* (New York, 1942), ch. 14; Paul A. Baran and Paul Sweezy, *Monopoly Capital* (New York, 1966); and Ernest Mandel, *Marxist Economic Theory*, 2 vols. (New York, 1969). For the Marxist argument that labor's contribution may not decrease in later capitalism, and that the rate of profit will not fall, see the excellent essay by Geoff Hodgson, "The Theory of the Falling Rate of Profit" (*New Left Review*, no. 84 [March–April 1974], pp. 55–82). For a speculative, neo-Marxist piece that takes these empirical developments as the basis for establishing a subjective, or "New Left," theory of revolution concurrent with the centrality of alienated consciousness, see Martin J. Sklar, "On the Proletarian Revolution and the End of Political Economic Society" (*Radical America* 3, no. 3 [May–June 1969]: 1–41).

166. The same self-consciousness might be ascribed to Marx's discussion of the movement toward joint-stock companies (*Capital*, 3: 427–429), where he points to the separation of ownership from control while fitting this development inside of his theory of economic contradiction.

167. See, e.g., McLellan (n. 7 above), pp. 290–304.

168. Marx, *The Grundrisse* (n. 5 above), pp. 704–705.

169. Ibid., p. 699.

170. Ibid.

171. Ibid., p. 705, italics added.

172. Ibid., p. 706, italics in original.

173. Ibid., pp. 705–706, italics in original.

174. Ibid., p. 708, italics in original.

175. Ibid., p. 708.

176. Ibid., p. 704. Marx's care in integrating potentially autonomous "science" into his theory of capitalist production directly parallels his treatment in *The Communist Manifesto* of the potentially free-floating revolutionary theorist (i.e., Marx himself). Both empirical elements are products of the mind—one in natural, the other in social science—and at certain points in both of his analyses Marx is sorely tempted to make each an independent determinant in the historical process. To observe his empirical strategy in these situations is to observe the formative impact of theoretical on empirical logic.

177. Ibid., p. 699.

178. Interpreters who have emphasized the empirical challenge of the *Grundrisse* have failed to take seriously the fact that Marx never links this supposed acceptance of affluent capitalism with a specific analysis of the means of overthrowing it. E.g., McLellan (n. 7 above) concludes his enthusiastic discussion of this empirical material by observing, without comment, simply that "it is noteworthy here [that] there is no allusion to the agent of this transformation—namely, the revolutionary

activity of the proletariat" (p. 300). But Marx could not make such an illusion without violating the entire thrust of his analytic work. I have tried to show that Marx's discussion in the *Grundrisse* makes reference to a different kind of revolutionary agent unnecessary: he returns to an external and conditional analysis of capitalist contradiction. (Wellmer [n. 5 above] points out that even if Marx's empirical speculations are taken seriously as propositional commitments, he has still economized his analysis of transformation, for he implies that the extreme shift in the organic composition of capital will inevitably bring a consciousness among workers of the new possibilities for leisure and free time [pp. 109, 113]).

179. The present use of historicism must be clearly distinguished from that of Karl Popper in *The Poverty of Historicism* (London, 1957), although some of the objections raised against Marxism are similar. Popper tries to evaluate Marxism purely from the level of its meta-methodological commitment, and he derives his definition of historicism from that level alone. But Popper's very differentiation of Marx's vision of science from other social scientific ones is incorrect. He begins by criticizing Marx's insistence on limiting scientific laws to specific historical periods; he concludes by condemning him for suggesting laws that are universal and transhistorical in scope. Still, whether or not Marx believed that historical laws were limited temporally, the meta-methodological status of his laws *within* any given historical period is no different from the status of laws in less historicist social science: they are predictions about the probability of events. To use Popper's terms, the status of law in "technological," or piecemeal science is no different from law in prophetic science.

When Popper's attack on "historicism" is examined more closely one sees that his objections are not really rooted in commitments that derive from this meta-methodological level at all, but rather from more substantive theoretical, ideological, and empirical issues. He objects to the notion that "historicism" does not allow that philosopher kings, ordinary individuals, and rational scientific knowledge can alter the course of history, and he criticizes its assumption of holism in favor of a more atomistic approach to social explanation. Finally, and most importantly for my purposes, he objects to the determinism of "historicism" on the grounds that it gives individual will little freedom or control. It should be clear, in light of the preceding discussion (including the analysis in vol. 1, passim), that these objections do not proceed from Marx's vision of the social world as bound by laws (particularly the probabilistic laws which Marx employs). These Marxian commitments derive, rather, from linking methodological orientations to other kinds of commitments. His theory is antivoluntaristic because, among other things, of its instrumental and collective assumptions about action and order.

My understanding of historicism refers to the relation between history and ethics, not history and method. Popper himself rarely refers to the ethical issue as such, except for his brief assertion that historicist morality assumes that what is morally progressive is morally good (*Poverty of Historicism*, p. 54). I would contend, rather, that the strict construction of Marx's theory holds that what is instrumentally expedient must be morally good. This is so not because of some commitment to "history," but because of how, precisely, this historical sociology is formulated.

180. Leon Trotsky, *Their Morals and Ours* (New York, 1939).

181. Maurice Merleau-Ponty, *Humanism and Terror* (Boston, [1947] 1969). For a strong criticism of Merleau-Ponty's argument for its relativistic ethics, see Leszek Kolakowski's review of the book in *The New York Review of Books* 15, no. 23 (Summer 1970).

182. In his impassioned *Plaidoyer pour l'Europe décadente* (Paris, 1977), Raymond Aron summarizes this distinctiveness very well when he writes that "the genius of Marx was to find the means of uniting these two condemnations [the moral and the scientific] and of founding each on the other" (p. 38).

The impossibility of building an antirelativistic ethical theory upon base-superstructural logic was forcefully stated by De Man, when he explained why, in his view, "socialism would be in a bad way" if the Marxist theory were taken as its only explanation. "Marxist theory," he wrote, "does not provide for the formation of new moral motives in the working class."

> In the present and future action of the workers, it sees nothing more than the mechanical continuation of the impulse born out of the antagonistic form of capitalist production. . . . To attempt to build up a new ethic upon the solidarity of proletarian interests is to march into a blind alley, for a sentiment which is only due to the awareness of an interest can have no ethical significance whatever. On the contrary, ethics presuppose a sentiment which finds expression in an inner impulse, independently of the consideration whether this impulse will or will not subserve an interest. We can even say that ethics do not begin until interest comes to an end, and that the worth of moral volition is measured by the strength of the opposing interest which this volition is able to overcome. (*Psychology of Socialism* [n. 162 above], p. 126.)

The crucial connection between the separation of Marx's actor from a subjective commitment to society and the impossibility of developing a theory of independent moral evaluation was sharply perceived by Robert Tucker when he wrote that Marx's "whole system . . . represented . . . a search for a way of transcendence that would entail no moral work of self-liberation on the part of the alienated individual."

> Marx exempted alienated man in particular from all moral responsibility for striving to change himself. Self-change was to be reached by a

revolutionary praxis that would alter *external* circumstances, and the war of the self was to be won through transference of hostilities to the field of relations between man and man. (*Philosophy and Myth in Karl Marx* [London, 1961], p. 241, italics in original.)

Daniel Bell argues according to a similar logic, but in a much more specifically political way, when he characterizes the result of Marx's later theory in the following way:

Individual responsibility is turned into class morality, and the variability of individual action subsumed under impersonal mechanisms. And the ground is laid for the loss of freedom in a new tyranny that finds its justification in the narrowed view of exploitation which Marx had fashioned. ("In Search of Marxist Humanism," *Survey*, no. 32 [April–June 1960], p. 26.)

183. The extensive debate over the status of the concept "dictatorship of the proletariat" in Marx's thought has focused too exclusively on the linguistic usage itself. Marx actually used the term rather infrequently—in his writings on the 1848–1850 revolutionary period (e.g., *Class Struggles in France*, 1848–1850, *MESW*, 1:223), in his famous letter to Weydemeyer in 1852 (*Selected Correspondence* [n. 78 above], p. 69), and in the *Critique of the Gotha Programme* in 1875. It is clear, moreover, as Marx's anti-Leninist defenders argue, that even when he used this term Marx did not envision dictatorship in the modern totalitarian sense. He employed it, rather, as part of his dialogue with the more conspiratorial Blanquists; it denoted, first, the general economic dominance the proletariat would assume after the revolution (creating a formal parallel to the capitalist "dictatorship" of the bourgeoisie) and, second, the necessity for some kind of force in bringing this revolution about. (See, e.g., Hal Draper, "Marx and the Dictatorship of the Proletariat," *New Politics* 4, no. 4 [1962]:91–104, as well as Avineri [n. 60 above], pp. 239–249, and idem, "How to Save Marx from the Alchemists of Revolution," *Political Theory* 4, no. 1 [1976]:35–44; both writers, however, underemphasize Marx's reference to the need for force.)

At the same time, however, it is equally clear that Marx envisioned force and terror as necessary components of most Communist revolutions. Although he made possible exceptions of democratic countries like the United States, England, and Holland, he emphasized that "force is the midwife of every old society pregnant with the new one" (*Capital*, 1: 751) and occasionally justified this midwifery in very specific terms. "The very cannibalism of the counterrevolution", he wrote in reference to the events of 1848, "will convince the nations that there is only one way in which the murderous death agonies of the old society and the bloody birth throes of the new societies can be shortened, simplified and concentrated, and that is *revolutionary terror"* (Marx and Engels, *The Revolution of 1848–9*, ed. Bernard Isaacs [Moscow, 1972], p. 124, italics in original). Most attempts at socialist revolution, Marx believed, would produce a civil war between classes, and the workers would have to be armed not simply for self-defense but to engage in revolutionary battle against the bourgeoisie. The purpose of this battle would be to expropriate private property and, more generally, to destroy the material basis of capitalism. Thus, Marx talked in the *Manifesto* about "despotic inroads on the rights of property and on the conditions of bourgeois production" that would have to be made (*MESW*, 1:53), and in *Class Struggles in France* he wrote that "socialism is the *declaration of the permanence of the revolution*, the *class dictatorship* of the proletariat as the necessary transit point to the abolition of *class distinctions* generally, to the abolition of all the social relations that correspond to these relations of production, to the revolutionizing of all the ideas that result from these social relations" (ibid., p. 223, italics in original). (For a related discussion of Marx's and Engels' strategy for arming the German workers during the phase of intense revolutionary activity in the spring of 1850, see Siegel [n. 6 above], p. 229; for Siegel's intelligent overview of the whole question of Marx's attitudes toward extrademocratic violence, see his review of Richard N. Hunt's *The Political Ideas of Marx and Engels*—the most recent argument for a purely social-democratic Marx—in *European Labor and Working Class History Newsletter*, no. 7 [May 1975], pp. 30–36.)

Marx justified this strategy of military struggle and terror—the particularistic application of force—by citing the practical and external exigencies of class interest. This rationalizing relativism comes through in his writings on the Paris Commune of 1871, even though he criticized it for its anarchistic failure to employ more strategic coercion in defense of the revolution: "With the savage warfare of Versailles outside, and its attempts at corruption and conspiracy inside Paris —would the Commune not have shamefully betrayed its trust by affecting to keep up all decencies and appearances of liberalism as in a time of profound peace?" (*MESW*, 1:528). Marx was confident, however, that once the material basis of reaction was eliminated, real democracy—and the universalistic application of force associated with the rule of law—would resume. The fact that he failed to see the danger that a real political dictatorship could emerge from this period of temporary "dictatorship" is, then, precisely the point. His relativistic moral theory gave him no theoretical sense of the enormous ethical problems that such a period could produce. If there is no insistence on any trans-situational moral codes, how would a ruling class or its political representatives ever decide that it was in their rational interest to refrain from the forceful imposition of their own will? Whether or not force may, in fact, empirically be necessary in revolutionary situations is not my concern here. The problem is how this force should be evaluated and what the theoretical resources are for making this evaluation.

184. E.g., Avineri (n. 60 above), pp. 220–238.

185. *MESW*, 2:24.

186. Marx, "Economic and Philosophical Manuscripts" in T. B. Bottomore, ed., *Karl Marx: Early Writings* (New York, 1963), p. 127.

187. *Capital*, 3:820.

188. Elie Halévy analyzed this relationship between Marx's sociology of communism and the pre-utilitarian theories of natural identity of interest in his brilliant short book, *Thomas Hodgkins* (London, [1903] 1956; see particularly pp. 175–176), an analysis of one of the radical British political economists who had some influence on Marx's early transition to political economy. In *The Growth of Philosophic Radicalism* (1901–1903) Halévy formulated the basic distinction between artificial and natural identity of interest that has been crucial to the present work.

In stressing the failure of constraint to operate in Marx's theory of true communism, I am agreeing on this specific point with the conservatives' criticism that Marx failed to develop a theory of the secondary institutions which are necessary for a democratic society (see, e.g., Robert A. Nisbet, *The Sociological Tradition* [New York, 1966], pp. 132–141). I stress, however, the theoretical reasons for what eventually came to be this moral problem in Marx's work, rather than any self-conscious political intention. Marcuse's early insight into the individualistic, postsociological structure of Marx's communism attests to this initial theoretical rather than ideological status:

> Reason, when determined by rational social conditions, is determined by itself. Socialist freedom embraces both sides of the relation between consciousness and social existence. The principle of historical materialism leads to its self-negation. (*Reason and Revolution* [n. 5 above], pp. 319–320; cf. Atkinson [n. 162 above], pp. 109–110.)

189. Marx and Engels, *The German Ideology* (n. 1 above), p. 41.

190. Ibid., p. 39.

191. *The Holy Family* (note 1, above), p. 379, italics in original.

192. *MESW*, 1: 363.

193. Marx, *The Grundrisse* (n. 5 above), p. 265. [*Grundisse der Kritique der Politischen Ökonomie* (n. 5 above), p. 176.]

194. Ibid., pp. 156–157, italics in original.

195. *The German Ideology*, p. 42, italics added.

196. Ibid., pp. 46–47 (*MEW*, 3: 25).

197. Ibid.

198. Marx, *The Poverty of Philosophy* (1847; New York, 1963), p. 109.

199. Ibid., p. 115.

200. Ibid.

201. Ibid., p. 83 (*MEW*, 4: 109).

202. It is precisely the failure to distinguish these two fundamental questions of action and order that has made much of the recent interpretation of Marx so vague and imprecise. E.g., after quoting the famous passage from Marx's Preface, Giddens suggests that "much calumny has been heaped upon Marx for this observation" and that it has largely been misplaced. "The operative term here," he insists, "is *social* being, and there can be little objection to the generalization that consciousness is governed by human activity in society." (*Capitalism and Modern Social Theory* [n. 114 above], p. 41, italics in original.) In a similar vein, Avineri (n. 60 above) argues that "whether change in individuals will precede change in circumstances" is "quite irrelevant." And he justifies this dismissal on grounds that simply take over Marx's own confusion of different kinds of social determinism: "As 'society' does not exist, according to Marx, as an entity distinct from the 'individuals,' change in individuals is *ipso facto* also change in society, and change in social circumstances is also change in individuals." (P. 92.)

This conflation of action and order, then, sometimes makes it difficult for critics to see the very distinctions about "social" order that Marx tried so hard to make. Giddens, e.g., argues that Marx insisted simply that "ideology must be studied in relation to the social relationships in which it is embedded" (p. 41). Ollman, similarly, suggests that Marx meant to include in his definition of determinate conditions "everything that the individual comes into contact with from the time of birth onward," including "family, friends, and one's very place on earth each moment of the day" (*Alienation* [n. 60 above], p. 125). And Nathan Rotenstreich takes "conditions" in such a general and undifferentiated way as to suggest that the only way to encompass voluntarism is to step outside the collectivist framework completely (*Basic Problems in Marx's Philosophy* [Indianapolis, 1965], pp. 32–34).

CHAPTER SEVEN

1. An intellectual who stood somewhat apart from the French academic scene, the Marxist Georges Sorel, testified to the immediate impact of the *Division of Labor* in the critical appreciation he wrote for the first issue of the Marxist journal *Le Devenir social* (April 1895, pp. 1–26): "M. E. Durkheim is professor of sociology at the faculty of letters of Bordeaux; he proposed, in 1893, a thesis on the *division of labor*, that created a great ado in the philosophical world" (p. 1), italics in original.

2. Emile Durkheim, "Course in Sociology: Opening Lecture," pp. 43–70 in Mark Traugott, ed., *Emile Durkheim on Institutional Analysis* (Chi-

cago, 1978), p. 57. Originally published in *Revue internationale de l'enseignement* 15 (1888): 23–42.

3. Ibid., p. 58.

4. Durkheim, "La Science positive de la morale en Allemagne," *Revue philosophique* 24 (1887): 33–58, 113–142, 275–284, esp. 114.

5. The first clause is taken from Durkheim's Latin dissertation (1892), "Montesquieu's Contribution to the rise of Social Science." pp. 1–64 in Durkheim, *Montesquieu and Rousseau* (Ann Arbor, Mich., 1960), p. 52; the quotation is from "La Science positive," p. 114.

6. "Course in Sociology: Opening Lecture," p. 49.

7. "La Science positive," p. 276.

8. "Course in Sociology: Opening Lecture," pp. 57, 58.

9. Durkheim, "The Principles of 1789 and Sociology," pp. 34–43 in Robert N. Bellah, ed., *Emile Durkheim on Morality and Society* (Chicago, 1973), p. 39. Originally published in *Revue internationale de l'enseignement* 19 (1890): 450–456.

10. "Course in Sociology: Opening Lecture," pp. 50, 53.

11. Ibid., p. 44.

12. Ibid., p. 46.

13. Ibid., pp. 47, 48, 52.

14. Durkheim, "Montesquieu's Contribution" (n. 5 above), p. 3.

15. Ibid., p. 12.

16. Emile Durkheim, *The Division of Labor in Society* (1893; New York, 1933), p. 37. Quotations are from the second Preface (1902).

17. Ibid., pp. 37–38.

18. E.g., in *The Rules of Sociological Method*, which marked a revolutionary break in his theoretical thinking, as will be seen, Durkheim still writes that "all preconceptions must be eradicated" (1895; New York, 1938, p. 31). In *Suicide* (1897; New York, 1951), Durkheim continually tries to make analogies between the precision of his own statistical analysis of social forces and those of thermodynamics (see, e.g., pp. 299, 309–310). More than a decade later he is still arguing that the scientist "must accept in principle the fact that he knows nothing about them [social phenomena] or about their characteristics or of the causes on which they depend." The scientist "must, in a word, place himself in a state of mind like that of physicists, chemists, physiologists, and today even psychologists when they enter a previously unexplored region of their scientific domain." ("Sociology and the Social Sciences," pp. 71–87 in Traugott [n. 1 above], pp. 86–87; first published in 1909 in *De la méthode dans les sciences.*) This self-conscious positivism, of course, did not mean that Durkheim's theoretical insights in his later writings were consistent with such instrumentalist thinking about science on the presuppositional level. By the time he had composed *Primitive Classification* with Marcel Mauss in 1902—a work I will discuss later—he had already demonstrated that sci-

ence could not proceed without strong a priori cultural assumptions. His fullest statement of this comes in 1912 in *The Elementary Forms of Religious Life*, where he actually applies this insight directly to science (New York, 1965, pp. 486 ff.).

The notion that Durkheim's instrumentalism on the presuppositional level was created by his methodological positivism has been widely accepted because it corresponds to an extremely deep-rooted error in the Western theoretical tradition. Elie Halévy, e.g., in his classical work on utilitarian theory, *The Growth of Philosophic Radicalism* (1901–1903; New York, 1972), argues that it was Bentham's intense desire to create a science of society that led him to see only egoistic motives in the creation of social order:

> The aim of Bentham, as of all Utilitarian philosophers, was to establish morals as an exact science. He therefore sought to isolate in the human soul that feeling which seems to be the most easily measurable. Now the feeling of sympathy seems to fulfill this condition less than any other. . . . Egoistic feelings, on the other hand, are better qualified than any other to admit an objective equivalent. (P. 15.)

Ironically, Halévy was one of Durkheim's first major critics in France; he accused him of theoretical utilitarianism and linked this with Durkheim's positivism. While Halévy was on safe grounds for the work of 1893 and before, subsequent developments in Durkheim's work were to prove him incorrect. Indeed, although there is no record of Halévy's ever withdrawing his critical evaluation of Durkheim, the conclusion of his own great work on utilitarianism treats Durkheim's later theory of symbolic representation somewhat more sympathetically. But the most important source for the belief in the crucial impact of positivism on Durkheim in particular is Talcott Parsons' interpretation in *The Structure of Social Action*. Parsons argues, first, that Durkheim mistakenly confused the scientific acceptance of natural laws with a mechanistic perspective on the nature of human action per se (New York, [1937] 1968, pp. 345, 348). Second, he sees Durkheim as moving away from his theoretical instrumentalism only insofar as he moves away from this methodological position, a movement propelled, Parsons believes, by the ineluctable force of empirical fact (pp. 249–251). For recent arguments for this inherent relationship between positivism and instrumentalism, see the work of Jürgen Habermas.

19. *Revue philosophique* 35 (1893): 290. Later in this review, Durkheim criticizes Richard's method as too "dialectical" and as insufficiently scientific, but this early statement still stands as a retrospective glance at the dangers of his own positivism.

20. Ibid., p. 292, italics added.

21. Ibid., p. 293.

22. Ibid., p. 296.

23. Durkheim, "Note sur la définition du socialisme," pp. 506–512 in *Revue philosophique* 36 (1893): 510.

24. Durkheim, review of Richard (n. 19 above), p. 291. Attention should be drawn here to the entirely different orientation Durkheim has given to *la lutte*, the French term employed frequently in the *Division of Labor* to denote the "struggle" for existence which he viewed as motivating society, and which Marx used in a similar way in the original French edition of *The Poverty of Philosophy*. Durkheim now uses *la lutte* to indicate the antisocial, anticollectivist dimension of society which he rejects as an object of social analysis.

25. Durkheim, *The Rules of Sociological Method* (n. 18 above), p. lx.

26. Ibid., pp. 1–3.

27. Ibid., p. 1.

28. Ibid., pp. 2, 9.

29. Ibid., pp. 3–4.

30. Ibid., p. 9.

31. Ibid., pp. 5, 4.

32. Ibid., p. 7.

33. Ibid., pp. 8, 5. "*L'âme*" is translated as "mind" throughout the *Rules*—and in other works as well—whereas it seems more appropriate, particularly as one begins to understand the direction of Durkheim's work, to translate it as "soul."

34. Ibid., p. 12.

35. Ibid. In subsequent chapters of *Rules*, which I will not consider at any length here, Durkheim confirms this position on the nature of social facts. In the third chapter, e.g., he writes:

> Social life consists ... of free currents perpetually in the process of transformation and incapable of being mentally fixed by the observer, and the scholar cannot approach the study of social reality from this angle. But we know [nonetheless] that it possesses the power of crystallization without ceasing to be itself. Thus, apart from the individual acts to which they give rise, collective habits find expression in definite forms. ... As these forms have a permanent existence and do not change with the diverse applications made of them, they constitute a fixed object, a constant standard within the observer's reach, exclusive of subjective impressions and purely personal observations. (P. 451.)

One could wish for no better example of the way that Durkheim has reconciled his positivistic desire to study only external, visible objects with his new understanding that these objects have a subjective rather than objective status.

36. Ibid., pp. 2, 4.

37. Ibid., p. 9.

38. Ibid., p. 6.

39. Ibid.

40. Ibid., p. 2.

41. Ibid., pp. 11–13, italics added.

42. I must insist here that I am not talking about any ideological distance between the *Division of Labor* and *Rules*, for Durkheim continues to maintain in the latter work his understanding of modern society as an individually oriented and differentiated social system that is distinguished by its capacity for critical rationality. On this issue, as will be noted in the chapter following, Durkheim's later writing is rooted in *Division of Labor's* fifth chapter, the single chapter where he had broken entirely free of the limited instrumentalism that characterized most of the rest of that book. It should also be noted, for the record, that there are, in fact, two or three instances in the *Rules* monograph where Durkheim reverts to the instrumentalist reasoning of his earlier work (see, e.g., pp. 3 and 92–93). This kind of occasional backward glance recurs throughout his later writing and is, I believe, entirely residual to the main thrust of the later work. It represents, perhaps, a bad conscience, a subliminal sense that something is lacking from the later theory in terms of its understanding of the material world.

43. Ibid., pp. 113–114.

44. Ibid., p. 115, n. 22.

45. Durkheim, *Socialism and Saint-Simon*, ed. Alvin W. Gouldner (Yellow Springs, Ohio, 1958), p. 19.

46. Ibid., p. 22.

47. Ibid., p. 25.

48. Ibid., pp. 18–19.

49. Ibid., p. 21.

50. Ibid., p. 199.

51. Ibid., p. 204.

52. Ibid., p. 197.

53. Ibid., p. 199.

54. Ibid., p. 200. Durkheim's reference to "social order" in this context is clearly conflationary, for he is equating the collective force that orders individual action with one that is sufficient also to produce empirical equilibrium. We noted this conflation as crucial to the transition that Durkheim made toward his materialist sociology in the earlier writings. A testimony, perhaps, to Durkheim's ideological commitment to stabilizing the French nation on its liberal path, it continues to play a dominant role in the later work as well, even when the nature of collective order is different. We shall also see, however, that this commitment to empirical equilibrium does not characterize every aspect of Durkheim's normative theory, and of course, in terms of theoretical logic, there is no reason for it to do so.

55. Ibid., p. 52.

56. Ibid.
57. Ibid., pp. 68–69.
58. Ibid., p. 7.
59. Ibid., pp. 41, 7.
60. Ibid., p. 25. The similarity between this later theorizing by Durkheim and the early work of Marx has already been noted (see the beginning of this section). As this statement about socialism indicates, Durkheim's sensitivity to the subjective and ideal aspects of socialism represents precisely the kind of emphasis on the nonalienated, "praxis"-inspired aspect of revolutionary struggle that Marx would have had to consider if he had continued the theoretical orientation of his earlier writings. It is interesting, in this respect, to quote more fully from the Durkheimian description of socialism and to compare it with Marx's famous early statement about religion as the product of a creative, if partly alienated, consciousness. Durkheim writes:

> It is fervor that has been the inspiration of all these systems; What gave them life and strength is a thirst for a more perfect justice, pity for the misery of the working classes, a vague sympathy for the travail of contemporary societies. . . . Socialism is not a science, a sociology in miniature—it is a cry of grief, sometimes of anger, uttered by men who feel most keenly our collective malaise. Socialism is to the facts which produce it what the groans of a sick man are to the illness with which he is afflicted, to the needs that torment him. (Ibid., p. 7.)

In 1843, Marx articulates the relative autonomy of rebellious consciousness, in this case a religious one, in a remarkably similar way:

> Man makes religion; religion does not make man. Religion is indeed man's self-consciousness and self-awareness so long as he has not found himself. . . . This state, this society, produce religion which is an *inverted world consciousness*, because they are an *inverted world*. Religion is the general theory of this world, its encyclopedic compendium, its logic in popular form . . . its general basis of consolation and justification. . . . *Religious* suffering is at the same time an *expression* of real suffering and a *protest* against real suffering. Religion is the sigh of the oppressed creature, the sentiment of a heartless world, and the soul of soulless conditions. "Contribution to the Critique of Hegel's *Philosophy of Right*," pp. 43–59 in T. B. Bottomore, ed., *Karl Marx: Early Writings* [New York, 1963], (pp. 43–44, italics in original.)

If the later Marx had been able to consider aspects of the socialist struggle in terms of this earlier understanding of religion, he would have been able to understand much more accurately the transition from "primitive" to "true" communism, for he would have seen that the desire for moral and affective association per se—the desire to overthrow the morality of exchange—is a part of socialist struggle from the beginning.

61. This is the general position that Gouldner takes in his "Introduction" to Durkheim's *Socialism and Saint-Simon* (n. 45 above, pp. i-xxiv). Gouldner attempts to point to this work as evidence for the fallacy of Parsons' interpretation of Durkheim as emphasizing mainly moral integration. Actually, this work clearly demonstrates exactly what Parsons said. (More correct is Gouldner's attempt to use these lectures as evidence for the left-leaning character of Durkheim's ideological views, a factor certainly neglected, although not denied, by Parsons.) A much more accurate reading of the lectures, in my opinion, is provided by Pierre Birnbaum in his article "Cadres sociaux et représentations collectives dans l'oeuvre de Durkheim: L'Exemple du *Socialisme*" (*Revue française sociologique* 10 [1969]: 3–11), where he argues for the importance of subjective factors and points to differences between Durkheim and Marx. I would, however, disagree with this important article in three respects. First, I do not think that Durkheim presents here an "ambiguous" portrait of the relation between base and superstructure, or substrate and representation, though he emphasizes at one point a more material causation and at another a more idealist one. I would contend, to the contrary, that the very notion of substrate has implicitly changed, and that this was already clearly marked in *Rules*. My second disagreement, which is related to this first point, concerns Birnbaum's argument that the lectures on socialism represent a "privileged" moment in Durkheim's theoretical development because immediately after this work he returned to a form of social determination from which "any form of independent consciousness disappeared." To contrary, as I will try to demonstrate in the remainder of this chapter, Durkheim was announcing in these lectures a fundamental change in his understanding of modernity, the empirical specification of the general position he had already worked out the year before. In fact, the autonomy of consciousness not only remains crucial but becomes even more important in the work which follows these lectures. Finally, and this is rather less important, I would insist, in contrast to Birnbaum, that the "Note sur la définition du socialisme" (n. 23 above), published in 1893, does indeed bear an important relationship not only to these later lectures but to Durkheim's later work as a whole.

62. Parsons' discussion presents the best example of this kind of judgment of *Rules* as primarily a book of the "old Durkheim," and as presenting a positivistic and primarily instrumentalist position (*Structure* [n. 18 above], pp. 344–350).

63. *Suicide* (n. 18 above), p. 299.

64. Ibid., p. 170.

65. Ibid., p. 310.

66. Ibid., p. 211.

67. Ibid., p. 201.

68. Ibid., p. 210.

69. Ibid., p. 212. Durkheim put this new position most succinctly in a footnote to a 1914 essay, "The Dualism of Human Nature and Its Social Conditions": "We see our *individuality* [as associated with physical desire] and not our *personality*. Although the two words are often used synonymously, they must be distinguished with the greatest possible care, for the personality is made up essentially of supra-individual elements." (Bellah [n. 9 above], p. 237, n. 6, italics altered.)

70. *Suicide*, p. 249.

71. Ibid., p. 252.

72. Ibid., p. 247.

73. Ibid., p. 299.

74. Ibid., p. 168.

75. Ibid., pp. 299–300.

76. Ibid., pp. 212, 213–214, italics added.

77. Ibid., pp. 256–257.

78. Ibid., pp. 250, 253.

79. Ibid., p. 242.

80. Ibid., pp. 243–245.

81. Ibid., pp. 381, 383. Durkheim's understanding of social reform, therefore, naturally follows his subjectification of the problem of anomy. This change in emphasis is signaled clearly in his Preface to the second edition of the *Division of Labor* (1902; New York, 1933). Durkheim spends most of the essay discussing the history and current strategy for recreating the moral solidarity of occupational groups. Only in the concluding pages does he mention that "objective" justice, the abolition of hereditary wealth, will also be necessary for a solution to the anomy of industrialism. Yet he immediately warns the reader that "the problems in the environment with which we were struggling would not be solved by that," and he goes on to emphasize "how much more important it is to put ourselves at once to work establishing . . . moral forces" (pp. 29–31). One might note here that contemporary sociological theory, in its stress on the theoretical consistency that supposedly derives from accurate insight into the empirical world, has usually ignored the differences between Durkheim's two theories of anomy. This is true, e.g., of Robert K. Merton's famous middle-range theory of anomie, set forth in a multidimensional essay which while paying obeisance to Durkheim effectively tries to transcend the two poles of his analysis (*Social Theory and Social Structure* [New York, 1968], pp. 185–214). For an insightful discussion of the differences that actually exist between the two theories of anomie, see Bernard Lacroix, "Emile Durkheim et la question du politique" (Ph.D. diss., University of Paris, 1976, pp. 167 ff., published as *Durkheim et le politique* [Montreal, 1981]).

82. By conflating the questions of action and order, these recent critics can, in other words, read Durkheim as arguing for an instrumentalist picture of order, something that is precisely the opposite of what he actually is moving toward in his middle-period writing. Peter M. Blau, e.g., takes Durkheim's emphasis on "constraint" and "externality" as referring to concrete group pressures, to the structuring of values through material sanctions, *as opposed to* an emphasis on the structuring of values through internalization. But this is exactly the kind of reification that Durkheim was trying to avoid. When Blau writes, in his article "Structural Effects" (*American Sociological Review* 25, no. 2 [1960]: 178–193), that Durkheim's structuralism allowed him to understand that "even socially acquired or socially defined attributes of individuals are clearly distinct in their effects from attributes of social structure" (p. 178), he reveals his inability to understand the very insight into the social individual that allowed Durkheim to move in his middle-period work to a more voluntaristic theory of order. Blau, in other words, is the same kind of "sympathetic" critic whose misinterpretation motivated Durkheim continually to move in a more self-consciously idealistic direction. Stimulated by the same kind of instrumentalist polemic, Gouldner (n. 45 above, pp. 23–27) makes the same kind of "structural" reading, arguing that because Durkheim views the interaction of concrete persons as necessary for the existence of social values and solidarity he has "converged" with the materialism of Marx. Yet Gouldner, like Blau, can cite no real evidence for this reading. He points only to the fact that Durkheim rejects the theological explanation of values as "divinely given and thus without a developmental history" (p. 24). This, of course, confuses Durkheim's empirical and ideological commitment to a postcosmological, i.e., secular, vision with a presuppositional commitment to materialism. (As will be seen later in this chapter, it was precisely a theory of posttheological idealism that characterized Durkheim's response to Marxian theory.) Raymond Aron makes the same kind of misinterpretation, though the polemical position from which his reading derives is more individualist and existentialist than instrumentalist. In discussion *Suicide*, e.g., Aron writes that "Durkheim tends to mistake the social milieu for a *sui generis* reality, objectively and materially defined, when in fact it is merely an intellectual representation" (*Main Currents in Sociological Thought* [New York, 1970], 2:103). This kind of mistaken reification, to the contrary, was precisely what Durkheim successfully overcame in this middle period of his work.

Among more recent interpreters, Whitney Pope has made the same kind of error. Pope writes, e.g., that Durkheim was not interested in the "value content" of culture but only in its ability to "control" individual action from without. Pope reads Durkheim as a determinist rather than as the voluntarist he is actually in the process of becoming, and makes this misinterpretation because of his own confusions about theoretical logic. He insists that voluntarism can be combined with constraint only if individual action is based upon "rational calculation" about the advantages of and disadvantages of society's rules. Thus Pope misreads Durkheim's attacks on "subjectivity" as the rejection of normative action rather than as the rejection of individualistic randomness as a solution to order ("Classic on Classic: Parsons' Interpretation of Durkheim," *American Sociological Review* 38 [1973]: 399–415). It should be noted that although there are some elements of truth in Pope's criticisms of Parsons' classical interpretation, his own interpretation represents a woeful lack of comprehension of the theoretical lessons that Parsons so brilliantly taught. The same misinterpretation of *Suicide* as an antisubjectivist exercise in social realism mars Pope's *Durkheim's "Suicide"* (Chicago, 1976; e.g., pp. 58–60), which, not surprisingly, also argues for the close continuity between the "morphological" emphases in *Suicide* and the *Division of Labor*. Stephen R. Marks makes the same kind of error when he reads Durkheim's middle-period work as maintaining two independent and potentially conflicting understandings of social order, the "structural"—based on the importance of social interaction—and the "normative"—reflecting cultural understanding alone ("Durkheim's Theory of Anomie," ibid., 80, no. 2 [1974]: 329–363). The problem for Durkheim, however, was the nature of social interaction, not the simple fact of its existence. By the middle period, Durkheim's approach to this social structural phenomenon has shifted decisively to a normative understanding. Finally, although it is difficult to understand the overall interpretive position of Durkheim's biographer Steven Lukes, it seems fair to say that he also views this middle-period work as not representing a substantial departure from the earlier writing. He insists, e.g., that Durkheim's understanding of morphology shifted only in 1899, whereas the evidence is clear that it shifted in *Rules* and that this shift determined the very character of *Suicide* (see Lukes, *Emile Durkheim* [New York, 1972], p. 235).

83. One of the first to make this argument for the complete continuity of Durkheim's normative theorizing was Harry Alpert in *Emile Durkheim and His Sociology* (New York, 1939). Alpert produced an elegant demonstration (pp. 134–163) that Durkheim's associational analysis is both normative and consistent with voluntarism, that it was an attempt to transcend both nominalist and realist claims. Yet the truth and value of this interpretation is mitigated by Alpert's contention that Durkheim always had this insight. More recently, Robert N. Bellah has advanced a sophisticated argument for the same claim; but while mistakenly arguing for the continuity of Durkheim's work, Bellah has produced the best single analysis of the relationship between interaction and symbolization

that Durkheim's middle-period work initiates ("Introduction" [n. 9 above]). Jean-Claude Filloux provides the best general discussion of the understanding of affective association in this middle-period work (see, particularly, pp. 69–79 in his *Durkheim et le socialisme* [Geneva and Paris, 1977]), though, once again, Filloux argues that such a perspective informs Durkheim's work throughout his life.

Perhaps the best single illustration of the discontinuity in Durkheim's work is the relationship between his first article on suicide, published in 1888, "Suicide et natalité: Etude de statistique morale," (*Revue philosophique* 26: 446–463), and the book *Suicide*, published almost a decade later. Lukes (p. 195) and Filloux (p. 32) argue for the complete continuity between the two studies, seeing the first as the logical and empirical precursor of the second. As the contrast revealed by my own accounts demonstrates, however, this is hardly the case. In the 1888 article (see the discussion in ch. 4, the third subsection of sec. 2.3.2), Durkheim invokes two quasi-instrumental factors as his principal explanatory devices: first, the objective disequilibrium of social groups; second, the difficulty of the struggle for existence—among the poor. In his later work, these explanations are replaced by the relative weakness or strength of subjective solidarity. Durkheim specifically argues, e.g., against the contention that the objective difficulty of the life struggle can be an explanation of suicide.

The most important argument that has been advanced for the discontinuity of Durkheim's work is Parsons' (*Structure* [n. 18 above]). It was Parsons who generated the first crucial insight into Durkheim's changing attitude toward the individual and to "external factors." The limits of Parsons' analysis are, first, his explanation of this change and its timing. He argues that Durkheim's theoretical evolution was motivated by the tension between his earlier theory and the nature of empirical fact—that *Suicide*, e.g., is internally contradictory because of the tensions that new empirical understanding has generated with Durkheim's lingering commitment to the deterministic framework produced by his methodological positivism (*Structure*, pp. 343, 376). Parsons sees subsequent theoretical advances as produced by Durkheim's movement away from his positivism, a movement more in keeping with his empirical insight. My position, to the contrary, is that Durkheim's methodological position never changed, and I believe that Parsons never produced any evidence that it actually did change. Further, what did change was not Durkheim's insight into the atheoretical empirical world but his general conception of action and order—which were generated for extra-empirical and extra-scientific reasons.

But Parsons' analysis contains a more important misunderstanding of Durkheim's normative position: he reads it not just as an important new insight into the basis of one dimension of social order but as an explanation of collective order itself. Unfortunately, this same reading is found in most of the interpretations (mainly American) which have so significantly illuminated the true normative status of Durkheim's middle-period understanding of association. More sensitive perhaps to the Marxian challenge, some recent French critics, like Filloux, have not made this error. The excellent 1976 dissertation of Lacroix (n. 81 above) develops the best discussion known to me of the discontinuity of Durkheim's work, both in its voluntaristic breakthrough and in its idealist problems, though the fact of discontinuity between *Division* and *Rules* has also been noted by Georges Gurvitch, "Le Problème de la conscience collective dans la sociologie de Durkheim," pp. 351–408 in his *La Vocation actuelle de la sociologie* (Paris, 1950; see, e.g., p. 365), and by M. J. Hawkins, "Continuity and Change in Durkheim's Theory of Social Solidarity," *Sociological Quarterly* 20 (1979): 155–164.

84. For an excellent discussion of this aspect of the French scene, and its relation to new and more idealist developments in Durkheim's work, see Edward A. Tiryakian, "Emile Durkheim," in T. B. Bottomore and Robert A. Nisbet, eds., *A History of Sociological Analysis* (New York, 1978) pp. 187–236; particularly, see n. 106, pp. 233–234.

85. This portrait of the impact of Marxian and socialist ideas on French intellectual circles relies on W. Paul Vogt, "The Confrontation of Socialists and Sociologists in Prewar France, 1890–1914," in Western Society for French History, Joyce Duncan Falk, ed., *Proceedings*, vol. 4, (1976), and Joseph R. Llobera, "Durkheim, the Durkheimians, and Their Collective Misrepresentation of Marx," paper presented at the 9th World Congress of Sociology, Uppsala, Sweden, August 1978.

86. Marcel Mauss, in the "Introduction" to the first edition of Durkheim's lectures on socialism, reprinted in *Socialism and Saint-Simon* (n. 45 above), pp. 2–3.

87. This attempt at the reconstruction of Durkheim's thought is, of course, not an estimation based on hard evidence. Whether or not I am correct in this exercise in *Verstehen* does not, however, affect the validity of the theoretical reading that I am attempting; I am merely trying to provide some social and individual context for understanding how Durkheim's theorizing could have gone through such dramatic shifts in such a short period of time.

88. In the first and probably most important review, "L'Année philosophique, 1893," in the 1894 *Revue de métaphysique et de morale*, pp. 564–590, Brunschvicg and Halévy wrote that even if Durkheim refused to accept all the consequences of his position, the *Division of Labor* was, in the last analysis, "mechanical and material" in its causal analysis (p. 565). They remark, quite rightly, that such an analysis actually excluded the very voluntarism that Durkheim referred to in his concluding call for social reform (pp. 568–569). But these reviewers read the *Division* into

the later *Rules,* arguing in the face of Durkheim's very explicit theorizing that his proposed method excluded all psychological elements from society (pp. 565–567; these critics, it should be noted, had access to the articles of 1894 that formed the substance of the monograph on *Rules* published in 1895). And in a series of concluding arguments that must have been especially grating to Durkheim, they offer suggestions that he had actually already taken up. Social laws, they write, should be studied in terms of the spontaneous interaction of the individuals whose spirit gives them life. Only in this way could these so-called laws be seen for what they really are, common ideas and sentiments (p. 571). (I cannot avoid noting the irony that while it was Halévy himself who shortly after writing this critical review developed one of the most penetrating critiques of instrumentalist theorizing ever written—*The Growth of Philosophic Radicalism*—it was the object of his early criticism, Durkheim himself, who developed the most sophisticated alternative to this utilitarianism. He was developing this understanding, moreover, in the very work which Halévy attacked. It might be noted also that although Halévy's later seminal insight into the conservatizing effects of British religion on working-class radicalism was inspired by Weber, it was not at all inconsistent with the later insights of Durkheim himself.)

The same perspective on Durkheim's sociology is expressed in the 1896 issue of the same review. Charles Andler finds the determinism and inevitability of Durkheim's analysis to be antithetical to the democratic culture he is trying to create. In concluding, he accuses Durkheim of the "Marxist error."

> The "conditions of economic production" present a situation in which Durkheim's theory could no doubt be better applied [than to society as a whole], without, however, still being completely relevant. M. Durkheim generalizes the economic "thingism" [*le choisisme*] of Marx while making of it a "thingism" that is specifically sociological. In doing so, he generalizes the Marxist error. ("Sociologie et démocratie," *Revue de métaphysique et de morale* 4: 252, n. 1.)

In a review published in Germany in 1897 by Paul Barth, Durkheim had evidence that this materialist misinterpretation had spread beyond the borders of France. A follower of Dilthey, Barth in his *Die Philosophie der Geschichte als Soziologie* discusses Durkheim's work in the chapter entitled "The Economic Conception of History" (4th ed.; Leipzig, 1922, Bk. 2, ch. 6). He attacks Durkheim for being, like Spencer, "an almost superstitious worshiper of the contract" and argues that Durkheim, in his early works at least, views morality as a "hindrance to economic progress" and as "unfavorable to the autonomy of the individual" (p. 612).

As if to confirm this materialist evaluation by his non-Marxist critics, Durkheim was hailed in 1895 by Georges Sorel, the major Marxist intellectual in France, as a sympathetic spirit. In the lead article of the first issue of the Marxist journal *Le Devenir,* "Les Théories de M. Durkheim" (pp. 1–25, 148–80), Sorel applauds *Rules* for its antipsychological emphasis on coercion and constraint (pp. 16–17). He neatly sums up the prevailing perspective on *Rules* as in complete continuity with the *Division of Labor* when he begins by noting that Durkheim had "just brought together in a small volume of very modest style, what is essential in his doctrine" (p. 1). As for the content of *Division*, he calls it an exposition of "great beauty" and makes a direct parallel between it and the theory of Marx. "With Durkheim," he writes, "we are placed on the ground of real science, and we see the importance of struggle [*la lutte*]" (p. 23). But Durkheim seems to hesitate, Sorel writes, before taking the final step toward a materialist history. In order to define the conditions of existence more specifically, "he would have to place himself on the ground of Marxist philosophy" (p. 177). If he could borrow from Marxism the conception of classes, "it would be for social philosophy a happy event." "I would be the first," Sorel affirms, "to acclaim him my master," for he is the "only French sociologist who possesses a sufficient philosophical preparation and well developed critical spirit to be able to perceive in historical change scientific laws and the material conditions of becoming." (Pp. 179, 180.)

This review by Sorel is a fascinating document because it reveals the reaction of a powerful intellect to Durkheim's sociology during its most important point of transition. Even for a self-conscious "historical materialist," Durkheim's theory seemed, at that time, impossible to fault on philosophical grounds. Indeed, at one point Sorel—the sympathizer of Bergson and later author of *The Myth of Violence*—actually chides Durkheim for being too objectivist, and for not taking consciousness sufficiently into account. Most of the time, however, Sorel accepts Durkheim's materialist project as his own, and his criticism focuses not on Durkheim's presuppositions but on his insufficiently critical understanding of capitalist society. He takes for granted that in emphasizing "*la lutte*" (struggle) as the vehicle for order, Durkheim is taking his stand on the same grounds as Marx; the question remains, however, "of knowing if the struggle is produced in conditions as simple as the author supposes" (p. 24). Socialist theory, Sorel argues, demonstrates that it is impossible to separate the division of labor from class conflict; "the latter, organized for struggle, exercises a fundamental influence on the division of labor, introducing into it forces very different from those of which M. Durkheim speaks" (p. 168). Sorel evidently had not read the *Division of Labor* closely enough, for he would have discovered that in the third book Durkheim himself realized that the division of labor is strongly affected by the nature of class relations. Sorel urged Durkheim to consider the empirical implications of economic classes, and believed that if he did so he could become the premier materialist scientist of his day. Ironically, however, it was, in part, Durkheim's very realization of the implications of the relation between divided labor and class struggle that had already led him to move away from materialism toward a more voluntaristic analysis.

Although there seems to be no reason to doubt the sincerity of Sorel's fellow feeling, this very sincerity testifies to the misperception against which Durkheim had mightily to struggle. Durkheim could only have read Sorel's essay with alarm, even astonishment, although by never acknowledging the break in his work he had in a certain sense brought such misperception on himself. (Some indirect evidence of Durkheim's displeasure with Sorel's reading can be seen in the fact that he decided, several years later, to participate in a sharply antagonistic dispute over the definition of socialism in which Sorel was involved. I will refer to this below.)

The sole exception to these negative reviews that I have been able to find is an essay by Paul Lapie ("L'Année sociologique, 1894," *Revue de métaphysique et de morale* 3 [1895]: 309–339, particularly 309–310). Lapie saw very clearly the subjective, normative basis that Durkheim gave to social facts in *Rules*, and applauded him for it. Later, as director of primary education in France, Lapie introduced Durkheimian sociology into the required curriculum. This movement toward subjectivity must have pleased Lapie, for he shared Durkheim's opinion that a scientifically-based Republican ethics was essential to the survival of French democracy.

89. Durkheim, *Rules* (n. 18 above) p. xxxix.

90. Ibid., p. xli. Durkheim complains that the most revolutionary message of his book had been completely misinterpreted:

> In our first chapter we gave a definition of social facts as ways of acting or thinking with the peculiar characteristic of exercising a coercive influence on individual consciousnesses. Confusion has arisen on this score which requires comment. . . . They [the critics] claimed that we are explaining social phenomena by constraint. This was far from our intention—in fact, it had never even occurred to us that it could have been so interpreted, so much is it contrary to our entire method. (P. liii.)

To identify "coercive influence" with material "constraint," however, does not seem to have been an unwarranted leap of faith for contemporary interpreters. Durkheim himself had made the very same equation in the *Division of Labor* (1893), the year before these articles on method appeared, and despite his later protestations he did nothing at all to dispel the apparent continuity between *Rules* and that earlier work.

91. This was in response to Andler's review. Durkheim wrote, in what was evidently his second letter of complaint: "Without wishing to prolong the discussion, I wish to declare that I regret absolutely the ideas

that are attributed to me by M. Andler, especially in his last note. He has been able to attribute them to me only by taking advantage of several isolated words, while I had myself taken great care to put the reader on guard against such an abuse." (Letter to the editor, *Revue de métaphysique et de morale*, vol. 4, suppl. of July 4, 1896, p. 20.)

92. The letter is cited in Lukes (n. 82 above), p. 234, n. 35. Bouglé's review is directed against Barth, and it is prominently displayed in the first issue of the Durkheimians' new journal, *L'Année sociologique* (1898, pp. 116–123). It is of great interest because it is simultaneously an attempt to defend Durkheim's earlier work and an admission that it was too instrumentalist to serve as the basis of future research. In the context of 1898, of course, the latter admission still served as a call to follow the new wave of (revised) Durkheimian sociology. Bouglé writes that Barth wrongly characterized Durkheim as belonging to the school of historical materialism, suggesting that the title of Durkheim's first book may have caused the confusion. Durkheim had wanted to study the division of labor for its moral, not economic, effects. Yet Bouglé then characterizes this argument of 1893 in purely material terms, as concerned with the growth of density that forces differentiation, and he admits that while this explanation is not economistic, "one could ... judge that his [Durkheim's] theory remains exterior or mechanistic." It now becomes apparent that Bouglé is, implicitly, suggesting that Barth's criticisms apply to the old Durkheim, not the new one (a point, incidentally, that Barth himself readily admitted). "That sociological systems," Bouglé writes, "have because of their naturalistic tendencies often misunderstood the value and proper character of the spirit, does not prove that one cannot determine scientifically the social role of spirit itself." To achieve this, he adds, it is only necessary to distinguish the "concepts" of natural science from the "methods" it employs. In other words, naturalistic methods do not necessarily imply the determination of actions by mechanical, physical force. This, of course, was, not coincidentally, precisely the insight that had already launched Durkheim's new sociological theorizing upon which, as will be shown later, *L'Année sociologique* was based.

93. Durkheim, *Suicide* (n. 18 above), p. 315, n. 12.

94. Durkheim, *The Elementary Forms of Religious Life* (n. 18 above), p. 239, n. 6; cf. p. 471.

95. Mauss (n. 86 above), p. 2. Lacroix (n. 81 above) has found historical evidence to verify this recollection by Mauss, at least to the extent that Durkheim did indeed make strenuous remonstrations in 1893 and again in 1897 to his contacts in the Parisian educational establishment to help procure for him positions that had opened up. Clearly, he could only have been extremely disappointed with the results. Lacroix's speculation that these rebuffs were pivotal in Durkheim's change of theoretical direction away from the quasi-Marxist analysis of his earlier work is, how-

ever, extremely overdrawn (see, in addition to Lacroix's dissertation, his article "A propos des rapports entre Durkheim et Marx: De l'analyze de texte à l'analyse sociologique," in *Etudes offertés au Professeur Emerentienne de Lagrange* [Paris, 1978], pp. 330–350). First, Durkheim's earlier collective materialism had never been unambiguous, and he himself had from the beginning defined his own ambition in a direction that ran counter to Marx's. Second, there was an enormous theoretical frustration, not just a practical one, involved in the shift that did occur. Finally, some genuine theoretical insight was also involved. Much in the same manner as Lacroix, Vogt and Llobera (both, n. 85 above) are equally incorrect in seeing anti-Marxist political considerations as the principal explanatory vehicle in Durkheim's development. There is no doubt that Durkheim's concern with Marxism was a major consideration, although by no means the only one, but it is incorrect to view this concern as a purely ideological one. Durkheim's very ideological antagonism rested upon a certain prior theoretical judgment of the implications of Marx's instrumentalism; it also never denied the need for "socialist" change of a different sort. A more vulgar example of this reduction of Durkheim's thinking to a conservative response to Marxism can be found in Irving Zeitlin's *Ideology and the Development of Sociological Theory* (Englewood Cliffs, N.J., 1968, pp. 234–280). The issue has been described by some of Durkheim's French critics more accurately as a reaction against the *perception* that his own theory was linked with Marx's in the public mind. Guy Aimard writes that "the very analogies between Durkheimian sociology and Marxist sociology incited Durkheim to demarcate strongly the differences between his method properly understood and Marx's" (*Durkheim et la science économique* [Paris, 1962] p. 231). In a similar vein, Armand Cuvillier argues that Durkheim had perceived the possibility that he would be taken as a Marxist and that it was against this that he promoted a more idealist picture in 1898 ("Durkheim et Marx," *Cahiers internationaux de sociologie* 4 [1948]: 75–97). Georges Kagan argues, similarly, that Durkheim "was accused of being a materialist, of having created a historical theory reducing all human development to the progress of the division of labor" ("Durkheim et Marx," *Revue de l'histoire économique et sociale* 24 [1938]: 233–245, quoting 233). Yet while sensitive to Durkheim's unease at the perception of his similarity with Marx, these critics vastly overestimate, once again, the extent to which Durkheim was reacting against Marxism alone. They do not see the independence of Durkheim's theoretical project, and the way its intellectual integrity extended back to his earliest work.

96. Filloux (n. 83 above) provides the best formulation of the subjective theory of association in Durkheim's work (pp. 112–113).

97. Durkheim, "The Dualism of Human Nature and Its Social Conditions," pp. 149–163 in Bellah (n. 9 above), p. 154.

98. Ibid., p. 150. The same point is made in Durkheim, *Moral Education* (New York, 1961), p. 223. (Durkheim died in 1917. This work was posthumously published in 1925.)

99. "Dualism of Human Nature," p. 151.

100. *Division of Labor,* p. 15. The irony, of course, is that in the monograph which this second Preface purports to introduce Durkheim usually operates with a utilitarian conception of action that is very different from the one he defines so forcefully here as affective and normative.

101. Durkheim, *Professional Ethics and Civic Morals* (Glencoe, Ill., 1958), p. 25. First published in 1950 (as *Leçons de sociologie: Physique des moeurs et du droit*), from lectures given in 1900.

102. *Moral Education,* p. 220; cf. pp. 224–225.

103. *Elementary Forms of Religious Life* (n. 18 above), p. 218.

104. *Suicide,* pp. 313–314.

105. Ibid., p. 130.

106. Ibid., p. 151.

107. Parsons (n. 18 above) is still the most perceptive analyst of this tension in *Suicide.* Compare his treatment, e.g., with that of Alpert (n. 83 above), which tries to explain Durkheim's continued reification of the social as a strategy that adopts utilitarian thinking in order better to refute it.

108. This quotation is from Durkheim's letter of November 8, 1907, to the director of the *Revue néo-scolastique* (14 [1907]: 612–614). I have used the translation in Lukes (n. 82 above, p. 237) with a few exceptions, the most important of which is that in the original Durkheim employs the verb *marquer* in the present tense, whereas Lukes translates it as "marked." The correct tense gives a more vivid sense of the fact that Durkheim feels as if the "revelation" about religion which he is recounting is still, in fact, occurring.

109. Although the sociology of Durkheim's theoretical knowledge, or its social psychology for that matter, is not the focus here, we might note, nonetheless, that there is some evidence to indicate that this period of transition and upheaval in Durkheim's life was accompanied by unusual symptoms of psychological strain. It may well have been initiated for personal, biographical reasons as much as for intellectual ones. A sensitive, if necessarily very circumstantial account of Durkheim's state of mind in these years is contained in Bernard Lacroix, "Emile Durkheim et la question du politique" (n. 81 above), ch. 3, pp. 150–251. Durkheim was raised in a patriarchal, highly authoritarian family, and he was expected to follow the vocation of his father and grandfather and become a rabbi in Alsace. At thirteen, however, he made a decisive rebellion against the rule of his father, deciding to give up rabbinical training for secular education and, eventually, for the "faith of science." Although the evidence can, at this point, only be indirect, it seems clear that Durkheim must

have felt a great deal of guilt for this unexpected change in his vocation. Durkheim's father died in February 1896, and it does not seem unwarranted to assume that this death, and the anticipation of it in the months preceding, was laden with not only emotional but also intellectual significance for the son. Can it be pure coincidence that it was in precisely this period that Durkheim reversed his long-standing belief—which he had taken up after his initial rebellion against his father—that modernity had to be perceived as immune to the attractions of religious thought and feeling? It seems quite possible, as Lacroix has argued, that the father's death "unblocked the possibility of another discourse" for Durkheim (p. 216). The link between his own theoretical evolution and the recovery, in some form, of the sensibilities of childhood, can perhaps be recognized in the juxtaposition of two sentences in the following passage from *The Elementary Forms of Religious Life* (n.18 above), written in 1912:

> It is readily seen how that group of readily repeated acts which form the cult get their importance. In fact, however, whoever has really practiced a religion knows very well that it is the cult which gives rise to these impressions of joy, of interior peace, of serenity, of enthusiasm which are, for the believer, an experimental proof of his beliefs. (P. 464.)

Who had "really practiced a religion" if not Durkheim himself? Would the younger, resolutely rationalist Durkheim have been ready to accept the self-report of such a fallen believer as "experimental proof" of the importance of some social practice?

110. After presenting Durkheim's understanding of religion at some length, I will return to discuss the impact that Robertson Smith's writings had on his development. See n. 176 below.

111. Durkheim, "De la définition des phénomènes religieux," *L'Année sociologique* 2 (1899): 1–28, quoting 20.

112. Ibid., p. 13.

113. Ibid., pp. 14–15.

114. Ibid., pp. 16, 14.

115. Ibid., p. 17, italics in original.

116. Ibid., p. 18.

117. Ibid.

118. Ibid., p. 13.

119. Ibid., pp. 16, 24.

120. Ibid., p. 20.

121. Ibid., p. 21.

122. Quoted from a letter to Gaston Richard, May 11, 1899, reproduced under the heading "Remarque sur la nature de la religiosité," in Emile Durkheim, *Textes* (Paris, 1975), 2: 9. The letter was in response to questions that Richard posed to Durkheim after reading "De la définition des phénomènes religieux."

123. "De la définition des phénomènes religieux," p. 25.

124. Durkheim, *The Elementary Forms of Religious Life* (n. 18 above),
p. 121, cf. p. 51.

125. Ibid., p. 236.

126. Ibid., p. 194.

127. Ibid., p. 140.

128. Ibid., p. 194, italics added.

129. Ibid., p. 217.

130. Ibid., p. 246.

131. Ibid., p. 217.

132. Ibid., p. 467. Nothing could indicate more clearly the distance
which Durkheim has traveled from the theoretical position of his earlier
writing that this inversion of the metaphor "external envelope." In 1887,
in his review of Guyau's book, Durkheim had written that it was mental
"representations" which were "only the symbol and superficial wrapping" (*l'enveloppe superficielle*—see ch. 4, n. 205, above) of the social conditions that created religion and the habits which had formed around
them ("Guyau, *L'Irreligion de l'avenir: Etude de sociologie*," *Revue philosophique* 23 [1887]: 299–311). Now it is the more habitual parts of the
religious ceremony, the patterns of the ritual, that are the envelope for
the mental operations themselves.

133. *Elementary Forms*, p. 252.

134. Ibid., p. 224.

135. Ibid., p. 252.

136. Ibid., p. 358; cf. p. 254.

137. Ibid., p. 338; cf. pp. 338–395.

138. Ibid., pp. 366–434.

139. Ibid., p. 420.

140. Ibid., p. 400.

141. Durkheim, "The Dualism of Human Nature and Its Social Conditions" (n. 97 above), pp. 159–160.

142. *Elementary Forms*, p. 13.

143. Durkheim, "The Determination of Moral Facts," pp. 35–79 in
Durkheim, *Sociology and Philosophy* (New York, 1974), p. 49; first published in 1906 in the *Bulletin de la Société de philosophie*.

144. Ibid., p. 57.

145. Ibid., p. 48.

146. Ibid.

147. Ibid., p. 69, italics added; cf. p. 36. Pp. 63–79 contain Durkheim's
replies to objections which were made in a discussion of his initial talk.

148. Durkheim, *Moral Education* (n. 98 above), p. 11. The first section, pp. 1–126, devoted to morality in general, including secular morality, represents the only extended discussion in Durkheim's later writing
of this central subject. Durkheim was working on a multivolume work

devoted to *"la morale"* when he died, and only a fragment remains. For a sensitive discussion of Durkheim's theory of symbolism as it relates to his sociology of religion, see Bellah, "Introduction" (n. 9 above), pp. xlviii–liii.

149. *Elementary Forms*, p. 243.
150. "The Determination of Moral Facts" (n. 143 above), p. 59.
151. *Elementary Forms*, p. 241.
152. Durkheim, "Value Judgments and Judgments of Reality," pp. 80–97 in Durkheim, *Sociology and Philosophy* (n. 143 above), pp. 91–92. This essay, given as a lecture to the general meeting of the International Congress of Philosophy, at Bologna, was first published in the *Revue de métaphysique et de morale* in 1911.
153. *Elementary Forms*, p. 240.
154. Ibid., pp. 474–475, italics added.
155. Ibid., p. 242.
156. In a footnote in the final book of *Suicide*, written in 1896, Durkheim expresses his frustration with the critical reception of his previous work and reveals the extent to which his increased emphasis on ordered subjectivity reverses his earlier position. In the text, he has just employed the inverse metaphor which has been noted above, arguing that legal and moral precepts, in their crystallized and "sacrosanct" form, are merely the "superficial envelope" for actual, living sentiments. In a note at the bottom of the page, in case his point is not sufficiently clear, he makes the following assertion:

> We do not expect to be reproached further, after this explanation, with wishing to substitute the exterior for the interior in sociology. We start from the exterior because it alone is immediately given, but only to reach the interior. Doubtless the procedure is complicated; but there is no other unless one would risk having his research apply to his personal feeling concerning the order of facts under investigation, instead of to this factual order itself. (*Suicide* [n. 18 above], p. 315, n. 12.)

In 1893, Durkheim's positivist desire to produce external and visible facts had paralleled his presuppositional commitment to materially coercive order. By the end of 1896, he has placed his positivism within a highly qualified context, warning his readers that his methodological concentration on exteriority must not be confused with concentrating on external order in presuppositional terms.

157. "The Determination of Moral Facts," pp. 48, 36.
158. Ibid., pp. 35–36, italics added.
159. *Moral Education*, p. 10; cf. *Elementary Forms*, p. 244.
160. *Moral Education*, p. 31.
161. "The Determination of Moral Facts," p. 47.
162. *Moral Education*, p. 41.

163. *Elementary Forms*, p. 238; cf. p. 244 and "The Dualism of Human Nature" (n. 97 above), p. 159.

164. *Moral Education*, p. 30; cf. *Elementary Forms*, p. 237.

165. *Elementary Forms*, p. 238; cf. *Moral Education*, p. 41.

166. The psychological understanding of representation, and its context in the sensationalist/rationalist debate, can be readily seen from this passage in the *Division of Labor.*

> A representation is not simply a mere image of reality, an inert shadow projected by things upon us, but it is a force which raises around itself a turbulence of organic and psychical phenomena. Not only does the nervous current which accompanies the ideation radiate to the cortical centres around the point where it originated and pass from one plexus to the next, but it gains a foothold in the motor centres where it *determines* movements, in the sensorial centres where it *arouses* images. (P. 97, italics added.)

The usefulness of this position to Durkheim's polemic against Tarde's theory of action as based on imitation—an antagonism which goes back to Durkheim's earliest sociological writings—is articulated in *Suicide:*

> An intellectual operation intrudes between the representation and the execution of [an] act, consisting of a clear or unclear, rapid or slow awareness. . . . Our way of conforming to the morals or manners of our country has nothing in common, therefore, with the mechanical, ape-like repetition causing us to reproduce motions which we witness. Between the two ways of acting, is all the difference between reasonable, deliberate behavior and automatic reflex. The former has motives even when not expressed as explicit judgments. The latter has not; it results directly from the mere sight of an act, with no other mental intermediary. (Pp. 128–129).

As this latter passage indicates, Durkheim's earlier understanding of "representation," firmly lodged in the debate over rationalism versus sensationalism, gave to it an exclusively intellectual, cognitive focus. This is clear, for example, in his early writings on German thought, where he uses the fact of representation to argue for the significance of conscious reflection about the ends of human action, e.g., "La Science positive de la morale en Allemagne" (n. 4 above, pp. 48, 51). This purely cognitive understanding is just as manifest in 1894, in *Rules*, where he identifies representations with the purely intellectual "ideas of things" (n. 18 above, p. 23; based on articles published in 1894). The fact that such a narrow reference could even appear in *Rules*, which in broader, presuppositional terms was truly revolutionary and which initiated Durkheim's middle-period theorizing, is perhaps one of the most compelling demonstrations that the effects of his encounter with religion must be separated from the earlier revision of instrumentalism that constituted his middle-period work. It might be added that Durkheim's belated understanding of the affective and moral dimensions of the representation of reality bears a striking similarity to Wundt's position, which Durkheim had strongly rejected in 1887 as much too antimaterialistic. Wundt had written that the individual need for solidarity produces a search for external objects that can serve a means of expression for this need. Society provides such objects, Wundt believed, and the value which individuals give to these objects accrues to them because they symbolize solidarizing beliefs. (See "La Science positive de la morale en Allemagne" [n. 4 above], p. 138.)

167. Durkheim, "Individual and Collective Representations," pp. 1–34 in Durkheim, *Sociology and Philosophy* (n. 143 above), p. 23. First published in 1898 in the *Revue de métaphysique et de morale*.

168. The significant role that "representation" played in the resolution of the problems that haunted Durkheim's middle-period work is revealed in an extremely interesting manner in his Preface to the second edition of *Rules*, in 1901. "When this book appeared for the first time," he begins, "it aroused [such] lively controversy . . . that for a time it was almost impossible for us to make ourselves heard." He goes on to claim, not simply that he had in fact presented a subjective theory in *Rules*, which would have been utterly correct, but that this theory had been based upon a notion of representations.

> On the very points on which we had expressed ourselves most explicitly, views were freely attributed to us which had nothing in common with our own; and our opponents held that they were refuting us in refuting these mistaken ideas. . . . Whereas we had expressly stated and reiterated that social life is constituted wholly of collective "representation," we were accused of eliminating the mental element from sociology. (P. xli.)

In fact, this is actually an attempt to rewrite intellectual history from the later perspective of Durkheim's religiously-informed theorizing. (The Preface to the second edition of *Division of Labor*, published the following year, attempts much the same thing.) Durkheim's utilization of the concept of representation in the original edition of *Rules* was actually a minimal and impoverished one, as I have indicated above. That he is now, in an effort to confute the critics' charges about his latent materialism, invoking an understanding of social reality as composed of such representations indicates not that this understanding had always been there, but rather that it had been invented precisely to serve this polemical function—to make the subjective, voluntaristic underpinnings of Durkheim's theory more visible and more sophisticated.

169. *Elementary Forms*, p. 149.

170. "Individual and Collective Representations," p. 33.

171. *Moral Education*, p. 215, italics added.

172. Ibid., p. 216; cf. "The Determination of Moral Facts," p. 57.

173. *Elementary Forms*, pp. 259–260; cf. p. 76.

174. *Moral Education*, p. 215. The point, in other words, is that if Marx had decided to sociologize—to specify—the normative theory of "praxis" that informed his early writings, he would have had to develop a notion of representation similar to Durkheim's own, for only in this way could he have connected the subjective intentions of praxis with the material and conceptual "things" that seem to populate the world. The only way to achieve the kind of interpenetration of subjective and objective forces that Marx saw as inherent in nonalienated human praxis is to see these forces as having a "representational" status. Although the term is never used as such, it is precisely such a notion of representation that underlies much of Marx's early writings. E.g.: "The criticism of religion disillusions man so that he will think, act and *fashion his reality* as a man who has lost his illusions and regained his reason" ("Contribution to the Critique of Hegel's *Philosophy of Right*," pp. 41–60 in Bottomore [n. 60 above], p. 44).

175. Durkheim, "Individual and Collective Representations," p. 34, italics added.

176. These last quotations, and more generally the entire argument in this section, should make abundantly clear how important these later insights into the nature of religion were to Durkheim's conception of modernity. My position on this issue could not be more different, for example, than the analysis of this religious writing proposed by Anthony Giddens, who argues that *Elementary Forms* contributed primarily to Durkheim's understanding of primitive societies, and that it implied no change in his view of modernity.

> The *Elementary Forms* fills, in some considerable detail, a major gap in *The Division of Labor*. In the latter work . . . Durkheim put himself the principal task of establishing the nature of the moral forms appropriate to the *modern* type of society, accepting that . . . the characteristics of mechanical solidarity had already been satisfactorily determined by other authors. But he came to see later that this was by no means the case, and *The Elementary Forms* provides a penetrating analysis of . . . basic features of the functioning of mechanical solidarity which were left aside in the former work. ("Introduction," to Giddens, ed., *Emile Durkheim: Selected Writings* [London, 1972], p. 24, italics in original.)

Only after presenting the analysis in this and the preceding section of Durkheim's sociology of religion and its relation to the middle-period work am I finally in a position to indicate the effect that Durkheim's "revelatory" reading of Robertson Smith's religious writings in 1895 may have had on his later work. I must first insist, at least on the evidence at present available, that Durkheim had already adopted a normative and affective mode of analysis—as demonstrated, for example, in his methodology articles of 1894—before he ever seriously encountered Smith's work. The eagerness with which he received it, therefore, could only have corresponded to the striking similarities between Smith's work and his own new direction, and it was this similarity that allowed Durkheim to begin to reinterpret his shifting understanding in the explicitly religious terms that Smith provided.

Although Robertson Smith was himself influenced by the new historical approach to religion that began in Germany earlier in the nineteenth century, his own contributions further revolutionized Biblical scholarship and religious history, and they did so because of their insistence on the role of religious "practice" over belief. One can see in Smith's definitions a close parallel to those Durkheim offered independently in 1894, and the adumbration, as well, of the language Durkheim employed in his article on religion in 1899. "In connection with every religion, whether ancient or modern," Smith writes in his introduction to his most important work, *Lectures on the Religion of the Semites*, "we find on the one hand certain beliefs, and on the other certain institutions [of] ritual practices and rules of conduct" (1887; New York, 1969, p. 16). Smith objected to religious study that focused exclusively on the nature of divinities (p. 23), and argued, at least for primitive religions, that rites were primary (pp. 17–18). The nature of rites, he further insisted, was not rational and purposive, but rather was designed to allow "communion" between God and man (p. 226). Smith argued, moreover, that this communion between God and man was also the occasion of greater emotional fellow-feeling among men themselves.

> The most important functions of ancient worship were reserved for public occasions, when the whole community was stirred by a common emotion. . . . In rejoicing before his god a man rejoiced with and for the welfare of his kindred, his neighbours and his country, and, in renewing by a solemn act of worship the bond that united him to his god, he also renewed the bonds of family, social, and national obligation . . . Every complete act of worship . . . had a public or quasi-public character. Most sacrifices were offered on fixed occasions, at the great communal or national feasts, but even a private offering was not complete without guests, and the surplus of sacrificial flesh was not sold but distributed with an open hand. Thus every act of worship expressed the idea that man does not live for himself only but for his fellows, and that this partnership of social interests is the sphere over which the gods preside and on which they bestow their assured blessing. (Pp. 260 265.)

"In ancient society," Smith concludes, "all morality . . . was consecrated and enforced by religious motives and sanctions" (p. 267). It is clearly not surprising, then, that Durkheim saw in this work that the affective association he had already placed at the center of society could be read also as a kind of religious rite.

But though the significance of rites over belief and the communality of ritual life were Smith's most developed ideas about religion, he sketched a number of other insights that also proved to be important to Durkheim's later work. Two are probably the most important. First, Smith defined sacredness as a relationship to divinity rather than an intrinsic quality of objects themselves (p. 91). The quality of holiness, he wrote, accrues to things, places, or animals that stand in a close relationship to gods and which "claim a special reverence from men" (p. 25). Second, Smith saw in ancient religion a tight relationship between material form and spiritual substance. "All acts of ancient worship," he wrote, "have a material embodiment" (p. 25); they are "wrapped up in [its] husk" (p. 439).

If Smith, then, did not provide Durkheim with his initial understanding of the normative and emotional basis of social order and association, his understanding of religion certainly allowed Durkheim to begin to visualize this order in a religious form. This was, however, only a general kind of stimulus. In terms of the specifically religious theory of his later work, Durkheim revised Smith in crucial ways, both in terms of the nature of primitive religion and in terms of its relationship to the modern world. In regard to the first issue, Durkheim conducted a radical revision of Smith's understanding of the relation between men and gods. Smith's own theorizing was rather vague, but he clearly believed that rituals were conducted with the communion with gods as their primary object. Durkheim saw, much more clearly, that social solidarity itself was the object of ritual and that the divine was a device for men to represent the human experience of society to one another. Durkheim understood, in other words, where Smith did not, the process of representation that transformed association into religious experience. Related to this was Smith's unacceptable temporal separation of rituals and mythical beliefs: he believed that rituals preceded myths in time, not only within the development of a single religion but within the history of religion itself. Durkheim saw, to the contrary, that belief and practice were interrelated in an analytical way in every moment of religious life. Both of these far-reaching challenges to Smith, I should add, emerged because of the independent nature of Durkheim's own theoretical concern with similar issues. By the time of his encounter with Smith, he had earlier already asserted the primary role of human solidarity in creating any institutional form. This, and his long-standing interest in securing voluntaristic action, made him concentrate on the creation of gods by men. Similarly, his commitment to the affective and moral power of crystallized forms, and their power to stimulate social action, made him sensitive to the role of belief as an equal partner in religious experience.

In terms of the "status" of primitive religion, Durkheim also made radical departures. While Smith had taken Semitic religion as the basis of all primitive religion, he had drawn a sharp line between this "materialistic" and "sensuous" religion and what he believed to be the more idealistic, spiritual, and antiritualistic religion of modern Christianity. Durkheim radicalized Smith by arguing, first, that primitive religion was basically the same as any advanced religion and, second, that such religious practices were characteristic of the operation of secular society as a whole. This last point would have been sharply opposed by Smith as well.

For an excellent background discussion of Smith and his relationship to modern sociological, psychological, and anthropological thinking about religion, see T. O. Beidelman, *W. Robertson Smith and the Sociological Study of Religion* (Chicago, 1974). Beidelman, however, overemphasizes Smith's effect on Durkheim, primarily because he is not aware of the movement of Durkheim's thought before he encountered Smith's work. Lukes (n. 82 above, pp. 238–239) is guilty of the same exaggeration when he tries to demonstrate the impact of Smith simply by comparing his religious theory with Durkheim's earlier writing on the narrow topic of religion itself—without considering the shifts that had taken place in Durkheim's general social theory in the immediately preceding years. While Filloux's (n. 83 above, pp. 91–92) assessment is more cautious on this point, he moves too far over to the other side by claiming that Durkheim knew "in principle that all is religious" as early as 1886 and 1887, and that Smith merely gave him a better understanding of how this permeation by religion could come about. Despite the great interest of his interpretation, Filloux, as noted earlier (ch. 5), errs in his belief that Durkheim's work is continuous from beginning to end. Robert Alun Jones also seems to underestimate Smith's impact on Durkheim ("On Understanding a Sociological Classic," *American Journal of Sociology* 83 [1977]: 279–319), for while his detailed scholarship clearly reveals the commonality, and differences, between these two thinkers in terms of specific empirical problems in the study of religion, e.g., the problem of sacrifice, this powerful microscopic focus ignores the relationship between the general, macroscopic frameworks of their theories. Thus, Jones finds no impact of Smith on Durkheim until after 1900 (p. 307), arguing because of a detailed propositional disagreement against any impact of Smith on the essay on religious phenomena in 1899. I would suggest, to the contrary, that without encountering Smith and his school in the mid-90's, Durkheim may not have made the transition from his middle-period associational theory to his more spiritualized, religious understanding, an understanding well in place by 1900. This is, of course, still an historical hypothesis: we don't know what would have happened without Smith's work—if Durkheim's statement about the "revelation" is, indeed, authentic in the first place. Nonetheless, even historians of social thought cannot avoid such counter-factual hypotheses, any more than they can afford to concentrate on intellectual detail at the expense of general frameworks.

Although I am not concerned here with an intellectual history of Durkheim's theory of religion, but rather with the specific inspiration for a crucial transition in his general theory of society, it should be noted that Fustel de Coulanges certainly also affected Durkheim's later thinking, although in much less significant ways than Smith. Specifically, Durkheim's emphasis on the "sacred" as a way of summarizing the effects of religious forces was probably indirectly derived from Coulanges rather than Smith. In Coulanges' *The Ancient City*, the sacred is a central part of his argument (see particularly bk. 1, "Ancient Beliefs").

Finally, this analysis of Durkheim's social and voluntaristic understanding of religion, and his discovery of the important role that the notion of active representational processes had in secular moral life, allows one to understand the basic error of those interpreters like Gurvitch (n. 83 above) who view Durkheim's later theory as presenting a reified and anti-individualistic theory of morality. For Gurvitch, Durkheim's movement toward the religious merely revealed the reified essence of his theory of the *collective conscience*, i.e., his view that social morality plays the same metaphysical role as the notion of the Divine Being in theological writings. I have tried to demonstrate, to the contrary, that instead of divinizing society Durkheim was, in fact, socializing religion: he utilized his newly discovered religious terminology to root morality more firmly in individual interaction and voluntaristic representation. The basis of Gurvitch's error can be found in his theoretical logic. Confusing the analytical with the concrete individual, he claims that Durkheim sees the individual conscience as closed and impenetrable, hence the reified and external quality, according to Gurvitch, of Durkheim's vision of the *collective conscience*. Yet for Durkheim, at least after the theoretical advances of *Rules* and *Suicide*, this closed individual conscience refers, for the most part, not to the concrete actor—who is clearly social in his individuality—but only to the private and asocial actor, that is, to the individual in the analytical sense. Some ambiguity does remain in Durkheim's theory of the individual conscience, but, as I will note in ch. 9, the residual insularity of Durkheim's individual pushes him in a quasi-utilitarian direction, not in the idealist direction that Gurvitch perceives.

177. For this information, see Vogt, "The Confrontation of Socialists and Sociologists in Prewar France, 1890–1914" (n. 85 above).

178. Durkheim, "Review of Gaston Richard, *Le Socialisme et la science sociale*," pp. 131–138 in Traugott (n. 1 above), p. 135. First published in 1897 in the *Revue philosophique*.

179. Ibid., p. 137.

180. Georges Sorel, "Preface," pp. 1–20, in Antonio Labriola, *Essais sur la conception matérialiste de l'histoire* (Paris, 1897), p. 19.

181. Durkheim, "Review of Antonio Labriola, *Essais sur la conception matérialiste de l'histoire,*" pp. 123–130 in Traugott, p. 126.

182. Ibid., p. 127.

183. Ibid., p. 128.

184. Ibid., pp. 129–130.

185. Perhaps the major failure in the interpretation of this crucial phase in Durkheim's theoretical development rests with the widespread inclination to describe the issue he was grappling with as exactly parallel to the Marxian concern with base versus superstructure. Thus, Emile Benoît-Smullyan writes about the crucial relationship for Durkheim of "material substratum" and "collective representation" ("The Sociologism of Emile Durkheim and his School," in H. E. Barnes, ed., *An Introduction to the History of Sociology* [Chicago, 1948], p. 511). Pope (n. 82 above, p. 410) talks about whether or not "material foundations" still play a significant role. Giddens tries to indicate the continuing impact, and therefore anti-idealist reference, of social institutions on ideas in Durkheim's sociology ("The 'Individual' in the Writings of Emile Durkheim," pp. 273–291 in Giddens, *Studies in Social and Political Theory* [New York, 1977], p. 290). This same dichotomy is the principal organizing rubric for Lukes' thinking (n. 82 above) about the shift in Durkheim's thinking initiated by religion, as it is for Dominick La Capra in *Emile Durkheim: Sociologist and Philosopher* (Ithaca, N.Y., 1972); for similar analyses of Durkheim couched in a base-superstructure frame of reference, see Marks (n. 82 above) and Gouldner (n. 45 above). These interpreters take different positions on whether or not a shift did occur, but the error is the same no matter what their conclusion. For the issue in this confrontation with religion is not whether or not the material base will be dominant. This issue had already been decided by Durkheim in 1894. The issue rather is what will be the nature of the normative order to which Durkheim is already committed.

Many interpreters, of course, have simply failed to appreciate the significance of this early encounter with religion altogether. In his influential earlier work on Durkheim, Parsons (n. 18 above, p. 409), e.g., viewed Durkheim's religious understanding as coming into play only after the publication of *Elementary Forms*. (It is an extraordinary testimony to the sensitivity of this early interpretation that Parsons was able to describe the transition to subjectivity in Durkheim's middle writings without comprehending the early significance of religion.) Yet even among those who have seen the importance of this encounter, none have adequately assessed its enormous impact on his later theory of society. Lukes, e.g., who is much more aware of this crucial biographical fact than most, basically considers this religious breakthrough as a separate line of analysis culminating in *Elementary Forms*, and integrates it hardly at all with Durkheim's writing on education, politics, and other institutions. The only important exceptions, to my knowledge, are Gianfranco Poggi, "The Place of Religion in Durkheim's Theory of Institutions" (*European Journal of Sociology* 12 [1971]: 229–260, esp. 252-254), and the important dissertation by Lacroix (n. 81 above). Poggi's insightful analysis, however, is mainly programmatic, and fails to link the importance of religion to any decisive break in Durkheim's work. Lacroix's work presents two problems, from my perspective. (1) Although it firmly exposes the "break" [*la coupure*] that Durkheim's religious revelation created in his theoretical development, it tries to tie this religion-inspired shift too closely to the middle-period work. Any definitive resolution of this question, of course, must await firmer historical evidence, but at this point it seems evident to me that Durkheim's theory underwent two shifts after the publication of the *Division of Labor*, not one. The first, which begins even as that work is published—in the "Note" (n.23 above) and review cited earlier—reorganizes his schema in a radically subjective manner without any particular reference to collective representations or religion. The second, which is barely visible in the lectures of 1895 and does not become explicit until 1897, brings spiritual considerations into the center of this newly subjectified theory. Only the latter development, it would seem, can be linked to the "revelation" of 1895. (2) Lacroix's analysis, valuable as it is, does not expose the "religious dimension" of Durkheim's later institutional theory in a systematic way. Bellah (n. 9 above) takes some initial steps in the direction in which such an analysis would have to go.

Lévi-Strauss has criticized Durkheim's theory of ritual on the grounds that, since Durkheim holds that the purely ideal social sentiments of individuals are always of a similar kind, he cannot explain the different kind of symbolism generated by religious life (*Totemism* [Boston, 1963], p. 76). This criticism has been taken up by other anthropologists, e.g. by Rodney Needham ("Introduction," pp. vii–xlviii in Emile Durkheim and Marcel Mauss, *Primitive Classification* [1903; Chicago, 1963], p. xxiv) and also by contemporary sociologists. It is, e.g., a continual criticism by J. Duvignaud in his introductory discussions to Durkheim's contributions on religion to *L'Année sociologique*, which Duvignaud collected in *Journal sociologique* (Paris, 1969). I hope that my analysis has demonstrated the fallacy of such a reading of Durkheim as an anti-individualistic idealist. Ritual, in his view, does involve sentiment and affect, but this emotion is always strongly affected by the specific ideational forms that have crystallized earlier association, and it is also structured in the particular situation by the process of cognitive ideation that Durkheim calls representation. The sense of active individual cognition that is asserted, though not elaborated, in Durkheim's analysis of ritual practice is evidenced by the fact that it is not inconsistent with certain central notions in the contemporary theories of the pragmatist-inspired tradition of "symbolic interactionism." Cf. Gregory P. Stone and Harvey A. Farberman, "On the Edge of Rapprochement: Was Durkheim Moving toward the Perspective of Symbolic Interaction?" *Sociological Quarterly* 8 (1967):149–164, esp. 154–155; see also the treatment of George Herbert Mead's thought by J. David Lewis and Richard L. Smith in *American Sociology and Pragmatism* (Chicago, 1980), which demonstrates that Mead, considered the founder of symbolic interactionism, was, for his part, more sensitive to the "realist" status of the symbolic order than is generally acknowledged. Lewis and Smith argue, on this basis, that the "activism" of Mead's symbolic theory is quite consistent with Durkheim's later theory of collective representation.

There are particularly significant parallels, in this regard, between Charles Pierce, the philosophical progenitor of pragmatic theory who created, along with it, a theory of signs, and Durkheim himself. The connection is not, in fact, simply hypothetical: Pierce's work has been extended, e.g., by Charles Morris, whose numerous writings in the theory of signs and symbols became important to theorizing which is considered prototypically "Durkheimian," e.g., Talcott Parsons and Edward Shils in their *Towards a General Theory of Action* (Cambridge, Mass., 1951). A rapprochement between Durkheim and contemporary, more individualistic traditions, in other words, depends not only on a greater appreciation of the cognitive activism of his representation theory but also on a more "realist" understanding of the collectivist dimensions of the founders of contemporary interactionism.

186. This review of Labriola has been seriously misread by Durkheim's interpreters, so much so that its theoretical meaning has become fundamentally obscured. Giddens, e.g., who never acknowledges the influence of religion on Durkheim's later view of contemporary society, discusses the review in a manner that makes it appear convergent with most if not all of the crucial aspects of Marx's thought (pp. 181–182 in "Durkheim as a Review Critic," *Sociological Review*, n.s. 18, no. 2 [1970]:181–182, esp. 171–196). But the same point is also maintained by those who know better the revolution that Durkheim's theory was in the process of undergoing. These critics recognize that Durkheim is self-consciously trying to separate himself from Marx's thought, but they argue that he is mistaken in doing so, that the emerging theory does not differ from Marx's in significant ways. Filloux and Cuvillier, e.g., argue that Durkheim has misread Labriola, who, they say, actually follows Marx's original emphasis on the relative autonomy of superstructural forms. In Cuvillier's opinion, by arguing against economic determinism Durkheim "fights against a phantom" ("Durkheim et Marx" [n. 95 above], p. 92). Filloux agrees, maintaining that on the point of the relative autonomy of representations, "Durkheim is much nearer to Marx than he believes himself to be" (*Durkheim et le socialisme* [n. 83 above], p. 132).

I believe that these interpretations are incorrect on both counts. First, Durkheim is trying specifically to differentiate himself from Marx's thought; second, he is correct in his understanding of what the differences are. True, at certain points in his review Durkheim misrepresents Marxism as a theory of technological determinism. Nonetheless, his general understanding of Marx's theoretical logic is an accurate one; and he gives a fair reading to Labriola's work, which was itself a fair representation of Marx's central tenets. Labriola was not, I agree, a vulgar Marxist. He was much more concerned than most of the other leading Marxists of his day with the organization of the superstructure and with the "mediations" by which it was produced from the base. He took Engels' later letter to Bloch, where Engels rejects the mechanical determination of superstructure by base, as an authoritative statement of Marx's ideas. Yet we have seen already, and will have occasion in the following chapter to see again, that Engels' statement on this matter must be read as an implicit rejection of Marxian logic, not as its elaboration: there are no theoretical resources within original Marxism to carry out this antideterministic program.

This internal dilemma of Marxist thought is the secret problem of Labriola's essay; it explains why his work and Durkheim's response to it have so often been misinterpreted. For while paying obeisance to an antideterministic position, the substance of Labriola's analysis is actually a highly reductionist one. His animating desire, in fact, is not to save the autonomy of the superstructure but to better explain how it is produced exclusively by the pressure of the economic base.

> We begin with motives religious, political, aesthetic, passionate, etc. but . . . we must subsequently discover the causes of these motives in the material conditions underlying them. Now the study of these conditions should be so specified that we may perceive indubitably not only what are the causes, but again by what mediations they arrive at that form which reveals them to the consciousness as motives whose origin is often obliterated. (*Essays in the Materialist Conception of History* [New York, 1966], pp. 110–111; cf. pp. 148–149.)

In the pursuit of these determining material conditions, moreover, Labriola often fails to achieve the level of analysis of Marx himself, sometimes barely distinguishing property relations—the relations of production—from the technical base that constitutes its forces. In other words, his theory does, in fact, often degenerate into a form of technological determinism. His analysis of Australian Aboriginal society focuses on the discovery of fire and the "many other artificial means by which the needs of life are satisfied"; he believes that "the canalization of Mesopotamia gives us the ancient pre-Semitic Babylonian state," while "the extremely ancient Egyptian civilization rests upon the application of the Nile to agriculture." "History," Labriola writes, "is the work of man in so far as man can create and improve his instruments of labor. . . .

Their [men's] discoveries, and their inventions, by creating artificial ways of living, have produced not only habits and customs . . . but relations and bonds of coexistence." (Pp. 116–120.)

Durkheim, then, was not wrong in his assessment. He saw clearly the essence of Labriola's argument if not his ambivalent desire to escape from the determinism within which he was caught; and if Durkheim had, in fact, been aware of the latter it would only have been grist for his mill. Durkheim was aware when he reviewed Labriola that he had found the best possible context in which to establish the independence of his new position vis-à-vis Marx.

187. Evidently, this "astonishment" was not limited to Durkheim's critics. Paul Lapie, the reviewer turned follower who had earlier applauded the subjective turn of Durkheim's *Rules*, complained in an 1897 letter to Célèstin Bouglé, one of Durkheim's collaborators on *L'Année*, that "Durkheim explains everything, at this time, by religion; the interdiction against marriages between parents is a religious affair, the punishment is a religious phenomenon, all is religious" (quoted in Lacroix [n. 81 above], p. 213, n. 2.)

188. Durkheim, "Preface," *L'Année sociologique* (2 [1889]: i–vi), pp. 347–352 in Kurt H. Wolff, ed., *Essays on Sociology and Philosophy by Emile Durkheim et al.* (New York, 1964), pp. 350–351. Precisely the same sentiment is expressed thirteen years later, in *Elementary Forms* (n.18 above), after Durkheim had largely carried this program out. "It is inadmissible," he writes, "that systems of ideas like religions, which have held so considerable a place in history, and to which, in all times, men have come to receive the energy which they must have to live, should be made up of a tissue of illusions." The truth, he wrote, is that "today we are beginning to realize that law, morals and even scientific thought itself were born of religion, were for a long time confounded with it, and have remained penetrated with its spirit." (P. 87.)

189. Durkheim, "Note on Social Morphology," pp. 88–90 in Traugott (n. 2 above), p. 88. First published in *L'Année sociologique*, vol. 2 (1899).

190. Ibid., p. 89, italics added.

191. In his 1909 essay on "Sociology and the Social Sciences," Durkheim makes the same point when he writes that "parallel to the substratum of collective life, there is this life itself" (Traugott, p. 79). It is "life itself," in other words, not the purely artificial forms of morphology in which it is imbedded, that must be the starting point for causal analysis of social morphology. Filloux (n. 83 above, pp. 107–108, 134) has put this issue into the language of structure and function. For Durkheim, he writes, the physiology of groups is their psychic life, but rather than seeing this physiology as effectively structured by the anatomy upon which it must rely, Durkheim views the anatomy, or structural "base," as merely the consolidation of physiological functioning.

192. Durkheim, review of Paul Merriot, *Des agglomérations urbaines*

dans l'Europe contemporaine, pp. 201–204 in Duvignaud (n. 185 above), p. 203. First published in *L'Année sociologique,* vol. 2 (1899).

193. Durkheim, review of Siegfried Rietschel, *Markt und Stadt in ihrem Rechtlichen Verhältniss,* pp. 196–199 in Duvignaud, quoting p. 196. First published in *L'Année sociologique,* vol. 2 (1899).

194. Durkheim, review of Karl Hegel, *Die Entstehung des deutschen städtswesens,* pp. 199–201 in Duvignaud, quoting p. 200. First published in *L'Année sociologique,* vol. 2 (1899).

195. Durkheim, review of A. Dumont, *Natalité et democratie,* pp. 237–240 in Duvignaud, quoting p. 239. First published in *L'Année sociologique,* vol. 3 (1900).

196. Although these writings will by no means go unmentioned in my remaining discussion, the essays on primitive anthropology in particular will not receive the theoretical attention they deserve. To my knowledge, they have never received it.

197. This position was first articulated in Durkheim's review of Heinrich Gunow, *Die oekonomischen Grundlagen der Mutterherrschaft,* pp. 165-168 in Duvignaud. First published in *L'Année sociologique,* vol. 2 (1899). This review foreshadows the more substantial article, "Sur l'organization matrimoniale des sociétés australiennes," *L'Année sociologique* 8 (1907):118–147.

198. Durkheim, "Two Laws of Penal Evolution," in Traugott, pp. 153–180. First published in *L'Année sociologique,* vol. 4 (1901).

199. Durkheim, "Note sur la sociologie criminelle et la statistique morale," pp. 293–296 in Duvignaud, esp. p. 294. This note was Durkheim's Introduction to a new section of *L'Année sociologique,* vol. 4 (1901).

200. Durkheim and Mauss (n. 185 above).

201. Durkheim and Mauss, "Sur la notion de civilization," *L'Année sociologique* 12 (1913):46–50. Translated as "Note on the Notion of Civilization," *Social Research* 38 (1971):808–813.

202. *Socialism and Saint-Simon* (n. 45 above), p. 180.

203. Ibid., p. 181.

204. Ibid., pp. 182–183.

205. Ibid., p. 231.

206. Ibid., pp. 194–195. In the Preface to the second edition of *Division of Labor,* in 1902, Durkheim reveals—without acknowledging it—that he himself has come to the same kind of realization that he has just described in Saint-Simon. While at first he repeats the claim of 1893 that integration can be achieved by organizing egoistic interest through the division of labor, he qualifies it sharply and argues that true integration must come from a very different source.

> In the body of this work, we have especially insisted upon showing that the division of labor cannot be held responsible, as is sometimes unjustly charged; that it does not necessarily produce dispersion and in-

coherence, but that functions, when they are sufficiently in contact with one another, tend to stabilize and regulate themselves. *But this explanation is incomplete.* For, if it is true that social functions spontaneously seek to adapt themselves to one another, provided they are regularly in relationship, *nevertheless this mode of adaptation becomes a rule of conduct only if the group consecrates it with its authority.* A rule, indeed, is not only an habitual means of acting; it is, above all, an *obligatory means of acting.* (*Division of Labor* [n. 81 above], p. 4, italics added.)

207. Ibid., pp. 231–233.

208. Ibid., p. 240. Edward A. Tiryakian has also referred to the possibly self-reflecting quality of these lectures on Saint-Simon in his excellent "Emile Durkheim," pp. 187–236 in T. B. Bottomore and Robert Nisbet, eds., *A History of Sociological Analysis* (New York, 1978).

209. Durkheim, *Division of Labor,* p. 168.

CHAPTER EIGHT

1. Paul Fauconnet and Marcel Mauss, "Sociologie," in *La Grande Encyclopédie* (1901) 30: 165–176.

2. Emile Durkheim, *The Rules of Sociological Method* (New York, 1938), p. lvi.

3. Fauconnet and Mauss, pp. 168–169.

4. Durkheim, *Rules,* p. lvi. To be more precise, Durkheim actually establishes two different levels of crystallization. In vol. 6 of *L'Année sociologique* (1903), when he was trying to locate the level of juridical phenomena, he realized that the law contained different degrees of systematization. He distinguished in this way between acts, institutions, and systems. Most of the studies he later embarked on are, in this sense, as much about "systems" as "institutions." (See "Note sur les systèmes juridiques," pp. 461–462 in J. Duvignaud, comp., *Journal sociologique* [Paris, 1969].) For other discussions of Durkheim's analysis of "institutions" that emphasize the affective and moral element, see Gianfranco Poggi, "The Place of Religion in Durkheim's Theory of Institutions," *European Journal of Sociology* 12 (1971):229–260; Jean-Claude Filloux, *Durkheim et le socialisme* (Geneva and Paris, 1977), pp. 112–113; and Talcott Parsons, *The Structure of Social Action* (New York, [1937] 1968), pp. 399–408. For a closely related discussion, see Georges Gurvitch's analysis of Durkheim's "sociology in depth," in his "Le Problème de la conscience collective dans la sociologie de Durkheim," pp. 351–408 in Gurvitch, *La Vocation actuelle de la sociologie* (Paris, 1950), esp. pp. 351–352.

5. Durkheim, *The Elementary Forms of Religious Life* (New York, 1965), p. 239, n. 6.

6. Durkheim, "Review of Antonio Labriola, *Essais sur la conception matérialiste de la histoire,*" pp. 123–130 in Mark Traugott, ed., *Emile Durkheim on Institutional Analysis* (Chicago, 1978), p. 130.

7. Durkheim, *Suicide* (New York, 1951), pp. 313–315.

8. Durkheim, "Sociology and the Social Sciences," pp. 71–87 in Traugott (n. 6 above), p. 84.

9. Ibid.

10. *Suicide*, p. 314.

11. None of the middle-period work—1894–96—was centrally informed by the religious theory, but it is possible, nonetheless, to find certain references that convince us that Durkheim was thinking about religion at this time. It is hard to determine whether or not the understanding of religion touches *Rules* at all. In the last few pages of the book, Durkheim talks about "ways of acting and thinking which it [society] has consecrated with its prestige" (p. 102), and it is possible, according to the timetable that Durkheim later provides us, that his lectures for the 1894/95 course on religion could already have affected his final considerations in *Rules*. (This phrase about consecration, however, was in the original 1894 article; it was not modified when Durkheim prepared the 1894 pieces for publication in 1895. See Durkheim, "Les Règles de la méthode sociologique [3° article]," in *Revue philosophique* 38 [1894]: 14–39, quoting 23). A much stronger case, we have seen (ch. 7, sec. 3, above), can be made for the 1895/96 lectures on socialism, where Durkheim concludes by confirming Saint-Simon's observation that industrial society needs a new religion (*Socialism and Saint-Simon* [Yellow Springs, Ohio, 1958], p. 239). Although the great bulk of *Suicide* represents, along with these other middle-period works, a subjective approach to solidary order that is religiously unconscious, in the concluding pages Durkheim makes several references to the religious dimension of modern society that demonstrate that by the end of 1896 he had begun to assimilate the insights of the sociology of religion in a serious way (pp. 312, 333–335). As for publications after 1906, there is, of course, *The Elementary Forms of Religious Life*, to which I have already referred and will discuss subsequently as well. There are also lectures and essays on science, education, and economics. Each of these areas of writing will also be part of the following analysis. I should mention, finally, that for the crucial period 1897–1906 I will be dealing with two central sets of Durkheim's lectures, those on the state and occupational and legal ethics, and those on education, which Durkheim gave throughout his career, beginning in the late 1880s. I will be dealing with the publications which resulted from the final sets of lectures, with publications, that is, from the "later" period of Durkheim's development. It would be extremely interesting to follow the evolution of these lectures over the entire course of Durkheim's intellectual life.

12. The Dreyfus affair, indeed, could only have fueled Durkheim's determination to produce a religious theory of modernity. Though he had already adopted a thoroughly religious model of society, Dreyfus

could only have made him even more convinced that the polarization of French society could be overcome only through the creation of a new morality. If sociology could convince the traditionalists that even rational and modern institutions had a religious dimension it could, perhaps, also convince them to support the liberal institutions of the Third Republic. I should stress, however, in opposition to some interpreters (e.g., Dominick La Capra in his *Emile Durkheim: Sociologist and Philosopher* (Ithaca, N.Y., 1972), my conviction that the critical intellectual changes in Durkheim's career occurred before the beginning of the Dreyfus affair (see the analysis of the transition from the middle to the late period in the preceding chapter).

That Durkheim employed the concepts of religion to understand—more accurately, to endorse—the structures of liberal modernity has been difficult for contemporary sociologists to understand, particularly those of the left and the right. While Robert Nisbet has formally maintained that Durkheim accepted ideological liberalism even though he utilized the analytic, or "philosophical," apparatus of French conservatism, there is, in fact, a clear elision in his work between the analytic and ideological dimensions. Nisbet argues, in effect, that the "religious" presuppositions Durkheim accepted made him reject the substance of modernity. "The kinds of society, constraint, and solidarity dealt with in all his later works—either in theoretical or practical terms—have nothing whatsoever to do with the attributes that he had laid down for an organic and (presumably) irreversibly modern society" ("Introduction," pp. 1–102 in Nisbet, ed., *Emile Durkheim* [Englewood Cliffs, N.J., 1965], p. 37). This statement, however, is still rather ambiguous, for it could refer to either analytic or ideological elements in Durkheim's work. In a subsequent work, Nisbet makes his point more specific. He claims that "Durkheim rejected individualism on every possible ground," that "he found it insupportable as a principle of social solidarity, as an ethic or moral value, as a cornerstone of the social order, and not least, as the vantage point of social analysis" (*The Sociology of Emile Durkheim* [New York, 1974], p. 16). Nisbet seems to believe, in other words, that Durkheim has reversed the ideological, not just the theoretical, position which he held in his earlier writing.

Radical writers often make the same kind of evaluation, conflating ideology and presuppositions to argue for the rejection of Durkheim rather than for his acceptance. Lewis Coser mistakes Durkheim's emphasis on organic ties of solidarity for a justification of hierarchical, organic society in "Durkheim's Conservatism and its Implications for His Sociological Theory" (pp. 211–232 in Kurt H. Wolff, ed., *Essays on Sociology and Philosophy by Emile Durkheim et al.* [New York, 1964]), although he seems to have modified his position in his later reconsideration of Durkheim's work in *Masters of Sociological Thought* (New York,

1971, pp. 129–174). On a somewhat less sophisticated plane, Irving Zeitlin exhibits the same kind of imcomprehension in *Ideology and the Development of Sociological Theory* (Englewood Cliffs, N.J., 1968), pp. 234–280.

But if contemporary left-liberal and radical thinkers have often had a difficult time understanding Durkheim's position, it could only have been more difficult in the polarized France of his time. "What were the defenders of 1789 to think of a sociologist," Joseph Neyer asks, "who claimed that he took his stand upon 'science and progress,' but who associated in friendship with Hamelin, the defender of Hegel, and who was able to utilize Hamelin's analyses of Kant, Charles Renouvier, and Hegel in his own sociological work?" ("Individualism and Socialism in Durkheim," pp. 32–76 in Wolff, *Essays*, p. 60, n. 6). Neyer presents a good antidote to the works I have mentioned here, as do Robert N. Bellah ("Durkheim and History," in Nisbet [n. 1 above, ch. 5], pp. 153–176), Anthony Giddens (*Capitalism and Modern Social Theory* [London, 1971]), and Edward A. Tiryakian ("Emile Durkheim," pp. 187–236 in T. B. Bottomore and Robert Nisbet, eds., *A History of Sociological Analysis* [New York, 1978]). For a powerful general analysis of the relationship of classical sociology to the Enlightenment and Reaction—one which disputes the claims of both left and right that the classical thinkers were conservative—see Steven Seidman, *Liberalism and the Origins of European Social Theory* (Berkeley and Los Angeles, 1983).

The relationship of ideology to presuppositions in Durkheim's later writing, it should be noted, bears a striking similarity to the critical idealism that permeated Marx's early work. The constant reference for the early Marx was universalistic morality, a standard for criticism that rested with the "public mind." Marx repeated time and time again that ideal sentiments were stronger than material chains, and for this reason believed that the central resource of any movement for reform must be "the sacredness and inviolability of subjective conviction." It would not be too farfetched to argue that the tension between sacred rationality and the profane world was the moving force in Marx's early works— indeed, the young Hegelians can all be viewed as radical secular Christians of a certain type. Contemporary "critical" social theorists, however, seem much more able to accept this ideological-theoretical combination in "Marxism" than in "bourgeois" theory. For an important exception, see Alvin W. Gouldner's *The Dialectic of Ideology and Technology* (New York, 1976), and his *The Two Marxisms* (New York, 1980).

13. Durkheim, *Professional Ethics and Civic Morals* (Glencoe, Ill., 1958) pp. 2–5; cf. Durkheim, *Moral Education* (New York, 1961), p. 74.

14. *Professional Ethics and Civic Morals*, p. 5.

15. *Rules* (n. 2 above), pp. 116, 117.

16. *Elementary Forms* (n. 5 above), p. 262.

17. Ibid., pp. 263, 262. This position is also clearly implied in Durkheim's "Individual and Collective Representations," pp. 1–34 in his *Sociology and Philosophy* (New York, 1974), passim.

18. Durkheim, "The Determination of Moral Facts," ibid., pp. 35–79, see p. 57.

19. *Suicide*, p. 169.

20. This quotation is from a comment Durkheim made in the course of a discussion on "Science and Religion" at a meeting of the Société française de philosophie, November 19, 1908, published in its *Bulletin*, vol. 9 (1909). The text of the comment can be found under the heading "Débat sur la possibilité d'une science religieuse," in Durkheim, *Textes* (Paris, 1975), 1: 142–146, see 144.

21. Durkheim and Mauss, *Primitive Classification* (1903; Chicago, 1963), p. 81.

22. *Elementary Forms*, p. 30.

23. *Primitive Classification*, pp. 85–87. Cf. *Elementary Forms*, p. 270; for a similar explanation of the cognitive category of "force," see pp. 232 ff.

24. *Primitive Classification*, p. 32. The enormous implications for Durkheim's earlier view of history of making the cognitive orientations of primitive peoples problematic is evident in this passage:

> Species of things, classed in a clan, serve it as secondary or sub-totems; i.e., within the clan a particular group of individuals, under the influence of causes which are unknown to us, comes to feel more specially related to certain things which are attributed, in a general way, to the whole clan. The latter, when it becomes too large, then tends to segment, *and this segmentation takes place along the lines laid down by the classification.* (Ibid., p. 32, italics added.)

We might recall that in the *Division of Labor*, bk. 2, Durkheim had made a residual reference to the importance of prior solidarity in determining whether societies would segment in response to external pressure. This later, self-confident, and consistent assertion of the importance of such an internal, voluntaristic reference takes up this suggestion, which was buried in the instrumentalism of the earlier work. It demonstrates, once again, how Durkheim found in the later phase the theoretical tools to express some of his earlier convictions.

25. *Moral Education* (n. 13 above), p. 75.

26. "Individualism and the Intellectuals," pp. 43–57 in Bellah, (n. 12 above), p. 44. First published in 1898 in the *Revue bleue*.

27. Durkheim, *The Evolution of Educational Thought* (London, 1977), p. 290. From lectures given in 1904/5, first published in French in 1938. Cf. *Elementary Forms*, p. 225.

28. "Individualism and the Intellectuals," pp. 45–46.

29. "The Determination of Moral Facts" (n. 18 above), p. 48.

30. "Individualism and the Intellectuals," p. 46.

31. *Professional Ethics and Civic Morals* (n. 13 above), p. 57.

32. "Individualism and the Intellectuals," p. 46.

33. Ibid., pp. 52–53.

34. Ibid., p. 54.

35. Ibid., pp. 54–55.

36. Ibid., pp. 53–54.

37. Ibid., pp. 48–49.

38. Ibid., pp. 49–50.

39. Ibid., p. 48; cf. Durkheim and Mauss, "Note on the Notion of Civilization," *Social Research* 38 (1971): 808–813. First published in *L'Année sociologique* 12 (1913): 46–50.

40. Ibid., pp. 811, 812.

41. *Professional Ethics and Civic Morals*, p. 50.

42. *Suicide*, pp. 202–208.

43. *Moral Education* (n. 13 above), p. 69.

44. Ibid.

45. Durkheim, in an invited response to an inquiry into "the religious question"—the problem of the separation of church and state—published in *Mercure de France*, vol. 67 (1907). Reprinted in *Textes*, 2: 169–170.

46. Ibid., p. 169.

47. Durkheim, *The Division of Labor in Society* (1893; New York, 1933), pp. 15, 16.

48. *Moral Education*, p. 230.

49. Review of A. Dumont, *Natalité et democratie*, in Duvignaud (n. 4 above), p. 240.

50. *Professional Ethics and Civic Morals*, pp. 20, 26.

51. Review of A. Dumont, pp. 239–240.

52. Durkheim, "Review of Marianne Weber, *Ehefrau und Mutter in der Rechtsentwickelung*," pp. 139–144 in Traugott (n. 6 above), p. 143. Originally published in *L'Année sociologique*, vol. 11 (1910).

53. Review of A. Dumont, pp. 239–240.

54. "Review of M. Weber . . . ," pp. 143, 144.

55. *Moral Education*, p. 147.

56. Ibid., pp. 147, 74.

57. *Professional Ethics and Civic Morals*, p. 62.

58. *Moral Education*, p. 74.

59. *Professional Ethics and Civic Morals*, p. 6.

60. Durkheim, "Pedagogy and Sociology," pp. 113–134 in Durkheim, *Education and Sociology* (New York, 1956), p. 117. This article, first published in the *Revue de métaphysique et morale* in 1903, was Durkheim's

inaugural lecture at the Sorbonne, when he assumed the chair in education and sociology.

61. *Professional Ethics and Civic Morals*, pp. 7–8.

62. Ibid., pp. 23–24.

63. Ibid., p. 8.

64. Ibid., pp. 5, 8.

65. *The Evolution of Educational Thought* (n. 27 above), pp. 88–100.

66. Durkheim, review of Wilhelm Jerusalem, *Soziologie des Erkennis*, *L'Année sociologique* 11 (1910): 44; quoted in La Capra (n. 12 above), p. 274.

67. "The Determination of Moral Facts" (n. 18 above), p. 53.

68. *Professional Ethics and Civic Morals*, pp. 20–21.

69. Ibid., p. 22; cf. second Preface, *Division of Labor.*

70. *The Evolution of Educational Thought*, pp. 88–100.

71. *Professional Ethics and Civic Morals*, p. 6.

72. Ibid., p. 5.

73. Ibid., p. 51.

74. Ibid., p. 72.

75. Ibid., p. 51.

76. Ibid., p. 49.

77. Ibid.

78. Ibid., p. 79.

79. Ibid., pp. 80–81.

80. Ibid., p. 50.

81. Ibid., p. 92.

82. Ibid., p. 88.

83. *Division of Labor*, pp. 77, 104.

84. *Professional Ethics and Civic Morals*, pp. 69–70.

85. Ibid., p. 70.

86. Ibid., pp. 55–57.

87. Ibid., p. 57.

88. Ibid., p. 62.

89. Ibid., p. 65; cf. pp. 65–76.

90. Ibid., p. 69.

91. Ibid., p. 110.

92. *Division of Labor*, pp. 4–5.

93. "Sociology and the Social Sciences" (n. 8 above), p. 80.

94. *Professional Ethics and Civic Morals*, pp. 28–29.

95. "The Determination of Moral Facts" (n. 18 above), p. 69.

96. Ibid., p. 43.

97. *Professional Ethics and Civic Morals*, p. 73.

98. Ibid., pp. 110–112; cf. Durkheim, "Two Laws of Penal Evolution," pp. 153–180 in Traugott (n. 6 above), p. 172. First published in *L'Année sociologique*, vol. 4 (1901).

99. Ibid., p. 171.

100. *Professional Ethics and Civic Morals*, p. 121.

101. Ibid., p. 162.

102. Ibid., p. 148.

103. Ibid., p. 172.

104. Ibid., p. 308.

105. Ibid., p. 143.

106. Ibid.

107. Ibid., pp. 150–153.

108. Ibid., p. 165. It is in this section of his analysis that Durkheim makes one of the few references in his lectures to the influence of economic developments on such moral development, citing the rise of movable property as another stimulus to more individualistic law (ibid., p. 167). Even here, however, this reference is treated in an ad hoc and basically residual way, for Durkheim usually speaks vaguely about the "chain of circumstances" that developed on the material side of the equation (ibid., p. 165).

109. Ibid., pp. 179–180.

110. Ibid., p. 180.

111. Ibid., p. 181.

112. Ibid., p. 182.

113. Ibid., p. 186.

114. Ibid., p. 193.

115. Ibid., pp. 193–194, 197.

116. Ibid., p. 219; cf. p. 212.

117. Ibid., p. 210.

118. "Two Laws of Penal Evolution," p. 164.

119. Ibid., p. 168. This is also the reference for all quotations in the preceding paragraph.

120. Ibid. In the 1960s and 1970s there developed a strong interest in the empirical codification and testing of Durkheim's theory of legal evolution. This empirical exercise, however, has unfortunately been informed by an instrumentalist, "structuralist" reading of Durkheim's theory. Thus, Richard Schwartz and James Miller ("Legal Evolution and Societal Complexity," *American Journal of Sociology* 70, no. 2 [1964]:159–160) make "organization" in the material sense of the existence of centralized police agencies the principal indicator, or independent variable, in their hypothetical "Durkheimian" theory of the development of modern crime and punishment—a hypothesis they proceed to refute. As has been shown, however, it is the progression of social solidarity, in an anti-instrumentalist sense, that is central to the latter version of Durkheim's theory. (As I will mention later in this chapter, Durkheim does include here some recognition of the importance of instrumental functions by discussing the growth of the repressive state as another cause of legal

evolution; this reference, however, is clearly residual to his main discussion.) A much more sensitive reading of Durkheim's theory of legal evolution is supplied by Upendra Baxi ("Durkheim and Legal Evolution: Some Problems of Disproof," *Law and Society Review* 8, no. 4 [1974]: 645–651), but Baxi fails even to mention the fact of social sentiments as the principal motor of development.

121. Durkheim, "Pedagogy and Sociology" (n. 60 above), pp. 113–134.

122. *Moral Education* (n. 13 above), p. 149.

123. Ibid., p. 103. Cf. Durkheim, "Education: Its Nature and Role," pp. 61–90 in *Education and Sociology* (n. 60 above), p. 70. First published in 1911 in the *Nouveau Dictionnaire de pédagogie et d'instruction primaire.*

124. "Pedagogy and Sociology," pp. 89–90.

125. Ibid., p. 90.

126. *Moral Education*, p. 4; cf. pp. 49, 52.

127. "Pedagogy and Sociology," pp. 121–124.

128. "Education: Its Nature and Role," p. 87.

129. "Pedagogy and Sociology," p. 121.

130. "Education: Its Nature and Role," p. 79.

131. Durkheim, "The Nature and Methods of Pedagogy," pp. 91–112 in *Education and Sociology*, p. 94. First published in 1911 in the *Nouveau Dictionnaire.*

132. *Moral Education*, p. 10.

133. Ibid., pp. 10–11.

134. "Education: Its Nature and Role," pp. 88–89.

135. *Moral Education*, p. 155.

136. Ibid., pp. 10–11.

137. Ibid., p. 155.

138. Ibid., p. 165.

139. Ibid., p. 159.

140. "The Nature and Methods of Pedagogy," p. 112; cf. *The Evolution of Educational Thought* (n. 27 above), p. 31.

141. *Moral Education*, p. 165.

142. Ibid., p. 175, italics in original. In keeping with the common ideological misreading of Durkheim as a conservative—and in keeping also with the common conflation of this supposedly conservative ideology with his presuppositional emphasis on the internalization of norms—Durkheim's education theory has often been misread as a repressive theory that teaches deference and obedience to authority at the expense of individualism, criticism, and rationality. This is, for example, the position of A. K. C. Ottoway, in one of the very few articles on Durkheim's educational theory in English ("The Educational Sociology of Emile Durkheim," *British Journal of Sociology* 6 [1955]:213–227.) Lewis A. Coser also points to Durkheim's theory of education as support for his

thesis that Durkheim was a conservative ("Durkheim's Conservatism and Its Implications for His Sociological Theory," pp. 211–232 in Wolff, *Essays* [n. 12 above]). The criticism of Durkheim by Jean Piaget, in his *The Moral Judgment of the Child* (New York, [1932] 1965), pp. 327–370, is more thoughtful and empirical. Piaget holds that Durkheim overemphasizes punishment, and he argues against Durkheim's understanding that the teacher must impose a preexisting system of authority on the student from the outside. Insofar as this is an interpretation of Durkheim's ideological intention, it is incorrect, for Durkheim was as committed as Piaget himself to an anti-authoritarian, rational, and critical form of morality. (For a good discussion of these issues, see Ernest Wallwork, *Durkheim: Morality and Milieu* [Cambridge, Mass., 1972], pp. 66–70, 148–149.) Empirically, Durkheim's analysis of the process of education suffered from the same problems as his understanding of socialization in general: he had little comprehension of the "personality" and could not, therefore, understand the true nature of the interaction between personality and social structure. In this, he was a victim of the psychology of France in his own day. Piaget, in other words, is often more empirically correct than Durkheim about what teachers should do to produce rational autonomy. More generally, Durkheim's writing on this area must be compared with Talcott Parsons' to see the enormous difference that a more empirically accurate understanding of personality makes for a theory of moral order. I will make such an examination in vol. 4.

143. *The Evolution of Educational Thought*, p. 18.

144. Ibid., p. 75.

145. Ibid., pp. 177, 180.

146. Ibid., p. 180.

147. Ibid., pp. 19, 24–25, 26, 27, 30–31; cf. pp. 92–93.

148. Ibid., pp. 33–34.

149. Ibid., p. 34; cf. p. 37.

150. Ibid., pp. 33–37.

151. Ibid., p. 40.

152. Ibid., p. 67.

153. Ibid., p. 68.

154. Ibid., p. 73.

155. Ibid., p. 79.

156. Ibid., p. 81.

157. Ibid., p. 95.

158. Ibid., p. 123.

159. Ibid., p. 130.

160. See, for the continuity of structure, ibid., p. 162; for the impact of the Jesuits' reforms, pp. 259–260, 263–264.

161. Ibid., pp. 281–283.

162. Ibid., pp. 168, 172, 291–293.

163. Ibid., pp. 170–171.

164. Ibid., pp. 180–181.

165. For the impact of Protestantism, see ibid., pp. 285–286; for that of the rationalization of economic and political developments, pp. 284, 336.

166. Ibid., p. 290.

167. Ibid., pp. 293, 305.

168. Ibid., p. 310.

169. Ibid., p. 337. I have changed the English translation from "human consciousness" to "human conscience." In the French, the term is *"la conscience humaine"* (*L'Evolution pédagogique en France* [Paris, 1938], p. 386). It is clear that Durkheim intended this phrase to refer to the sacralization of the individual conscience which had been the point of his moral history in his other writings. The French *conscience* has both a moral and cognitive meaning, implying either conscience or consciousness. In this context, as in many others, this double meaning is not, of course, entirely misleading, for Durkheim does not think that the emergence of individual conscience as a guiding principle is in any way antithetical to the contemporary emphasis on rational consciousness.

This analysis of Durkheim's history of education should demonstrate that an emphasis on conflict and change is in no way incompatible with an emphasis on normative order. This lesson is brought out particularly well by Mohamed Cherkaoui ("Socialisation et conflit: Les Systèmes éducatifs et leur histoire selon Durkheim," *Revue française de sociologie* 17, no. 2 [April-June, 1976]: 197–212), who emphasizes that Durkheim sees the distinct possibility that education will be part of the struggle for domination between different social groups. I strongly agree with this point, although I disagree with Cherkaoui's tendency to instrumentalize what is, for all its emphasis on conflict, a fundamentally cultural and anti-instrumental analysis of educational development. Although Durkheim ususally tied his theoretical and ideological positions to an equilibrium model, this historical analysis demonstrates that at least on certain occasions he was able to explore the wider empirical possibilities open to him. That he was aware of the relative autonomy of these different levels of analysis is clear even in his earliest writings, despite the fact that he often violated in practice this conscious theoretical knowledge. In his 1892 Latin dissertation, for example, Durkheim chided Montesquieu because "he fails to see that every society embodies conflicting factors, simply because it has gradually emerged from a past form and is tending toward a future one" (*Montesquieu and Rousseau* [Ann Arbor, Mich., 1960], p. 59).

170. *Professional Ethics and Civic Morals* (n. 13 above), p. 153.

171. "Two Laws of Penal Evolution" (n. 98 above), passim.

172. *Professional Ethics and Civic Morals*, p. 69.

173. For a criticism of Durkheim's failure to consider the "mechanisms of legitimation in politics," see Anthony Giddens, "Durkheim's Political Sociology," pp. 233–272 in his *Studies in Social and Political Theory* (New York, 1977), p. 267; for a comment on Durkheim's treatment of bureaucracy as an anomalous exception to political development, see Melvin Richter, "Durkheim's Politics and Political Theory," pp. 170–210 in Wolff (n. 12 above), p. 198; for a general criticism of Durkheim's failure to consider the instrumental nature of political action, see Raymond Aron, *Main Currents in Sociological Thought* (New York, 1970), 2: 11–118. The most extensive recent criticism of Durkheim's political sociology is Pierre Birnbaum's in "La Conception durkheimienne de l'état: L'Apolitisme des fonctionnaires," *Revue française de sociologie* 17, no. 2 [April-June, 1976]: 247–258. Birnbaum justly accuses Durkheim of an apolitical, rather naïve understanding of political functionaries, of believing that the holders of state power will exercise this control in a neutral and rational manner, independently of social conflicts and interests. Durkheim's political functionaries, Birnbaum insists, are less holders of power than exercisers of reason. I would, nonetheless, disagree with several additional points Birnbaum makes about Durkheim's general political theory: that Durkheim establishes no links between the state and "social structure," that the state's capacity for exercising reason is a Hegelian kind of natural "aptitude," that the political elite makes decisions for an essentially "irrational" and passive people, and, finally, that this political vision is essentially comparable with the understanding of the *Division of Labor.* I would insist, to the contrary, that Durkheim's political theory is thoroughly sociological. It is concerned with the state's mediation of cultural meanings, both universalistic symbolic currents and the more particularistic cultures of concrete social groups. In reducing the later writings to the *Division of Labor,* Birnbaum misses this symbolical function, a function which also makes clear that Durkheim does not view politics as inherently rational. True, its contribution is to "universalize" collective particularism, but it always does so within the context of broader cultural directives: these directives, moreover, could conceivably be rather antirational and particularistic. Birnbaum has not separated, in other words, Durkheim's empirical analysis of a particular society from his model of politics generally. Finally, Durkheim's emphasis on the clarifying rationality of the state is not antidemocratic or elitist in a conventional sense, since he emphasizes that the state acts mainly to clarify issues for the discussion and communication that occurs among the people themselves. Yet these qualifications notwithstanding, Birnbaum's initial criticism is well taken. Within the "universalistic" cultural context which he accepted as characterizing his own time, and within the framework of his anti-instrumentalist assumptions, Durkheim's theory was much too optimistic about the capacity of the state to

avoid particularism and to be separated from conflicts of interest. (Cf. Filloux: "It seems to us that Fascism would . . . bear witness against the somewhat naïve trust of Durkheim in the individualizing vocation of the state" [J.-C. Filloux, "Durkheim and Socialism," *The Review: A Quarterly Journal of Pluralistic Socialism* 5 (1963): 66–85, quoting 83].)

174. This quotation from Durkheim's statement in the debate is in *Textes*, 1:220. It is not clear from the text whether the statements attributed to Durkheim are direct and literal quotations or are paraphrases made by a stenographer.

175. Ibid.

176. *Suicide* (n. 19 above), pp. 249–250; "The Determination of Moral Facts" (n. 18 above), p. 57; *Professional Ethics and Civic Morals*, p. 209; *Elementary Forms* (n. 5 above), p. 255.

177. "Unfair," of course, is the term used by Durkheim to refer to the wages of capitalist society, not by Marx. It will be recalled that Marx went to great lengths to argue that in terms of the order that governed the exchange of commodities, the exchange of wage for service was objectively reciprocal.

178. *Professional Ethics and Civic Morals*, p. 212.

179. Ibid.

180. Ibid., p. 214.

181. Ibid., p. 219. It is interesting to compare this position with Durkheim's understanding of change in economic value in the two phases of his development that preceded his later turn to subjective order. In the *Division of Labor*, it is clear, he accepted an objective determination of labor value as determined by the forces of supply and demand. But in 1887, before his shift to the empirical sociology that marked the onset of an instrumentalist framework, he laid out a theory of value change that is similar in most respects to the one he offers in his later work. In "La Science positive de la morale en Allemagne," Durkheim offers what is, in effect, an alternative to Marx's explanation of the changing organic composition of capital. He asserts that the gradual substitution of machines for labor of men, women, and children occurs because of the growing moral revulsion against exploitation. (*Revue philosophique* 14 [1887]: 33–58, 113–142, 275–284, esp. 41). The similarity between this early account of value change and the later one shows how the accomplishments of the later theory lay, not in an entirely novel understanding of society, but rather in finding a more satisfactory theoretical framework within which to translate many of the empirical insights, and ideological commitments, that Durkheim had from the beginning of his career.

Filloux puts Durkheim's subjective treatment of the economy very well when he writes that "if men unite, in the Durkheimian model, it is not to produce goods but for the pleasure of communing" (*Durkheim et le socialisme* [n. 4 above], p. 130). For similarly critical treatments of

Durkheim's economic sociology, see Guy Aimard, *Durkheim et la science économique* (Paris, 1962), pp. 232 ff.; Armand Cuvillier, "Durkheim et Marx," *Cahiers internationaux de sociologie* 4 (1948): 75–97, esp. 84, 96; and Poggi (n. 4 above), p. 256. For an excellent analysis of the discontinuity between Durkheim's discussion of economic value in *Division of Labor* and his later writings, see Joseph Neyer, "Individualism and Socialism in Durkheim," pp. 32–76 in Wolff (n. 12 above), pp. 75–76, n. 114.

182. "Sociology and the Social Sciences" (n. 8 above), p. 75.

183. "The Dualism of Human Nature and Its Social Conditions," pp. 149–163 in Robert N. Bellah, ed., *Emile Durkheim on Morality and Society* (Chicago, 1973), p. 151.

184. Ibid., n. 3 (p. 236).

185. *Suicide*, p. 211.

186. Ibid., p. 252, italics added.

187. Ibid., pp. 246–249.

188. *Division of Labor*, pp. 5–6.

189. *Professional Ethics and Civic Morals*, p. 14.

190. "Pedagogy and Sociology" (n. 60 above), p. 125.

191. "Sociology and the Social Sciences," p. 81.

192. "De la définition des phénomènes religieux," *L'Année sociologique* 2 (1899):25–26.

193. "The Dualism of Human Nature and Its Social Conditions," p. 160.

194. *Socialism and Saint-Simon* (n. 11 above), p. 18.

195. *Elementary Forms* (n. 5 above), p. 246. For a critique of Durkheim's economic theory as "outside" his moral theory of society, resembling the one I make here, see Poggi (no. 4 above), p. 255; also Poggi, *Images of Society* (Stanford, Calif., 1972), p. 245.

196. Durkheim took this position in a debate sponsored by the "Union pour la vérité" about the relative internationalism of different social classes, published in the Union's *Libres Entretiens* in 1905. Reprinted as "Débat sur le patriotisme et l'internationalisme des classes sociales" in *Textes*, 3: 186–188.

197. This review of Célèstin Bouglé's *Essai sur le régime des castes* appeared in *L'Année sociologique*, vol. 11 (1910). Reprinted as "Le Régime des castes" in *Textes*, 3: 293–296.

198. Ibid., pp. 187–188.

CHAPTER NINE

1. Thomas Kuhn, *The Structure of Scientific Revolutions* (Chicago, 1963).

2. A similar process of covert revision in the theoretical writings of Talcott Parsons' students is traced in my "Paradigm Revision and 'Parsonianism,'" *Canadian Journal of Sociology* 4 (1979):343–358. See also

the concluding chapters of volumes 3 and 4 of the present work, where I discuss this issue in terms of Weber and Parsons.

3. For background on these developments, see Koenraad W. Swart, "'Individualism' in the Mid-Nineteenth Century," *Journal of the History of Ideas* 23, no. 1 (1962): 77–90; also Steven Lukes, "The Meaning of 'Individualism,'" *Journal of the History of Ideas* 32, no. 1 (1971):45–66.

4. Emile Durkheim, *Suicide* (1897; New York, 1951), p. 364.

5. Durkheim, Review of Alfred Fouillée, *La France au point de vue moral*, *L'Année sociologique* 5 (1901): 443–445, quoted in Steven Lukes, *Emile Durkheim* (New York, 1972), pp. 354–355.

6. Durkheim, "Divorce by Mutual Consent," in Mark Traugott, ed., *Emile Durkheim on Institutional Analysis* (Chicago, 1978), pp. 240–252. First published in *Revue bleue*, 1906, pp. 549–554. The existence of such an amoral perspective on the individual has been recognized by Georges Gurvitch ("Le Problème de la conscience collective dans la sociologie de Durkheim," pp. 351–408 in his *La Vocation actuelle de la sociologie*, Paris, 1950, passim), but he made the very serious error of viewing it as Durkheim's principal perspective rather than as a minor and deviant theme.

7. Durkheim, *The Division of Labor in Society* (1893; New York, 1933), p. 34. The strains in the master's work are usually more apparent in the works of his students, because the latter usually lack the master's complicating subtlety. This is certainly true for Durkheim's conflation of ideology and presuppositions. There can be no question that Durkheim's followers continued to sociologize in a manner that buttressed the ideological hopes of the Third Republic in France, yet they themselves maintained that, to the contrary, their application of Durkheimian sociology, like Durkheim's own, was completely free from nonobservational judgment. Thus, in an account of "The Durkheim School in France" written in 1927, one of Durkheim's major collaborators, Paul Fauconnet, wrote:

> First of all, he [Durkheim] wishes that sociology be a pure science, without a mingling of philosophy or politics. Putting aside all ideas of application or of social action, taking the various societies exactly as they are, he seeks only to know them, that is to describe and explain them. As a savant he has no politics, no detailed program of action; he does not fall into the error of Comte, passing ostensibly from social dynamics to the institutions of a politics and a religion of the future. (*Sociological Review* 19 [1927]:15–20, quoting 15.)

To the contrary, Durkheim did seek to know in order to act. He mingled pure science decisively with philosophy and politics, and he had a self-conscious politics and a fairly detailed program for action, as will be seen. He was also, quite clearly, very much concerned with the religion of the future. That even some of his closest students apparently were not aware of these facts is testimony to the power of Durkheim's original conflation of these two different levels of his science.

8. The residual category of utilitarian modernity, one should note, is the most generalized, theoretical reason for Durkheim's invocation of the "normal-pathological" distinction throughout his empirical work. I earlier tried to demonstrate that the social formations that Durkheim designated as pathological were in fact, never demonstrated to be so "exceptional" in empirical terms. Now a presuppositional reason for this anomalous situation can be seen: the theoretical assumptions that Durkheim used to explain the pathological elements of society were themselves unintegrated with this major emphasis of his theoretical work.

9. Ibid., p. 408.

10. *Suicide*, pp. 158–159, 209–210.

11. Ibid., p. 253.

12. Ibid., p. 389.

13. Durkheim, *Professional Ethics and Civic Morals* (London, 1957), p. 96 (first published in French in 1950); Durkheim, *Moral Education* (1925; New York, 1961), p. 235.

14. Durkheim, "A Durkheim Fragment: The Conjugal Family," pp. 527–36 in *American Journal of Sociology* 70 (1965):527–536; see 534–536. First published in 1921 as "La Famille conjugale: Conclusion du cours sur la famille," in the *Revue philosophique*. See also *Suicide*, pp. 377, 202.

15. *Division of Labor*, p. 4 (from the second preface, first published in 1902); cf. *Professional Ethics and Civic Morals*, p. 12.

16. Ibid., pp. 93, 94, 105.

17. Durkheim, *The Elementary Forms of Religious Life* (1912; New York, 1965), p. 475.

18. Durkheim's first substantial discussion of the occupational group appears in *Suicide*, bk. 3, ch. 3. His most famous discussion is in the second preface to *Division of Labor*. References also appear throughout most of his subsequent work, for example in *Professional Ethics and Civic Morals*.

19. Durkheim, "Course in Sociology: Opening Lecture" (1888), in Traugott (n. 6 above), pp. 43–70, quoting p. 49.

20. In the liberal tradition, Talcott Parsons leaves this reference out of his interpretation of Durkheim in *The Structure of Social Action* (New York, [1937] 1968); in the Marxist, Irving Zeitlin makes a similar mistake in *Ideology and the Development of Sociological Theory* (Englewood Cliffs, N.J., 1968).

21. The most conspicuous example of this approach is Stephen R. Marks' "Durkheim's Theory of Anomie" (*American Journal of Sociology* 80 [1974]:329–363), which views Durkheim's entire theoretical development as derived from his concern for anomie, virtually ignoring Durkheim's independent analytical concerns. Not surprisingly, Marks equates the instrumental aspect of Durkheim's anomie theory—and, therefore, Durkheim's theory as a whole—with Marx's view of "alienation" in mod-

ern capitalist society. Anthony Giddens makes a similar argument, asserting that the theory of egoism and anomie provides a quasi-Marxist understanding of industrial society as a war of all against all (*Capitalism and Modern Social Theory* [London, 1971], p. 232). Giddens argues that the only difference between Durkheim and Marx on this point is that Durkheim takes a more resigned attitude to the condition of anomie than Marx, who thinks that under different productive conditions industrialization would not produce anomie.

22. This was the view taken, e.g., by Georges Davy in 1926 ("La Sociologie française de 1918 à 1925," in the *Monist*, reprinted in Davy, *Sociologues d'hier et d'aujourd'hui*, 1931) and by Célestin Bouglé in 1930 ("The Present Tendency of the Social Sciences in France," in L. D. White, ed., *The New Social Sciences* [Chicago, 1930]). Among observers outside the school, this emphasis on internal unity is asserted, e.g., by Terry Clark in *Prophets and Patrons: The French University and the Emergence of the Social Sciences* (Cambridge, Mass., 1973).

23. For an excellent recent example of this approach, see Philippe Besnard, "La Formation de l'équipe de *L'Année sociologique*," *Revue française de sociologie* 20 (1979): 7–31.

24. That the master himself was aware of the incompatibility between the phases in this work which his students sought to combine was, of course, more explicitly true for Marx than for Durkheim. It is undoubtedly true that Durkheim's continued overt support for the sociology of the *Division of Labor* made his students feel on more secure ground when they tried to combine this early sociology with Durkheim's later work. I have tried to show, nonetheless, that Durkheim was more or less aware of the break in his oeuvre, and he made a series of statements about the course of his intellectual development which, for those who were so inclined, would have revealed the strains involved. My point, of course, is that his students were not so inclined. Their intention, conscious or unconscious, was to bridge the gaps in Durkheim's development, not to reproduce them.

25. Halbwachs, "Introduction," in Durkheim, *The Evolution of Educational Thought* (London, [1938] 1977), pp. xi–xv, esp. p. xii.

26. Mauss, "Introduction," in Durkheim, *Socialism and Saint-Simon* (1928; Yellow Springs, Ohio, 1958), pp. 1–4.

27. Cf. Davy, *Le Droit, l'idéalisme, et l'experience* (Paris, 1922).

28. Hertz, *Death and the Right Hand* (1907, 1909; London, 1960); Granet, *The Religion of the Chinese People* (New York, [1922] 1975).

29. Davy, "Introduction," xiii–xliv in Durkheim, *Professional Ethics and Civic Morals* (n. 13 above), pp. xiii–xliv, quoting p. xviii.

30. Ibid., pp. xviii–xix.

31. Mauss and Fauconnet, "Sociologie," in *La Grande Encyclopédie* (1901), 30: 165–176, see 172.

32. Ibid.

33. Ibid., p. 166–167.

34. Ibid., p. 167.

35. Ibid., p. 171.

36. Unfortunately, only a small portion of the writing of these French sociologists has been translated—at the time of this writing. Mauss is a partial exception, for his two most important essays, on gift exchange and Eskimo society, are in English (see nn. 41, 45). Bouglé's work is almost completely untranslated. (The only monograph in English, *The Evolution of Values* [1922], is not an important work.) Two of Halbwachs' works are translated (one on class, the other on demography), although the bulk of them remain only in French. I have not been able to find any of Simiand in English. Two dissertations that should be helpful to English readers are Perry Mackay Sturges, "Social Theory and Political Ideology: Célèstin Bouglé and the Durkheim School" (City University of New York, 1978), and Suzanne Vromen, "The Sociology of Maurice Halbwachs," (New York University, 1975). Sturges' work is particularly illuminating, and deserves to be widely read. Because of the paucity of English translations, the volume that Edward Tiryakian is preparing on the Durkheim school for the Heritage of Sociology series (University of Chicago Press) will be especially valuable.

37. Halbwachs, *Les Causes du suicide* (Paris, 1930), ch. 15.

38. See, for example, Halbwachs, *La Mémoire collective* (Paris, 1950).

39. Mauss, "Rapports réels et practiques de la psychologie et de la sociologie," *Journal de psychologie* 21 (1924): 892–922.

40. The influence of Simmel is clear from the very first of Bouglé's works, *Les Idées égalitaires* (1899), where he places alongside of Durkheim's explanation of modern individualism Simmel's understanding of the individual experience of cross-cutting ties, a cross-cutting that Bouglé calls *"la complication."* It is worthwhile to note that some of these objections which Durkheim's students make to his apparent anti-individualism were raised directly with Durkheim himself. Between 1895 and 1897, in preparation for the launching of *L'Année sociologique*, both Bouglé and Paul Lapie engaged in lengthy correspondence with Durkheim over the status of "social psychology" and the relation between society and the individual (see the letters in Durkheim, *Textes* [Paris, 1975], 2:393–402). The students wanted to adopt a more ecumenical attitude to psychological explanation. Durkheim did not. In a letter written to his young interlocutors, Durkheim insisted on "the necessity of doing sociology *sociologically*," (italics in original), but he diplomatically assured them that "I see in sociology not only a psychology, but a psychology *sui generis*" (letters of March 14, 1897, and January 24, 1897, in *Textes*, reprinted in *Revue française de sociologie*, vol. 20, no. 1 (1979); cited also by Besnard (n. 23 above, p. 12). These letters are direct historical evidence

for the kind of intra-paradigm tensions and disagreements which I try to demonstrate in purely analytical, unhistorical terms. It is interesting, in this regard, to note that after Durkheim's *Suicide* appeared in 1897, these students regarded it partly as a response to their criticisms—a perception, however, which failed to appreciate the broader reasons for the shift in Durkheim's work, and which also failed, incidentally, to note its full significance. E.g., Lapie perceived in *Suicide* "the desire to make concessions to us" about the importance of psychological causes (letter of July 9, 1897, reproduced in *Revue française de sociologie*, loc. cit., p. 40).

41. Marcel Mauss, *The Gift* (New York, [1925] 1967), pp. 46, 49, 63; cf. pp. 73–74.

42. Ibid., pp. 4, 10, 37, 39, 41, 43, 71–72.

43. Ibid., p. 6.

44. Ibid., p. 70.

45. Mauss, *Seasonal Variations of the Eskimos* (1906; London, 1979), p. 55.

46. Ibid., p. 20; cf. p. 32.

47. Ibid., pp. 34, 55.

48. Ibid., pp. 46, 48.

49. Ibid., p. 76.

50. Ibid., p. 56.

51. Ibid., pp. 80, 62.

52. Ibid., p. 80. This confusion on Mauss's part may help illuminate a perplexing problem in the essay on *Primitive Classification*, which Mauss co-authored with Durkheim three years before this work on Eskimo society appeared. The earlier work, as has been noted, was ambiguous about the place it assigned to religious phenomena. For most of the earlier sections, collective representations are treated as reflections of social structure, but in the latter part of the essay there is a determined attempt to argue that these "structural" (usually geographical and familial) features themselves represented the formalization of certain religious divisions of sacred and profane. On these latter grounds, the essay concludes that primitive classifications reflect, ultimately, certain religious categorizations. In the light of the preceding analysis, I might now suggest that possibly Mauss was more responsible for the first part of the essay, Durkheim for the latter part. It is also possible that Mauss took the major role for the entire essay, and that it reflects the ambivalence that marks his own later work. Unfortunately, this is pure speculation; as far as I am aware, the actual distribution of the formally joint effort is unknown.

53. Ibid., p. 21.

54. Ibid., p. 80.

55. Ibid., pp. 46, 79.

56. Ibid., pp. 55 ff.

57. Oscar Jaszi, "An Inductive Vindication of Historical Materialism," *The Review: A Quarterly of Pluralist Socialism* 5, no. 2 (1963):51–65, quoting 57, 65, italics in original. Originally published in *Huszadik Szazad* in Budapest in 1906.

58. Claude Dubar, "Rétour aux textes," *L'Arc* 48 (1972):23–27, see 25. See also the insightful argument for the closeness of Mauss's argument in *The Gift* to the instrumental theorizing of Hobbes and Marx by Marshall Sahlins in "The Spirit of the Gift," pp. 149–184 of his *Stone Age Economics* (Chicago, 1972), particularly pp. 168 ff.

59. For a sensitive discussion of the relation between Bouglé's pragmatic liberalism and his scientific theorizing, see the dissertation by Sturges (n. 36 above).

60. Célèstin Bouglé, *Qu'est-ce que la sociologie?* (Paris, [1907] 1921), p. 27.

61. Ibid., p. 29.

62. Durkheim expressed these views in the dozen letters he wrote to Bouglé in the months preceding publication of the first volume of *L'Année sociologique* in 1898, in the production of which Bouglé played a central role. See, e.g., the letters of July 6 and September 27, 1897, discussed in Sturges (n. 36 above), pp. 47–48.

63. Bouglé, *Les Idées égalitaires*, pp. 60, 66, 239. As noted earlier (ch. 7, sec. 1.3), Halévy wrote with Brunschvicg, in 1894, one of the most important critical reviews of the *Division of Labor.* Halévy took Durkheim to task precisely for the problems that Bouglé is responding to, the conflation of positivistic method with collective presupposition. However, Halévy was not aware of the movement against the instrumental version of collective order upon which Durkheim was already embarked by the time this review was published. Bouglé, on the other hand, was probably more conscious of this development, though he never explicitly discussed it.

64. Ibid., pt.2.

65. Ibid., pp. 91–167. The reservation expressed indirectly about Durkheim's work in 1896 is reiterated by Bouglé in an essay of 1900, after the publication of *Les Idées égalitaires.* "Because they are men," he writes, ". . . the elements of the social group are capable of reasoning about the outcomes of differentiation as it affects them, and working to limit or change its effects if they consider them unjust" ("La Sociologie biologique et le régime des castes," *Revue philosophique* 49:337–353, quoting 344). This essay, however, already points the way to later developments in Bouglé's thought which I will discuss farther on.

66. Ibid., p. 207 and, more generally, pt. 2, ch. 3.

67. Ibid., p. 240.

68. Ibid., pp. 241–242.

69. Bouglé, *Qu'est-ce que la sociologie?* p. 140.

70. Bouglé, *Essais sur le régime des castes* (Paris, 1908), e.g., pp. 164–166.

71. Ibid., pp. 168, 171.

72. Ibid., pp. 171–172.

73. Letter, July 23, 1907, reprinted in *Revue française de sociologie* 20, no. 1 (1979): 46.

74. Letter, undated, but clearly from approximately the same period. Quoted in Besnard (n. 23 above), p. 24.

75. *Essais sur le régime des castes*, p. 169, n. 3.

76. It is ironic that Mauss should have been the "official representative" of the religious perspective vis-à-vis Bouglé, since in his own work he made an effort to avoid following Durkheim on his path toward a religious sociology. It is clear, however, that in matters having to do with *L'Année sociologique*, Mauss often functioned as Durkheim's official representative, formally adopting his uncle's viewpoint.

77. Marcel Mauss, "Avant-Propos," pp. vii–viii in Halbwachs, *Les Causes du suicide* (n. 37 above).

78. Ibid., ch. 8.

79. Ibid., p. 6.

80. Ibid., p. 502.

81. Ibid., p. 328.

82. Ibid., p. 291.

83. Halbwachs, *Morphologie sociale* (Paris, 1938), p. 19. Published in English as *Population and Society* (Glencoe, Ill., 1960).

84. Halbwachs, *Le Topographie légendaire des évangiles en Terre Sainte.* (Paris, 1941).

85. Halbwachs, *La Mémoire collective* (Paris, 1950).

86. This concern for material factors can be seen from the very beginning of Halbwachs' career—e.g., in his first known publication, "La Psychologie de l'ouvrier moderne d'après Bernstein," *Revue socialiste* 41 (1905):46–57. He published six monographs on material conditions and social classes, as well as a number of articles. Beginning in the second year of his professorship in sociology at Strasbourg, he offered a regular course on "Social Classes" (see John E. Craig, "France's First Chair of Sociology: A Note on the Origins," *Etudes durkheimiennes*, December 1979, pp. 8–13).

87. Halbwachs, *The Psychology of Social Class* (Glencoe, Ill., 1958), pp. 16–19. Originally published as *Analyse des mobiles qui orientent l'activité des individus dans la vie sociale* (Paris, 1938).

88. Ibid., pp. 115–116; cf. p. 155.

89. Halbwachs, *La Classe ouvrière et les niveaux de vie* (Paris, 1913), chs. 1, 2; cf. p. 125. "Alienation" is my word, not Halbwachs'.

90. Ibid., p. 416.

91. Halbwachs, *The Psychology of Social Class*, pp. 96–97.

92. Halbwachs, *L'Evolution des besoins dans les classes ouvrières* (Paris, 1933), p. 152 and passim.

93. Michel Verret, "Halbwachs ou le deuxieme âge du Durkheimisme," *Cahiers Internationaux de Sociologie* n. 5, 53 (July-December 1972): 316. Georges Friedmann makes much the same kind of claim in his "Foreword" to Halbwachs' *The Psychology of Social Class* (n. 87 above), pp. vii–xviii, arguing that Halbwachs "approaches Marxist sociology" (p. xiii).

94. François Simiand, *La Méthode positive en science économique* (Paris, 1912), pp. 13–14.

95. Simiand, "Essai sur le prix du charbon en France et au XIXᵉ siècle," *L'Année sociologique* 5 (1902): 1–81, see p. 74.

96. Ibid., p. 35.

97. Ibid., p. 2.

98. Simiand, *La Méthode positive*, pp. 204–205; cf. p. 201.

99. Simiand, "Essai sur le prix du charbon," p. 35.

100. Ibid., pp. 74, 78.

101. Ibid., p. 75.

102. Ibid., p. 40.

103. Ibid., p. 42.

104. Ibid., p. 75.

105. Ibid., p. 74.

106. Ibid., pp. 77–78.

107. Simiand, "La Monnaie, réalité sociale," *Annales sociologiques*, ser. D (Paris, 1934), pp. 1–86, see pp.18–19.

108. Ibid., pp. 23–24.

109. Ibid., pp. 30–31.

110. Ibid., pp. 46, 35.

111. These social conditions that undermined the influence of Durkheimian sociology are mirrored in the career of Célèstin Bouglé. Personally committed to using sociology to develop common political ground between the liberalism of the middle classes and the socialism of the working classes, Bouglé had some success before World War I. After the war, though his own public prestige increased, his ability to effect this reform of French public life dramatically declined, and he became increasingly isolated from the mainstream of political events. For an excellent discussion of Bouglé's public career, see Perry Mackay Sturges, "Social Theory and Political Ideology: Célèstin Bouglé and the Durkheim School" (Ph.D. diss. City University of New York, 1978).

112. This is how Pierre Bourdieu and Jean-Claude Passeron characterize the feelings of the pre-World War II generation of French intellectuals vis-à-vis Durkheimianism in "Sociology and Philosophy in France since 1945: Death and Resurrection of a Philosophy without Subject," *Social Research* 34 (1967):162–212, esp. p. 172.

113. Jean-Paul Sartre, in F. Jeanson, *Sartre par lui-meme* (Paris, 1958), p. 12, quoted in Bourdieu and Passeron, p. 174.

114. Raymond Aron, "La Sociologie," pp. 13–48 in Bouglé, Aron, et al., *Les Sciences sociales en France*, Centre d'Etudes de Politique Etrangère, publication no. 5 (Paris, 1937), p. 16.

115. Ibid., p. 47. Although this response by Aron to Durkheimian sociology is understandable in a historical sense, it is clearly a fundamental distortion of Durkheim's actual work. It is noteworthy, in this regard, that in Aron's later, usually perceptive, discussions of sociological theory, Durkheim is the only major theorist whom he simply cannot accurately explicate. (See his *Main Currents in Sociological Thought* [New York, 1970], 2:11–118.) In other words, the lectures that he gave on Durkheim later in life still reflect the cultural and political circumstances under which his generation's understanding of Durkheim was formed. Georges Gurvitch is another major figure in postwar French sociology whose anti-Durkheimian position is based on a heightened and sometimes misdirected individualism, a position which—like Aron's—has been legitimated by a drastic misreading of Durkheim's work (e.g., in his "Le Problème de la conscience collective" [n. 6 above]).

116. A. R. Radcliffe-Brown, *A Natural Science of Society* (Glencoe, Ill., [1937] 1957) pp. 80–86.

117. Ibid., p. 106.

118. Radcliffe-Brown, *Structure and Function in Primitive Society* (Glencoe, Ill., 1952), p. 177.

119. E. E. Evans-Pritchard, "Social Anthropology: Past and Present" (1950), pp. 139–157 in his *Social Anthropology and Other Essays* (Glencoe, Ill., 1962), quoting p. 152.

120. Evans-Pritchard, *Nuer Religion* (London, 1956), p. viii.

121. Ibid., p. 92.

122. Claude Lévi-Strauss, "French Sociology," pp. 503–537 in Georges Gurvitch and Wilbert E. Moore, *Twentieth Century Sociology* (New York, 1945), pp. 526–527; cf. idem, "Introduction à l'oeuvre de Marcel Mauss," pp. ix–lii in Mauss, *Sociologie et anthropologie* (Paris, 1968).

123. Lévi-Strauss, "French Sociology," p. 518.

124. Lévi-Strauss, *Totemism* (London, 1962), p. 97.

125. Lévi-Strauss, *The Savage Mind* (Chicago, 1966), p. 214.

126. There were, of course, other influences on Lévi-Strauss's model of cultural opposition (e.g., the work of Saussure and modern information theory).

127. This is not to say that there are no other Durkheimian strains in modern anthropology than those described. There are none, however, which explicitly align themselves with the formulation of a "Durkheimian" theory. Certainly the revival of symbolic anthropology in the last decade in the works of writers like Victor Turner, Mircea Eliade, Clifford

Geertz, Mary Douglas, and Louis Dumont is ultimately inspired by Durkheim's later thought.

128. Parsons laid out the basis for this understanding in *The Structure of Social Action* (n. 20 above), and he refined the approach to socialization and individual freedom in *Towards a General Theory of Action* (with Edward Shils; New York, 1950) and in *Social Structure and Personality* (New York, 1964).

129. E.g., Parsons, "Introduction to Culture and the Social System," pp. 963–993 in Parsons et al., eds., *Theories of Society* (New York, 1961). See the application of this later theory to Durkheim in Parsons' important essay, "Durkheim's Contribution to the Theory of Integration of Social Systems," pp. 118–153 in Kurt Wolff, ed., *Essays on Sociology and Philosophy by Emile Durkheim et al.* (New York, 1960). It should be noted here that Parsons achieved this multidimensional clarification only by integrating Durkheim's with Weber's work.

130. In one sense, Parsons' theory allows for the incorporation into a more general framework of the search that Durkheim's students launched for a compromise between *Division of Labor* and the later cultural emphasis. One the other hand, insofar as Parsons' work itself reveals an idealist reduction, he leaves their search unfulfilled. There seem today to be no self-conscious representatives of the more materialistic Durkheimianism propounded, at times, by Durkheim's students, and by his own early work as well. Critics who have purposely drawn attention to this dimension in Durkheim's theory—such as Alvin W. Gouldner, Georges Friedmann, David Lockwood—usually have chosen to pursue this orientation within the framework of Marx or Weber, rather than that of Durkheim himself.

CHAPTER TEN

1. For Marx's reference to the proletarian revolution as the "old mole," see *The Eighteenth Brumaire of Louis Bonaparte* (1852), in Karl Marx and Frederick Engels, *Selected Works* (Moscow, 1962), 1:332; hereafter cited as *MESW*.

2. Marx, *Capital*, vol. 1 (1867; Moscow, n.d.), p. 9.

3. Ibid., pp. 734–737.

4. Ibid., p. 559.

5. Ibid., p. 171.

6. Ibid., p. 232. It is perhaps revealing of the Marxist embarrassment with this residual category that Samuel Moore and Edward Aveling—who made the English translation in 1887 upon which this edition of *Capital*, vol. 1, is based—chose to translate *Kulturzustand* as the "state of social advancement" rather than as the state of culture or civilization. The German reference is in *Marx-Engels Werke* (Berlin, 1962), 23:246.

7. These occasional references to normative factors in Marx's theory of wages have been noticed by a number of analysts, but they have rarely been seen for the theoretical contradictions which they really are, either by Marx's supporters or his critics. Thus, a critic, Raymond Aron, in his account of Marx's wage formula, simply reproduces the incongruous analysis without giving it any particular scrutiny:

> Now to produce labor power, the worker and his family must be assured the indispensable means of existence. Can one determine the *indispensable* amount of these means? Marx answers that the amount varies with the social conscience but that the worker's salary in his time was approaching a point at the physiological minimum. (*Plaidoyer pour l'Europe décadente* [Paris, 1977], p. 39, italics in original.

A few interpreters, however, have been sensitive to the problem that such a double reference raises. The Frankfurt school Marxist Jürgen Habermas recognizes its residual status: "Marx . . . did not systematically take into consideration that capitalism itself could revolutionize the 'historical and moral element' that enters into determining the value of labor power." Because of this failure, he believes, Marx failed to develop a consistent theory of the value of labor itself, something he could not do "without introducing the dimension of the 'historical and moral element' explicitly into the method of determining the value of labor power" (*Theory and Practice* [Boston, 1973], pp. 230–231; cf. Alvin W. Gouldner's comment that for Marx "this *social* element, this symbolic and cultural aspect, is an untheoretized *residual* factor" [*The Two Marxisms* (New York, 1980), p. 208, italics in original]). Very much the same critical observation is offered by Noel Annan in his discussion of a similar normative reference in the wage theory of Marx's great predecessor, Ricardo:

> [Ricardo] was forced to admit that he could not account by the Iron Law of wages [for the fact that] Irish labourers had a lower level of wages than English labourers. . . . Like Malthus he fell back on an explanation—that the habits and customs of the two peoples were different—which was outside the positivist system of rational individuals calculating their welfare. (*The Curious Strength of Positivism in English Political Thought* [London, 1959], p. 7.)

Marx's political economy shared the same instrumental assumptions about action as Ricardo's. For this reason, his reference to normative pressure on wages assumes the same residual status.

8. Letter to L. Kugelmann, November 29, 1869 (Marx and Engels, *Selected Correspondence* [Moscow, n.d.], p. 277), hereafter cited as *MESC*. Cf. letter to S. Meyer and A. Vogt, April 9, 1870, p. 285.

9. Letter to Kugelmann, p. 277.

10. Letter to Meyer and Vogt, p. 285.

11. Ibid.

12. Ibid., p. 286. References to the power of "national character" on events occur throughout Marx's letters and informal writing. At one point, for example, he writes about the "sound aesthetical common sense" of the British people—a trait that in his view made them less susceptible to upper-class deceit. At another point he discusses the great achievements of German science as "something an individual German can avow since it is in no way *his* merit, but belongs much more to the *nation*," which otherwise "is the *silliest nation* under the sun!" (quoted in Jerrold Siegel, *Marx's Fate: The Shape of a Life* [Princeton, N.J., 1978], pp. 224, 329, italics added). Other references to the irrational relation between ruling and dominated classes can also be found in the letters. Marx writes, e.g., about the English public, usually practical, "falling in love" with the politician Palmerston, whereby Palmerston's "views on all things spread to others like a contagion," an effect which "contributed more to confuse the judgment of his hearers than the most ingenious perversion could have done" (quoted, ibid., p. 224).

13. E. Priester, "Karl Marx in Wien," *Zeitschrift für Geschichtswissenschaft*, 1953, p. 723, quoted in David McLellan, *Karl Marx* (New York, 1973), p. 206.

14. Marx, "Address of the Central Committee to the Communist League," *MESW*, 1:117.

15. Letters to F. Bolte, November 23, 1871, and F. A. Sorge, September 27, 1873, *MESC*, pp. 327, 348.

16. Marx and Engels to A. Bebel, W. Liebknecht, W. Bracke, and others ("Circular Letter"), September 17–18, 1879, *MESC*, pp. 388–395.

17. Letter, summer 1870, quoted in McLellan, p. 389.

18. Letter to Sorge, October 19, 1877, *MESC*, pp. 375–376.

19. Marx, "Inaugural Address of the Working Men's International Association," September 28, 1864, pp. 377–385 in *MESW*, 1:381.

20. Ibid., p. 382.

21. Ibid.

22. Ibid., p. 383.

23. Ibid.

24. Ibid., p. 384.

25. Ibid., p. 385.

26. Writing to Engels about his struggle to get his draft of the rules accepted, in 1864, Marx insisted, "I was obliged to accept into the preamble of the Statutes two phrases on 'duty' and 'right,' and also on 'truth, morality and justice'; but they are placed so that they cannot do harm" (quoted in McLellan, *Karl Marx* p. 365). My analysis, however, refers not to these phrases but to the general structure of Marx's argument about the requisites of revolutionary struggle—a structure which, evidently, he did not perceive as in any way anomalous. In what follows, moreover, I

refer to the implicitly sociological theory in the very rules that Marx had devised his "phrases" to legitimate. He viewed them, in other words, as strictly orthodox.

27. Marx, "General Rules of the International Working Men's Association," adopted September 1871 (based upon the provisional rules drawn up by Marx in 1864), pp. 386–389 in *MESW*, 1:386.

28. Ibid., p. 388.

29. Ibid.

30. Ibid.

31. Marx to Engels, March 1869, quoted in Siegel (n.12 above), p. 237.

32. There are, of course, a number of similar pamphlets that Marx produced as a political journalist, most notably *The Class Struggles in France* (1850) and *The Civil War in France* (1871). I discuss none of these others here, though I have referred to them at various points in my earlier analyses (e.g., ch. 6, sec. 1 and n.183; cf. n.57 below). Generally, they contain the same kind of anomalies as are to be found in *The Eighteenth Brumaire*.

There is one little-known pamphlet, however, to which I would like to call some special attention, *The Secret Diplomatic History of the Eighteenth Century*, comprising articles which Marx published in 1856 in an English newspaper, the Sheffield *Free Press*, and later in the London *Free Press*, both papers owned by the radical Tory journalist and politician David Urquhart. The articles—which Marx initially undertook because he needed the money but to which he devoted, nonetheless, serious intellectual and political effort—represent Marx's attempt to explain the roots of what he regarded as England's long-standing diplomatic subservience to Russia.

First, Marx dismisses any objectivistic explanation, one that would look to "mutual material interests of the two countries" (*The Secret Diplomatic History of the Eighteenth Century and The Story of the Life of Lord Palmerston*, ed. Lester Hutchinson [London, 1969], p. 63). Although such a materialist explanation was promulgated by some misguided publicists and historians, Marx insists that such "economic" factors were only a pretext that the English *political* oligarchy worked out, in the seventeenth century, to hide its real motives.

> They wanted to give . . . the appearance at least of being altogether regulated by the mercantile interest, an appearance the more easily to be produced, as the exclusive interest of one or the other small fraction of that class would, of course, be always identified with this or that Ministerial measure (p. 91).

In fact, it was a complicated mixture of political and national-psychological factors that led England, from an early point, to "abject servility and cynical submission" to Russia (p. 61). Marx insists that Russia

522 Notes to Pages 336–340

was not at the present time, nor had ever been, a truly powerful nation in an objective sense. He contrasts those who take the "materialist" position on Russia's power, viewing it "as palpable fact," with those "spiritualists" who view it as "the mere vision of the guilt-stricken conscience of Europe" (p. 108). He clearly places himself in the latter spiritual camp. England was psychologically and diplomatically defeated by Russia. Russia had attained its subjective power to dominate because it had learned the role of "slave as master" from its centuries-long subjugation by the Tartars (p. 121). When Russia had been conquered by these Mongols, it had lost its "soul" (p. 111), and through a symbiotic process it began to imitate the unscrupulous behaviour of the Mongols themselves. Eventually, it "generalized" the Mongols' deceitful actions and developed a self-conscious methodology for expelling them. Subsequently, the Russians turned this method on Europe (p. 121). By their own internal corruption and hypocrisy, aided by the servility and guilt of England, Russia established a relationship that was inexplicable in material terms.

Surely this is an astonishing analysis from the author of scientific historical materialism. But its anti-instrumental logic is not, in fact, untypical of his explicitly political writings, as we will see farther on.

33. Marx, *The Eighteenth Brumaire of Louis Bonaparte* (1852), *MESW*, 1:247–344, see 247–249.

34. Ibid., p. 255.
35. Ibid., p. 247.
36. Ibid., passim.
37. Ibid., p. 257.
38. Ibid., p. 278.
39. Ibid., pp. 334–335.
40. E.g., ibid., p. 311.
41. Ibid., p. 257.
42. Ibid., p. 275, italics added.
43. Ibid., p. 302.
44. Ibid., pp. 317, 327.
45. Ibid., p. 310.
46. Ibid., p. 308.
47. Ibid., p. 306.
48. Ibid., p. 307.
49. Ibid., pp. 289, 302.
50. Ibid., p. 254.
51. Ibid., p. 253.
52. Ibid., p. 334.
53. Ibid., p. 286.
54. Ibid., pp. 334, 335, 336.
55. Ibid., p. 257.
56. Ibid., p. 288, italics added.

57. Ibid. Marx takes basically the same attitude to the independent effects of universal suffrage in *The Class Struggles in France*: "If universal suffrage was not the miraculous magic wand for which the republican duffers had taken it, it possessed the incomparably higher merit of un-chaining the class struggle, of letting the various middle sections of petty-bourgeois society rapidly live through their illusions and disap-pointments, of tossing all the fractions of the exploiting class at one throw to the head of the state, and thus tearing from them their treach-erous mask" (*MESW*, 1:158).

58. *Eighteenth Brumaire*, in *MESW*, 1:257.

59. Ibid., p. 306.

60. Ibid., p. 285.

61. Ibid., pp. 300, 267.

62. Ibid., p. 306.

63. Ibid., p. 270.

64. Ibid., p. 290.

65. Ibid., p. 261.

66. Ibid., pp. 264, 273, 312.

67. Ibid., p. 260.

68. Ibid., p. 316.

69. Ibid., p. 332.

70. Ibid., pp. 284, 333. Elsewhere, in an account of the failure of Ger-man revolution of 1848, Marx makes a similar point about the indepen-dent power of the state from social class. The March revolution in Germany, he declared in a speech in 1849, failed because while it "re-formed the political summit," it "left untouched all the foundations of this summit—the old bureaucracy, the old army, the old courts, the old judges born, educated and grown grey in the services of absolutism" (quoted in McLellan [n.13 above], p. 215).

71. *Eighteenth Brumaire*, in *MESW*, 1:263–264.

72. Ibid., pp. 262–263.

73. Ibid., pp. 285, 293; cf. p. 303.

74. Ibid., p. 250.

75. Ibid., p. 271.

76. Ibid., p. 272.

77. Ibid., p. 272, italics in original.

78. For Marx's remarks on the constitution, see ibid., p. 259; his com-ments on the other issues are scattered throughout the essay.

79. Ibid., p. 272, italics added.

80. My reading of *The Eighteenth Brumaire* depends, of course, on separating the normative aspects of this treatment from what I have called Marx's more systematic, "scientific" theory, which, I believe, con-stitutes the main line of his self-conscious theorizing. I have pointed out the ad hoc and often self-contradictory character of the argument in *The*

Eighteenth Brumaire, and have also indicated its antipathy to the presuppositions, models, and propositions that Marx developed in the writings he thought represented his scientific work. Other interpreters of Marx have disagreed with such a reading of the relation between this essay and the rest of Marx's work. The first to do so was Engels, who claimed in his famous "Letter to Bloch" (1890; *MESW*, 2:488–490) that *The Eighteenth Brumaire* was representative of the "true" Marxist approach to history. (I will discuss this letter at some length below.) Engels' position has been taken up by many contemporary Marxists. The issue at stake is demonstrated by Bertell Ollman, who, after citing Engels' original argument about *The Eighteenth Brumaire*, insists that "practically at every turn" Marx "strayed from his general conception" of materialist history (*Alienation* [London, 1971], pp. 9–10; to some extent, this is also the argument of Anthony Giddens, in his *Capitalism and Modern Social Theory* [London, 1971], pp. 36–45).

In earlier chapters devoted to Marx's thought, e.g., chs. 3 and 6, I have tried to show the very opposite, namely, that Marx was among the most consistent of thinkers—at least in the works to which he devoted long and considered attention and which he wanted the world to accept as his scientific work. In this respect, I fully agree with Smelser's judgment that Marx's "work is a genuine synthesis, precisely because he was able to weld together . . . diverse ingredients . . . into a systematic whole." "It must be appreciated," Smelser continues, "that Marx's theory—in contrast to so many of the bodies of thought from which he borrowed and which have borrowed from him—does indeed consist of an attempt to derive all its important ingredients from first theoretical principles, and thereby an attempt to create an original, independent, and integrated *theoretical structure*." ("Introduction," pp. vii–xxxviii, in Neil J. Smelser, ed., *Karl Marx on Society and Social Change* [Chicago, 1973], pp. xi–xii, italics in original.)

My general approach to *Eighteenth Brumaire* as anomalous vis-à-vis the main sections of Marx's theorizing is also supported by Raymond Aron in *Main Currents in Sociological Thought* (New York, 1970), 1:318–332), and, more recently and elaborately, by Martin E. Spencer in his article "Marx on the State: The Events in France between 1848–1850," *Theory and Society* 7 (1979): 167–198. See also the remark by Dick Atkinson that "unfortunately, the methodology of explanation which is involved [in 'historical' works like *Eighteenth Brumaire*] was not worked out [by Marx], and though the history he wrote often contradicted his theoretical models and presuppositions, he did not modify them" (*Orthodox Consensus and Radical Alternative* [New York, 1972], p. 153). Cf. Gouldner's remark that in *Eighteenth Brumaire* the "new role of the superstructure is not really theoretized" (n. 7 above), p. 308.

Aside from the argument that the theoretical voluntarism and multi-dimensionality which can be found in *Eighteenth Brumaire* and the other political writings is characteristic of Marx's work, the argument is often advanced that such writings indicate theoretical voluntarism in another way: they show Marx's acceptance of the role of contingency and accident in historical events and his understanding of the complexity of empirical class relations. (See, e.g., Henri Lefebvre, *The Sociology of Marx* [New York, 1969], pp. 54–55.) Although this interpretation is considered to be another demonstration of the centrality of "praxis" in Marx's writing, this argument is not valid if we understand by "voluntarism" a commitment at the level of theoretical presuppositions. Marx, of course, certainly does emphasize the importance of events and contingency, not just in his political writings but at many points in his "scientific" work as well. He could do so because he never confused the problem of free will in a particular situation with the "determinism" that accrues from probability derived from aggregate cases. In other words, Marx accepted "scientific determinism" on the methodological level, an acceptance of aggregate probabilities that never challenged the free will of unique and specific acts. This, then, is not the problem of Marx's voluntarism, as I view it here. Rather, the problem as I have defined it derives from Marx's presuppositional judgments, not his methodological ones. Durkheim, too, shared Marx's methodological assumptions about probabilistic predictability, but he could maintain a voluntaristic theory in his later work only because he departed from Marx presuppositionally. It is, therefore, the presuppositional departures of *The Eighteenth Brumaire*, not the acceptance of contingency, that mark it as an anomalous, voluntaristic work.

As for the argument about specificity in class analysis, this is an issue on the propositional level, not on more generalized ones. Marx's scientific writings created general concepts, and although this corpus often contained applications of these concepts to specific instances it did not try to cover every conceivable historical possibility. The specificity of the political writings, then, has nothing to do with their relative determinateness or voluntarism in a general theoretical sense.

81. By emphasizing the independent and crucial importance of the preexisting strains in Marx's work on the theoretical level, I am departing from a purely "social" explanation for the course of Marxist revisionism, as suggested, e.g., by Lewis A. Coser in "Marxist Thought in the First Quarter of the 20th Century," pp. 173–201 in his *Varieties of Political Expression in Sociology* (Chicago, 1972).

In my terms, Coser emphasizes the ideological level of the scientific continuum, and while I agree with much of his very interesting effort to explain the voluntarist aspect of early Marxist revisionism by reference to the social location of major early revisionists (e.g., Lenin, Lukács, Gramsci) in less industrialized nations, I would emphasize that even this early twentieth-century revisionism occurred against a background of the more generalized strains in Marx's thought. Although an ecology of Marxism does not in itself contradict the possibility that strains could also be important on the presuppositional level, it is interesting to note that in Marxism's postwar period, which Coser does not discuss, voluntaristic Marxism spread to—and became centered in—the most developed countries.

My approach more closely resembles Perry Anderson's *Considerations on Western Marxism* (London, 1976) in its concern with internal, analytic issues in the history of Marxism. Yet I differ fundamentally with Anderson in my understanding of the status of "classical Marxism" vis-à-vis its subsequent revisers, and about the reasons for this relation. Anderson takes "classical Marxism" (primarily that of Marx, Engels, and Lenin) as being generally unproblematic, and he ascribes this to the close interweaving in this early period of theory and practice. Later revisions of Marx, then, are weakened by their isolation from political practice; in Anderson's view, they introduce revisions that are overly abstract and philosophical, and, therefore, they make no decisive theoretical advance. Politicizing their contributions in a particularly extreme way, he relates the renewed interest in superstructure to the climate of political defeat. The intrusion of Western idealism, in this view, represented merely an indication of this objective political defeat.

My understanding, as it will unfold in the following pages, could not be more different. I start with fundamental theoretical problems in the work of classical Marxism, with errors which I attribute to certain theoretical, not political, circumstances. The revisions offered to this orthodoxy, therefore, were in my view largely correct; indeed, the isolation from practice and the frustration of Marxian socialism presented "anomalies" that demanded such theoretical revision at the most general level. The "intrusion" of Western idealism was an adaptive response to *meet* this crisis, and the great abstraction of late Marxist theorizing represented not an escape from reality but an attempt to rethink Marxist theory at the most general level. It is worth noting that in his "Afterword" to *Considerations on Western Marxism*, Anderson modifies his claims, particularly his demand for the close connection of theory to practice as the principal validating mechanism, and his uncritical embrace of classical Marxism.

For a treatment of Marxist revisionism that more closely resembles my own analytic emphasis—though not, necessarily, my substantive conclusions—see Daniel Bell's essay "The Once and Future Marx," *American Journal of Sociology* 83, no. 1 (1977): 187–197.

In terms both of analytic focus and substantive argument, there is a striking convergence between the present work and Gouldner's *The Two Marxisms* (n.7 above). Gouldner focuses in his excellent book on many of the same presuppositional problems—instrumental and deterministic orientations versus normative and voluntaristic ones—and also reveals very clearly the way in which Marxist paradigm revision has been motivated by theoretical anomalies and by the desire to "normalize" this revision by reading Marx's writing in an apparently orthodox way. My account differs from Gouldner's, however, in at least three general ways. (1) In discussing the voluntaristic and deterministic strands of Marx and Marxism, Gouldner has a tendency to conflate ideological and epistemological issues. The evolutionary Marxists, like Bernstein, are considered to be instrumental and deterministic, and the revolutionary are normative. There is also a tendency in Gouldner's account to conflate both ideology and epistemology with meta-methodological commitment—so that "scientific," or positivistic Marxism is identical with instrumental and conservative Marxism. (2) With regard to the presuppositional issues of voluntarism and determinism, Gouldner does not enter deeply enough into the actual theoretical structure of Marx's text. The difficulty that results from this lack of attention is that he never sufficiently clarifies the relationship between the "two Marxisms" which are the subject of his account. He gives the impression, at times, that both strands in Marx's work are equally important on both analytic and ideological levels, at other times that the instrumental strand is, in fact, the core of the "scientific" theory that Marx consciously articulated. In this regard, the archaeological metaphor employed—that "critical Marxism" is less articulate but "deeper" than the scientific Marx, supplying its archeological foundations—is overly simplified and diffuse. Gouldner's major contribution to textual-theoretical analysis is his penetrating illumination of the tensions in Marx's account of the state in his theory of the Asiatic Mode of Production. Yet although this theory is of vital concern for empirical, ideological, and model issues, it is not central to the epistemological problem. (3) Finally, I would regard Gouldner's model of scientific development as too Kuhnian, suggesting as it does the linear movement from paradigm consistency to anomaly to normalization to the resurgence of anomaly (pp. 291 ff.).

82. Korsch, "Marxism and Philosophy" (1923), pp. 29–85 in his *Marxism and Philosophy* (London, 1970), quoting p. 48.

83. This is not to say, of course, that there is not a Marxism that can be distinguished as more "vulgar" from other, more refined and subtle exercises in Marxist analysis. My point, rather, is that the division between these vulgar and refined Marxisms—which may in fact correspond to more instrumental versus more normative forms of critical theorizing—

is not isomorphic with the division between Marx and his late-nineteenth-century followers. Although he was certainly a much more sophisticated and supple thinker than Kautsky or Engels or Plekhanov, Marx, in his systematic "scientific" work, was just as "vulgarly" instrumental.

84. Karl Kautsky, *The Class Struggle* (1891; New York, 1971).

85. Engels to J. Bloch, September 21–22, 1890, in *MESW*, 448–490, see 488. All quotations in the following discussion are from this letter; italics added.

86. The Marxist critic E. P. Thompson has pointed to the logical difficulties of these linguistic ambiguities in his polemical statement, *The Poverty of Theory and Other Essays* (London, 1978). The notion of "determination in the last instance," Thompson insists, eventually leads "to the good old utilitarian assumption that it [the material world of the economy] is therefore somehow more 'real' in all ways." If, for example, "the decisive region appears to be noneconomic (kinship, military power), then this can simply be redefined as the area to which the 'economic instance' has been 'assigned.'" More commonly, however, "other areas are simply regarded as being *less* real—as second- or third-order problems, as the concern of another 'region' of theory ... or simply as nonproblems, which may be spirited away with the want of 'relative autonomy.'" These problems, Thompson insists, "are so severe as to call in question the effectivity of Marx's general notions," for "very few of the critically-significant (the most 'real') problems which we confront in our actual lives appear to be *directly* and causally implicated in this field of correspondence ..." (Pp. 351–353, italics in original.) Even more pointedly, Gouldner (n.7 above) calls Marxism's last instance argument its "analytic millenium" (p. 240).

87. In terms of theoretical logic, the strategic importance of this contradictory letter by Engels to Bloch can hardly be overestimated: it has been used to legitimize a fantastic range of different readings of Marx's work. The most interesting and instructive of these, for my present purposes, are arguments that claim there is a basic similarity between Marx's theories and those of other classical theorists. The clearest example of this is the manner in which French theorists sympathetic to both Marx and Durkheim have employed Engels' letter to argue that, despite Durkheim's own understanding, his theory was not actually in conflict with the more normatively-sensitive Marxism of Marx himself.

Thus Cuvillier, in 1948, after discussing at some length Engels' letters, excuses himself "for having insisted at such length on these texts." This lengthy discussion "was necessary," he declares, "to appreciate Durkheim's position in regard to Marxism." It should now be clear, Cuvillier believes, that while "believing himself to be combating authentic Marxism," Durkheim was actually attacking "precisely the false interpretation of historical materialism that . . . Engels [declared] 'absurd'; it is, in sum, the vulgar interpretation." ("Durkheim et Marx," *Cahiers internationaux de sociologie* 5, no. 4 (1948): 75–97, see 89.)

In 1962, Aimard argued, similarly, that the "autonomy given to collective representations" by Durkheim "is not in contradiction with certain more nuanced forms of Marxism," and he cites Engels' letter to Bloch as indicating a position "very near to that of Durkheim" (Guy Aimard, *Durkheim et la science économique* [Paris, 1962], p. 234). A decade later, the argument is made yet again by Jean-Claude Filloux in *Durkheim et le socialisme* (Geneva, 1977), pp. 120 ff.

88. Edward Bernstein, *Evolutionary Socialism* (1899; New York, 1963).

89. Otto Bauer, *Die Nationalitätenfrage und die Sozialdemokratie* (1907), translated, in part, in "The Concept of the 'Nation,' " pp. 102–109 in Tom Bottomore and Patrick Goode, eds., *Austro-Marxism* (London, 1978), which I quote from p. 102.

90. See the translated section "Socialism and the Principle of Nationality," ibid., pp. 109–117.

91. V. I. Lenin, *What Is to Be Done?* (1902; New York, 1929), p. 31.

92. Ibid., p. 26.

93. Ibid., p. 28.

94. Leon Trotsky, *The Russian Revolution* (1930; New York, 1932), ch. 1, "Peculiarities of Russian Development," particularly pp. 4–11.

95. Ibid., ch. 15, "The Bolsheviks and Lenin," esp. pp. 232–239.

96. Ibid., ch. 16, p. 240.

97. Leon Trotsky, *The Revolution Betrayed*, selection, pp. 216–222 in Irving Howe, ed., *The Basic Writings of Trotsky* (New York, 1976), p. 216.

98. Ibid., p. 217.

99. Ibid.

100. Ibid., p. 219.

101. Ibid., pp. 217, 222.

102. Ibid., p. 222.

103. Mao Tse-tung, "Analysis of the Classes in Chinese Society" (1926) and "Report of an Investigation into the Peasant Movement in Hunan" (1927), in *Selected Works of Mao Tse-tung* (London, 1954), 1:13–21, 21–59, respectively.

104. Mao Tse-tung, "On Contradiction" (1937), pp. 214–241 in Anne Fremantle, ed., *Mao Tse-tung: An Anthology of his Writings*, (New York, 1962), p. 223.

105. Ibid., p. 225.

106. Ibid., pp. 232–233.

107. Ibid., p. 232.

108. Ibid., pp. 232–233, italics added.

109. Mao Tse-tung, "On the Correct Handling of Contradictions among the People" (1957), pp. 264–297, in Fremantle, *Anthology*, p. 271.

110. Ibid., p. 269.

111. Ibid., p. 270.

112. Georg Lukács, "What Is Orthodox Marxism?" pp. 1–26 in his *History and Class Consciousness* (1923; Cambridge, Mass., 1971), p. 6.

113. Lukács, "Reification and the Consciousness of the Proletariat," ibid., pp. 83–222, see p. 93.

114. Ibid., pp. 88, 91, italics added.

115. Ibid., pp. 98–110.

116. Ibid., p. 93.

117. Ibid., p. 84.

118. Lukács, "What Is Orthodox Marxism?" p. 14.

119. Lukács, "The Marxism of Rosa Luxemburg," ibid., pp. 27–45, quoting p. 41, italics in original.

120. Ibid., p. 42.

121. Ibid.

122. Lukács, "Reification and the Consciousness of the Proletariat," p. 83.

123. Ibid., p. 91.

124. Ibid., pp. 91–92.

125. Ibid., p. 109; cf., more generally, pp. 109–111.

126. Ibid., p. 89.

127. Ibid., p. 149.

128. Ibid., p. 168.

129. Ibid., p. 166.

130. Ibid., p. 162.

131. Ibid., italics in original.

132. Ibid., p. 163.

133. Antonio Gramsci, "The Programme of Ordine Nuovo" (1920), pp. 22–27 in Gramsci, *The Modern Prince and Other Writings* (New York, 1957), see p. 24.

134. Gramsci, "The Study of Philosophy," pp. 321–376 in Gramsci, *Selections from the Prison Notebooks (1929–1937)*, ed., Quintin Hoare and Geoffrey Nowell Smith (New York, 1971), p. 339.

135. Ibid.

136. Gramsci, "Critical Notes on an Attempt at a Popular Sociology," ibid., pp. 419–472, quoting p. 441.

137. Ibid., p. 447.

138. Gramsci, "The Study of Philosophy," p. 333.

139. Ibid., p. 328.

140. "The Study of Philosophy," p. 336.

141. Gramsci, "Notes on Italian History," pp. 44–122 in *Prison Notebooks*, p. 57.

142. Ibid., pp. 58, 61.

143. Gramsci, "The Intellectuals," pp. 3–23 in *Prison Notebooks*, p. 12.

144. For "complex structure," see Gramsci, "State and Civil Society," pp. 206–276 in *Prison Notebooks*, p. 235; for "ensemble of relations," see ibid., pp. 12, 352–353, 359–360, 366, 466.

145. Gramsci, "State and Civil Society," p. 235.

146. Ibid., p. 210.

147. Ibid.

148. Ibid., p. 276.

149. Gramsci, "Marxism and Modern Culture," pp. 82–89 in *The Modern Prince and Other Writings*, p. 85.

150. Gramsci, "The Modern Prince," pp. 123–205 in *Prison Notebooks*, pp. 132–133.

151. Ibid., p. 133.

152. "The Study of Philosophy," p. 334.

153. Gramsci, "La Rivoluzione contro il 'Capitale,' " *Avanti*, November 24, 1918, quoted in Carl Boggs, *Gramsci's Marxism* (London, 1976), p. 25. See also Giuseppi Fiori, *Antonio Gramsci: Life of a Revolutionary* (London, 1970) for this thread that runs through Gramsci's career.

154. Gramsci, "Critical Notes on an Attempt at Popular Sociology," p. 438.

155. Gramsci, "The Intellectuals," pp. 12, 11.

156. Ibid., p. 8.

157. Gramsci, "The Study of Philosophy," pp. 329, 394–395.

158. Gramsci, "Americanism and Fordism," pp. 277–320 in *Prison Notebooks*, p. 281.

159. Ibid., pp. 299, 303.

160. Ibid., pp. 286, 279.

161. Jean-Paul Sartre, *Search for a Method* (1960; New York, 1963), p. 48.

162. Ibid., p. 133.

163. Ibid., pp. 133, 152.

164. Ibid., pp. 91, 152.

165. Ibid., pp. 42, 78.

166. Ibid., pp. 42, 115–116.

167. Ibid., pp. 37–38, 123–127, 133.

168. Ibid., pp. 62–63, 97.

169. Jean-Paul Sartre, *Critique of Dialectical Reason* (London, 1976). In France, this book was published simultaneously in 1960 with *Search for a Method (Question de Méthode)*. While the latter essay formed only a

preface to the *Critique*, the larger and more important work was translated into English only in 1976.

170. Sartre, *Critique of Dialectical Reason*, p. 317.

171. Ibid., p. 710. Cf. Mark Poster's comment: "In Marx . . . the capitalist mode of production generated the appearance that human beings were things and things were human. The fetish of the commodity produced the illusion of the reversal of subject and object. In Sartre's *Critique* this reversal is not . . . merely an objective feature of a social system. Human beings do not become things only in appearance. They undergo . . . a profound interior alteration." (*Sartre's Marxism* [London, 1979], p. 53.)

172. *Critique of Dialectical Reason*, pp. 739, 748.

173. Ibid., p. 346.

174. Ibid., p. 348.

175. Ibid., pp. 353–380; quoted phrases from pp. 353, 357, 358, 369, 380, 399.

176. Ibid., p. 358.

177. Ibid., p. 414.

178. Ibid., pp. 417, 412.

179. Ibid., pp. 591–608; the quotation is from p. 608.

180. Ibid., p. 591.

181. Ibid., p. 608.

182. To be sure, Sartre acknowledges only his debt to Freud, not to Durkheim. His only references to the latter in *Critique of Dialectical Reason*—and, as might be expected from the French intellectual generation of the 1930s, in his earlier existentialist work as well—are uniformly critical. Nonetheless, the parallels between Sartre's understanding of the community-dispersion cycle and Durkheim's theory of solidarity are too significant to overlook. Sartre misunderstood Durkheim's thought, as Durkheim no doubt would have misunderstood Sartre's. Both thinkers, however, reflect the concern with spontaneous community that has been such a distinctive part of the French political and intellectual tradition. That in Sartre's reading this common concern should be crystallized in a theory that is so strikingly similar to Durkheim's is a testimony to the universal element in theoretical structure, and to the continuities in the French cultural tradition, rather than to any conscious intention to model his theory on Durkheim's own.

183. See *Search for a Method*, pp. 111–140.

184. Ibid., p. 21.

185. *Critique of Dialectical Reason*, p. 713.

186. *Search for a Method*, p. 103.

187. Ibid., p. 102.

188. *Critique of Dialectical Reason*, p. 132.

189. Ibid., pp. 124, 737–738.

190. Ibid., p. 779, italics altered.

191. Ibid., p. 680.

192. Ibid., p. 673, italics in original.

193. The manner in which this single sentence embodies the contradictions of Marxian theory recalls also the ambiguous statement by Marx in *The Eighteenth Brumaire* with which I concluded the discussion of that work in sec. 1 above (see the first quotation [n.79] in the final paragraph of that section).

194. In *The Dialectical Imagination* (Boston, 1973), p. 272, Martin Jay has viewed this profound ambiguity—this aspect of retrenchment in the Frankfurt tradition—as stemming from its ideological reluctance to embrace any part of the "bourgeois society" that it critiqued. Although this is certainly one aspect of the writings of the Frankfurt Marxists, I would stress the independence of the problems they encountered on the level of general theoretical logic. Their ideological commitments, of course, were one reason for their continued commitment to certain elements of orthodox Marxist theorizing.

195. Herbert Marcuse, *An Essay on Liberation* (Boston, 1969) and *The Aesthetic Dimension* (Boston, 1978).

196. Jürgen Habermas, *Knowledge and Human Interests* (Boston, 1972), p. 42.

197. Ibid., pp. 326–329, n.14.

198. Habermas, "Science and Technology as Ideology," pp. 81–122 in his *Towards a Rational Society* (Boston, 1970), is an early statement of this position on action and order, particularly insofar as the latter is discussed in terms of "system" models.

199. Habermas, *Knowledge and Human Interests*, p. 54.

200. Habermas, *Theory and Practice* (Boston, 1973), p. 238.

201. *Knowledge and Human Interests*, p. 30.

202. Ibid., p. 52.

203. Ibid., p. 61.

204. Habermas, *Theory and Practice*, p. 30.

205. *Knowledge and Human Interest*, p. 42.

206. For this strand of communications analysis, see, e.g., the Appendix to *Knowledge and Human Interests*, "Knowledge and Human Interests: A General Perspective"; the Introduction to *Theory and Practice*, "Some Difficulties in the Attempt to Link Theory and Practice"; and "The Relation of Practical Questions to Truth," pp. 102–110 in Habermas, *Legitimation Crisis* (Boston, 1975).

207. For the model of therapy, see Habermas, "Self-Reflection as Science: Freud's Psychoanalytic Critique of Meaning," pp. 214–245 in *Knowledge and Human Interests*.

208. Habermas, *Legitimation Crisis*, p. 73.

209. For a more detailed examination of the indeterminacy of Haber-

mas' insistence on the ultimately contradictory character of the "capitalist system," see Axel van den Berg, "Critical Theory: Is There Still Hope?" *American Journal of Sociology* 86, no. 3 (1980): 449–478, and Jeffrey C. Alexander, "Looking for Theory: 'Facts' and 'Values' as the Intellectual Legacy of the 1970's," *Theory and Society* 10 (1981): 279–292.

210. For the earliest and most general statements of this position, see Althusser's essays "Contradiction and Overdetermination" and "On the Materialist Dialectic," in Louis Althusser, *For Marx* (London, 1969).

211. Althusser, "The Errors of Classical Economics," in his and Etienne Balibar's *Reading "Capital"* (London, 1970), p. 97, italics in original.

212. For "structured whole" and "synchronicity," see ibid., pp. 97, 107; for "totality," see *For Marx*, pp. 202–204.

213. *For Marx*, p. 113.

214. For the convergence between Marxist structuralism and Parsonian systems theory and functionalism generally, see particularly Althusser's follower, Maurice Godelier, "Functionalism, Structuralism, and Marxism," the Introduction to his *Rationality and Irrationality in Economics* (London, 1971), and "The Idea of a System," ibid., 257–259. See also vol. 1, ch. 3, sec. 4.

215. *Reading "Capital"*, p. 97.

216. Ibid., p. 99.

217. Ibid., p. 179, italics in original.

218. Balibar, "The Basic Concepts of Historical Materialism," pp. 199–308 in *Reading "Capital,"* pp. 265–266.

219. Ibid., pp. 265, 259. To see precisely what Balibar is trying to prevent—a relative autonomy argument that really takes seriously the "independence" of reproductive consumption—one can refer to the pointed discussion in Marshall Sahlin's *Culture and Practical Reason* (Chicago, 1976). Sahlins argues, as I did above, that Marx cannot understand the true empirical nature of proletarian consumption because he has argued for the total domination of exchange over use value in capitalist society (p. 134). But material goods have a *qualitative* meaning for the buyer even in capitalism, Sahlins argues, and he presents the kind of symbolic, quasi-Durkheimian analysis of normative order that Marx would have had to evoke if he were to have considered reproductive consumption in anything more than a purely instrumental way (pp. 148–149). In dissecting the cultural codes within which various kinds of consumption occur, he analyzes, e.g., the antipathies of sacred and profane which organize food preferences and taboos in the consumption of animal meat in America (pp. 170–179).

220. Althusser, "Ideology and Ideological State Apparatuses," pp. 127–186 in his *Lenin and Philosophy and Other Essays* (New York, 1971), p. 132.

221. Ibid., p. 143.

222. Ibid., p. 132.

223. Cf. Martin Jay's statement about the intellectual origins of the Frankfurt school:

> The members of the Frankfurt School were fortunate in having had philosophical training outside the Marxist tradition. Like other twentieth century contributors to the revitalization of Marxism—Lukács, Gramsci, Bloch, Sartre, Merleau-Ponty—they were influenced at an early stage in their careers by more subjectivist, even idealist philosophies. (*The Dialectical Imagination* [Boston, 1973], p. 44.)

224. This is not to say, of course, that these idealist influences by any means exhaust the intellectual resources of these students. In Althusser's case, e.g., one would have to note the counterbalancing impact of the determinism of Spinoza.

225. In a survey in *The Socialist Register* of Marxist treatments of revolutionary consciousness, H. Wolpe concludes with the question "What elements of the superstructure must be taken into account and in what way?" He answers that "for Marx and Engels [and for the others he has examined] no theoretical answer can be given to these questions." "This suggests," he remarks dryly, "the need to develop a theory of the superstructure." ("Some Problems Concerning Revolutionary Consciousness," pp. 251–280 in Ralph Miliband and John Saville, eds., *The Socialist Register, 1970* [London], p. 274.)

Another critical admonishment from within the Marxist movement is Norman Birnbaum's essay, "The Crisis of Marxist Sociology" (pp. 95–129 in his *Toward a Critical Sociology* [London, 1971]). Arguing from the position that an understanding of the superstructure is vital to any revitalized Marxism, Birnbaum warns his radical colleagues that "the multiple theoretic traditions and the techniques of inquiry developed in bourgeois sociology pose grave problems for a Marxist sociology, problems which are far from resolved and often enough hardly acknowledged" (p. 99). He points out, for example, that a "good deal of Marxist analysis . . . is particularly insensitive to . . . specific cultural traditions" (p. 107). He concludes that "the crisis in Marxist sociology may mark the beginning of the end of Marxism" (p. 129). This last prediction is doubtful. For a number of complex reasons which I have laid out very briefly above, the "crisis" of Marxism will principally lead to continued revisionism.

Works of Marx and Durkheim

Following are the works cited in the text and notes, listed chronologically according to date of original publication or, if unpublished, date of composition. I have included the original language edition only when it was a primary reference.

Marx

"Preparatory Notes" to *The Difference between the Democritean and Epicurean Philosophy of Nature*, [1842], in Loyd D. Easton and Kurt H. Guddat, eds., *Writings of the Young Marx on Philosophy and Society*, 1967.

"The Philosophical Manifesto of the Historical School of Law," [1842], in Easton and Guddat, eds., *Writings of the Young Marx on Philosophy and Society*, 1967.

"On a Proposed Divorce Law," [1842], in Easton and Guddat, eds., *Writings of the Young Marx on Philosophy and Society*, 1967.

"Communism and the Augsburg *'Allegemeine Zeitung'*," [1842], in Easton and Guddat, eds., *Writings of the Young Marx on Philosophy and Society*, 1967.

"Religion, Free Press, and Philosophy," [1842], in Easton and Guddat, eds., *Writings of the Young Marx on Philosophy and Society*, 1967.

"Comments on the Latest Prussian Censorship Instruction," [1843], in Easton and Guddat, eds., *Writings of the Young Marx on Philosophy and Society*, 1967.

"Cologne, in May 1843," [1843], in Easton and Guddat, eds., *Writings of the Young Marx on Philosophy and Society*, 1967.

"Defense of the Moselle Correspondent: Economic Distress and Freedom of the Press," [1843], in Easton and Guddat, eds., *Writings of the Young Marx on Philosophy and Society*, 1967.

"Contribution to the Critique of Hegel's *Philosophy of Right*," [1844], in T. B. Bottomore, ed., *Karl Marx: Early Writings*, 1963.

537

"On the Jewish Question," [1844], in T. B. Bottomore, ed., *Karl Marx: Early Writings*, 1963.

"Kreuznach, in September 1843," [1844], in Easton and Guddat, eds., *Writings of the Young Marx on Philosophy and Society*, 1967.

"Economic and Philosophical Manuscripts," [1844], in T. B. Bottomore, ed., *Karl Marx: Early Writings*, 1963.

"Theses on Feuerbach," [1845], in Nathan Rotenstreich, *Basic Problems of Marx's Philosophy*, 1965.

Holy Family, 1845.

The German Ideology, 1846.

The Poverty of Philosophy, [1847], 1963.

Manifesto of the Communist Party, [1848], in *Marx and Engels: Selected Works*, 1962.

The Revolution of 1848–9, ed. by Bernard Isaacs, 1972.

Wage-Labour and Capital, [1849], in *Marx and Engels: Selected Works I*, 1962.

"Address of the Central Committee to the Communist League," [1850], in *Marx and Engels: Selected Works I*, 1962.

The Class Struggles in France, 1848–1850, [1850], in *Marx and Engels: Selected Works I*, 1962.

The Eighteenth Brumaire of Louis Bonaparte, 1852.

The Secret Diplomatic History of the Eighteenth Century and *The Story of the Life of Lord Palmerston*, [1856], ed. by Lester Hutchinson, 1969.

"Preface" to *The Critique of Political Economy*, [1859], in *Marx-Engels Werke*, 1962.

The Grundrisse: Foundations of the Critique of Political Economy, [1858–9], 1974.

"Inaugural Address of the Working Men's International Association," [1864], in *Marx and Engels: Selected Works I*, 1962.

"General Rules of the International Working Men's Association," [1864], in *Marx and Engels: Selected Works I*, 1962.

Value, Price, and Profit, [1865], 1935.

Capital, vol. 1, [1867], 1962.

Capital, vol. 2, [1885], 1971.

Capital, vol. 3, [1894], 1972.

The Civil War in France, [1871], in *Marx and Engels: Selected Works I*, 1962.

"Critique of the Gotha Programme," [1875], in *Marx and Engels: Selected Works II*, 1962.

Marx-Engels Werke, 1962.

Karl Marx and Frederick Engels: Selected Correspondence, n.d.

Durkheim

"Address to the Lyceens of Sens," [1883], in Robert N. Bellah, ed., *Emile Durkheim on Morality and Society*, 1973.

Review of Albert Schaeffle, *Bau und Leben des Sozialen Körpers*, first volume, [1885], in Mark Traugott, ed., *Emile Durkheim on Institutional Analysis*, 1978.

Review of Ludwig Gumplowicz, *Grundrisse der Soziologie*, [1885], in *Emile Durkheim: Textes (1)*, 1975.

"A. Fouillée, *La Propriété sociale et la democratie*," *Revue philosophique* 19 (1885): 446–453.

"Les Etudes de science sociale," *Revue philosophique* 22 (1886): 61–80; one section translated as "Durkheim's Critique of Spencer's *Ecclesiastical Institutions*," *Sociological Inquiry* 44, no. 3 (1974): 205–214.

"La Science sociale selon De Greef," *Revue philosophique* 22 (1886): 658–663; in *Textes* (1), 1975.

"Guyau, *L'Irreligion de l'avenir: Etude de sociologie*," *Revue philosophique* 23 (1887): 299–311.

"La Science positive de la morale en Allemagne," *Revue philosophique* 24 (1887): 33–58, 113–142, 275–284.

"Notice biographique sur Victor Hommay," *L'Annuaire de l'association des anciens élèves de l'Ecole normale supérieure*, January 9, 1887: 51–55; in *Textes* (1), 1975.

"La Philosophie dans les universités allemandes," *Revue internationale de l'enseignement* 23 [1887]: 313–338, 423–440; in *Textes* (3), 1975.

"Introduction to the Sociology of the Family," [1888], in Traugott, ed., *Emile Durkheim on Institutional Analysis*, 1978.

"Course in Sociology: Opening Lecture," [1888], in Traugott, ed., *Emile Durkheim on Institutional Analysis*, 1978.

"La Programme économique de M. Schaeffle," *Revue d'économie politique* 11 [1888]: 3–7; in *Textes* (1), 1975.

"Suicide et natalité: Etude de statistique morale," *Revue philosophique* 26 [1888]: 446–463; in *Textes* (2), 1975.

Review of Ferdinand Tönnies, *Gemeinschaft und Gesellschaft*, [1889], in Traugott, ed., *Emile Durkheim on Institutional Analysis*, 1978.

"Preface," *L'Année sociologique*, (2[1889]: i–vi), in Kurt H. Wolff, ed., *Essays on Sociology and Philosophy by Emile Durkheim et al.*, 1964.

"The Principles of 1789 and Sociology," [1890], in Bellah, ed., *Emile Durkheim on Morality and Society*, 1973.

"Montesquieu's Contribution to the Rise of Social Science," [1892], in Durkheim, *Montesquieu and Rousseau*, 1960.

The Division of Labor in Society, [1893; 1903], 1933.

"G. Richard, *Essai sur l'origine de l'idée de droit*," *Revue philosophique* 35 (1893): 290–296.

"Note sur la définition du socialisme," *Revue philosophique* 36 (1893): 506–512.

"Les Règles de la méthode sociologique [3° article]," *Revue philosophique* 38 (1894): 14–39.

The Rules of Sociological Method, [1895], 1938.

Suicide, [1897], 1951.

Review of Gaston Richard, *Le Socialisme et la science sociale*, [1897], in Traugott, ed., *Emile Durkheim on Institutional Analysis*, 1978.

Review of Antonio Labriola, *Essais sur la conception matérialiste de l'histoire*, [1897], in Traugott, ed., *Emile Durkheim on Institutional Analysis*, 1978.

"Individualism and the Intellectuals," [1898], in Bellah, ed., *Emile Durkheim on Morality and Society*, 1973.

"Individual and Collective Representations," [1898], in Durkheim, *Sociology and Philosophy*, 1974.

Review of Siegfried Rietschel, *Markt und Stadt in ihrem Rechtlichen Ver-hältniss*, [1899], in J. Duvignaud, ed., *Journal sociologique*, 1969.

"De la définition des phénomènes religieux," *L'Année sociologique* 2 (1899): 1–28.

Review of Heinrich Gunow, *Die oekonomischen Grundlagen der Mutterherrschaft*, [1899], in Duvignaud, ed., *Journal sociologique*, 1969.

Review of Paul Merriot, *Des agglomérations urbaines dans l'Europe contemporaine*, [1899], in Duvignaud, ed., *Journal sociologique*, 1969.

Review of Karl Hegel, *Die Entstehung des deutschen städtswesens*, [1899], in Duvignaud, ed., *Journal sociologique*, 1969.

"Remarque sur la nature de la religiosité," [1899], in *Textes* (2), 1975.

"Note on Social Morphology," [1899], in Traugott, ed., *Emile Durkheim on Institutional Analysis*, 1978.

"Sociology in France in the Nineteenth Century," [1900], in Bellah, ed., *Emile Durkheim on Morality and Society*, 1973.

Review of A. Dumont, *Natalité et démocratie*, [1900], in Duvignaud, ed., *Journal sociologique*, 1969.

"Note sur la sociologie criminelle et la statistique morale," *L'Année sociologique* 4 [1901]: 433–436; in Duvignaud, ed., *Journal sociologique*, 1969.

"A. Fouillée, *La France au point de vue moral*," *L'Année sociologique* 5 (1901): 443–445.

"Two Laws of Penal Evolution," [1901], in Traugott, ed., *Emile Durkheim on Institutional Analysis*, 1978.

Primitive Classification, [1902], 1963.

"Pedagogy and Sociology," [1903], in Durkheim, *Education and Sociology*, 1956.

"Note sur les systèmes juridiques," *L'Année sociologique* 6 [1903]: 305; in Duvignaud, ed., *Journal sociologique*, 1969.

"The Determination of Moral Facts," [1906], in Durkheim, *Sociology and Philosophy*, 1974.

"Débat sur le patriotisme et l'internationalisme des classes sociales," *Libres Entretiens* [1905]; in *Textes* (3), 1975.

"Débat sur les conséquences religieuses de la séparation des églises et de l'état," *Mercure de France* 67 [1907]; in *Textes* (2), 1975: 165–169.

"Sur l'organization matrimoniale des sociétés australiennes," *L'Année sociologique* 8 (1907): 118–147.

"Sociology and the Social Sciences," [1909], in Traugott, ed., *Emile Durkheim on Institutional Analysis*, 1978.

"Débat sur la possibilité d'une science religieuse," *Bulletin of the Société française de philosophie* 9 [1909]: 56–60; in *Textes* (1), 1975.

Review of Marianne Weber, *Ehefrau und Mutter in der Rechtsentwickelung*, [1910], in Traugott, ed., *Emile Durkheim on Institutional Analysis*, 1978.

"W. Jérusalem, *Soziologie des Erkennens*," *L'Année sociologique* 11 (1910): 42–45.

Review of Célèstin Bouglé, *Essai sur le régime des castes*, [1910], in *Textes* (3), 1975.

"The Nature and Methods of Pedagogy," [1911], in Durkheim, *Education and Sociology*, 1956.

"Education: Its Nature and Role," [1911], in Durkheim, *Education and Sociology*, 1956.

"Value Judgments and Judgments of Reality," [1911], in Durkheim, *Sociology and Philosophy*, 1974.

The Elementary Forms of Religious Life, [1912], 1965.

"Note on the Notion of Civilization," [1913], *Social Research* 38 (1971): 808–813.

"The Dualism of Human Nature and Its Social Conditions," [1914], in Bellah, ed., *Emile Durkheim on Morality and Society*, 1973.

"A Durkheim Fragment: The Conjugal Family," [1921], *American Journal of Sociology* 70 (1965): 527–536.

Moral Education, [1925], 1961.

Socialism and Saint-Simon, [1928], 1958.

The Evolution of Educational Thought, [1938], 1977.

Professional Ethics and Civic Morals, [1950], 1958.

Education and Sociology, 1956.

Author-Citation Index

This index is intended as a combination bibliography/name index. Every article and book referred to in the text and notes is included here (with the exception of works by Marx and Durkheim), but authors are included only if their work is specifically cited. If the work of an author mentioned in the text is cited only in the notes, the page of both text and note references is indexed.

Subject Index